*This book
is dedicated to my wife
Barbara*

Dr. Rüdiger Riehl

Coverphotos:
Title: *Melanotaenia boesemani*
                Arend van den Nieuwenhuizen,

Backcover: *Aphyosemion [Diapteron]* sp.   *Corydras adolfoi, C. imitator*
                Arend van den Nieuwenhuizen   David Sands

                Aulonocara hansbaenschi   *Hygrophyla stricta*
                Manfred K. Meyer   Kurt Paffrath

Page 3:   *Aphyosemion huwaldi* "Fullaba"
                Steffen Hellner

Publisher:
Hans A. Baensch

Editor:
Dr. Rüdiger Riehl

Translated and revised by:
Gero W. Fischer, Ph.D.
Shellie E. Borrer, M.S.

© Copyright 1996/1997 MERGUS®-Verlag, 49302 Melle, Germany
® MERGUS is a registered trademark in USA

ISBN: 1-890087-07-6 (U.S.A. only)
ISBN: 3-88244-503-3 (For other countries)

First English Edition, 1996
Second Revised English Edition, First Paperback Edition, 1997

Published in the United States by:
Microcosm Ltd., 2085 Shelburne Road, Shelburne, Vermont 05482

Distribution
USA: Microcosm Ltd., 2085 Shelburne Road, Shelburne, Vermont 05482
Canada: Rolf C. Hagen Inc., 3225 Sartelon Street, Montreal, Que. H4R 1E8
Great Britain: Rolf C. Hagen (U.K.) Limited, California Drive, Whitwood Industrial
                Estate, Castleford WF 10 50H, West Yorkshire, England.
Australia: Pet Pacific Pty Ltd., Unit C, 30 Skarratt Street, Auburn NSW 2144,
                P.O. Box 398, Rydalmere NSW 2116, Australia

Printed in Singapore

Dr. Rüdiger Riehl   Hans A. Baensch

AQUARIUM ATLAS

Volume 3
Paperback Edition

MERGUS

Publishers of Natural History and Pet Books
Hans A. Baensch • Melle • Germany

Preface

Preface to Volume 3

After Aquarium Atlas Volumes 1 and 2, no enhancement seemed possible. However, after laborious work we have again successfully collected over 1,000 color photographs of species not presented in the previous volumes of the Aquarium Atlas. It was then merely a question of time and detective work to collect the necessary textual information. A newly installed computer significantly eased this task. Today we can print out the names of over 6,500 freshwater fishes and search and sort them by scientific data and photos.

Your help in improving and augmenting our texts is always welcome, since pertinent literature is often scant. Only experience helps further. Hobbyists frequently work hand in hand with science.

This volume again emphasizes catfishes, killifishes and, naturally, the cichlids—the eternal favorites of most aquarists. But Russian species, hereto almost unknown in Western Europe, the United States, Canada, and the Far East, have been included to a larger degree than previously. It will probably be several years more until these species appear in our aquaria. The sometimes exotic beauty of species from the Amur River (the "Russian Amazon") will fascinate some western aquarists. Garden ponds and coldwater aquaria will be enriched by their presence. The aquarium hobby has a never ending diversity to draw upon. This diversity complemented with breeding efforts and information gained—from aquarists—will help ensure that we have the knowledge and ability to protect species from outside pressures threatening extinction.

Hans Frey, the old master of aquarium literature since 1950, once wrote the following to me in a book dedication:

> Aquarism is merry science
> and serious hobby.

This is the vein in which we published Aquarium Atlas 3. It is not lacking—yet makes a lovely and enjoyable addition.

For help with this extensive volume we especially want to extend our thanks to the following persons:

Hans-Joachim Herrmann (Cichlids)
Harro Hieronimus (Catfishes and many other species)
Hans Horsthemke (Gobies)
Manfred K. Meyer (Livebearers)
Gerhard Ott (Cyprinids)
Kurt Paffrath (Plants)
Gina and Mike Sandfort—British Catfish Ass. (Catfishes)
Jürgen Schmidt (Labyrinth fishes, characins, and other species)
Lothar Seegers (Killifishes and other species)
Andreas Spreinat (Cichlids)
Rainer Stawikowski (Cichlids)
Uwe Werner (Cichlids)
Axel Zarske (Cyprinids)
—and the many unnamed aquarists

We are presently working on Aquarium Atlas Volume 4, and we appreciate all contributions our readers care to make in regard to photographs and additional textual information. Only with your help can the Aquarium Atlas continue to present a continuously expanding and up-to-date knowledge base.

Rüdiger Riehl   Hans A. Baensch
Düsseldorf   Melle

Spring 1997

Table of Contents

Eichhornia sp. cf. *diversifolia* : east Brazil

Selection of Plants (Definition of the Groups)

GROUP 1

Plants with Upright Stems

The common characteristic of these plants is the upright main axis with alternate, opposite, or whorled leaves at the nodes.

This group is comprised of 41 genera, 85 species with 18 varieties and forms as well as one hybrid. These are subdivided according to their different leaf arrangements.

Subgroup 1

Leaves Alternate

Single leaves originate from each node and are usually arranged in a spiral around the stem. The following genera fall into this subgroup: *Cardamine, Eichhornia, Fontinalis, Heteranthera, Houttuynia, Hydrocotyle, Lagarosiphon, Lobelia, Mayaca, Polygonum, Potamogeton, Proserpinaca* (or *Hottonia*), *Saururus, Zosterella.*

1.1.
Lobelia

Subgroup 2

Leaves Opposite

Two leaves emerge from each node directly opposite to each other. Included in this subgroup are the following genera:
Althernanthera, Ammannia, Bacopa, Cabomba, Crassula, Didiplis, Gymnocoronis, Hydrotriche, Hygrophila, Ilysanthes, Ludwigia, Lysimachia, Micranthemum, Najas, Nesaea, Rotala, Shinnersia.

1.2.
Hygrophila

Subgroup 3

Leaves in a Whorl

Three or more leaves originate from a node at the same height around the stem. This subgroup includes the following genera:
Egeria, Elodea, Eusteralis, Hemianthus, Hydrilla, Hydrothrix, Limnophila, Myriophyllum, Nitella, Rotala.

1.3.
Eusteralis

Group 2
Plants with Leaves in a Rosette

The leaves grow upward from a thick root stock (rhizome) in the ground and are very differently shaped, either with or without a petiole. In total, this group is comprised of 22 genera with 126 species and 24 varieties.

2.1.
Sagittaria

Subgroup 1
Narrow-Leaved Rosettes

Predominately tall forms with sessile, thin, ribbon- or thread-shaped leaves. This subgroup includes the following genera:
Acorus, Blyxa, Crinum, Eleocharis, Isoetes, Ranalisma, Sagittaria, Spiranthes, Vallisneria.

2.2.
Nuphar

Subgroup 2
Broad-Leaved Rosettes

Special characteristics are the roundish, usually cordate, incised leaves and its often compact growth form. This subgroup includes the following genera:
Anubias, Barclaya, Ceratopteris, Lagenandra, Nuphar, Nymphaea, Nymphoides, Ottelia, Samolus, Spathiphyllum.

2.3.
Echinodorus
(round-leaved)

Subgroup 3
Amazon Sword Plants (*Echinodorus*)

Native to the American continent and variable in form. There are 47 species and 12 varieties.
About 25–30 species can be kept in an aquarium. Their requirements and uses are varied.

2.3.
Echinodorus
(slender-leaved)

Subgroup 4

Aponogetons (*Aponogeton*)

The 42 described species in this subgroup are found in Africa (15), Madagascar (11), southeast Asia (13), and Australia (4). 13 species and 3 varieties are more or less suited for the aquarium. These are rapid growing plants that easily flower and fruit in an aquarium.

Subgroup 5

Cryptocorynes (*Cryptocoryne*)

This genus has over 60 described species and is widely distributed in southeast Asia. About 30 species are suited for aquarium cultivation in varying degrees. Their living requirements in an aquarium are usually more demanding than those of numerous other aquarium plants.

2.4.
Aponogeton

GROUP 3

Creeping-Shoot Plants

This small group of 16 species from 10 genera is characterized by a creeping shoot with leaves of different shapes. Some species can be fastened on stones or wood and will continue to grow there. The following genera are included in this group: *Bolbitis, Elatine, Glossostigma, Hydrocotyle, Lilaeopsis, Marsilea, Microsorium, Pilularia, Selliera, Vesicularia*.

2.5.
Cryptocoryne

GROUP 4

Floating Plants

These 15 genera contain 30 species which can be divided into 3 biological types.

1. Genera producing totally submersed plants without roots: *Lemna, Utricularia*, and *Riccia*.

2. Free floating plants with either the upper side or the entire leaf above the water. The following genera are included in this category: *Azolla, Ceratopteris, Eichhornia, Lemna, Limnobium, Pistia, Salvinia*, and *Wolffia*.

3. Rooted plants with floating leaves: *Heteranthera, Hydrocleys, Nymphaea, Nymphoides*, and *Trapa*.

3.
Hydrocotyle

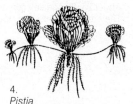

4.
Pistia

Jungle creek in Borneo

Explanation of the Symbols

D = Degree of Difficulty

This symbol indicates whether a species has basic or specific demands for successful growth. Degrees 1 and 2 are recommended for beginners. Plants in group 3 demand somewhat more experience, while those rated a 4 demand optimal water conditions (usually soft) and should only be kept by advanced aquarists.

D: 1 Robust and adaptable species; hard water and less than optimal nutrient conditions are tolerated. Light requirement is low to moderate, about 1 watt per 3–4 liters (1 gal).

Propagation is usually straightforward.
pH 6.0–8.0
Hardness up to 20° KH

D: 2 Robust and enduring species, but somewhat more demanding of water quality than those in D:1. Light requirement is moderate, about 1 watt per 2–3 liters ($^3/_4$ gal).

Propagation is possible.
pH 6.0–7.5
Hardness up to 15° KH

D: 3 These plants prefer soft to medium-hard water with balanced nutrients. However, it can remain healthy and grow in water with higher carbonate hardness levels when carbon dioxide is added. Light requirement is medium to high, about 1 watt per 1.5–2.0 liters ($^1/_2$ gal).

Propagation not always easy.
pH 6.0–7.2
Hardness up to 10° KH

D: 4 Plants within this group are not very adaptable and generally require soft water. They normally have a high light requirement of about 1 watt per 1.5 liters ($^2/_5$ gal).

Propagation usually difficult.
pH 6.0–6.8
Hardness up to 4° KH

KH = Carbonate Hardness

The proportion of carbonate hardness in the water often determines the well-being of the plants. Very soft water, below 2° KH, is usually less suitable for plant growth, but the overall ability of the plant to adapt to a certain hardness range decides the issue. Some plants have to have soft water. Numerous plants, although tolerant of higher carbonate hardnesses, respond to a higher pH or low carbon dioxide concentrations by diminished growth.

Information in the data line below each species shows the most favorable range for plant growth. Minor fluctuations are possible, as many factors are interrelated. It is best not to combine plants with widely differing requirements.

pH = Acidity and Alkalinity of the Water

This is the acidity or alkalinity at which the plant grows best. Most plants prefer the favorable range of 6.5–7.2. While the pH can fluctuate above or below the suggested value, many species or genera may be harmed by values too deviant from the suggested range. If problems in growth are noted, pH can easily be measured to identify or eliminate it as the source of the problem.

Plants with widely differing preference should not be planted in the same tank.

T = Temperature

The range in which the plant grows best under normal conditions is indicated. The optimum is usually slightly above the middle value. In certain species, 2°C above the listed values is possible, but higher levels of nutrients and light have to be provided to compensate for increased respiration.

AH = Aquarium Height

The appropriate aquarium height for the species is listed. Tall plants, large rhizome plants, and rapid growing stalked plants should be placed in aquaria which are as roomy and tall as possible. In shallow aquaria, such plants are out of place or have to be pruned too often. Plants that are low or moderately tall are suitable for any tank in regard to height, but keep in mind the light-attenuating effect of water which may result in small or small-leaved stalked plants languishing from lack of light in tall aquaria. For brevity, tank heights are grouped into three types.

AH = 1   Small aquaria up to 35 cm (14") in height.
AH = 2   Medium aquaria up to about 45 cm (18") in height.
AH = 3   Large aquaria more than 45 cm (18") in height.

1. Plants with Upright Stems

1.1 Leaves Alternate

Eichhornia natans   (BEAUVOIS) SOLMS-LAUBACH (1882)

Fam.: Pontederiaceae

Hab.: Tropical Africa.

Main axis is erect, later becoming natant. Aquatic leaves are alternate (opposite) with those at the apex usually arranged in a spiral. Blade is entire and clasping, up to 6 cm long, 0.7 cm wide, and narrowing uniformly towards its obtuse tip. There are 3–4 fine veins between each of the 5 main veins. Floating leaves are broad, cordate, and 4 cm long and wide with a cordate and overlapping base. Peduncle grows up to 6 cm long and has a 3 cm sheath at its base. Inflorescences are situated in the axils and are reduced to one small, blue, 6 petaled flower on each.

Either suitable as a submersed aquatic plant or in its natant form. It is extremely difficult to cultivate, quickly perishing in hard water. Very soft water is a prerequisite. Under proper conditions, the submersed leaves are long-lived. However, it tends to regularly develop floating leaves. Small flowers are produced in its natant form under strong illumination. *Eichhornia diversifolia* is a significantly better aquarium plant. It was presented in Vol. 2, p. 48.

Prop.: Lateral shoots.

D: 4, **KH**: 2–4, **pH**: 5.5–6.5, **T**: 22°–25°C, **AH**: 1–2

Hydrocotyle lemnoides   BENTHAM (1868)

Fam.: Apiaceae

Hab.: Australia.

The thin shoot is upright when submersed. Leaves are alternate, reniform to roundish, indented at the base, and up to 1 cm wide with 3 notched cuneate lobes. Each blade is supported by a short petiole. There are tiny umbels in the axils with 4–5 small, often imperfect flowers. An adaptable, easily grown aquarium plant. Even new water rarely causes problems. Although the stems are not expressly light-demanding, they should nevertheless be exposed to direct light. Besides the submersed form, there is a floating form. Its thin, creeping, emersed shoots make a good ground cover in bog aquaria.

Prop.: Self-branching of the shoots.

D: 1, **KH**: 2–15, **pH**: 6.0–7.8, **T**: 22°–28°C, **AH**: 1–3

Eichhornia natans

Hydrocotyle lemnoides

1. Plants with Upright Stems

1.1 Leaves Alternate

Mayaca sellowiana KUNTH (1843)

Fam.: Mayacaceae

Hab.: South America.

Leaves are linear, pointed, up to 1.5 cm long, 0.15 cm wide, and arranged in alternate spirals. Blade is single veined. The upper side of the leaf is light green, while the underside is light pink. The land form is prostrate with needle-shaped aerial leaves. Flowers are single and axile with 3 white petals, 3 yellow short filamented stamens, and a very short style with a tiny stigma.

A delicate plant for moderately tall aquaria that fulfill its requirements. Soft water is preferred; light requirement is high. Let it grow undisturbed, regularly trimming the surface-reaching shoots and planting anew. In time, dense decorative bunches form.

Prop.: Self-branching.

D: 3, KH: 2–5, pH: 5.5–6.8, T: 24°–26°C, AH: 1–2

Potamogeton pusillus LINNE (1753)

Fam.: Potamogetonaceae

Hab.: Europe, Asia, Africa, America.

The thin elongated main shoot is richly branched. Leaves are slender, up to 6 cm long, 0.2 cm wide, and pointed with 1–3 fine, longitudinal veins emerging from the base. The spike grows up to 0.7 cm long and bears few blooms. This is one of the few *Potamogeton* of temperate latitudes that can be kept in the aquarium for extended periods of time, largely due to the fact that these plants are often found in warm subtropical regions. Intense illumination is suggested. Grouped shoots will soon develop lateral shoots which grow into an extensive stand. Densely intertwined mats result in the garden pond, where this hardy aquatic plant grows well.

Prop.: Lateral shoots.

D: 2, KH: 5–12, pH: 6.0–7.5, T: 10°–25°C, AH: 1–3

Polygonum javanicum DE BRUYN

Fam.: Polygonaceae

Hab.: Southeast Asia.

Aquatic shoots are erect with divided, slender leaves. Blade is up to 9 cm long, 1.5 cm wide with a pointed tip, cuneate base, and finely serrate or ciliate edges. Running next to the main vein are 15 pairs of finer lateral veins. The inflorescence is branched and each short spike bears up to 20 small white blooms.

It is best to only use moderately long cuttings. These are introduced shallowly and left undisturbed to root. Aerial leaves, if present, quickly die. But by that time, sufficient aquatic leaves are generally present so that the plant can continue to grow.

The light requirement is high. Under moderate light, the shoots become excessively elongated and the leaves remain small.

Prop.: Lateral shoots.

D: 2, KH: 5–10, pH: 6.0–7.5, T: 22°–26°C, AH: 2

Mayaca sellowiana

Potamogeton pusillus

Polygonum javanicum

1. Plants with Upright Stems
1.1 Leaves Alternate

Saururus cernuus LINNE (1753)   Lizard-tail, water dragon, swamp lily

Fam.: Saururaceae — Lizard-tails

Hab.: States along the Atlantic seaboard of North America.

Leaves grow alternately on an erect axis. The variable-sized blade is between 5 and 10 cm long and 3–5 cm wide with a pointed tip.

A decorative, appreciated group plant that needs intense illumination. Other requirements are moderate. When decorating the aquarium, this plant can be used in a variety of ways. The simplest use for this species is to plant it in groups, but another method involves taking cuttings of various lengths and densely planting them with the shortest in the foreground and the tallest in the back, creating a "plant street." However, the latter method demands regular and intense care.

Prop.: Lateral shoots after cutting

D: 2, KH: 5–12, pH: 6.0–7.5, T: 22°–30°C, AH: 1–3

Zosterella dubia (JAQUIN) SMALL (1913)

Syn.: *Heteranthera dubia, Heteranthera graminea*

Fam.: Pontederiaceae

Hab.: Central America, southern North America.

The main axis is thin and elongated with long internodes. Leaves are linear, alternate, sessile, up to 12 cm long and 0.5 cm wide, entire, green to brown in color, and long tipped. The central vein is pronounced, while the lateral veins are faint. In the axils of floating shoots, there are single, pedunculated blooms. The flower is about 2 cm in diameter and has six linear, yellow petals. Terrestrial shoots creep in shallow water and produce fleshy aerial leaves. Undemanding plant when provided with unobstructed illumination, temperate temperatures, and water that is not overly soft water. Its elongated internodes allow for rapid upward growth, meaning shoots reach the water surface even in tall aquaria. Once the shoot reaches the surface, it continues growing in a natant fashion, providing a green zone in the upper water strata with its many lateral shoots. This rapidly growing plant has to be regularly trimmed. During the summer, *Zosterella* grows in the shallows of warm, bright ponds. There the dense mats produce numerous flowers.

Prop.: Cuttings from lateral shoots, self-branching.

D: 2, KH: 5–15, pH: 6.0–7.5, T: 15°–25°C, AH: 3

Saururus cernuus

Saururus cernuus, inflorescence

Zosterella dubia

Alternanthera philoxeroides GRISEBACH (1879)

Fam.: Amaranthaceae

Hab.: Argentina.

The main axis and leaves are green. Blades are petiolate, lanceolate, up to 4 cm long and 2 cm wide with a pointed base and tip. Several curved lateral veins emerge from the pronounced central vein. Short capitate (head-shaped) spikes with ca. 20 small white blooms are borne in the leaf axils.

This species sometimes appears in the trade mixed among other imported plants, as it is easily confused with *Hygrophila polysperma*. Little suited for aquaria, since submersed shoots become highly elongated and break the water surface in a few weeks. This process is postponed if the water is kept cool. Generally considered a plant for either bog aquaria or garden ponds. There it forms beautiful, bushy specimens.

Prop.: Lateral shoots.

D: 4, KH: 2–15, pH: 6.0–8.0, T: 15°–20°C, AH: 3

Alternanthera reineckii BRIQUET (1899)

Type: Slender red

Syn.: *Alternanthera sessilis* red

Fam.: Amaranthaceae

Hab.: South America.

This plant was erroneously identified as *A. sessilis* and presented as such in earlier editions of Vol. 1, pp. 92–93.

Aquatic leaves are slender, up to 10 cm long, about 1 cm wide with sinuate edges, a pointed tip, and a base that elongates into a short petiole. Its blade is olive green to brown-red superiorly and wine red inferiorly. This is the best variety of *A. reineckii* for aquaria. Easily adapts to various conditions. Under intense illumination, the plant is more compact and darker red. Large aquaria are more effective for group plants, where they can serve as an excellent point of emphasis in the decor.

Prop.: Cuttings.

D: 2, KH: 2–12, pH: 5.5–7.2, T: 24°–30°C, AH: 2–3

Alternanthera reineckii BRIQUET (1899)

Type: Red-green

Fam.: Amaranthaceae

Hab.: Tropical South America.

An extremely variable species which is divided into different varieties based on leaf shape and color. The variety presented here has characteristic aquatic leaves that are distinctly divergent in color with a green center and dark red edges. Blade is about 8 cm long and 3 cm wide with a pointed tip and base. Because of the green portions of the leaves, this variety is less demanding than, for example, the red *Alternanthera "lilacina,"* which is likewise a variety of *A. reineckii*. See Vol. 1, pp. 92–93.

A large terraced group provides a striking decorative effect. Refrain from planting the cuttings too close to one another.

Prop.: Lateral shoots after cutting.

D: 2, KH: 2–10, pH: 5.5–7.2, T: 24°–30°C, AH: 2–3

Alternanthera philoxeroides

Alternanthera rulnockii, slender red

Alternanthera reineckii, red-green

21

Alternanthera sessilis   (LINNAEUS) DE CANDOLLE (1836)

Fam.: Amaranthaceae

Hab.: Tropics of the Old and New World.

Basically it has to be said that this plant will not adapt to submersed life and is therefore totally unsuited for aquaria. Its inappropriateness will not be readily apparent, since it maintains its beauty for several weeks before it begins to dissolve. The bog aquarium represents a better environment. The main axis and leaves are naked, bright red, and shiny. Blades are obtuse, up to 10 cm long and 1 cm wide. Small blood-red clusters of blooms develop in their axils.

Prop.: Cuttings.

D: 4, **KH**: 2–15, **pH**: 6.0–8.0, **T**: 20°–25°C, **AH**: 2–3

Bacopa lanigera   (CHAMISSO et SCHLECHTENDAHL) WETTSTEIN (1891)

Type: Green-leaved

Fam.: Scrophulariaceae

Hab.: Brazil.

Leaves and stems of the terrestrial form are densely pilose. Blades are sessile, round-ish-oval, up to 3 cm long and 2.5 cm wide, and light green. The leaf base clasps and overlaps the stem. The single pedunculated blooms are 0.5 cm in diameter with a violet upper labia and a lower labia that is either white with violet venation or totally violet. There is a variety with yellow-veined blades which was previously introduced in Vol. 2, pp. 30–31. That variety as well as this one is virtually impossible to adapt to aquatic life. Successful cultivation is contingent on intense illumination and CO_2 and iron fertilization.

Prop.: Cuttings.

D: 4, **KH**: 2–8, **pH**: 6.0–7.0, **T**: 20°–24°C, **AH**: 1–2

Bacopa monnieri   (LINNE) PENNELL (1891)

Type: Crenate

Fam.: Scrophulariaceae

Hab.: Africa.

Blades are oval, up to 2 cm long and 0.8 cm wide, with a petiolelike slender base and a rounded tip. Unlike the nominate form with entire leaves, this type has crenate blades. It was first imported from Africa in 1975. This plant does not have the status of species or variety. However, it is more suitability as an aquarium plant than the familiar nominate form. An excellent subject for dense terraces, but intense illumination is needed for tight growth.

Prop.: Cuttings, lateral shoots after cutting.

D: 1, **KH**: 2–15, **pH**: 6.0–7.5, **T**: 22°–30°C, **AH**: 1–3

Crassula aquatica   (LINNE) SCHÖNLAND (1891)

Fam.: Crassulaceae

Hab.: Europe, North America, Siberia.

The slender clasping submersed leaves are up to 2 cm long, 0.15 cm wide, sessile, and slightly arched. They are supported by a thin elongated axil. Aerial leaves are shorter, succulent, smooth, and shiny. Almost extinct in nature. Occasionally, pond-cultivated plants are sold in pet stores. This is a delicate group plant for cold to temperate aquaria. At higher temperatures, the shoots become progressively weaker. A good addition for the garden pond. Bog plants are annuals, while aquatic plants are perennials.

Prop.: Cuttings.

D: 3, **KH**: 2–15, **pH**: 6.0–7.8, **T**: 15°–22°C, **AH**: 1–2

Alternanthera sessilis

Bacopa lanigera green-leaved

Bacopa monnieri crenate

Crassula aquatica

Hygrophila polysperma   ANDERS (1867)   Dwarf Hygrophila

Type: Brown-red

Fam.: Acanthaceae — Acanthus

Hab.: India.

Aquatic leaves are narrowly lanceolate, up to 8 cm long, 0.6 wide, and have a short petiole and a pointed tip. Depending on the illumination, leaf color varies from dark green to brown to olive green. This type was imported for the first time in 1977 and positively identified based on flowering specimens. It differs from the green nominate form that has been imported since 1948 and was introduced in Vol. 1, pp. 98 and 99. Aerial leaves are shorter, lanceolate, brown to dark green, and wavy to crisp. Both the short-bracteate terminal spike and the flowers correspond in morphology to the nominate form.

When this plant receives strong, unobstructed light, its leaves are dark brown, creating an interesting color contrast to green plants. The main shoots have numerous branches and quickly create a dense bush. Insure that the plant receives direct light. Prune the shoots regularly and plant anew.

Prop.: Lateral shoots, cuttings, self-branching.

D: 2, KH: 2–10, pH: 6.0–7.5, T: 22°–28°C, AH: 2–3

Hygrophila corymbosa   (BLUME) LINDAU (1885)   Afrikanischer Wasserfreund

Fam.: Acanthaceae — Acanthus   Syn.: *Hygrophila stricta*

Hab.: Africa (Senegal).

This plant was imported for the first time in 1977. Aquatic leaves are lanceolate, short-stalked, up to 17 cm long and 2.5 cm wide, uniformly tapering from the center to both ends. The relation of length to width is about 5.5 to 1. In comparison thereof, the blades of the Asian form are about 7 times as long as wide (15 x 2 cm). Emersed leaves are about 7 x 1.8 cm in size, pointed on both ends, and dark green. Like the Asian form, this plant has clusters of blooms in the leaf axils. However, the clusters only consist of 5–7 blooms. Young leaves are slightly reddish and pilose along the edges, but otherwise naked. The aquatic form is difficult to identify. Some of the other *Hygrophila* species are very similar. The Asian form of *H. stricta* has narrower leaves, and *H. corymbosa* has shorter, broader aquatic blades.

Excellent aquatic plant that adapts well to almost all conditions. The fast growing shoots have short internodes, producing a leafy, compact solitary plant. Its easy propagation makes this plant eminently suitable for extensive groups in roomy aquaria.

Prop.: Lateral shoots.

D: 1, KH: 2–15, pH: 6.5–7.5, T: 24°–30°C, AH: 2–3

Hygrophila polysperma, brown-red

Hygrophila corymbosa, Africa

Ludwigia palustris   (LINNE) ELLIOTT (1821)

Fam.: Onagraceae — Evening primroses

Hab.: Europe, western Asia, Mediterranean region, North America.

The axis bears paired, lanceolate to ovate, pointed aerial leaves. Yellow-green, small, crownless blooms are borne in the leaf axils. Different varieties, primarily distributed in North America, are described for this species: var. *elongata* with large leaves, var. *longifolia* with long, slender leaves, and var. *rotundifolia* with round leaves.

While European *Ludwigia* is not normally used as an aquarium plant, it can nevertheless be easily cultivated. Provide the plant with intense light and moderate temperatures. Cuttings off terrestrial plants generally adapt to the aquatic environment without major difficulties.

Prop.: Lateral shoots.

D: 2, KH: 2–10, pH: 6.0–7.5, T: 20°–25°C, AH: 1–3

Ludwigia repens   FORSTER (1771)   Creeping ludwigia, false loosestrife

Fam.: Onagraceae — Evening primroses

Hab.: Southern North America, Central America, Caribbean.

This species has several geographical morphs or types that do not have the status of variety. For our purposes, the forms are differentiated according to leaf morphology and coloration.

1. Slender-leaved reddish form.
Leaves are lanceolate, elliptical, 3 cm long and 1 cm wide, with a pointed tip and a base that narrows into the petiole. Upper side of the leaf is olive green or, depending on the light, partially reddish. Underside is reddish.

2. Slender-leaved green form.
Leaves are similar to the form above, but they are dark green superiorly and green, not reddish, inferiorly.

3. Round-leaved reddish form.
Leaves are elliptical to roundish, up to 4 cm long and 3.5 cm wide, with a roundish base that narrows into the petiole. The leaf tip is short and curved. Upper side of the leaf is olive green or, depending on the light, partially dark red. Underside is dark red. This form was presented in Vol. 1, pp. 98 and 99.

4. Round-leaved green form.
Leaves elongated to roundish, up to 3 cm long and 2 cm wide, with an arched base and a short, pointed, arched tip. Upper side of the blade is green, rarely light olive green, and lacks red tones. The lower side of the blade is a light green, not reddish.

All forms are undemanding and adaptive aquarium plants and recommended for the aquarium without reservations. Reddish forms seem to be more light requiring than green forms. Plant this species in groups, since the fast growing shoots branch readily and form a dense stand. Regularly shorten and plant the cuttings.

Prop.: Cuttings, self-branching.

D: 1, KH: 2–15, pH: 5.5–7.5, T: 20°–30°C, AH: 2–3

Ludwigia palustris

Ludwigia repens, slender green form

Ludwigia repens, slender red form

Najas flexilis (WILLDENOW) ROSTKOVIUS et SCHMIDT (1824)

Fam.: Najadaceae

Hab.: Europe, Mediterranean.

Main axis thin, smooth, and flexible. Leaves are linear, occasionally arched back, up to 2 cm long and 0.1 cm wide, with a pointed tip, 2 longitudinal veins, and up to 40 fine teeth along the edge. The angular sheath at the base of the leaf has 5 tiny, pointed teeth. Annuals in nature, but perennials in aquaria. Recommended for cool to moderately warm, brightly lit aquaria. Dense bunches will form in time. This plant will also form a natant mat just beneath the water surface, providing a spawning substrate for many fish species. Adapts easily to different water values. Rarely cultivated in aquaria.

Prop.: Self-branching.

D: 2, KH: 2–15, pH: 6.0–7.8, T: 15°–22°C, AH: 1–3

1. Plants with Upright Stems

1.3 Leaves in a Whorl

Hydrilla verticillata var. *crispa* CASPARY

Fam.: Hydrocharitaceae

Hab.: Southeast Asia, Indonesia, Australia, Africa, Europe.

Main shoot is thin and slightly brittle with whorls of 3–9, sessile, slender lanceolate, acuminate, up to 2.5 cm long and 0.6 cm wide, coarsely dentate leaves. This variety has very arched blades with crisp (curled) edges. It has been described as an autonomous species (*Udora lithuanica*). Short cuttings can be used in an open site in the foreground. Under bright illumination, the shoots grow horizontally, later developing into dense moderately high stands.

Prop.: Cuttings, lateral shoots.

D: 1, KH: 2–15, pH: 5.0–7.8, T: 15°–28°C, AH: 1–3

Ludwigia repens, roundish-green

Najas flexilis

Hydrilla verticillata var. *crispa*

Limnophila heterophylla   BENTHAM (1835)

Fam.: Scrophulariaceae

Hab.: India, Pakistan, Sri Lanka, Indonesia, south China.

The main shoot bears whorls of 5–13 leaves that are pinnate and opposite with lower pinna pinnate and upper pinna forked. Tips are up to 0.2 cm wide, not broadened. The length of the last segment surpasses both tips below. Leaf segments are twisted, often resulting in the light underside of the leaf being partially turned up. Under insufficient illumination, this plant deteriorates into the nominate form, presented in Vol. 2, pp. 22 and 23.

Excellent group plant for an open central section of the aquarium. The older stand is opportunely rejuvenated with cuttings of the new tips.

Prop.: Cuttings from lateral shoots, runner-like lateral shoots.

D: 2, **KH:** 2–10, **pH:** 6.0–7.2, **T:** 22°–28°C, **AH:** 2–3

Limnophila indica   (LINNE) DRUCE (1923)   Indian Ambulia

Fam.: Scrophulariaceae

Hab.: Tropical regions of Africa, Southeast Asia, Australia.

Several forms of this widely distributed species have been described. The plant presented in Vol. 2, p. 23 is a delicate form of *L. indica*. The type species is pictured and briefly described here. Whorls are up to 5 cm wide and are composed of 6–12 leaves that are simple pinnate with forked proximal segments. These segments are about 2 mm wide, and the final segment surpasses both of those below by almost half their length. An adaptive, decorative aquarium plant that makes an excellent point of contrast.

Prop.: Cuttings from lateral shoots.

D: 2, **KH:** 2–12, **pH:** 6.0–7.5, **T:** 22°–28°C, **AH:** 3

Nitella flexilis   (LINNE) AGARDH (1824)

Fam.: Characeae

Hab.: Europe, Asia, America.

The slender, stalklike main axis has short shoots that in turn have whorls of 1–6 leaves. But these "leaves" are actually lateral shoots which are either bifurcate or trifurcate. The leaves are apiculate.

An extremely easily cultivated aquatic plant that is even suitable for very hard water. *Nitella* is generally used in coldwater tanks, but higher temperatures are also tolerated. However, when grown under the latter conditions, the shoots are very thin and weak. Planted shoots will take root, but their brittle nature makes them better kept natant. Lateral shoots help form dense drifting mats that serve as a spawning substrate and a subsequent shelter for young fishes. Supposedly they also condition the water.

Prop.: Lateral shoots.

D: 1, **KH:** 2–15, **pH:** 5.5–7.5, **T:** 10°–22°C, **AH:** 1–3

Limnophila heterophylla

Limnophila indica

Nitella flexilis

Acorus gramineus SOLANDER (1789) Japanese rush

Fam.: Araceae

Hab.: East Asia.

Rhizome is elongated and up to 1 cm thick. Leaves are basal, linear, 50 cm long, 1 cm wide, dark green, with a long, pointed tip, and arranged in a fanlike fashion. An upright 20 cm stem supports the 10 cm spadix and its pointed bract. Small, whitish perfect flowers densely cover the spadix.
Use of this plant is limited, since it will not grow submersed. Therefore, to maintain this plant as a decorative aquarium addition, it must be regularly exchanged for fresh specimens that have been growing terrestrially. Rooted, potted plants are buried in the substrate, pot and all.

Prop.: Lateral shoots off the rhizome.

D: 4, KH: 2–15, pH: 5.5–8.5, T: 15°–20°C, AH: 1–3

Acorus gramineus SOLANDER (1789) Japanese rush

Type: *Aureovariegatus*

Fam.: Araceae

Hab.: Cultivated plant.

Leaves are linear, 40 cm long, 1 cm wide with a long pointed tip and arranged in a fanlike fashion. The main characteristic is the golden to light yellow longitudinal striation along the blade. Like the nominate form, this type is only suitable as an exchange plant. It is usually sold for coldwater aquaria, where it remains alive for extended periods of time. A good winter hardy pond plant. Type *argenteostriatus* is similar but has silver-white stripes along the blade.

Prop.: Lateral shoots on the rhizome.

D: 4, KH: 2–15, pH: 5.5–8.5, T: 15°–20°C, AH: 1–3

Blyxa octandra (ROXBURGH) PLANCHES ex THWAITES (1902)

Fam.: Hydrocharitaceae

Hab.: Sri Lanka, India, Burma, southeast Asia, northern Australia.

The basal rhizome produces a dense rosette. In its natural biotope, the grasslike leaves are up to 60 cm long and 1 cm wide. However, the leaves are considerably smaller on aquarium forms, reaching a mere 15 cm in length and 0.5 cm in width. Flowers are imperfect. Male blooms have 9 stamens. Seeds have 8 rows of tiny hook-shaped thorns.
Very difficult to grow, usually only enduring a few months in the aquarium. Soft water and intense illumination of about 100 watts per 100 l of water are mandatory. Due to its extremely brittle leaves, handle with care and only associate with sedate fishes.

Prop.: Lateral shoots off the rhizome.

D: 4, KH: 1–3, pH: 5.5–6.5, T: 22°–26°C, AH: 1–2

Acorus gramineus

Acorus gramineus, aureovariegatus

Blyxa octandra

2. Plants with Leaves in a Rosette
2.1 Narrow-Leaved Rosettes

Crinum sp. "Tortifolia"
Fam.: Amaryllidaceae
Hab.: Africa.

The up to 5 cm thick tuber has a bulblike 20 cm long projection. Leaves are light green, thin, and up to 50 cm long and 2 cm wide. As the plant grows, the leaves begin to curl from the bottom. The first specimens were imported in 1974, but the species has not been identified. In nature, it is constantly submersed. This notorious plant should be planted totally in the open and further accented with contrasting plants. Water depth should be at least 45 cm; otherwise, young leaves grow above the water surface and wither. Moderate requirements generally lead to uncomplicated care.

Prop.: Lateral tubers on the rhizome.

D: 2, KH: 2–15, pH: 6.0–7.5, T: 24°–28°C, AH: 3

Isoetes lacustris LINNE (1753)
Fam.: Isoetaceae — Quillworts
Hab.: Europe, northern Asia, North America.

Leaves are dark green, widely spread, 25 cm long and 0.3 cm wide, with a cylindrical cross-section. Tapered. The tip is slightly hooked, while the base is somewhat spoon-shaped.
This is a small plant for the foreground of shallow temperate aquaria. The very brittle leaves require cautious handling, so do not associate with robust fishes. Best kept in aquaria that house peaceful, cool water characins.
Acid water is required for continued healthy growth.

Prop.: Unknown for aquarium plants; otherwise through spores.

D: 4, KH: 2–5, pH: 5.0–6.0, T: 18°–22°C, AH: 1–2

Isoetes velata var. *sicula* CESATI et DE NOTARIS apud GENNARI (1861)
Fam.: Isoetaceae — Quillworts
Hab.: Western Mediterranean region.

The name has now been corrected (Kasselmann). Vol. 2, pp. 58 and 59 lists the plant as being *Isoetes malinverniana,* which is incorrect. That species is little suited for tropical aquaria. The medium green leaves usually grow to a length of 40 cm and a width of ca. 2 mm in the aquarium. Cross-section of the leaf is roundish to semicircular, not angular. Exterior leaves are laterally bent towards the bottom before they rise again in a slight spiral. Easiest quillwort to cultivate in an aquarium.

Prop.: Spores; extremely difficult.

D: 2, KH: 2–10, pH: 5.5–7.0, T: 22°–28°C, AH: 3

Isoetes lacustris

Crinum sp. "Tortifolia"

Isoetes velata

2. Plants with Leaves in a Rosette
2.1 Narrow-Leaved Rosettes

Vallisneria americana var. *biwaensis*   MICHAUX (MIKI) LOWDEN (1982)

Type: Broad-twisted   Syn.: *Vallisneria asiatica*

Fam.: Hydrocharitaceae

Hab.: Southeast Asia.

Leaves are ribbonlike, twisted several times, 25–30 cm long and up to 2 cm wide, with an obtuse and rounded tip. Usually only dentate along the edges near the tip. First imported into Germany in 1975. This species has not yet been identified. It could be a variant of *V. asiatica*. Adaptive group plants that can also be used in shallow aquaria. Growth tends to be compact when the plants are loosely planted and grown under moderate temperatures and intense illumination. When one or more of these criteria are not met, the plants grow taller and no longer have their characteristic twisted leaves. Numerous adventitious plants form intertwined dense groups that will need to be thinned occasionally. Insure proper iron levels and do not cultivate in extremely soft waters.

Prop.: Runners with numerous daughter plants.

D: 1 KH: 5–12, pH: 6.0–7.5, T: 22°–25°C, AH: 2–3

Vallisneria spiralis var. *spiralis*   LINNAEUS (1753)

Fam.: Hydrocharitaceae   Syn.: *Vallisneria aethiopica*

Hab.: Africa (central and east Sudan)

Blades are linear, usually somewhat twisted distally, 5–12 cm long and up to 0.4 cm wide, with serrate, undulate edges, and an acute tip. This species was first imported into Germany in 1977, but identification has not been confirmed with flowering specimens. In nature it grows in shallow, cool waters.

This *Vallisneria* enriches the assortment of available small plants for the foreground. Adapts to general aquarium conditions quite well, but demands bright light. When brightly illuminated, growth is compact and the plants reproduce copiously. Seldom cultivated.

Prop.: Daughter plants from runners, but less numerous than those of most other species of the genus.

D: 2, KH: 5–12, pH: 6.0–7.5, T: 22°–28°C, AH: 1–2

Vallisneria americana var. *biwaensis*

Vallisneria spiralis var. *spiralis*

Anubias barteri var. *glabra*   N. E. BROWN (1901)

Type: "Minimus"

Syn.: *Anubias minima*

Fam.: Araceae

Hab.: Tropical west Africa.

The flat, creeping rhizome grows up to 5 mm in diameter. Blades are lanceolate, 5–10 cm long and 2–5 cm wide, with a pointed tip, and a cuneate base. Short petioles. *A. minima* CHEVALIER, 1909 was previously considered an autonomous species. Crusio, who published a revision of the genus *Anubias,* did not recognize *A. minima.* Instead, he classified the plant as a type, not a variety, of *A. barteri* var. *glabra.* Its height of 10–15 cm makes it suitable for small, shallow tanks. Well-rooted specimens grow well.

Prop.: While its natural tendency is not to grow lateral shoots, cutting the rhizome induces the back part of the rhizome that remains in the substrate to generate a new shoot.

D: 2, KH: 2–12, pH: 6.0–7.5, T: 22°–28°C, AH: 1–3

Anubias heterophylla   ENGLER (1879)

Syn.: *Anubias congensis*

Fam.: Araceae

Hab.: Tropical west Africa.

The blade is narrow to broadly lanceolate, up to 20 cm long, 10 cm wide (aerial leaves 30 x 15 cm), and tapered to slightly rounded towards the base, with a short pointed tip. Spathe up to 5 cm long and whitish on the inside. Spadix about equal in length to the spathe with the female part slightly shorter than the male segment. When left undisturbed and provided with favorable living conditions, this plant will become quite large. In shallow aquaria, the leaves readily break the water surface. General adaptation is good. Appropriate illumination and a correct photoperiod should be provided.

Prop.: Lateral shoots off the rhizome.

D: 2, KH: 2–15, pH: 6.0–7.5, T: 22°–26°C, AH: 3

Nymphaea lotus x *lotus*

Fam.: Nymphaeaceae

Hab.: Southeast Asia (Thailand).

Both the green and red tiger lotus (*Nymphaea lotus*) are common aquarium plants that can adapt to submersed growth. This plant, a cross between the green and red tiger lotus, is likewise adaptable to life in aquaria. Blade coloration is not always uniform. It tends to be a faded brown-red with dark spots. Hybrid flowers produce seeds that germinate and yield 25% green, 25% red, and 50% hybrids (a textbook example of Mendel's hereditary laws). The solid color plants are homozygous and therefore generate solid-colored offspring. The hybrid plants again produce a variety of offspring when sexually reproduced.

D: 2, KH: 2–10, pH: 5.5–7.5, T: 22°–28°C, AH: 2–3

Anubias barteri var. *glabra*, "Minimus"

Anubias heterophylla

Nymphaea lotus x *lotus*

2. Plants with Leaves in a Rosette

2.1 Broad-Leaved Rosettes

Nymphoides cordata (ELLIOT) FERNALD

Fam.: Menyanthaceae

Hab.: Newfoundland to Florida.

The cylindrical, banana-shaped dark green tubers at the base of the plant are much more slender and pointed than those of *N. aquatica*. Aquatic leaves are shiny green, occasionally with brownish speckles, up to 15 cm wide, roundish with a cordate base, and borne on short petioles. Floating leaves—similar to those of *N. aquatica*— are up to 20 cm wide and supported by long petioles.

This species can exist very well in its aquatic form without immediately growing floating leaves, but the plant will need to be placed in a free area and left to produce its decorative aquatic leaves undisturbed. Soft water and intense illumination are additional conditions for submersed growth. Remove the floating leaves at the base as they form.

Prop.: Adventitious shoots off flowered petioles from the floating leaves.

D: 3, KH: 3–8, pH: 5.5–7.0, T: 20°–27°C, AH: 2–3

Spathiphyllum grandifolius

Fam.: Araceae

Hab.: South America.

Since *Spathiphyllum* are very difficult to identify, the systematics of this species are not definite. Petiolate leaves emerge off a stout rhizome. Blades are elongated to broadly-lanceolate, up to 40 cm long, 25 cm wide, with both ends pointed, and a slightly undulate edge. Petiole about 40 cm long. Spathe is white, 15 cm long, and wide open.

Terrestrial specimens are often unable to adapt to submersed life, loosing their leaves after just a few days. Young specimens rooted in a pot and maintained in sunlight for about 4 weeks in a plastic bag usually have less problems and, since they are capable of maintaining their leaves for a longer period underwater, it allows the plant more time to form new leaves.

D: 4, KH: 2–10, pH: 6.0–7.0, T: 20°–25°C, AH: 3

Spiranthes odorata (NUTALL) LINDLEY (1840)

Fam.: Orchideaceae   Syn.: *Spiranthes cernua*

Hab.: Southern North America.

Small rosette plant with blades that are lanceolate, medium green, 10–15 cm long and 1–2 cm wide, with a pointed tip, and a tapered stalklike base. Flowers are generally produced by terrestrial plants, but they have been known to form on submersed aquarium plants as well. The 40 cm peduncle pushes the bud above the water. The spiral, 10 cm spike bears numerous small white blooms (orchids). Afterwards the leaf rosette dies. New plants arise from the rhizome. An appropriate small plant for the foreground. Healthy growth requires medium-hard water, sufficient illumination, and a moderately coarse substrate.

Prop.: Daughter plants on the rhizome after flowering and the root tips.

D: 2, KH: 2–12, pH: 6.0–7.0, T: 22°–26°C, AH: 1–3

Nymphoides cordata

Spathiphyllum grandifolius

Spiranthes odorata

2. Plants with Leaves in a Rosette

Echinodorus tenellus   (MARTIUS) BUCHENAU (1868)   Red tenellus

Fam.: Alismataceae

Hab.: Central America, southern Brazil.

The dwarf form of this plant (*E. t.* var. *parvulus*), which is the more difficult of the two to cultivate, was presented in Vol. 1, pp. 126 and 127.
This aquarium plant was identified as variety *tenellus* in 1975 based on its flowers and seeds. Aquatic leaves are up to 12 cm long, 0.2 cm wide, and dark green, occasionally red when young (known as red tenellus to aquarists). The up to 5 cm long aerial leaves are about 0.5 cm wide and are clearly more slender at the tip than the base. Peduncle is usually 1.5 times as long as the blade, but equal or shorter than the blade in the dwarf form. Extremely adaptive aquarium plant which is becoming more common in the aquarium hobby. At a height of about 10 cm, this variant is appropriate for the foreground and to create large green areas. Adapts well to hard water, and its light requirement is normal.

Prop.: Runners with numerous daughter plants.

D: 1, **KH:** 2–15, **pH:** 6.5–7.5, **T:** 22°–28°C, **AH:** 1–3

Echinodorus pellucidus   RATAJ (1974)

Fam.: Alismataceae

Hab.: Paraguay, Argentina, southern Brazil.

This rare, medium-sized bog plant does not always make a good aquarium plant. Only recommended for plant specialists. Aerial leaves are elliptical, up to 11 cm long and 5 cm wide, with a base that is occasionally cordate, and a long petiole. Inflorescence is erect, infrequently branched basally, up to 60 cm long with a row of 1.5 cm blooms that have 24–28 stamens. Aquatic leaves are elliptical, up to 12 cm long and 3 cm wide, with a pointed, rarely rounded, base, and a short, obtuse tip. Petioles are frequently significantly longer than the blades. Usually 3 very faint longitudinal veins emerge from the base. Young developing leaves have irregular brown spots, while older leaves are olive green to dark green. Some specimens will grow to be 35 cm tall. Large plants such as this must be placed in the open. If grown under crowded conditions, the blades grow above the water surface and are borne on overly long petioles. Cut these stems, but do not transplant at the same time.

Prop.: Separate lateral shoots from the rhizome and plant singly. Such juveniles usually grow short-stalked leaves for an extended period of time.

D: 3, **KH:** 5–12, **pH:** 6.5–7.2, **T:** 22°–28°C, **AH:** 3

Echinodorus tenellus

Echinodorus pellucidus

2. Plants with Leaves in a Rosette

Cryptocoryne aponogetifolia MERRIL (1919)

Fam.: Araceae

Hab.: Philippines.

This species was incorrectly identified as *Cryptocoryne usteriana* and introduced as such in Vol. 1, pp. 136 and 137. Research done by J. Bogner (Munich) proved the autonomy of the species. The linear leaves of *C. aponogetifolia* grow 100 cm long and 5 cm wide and are pilose over their entire length. Even aquarium specimens may flower. The spathe, depending on the water level, reaches a height of 30–50 cm and sits on a 20 cm peduncle. Flag is about 8 cm long, purple-red, wrinkled, lighter through the throat region, and lacks a collar.

Robust plants that adapt well to captivity. This plant, which becomes quite voluminous, requires a roomy tank with at least 60 cm of water. Best placed on the side or in the back section of the tank. Generally the long leaves drift along the water surface.

Prop.: Daughter plants from runners are numerous and fast growing.

D: 2, **KH:** 2–15, **pH:** 6.0–7.8, **T:** 20°–30°C, **AH:** 3

Cryptocoryne auriculata ENGLER (1897)

Fam.: Araceae

Hab.: Northeast Borneo, southwest Philippines.

Small bog plant with elongated oval or small ovate leaves that are up to 9 cm long and 3 cm wide with a round to cordate base and a long, tapered acute tip. Superior side of the leaf is light green with dark crossbands. Spathe is 3 cm long, flag 2 cm, wide open, somewhat twisted, white, throat equally colored, without collar. Aquatic leaves are elongated, ovate, somewhat bullate, up to 5 cm long, 3 cm wide, and slightly cordate at the base, with an obtuse, pointed tip. These dark green leaves have an even darker green design when placed under strong illumination from above.

Aquarium plants are only a few centimeters tall; the leaves frequently lie almost prostrate. Due to its reduced ability to adapt, it is quite difficult to cultivate, especially under weak illumination. Little growth will occur under these conditions. Sensitive to suboptimal water values. Rarely imported. In its native waters, it grows in the cracks of rock terraces in river beds and in humid shady clefts on sites that are periodically inundated.

Prop.: Daughter plant production is very moderate. Growth is slow.

D: 4, **KH:** 2–8, **pH:** 5.5–6.8, **T:** 25°–28°C, **AH:** 1–2

Cryptocoryne aponogetifolia

Cryptocoryne auriculata

Cryptocoryne ciliata var. *latifolia*   RATAJ (1975)

Fam.: Araceae

Hab.: Southeast Asia (Celebes).

Blade is broadly lanceolate, short-stalked, solid green, up to 15 cm long and 8 cm wide, with a cordate base, and a short, pointed tip. The petiole, as a rule, is equal in length to the blade. Spathe is similar to that of *C. ciliata* var. *ciliata,* but the cilia along the edge of the blade are simple, according to Rataj. In comparison to the taller nominate form (see Vol. 1, pp. 132 and 133), this broad-leaved variant remains more compact. Acclimating the land form to an aquatic environment is somewhat time consuming, largely due to its high light requirement.

Prop.: Daughter plants are rare, and runners are not produced. In the axils of older leaves, short lateral shoots grow, which can be removed and planted; however, they are very slow growing.

D: 2, KH: 2–12, pH: 6.0–7.0, T: 22°–26°C, AH: 2–3

Cryptocoryne crispatula   ENGLER (1920)

Fam.: Araceae

Hab.: Northeast India, Thailand.

Erroneously identified as *C. retrospiralis,* a name it has become known by in aquarium literature. However, that species is an entirely different plant with extremely slender leaves (3 mm) and is totally unsuitable for aquaria. *C. crispatula*'s linear leaves are 60 cm long and 1.5 cm wide with a relatively broad central vein. Submersed plants occur in deep, fast-flowing waters. Well suited for the background of tall aquaria. Adapts to general conditions well, and cultivation has proven to be unproblematic.

Prop.: Daughter plants on runners are numerous and fast growing.

D: 1, KH: 2–15, pH: 6.0–7.5, T: 25°–28°C, AH: 3

Cryptocoryne x *willisii*   REITZ (1908)

Fam.: Araceae   Syn.: *Cryptocoryne lucens*

Hab.: Sri Lanka.

The lanceolate leaves are solid green, up to 10 cm long, 0.6 cm wide, and uniformly tapered distally into a long tip. Spathe up to 7 cm long, flag up to 2 cm long, roundish, broad and obtuse, slightly twisted, warty, dark purple, throat darker, with a collar. This small species is used as a foreground plant. Substrate heating, fertilization, and strong illumination greatly foster growth.

Prop.: Moderate formation of daughter plants on runners and only off well-rooted mother plants.

D: 2, KH: 2–10, pH: 6.0–7.2, T: 25°–28°C, AH: 1–2

Cryptocoryne ciliata var. *latifolia*

Cryptocoryne crispatula

Cryptocoryne x *willisii*

Cryptocoryne minima RIDLEY (1910)

Fam.: Araceae

Hab.: Malay Peninsula.

Aerial leaves are ovate to narrowly ovate, pointed, rounded at the base, up to 4 cm long, 2.5 cm wide, matte green, slightly bullate, and purple on the inferior side. Spathe remains very small, tube about 1 cm long, flag somewhat longer and matte yellow with brown dots. Throat is darker, shiny, with a collar.

Leaf shape in aquatic specimens and terrestrial plants is largely the same. However, aquatic blades are smooth and slightly olive green with a dark design. Decorative small plants for the foreground and very small aquaria. When compared to other species, its requirements are stringent and growth is slow.

Prop.: Due to the moderate formation of daughter plants on runners, it is not easy to produce a large group. Therefore, it is recommendable to procure several speci-mens simultaneously to use in a group. Rarely cultivated.

D: 3, KH: 2–8, pH: 5.5–6.8, T: 25°–28°C, AH: 1–2

Cryptocoryne nurii FURTADO (1935)

Fam.: Araceae

Hab.: Malay Peninsula.

Small amphibious bog plant with hard, somewhat thick, 18 cm long, 3 cm wide, red-brown aerial leaves. Spathe 10 cm long, flag about 5 cm, straight, roundish and brown with a 2 cm tip. Throat darker and lacks a collar. Aquatic leaves are narrowly lanceolate, up to 10 cm long and 2 cm wide, olive green bronze with dark red striations, and finely dentate edges.

Extremely difficult to cultivate due to its limited adaptability. Very soft water with a low mineral content is needed. Light requirement is extremely high, and the substrate should contain quite a bit of clay. Imported specimens usually lose their leaves; rhizomes undergo moderate growth, and new blades initially remain quite small. Very rare and only suggested for experienced hobbyists whose aquaria have the required living conditions.

Prop.: Daughter plants on runners are rarely formed.

D: 4, KH: 1–3, pH: 5.5–6.5, T: 25°–28°C, AH: 1–2

Cryptocoryne minima

Cryptocoryne nurii

Cryptocoryne wendtii   DE WIT (1958)

Type: Latifolius

Fam.: Araceae

Hab.: Sri Lanka.

Five different varieties of this extremely variable species were presented in Vols. 1 and 2. This form was described as a type and imported in 1978. It has not been scientifically described. There are probably more types and transitional forms. Latifolius refers to the fact that these plants have broader, shorter blades than the nominate form. Leaves are ovate, up to 5 cm long, 3.5 cm wide, short-stalked, with a cordate base, and slightly sinuate edges. Upper side of the leaf is olive green to reddish brown with a faint green angular design; underside is brown. This compact plant is suitable for the foreground. While not difficult to cultivate, it does demand a certain amount of light.

Prop.: Daughter plants on runners.

D: 2, KH: 2–12, pH: 6.0–7.2, T: 22°–28°C, AH: 1–3

Cryptocoryne undulata, see Vol. 2, page 124

Cryptocoryne wendtii, latifolius

Cryptocoryne x *willisii*, see page 46

3. Creeping-Shoot Plants

Elatine macropoda GUSSONE (1827)

Fam.: Elatinaceae

Hab.: Mediterranean region, east Africa.

Thin creeping shoot with roots that are about 4 cm long. Leaves are opposite, spade-shaped, up to 1.7 cm long, 0.3 cm wide, entire, with an elongated base, an obtuse tip, and a pronounced central vein. Very small, whitish green blooms with exposed sepals and petals are borne in the leaf axils. *E. macropoda* can only be distinguished from *Glossostigma elatinoides* by its flowers. Under favorable conditions, this species proves to be a good aquarium plant which, through branching of the creeping shoot, produces flat, dense growth suitable for the foreground. Plant the shoots shallowly and horizontally in a medium-grained substrate. Situate in an open site that receives direct light. High carbonate hardness usually results in poor growth, but this can be overcome with carbon dioxide fertilization. Certain medications against algae and fish diseases are not tolerated, and snails show a particular fondness for the tender leaves of this plant.

Prop.: Removal of branches.

D: 3, **KH**: 2–10, **pH**: 6.0–7.0, **T**: 22°–26°C, **AH**: 1–2

Glossostigma diandra KUNTZE (1891)

Fam.: Scrophulariaceae

Hab.: Australia.

Thin creeping shoot with short roots. Leaves are opposite, paliform, entire, up to 0.8 cm long, 0.3 cm wide, with an obtuse rounded tip. The blade tapers into a petiole of similar length. Single blooms on short peduncles sit in the axils of the aerial leaves. The crown is 0.3 cm in diameter and white with 5 petals and 2 stamens. The number of stamens will differentiate this species from the very similar *Glossostigma elatinoides*. Shallowly introduce shoots in the upper layers of the sand substrate, planting them uniformly throughout the area where the stand is desired. Coarse-grained gravel should be avoided, and due to the high light requirement, floating plants should be absent. Usually the shoots tend to grow more or less upright. Do not look for a lawn of these plants to develop with their creeping shoots, as this type of growth demands intense light, making it a rare occurrence in aquaria. To keep the stand low, the shoots must be regularly pruned and replanted. In general, this species is not very adaptable to submersed life.

Prop.: Lateral shoots.

D: 3, **KH**: 2–12, **pH**: 6.0–7.0, **T**: 22°–25°C, **AH**: 1–2

Elatine macropoda

Glossostigma diandra

3. Creeping-Shoot Plants

Hydrocotyle vulgaris LINNE (1753)   Pennywort, umbrella plant

Fam.: Hydrocotylaceae

Hab.: Europe, around the Mediterranean.

Thin creeping main shoot grows along the substrate. Peltate, almost round, petiolate leaves are 1–4 cm in diameter. Veins radiate like the spokes of a wheel from the cup-shaped center towards the indented edge. Each small, capitate inflorescence produces an umbel with 3–5 flowers; though rare, occasionally 2 flower whorls will be found, one superior to the other. Though decorative, its limited ability to adapt to submersed life restricts its use. Constant elevated temperatures found in tropical aquaria are hardly suitable for this species. Maintaining short petioles is virtually impossible. Generally the petioles elongate, while the blades become smaller, totally degenerating after a while. Small, unheated aquaria that are illuminated with natural sunlight are moderately appropriate. An attractive perennial bog plant for the garden pond.

Prop.: Lateral shoots.

D: 4, KH: 2–10, pH: 6.0–7.0, T: 15°–20°C, AH: 1–2

Lilaeopsis brasiliensis (GLAZIOU) AFFOLTER (1985)

Fam.: Apiaceae

Hab.: Brazil.

The thin creeping shoot bears petiolate leaves. Blades are lanceolate, 5–12 cm long, 0.5 cm wide, and have an obtuse tip. Several very fine veins run along the midrib; a few crossveins extend to the faintly incised edge. Aquatic leaves are more slender, up to 0.3 cm wide, with an acute tip. Only the midrib is pronounced.

It seems that both *L. polyantha* and *L. novae-zelandiae* are synonyms of *L. brasiliensis*.

A decorative, low-growing foreground plant that can green large surfaces. Adapts well to submersed life. Bunches planted in the upper layers of the substrate produce numerous elongated lateral shoots, creating an extensive stand which looks like a small lawn.

Prop.: Branchings off shoots; removal of lateral shoots.

D: 2, KH: 2–15, pH: 6.0–7.5, T: 20°–28°C, AH: 1–3

Hydrocotyle vulgaris

Lilaeopsis brasiliensis

3. Creeping-Shoot Plants

Marsilea crenata   K. B. PRESL (1830)   Dwarf four-leaf clover
Fam.: Marsileaceae
Hab.: Australia.

For a long time, this species was confused with *M. drummondii* in aquarium literature. The two can only be positively identified by their infrequently formed sporocarp,
which is ribbed in *M. crenata,* but smooth in *M. drummondii.*
The four-lobed aerial leaves grow up to 2 cm in diameter on a thin, creeping shoot.
Aquatic leaves are predominately unilobed, usually roundish-ovate, and up to 0.6 cm
wide. Only when aerial shoots are planted under water are the more or less divided
aquatic leaves generated. Cultivating this plant as an aquarium plant has proven
somewhat tricky, since its general adaptation to submersed life is poor. Soft water,
strong light, and the addition of carbon dioxide favor submersed growth. Nevertheless, *M. crenata* cannot be constantly maintained as a submersed plant, but for a
limited time, a beautiful low lawn results which can be placed in the open foreground.

D: 3, KH: 2–8, pH: 6.0–7.0, T: 22°–25°C, AH: 1–2

Pilularia globulifera   LINNE (1753)
Fam.: Marsileaceae
Hab.: Europe.

The creeping shoot supports upright leaves that are soft, grass green, awl-shaped,
about 1 mm thick, up to 10 cm long, with a pointed tip, and a roundish cross-section.
Pea-sized short peduncled brown sporocarps are borne in the axils on bog plants.
Occasionally found in deeper waters of its natural habitat. There its leaves may reach
lengths of 100 cm. A lawnlike plant for the foreground of shallow aquaria. Culture in
sand substrates at low temperatures. Higher temperatures of up to ca. 25°C are
tolerated for short periods of time, but a corresponding increase in illumination will be
required. An extremely rare aquarium plant. Generally used along marshy pond
shores.

Prop.: Lateral shoots.

D: 4, KH: 2–5, pH: 6.0–7.0, T: 15°–20°C, AH: 1–2

Marsilea crenata

Pilularia globulifera

3. Creeping-Shoot Plants

Selliera radicans CANAVILLES (1799)

Fam.: Goodeniaceae

Hab.: East Australia, Tasmania, New Zealand, Chile.

The thin shoot has roots at the nodes and grows simple petiolate leaves. Blade is slightly succulent, lanceolate, up to 6 cm long, 1.5 cm wide, with an elongated base, and an obtuse rounded tip. In the axils of aerial leaves are single blooms that are 0.7 cm in diameter with 5 petals on a white crown. Rarely kept in aquaria today. To separate the genus from the nonflowering state of *Lilaeopsis*, note *Selliera's* leaf morphology, which is broader and more bladelike.

Suitable for the foreground of shallow, long, roomy aquaria. Only recommended for cooler temperatures; higher temperatures tend to cause the internodes to elongate and the leaves to become thin and degenerate. Strong illumination and an open area are demanded. The terrestrial form is easily grown around the garden pond during the summer months.

Prop.: Removal of lateral shoots.

D: 3, KH: 2–10, pH: 6.0–7.0, T: 18°–22°C, AH: 1–2

4. Floating Plants

Aponogeton distachyos LINNE filius (1781)

Fam.: Aponogetonaceae

Hab.: South Africa.

The tuber grows up to 3 cm thick. The blade is elliptic, leathery, up to 25 cm long, 3–7 cm wide, and floats on the water surface. It is attached to the tuber by a long petiole. The superior side of the blade is light green with occasional dark spots. Inflorescence has 2 spikes that are about 6 cm long with 5–10 flowers on each. Each flower has 25 stamens, 6 carpels, and one white petal that is 10 x 5 cm.

This aponogeton can be kept in intensely illuminated aquaria as long they are not too tall. Temperatures should be moderate. Not a perennial plant. After a period of speedy growth, its growth slows and the plant becomes dormant. At that time the tuber should be removed and stored in a cool, moist place for about 2 months. Not a suggested aquarium plant, but on the other hand, it does well along shallow pond edges during the summer, even surviving mild winters in this setting.

Prop.: Seeds.

D: 3, KH: 2–8, pH: 6.0–7.5, T: 18°–23°C, AH: 1–3

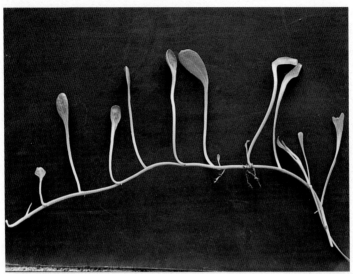

Selliera radicans

Aponogeton distachyos

4. Floating Plants

Limnobium spongia   (BOSC) STEUDEL (1841)
Fam.: Hydrocharitaceae
Hab.: North America.

Free floating rosette plant that has 2–4 cm cordate to circular blades supported by 10 cm petioles. Upper side of the leaf is slightly arcuate to flat, light green, and occasionally has red spots; the lower side is spongy, lighter green, and slightly violet or spotted. Roots that hang into the water are long, pilose, and whitish or violet. Male blossoms are arranged in groups and have a singly bract, 3 sepals, 3 green-white petals, and 9–12 stamens. Female blossoms have 6 styles with bicleft, wide, awllike stigmas.

An excellent floating plant for either slightly heated or unheated aquaria. Adapts well to various water values; however, it has a high light requirement. An appropriate plant for bog aquaria. During the summer, these plants can be grown in the open, either floating or rooted in a bog. Requires full sunlight to flower.

Prop.: Through prolific production of daughter plants on runners, a dense stand is quickly formed; thin the stand regularly.

D: 2, KH: 2–15, pH: 6.0–7.5, T: 15°–20°C, AH: 1–3

Riccia rhenana   LORBEER ex. K. MÜLLER (1941)   Sinking riccia
Fam.: Ricciaceae
Hab.: Cosmopolitan.

This plant looks like *Riccia fluitans,* though the tips of the thallus are shorter and slightly finer. Shoots frequently sink to the substrate in aquaria and anchor themselves with their rhizoids to rocks or grains of sand. This species is occasionally found with *Riccia fluitans*. If such a cluster, having been exposed to intense illumination, is separated, *R. rhenana* sinks to the bottom. With dim lighting, *R. rhenana* drifts just beneath the water surface. With continuous dichotomous splitting, the single, benthic plant segments grow into dense spherical mats. An interesting foreground decoration is created near the bottom.

Prop.: Dividing the group.

D: 1, KH: 5–15, pH: 6.0–8.0, T: 15°–30°C, AH: 1–2

Limnobium spongia

Riccia rhenana

4. Floating Plants

Salvinia natans   LINNE (1753)

Fam.: Salviniaceae

Hab.: North Africa, temperate Asia, Europe.

This plant has a horizontal main shoot and floating leaves borne on short stalks. The blade is oval, up to 2 cm long, 1 cm wide, usually twice as long as wide, with a cordate base, and an emarginate tip. Upper side is warty and loosely pilose with free, upright bristles in semi-regular rows. In nature, this is a protected species on the brink of extinction. Conditionally recommended for tropical aquaria because the high humidity under the cover of the tank rots the plants. Appropriate for brightly illuminated, unheated tanks. Growing *S. natans* in the open is undoubtedly optimal. During the winter, this annual floating fern dies. Sporocarps are formed which sink to the bottom when the plants disintegrate in the winter. In the following spring, the spores germinate, float to the water surface, and develop into new individuals.

Prop.: Separation of lateral shoots and sowing the rare sporocarps.

D: 4, **KH**: 2–8, **pH**: 6.0–7.5, **T**: 15°–20°C, **AH**: 1–3

Salvinia oblongifolia   VON MARTIUS (1834)

Fam.: Salviniaceae

Hab.: Brazil, Amazon Basin.

Horizontal main shoot with floating leaves that are elongate-ovate, up to 3 cm long, 1 cm wide, frequently smaller, but usually 3 times as long as they are wide, with a cordate base, and a faintly indented tip. Upper side is warty and very densely and finely pilose; the free standing bristle clusters are pointed forward. There is a degenerate form that appears in aquaria which is easily confused with *S. auriculata*. Note the narrower leaves whose clustered bristles do not converge in an arch.

Extremely rarely cultivated and therefore unfamiliar to aquarists. This photophilous floating fern should, if possible, be kept in loose formations; this means that they must be occasionally thinned. The finely divided aquatic leaves that hang down from the clusters are up to 10 cm long and provide a good spawning substrate for some fish species and shelter for fry. Excessive current at the water surface is not tolerated.

Prop.: Separation of lateral shoots which develop in great numbers.

D: 3, **KH**: 2–12, **pH**: 6.0–7.5, **T**: 18°–25°C, **AH**: 1–3

Salvinia natans

Salvinia oblongifolia

4. Floating Plants

Salvinia rotundifolia WILLDENOW (1810)

Fam.: Salviniaceae

Hab.: Tropical America.

Horizontal main axis with floating leaves that are roundish-ovate, up to 0.7 cm long and 0.6 cm wide, usually almost as long as wide, with a rounded, weakly concave tip. The upper side of the leaf is warty, whereby each papillose projection has 1–2, upright, short, light setae. Under bright light, the leaves are tomentose; however, artificial lighting generally results in less pilose specimens. Sometimes similar to a degenerate form of *S. auriculata*, so note the number of setae on the warts. *S. auriculata* has 4 setae per wart. Free floating plant for aquaria that meet its requirements. It seems that hard water and dripping condensation is tolerated better by this species than by many other floating ferns.

Prop.: The numerous lateral shoots soon form new plants, producing a dense mat. Ensure that rooted plants receive sufficient illumination by occasionally thinning the stand.

D: 2, **KH:** 2–15, **pH:** 6.0–7.5, **T:** 18°–25°C, **AH:** 1–3

Utricularia aurea LOUREIRO (1790)

Fam.: Utriculariaceae

Hab.: Tropical southeast Asia.

The elongated main shoot grows to a length of 100 cm and is about 0.3 cm thick. The four-part leaf grows up to 8 cm in size and has 24 pinna. These divide further into as many as 12 filiform tips until there are up to 700 threadlike tips. Leaves have small capture bladders (utricles), which the plant uses to catch and digest aquatic insects. What determines the presence or absence of these utricles is unknown. Newly imported shoots might not have utricles, but develop them in an aquarium. But wild specimens that have utricles may spontaneously cease to grow them in an aquarium. Besides adaptive characteristics influenced by environment, species-specific factors must also play a role.

This delicate surface plant adapts well and forms extensive mats with its numerous lateral shoots and rapid growth. Its uncommonly rapid initial growth, however, diminishes over time, and older aquarium specimens grow slower and become weaker.

Prop.: Lateral shoots, dividing of shoots, leaf cuttings.

D: 1, **KH:** 2–15, **pH:** 5.5–7.5, **T:** 22°–30°C, **AH:** 1–3

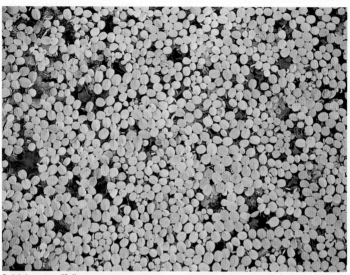

Salvinia rotundifolia

Utricularia aurea

Utricularia aurea (flowers)

Unsuitable "Aquarium Plants"

In the following chapter, a number of plant species are introduced which have appeared in aquarium stores more frequently of late. Some of these so-called "aquarium plants" are regularly offered, and the selection of this type of plant is constantly increasing. The first question to ask is whether or not these plants are aquatic plants in their natural habitat. A few are found in moist locals, but they are not aquarium plants in the traditional sense of the word. In other words, they cannot grow submersed. Vendors rarely feel guilty, because clients are usually informed of the limited suitability of these plants. On the positive side, some of these plants are attractive and very different from common aquatic plants that are offered, providing a special accent without having to resort to plastic plants. Another point in their favor is that—terrestrial or not—they often have a longer life span in the aquarium than even true aquatic plants, since many aquatic plants quickly decompose under suboptimal water conditions.

Each aquarist must decide how to weigh these aspects and decide whether to place the following plants in the aquarium or on the window sill—or refrain from buying them altogether. Since these plants are found in retail stores and find appropriate use in bog, amphibious, and other specialty aquaria, we deemed it apropos to include a brief introduction here.

Iresine lindenii

Iresine lindenii VAN HOUTTE

Hab.: Ecuador.

A foxtail from the family Amaranthaceae. Stalked plants with opposite leaves. Blades are about 8 cm long, 3 cm wide, brown-red, with dark red veins. These soft plants live a short time underwater. Better suited for flower pots, balconies, or gardens during the summer.

5. Unsuitable "Aquarium Plants"

Alternanthera ficoides   (LINNE) BRAUN ex ROEMER et Schultes
Type: "Bettzickiana"
Hab.: South America.

This compact, stalked plant reaches a height of 10–15 cm. Blades are slender and normally rolled upwards along the sides. Depending on the type, blades are red-green or yellow-green. In the aquarium, the plant remains green for a few weeks before decomposing. Grows well in the yard during the summer.

Chamaedorea elegans   MARTIUS
Hab.: Mexico, Guatemala.

Usually 20–30 cm tall seedlings are sold. These have about 6 leaves that are simple pinnate. This palm is very resistant and can live for long periods of time submersed. To keep alive, regularly fortify the plant by removing it from the water.

Cryptanthus bivittatus   (HOOKER) REGEL
Hab.: Brazil.

Small leaf rosettes are grown on short shoots. Blades are green, about 5 x 1 cm, and have two light green striations. Its hard leaves make it resistant to submersed conditions. Very appropriate in bog aquaria as an epiphyte fastened to wood.

Chlorophytum comosum   (THUNBERG) JAQUES   Spider plant, airplane plant
Hab.: South Africa.

A common indoor plant which is almost indestructible. Leaves of the rosette are slender with green striations along the outer edge and white stripes along the midrib. Long peduncles later develop adventitious plants. As robust as this plant is in its terrestrial environment, it is totally inappropriate for submersed life.

Chlorophytum bichetii   (KARRER) BAKER
Hab.: Gabon.

This 15 cm plant has a rosette of lanceolate leaves. Blades have white to yellowish edges and occasionally have thin light stripes through the middle. Its maintenance underwater is extremely precarious. Appropriate as an indoor plant or for the bog aquarium. Propagated through adventitious plants.

Dracaena sanderiana   SANDER ex MAST
Hab.: Cameroon.

An attractive representative of the agave plants. The upright, almost 1 cm thick stem supports leaves that are white and green striped along the edges, up to 15 cm long, and quite hard. Young, 30 cm shoots live about 8 weeks underwater before they begin to decompose. Grows well in brightly lit windows.

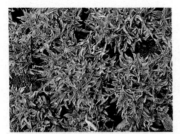

Alternanthera ficoides

Cryptanthus bivittatus

Chamaedorea elegans

Dracaena sanderiana

Chlorophytum comosum

Chlorophytum bichetii

5. Unsuitable "Aquarium Plants"

Dracaena marginata LAMARCK
Hab.: Madagascar.

Upright stem has leaves from top to bottom. Broad, lanceolate blades around the terminal tip are dark red with a green center. Older leaves keep the red margins. The plant lives for about 2 months submersed. Decorative plant when grown on the window sill; it tolerates wet roots in the bog aquarium.

Fittonia verschaffeltii (LEMAIRE) VAN HOUTTE
Hab.: Columbia, Bolivia.

The prostrate shoot has opposite, ovate leaves that are up to 15 cm long, 10 cm wide, and brownish with red veins. Offered for the aquarium, but they cannot live for any length of time underwater. Beautiful low-growing contrast plant. Good ground cover in the bog aquarium.

Fittonia verschaffeltii (LEMAIRE) VAN HOUTTE
Type: "Argyroneura"
Hab.: Colombia, Bolivia.

Main shoot grows prostrate. Leaves are opposite, up to 10 cm long, and 5 cm wide. Blade is light green with a dense net of silver white veins. Its beautiful leaf design is a temptation to anyone looking for plants, but it lives only a few weeks underwater.

Maranta leuconeura MORREN
Type: "Kerchoviana"
Hab.: Brazil.

Attractive plant with oval leaves on a short prostrate shoot. Blade is 15 x 8 cm, dark green, velvety, with red veins, and light spots along the midrib. Not suitable for aquaria, but potted specimens can be propagated in hot, humid bog aquaria or window sills.

Selaginella martensii SPRINGER
Hab.: Mexico.

Small (15 cm) rosette plant with short-stalked leaves. Very small pinna sit in dense rows next to each other. Life underwater is limited to about 2 weeks. Afterwards, the plant begins to disintegrate. Maintain in humid, warm bog aquaria and mist with rain water.

Selaginella willdenowii BAKER
Hab.: Tropical Asia.

Sold as an aquatic fir, but it is not at all aquatic. As a rule, they have single leaves which are about 30 cm in size and borne on equally long petioles. The trilobed blade is dark green and rigidly structured. Remains attractive for about 6 weeks submersed.

Syngonium auritum (LINNE) SCHOTT
Hab.: Jamaica, Honduras.

The climbing shoot has dark green leaves which are hastate (spearlike) in their juvenile form. Venation is lighter green. Totally worthless for the aquarium, since the plant decomposes rapidly in water. Use it as a climbing plant in large bog aquaria or support it with a small trellis in the window sill.

Dracaena marginata

Maranta leuconeura

Selaginella martensii

Fittonia verschaffeltii

Selaginella willdenowii

Fittonia verschaffeltii

Syngonium auritum

River in Borneo

Symbols Used in the Illustrated Fish Section:

Fam.:   = Family.
Subfam.: = Subfamily.
Syn.:   = Synonym = additional names for the same species.
             In the systematics of faunal nomenclature, only the name
             given by the original describer is valid. Subsequent de-
             scriptions of the same species using another name create
             so-called synonyms.
Hab.:   = Habitat; the natural region of origin.
F.I.:   = First import. It is often interesting to know how long a
             particular species has been known in the hobby.
Sex.:   = Differences between the sexes.
Soc. B.: = Social behavior.
M: = Conditions recommended for maintenance.
             A specific value placed in parentheses following a range
             for pH, degrees German total hardness (° dGH), and
             degrees German carbonate hardness (° dKH) indicates
             the optimal value within the range for the species.
B: = Breeding. Recommendations under this heading are merely
             meant to be used as a guideline. Complete breeding ac-
             counts should be obtained from fish journals or relevant
             specialized books.
F: = Feeding. Under this heading you will see the abbrevia-
             tions C, H, L, O. These stand for:
             C = Carnivore = meat/fish eater
             H = Herbivore = plant/vegetable eater
             L = Limnovore = aufwuchs/detritus eater
             O = Omnivore = eats foods from all above categories
S: = Special observations.
T: = Temperature.
L: = Maximal length of the adult fish. A value in parenthesis
             refers to maximal length achieved in aquaria.
A: = Recommended aquarium length.
R: = Water region preferred by the fish in an aquarium: t = top,
             m = middle, b = bottom.
D: = Degree of difficulty. For explanations refer Vol. 1, p. 203.
             D: 1 = species for the beginning hobbyist.
             D: 2 = species for novices with some basic knowledge.
             D: 3 = species for advanced hobbyists.
             D: 4 = species for experts and specialists.
             H = Herbivore; Ch = Water chemistry; C = Carnivore;
             S = Size
WC   = Wild caught specimen.

* Detailed explanations can be found in Aquarium Atlas, Vol. 1, p. 200.

Group 1
Fam.: Acipenseridae

Acipenser baeri
Siberian sturgeon

BRANDT, 1869

Syn.: *Acipenser stenorhynchus, A. stenorhynchus* var. *baicalensis*.

Hab.: Asia: former Soviet Union, in the rivers of Siberia from the Ob River to the Kolyma River, including their mouths.

F.I.: Has not been imported.

Sex.: None known.

Soc. B.: Despite its size, this is a peaceful species. *A. baeri* digs as it searches for food.

M: Only juveniles are suitable for home aquaria. The aquarium should be as roomy as possible with a large surface area. Provide open swimming areas and a sand or fine-grained gravel substrate; sharp stones should be avoided so that the fish do not injure their mouth while digging. The water should be clear, clean, and oxygen-rich with a pH of 7.0–7.5 and a hardness up to 20° dGH. *A. baeri* finds water movement and sea salt added to its water beneficial. Best kept in a species aquarium.

B: Its mature size and the limited space of an aquarium make it impossible to bred these animals in captivity. *A. baeri* requires many years to attain sexual maturity: ♂♂ need at least 11 years, whereas ♀♀ require 17 years! The animals are anadromous, spending most of their lives at sea, but entering rivers to spawn. The spawning season extends from June to July. Up to 420,000 eggs are laid. The ♀ only spawns once over the course of several years.

F: C; live foods, benthic invertebrates (insect larvae, crustacea, molluscs, worms), and sometimes small fishes.

S: *A. baeri* has two geographic races, one eastern and one western. While this is considered a migratory species, some large Siberian lakes (e.g., Lake Baikal) contain nonmigrating strains.

T: 10°–20°C (coldwater fish), **L:** 200 cm, **A:** 80 cm, **R:** b, **D:** 3–4

Acipenser gueldenstaedti

BRANDT, 1833

Syn.: None.

Hab.: Europe and western Asia: the Black, Azov, and Caspian Seas. The species enters the mouths of rivers to spawn. Known to migrate up to Pressburg (Bratislava) in the Danube.

F.I.: Unknown.

Sex.: No definite external differentiating characteristics are known.

Soc. B.: Despite its size, quite peaceful. It digs as it searches for food. They live in localized schools in their natural habitat.

M: As for *Acipenser sturio* (p. 81). Only juveniles are suitable for home aquaria; only public aquaria can meet the spatial requirements of adults.

B: Probably impossible in aquaria because of its size. In nature they spawn in June. The species is anadromous; that is, it enters freshwater to spawn. At least eight years are needed to reach sexual maturity. More than 800,000 eggs can be laid over rubble substrates. The eggs develop in about 90 hr.

F: C; live foods such as fishes (gobies, etc.) and all kinds of invertebrates, e.g., chironomid larvae, molluscs, and *Daphnia*.

S: Because it is an important source of caviar, *A. gueldenstaedti* is of great economic consequence. The meat is also tasty and valuable. Beside the nominate form, there are two additional subspecies: *A. g. persicus* BORODIN, 1897 and *A. g. colchius* MARTI, 1940.

T: 10°–20°C, **L:** to 400 cm, **A:** over 200 cm, **R:** b, **D:** 3–4 (C)

Acipenser baeri

Acipenser gueldenstaedti

Acipenser medirostris
Green sturgeon

AYRES, 1854

Syn.: *Acipenser micadoi, A. acutirostris.*

Hab.: America and Asia: along the east and west coasts of the northern Pacific Ocean. Also enters mouths of rivers.

F.I.: Has not been imported into Germany.

Sex.: None known.

Soc. B.: Anadromous.

M: There is no information available concerning caring for this sturgeon in captivity.

B: Little is known about *A. medirostris'* reproductive behavior in its natural habitat. This anadromous fish leaves the sea and moves up rivers to spawn. In the Datta River (former Soviet Union) it spawns from mid-June to mid-July. All other information about this species is based on suppositions.

F: C; live foods, but primarily benthic invertebrates.

S: This rare species can easily be distinguished from other sturgeons by its olive green coloration.

T: 10°–20°C (coldwater fish), **L:** to 210 cm, **A:** from 200 cm, **R:** b, **D:** 3–4

Acipenser nudiventris

LOVETZKY, 1828

Syn.: *Acipenser glaber, A. schipa, A. schypa.*

Hab.: Asia and Europe: Caspian, Aral, and Black Seas. From there it also enters rivers such as the Danube.

F.I.: Has probably not been imported into Germany.

Sex.: None known.

Soc. B.: Despite its size, this is a peaceful fish. It digs as it searches for food.

M: Only juveniles are suitable for aquaria. Furnish the aquarium as you would for *Acipenser sturio* (p. 81).

B: Not possible in aquaria due to its size. In nature *A. nudiventris* is anadromous, entering rivers from the sea to spawn. Spawning season extends from March to May. Water temperature at that time is between 10°–15°C. The 200,000 to 1.3 million eggs are laid on rubble substrates. Egg diameter varies between

1.5 and 3 mm. At temperatures of about 20°C, the eggs take 5 days to develop.

F: C; live foods such as benthic invertebrates (e.g., crustacea, mussels, worms, and insect larvae).

S: Unlike other sturgeons, *A. nudiventris* has a solid lower lip. *A. nudiventris* and *A. stellatus* will hybridize.

T: 10°–20°C (coldwater fish), **L:** 200 cm, **A:** from 200 cm, **R:** b, **D:** 3–4

Acipenser medirostris

Acipenser nudiventris

Acipenser schrencki
Amur sturgeon

BRANDT, 1869

Syn.: None.

Hab.: Asia: China and former Soviet Union, in the Amur system from its estuary to the headwaters of the Argun and Schilka Rivers.

F.I.: Has not been imported into Germany.

Sex.: None known.

Soc. B.: In nature, A. schrencki form localized schools which remain in certain regions. Despite its size, this is a peaceful fish.

M: As suggested for Acipenser sturio.

B: Its respectable mature size makes reproduction in an aquarium impossible. In nature, the spawning season extends from the end of May to the end of June, sometimes to mid-July. Between 29,000

and 435,000 eggs are laid over rubble or sand substrates. ♀♀ do not spawn every year.

F: C; all kinds of invertebrates e.g., crustacea, worms, insect larvae, and molluscs. Large specimens also eat fishes.

S: Morphologically, A. schrencki is very similar to Acipenser baeri.

T: 10°–20°C (coldwater fish), L: to 290 cm, A: from 200 cm, R: b, D: 3–4

Acipenser stellatus
Star sterlet

PALLAS, 1771

Syn.: Acipenser hellops.

Hab.: Europe and western Asia: Black, Azov, and Caspian Seas. Rarely encountered in the Adriatic Sea, but sometimes found in the Aral Sea. Enters rivers.

F.I.: Could not be determined.

Sex.: No definite external differentiating characteristics are known. ♀♀ are somewhat fuller during the spawning season.

Soc. B.: See Acipenser sturio (p. 81).

M: Follow recommendations for A. sturio.

B: Has not been accomplished in an aquarium, largely because of its mature size. In nature, A. stellatus is anadromous. It spawns from June to September in the mouths of rivers or often on banks in the sea. The 20,000–350,000 eggs adhere to stones. Depending on temperature, the young hatch after 2–4 days, rise to the surface and, either im-

mediately or after a maximum of 3 months, follow the current into the sea.

F: C; live foods, particularly chironomid larvae and small crustacea. Small fishes are occasionally accepted.

S: After migration, A. stellatus can be classified into a winter and a summer form. The winter form enters rivers to spawn, while the summer form tends to spawn at the river's mouth.

T: 10°–20°C (coldwater fish), L: to 190 cm, A: from 150 cm, R: b, D: 3

Acipenser schrencki

Acipenser stellatus

Lake Baikal, former Soviet Union

This lake in southern Russia, considered the deepest on earth (1,620 m), is situated 455 m above sea level. With its 31,500 km² of surface area, it is about 60 times larger than Lake Constance. Several species from this ancient lake, such as the oil fishes, have persevered in this environment since the Tertiary Period.

Acipenser sturio
Sturgeon

LINNAEUS, 1758

Syn.: None.

Hab.: European coasts from North Cape to the Mediterranean and Black Seas, northern Atlantic, along both the European and American Coasts and the Baltic Sea and Lakes Onega and Ladoga.

F.I.: Native to Europe.

Sex.: None known.

Soc. B.: Peaceful despite its size. The animals dig as they search for food. Hardy when appropriately cared for.

M: Only juveniles are suitable aquarium inhabitants. The tank should have a large surface area and a soft sand substrate. Do not use sharp gravel as substrate lest it proves injurious to the animals as they dig for food. Leave plenty of free swimming space. The water should be clear, cold, oxygen-rich, medium-hard to hard (10°–20° dGH), and slightly alkaline (pH about 7.5). Good filtration is required, and as a secondary consider-

ation, the fish may find pump-generated current beneficial. Likewise, salt can be added to the water. Best kept in a species tank.

B: The mature size of the animals circumvents successfully breeding *A. sturio* in an aquarium. Anadromous fish; that is, it leaves the sea and enters rivers to spawn. From June to July it spawns in deep channels in fast-flowing sections of the river proper. Between 400,000 and 2.5 million eggs are laid. The fry hatch in 3–5 days. There are conflicting reports on how long the juveniles remain in freshwater before migrating to the sea.

F: C; live benthic invertebrates (crustacea, mussels, worms) and the occasional small fish.

S: *A. sturio* is an important source of caviar. Due to environmental degradation of rivers, the species is virtually extinct in Germany. Occasionally an individual specimen is caught.

T: 10°–18°C (coldwater fish), **L:** max. 6 m, **A:** from 200 cm, **R:** b, **D:** 4 (S)

Huso dauricus (GEORGI, 1775)

Syn.: *Acipenser dauricus, A. orientalis.*

Hab.: Asia: former Soviet Union and China, in the Amur system from its estuaries to the head waters of the Schilka and Argun Rivers.

F.I.: Has not been imported into Germany.

Sex.: No definite external differentiating characteristics are known.

Soc. B.: Localized schools are frequently found in the Amur. Peaceful as juveniles, turning predacious as they age.

M: Only juveniles are suitable for aquaria. See *Acipenser sturio.*

B: Impossible in aquaria due to its mature size. In its natural habitat, these sturgeons spawn for several days in May and June when temperatures are 12°–

14°C. The 600,000 to 4.1 million eggs are laid over sand or rubble substrates at depths of 2–4 m. Eggs are slightly adhesive, 3.2–4.0 mm in diameter, and dark gray when mature. After the yolk sac is absorbed, the juveniles become benthic.

F: C; juveniles consume all live foods, e.g., worms, mosquito larvae, mussels, and crustacea. Adults primarily feed on fishes.

S: Unlike *Huso huso, H. dauricus*'s first dorsal shield is larger than the rest, and the dorsal fin has less than 60 rays.

T: 10°–20°C (coldwater fish), **L**: to 5.6 m, **A**: from 200 cm, **R**: b, **D**: 4

Huso huso (LINNAEUS, 1758)

Syn.: *Acipenser huso.*

Hab.: Asia and Europe: Caspian, Black, Azov, and Adriatic Seas as well as their tributaries (Po River).

F.I.: Could not be determined; sometimes kept in show aquaria.

Sex.: According to BERG there is slight sexual dimorphism, but how it is manifest is not given.

Soc. B.: Anadromous fish which may be found in upper river courses. Adults are predators.

M: See *Acipenser sturio.* Only juveniles are suitable for home aquaria.

B: Impossible in aquaria. In nature, there are several races, each of which undergoes spawning migrations at different times of the year (fall and spring). Usually the spawning sites are in the lower to central courses of the rivers. Spawning occurs along the river bed. The num-

ber of eggs laid correlates to the size of the fish, fluctuating between 360,000 and 7.7 million. At temperatures of about 13°C, egg development takes about 8 days. After hatching, the young soon proceed to the sea.

F: C; all kinds of live invertebrates; larger animals predominately feed on fishes.

S: At a length of 9 m and a weight of up to 1.5 tons, this is one of the largest fishes. *H. huso* produces the world famous Beluga caviar.

T: 10°–20°C (coldwater fish), **L**: to 9 m, **A**: from 200 cm, **R**: b, **D**: 4

Huso dauricus

Huso huso, adult

Pseudoscaphirhynchus kaufmanni (BOGDANOW, 1874)

Syn.: *Scaphirhynchus kaufmanni.*

Hab.: Former Soviet Union: from the lower course of the Amu Darya River to Pjandsha.

F.I.: Has probably not been imported into Germany.

Sex.: ♂♂ have a pointed mouth and a much more elongated tail fin; ♀♀ have rounded mouths.

Soc. B.: Unknown.

M: As for *Acipenser sturio* (p. 81).

B: Has not been successfully accomplished in aquaria. In nature, the animals spawn in mid-April. Sexual maturity is attained at a length of ca. 45 cm.

F: C; live foods of all kinds. In nature, these animals primarily feed on fishes from the genera *Nemacheilus*, *Barbus*, and *Capoetobrama*. Insect larvae are also appreciated.

S: In contrast to the American shovel sturgeons of the genus *Scaphirhynchus*, *Pseudoscaphirhynchus* has a shorter caudal peduncle which is not completely covered with plates.

T: 10°–20°C, **L:** 75 cm, **A:** 150 cm, **R:** b, **D:** 3–4 (C)

Amu Darya River at Tschadshou

Pseudoscaphirhynchus kaufmanni ♂

Pseudoscaphirhynchus kaufmanni ♀

Protopterus aethiopicus aethiopicus
Ethiopian lungfish
HECKEL, 1851

Syn.: *Lepidosiren arnaudii.*

Hab.: Africa: the Nile, but particularly Lakes Albert, Edward, Victoria, Nabugabo, Tanganyika, Kyoga, and No.

F.I.: Unknown.

Sex.: None known.

Soc. B.: Quarrelsome, indolent, voracious predator. It practices broodcare (paternal family).

M: As for *Protopterus annectens annectens.* Solitary maintenance is best. Only juveniles are suitable for home aquaria.

B: Lack of adequate space precludes breeding in aquaria. In nature, spawning generally occurs during the rainy season in muddy, deep holes. ♂♂ guard the eggs and the hatching young. The eggs are large with a large yolk and a gelatinous cover, reminiscent of that found on amphibian eggs. Juveniles have branched external gills very similar to those of newts. After 2–3 months, the larvae undergo a transformation (metamorphosis) and adopt the adult morphology.

F: C; all kinds of hardy live foods such as fishes, worms, snails, mussel meat, crustacea, and insects and their larvae. The species can also be trained to accept pieces of meat.

S: Besides this nominate form, two other subspecies have been described: *P. a. congicus* POLL, 1961 (Zaïre Basin from the upper Lualaba to Kinshasa) and *P. a. mesmaekersi* POLL, 1961 (lower Zaïre Basin).

T: 25°–30°C, L: 200 cm, A: from 200 cm, R: b, m, D: 4 (C)

Protopterus annectens annectens (no photo)
African lungfish
(OWEN, 1839)

Syn.: *Lepidosiren annectens, L. tobal, Protopterus anguilliformes, P. rhinocryptis, Rhinocryptis amphibia, R. annectens.*

Hab.: Africa: Senegal, Niger, Gambia, Volta, and Chad Basins. Occasionally found in the tributaries of the Chari River in western Sudan.

F.I.: 1910.

Sex.: None known.

Soc. B.: This predator is antagonistic and waspish with congeners and other species. ♂♂ guard the eggs and fry (paternal family).

M: Maintaining these fish is limited to those persons or institutions having large show aquaria. Only young specimens are suitable for the home aquarium. A muddy substrate and dense vegetation are advantageous. The water does not need to be very deep; 30 cm is plenty. No demands are placed on water chemistry. Since this voracious fish frequently bites, individual maintenance is strongly recommended.

B: Has not been accomplished in an aquarium.

F: C; hardy live foods such as fishes, snails, earthworms, and insects and their larvae. Sometimes these animals will learn to eat pieces of meat.

S: Besides the nominate form, another, smaller (60 cm) subspecies has been described, *P. annectens brieni* POLL, 1961. The life history of *Protopterus* species was addressed on p. 208 of Vol 1 (S.).

T: 25°–30°C, L: 82 cm, A: from 120 cm, R: b, m, D: 4 (C)

Protopterus aethiopicus, white form

Protopterus aethiopicus aethiopicus

Moenkhausia colletti, ♀ above, ♂ below

Hemigrammopetersius barnardi ♀

Hemigrammopetersius barnardi   (HERRE, 1936)

Syn.: *Rhabdalestes barnardi, Hemigrammopetersius intermedius*. Not to be confused with the "true" *H. intermedius*.

Hab.: East Africa: Tanzania, coastal regions.

F.I.: 1983 by SEEGERS and WISCHNATH.

Sex.: ♀♀ have a small anal fin (picture); ♂♂ have an anal fin that broadens into a round lobe.

Soc. B.: Peaceful schooling fish that is suitable for large community aquaria.

M: The aquarium must have a volume of at least 160 l. Maintain plenty of free swimming space. Keep vegetation confined to the edges. *H. banardi* should always be kept in schools.

B: Unknown.

F: C, O; live and flake foods.

T: 24°–27°C, **L**: 6 cm, **A**: 100 cm, **R**: m, **D**: 2

S: According to GÉRY, this fish should be classified into its own genus, but despite its peculiarities, it remains in the genus *Hemigrammopetersius*. The pictured animal is probably not *H. barnardi*, but an undescribed species.

Micralestes stormsi
True red Congo tetra

BOULENGER, 1902

Syn.: *Alestes imberi*. Often confused with *Micralestes humilis*.

Hab.: Africa: Zaïre Basin and southern Lake Chad.

F.I.: Unknown.

Sex.: ♂ ♂ can easily be recognized by their red adipose fin and iris. ♀ ♀ have a silver iris.

Soc. B.: Peaceful schooling fish which should always be maintained in groups. Well suited for large community tanks.

M: House in long aquaria and confine vegetation to the tank's fringes to insure plenty of swimming space. There are no particular demands placed on water quality: pH 6.0 to 7.6; hardness to 18° dGH. With careful adaptation, these fish can be acclimated to water with a hardness of 25° dGH.

B: Unknown. Probably similar to the blue Congo tetra, *Phenacogrammus interruptus*, Vol. 1, p. 222.

F: C, O; live and flake foods.

S: Like other *Micralestes* species, *M. stormsi* is rarely imported, although these fish are common in the Zaïre Basin.

T: 22°–26°C, **L:** 7.5 cm, **A:** 100 cm, **R:** m, **D:** 2

Petersius conserialis

HILGENDORF, 1894

Syn.: None.

Hab.: East Africa: Tanzania, Dar es Salaam to Morogoro, in small flowing waters.

F.I.: 1982 by CLASSEN and SEEGERS.

Sex.: The ♂ has a convex anal fin.

Soc. B.: Peaceful schooling fish.

M: Provide a large aquarium with plenty of swimming space, good filtration, and water movement. Limit tall vegetation to the edges.

B: Unknown.

F: O.

S: *Petersius* is a monotypic genus containing only *P. conserialis*. Very little is known about this species.

T: 22°–26°C, **L:** 14.5 cm, **A:** 100 cm, **R:** m, **D:** 3

Micralestes stormsi ♀

Petersius conserialis ♂, Ngerengere near Morogoro, Tanzania

Phenacogrammus altus   (BOULENGER, 1899)

Syn.: *Hemigrammalestes altus, Nannopetersius altus, Petersius altus, Phenacogrammus nummifer.*

Hab.: West Africa: Zaïre Basin.

F.I.: Not known.

Sex.: ♂♂ are more colorful, while ♀♀ tend to be rounder.

Soc. B.: Friendly schooling fish.

M: Needs a moderate-sized, well-planted aquarium. Maintain high water quality. Water: pH 6.2–7.0; hardness up to 15° dGH. Insure the presence of plenty of swimming space in the foreground. Keep a large group if possible.

B: Unknown. Probably similar to the blue Congo tetra, *Phenacogrammus interruptus* (see Vol. 1, p. 222).

F: C, O; live and flake foods.

S: This rarely imported species is difficult to keep and especially problematic to breed.
Additional members of the *P. altus* group are *P. notospilus, P. huloti, P. pseudonummifer, P. cadwaladeri,* and *P. gabonensis.* All of these species are very similar.

T: 24°–27°C, **L:** 6.5 cm, **A:** 80 cm, **R:** m, **D:** 3

Bathyaethiops caudomaculatus, Buta-Buma, Zaïre, compare to p. 95.

Phenacogrammus altus

Phenacogrammus altus ?, Kindu (Zaïre)

Phenacogrammus ansorgii
Ansorg's blue Congo tetra

(BOULENGER, 1910)

Syn.: *Petersius ansorgei, P. ubalo, Nannopetersius ansorgei, Phenacogrammus ansorgei.*

Hab.: West Africa: Gabon, Zaïre, and Angola.

F.I.: Ca. 1913.

Sex.: ♂♂ have a comma-shaped spot behind the operculum and long threadlike dorsal and anal fins. ♀♀ do not have a spot behind the operculum, and they are generally smaller with shorter fins. BOULENGER erroneously described the ♀♀ as a different species, *Petersius ubalo.*

Soc. B.: Peaceful schooling fish suitable for large community aquaria containing fishes such as *Phenacogrammus interruptus* or *Brycinus longipinnis.* Always keep a small group, since individual specimens wane.

M: Needs a large aquarium with dense vegetation yet plenty of free swimming space. Suitable for "Dutch" aquaria. When the tank is illuminated from the front, the notorious blue dorsal section becomes obvious. Soft and slightly acid water (up to 12° dGH and pH 6.5, respectively) is recommended. Its requirements closely mirror those of the blue Congo tetra, *Phenacogrammus interruptus* (see Vol. 1, p. 222).

B: Rarely successful. According to FRANKE, the species' reproductive biology is similar to that of the blue Congo tetra, *P. interruptus.*

F: C, O; all types of live foods, especially those that float on the water surface (*Drosophila*), and flake foods.

S: Infrequently kept in aquaria. *P. lamberti* is the only similar species from the *P. ansorgii* group.

T: 24°–28°C, L: 7.5 cm, A: 80 cm, R: m, t, D: 2–3

Bathyaethiops breuseghemi
African moon characin

(POLL, 1945)

Syn.: *Phenacogrammus breuseghemi, Micralestes breuseghemi.*

Hab.: Africa: Zaïre Basin.

F.I.: Ca. 1980 to the United States, but only imported into Europe as unidentified by-catch.

Sex.: ♀♀ are deeper-bodied and fuller than ♂♂. ♂♂ have a more colorful dorsal fin.

Soc. B.: Friendly schooling fish which should either be kept in a species tank or with other delicate fishes.

M: *B. breusegheni* needs free swimming space, a dark substrate, and a corner of floating plants. Filter over peat. Water: pH 6.0–7.2; hardness to 15° (6°) dGH. Exchange water every 2–3 weeks, and add a good water conditioner.

B: Eggs are scattered among plants. The morning sun or a strong incandescent light directed into a dark aquarium stimulates spawning. Breeders must be conditioned with live foods.

F: C, O; small live foods of all kinds, flake and FD foods, frozen mosquito larvae, etc.

S: This seldom imported species only develops into a beautiful fish under optimal water conditions. A rewarding species for the specialist. Very similar to *Bathyaethiops caudomaculatus.*

T: 22°–25°C, L: 7 cm, A: 80 cm, R: m, D: 2–3

Phenacogrammus ansorgii

Bathyaethiops breuseghemi

Citharinus citharus

(GEOFFROY, 1809)
Subfam.: Citharininae

Syn.: *Citharinoides citharus, Citharops citharus, Citharinus citharinus, C. geoffroyi.*

Hab.: Africa: from Senegal to the Nile Basin.

F.I.: Ca. 1970.

Sex.: Unknown.

Soc. B.: Peaceful schooling fish.

M: This characin's rapid growth limits its suitability to show aquaria. Its high food intake challenges most filter systems, so use a powerful filter and bolster its effectiveness with frequent water exchanges.

B: Unknown. Due to its size, breeding is very unlikely in an aquarium.

F: O; live foods, plant fare, and flake foods. Goldfish foods can be fed sparingly.

S: In Africa, *Citharinus* species are widely distributed and very important food fishes. Juveniles have many black longitudinal striations, whereas adults are uniformly silver. It weighs up to 7 kg.

T: 22°–28°C, **L**: 58 cm, **A**: from 120 cm, **R**: m, **D**: 3

Nannaethiops unitaeniatus
African single-line characin

GÜNTHER, 1871
Subfam.: Distichodinae

Syn.: None.

Hab.: Africa: Sudan, Chad, Nigeria, the Gold Coast, Cameroon, Gabon, in the Loange and Kabinda Rivers. Widely distributed from the Zaïre River to the Niger River and the White Nile.

F.I.: By "Platy-Tischrunde" from the "Niger region," in 1931.

Sex.: ♂♂ are more slender and brighter orange than ♀♀.

Soc. B.: Peaceful, timid schooling fish.

M: House in a species tank that has a fine-grained substrate, sparse vegetation, and lots of light! Water: pH 6.5–7.5; hardness up to ca. 12° dGH.

B: Easily accomplished. See Vol 1, p. 228.

F: C, O.

S: This fish's colors quickly fade when it is disturbed or maintained in an unfavorable environment. It usually leads a secluded life. While *N. unitaeniatus* was presented in Vol. 1, the pictured animal was a ♀. The more attractive ♂ is shown here.

T: 23°–26°C, **L**: 6.5 cm, **A**: 60 cm, **R**: b, m, **D**: 2–3

Citharinus citharus

Nannaethiops unitaeniatus

Neolebias ansorgii, red form

Neolebias ansorgii   BOULENGER, 1912

Syn.: *Neolebias landgrafi, Micraethiops ansorgii*.

Hab.: Africa: Cameroon, Angola, Central African Republic, and Zaïre (Tshilenge). Though it prefers to inhabit swamps, it has been found in the rivers Luculla and Luali.

F.I.: By McEVOY of Hamburg, Germany, in 1924.

Sex.: ♂♂ are darker. ♀♀ have a fuller ventral area. In the picture, the top fish is a ♀ and the lower two are ♂♂.

Soc. B.: This peaceful fish is often shy when kept under suboptimal conditions. Pair maintenance is possible. Not suitable for community aquaria!

M: This problematic species demands high water quality. Frequent small water exchanges are necessary.

B: Possible but not easy. Spawning occurs in peat substrates. The young hatch after one day and must be fed the tiniest live foods as they become free-swimming.

F: C, O; small live foods, flake foods.

S: This is a rare color morph. The common green form is pictured in Vol. 1, p. 231.

T: 24°–28°C, L: 3.5 cm, A: 50 cm, R: b, m, D: 2–3

Fam.: Distichodidae
Subfam.: Ichthyborinae

Ichthyborus ornatus
Ornate fin-nipper

(BOULENGER, 1899)

Syn.: *Neoborus ornatus, Phago ornatus, Ichthyborus taeniatus, Phagoborus ornatus.*

Hab.: Tropical Africa: Zaïre Basin.

F.I.: Ca. 1980.

Sex.: Unknown.

Soc. B.: Specialized fish and fin predators. Maintenance should be limited to a species tank. Provide plenty of food to prevent cannibalism.

M: Needs a dark-bottomed species tank rich in plants and hiding places. Cover the surface with floating plants. Bogwood and bamboo will provide additional hiding places and can serve to subdivide the aquarium. Water: pH 5.8–7.0; hardness up to 15° dGH. Strong filtration and frequent water exchanges are needed to keep dissolved metabolite concentrations low.

B: Unknown.

F: C; fishes or pieces thereof. Juveniles also accept insect larvae.

S: This species is similar to the rarely imported (only as by-catch) *Phago maculatus.* According to GÉRY, there is an additional smaller species, *Phagoborus quadrilineatus,* from the Casamance River in Senegal.

T: 22°–26°C, **L:** 20 cm, **A:** 100 cm, **R:** m, t, **D:** 4 (C)

Abramites solarii

HOLMBERG

Syn.: *Leporinus ternetzi, L. solarii, Abramites nigripinnis.*

Hab.: South America: Rio Paraguay Basin.

F.I.: 1984 by BLEHER, Frankfurt (Germany).

Sex.: Have not been described.

Soc. B.: Occasionally consumes tender plant shoots when sufficient plant fare is not provided. Older specimens may be rough towards conspecifics.

M: Provide good filtration and illumination. The substrate should consist of pebbles and rock fragments. Crevices are thoroughly searched for edibles. Only use tough plants such as Java fern, etc., and just remove algae from the front pane. Water: pH 6.5–7.8; hardness up to 20° dGH.

B: Not known.

F: L, H; algae, lettuce, spinach, and frozen peas. Offer small live foods for variety. Juveniles will also eat tablet and flake foods (e.g., Tetra Conditioning Food).

S: A beautiful species that should be imported more frequently. There is an additional *Abramites* species from the Rio Magdalena in Colombia (*A. egnes*), but to the best of our knowledge, it has not been imported.

T: 22°–25°C, **L**: 12 cm, **A**: 120 cm, **R**: m, b, **D**: 3

Anostomus plicatus

EIGENMANN, 1912

Syn.: None.

Hab.: South America: Guyana and Suriname.

F.I.: Unknown.

Sex.: Unknown.

Soc. B.: A congenial fish which can be appropriately cared for either in large schools or in community with heterospecifics. Loners may become quarrelsome.

M: Strongly illuminate the aquarium to provide the densely planted, somewhat algae-covered biotope these fish favor. Algae and vegetable fare are dietary necessities for long term care. *Anostomus plicatus*'s natural habitat is rich in plant life. Water: pH around 6; hardness up to 12° dGH, but lower values are better. Strong filtration helps insure the high water quality this fish demands.

B: Unknown.

F: H, O; vegetable fare is necessary, as are algae and small organisms such as water fleas and mosquito larvae.

S: At times, this species has four dark spots along its sides, recognizable as light areas in the photo. Their intensity is mood related.

T: 24°–28°C, **L**: 15 cm, **A**: 100 cm, **R**: b, m, **D**: 2–3

Abramites solarii

Anostomus plicatus

Anostomus spiloclistron

WINTERBOTTOM, 1974

Syn.: None.

Hab.: South America: Guyana and Suriname.

F.I.: Unknown.

Sex.: Unknown.

Soc. B.: When 6 or more animals are kept in a school, they are quite peaceful. Individuals wane and disturb other fishes. Suitable for community aquaria that are not overstocked.

M: This is a somewhat problematic species. See *Anostomus plicatus* and *Anostomus anostomus*, Vol. 1, p. 234.

B: Unknown.

F: H, O; plant fare, small live or frozen foods, and flake foods.

S: The genus *Anostomus* is divided into the subgenera *Anostomus* and *Laemolyta*. Only *Anostomus taeniatus* (see Vol. 1, p. 234) belongs to the subgenus *Laemolyta*. *A. anostomus, A. gracilis, A. plicatus, A. spiloclistron, A. ternetzi,* and *A. trimaculatus* belong to the subgenus *Anostomus* GRONOW, 1763.

T: 24°–28°C, **L:** 16 cm, **A:** 100 cm, **R:** b, m, **D:** 3

Leporinus granti
Grant's leporinus

EIGENMANN, 1912

Syn.: *Hypomasticus granti, Leporinus "maculatus."*

Hab.: South America: Guianas and the Amazon Basin.

F.I.: Unknown.

Sex.: None.

Soc. B.: Peaceful schooling fish which makes an appropriate addition for large community tanks. If the school is excessively small, they may turn belligerent towards conspecifics.

M: *Leporinus* species require large tanks with clear, well-filtered water, but the current should not be overly strong. Its captive environment should have a fine, dark gravel substrate, bogwood, and hardy, tough plants such as Java fern. All plants must be omitted from tanks containing adult specimens. Since most *Leporinus* species attain a respectable size, the aquarium should have a capacity of at least 200 l. Exchange $1/2$ to $1/3$ of the water volume every 2 to 3 weeks. While filtering over peat or adding peat extract increases the well-being of the fish, it is not necessary for successful maintenance. Water: pH 5.5 to 7.5; hardness up to 20° dGH with a dKH of 10°, but less is better.

B: Has not been successful.

F: H; flake foods, fruits, algae, lettuce, spinach, and chickweed. Various fruits or soft vegetables should be tried. Live or frozen foods should occasionally be offered.

S: Spotted *Leporinus* species are difficult to tell apart. *Leporinus badueli, L. granti, L. marcgravi, L. megalepis,* and *L. steyermarki* all hail from the same region and are often confused.

T: 22°–26°C, **L:** 20 cm, **A:** 100 cm, **R:** b, m, **D:** 2

Anostomus spiloclistron

Leporinus granti

Leporinus lacustris
Lake leporinus

MARAL-CAMPOS, 1945

Syn.: None.

Hab.: South America: Sao Paulo Province of Brazil and Laguna Negra in Paraguay (see MAHNERT,1987. Das Aquarium, 11: 221).

F.I.: Ca. 1980.

Sex.: There are no external differentiating features.

Soc. B.: This peaceful schooling fish is suitable for large community aquaria.

M: House in large aquaria that have clear water, a gravel bottom, roots, and very tough plants (e.g., Java fern) or those of plastic. *Leporinus* are usually unappreciated aquarium fishes because of their nasty habit of consuming any and all plants. They live in deep sections of sandy-bottomed creeks, often in the strongest currents, and feed off foods such as aquatic plants, fruits, and leaves carried to them in the current. Trees that have fallen into the water are "grazed." Since most species reach a respectable size, prospective purchasers should beware of the increasing demands these fishes will place. Water: pH 5.8–7.8; hardness up to 20° dGH.

B: Has not been successful.

F: H (O); vegetable fare. Live or frozen foods should occasionally be offered.

S: The pictured specimen is a young fish from Laguna Negra. The dark spots disappear with age.

T: 22°–27°C, L: 20 cm, A: 100 cm, R: b, m, D: 2

Leporinus megalepis
Large-scaled leporinus

GÜNTHER, 1863

Syn.: *Hypomasticus megalepis.*

Hab.: South America: Guayas and Amazon Basins.

F.I.: Unknown.

Sex.: There are no external differentiating features.

Soc. B.: While considered to be a schooling fish, single specimens can be kept. Conspecifics and heterospecifics are not disturbed, making it a good species for community tanks.

M: See *Leporinus granti* or *Leporinus friderici,* Vol. 2, p. 238.

B: Unknown.

F: H, O; herbivore that will appreciate frozen or FD foods occasionally being added to the diet. Flake and tablet foods will be accepted.

S: Very similar to *Leporinus megalepis, L. friderici, L. granti,* and *L. "maculatus."*

This species, though quite common in its natural habitat, is rarely imported.

T: 22°–27°C, L: 30 cm, A: 120 cm, R: b, m, D: 3

Leporinus lacustris

Leporinus megalepis

Leporinus nigrotaeniatus
Black-band leporinus

SCHOMBURGK, 1841

Syn.: *Chalceus nigrotaeniatus, Leporinus margaretaceus, Salmo biribiri.*

Hab.: South America: the Guianas and the Amazon Basin (?).

F.I.: Unknown.

Sex.: Sexes cannot be differentiated by external characteristics.

Soc. B.: Peaceful schooling species which may tend to be aggressive towards conspecifics if maintained in schools that are too small. Suitable for very large community aquaria.

M: Refer to Vol. 1, p. 240, or *Leporinus granti.*

B: Unknown.

F: H.

S: Because of its size, *L. nigrotaeniatus* is conditionally suitable for aquaria. This fish can be easily maintained in sizeable aquaria housing large cichlids. The pictured animal is an adult; a juvenile can be found in Vol. 1 on p. 241.

T: 23°–26°C, **L:** 40 cm, **A:** 150 cm, **R:** b, m, **D:** 3

Leporinus steyermarki
Gray leporinus

INGER, 1956

Syn.: None.

Hab.: South America: Venezuela (?) and Paraguay.

F.I.: Not known.

Sex.: Sexes cannot be differentiated by external characteristics.

Soc. B.: Peaceful schooling fish that can be kept in large aquaria.

M: See *Leporinus granti.*

B: Has not been successfully accomplished in an aquarium.

F: H, O; plants as well as live foods.

S: The pictured fish is a juvenile. As the fish ages, the design fades. There are several similar species. See *Leporinus granti*, p. 102.

T: 22°–26°C, **L:** 30 cm, **A:** 120 cm, **R:** b, m, **D:** 3

Leporinus nigrotaeniatus

Leporinus steyermarki

Brycon cephalus
South American trout

(GÜNTHER, 1869)

Syn.: *Megalobrycon cephalus, M. erythropterus* (?), *Chalceus cephalus*.

Hab.: South America: Amazon Basin.

F.I.: Only imported as by-catch.

Sex.: There are no external distinguishing features.

Soc. B.: Juveniles are peaceful schooling fish and suitable for community aquaria. Adults maintain their schooling behavior but are predators, which limits tankmates to equal-sized fishes.

M: House in a large, strongly filtered aquarium. Cover the aquarium well, since this species is an excellent jumper. Water: pH 5.5 to 7.5; hardness up to 20° dGH. Plants, if sufficiently robust, are possible. Always keep plenty of free swimming space.

B: Unknown. Its mature size is probably the only reason breeding has been unsuccessful.

F: C, O.

S: See the similar *Brycon falcatus* in Vol. 1, p. 244, and *Brycon melanopterus* in Vol. 2, p. 246.
This is the type species for the subgenus *Megalobrycon*.

T: 22°–26°C, **L:** 22 cm, **A:** 120 cm, **R:** m, **D:** 3

Chalceus erythrurus
Yellow-finned chalceus

COPE, 1870

Syn.: *Brycon erythrurus, Chalceus macrolepidotus, Plethodectes erythrurus*.

Hab.: South America: Amazon Basin.

F.I.: 1913 (?).

Sex.: There are no external differences between the two sexes.

Soc. B.: A schooling fish whose appearance deceives one into believing it is a predator. However, it is only predacious towards significantly smaller fishes, making it easy to house with other, somewhat larger fishes.

M: Use a large aquarium that has sufficient free swimming space and a good cover to prevent it from leaping out. Plants can be included in the decor.

B: Unknown.

F: C, O; hardy foods such as earthworms, beef heart, or shrimp (frozen) are necessary to satisfy its voracious appetite.

S: This species is a particularly relished food fish in its native land; their meat is reputed to be better tasting than that of trout.
C. erythrurus is easily confused with *C. macrolepidotus*, see Vol. 1, p. 244; however, *C. erythrurus* is easily identified by its yellow ventral fins.
If more irrefutable methods are called for, the two species can be identified by their dentition.

T: 22°–26°C, **L:** 25 cm, **A:** from 100 cm, **R:** m, t, **D:** 3

Brycon cephalus

Chalceus erythrurus

Gymnocharacinus bergi
Patagonian characin

STEINDACHNER, 1903

Syn.: None. *Gymnocharacinus "fugi"* is a trade name for ♂♂.

Hab.: South America: Argentina. Endemic to the headwaters of Valcheta Creek in northern Patagonia, south of the Rio de la Plata.

F.I.: 1978 by Dr. K. H. LÜLING, Bonn, Germany.

Sex.: ♂♂ are smaller than ♀♀. The upper and lower edges of the ♂♂'s forked caudal fin are outlined in white.

Soc. B.: Nimble, even hectic characins which are often found swimming against the current and jumping rapids like trout to gain access to other water regions. Does not form pairs or schools.

M: Use a substrate of sand or fine-grained gravel with a few flat stones or large pebbles on top. This fish needs a long aquarium with a lot of swimming space and a fast current. Maintain a low water level that allows clearance between it and the cover ("jumping space"). Correspondingly, an effective cover is needed to keep the fish from leaping out. Plants that rise above the water surface can be included in the decor. Because of the fish's predilection for swimming countercurrent, air-driven interior filters are inappropriate, since the fish swim into the tube.

B: *G. bergi* spawns in gravel substrates below stones. First the gravel is removed and then, after spawning, the spawn is covered using the same gravel. Suction the gravel up with the spawn and hatch in a container. The larvae emerge after 36–48 hr and are free-swimming after an additional 6 days. Feed with plankton. Growth is slow. Water values do not seem to be important, but the temperature should neither be below 18°C nor above 22°C.

F: O; omnivore with a seasonal, voracious appetite. For about 3 months of the year it, needs little nourishment.

S: *G. bergi* has the southernmost distribution of any South American characin.

The Valcheta Creek originates in a volcanic region and has a temperature of 22°C throughout the year, even in winter as snow falls (period of no food). The Patagonian characin is in danger of extinction, since trout have been introduced into the creek; currently there are only about 250 specimens!

T: 22°C, L: ♂ 4 cm, ♀ 6 cm, A: from 60 cm, R: b, D: 4

Gymnocharacinus bergi ♂

Gymnocharacinus bergi ♀

Acestrorhynchus altus
Red dog characin

MENEZES, 1969

Syn.: None.

Hab.: South America: Amazon and Paraguay Basins, predominantly in large rivers.

F.I.: Has not been imported alive(?).

Sex.: Unknown.

Soc. B.: A true predator that can only be kept with equal-sized fishes.

M: Subdivide the tank with wood and rocks and plant dense vegetation along the edges to prevent this very nervous fish from swimming against the glass. The surface should be partially covered with floating plants. Strong filtration and good water movement are required. Water: pH 5.5–7.2; hardness up to 18° dGH.

B: Unknown.

F: C; small fishes, meat, earthworms, and large insects and their larvae.

S: In Paraguay, this is an appreciated food fish. Its appropriateness as an aquarium specimen is rather limited; more suited for large show aquaria.

T: 22°–26°C, **L:** 35 cm, **A:** 120 cm, **R:** m, **D:** 4 (C)

Charax pauciradiatus
Glass headstander

(GÜNTHER, 1864)

Syn.: *Anacyrtus pauciradiatus, Characynus pauciradiatus, Cynopotamus pauciradiatus, Epicyrtus pauciradiatus.*

Hab.: South America: Amazon Basin and Paraguay.

F.I.: Ca. 1910.

Sex.: ♂♂ have gold patches during the spawning season (see picture). ♀♀ are larger and have a rounded ventral area.

Soc. B.: *C. pauciradiatus* is a peaceful, somewhat timid species which readily retires among water plants. Wanes when associated with active fishes. Small fishes and tender plants are unceremoniously eaten

M: Dense vegetation consisting of robust, fast-growing species. Roomy aquaria. While water movement is not necessary, good filtration is. Water: pH 6.2 to 7.5; hardness up to 25° dGH.

B: Unknown, but it should be similar to *Charax gibbosus*; see Vol. 2, p. 252.

F: O.

S: Though not a predator, its size and sporadic import make it a rarely kept species.

T: 22°–27°C, **L:** 15 cm, **A:** 100 cm, **R:** m, **D:** 2

Acestrorhynchus altus

Charax pauciradiatus ♂

Roeboides meeki
Meek's predatory characin

EIGENMANN, 1922

Syn.: None.

Hab.: South America: Colombia, Rio Cauca.

F.I.: Ca. 1950.

Sex.: ♂♂ are slender; ♀♀ are deeper-bodied.

Soc. B.: This predaceous species is unsuitable for community aquaria because of its diet of scales and eyes of larger fishes.

M: Needs clear, oxygen-rich water and a strong filter. Good nutrition is important. No particular demands are placed on water quality. This small, delicate-looking species is capable of devouring all its tankmates within a few weeks.

B: Unknown; other species of this genus are open spawners that spawn among plants near the water surface at a temperature of 25°C. Young hatch after 2 days and require live plankton. Juveniles are very cannibalistic if their dietary needs are not met.

F: C; live foods, fish scales, and flake foods.

S: There are several very similar species that are difficult for even scientists to differentiate.

T: 22°–26°C, **L**: 6 cm, **A**: 60 cm, **R**: m, **D**: 3

Roeboides paranensis
Paraguayan predatory characin

UJ, 1987

Syn.: None.

Hab.: South America: Paraguay.

F.I.: Ca. 1970.

Sex.: Unknown.

Soc. B.: Predator. Only equal-sized conspecifics make suitable tankmates.

M: See *Roeboides meeki*.

B: Unknown; see *R. meeki*.

F: C; live foods. Flake foods are occasionally accepted.

T: 22°–26°C, **L**: 6.5 cm, **A**: 60 cm, **R**: m, **D**: 3

Roeboides meeki

Roeboides paranensis

115

Brittanichthys myersi
Myers' blood tetra

GÉRY, 1965

Syn.: None.

Hab.: South America: Rio Negro and Rio Xeriuni, in sluggish black waters over shallow sand banks.

F.I.: 1964.

Sex.: ♂♂ have hooklets on the first rays of the anal fin and modified rays in the caudal fin.

Soc. B.: Peaceful schooling fish. Makes a good tankmate for other small, peaceful fishes. Very sensitive to stress.

M: A lot of free swimming space and resting places among plant thickets are needed. Plant the edges with natant creeping-shoot vegetation, and limit plants in the front quadrant to low-growing specimens. Hiding places among bogwood are important. As per its natural biotope, this sensitive species must

be kept in black water: pH 4.5 to 6.0; hardness up to 8° dGH; carbonate hardness immeasurably low. Either add peat extract or filter over peat. Keep illumination moderate; use water values that fall between the fish's requirements and those of the plants.

B: Unknown; probably difficult.

F: C, O; small live foods, *Artemia*, and flake, freeze-dried, and frozen foods.

S: *B. myersi* is very sensitive to transport-related stress and demands much attention when imported.
Brittanichthys axelrodi and *B. myersi* have unusual shaped anal and caudal fins which assumedly play a role in reproduction. Fin morphology is used to identify this species.

T: 22°–24°C, **L:** 4 cm, **A:** 80 cm, **R:** m, **D:** 3

Holoshestes pequira
Orange spot characin

(STEINDACHNER, 1882)

Syn.: *Cheirodon pequira, Odontostilbe pequira, O. trementina.*

Hab.: South America: Rio Guaporé and Rio Paraguay.

F.I.: Unknown.

Sex.: ♂♂ are more slender and colorful.

Soc. B.: Friendly schooling fish.

M: House in a large aquarium that is equipped with a filter strong enough to provide a constant current and, at the same time, maintain the water clean and clear. Use a dark substrate. Filtering over peat is advantageous. Water: pH 6.2 to 7.5; hardness up to 20° dGH.

B: Unknown, but it should be similar to that of *Paracheirodon innesi*; see Vol. 1, p. 307.

F: C, O; flake foods, *Artemia*, FD foods, and small live foods.

S: Fishes of the genus *Holoshestes* and the very similar genus *Saccoderma*

would make good aquarium fishes, but they are rarely imported.

T: 22°–26°C, **L:** 5.5 cm, **A:** 80 cm, **R:** m, **D:** 2

Brittanichthys myersi

Holoshestes pequira

Odontostilbe fugitiva
Fugitive characin

COPE, 1870

Syn.: *Cheirodon fugitiva, Odontostilbe caquetae, O. drepanon, O. madeirae.*

Hab.: South America: Amazon Basin and Colombia.

F.I.: Unknown.

Sex.: ♂♂ are slender, whereas ♀♀ are full through the ventral area.

Soc. B.: This peaceful schooling fish is only suitable for community tanks that have a population of small, tranquil species. Maintain in groups of at least 6; individuals wane.

M: This demanding species prefers clear water with a slight current. Its oxygen requirement is slightly above average. Peat filtration is beneficial. It can be slowly acclimated to slightly harder water. Water: pH 5.8 to 7.5; hardness up to 20° dGH.

B: Unknown.

F: C, O; live, flake, and FD foods are accepted.

S: Repeatedly imported into North America; probably has not been kept by European hobbyists.
O. fugitiva is the type species of the genus. FINK & WEITZMAN consider this fish a member of the genus *Cheirodon.*

T: 22°–26°C, **L:** 5 cm, **A:** 60 cm, **R:** m, **D:** 2–3

Phenacogaster pectinatus
Pectinatus

(COPE, 1870)

Syn.: *Astyanax pectinatus, Tetragonopterus pectinatus, T. bairdii, T. tabatingae, Phenawgastier bairdii.*

Hab.: South America: quite common in the upper and central regions of the Amazon Basin.

F.I.: Uncertain, since this fish has often been imported as by-catch. Definitely imported before 1968.

Sex.: The anal fin of the ♀ is slightly concave; the anterior part of the ♂'s anal fin is either strongly curved or a long lobelike entity—or something in between.

Soc. B.: Very peaceful schooling fish. It swims with its head slightly inclined. Greatly similar to the *Roeboides* characins.

M: This relatively undemanding species exhibits a humble amount of color when placed in tanks having sufficient vegetation to dim light penetration, a dark substrate, and good filtration. Fins turn red-brown, the golden band on the lateral line becomes more pronounced, and the two black spots become more intense than those seen on the picture. Water: pH 6.0–7.8; hardness up to 25° (12°) dGH.

B: Has not been described. It is probably similar to *Hemigrammus* species.

F: O; flake, FD, and frozen foods.

S: *Phenacogaster megalostictus*, a similar fish from the Rio Negro and the Guianas, has a larger black spot on its side.
P. pectinatus is the type species for the genus. Two rows of unusual genus-typical scales run ventrally along its sides. These scales form a double protruding keel that extends on both sides.

T: 23°–27°C, **L:** 8 cm, **A:** 80 cm, **R:** m, **D:** 1

Odontostilbe fugitiva

Phenacogaster pectinatus

Coelurichthys microlepis
Croaking tetra, small-scaled tetra

Syn.: *Mimagoniates microlepis, Paragoniates microlepis.*

Hab.: South America: southeast Brazil, Joinville.

F.I.: 1907 by O. KITTLER, Hamburg, Germany.

Sex.: ♂♂ are larger, more colorful, and have elongated fins. ♀♀ are somewhat fuller through the ventral area. Sexual differences are frequently difficult to impossible to see in animals that are not full-grown.

Soc. B.: Not a marked schooling animal, but it does like to live in a group.

M: Easily kept, even in community aquaria. Although soft, slightly acid to slightly alkaline water is probably preferred, water values seem to play a subordinate role. The blue iridescence of the fish is more pronounced when the illumination is not excessively bright. The aquarium should have plenty of vegetation along the edges, but also open areas since the animals are tireless swimmers.

T: 18°–23°C, **L:** 6 cm, **A:** 80 cm, **R:** t, m, **D:** 3–4

(STEINDACHNER, 1876)

B: These animals spawn on plants or similar substrates. The following method has been successful: In a 60 cm aquarium with soft, slightly acid water, a large bundle of loose, green synthetic floss is introduced. Two pairs are placed into the tank. If the animals do not spawn within 2 days, an intense diet of mosquito larvae should be instigated. After spawning, the parents have to be removed. The whitish eggs are distributed throughout the floss. Young hatch after 2–3 days and are fed with infusoria after they become free-swimming. Later, *Artemia* nauplii and other small foods are fed.

F: C; live, frozen, and flake foods.

S: This species is constantly confused with *C. tenuis* and *Glandulocauda* (= *Coelurichthys?*) *inaequalis*. Even the animal pictured in Vol. 2, p. 255, is a ♂ *C. microlepis*. Caudal fin morphology can be used to identify the species.

Coelurichthys tenuis
Barberos characin

NICHOLS, 1913

Syn.: *"Mimagoniates barberi;"* not REGAN.

Hab.: South America: southeast Brazil, Paraguay, and northern Argentina.

F.I.: 1907 by Oskar Kittler, Hamburg, Germany.

Sex.: ♀'s dorsal fin is rounded, whereas that of the ♂ is elongated. The anal fin of the ♂ reaches beyond the caudal peduncle (elongated into a tip), while that of the ♀ is rounded and terminates at the center of the caudal peduncle.

Soc. B.: This peaceful schooling fish is suitable for cool community aquaria.

M: Difficult to maintain. It comes from small, swift, shady creeks in hilly terrain. The water is clear, slightly peat-brown, and oxygen-rich. These conditions can only be simulated in tanks that are slightly heated (cooled during the sum-

mer). Water: pH 5.5–6.5; hardness up to 4° dGH. The tank should be immaculate and dimly lit with pronounced water current.

B: 24°C. Fertilization is internal. The semen package is transferred after intense courtship and the ♂'s unflagging trials to embrace the ♀. Once insemination is successful, the ♀ can, even weeks afterwards, lay fertilized eggs. The underside of water plants or grasses is preferred. Larvae hatch after 1 day, but are difficult to raise because of their diminutive size. The smallest freshwater plankton is necessary for even moderate success.

S: This species has been discussed under the name *"Mimagoniates barberi."* However that is a totally different, yet to be imported, species.

T: 19°–22°C, **L:** 5 cm, **A:** 80 cm, **R:** t, **D:** 3–4 (C)

Coelurichthys microlepis

Coelurichthys tenuis

Xenurobrycon macropus   MYERS & MIRANDA-RIBEIRO, 1945

Syn.: None.

Hab.: South America: Rio Paraguay.

F.I.: Unknown.

Sex.: ♂♂ have conspicuously shaped anal and tail fins.

Soc. B.: This peaceful schooling fish is suitable for community aquaria containing small tranquil fishes. A species tank is better, however, since *X. macropus* is somewhat prone to diseases.

M: Floating plants provide the cover this species requires. Water: pH 6.0 to 7.5; hardness up to 20° dGH.

B: Unknown.

F: O; live and flake foods.

S: The vitreous *X. macropus* is readily identified by the uncommon shape of its fins. Fishes of the genus *Tyttocharax* are very similar.

T: 22°–28°C, **L:** 5 cm, **A:** 70 cm, **R:** m, **D:** 2

Rachoviscus crassiceps   MYERS, 1926
Thick-head characin

Syn.: None.

Hab.: South America: Brazil, near Rio de Janeiro, Paraná.

F.I.: Ca. 1940.

Sex.: ♂♂ have hooklets and white-edged fins. ♀♀ remain smaller than ♂♂.

Soc. B.: This peaceful schooling fish is well suited for community aquaria stocked with small fishes. However, single specimens are reputed to be aggressive and will not live long.

M: Good swimmer, so be sure to leave plenty of swimming space. Insure that the water is well-filtered and the tank is bright and heavily planted. Water: pH 5.6 to 7.2; hardness up to 18° dGH. Always keep a small school of at least 8. *R. crassiceps* is rheotactic, often found in front of the filter discharge.

B: Unknown.

F: C, O; flake, FD, and small live foods, including water fleas and mosquito larvae.

S: This small and, unfortunately, rarely imported species makes a good aquarium fish, even for beginners. *Rachoviscus* is closely related to the genera *Aphyocharax* and *Prionobrama*.

T: 20°–25°C, **L:** 4.5 cm, **A:** 70 cm, **R:** m, **D:** 1–2

Astyanax fasciatus fasciatus
American stripe tetra, silvery tetra

(CUVIER, 1819)

Syn.: *Anoptichthys fasciatus, Poecilurichthys fasciatus.*

Hab.: South and Central America: from Argentina up to Mexico. Widely but sporadically distributed.

F.I.: Ca. 1920.

Sex.: ♂♂ are slimmer than ♀♀.

Soc. B.: Peaceful schooling fish. Good addition for community tanks containing large fishes.

M: This relatively undemanding species requires little attention. Water values are not particularly important, but soft water is advantageous. A lot of open swimming space is important for these active fish. Since flora is not eaten, the aquarium can contain plants.

B: Easy to breed. Either pairs or, more naturally, schools should be placed in a breeding tank. These characins spawn on plant bundles. A mesh over the bottom is beneficial, since the parents are distinctly predacious towards their spawn. Remove the parents after spawning is concluded. Young hatch after 1–2 days, but 6 days pass before the young are free-swimming. Larvae can be immediately fed *Artemia* nauplii. Copious feedings and frequent partial water exchanges are important factors when rearing this species.

F: C, O.

S: Nine subspecies of *A. fasciatus* have been described. The blind cave form was presented in Vol. 1, p. 256. *Astyanax bimaculatus* and *A. schubarti* are very similar.

T: 20°–25°C, **L:** 14 cm, **A:** 100 cm, **R:** m, **D:** 1

Astyanax giton

EIGENMANN, 1908

Syn.: None.

Hab.: South America: eastern Brazil.

F.I: Ca. 1980.

Sex.: Unknown.

Soc. B.: Schooling fish.

M: See *Astyanax fasciatus fasciatus*.

B: Unknown. Probably similar to that of the above species.

F: C, O.

S: This species is difficult to identify. The pictured animal could be *Hemigrammus schmardae* (STEINDACHNER, 1882). See Vol. 2, p. 274.

T: 20°–25°C, **L:** 8 cm, **A:** 80 cm, **R:** m, t, **D:** 1

Astyanax fasciatus

Astyanax giton

Astyanax guianensis
Guyana tetra

EIGENMANN, 1909

Syn.: None.

Hab.: South America: Guyana and Venezuela.

F.I.: Unknown.

Sex.: ♂♂ are slimmer, and their anal fin is more curved.

Soc. B.: Peaceful schooling fish. Suitable for any community tank of sufficient size.

M: Cover part of the water surface with floating plants and make sure there is plenty of free swimming space below. Dense edge vegetation. Peat filtration is preferred, but not necessary. Water: pH 5.8–7.5; hardness up to 20° (8°) dGH.

B: Spawns in schools among fine-leaved plants.

F: C, O; flake, frozen, and FD foodstuffs.

S: Rarely imported because of the nondescript appearance of juveniles.

T: 23°–27°C, **L:** 6 cm, **A:** 80 cm, **R:** m, **D:** 1–2

Astyanax scabripinnis
Rough-finned tetra

(JENYNS, 1842)

Syn.: *"Astyanax fasciatus,"* *Tetragonopterus scabripinnis*.

Hab.: South America: east and southeast Brazil.

F.I.: Unknown.

Sex.: ♀♀ are noticeably fuller through the ventral area.

Soc. B.: Peaceful schooling fish that are suitable for community tanks containing hardy plants. Tender plant shoots are nibbled on.

M: Offer plenty of free swimming space. Provide good filtration and water movement. Water: pH 6.5–7.5; hardness up to 18° dGH.

B: Open spawner. Schools as it lays its eggs among plants.

F: O; omnivore that consumes plants as well as any live foods it can catch. Vegetable flakes.

S: The genus *Astyanax* encompasses most species within the subfamily Tetragonopterinae. They are probably the most typical and basic of all tetras. The scales are clearly reminiscent of cyprinids. One subspecies of *A. scabripinnis* has been described by EIGENMANN, 1914: *A. scabripinnis paranae* from the Rio Paraná and the Rio Grande. Both of these rivers drain south into the junction between Brazil, Paraguay, and Argentina through the legendary Iguazu Waterfalls.

T: 22°–26°C, **L:** 10 cm, **A:** 100 cm, **R:** m, **D:** 2

Astyanax guianensis

Astyanax scabripinnis

Bryconamericus sp. aff. *stramineus*   EIGENMANN, 1908

Syn.: None; since the species name could not be unequivocally determined, perhaps it is still an undescribed species.

Hab.: South America: Paraguay.

F.I.: Not known.

Sex.: Unknown.

Soc. B.: Schooling fish.

M: Demands plenty of peace and quiet, particularly when only a few specimens are kept. Therefore, do not house with lively fishes. Dense vegetation increases their coloration, especially if part of the surface is also overgrown. A dark substrate and filtering over peat, while not necessary, are certainly helpful. Water: pH 5.5 to 7.2; hardness up to 25° (10°) dGH; not above 8° dKH.

B: Unknown, but probably similar to *Nematobrycon lacortei* and *N. palmeri*. See also *N. "amphiloxus" palmeri*.

F: C, O; small live foods are its preferred choice.

S: Rarely do fishes from the species-rich genus *Bryconamericus*, which GÉRY says require an urgent revision, reach our aquaria. Additionally, they are often unidentifiable. Fishes of this genus require high oxygen levels, since they live in fast-flowing creeks.

T: 22°–26°C, **L:** 6 cm, **A:** 70 cm, **R:** m, **D:** 2

Ceratobranchia obtusirostris   EIGENMANN, 1914

Syn.: *Ceratobranchia binghami. C. elatior* belongs to a different genus. The genus *Microgenys* has a similar body morphology, but totally different dentition.

Hab.: South America: Peru, Colombia.

F.I.: Has not been imported into Europe alive; the picture was taken in the United States.

Sex.: Unknown.

Soc. B.: Schooling fish.

M: As for *Bryconamericus*.

B: Unknown.

F: O.

S: The genus *Ceratobranchia* is monotypical; hence, the only species contained therein is *C. obtusirostris*. *Ceratobranchia* and *Microgenys* are very hard for the layperson to distinguish. See Syn.

T: 20°–24°C, **L:** 7 cm, **A:** 80 cm, **R:** m, **D:** 2

Bryconamericus sp. aff. *stramineus*

Ceratobranchia obtusirostris

Hemigrammus bellottii
Dash-dot tetra

STEINDACHNER, 1882

Syn.: *Hemigrammus agulha, H. bellottii, H. orthus, Tetragonopterus bellottii.*

Hab.: South America: the Guianas and the Amazon region.

F.I.: Unknown.

Sex.: ♂♂ are smaller and thinner in comparison to ripe ♀♀.

Soc. B.: Peaceful schooling fish that are suitable for community tanks housing active fishes.

M: In order for it to display its beauty, this species must be kept in schools and housed in tanks whose light is filtered through floating plants or leaves. Peat filtration and a slight water current are advantageous. Water: pH 5.8 to 7.5; hardness up to 15° dGH, but less than 10° is better.

B: Spawns in bunches of fine-leaved plants at 27°C. Either breed in pairs or schools. The breeding tank should have a spawning mesh and soft, peat-filtered water. Feed the young live plankton and rotifers.

F: C, O; small live foods and flake foods. Feed small portions several times a day.

S: This fish might actually be a *Hyphessobrycon*.

T: 23°–27°C, **L**: 4 cm, **A**: 60 cm, **R**: m, **D**: 2

Hemigrammus bleheri
Brilliant rummy-nose

GÉRY, 1986

Syn.: None.

Hab.: South America: Colombia, Rio Vaupes; Brazil, Rio Negro.

F.I.: 1965 by Heiko BLEHER, Kelsterbach, Germany.

Sex.: ♂ is slimmer. ♀ is fuller and has a rounded ventral area at spawning time.

Soc. B.: Peaceful, nimble schooling fish. Easily associated with similar species.

M: Not always easily maintained because of the attention to water quality it demands. Keep nitrate concentrations low with frequent water exchanges. Use a good water conditioner. Tap water that contributes a nitrate concentration above 30 mg/l is detrimental.

B: 25°–28°C; soft, peat-filtered water; pH 6.0–6.5; hardness less than 4° KH. Schools in large tanks are easier to spawn than pairs. Small-leaved plants are the substrate of choice. Eggs are frequently eaten. The fry hatch after 30–36 hr and are free-swimming after the fourth day. Feed the smallest freshwater plankton at first, since the fry are very tiny.

F: C, O; flake foods with FD components, FD tablets, and small live foods.

S: Compare to *Petitella georgiae* and *Hemigrammus rhodostomus* (Vol. 1, pp. 308 and 272, respectively).
H. bleheri was previously identified as *H. rhodostomus* AHL, 1924. However, after further consideration, the differences in coloration and cranial bone morphology established this fish as an autonomous species. *H. bleheri* and *H. rhodostomus* are black water fishes, while *Petitella* prefers white waters.

T: 23°–26°C, **L**: 4.5 cm, **A**: 80 cm, **R**: m, **D**: 2–3

Hemigrammus bellottii

Hemigrammus bleheri

Hemigrammus micropterus

MEEK, 1907

Syn.: None. It is possible that *Hemigrammus boesemanni* is a subspecies of *H. micropterus*.

Hab.: South America: Venezuela.

F.I.: Unknown.

Sex.: ♂♂ are smaller and slimmer.

Soc. B.: Peaceful schooling fish.

M: See *Hemigrammus bellottii*.

B: Unknown, but probably similar to other *Hemigrammus* species.

F: C, O; an omnivore that is particularly appreciative of small live foods.

S: *Hemigrammus* species with a spot on the caudal peduncle are unusually difficult to identify.

T: 23°–27°C, **L:** 3.5 cm, **A:** 50 cm, **R:** m, **D:** 2

Hemigrammus tridens
Cross-spot tetra

EIGENMANN, 1907

Syn.: None.

Hab.: South America: Rio Paraguay, Paraguay.

F.I.: Ca. 1980.

Sex.: ♂♂ are smaller and slimmer.

Soc. B.: Peaceful schooling fish.

M: See *Hemigrammus bellottii*.

B: Unknown, but probably similar to other *Hemigrammus* species.

F: C, O; flake and live foods.

S: According to GÉRY, this is a very colorful species.

T: 23°–25°C, **L:** 3.5 cm, **A:** 50 cm, **R:** m, **D:** 2

Hemigrammus micropterus

Hemigrammus tridens ♂

Hyphessobrycon compressus (MEEK, 1904)

Syn.: *Hemigrammus compressus*.

Hab.: Central America: Guatemala, Honduras, and Mexico.

F.I.: Ca. 1970.

Sex.: Full-grown ♂♂ are slightly larger and slimmer.

Soc. B.: Peaceful schooling fish.

M: See *Hyphessobrycon werneri* (p. 140).

B: Unknown, but probably similar to other *Hyphessobrycon* species.

F: C, O; flake and live foods.

S: *Hyphessobrycon milleri* is a very similar species from the same geographic area.

T: 23°–26°C, **L:** 3.5 cm, **A:** 50 cm, **R:** m, **D:** 2

Hyphessobrycon elachys
Reed tetra

WEITZMAN, 1985

Syn.: None. Frequently seen in books as *Cheirodon kriegi*.

Hab.: South America: Brazil, Paraguay. In the Rio Paraguay Basin, upper Rio Guaporé, and the Laguna Blanca. Usually found along reed-choked shores.

F.I.: Ca. 1935 as *Cheirodon kriegi*.

Sex.: ♂♂ have very elongated dorsal and ventral fins, a larger anal fin, and a noticeably white adipose fin. ♀♀ are normally thicker than ♂♂.

Soc. B.: A peaceful, active schooling fish which makes a good addition to the community aquarium.

M: Clean, well-filtered water with little current is best. Water: pH 6.0–7.2; hardness up to 15° dGH. The shy demeanor of this fish can be overcome to a large extent by using floating plants and dim lighting.

B: Like most characins, these animals prefer to spawn among fine-leaved plants.

F: C, O; flake, live, and frozen foods.

S: The black spot on the anal area only appears in ♀♀, despite indications to the contrary. However, it does not imply ripeness. *H. elachys* ♀♀ were first described as an autonomous species. Unfortunately, Vol. 2 contains this error. MAHNERT (1987) exhaustively described the Paraguayan habitat of *H. elachys* and its fellow species in Das Aquarium, 11, 221.

T: 24°–27°C, **L:** 5 cm, **A:** 80 cm, **R:** m, **D:** 2

Hyphessobrycon compressus

Hyphessobrycon elachys

Hyphessobrycon igneus   MIQUELARENA, MENNI, LOPEZ & CASCIOTTA, 1980
Firefin tetra

Syn.: None.

Hab.: South America: Argentina and Paraguay, in mountain creeks.

F.I.: 1984.

Sex.: ♂♂ are colorful and slim.

Soc. B.: An active, peaceful schooling fish.

M: The water should be slightly cool, meticulously clean, with a swift current. Good water quality is important, requiring good filtration and frequent partial water exchanges. Healthy, profuse plant growth helps insure low levels of dissolved metabolites. Water values play a subordinate role in maintaining this fish.

B: Unknown.

F: C, O; live and flake foods. If flakes are frequently fed, this characin should be housed with scavengers such as catfishes so leftovers will be eaten.

S: An interesting and beautiful new import for the hobby.

T: 20°–24°C, **L:** 5 cm, **A:** 80 cm, **R:** m, **D:** 2–3

Hyphessobrycon inconstans
Fickle tetra

EIGENMANN & OGLE, 1907

Syn.: None.

Hab.: South America: east Brazil, Paraguay, and Colombia, in flood plains of the Magdalena. Thanks to MÖRTH, its presence in Clemencia, Arjona, Repelon, Magdalena, Gambote, and Lake Cinga de Gambote has been determined.

F.I.: Unknown.

Sex.: With the exception of the more convex ventral profile of ♀♀, there are no differentiating characteristics.

Soc. B.: This peaceful schooling fish makes an appropriate addition to community aquaria.

M: Undemanding, somewhat shy fish. Good vegetation is necessary. Water: hardness of 2°–20° dGH; temperature 20°–28°C.

B: Only possible in aquaria at least 50 cm long. BÖHM was the first to successfully breed this fish. His conditions were as follows: pH 6.5; hardness 7° dGH; temperature 26°C. The young hatched after 24 to 30 hr. For an additional 3 days they hung on the glass and plants or laid on the substrate. After they were free-swimming, they could eat *Artemia* nauplii. This very fecund species lays about 600 eggs per set-up and per ♀.

F: C, O; small live foods as well as flake foods.

S: There are several geographical variants.

T: 22°–28°C, **L:** 4.5 cm, **A:** 60 cm, **R:** m, **D:** 1

Hyphessobrycon igneus

Hyphessobrycon inconstans

Hyphessobrycon luetkeni

BOULENGER, 1887

Syn.: None.

Hab.: South America: Paraguay and southeast Brazil.

F.I.: Ca. 1980.

Sex.: ♂♂ are slimmer.

Soc. B.: Peaceful schooling fish.

M: See *Hyphessobrycon inconstans* (previous species).

B: Not known.

F: O, C.

T: 22°–26°C, L: 4 cm, A: 60 cm, R: m, D: 2

Hyphessobrycon peruvianus
Peruvian tetra, blue Loreto tetra

LADIGES, 1938

Syn.: None.

Hab.: South America: Peruvian Amazon region around Iquitos and Tabatinga.

F.I.: 1938 by Aquarium Hamburg, Germany.

Sex.: ♂♂ are slimmer than ♀♀. Juveniles cannot be sexed.

Soc. B.: Lively, peaceful schooling fish. Other small tetras, *Corydoras* species, small labyrinth fishes, dwarf cichlids, and similar fishes make fitting tankmates.

M: Aquaria with dim lighting, peat filtration, and a dark substrate are ideal. Fine-leaved plants can be included in the decor. Partially covering the water surface with floating plants enhances the fish's well-being. Water: pH 6.0–7.0; hardness 5°–10° dGH. Regular water exchanges with the addition of peat extract every 3–4 weeks are recommended.

B: Reports on successfully reproducing this species are sparse. WOLF wrote about *Hyphessobrycon metae* in DATZ 1963, pp. 33 ff. According to this report, these fish have a notoriously bright red tail fin. However, this is only the case with *H. loretoensis*. In contrast, *H. peruvianus* has a colorless, translucent caudal fin. Furthermore, *H. metae*'s tail fin is only reddish along the base; the rest is colorless.

WOLF's breeding report is of interest, since *H. peruvianus* and *H. loretoensis* are closely related. It can therefore be assumed that breeding methods would

be similar: A suitable breeding pair was selected from a school. The ♂ spread his fins and commenced to intensely court his chosen ♀. WOLF used a "trial" combination of water parameters to breed this fish, which happened to be the same he uses to breed cardinal tetras. Exact specifications are not given. However, it was probably soft water (2°–4° dKH) with a pH of around 5–6. Peat filtration and deionized water are surely advantageous.

The ♀ spawned among fine-leaved plants. Considering the animal's timid nature, the breeding tank should be dark. Use Enchytraeidae and glassworms to ripen the animals. Two days after spawning, the larvae hatched and were fed small infusoria from the 5th day. After another 5 days, *Artemia* can be fed. These fish are not very fecund, which is why this species is rarely encountered in pet shops. Nevertheless, WOLF had 41 young the first spawn and 84 young in the second.

F: C, O; small live, flake, and FD foods. Frozen *Cyclops*. Bloodworms are only suitable for full-grown specimens. Young glassworms and mosquito larvae are better.

S: GÉRY assumes that this species is a *Hemigrammus*. Renaming many *Hyphessobrycon* species is still pending. Compare this species to *H. metae* and *H. loretoensis* (Vol. 2, p. 278 and Vol. 1, p. 290, respectively).

T: 24°–26°C, L: 4.5 cm, A: 60 cm, R: m, D: 2–3

Hyphessobrycon luetkeni

Hyphessobrycon peruvianus

Hyphessobrycon werneri
Werner's tetra

GÉRY & UJ, 1987

Syn.: None.

Hab.: South America: Brazil. In a forest creek between Maria do Para and Sao Miguel de Guama, 120 km from Belem (Para), road BR 010.

F.I.: In 1986 by A. WERNER, H. BLEHER, and others.

Sex.: ♂♂ have a larger dorsal fin and more intense coloration; ♀♀ are usually fuller.

Soc. B.: Peaceful schooling fish. Suitable for community tanks containing small species.

M: Moderate-sized aquaria with dense vegetation along the edges and sparse vegetation in the center quadrant. Insure that the foreground is free so that courtship and the display behavior of the ♂♂ can be observed. A dark sub-strate is preferred, as are a slight current and peat filtration. Water: pH 5.6 to 7.0; hardness up to 20° dGH; up to 7° dKH.

B: Unknown. Presumably similar to *Hyphessobrycon bentosi bentosi*. Surely soft water with a slightly acid pH will be required for reproduction.

F: C, O; all small live foods, including mosquito larvae, *Cyclops*, and *Artemia*. Flake and FD foods are also accepted.

S: This new species is part of the *H. bentosi* group, but it is also related to *Megalamphodus*. The dentition is species-typical, but aquarists can use its distinctive shoulder spot as an identifying characteristic. The species description can be found in DATZ, 12-1987, p. 546.

T: 22°–27°C, **L:** 4 cm, **A:** 60 cm, **R:** m, **D:** 1–2

Moenkhausia dichroura
Spot-tailed moenkhausia

(KNER, 1858)

Syn.: *Tetragonopterus dichrourus.*

Hab.: South America: Paraguay, Guyana, Brazil. In the Amazon Basin and the Ríos Paraguay and Paranagua.

F.I.: Ca. 1980.

Sex.: ♂♂ are slimmer and have a ventrally pointed swimbladder.

Soc. B.: Very peaceful schooling fish. Suitable for well maintained aquaria. It can be kept with other fishes.

M: Requires soft water with a hardness of up to 12° dGH. It does not live long in hard water. Peat filtration is advantageous. In subdued light—floating plants and a dark substrate will provide this ambient—*Moenkhausia* species display better.

B: Although as yet unsuccessful, it will probably prove similar to other *Moenkhausia* species and other characins.

F: C, O; small live foods, flake foods, and FD items. Plants are ignored.

S: Very similar to *Moenkhausia intermedia* (Vol. 1, p. 300).

T: 22°–26°C, **L:** 4.5 cm, **A:** 60 cm, **R:** m, **D:** 2–3

Hyphessobrycon werneri from the type locality

Moenkhausia dichroura

Moenkhausia hemigrammoides
Signal tetra

Syn.: None.

Hab.: South America: throughout the Guianas.

F.I.: Unknown, but identified in 1984 (see G. OTT in DATZ, **6**).

Sex.: Unknown.

Soc. B.: Peaceful and harmless towards all fishes.

M: Relatively hardy. Easily endures a hardness of 15° dGH and a pH of 7.5. Of course, this species is more colorful in soft, slightly acid water. Not a typical schooling fish; nevertheless, keep several specimens. It prefers dim tanks and a layer of floating plants.

B: Unknown, but probably similar to other small characins.

GÉRY, 1966

F: O; small live foods and flakes.

S: *M. hemigrammoides* is difficult to distinguish from *Hemigrammus unilineatus unilineatus* (GILL, 1858) and *H. unilineatus cayaennensis* GÉRY, 1959. *Moenkhausia* have a complete lateral line. See OTT for details (DATZ, 6-1984); additional references can also be found there.

T: 22°–25°C, **L:** 3.5 cm, **A:** 50 cm, **R:** m, b, **D:** 1

Moenkhausia sp. aff. *intermedia*
False spot-tailed tetra

Syn.: None.

Hab.: South America: Paraguay and southeast Brazil.

F.I.: Unknown.

Sex.: The ♂'s swimbladder is more pointed posteriorly, and the anal fin has a white tip and is slightly more elongated. ♀ does not have a white-tipped anal fin.

Soc. B.: Friendly schooling fish. Suitable for lightly- to moderately-stocked community tanks.

M: See *Moenkhausia dichroura,* p. 140.

B: Unknown.

F: C, O; live foods as well as high quality flake foods.

S: Very similar to *M. dichroura* and *Hemigrammus marginatus*. This species has a different design on the caudal fin than *M. intermedia* and is probably an as yet undescribed species.

EIGENMANN, 1908

T: 23°–27°C, **L:** 4.5 cm, **A:** 60 cm, **R:** m, **D:** 2–3

Moenkhausia hemigrammoides

Moenkhausia sp. aff. *intermedia*

Piabarchus analis
Piaba glass·tetra

Syn.: *Hemibrycon analis.*

Hab.: South America: Paraguay, in the Rio Paraguay and others.

F.I.: Ca. 1984.

Sex.: Unknown.

Soc. B.: A solitarily living fish.

M: Clear, clean water with reedlike vegetation such as *Vallisneria* or *Sagittaria.*

B: Unknown.

F: C, O; small live foods, but it can probably be trained to flakes.

S: Few specimens have reached scientists. Likewise, only individuals were captured in Paraguay (see MAHNERT, Das Aquarium, 221, 11-1987). For a long time the genus was considered monotypic, but a more slender *Piabarchus* species has been found.

T: 20°–26°C, **L:** 4 cm, **A:** 80 cm, **R:** m, **D:** 3

Psellogrammus kennedyi
Kennedy's astyanax, Kennedy's tetra

Syn.: *Astyanax kennedyi.*

Hab.: South America: Paraguay, in the Rio Paraguay and Rio San Francisco.

F.I.: Ca. 1984.

Sex.: Unknown.

Soc. B.: Sedate, rather reclusive animals that· predate on very small fishes. Not suitable for community aquaria.

M: Small aquaria with a capacity of about 50 l are sufficient. Soft, slightly acidic water is commiserate to its needs (hardness up to 12° dGH and pH 5.5–6.8, respectively). Do not overstock the tank; 5 to 7 animals are optimal.

B: Unknown.

F: C; small to large live foods, e.g., mosquito larvae, water fleas, *Tubifex,* and small fishes. Can also be trained to flakes, but regular meals of live foods will always be indispensable. During the winter, *Artemia* can be fed.

S: Seldom imported because of the lack of aquaristic interest.

T: 22°–28°C, **L:** 6.5 cm, **A:** 50 cm, **R:** m, **D:** 3

Piabarchus analis

Psellogrammus kennedyi

Odontocharacidium aphanes   (WEITZMAN & KANAZAWA, 1977)

Syn.: *Klausewitzia aphanes*.

Hab.: South America: Rio Negro and the Amazon River.

F.I.: 1969 by ESPE, Bremen, Germany.

Sex.: Sexes cannot be differentiated by external characteristics.

Soc. B.: Pacific loner. Limit tankmates to very small, peaceful fishes. If several animals are being cared for, territories are established.

M: Provide a large aquarium that is heavily planted with fine-leaved plants and Java moss. Water: pH between 5.8 and 7.0; hardness up to 12° dGH.

B: According to PINTER, these fish will breed in a 200 l aquarium that has plenty of Java moss without the active intervention of the hobbyist.

F: C, O; small live and FD foods, *Artemia*.

S: Very small member of a recently described genus. The species name of the pictured fish has not been confirmed. *K. aphanes* is almost identical to *Characidium voladorita* SCHULTZ, 1944. However, that species reaches a length of more than 4 cm and lives in the Maracaibo Basin in Venezuela. Eye diameter in relation to body length is greater in *K. aphanes*. See DATZ 1969, p. 100 and TI 6/1989, p. 12.

T: 22°–26°C, **L:** 2 cm, **A:** 30 cm, **R:** all, **D:** 3

Poecilocharax weitzmani
Black darter tetra

GÉRY, 1965

Syn.: None, but frequently written incorrectly as *Poeciliocharax*.

Hab.: South America: the Amazon Basin, upper Orinoco River, and upper Rio Negro.

F.I.: Unknown because it is often imported as unidentified by-catch in cardinal tetra shipments.

Sex.: ♂♂ are large and slender to "skinny" with beautiful finnage. The above photo shows 2 ♂♂.

Soc. B.: In contrast to *Crenuchus spilurus*, this is a peaceful schooling fish. It is somewhat shy, which makes it unsuitable for community aquaria. The ♂ cares for the spawn.

M: Difficult to keep. It places high demands on water quality and live foods are obligatory. Water: pH 5.2 to 6.5; hardness up to 5° dGH; no carbonate hardness! Totally deionized water filtered through peat is best. A little tap water must be added, however, to maintain the animal's mineral balance. *Ceratopteris thalictroides* (Indian fern = water sprite) tolerates these extreme water values and affords the necessary shade for the aquarium. Provide hiding places among bogwood, stones (slate), and floating plants. Immoderate illumination prevents the fish from displaying their marvelous colors.

B: Not precisely known. The ♂ practices broodcare. Read PINTER in DATZ, 1-1988.

F: C; small live foods such as mosquito larvae, water fleas, *Cyclops*, and *Artemia*. In the winter they can be fed *Tubifex* and frozen foods.

S: Often imported as by-catch among cardinal tetras where it "disappears" unfortunately. *Crenuchus spilurus* is similar but unsociable. *P. weitzmani* was presented previously on p. 279 of Vol. 1, but without accompanying text. An additional species, *Poecilocharax bovalli* EIGENMANN, 1909, has also been described.

T: 24°–28°C, **L:** 4 cm, **A:** 60 cm, **R:** m, b, **D:** 3

Curimata gillii
Gill's curimata

EIGENMANN & KENNEDY, 1903

Syn.: *Rivasella gillii.*

Hab.: South America: Paraguay.

F.I.: Ca. 1980.

Sex.: Unknown.

Soc. B.: Peaceful schooling fish.

M: Similar to *Curimata nasa.* Provide soft to medium-hard water.

B: Unknown.

F: H, O.

S: The silver *Curimata* and *Curimatopsis* species are especially difficult to distinguish. More information on curimatas can be found in MAHNERT, 1987, Das Aquarium, 11, 221.

T: 20°–28°C, **L:** 10 cm, **A:** 80 cm, **R:** m, **D:** 2

Curimata nasa
Nose curimata

STEINDACHNER, 1882

Syn.: *Cruxentina nasa.*

Hab.: South America: Paraguay.

F.I.: Ca. 1980.

Sex.: Unknown.

Soc. B.: Peaceful schooling fish. Possible suitable tankmates for other sedate species.

M: Soft substrate that allows the fish to dig, e.g., sand. Only tough or hardy, fast-growing plants can be used, preferably potted. A wide range of water values are tolerated. Water: pH 5.5 to 7.5; hardness up to 20° dGH. Since plants are normally chewed on, the decor should mainly consist of rocks and wood. Floating plants and filtering through peat are both advantageous. Strong filtration with little water movement and frequent water exchanges are important.

B: Unknown. Normally spawns after the rainy season in its natural habitat.

F: H, O; plant fare, live foods, and flake foods.

S: The numerous, very similar members of the family Curimatidae are difficult to differentiate, even for specialists.

T: 20°–28°C, **L:** 10 cm, **A:** 80 cm, **R:** m, **D:** 2

Curimata gillii

Curimata nasa

Curimatopsis myersi   VARI, 1982
Myer's curimata   Subfam.: Curimatinae

Syn.: None.

Hab.: South America: Paraguay.

F.I.: Ca. 1980.

Sex.: Unknown.

Soc. B.: Peaceful schooling fish.

M: See *Curimata nasa*.

B: Unknown, but probably similar to *Curimatopsis macrolepis*; see *Curimata nasa*.

F: H, O.

S: Another new species for the already populous *Curimata* and *Curimatella* genera.

T: 20°–26°C, **L:** 5 cm, **A:** 60 cm, **R:** m, **D:** 2

Prochilodus ortonianus   COPE, 1878
Gray prochilodus   Subfam.: Prochilodinae

Syn.: *Prochilodes cephalotes, Chilodus cephalotes.*

Hab.: South America: Amazon Basin.

F.I.: Ca. 1960.

Sex.: Unknown.

Soc. B.: Peaceful schooling fish.

M: Large aquarium with black water. Provide hiding places among bogwood. Water: pH 6.0 to 7.2; hardness up to 12° dGH.

B: Unknown.

F: H.

S: *P. ortonianus* is very similar to *Prochilodus nigricans*. The pictured fish is a juvenile. Adults are solid gray.

T: 22°–28°C, **L:** 25 cm, **A:** 120 cm, **R:** m, **D:** 3 (H)

Curimatopsis myersi

Prochilodus ortonianus

Semaprochilodus insignis

Semaprochilodus insignis
Flag prochilodus

(SCHOMBURGK, 1841)

Syn.: *Chilodus insignis, Prochilodus insignis.*

Hab.: South America: the Guianas, in the Rio Branco.

F.I.: Ca. 1960.

Sex.: Not known.

Soc. B.: Peaceful schooling fish for large aquaria. They can be associated with other herbivores.

M: A shallow, roomy aquarium with plenty of swimming space is needed. Its high metabolic rate makes a good filtration system compulsory. Water: pH 5.5 to 7.2; hardness up to 15° dGH. Waive plants and center the decor around plastic plants and wood.

B: Unknown.

F: H, O; an omnivore with a predilection for plants. Spinach, lettuce, etc., are accepted.

S: Not as colorful as *S. taeniurus* (opposite page).

T: 22°–26°C, **L:** 30 cm, **A:** 120 cm, **R:** m, **D:** 3 (H)

Semaprochilodus taeniurus

Semaprochilodus taeniurus
Plain-body prochilodus

(VALENCIENNES, 1817)

Syn.: Because of uncertain species identification, there are no synonyms to date.

Hab.: South America: west Brazil and Colombia, in the Rio Purus.

F.I.: Unknown.

Sex.: ♀♀ are fuller during spawning season; only distinguishable in large aquaria.

Soc. B.: Schooling fish. Its congenial nature towards fishes does not extend to vegetation.

M: Because this fish is an adept jumper, a cover is suggested. Provide strong filtration, current, and a substrate of fine-grained sand or mulm and mud. Hardly any requirements are placed on water: pH 5.8–7.8; hardness up to 25° dGH.

B: Difficult to breed in aquaria. The animals spawn during the rainy season in inundated areas. Like salmon, the fish migrate upcurrent during the spawning season, ascending rapids and small waterfalls.

F: O, H; algae, plant shoots. Peas (raw or frozen), lettuce, and chickweed are suitable substitutes. This species has two stomachs, one of which is generally full of mud. It seems that detritus is digested from the mud.

S: *S. taeniurus* was previously presented in Vol. 1, p. 320. However, the authors doubt that the color differences between the juvenile pictured in Vol. 1 and the animal pictured here are due to age. They suspect that these are two different species.
Aquarists who have had an opportunity to observe these animals are asked to please divulge information concerning any color changes that these fishes may undergo. In their native habitat, they are frequently consumed.

T: 23°–26°C, **L:** 30 cm, **A:** 180 cm, **R:** m, b, **D:** 2–4 (H)

Hemiodopsis quadrimaculatus vorderwinkleri
Torpedo characin

(PELLEGRIN, 1908)
Subfam.: Hemiodinae

Syn.: *Hemiodus quadrimaculatus.*

Hab.: South America: upper Amazon, Guyana, and Suriname.

F.I.: 1967 by BLEHER, Frankfurt (Germany).

Sex.: Unknown.

Soc. B.: Agile, peaceful schooling fish.

M: This very active schooling fish requires a lot of room, oxygen, and tough vegetation. Usually plants are spared. The animals are initially shy and constantly move nervously about. House them with bottom-dwelling fishes such as *Corydoras*. Use a plastic cuplike container in lieu of a net to catch these animals, as exposure to air quickly proves fatal. While its water chemistry requirements are not stringent, frequent water exchanges are a must. Water: pH 6.0–7.5; hardness up to 20° dGH.

B: Unknown.

F: O; flake and live foods and plenty of plant fare (peas, etc.).

S: Easily distinguished from *H. q. quadrimaculatus*. See the drawings in Vol. 2, p. 216.

T: 23°–27°C, **L:** 10 cm, **A:** 100 cm, **R:** m, **D:** 2–3

Parodon tortuosus tortuosus
Blue darter tetra

EIGENMANN & NORRIS, 1900
Subfam.: Parodontinae

Syn.: *Parodon pirassununguae* (*P. carrikeri* and *P. gestri* may also be synonyms).

Hab.: South America: upper Rio Paraguay, Rio Alto Paraná, Rio Apa, and Mato Grosso.

F.I.: Ca. 1985.

Sex.: Mature ♀♀ are fuller through the ventral area.

Soc. B.: Juveniles are peaceful schooling fish, but adults are territorial.

M: Requires current and oxygen-rich water. Therefore, well-filtered, clean water is conditional for *P. t. tortuosus*'s continued health. Algae growth is highly beneficial. With the exception of very fine-leaved plants such as *Myriophyllum*, plants are not damaged. Water: pH 6.2 to 7.2; hardness up to 20° dGH (high hardness values are only tolerated after careful acclimation).

B: Unknown.

F: H, O; algae, vegetable fare, small live foods, and flakes.

S: There is another subspecies, *P. t. caudalis*. *Parodon suborbitale* is a similar species (Vol. 2, p. 318).

T: 22°–26°C, **L:** 10 cm, **A:** 80 cm, **R:** b, m, **D:** 2

Hemiodopsis quadrimaculatus vorderwinkleri

Parodon tortuosus tortuosus

Lebiasina bimaculata

Lebiasina bimaculata
Two-spot lebiasina

VALENCIENNES, 1846

Syn.: None.

Hab.: South America: western Ecuador and Peru.

F.I.: Unknown, since most *Lebiasina* species are very similar.

Sex.: ♂♂ are slimmer and more colorful.

Soc. B.: Predacious. Restrict tankmates to larger fishes; a species tank is best.

M: Undemanding. Water: pH between 6.2 and 7.5; hardness up to 25° dGH. Hiding places created with wood, stones, or plants are appreciated.

B: Unknown.

F: C; live and frozen foods.

S: As with most *Lebiasina* species, this species lacks an adipose fin. In some species, individuals or populations with and without an adipose fin can be found.

T: 22°–26°C, **L:** 20 cm, **A:** 120 cm, **R:** m, **D:** 2–3

Nannostomus marylinae
Marylin's pencilfish

WEITZMAN & COBB, 1975

Syn.: None.

Hab.: South America: from the same regions as the cardinal tetra, *Paracheirodon axelrodi*.

F.I.: Unknown, since it is usually imported as unnoticed by-catch.

Sex.: ♂♂ are slender, whereas ♀♀ are roundish.

Soc. B.: Peaceful schooling fish. ♂♂ establish tiny subterritories within the school's territory. Only house with small, peaceful species.

M: A densely planted aquarium at least 50 cm in length. Water must be clean with a pH of 5.5–6.5, a hardness of less than 4° dGH, and no dKH. Dark substrate and a few aquatic plants provide a secure, darkened habitat, as preferred by this pencil fish. Avoid fluctuating water values during and after the necessary water exchanges.

B: Can be bred as a continuous spawner or in a pairwise set-up. A small yield, 20 to 30 juveniles per pair, is to be expected. Very soft water is a prerequisite for breeding. See PINTER, DATZ, 5-1987, for details.

F: C, O; small live and flake foods.

S: Very similar to *Nannostomus trifasciatus* but without the bright red in the fins. *N. marylinae* has an adipose fin. Rarely imported, beautiful species which sometimes reaches the aquarium trade as by-catch in cardinal tetra shipments.

T: 24°–26°C, **L:** 5 cm, **A:** 50 cm, **R:** m, t, **D:** 2–3

Pyrrhulina spilota
Blotched pyrrhulina

WEITZMAN, 1960

Syn.: *Copella spilota.*

Hab.: South America: no specific geographic distribution areas are known.

F.I.: Ca. 1970.

Sex.: ♂♂ are somewhat larger with a brighter white fringe on the caudal fin. ♀♀ are fuller.

Soc. B.: A peaceful species which makes a highly suitable tankmate for equal-sized fishes. In nature it is found in groups or schools. Nevertheless, this is not a schooling fish. Keep a group of 6–8 animals.

M: Large, moderately lit tank with good vegetation and an open swimming area in the foreground. Good filtration and current are important. Filter over peat. Water: pH 5.8 to 7.0; hardness up to 15° dGH.

B: As for *Pyrrhulina stoli*.

F: O; live foods are preferred.

S: Very similar to *Pyrrhulina vittata* (Vol. 1, p. 348).

T: 23°–26°C, **L:** 6 cm, **A:** 60 cm, **R:** m, t, **D:** 3

Pyrrhulina stoli

BOESEMAN, 1953

Syn.: *Copella stoli.*

Hab.: South America: Suriname, Guyana, in the upper Rio Meta.

F.I.: Around 1960.

Sex.: ♂♂ are larger, frequently darker, with more elongated fins; ♀♀ are smaller.

Soc. B.: Small groups of these peaceful animals can be maintained in community aquaria. At spawning time, ♂♂ establish small territories, becoming intolerant of rivals in their proximity.

M: Easily kept species. Large, densely planted tanks that have sufficient swimming space make an appropriate captive environment. Since the species is an excellent jumper, the aquarium must be well covered. Soft, slightly acid water.

B: Eggs are laid on large-leaved water plants, sometimes even in community aquaria. The ♂ guards the spawn and fans fresh water over the eggs. If you mean to reproduce this species, it is best to put a pair in a breeding tank and to remove the eggs (the entire leaf and accompanying eggs). Slight aeration promotes better egg development.

F: O; flake, live, and frozen foods. *Drosophila* and other floating insects play a vital role towards bringing pairs into breeding condition.

S: According to GÉRY, this species is closely related to *Pyrrhulina eleanorae* FOWLER, 1940. It can be distinguished by its greater number of predorsal scales, 12–13 vs. 11. *P. eleanorae* is native to the Rio Ucayali in Peru.

T: 20°–24°C, **L:** 8 cm, **A:** 60 cm, **R:** m, t, **D:** 1–2

Pyrrhulina spilota

Pyrrhulina stoli

Metynnis maculatus *
Red-bellied pacu

KNER, 1860

Syn.: *Myletes maculatus, Methynnis maculata, Metynnis roosevelti* (not EIGENMANN, 1915).

Hab.: South America: Brazil and Bolivia, in the Rio Guaporé Basin, and Rio Madeira.

F.I.: 1910 by Arthur Rachow.

Sex.: ♂'s anal fin is more intensely colored, and the anterior half is broader (convex); ♀'s anal fin is straight and equally wide over its entire length.

Soc. B.: Peaceful schooling fish, but not an appropriate addition for planted community tanks. Can be kept with *Leporinus* and other fishes, even small specimens.

M: When the diet includes sufficient vegetable fare, most aquatic plants are ignored. Java fern and Java moss are not molested. Otherwise, decorate with roots, plastic plants, and stones. The aquarium should not be densely stocked, since excessive nitrate concentrations (over 50 mg/l) cause the fins to deteriorate and fungus. Peat filtration or the addition of peat extract is advantageous. Water: up to 10° dGH; pH 6.0–7.2.

B: Breeding is typical for characins. After intense pursuit among fine-leaved plants (Java moss, perlon fibers), the approximately 150, nonadhesive eggs are released and fall to the bottom among the spawning substrate. The larvae hatch after 4 days, and 4–5 days later, the young are free-swimming. Remove the parents. Feed *Cyclops* nauplii, bosmids, *Artemia*, and finely ground flake foods (MicroMin, etc.).

*S: Species identification based on just a photograph is virtually impossible. The species name should therefore read *Metynnis* sp. aff. *maculatus*.

T: 20°–28°C, L: 18 cm, A: 100 cm, R: m, D: 2–3

Metynnis mola

EIGENMANN & KENNEDY, 1903

Syn.: *Metynnis otuquensis, Myletes mola*.

Hab.: South America: Rio Paraguay Basin.

Sex.: ♂♂ have a longer, rounded anal fin, whereas ♀♀ have a straight anal fin.

Soc. B.: Peaceful schooling fish. Suitable for community aquaria.

M: *Metynnis* species require large, shallow aquaria, dim illumination, plenty of free swimming space, and hiding places among bogwood or plastic plants. Filter over peat. Water: pH 5.0–7.0; hardness up to 12° dGH.

B: Unknown, but probably like other *Metynnis*.

F: H; all types of soft vegetation such as lettuce, spinach, watercress, chickweed, and vegetable flakes.

S: A rarely imported species, since hardly any imports are received from Paraguay. Full-grown animals are significantly more colorful than the pictured specimen.

T: 20°–26°C, L: 15 cm, A: 100 cm, R: m, D: 2–3

Metynnis maculatus

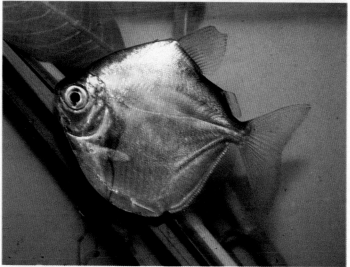

Metynnis mola, juvenile

Myleus gurupyensis

STEINDACHNER, 1911

Syn.: *Myleus arnoldi, M. maculatus, Myloplus gurupyensis.*

Hab.: South America: the Guianas and the Amazon Basin.

F.I.: Unknown.

Sex.: None.

M: Proper nitrogen cycle management and high oxygen levels are imperative. Water quality aside, requirements are minimal. Furnish a large aquarium with rocks, wood, and plastic plants. Real plants will be eaten

B: Unknown.

F: H; lettuce, spinach, aquatic plants, etc.

S: *M. gurupyensis* is a member of the valid subgenus *Myloplus.*

T: 23°–27°C, **L:** ca. 25 cm, **A:** 100 cm, **R:** m, **D:** 3

Myleus pacu
Brown pacu

(SCHOMBURGK in JARDINE, 1841)

Syn.: *Myletes pacu, Myleus setiger, M. doidyxodon, M. divaricatus, M. trilobatus, M. unilobatus.*

Hab.: South America: the Guianas and the Amazon Basin.

F.I.: Unknown.

Sex.: None.

Soc. B.: Peaceful schooling fish.

M: Rocks, roots, and perhaps tree bark make suitable appointments for the required large aquarium. Plants should be waived, since they will be chewed on.

B: Unknown.

F: H; lettuce, spinach, and fruit.

S: *Myleus* species, like some other characins, migrate upriver to spawn in the headwaters of their rivers. At that time, they develop large red spots on their sides. The brown spotted juvenile coloration is beautiful in its own right; it probably serves as camouflage.

T: 22°–26°C, **L:** 50–60 cm, **A:** from 100 cm, **R:** m, **D:** 3 (S)

Steel engraving of *Myleus pacu* from JARDINE.

Myleus gurupyensis

Metynnis hypsauchen ♂, spawning coloration, see Vol. 1, p. 353

Botia sp. aff. *striata* = probably a variety of *Botia striata*. Becomes progressively more similar to *B. striata* as it ages.

Continuation of *Abottina rivularis* (p. 168):

F: H, C; juveniles are herbivores (algae, including diatoms), but·adults are carnivores (small crustacea, aquatic insects).

S: *Abbottina rivularis* lives on sand or mud/sand bottoms in slow-flowing rivers, ponds, and swamps in its natural habitat. This species requires warmer temperatures than any other member of the subfamily Gobioninae from the Amur Basin.

T: 18°–23°C, **L:** ♂ 13.5 cm, ♀ 8.5 cm, **A:** 80 cm, **R:** b, **D:** 2–3

Catostomus commersonii
Commerson's sucker

(LACÉPÉDE, 1803)

Syn.: *Cyprinus commersonii, Catostomus alticolus, C. chloropteron, C. communis, C. flexuosus, C. gracilis, C. pallidus, C. reticulatus, C. sucklii, C. teres, Cyprinus teres, Myxostoma trisignatum.*

Hab.: North America: Canada and the United States, in rivers and lakes of Quebec and from the Great Lakes to Montana, Colorado, Missouri, and Georgia. It can be found in all types of water.

Sex.: Mature ♂♂ have a beautiful pink-purple-orange sheen on their sides. They also have large knots on the anal fin rays and are usually smaller than ♀♀.

Soc. B.: Peaceful, active schooling fish. Associating these animals with *Notropis* species seems logical.

M: Use sand or fine-grain gravel as substrate. Some stones and roots should be included in the tank's furnishings. Vegetation such as *Egeria* (*Elodea*) or *Myriophyllum* can be planted along the edges, but make sure there is still an open area for swimming. Water must be clear and clean; however, its chemistry is of secondary importance.

B: In nature the animals spawn in April and May. The ♂♂ arrive at the spawning sites first. They are neither nest builders nor territorial. Often two ♂♂ are found side-by-side with one ♀. The sperm and more than 20,000 adhesive eggs are released simultaneously. At 10°C, the 8 mm long larvae hatch after 2–3 weeks. and at that time are 8 mm long. First foods are protozoans, diatoms, and minute crustacea.

F: O; live foods of all kinds as well as shrimp, scraped meats, algae, and flake and tablet foods.

S: *C. commersonii* is the most common species within the genus. It can reach a weight of 3 kg.

T: 4°–20°C, **L:** 30 (45) cm, **A:** 120 cm, **R:** b, **D:** 2

Botia dario
Bengal loach

(from DAY, 1878) HAMILTON, 1822

Syn.: Cobitis dario, Botia macrolineata.

Hab.: India: Bengal and Assam, Bihar and Cachar. In the tributaries of the Bramaputra and Ganges Rivers.

F.I.: 1987.

Sex.: Only full-grown ♀♀ can be recognized by their large girth (eggs).

Soc. B.: Peaceful schooling fish that can be kept in community tanks, even those housing small fishes or large cichlids.

M: Soft water (up to 10° dGH) with a pH of 6.5 to 7.5. Caves and secluded areas

among plants are appreciated. Active during twilight hours, remaining hidden during the day. If associated with unsuitable tankmates (e.g., large predatory catfishes or fishes that dig), B. dario hides in the substrate.

B: Unsuccessful.

F: C, O; fine live foods, frozen foods, flake foods, and TetraTips.

S: A gorgeous, initially shy fish.

T: 23°–26°C, **L:** 6.5 cm, **A:** 70 cm, **R:** b, **D:** 3

Botia rostrata
Ladder loach

(HAMILTON, 1822)

Syn.: Cobitis geto, C. geta, Schistura geto, Botia geto, B. histrionica, B. birdi.

Hab.: Asia: Burma and India, in Punjab, the Himalayas, Ganges Valley, Assam, Sind, Sone River.

F.I.: 1986.

Sex.: ♀♀ are larger and barely have a light stripe between the dark double striations.

Soc. B.: Contrary to Botia dario, B. rostrata is an absolutely peaceful schooling fish. A group of at least 6 specimens makes an excellent addition to soft water community aquaria.

M: Though maintainable, it, like all Botia, is very sensitive to chemical pollutants in the water. Adapted B. rostrata are diurnal and only slightly bashful.

B: Unsuccessful to date, but indications that water exchanges trigger energetic swimming and courtship behavior could be interpreted to mean that this species is easier to breed than other Botia species.

F: C, O; small live foods are preferred. However, flake and tablet foods are readily accepted as well.

S: The species name, according to HUNTER (1877), is derived from the native name "Gengto" in Goálpárá. In Assam,

these loaches are generally called "Bottia." This is definitely the origin of the genus name.
Botia dario (HAMILTON, 1822), B. dayi (HORA, 1932), and B. rostrata (HAMILTON, 1822) are only superficially similar. Ichthyologists working exclusively with preserved specimens have classified these species and others as synonymous. From a contemporary viewpoint, this is almost inexplicable. Equally problematic is when an autonomous species is declared to be the juvenile form of another. B. dario has 8 to 10 dark crossbands on the body which may be connected in places by longitudinal bands. The head profile is steeply sloped, clearly convex. B. dayi has about 10 paired crossbands which are only connected in the dorsal region. The species is slightly similar to B. striata and likewise grows to be more than 10 cm long. B. rostrata has 8 to 10 dark crossbands as well with either paired or single, ocelluslike light areas, particularly along the lateral line. The forehead is steep, and the head profile is angular. Identifying live loaches to species is not always simple, even for those familiar with the distinguishing characteristics.

T: 22°–25°C, **L:** 6 cm, **A:** 70 cm, **R:** b, **D:** 1

Botia dario

Botia rostrata ♀

Abbottina rivularis

Abbottina rivularis   (BASILEWSKI, 1855)

Syn.: *Gobio rivularis, Abbottina sinensis, Pseudogobio rivularis, P. sinensis, Tylognathus sinensis.*

Hab.: Asia: former Soviet Union, central Amur Basin; Korea, Khan, Kun, and Suwon Rivers; Japan, with the exception of Hokkaido and the northern half of Hondo; northern China, the drainage basin of the central Yangtse and the Minkiana.

F.I.: Has not been imported into Germany.

Sex.: ♂♂ are larger and have a strongly convex dorsal fin. Nuptial tubercles appear on the first ray of the pectoral fins and the lower half of the head. ♀♀ are smaller, have a slightly convex dorsal fin, and do not have nuptial tubercles during the spawning season.

Soc. B.: Agile, peaceful schooling fish. ♀ practices broodcare.

M: Roomy aquaria with a sand or gravel substrate, some hiding places among stones, and sparse vegetation along the edges. Water should be clear and clean with a neutral pH and a hardness of up to 20° dGH. The species can be kept with other peaceful fishes.

B: Probably has not been bred in an aquarium. In nature, the animals spawn in June and July. Sexual maturity is reached at a length of 4 cm. The round nests the ♂♂ construct in the substrate are 5 mm deep with a diameter of 12-43 mm. ♀♀ can spawn several times, laying up to 2,000, 2–2.5 mm eggs. The ♀ guards the nest. At 18°C, the larvae hatch after 6–8 days. They lay barely moving on the bottom of the nest. Active feeding only starts after the yolk sac has been absorbed.

Continued on p. 164.

Abramis brama

Abramis brama
Bronze bream

(LINNAEUS, 1758)

Syn.: *Cyprinus brama.*

Hab.: Europe: from the Atlantic to the Urals north of the Pyrenees and Alps. The species also inhabits the Dwina, Volga, and Terek Rivers, as well as Lake Aral. It is not found in Iceland, northern Scotland, northern Norway, Sweden, Finland, or the western or southern Balkans. Can also be found in brackish Baltic Sea rivers, e.g., the Schlei.

F.I.: European species.

Sex.: ♂♂ have pronounced nuptial tubercles during the spawning season, whereas ♀♀ are much fuller during that time.

Soc. B.: During the spawning season and winter months, *A. brama* schools. The rest of the time the animals limit themselves to small groups.

M: Requires a roomy, tall aquarium, a substrate of fine sand, and some roots as decoration. Because the animals relish dense plant growth, the edges and back of the tank should be planted with native species. No special demands are placed on water composition; water values should be similar to those provided for other coldwater cyprinids (hardness ca. 15° dGH, pH 7.0–7.5). While higher temperatures are tolerated, the tank will have to be well-aerated.

B: Has not been successful in an aquarium. In nature, the bronze bream forms schools during the spawning season (May and June). Spawning usually occurs at night along shallow, vegetated shores. Large ♀♀ can lay up to 300,000 eggs which take 3 days to develop at 18°–20°C. The hatching larvae are about 4 mm long and remain motionlessly adhered to plants until their yolk sac is absorbed.

Continued on p. 172.

Acanthalburnus microlepis
Napotta

(FILIPPI, 1863)

Syn.: *Abramis microlepis, Acanthalburnus punctulatus, Alburnus punctulatus.*

Hab.: Asia: former Soviet Union, drainage basins of the Kura and the Arak Rivers; in rivers and lakes.

F.I.: Has not been imported to Germany.

Sex.: ♀♀ are fuller during the spawning season.

Soc. B.: Peaceful, lively schooling fish.

M: As indicated for *Alburnoides oblongus*.

B: To the best of our knowledge, this fish has not been bred in an aquarium. Little information is available concerning the reproductive biology of this species.

F: C, O; live foods of all kinds, flake foods, and sometimes vegetable fare.

S: The monotypic genus *Acanthalburnus* is closely related to the genus *Alburnoides* but the last unbranched ray of the dorsal fin is enlarged into a soft spine (genus name!).

T: 10°–20°C (coldwater fish), **L**: 25 cm, **A**: 80 cm, **R**: m, **D**: 2

Alburnoides oblongus

(BULGAKOV, 1923)

Syn.: *Squalalburnus oblongus.*

Hab.: Asia: former Soviet Union, in the basin of the Syr-Darya River.

F.I.: Has not been imported into Germany.

Sex.: ♀♀ are fuller during the spawning season.

Soc. B.: A surface-oriented schooling fish. Associate with other coldwater species that have similar requirements (other cyprinids).

M: Needs a substrate of sand or gravel; plant the edges with coldwater species; preserve sufficient swimming space; provide good aeration for the aquarium. Water: hardness of 10°–20° dGH; pH 7.0–7.5.

B: Probably has not been bred in an aquarium.

F: C, O; live foods of all kinds such as plankton and floating foods. Flake foods are also consumed.

S: *A. oblongus* is closely related to *Alburnoides taeniatus* (KESSLER, 1874); see Vol. 2, p. 360.

T: 10°–20°C (coldwater fish), **L**: 14 cm, **A**: 80 cm, **R**: t, m, **D**: 2

Acanthalburnus microlepis

Alburnoides oblongus

Continuation of *Abramis brama* (p. 169):

F: O; live foods of all kinds: benthic insect larvae (particularly chironomid larvae), small crustacea, molluscs, and worms. Flake and tablet foods are also eaten.

S: *A. brama* is the main fish of the metapotamons (= the lower courses of the cyprinid region = barb region). The bronze bream has a protrusile mouth. When searching for food, the fish plunges its mouth into the substrate, forming "bream holes."

T: 10°–24°C (coldwater fish), L: up to 75 cm, A: from 100 cm, R: b, m, D: 1–2

A scenic lowland river. Habitat of bleaks, breams, pikes, etc.

Continuation of *Alburnus alburnus* (p. 173):

S: The scales of *Alburnus alburnus* are used to produce artificial pearls (Essence d'Orient).

T: 10°–20°C (coldwater fish), L: 25 cm, A: 100 cm, R: t, D: 2

Fam.: Cyprinidae
Subfam.: Leuciscinae

Alburnus alburnus

Alburnus alburnus
Bleak

(LINNAEUS, 1758)

Syn.: *Cyprinus alburnus, Alburnus lucidus, A. lucidus* var. *lacustris*.

Hab.: Europe: north of the Pyrenees and Alps to the Urals; England, southeast Norway, Sweden, and Finland. Not found in Ireland or Scotland. Inhabits slow-flowing, static waters.

F.I.: Native species.

Sex.: Outside of the spawning season, difficult to distinguish. ♂♂ have numerous white knots on their head and body (nuptial tubercles) during the spawning season. ♀♀ are fuller at that time.

Soc. B.: Surface-oriented, lively, amiable schooling fish. Very skittish about shadows thrown from above.

M: Offer the largest aquarium possible, a substrate of fine sand, and edge and background vegetation predominately of fine-leaved species (e.g., *Myriophyllum*).

Sufficient free swimming space is very important for these active fish. Water should be clear, clean, and well-aerated with a hardness of about 10° dGH and a pH of 7.0. Associate with coldwater fishes that have similar lifestyles (such as *Alburnoides bipunctatus*).

B: 20°–22°C; possible in aquaria. In nature, the animals spawn from April to June. They form large schools and migrate upriver. Spawning occurs among stones or on twigs that extend into the water. Egg development takes 1 week. Fry feed on zooplankton and grow rapidly. The animals are sexually mature at 2 years of age.

F: C, O; in nature the animals feed on insects and their larvae, plankton (small crustacea, glassworms), and worms. Flake foods are also accepted.

Continued on p. 172.

Alburnus charusini hohenackeri
Transcaucasian bleak

KESSLER, 1877
Subfam.: Leuciscinae

Syn.: *Alburnus hohenackeri, A. alburnus hohenackeri.*

Hab.: Asia: former Soviet Union, in the Kura and Draks Basins and the rivers of the Lenkoran region.

F.I.: Has not been imported to Germany.

Sex.: Outside the spawning season, the sexes cannot be distinguished. During the spawning season, ♂ ♂ have nuptial tubercles and ♀ ♀ are fuller due to the eggs.

Soc. B.: Active, peaceful, surface-oriented schooling fish.

M: As indicated for *Alburnus alburnus*.

B: Has not been bred in an aquarium. Likewise, its spawning biology in nature is virtually unknown.

F: C; in their natural biotope, they feed on organisms that fall onto the water surface, all kinds of insects and insect larvae, and *Daphnia*.

S: The nominate form, *A. c. charusini* HERZENSTEIN, 1889, inhabits Lake Kamusch-Samarskije between the Volga and the Ural Rivers and the Terek, Sulak, Dagestan, and Kuban Rivers.

T: 10°–20°C (coldwater fish), **L:** 12 cm, **A:** 80 cm, **R:** t, m, **D:** 2–3

Alburnoides bipunctatus fasciatus
Striped tailorfish

(NORDMANN, 1940)
Subfam.: Abraminae

Syn.: *Aspius fasciatus, Alburnus maculatus.*

Hab.: Asia: former Soviet Union, at the Crimea and the western Caucasus Mountains.

F.I.: Has not been imported into Germany.

Sex.: ♀ ♀ are heavier-bodied than ♂ ♂.

Soc. B.: A surface-oriented, active schooling fish.

M: A substrate of fine sand, coldwater plants along the edge and background, and plenty of swimming space represent agreeable maintenance conditions. Provide good aeration, since *A. b. fasciatus* requires a lot of oxygen. This fish can be associated with other coldwater species that have similar requirements.

B: To the best of our knowledge, this fish has not been bred in an aquarium.

F: C, O; flake foods and small live foods such as planktonic organisms, insects, and mosquito larvae.

S: There are a number of subspecies of the nominate form *A. b. bipunctatus* (BLOCH, 1782). Classification of all the subspecies is under discussion by many ichthyologists.

T: 10°–20°C (coldwater fish), **L:** 12.5 cm, **A:** 80 cm, **R:** t, m, **D:** 2–3

Alburnus charusini hohenackeri

Alburnoides bipunctatus fasciatus

Aristichthys nobilis p. 226

Aspius aspius aspius   (LINNAEUS, 1758)
Asp

Syn.: *Cyprinus aspius, Aspius rapax, Cyprinus rapax.*

Hab.: Central Europe and west Asia: prefers the barb region of flowing waters, but found in large lakes as well.

Sex.: ♂♂ have nuptial tubercles.

Soc. B.: Social fish when young. Older specimens are territorial predators that lead a solitary lifestyle.

M: Place the tank in a cool local so the aquarium's temperature always stays below 20°C, even during the summer. Decorate with roots, stones, and reeds. Background vegetation is possible, but maintain plenty of swimming space. Good filtration, aeration, and regular water exchanges are needed. Generally, only juveniles are suitable aquarium specimens.

B: *A. aspius* spawn from April to June in swiftly flowing creeks having a gravel substrate. Fish living in lakes or bays migrate into tributaries to spawn. Courtship is intense. The eggs sink to the bottom and adhere to stones. Large ♀♀ can lay up to 100,000 eggs. They hatch in 10–16 days at 8° to 12°C. Hatching larvae hide among stones; later they migrate upriver. Four to five years are needed before the animals are sexually mature.

F: C; all kinds of live foods. Adults almost exclusively feed on small fishes. Amphibians and young water birds are also eaten.

S: Due to man altering the water courses and the accompanying decline in the populations of tailorfish, bleaks, and other small fishes, *A. aspius*, which depends on these fishes as a source of nourishment, has become scarce.

T: 4°–20°C, **L**: 100 (55) cm, **A**: from 120 cm, **R**: m, t, **D**: 2

Aspius aspius taeniatus   (EICHWALD, 1831)
Caspian asp

Syn.: *Cyprinus taeniatus, Aspius erythrostomus, A. transcaucasicus.*

Hab.: Asia: former Soviet Union, the southern section of the Caspian Sea and the Kura and Araks Rivers. Occasionally found at the mouth of the Volga and Terek Rivers.

F.I.: Has not been imported.

Sex.: ♂♂ have dermal knots (nuptial tubercles) during the spawning season.

Soc. B.: A predatory cyprinid. Juveniles live in schools, while larger specimens become progressively more solitary.

M: As indicated for *Leuciscus cephalus.* Perhaps sea salt should be added (brackish water).

B: Has not been bred in an aquarium. In its natural biotope, *A. a. taeniatus* begins to migrate into rivers in the autumn. Once there, it proceeds far upriver. Spawning occurs from March to April in fast-flowing river segments over stone bottoms at temperatures of 4.5° to 15°C. The number of eggs fluctuates between 58,000 and 483,000. At 12°C, egg development takes 11 days. In July and August, the 5–10 cm long juveniles migrate to the sea.

F: C; all kinds of live foods. Juveniles feed on planktonic and benthic organisms. Older specimens almost exclusively eat fishes.

S: This fish is of great economic importance in the southern waters of the former Soviet Union where it is an important food fish.

T: 10°–20°C (coldwater fish), **L**: 77 cm, **A**: from 120 cm, **R**: m, t, **D**: 2–3

Aspius aspius aspius

Aspius aspius taeniatus

Barbus semifasciolatus, see Vol. 1, p. 399

Barbus sp. cf. *bimaculatus* from west Africa

Fam.: Cyprinidae
Subfam.: Cyprininae

Barbodes altus

Barbodes altus
Tall barb

(GÜNTHER, 1863)

Syn.: *Puntius altus, Barbus bocourti, Barbus altus.*

Hab.: Asia: Thailand, Laos, Cambodia, Vietnam.

F.I.: Ca. 1980 as by-catch.

Sex.: Unknown. ♀♀ are significantly fuller during the spawning season.

Soc. B.: Peaceful schooling fish.

M: Undemanding, congenial charges. No special demands are placed on water composition. However, maintain in large aquaria to provide sufficient swimming space. The species does not burrow, and according to current experiences, it does not bother water plants.

B: Has not been breed.

T: 22°–27°C, **L:** 15 cm, **A:** 150 cm, **R:** m, b, **D:** 1–2

F: O; peaceful omnivores. Live foods of all types, dry commercial foods.

S: Not particularly attractive. To date, this fish has only been imported to central Europe as by-catch.

Barbus sp.

Barbus "kuda" = *B. asoka*, p. 182

Fam.: Cyprinidae
Subfam.: Cyprininae

Barbus amphigramma   BOULENGER, 1903

Syn.: *Barbus thikensis, B. longicauda* (partially), *B. macropristis meruensis, B. helleri.*

Hab.: East Africa: Kenya, Uganda, Tanzania.

F.I.: Unknown.

Sex.: ♂♂ are slimmer. ♀♀ have a notably fuller anterior body.

Soc. B.: Active, amiable fish which prefers to school. Some water holes may contain hundreds of *B. amphigramma.*

M: Care is totally unproblematic, even in community aquaria as long as overly aggressive fishes are excluded. The aquarium should be well-planted, especially around the edges. Maintain plenty of free swimming space. In nature, *B. amphigramma* is frequently found in plant-free water holes, along shores of drying bodies of water, and in muddy waters. When found in the latter, the fish are usually a yellowish silver color over their entire body and have little color or design; *B. amphigramma* from clear waters have more contrasting colors.

B: Has probably not been achieved in an aquarium. But since this species has little aesthetic appeal, there is little demand, which makes an attempt at breeding a rather uninteresting proposition. Those who desire to maintain these fish will probably have to either import the fish themselves or wait for an opportune by-catch.

F: C; live foods of all types as well as frozen, dry, and flake foods.

T: 19°–26°C, **L:** 7.5 cm, **A:** 80 cm, **R:** m, t, **D:** 2

Barbus apleurogramma

BOULENGER, 1911

Syn.: *Agrammobarbus babaulti, Barbus aphantogramma, B. babaulti, B. lapsus, B. mohasiensis, B. rufua, B. scheemanni, B. zanzibariensis* var. *paucior.*

Hab.: Africa: Uganda, widely distributed in Lakes Victoria and Edward; Rwanda and Burundi, in Lakes Kivu and Mohasi; Tanzania.

F.I.: Not known.

Sex.: None known. ♀♀ are probably fuller during the spawning season.

Soc. B.: Active, extremely peaceful schooling fish.

M: Dark substrate (e.g., Lavatit). The aquarium does not necessarily have to be very large or very deep. Always keep a school of at least 6–8 specimens. Plant *Anubias* and *Crinum* species. Bright il-lumination is not appreciated, so cut light penetration with floating plants; its colors are more pronounced during twilight hours. Cover the tank well. Water: hardness up to 12° dGH; pH 6.0–6.5.

B: To the best of our knowledge, this species has not been bred in captivity. Breeding is probably similar to other African barbs.

F: O; small live, frozen, and flake foods.

S: *B. apleurogramma* does not have a lateral line.

T: 23°–26°C, **L**: 5 cm, **A**: 60 cm, **R**: m, b, **D**: 2

Puntius asoka

(KOTTELAT & PETHIYAGODA, 1989)

Syn.: *Barbus asoka.* "*Barbus kuda*" is a trade name.

Hab.: Asia: Sri Lanka.

F.I.: 1976.

Sex.: No external differentiating characteristics.

Soc. B.: Usually lives in small groups. Scuffles may occasionally occur, but they are generally not injurious (most likely only ♂♂ fight).

M: Offer an aquarium that has swimming space and secluded areas among roots and plant groups. No particular water chemistry requirements have to be met: hardness 1°–18° dGH; pH 6.5–7.5.

B: Probably has not been successfully bred in a captive environment.

F: O; live and flake foods of all kinds as well as vegetable fare (lettuce, spinach, etc.).

T: 25°–30°C, **L**: 15 cm, **A**: 100 cm, **R**: b, m, **D**: 2–3

Barbus apleurogramma

Puntius asoka

Barbus atakorensis

DAGET, 1957

Syn.: None.

Hab.: Africa: Ghana, coastal rivers; north Benin, Oti River; Nigeria, Ogun and Kaduna Rivers.

F.I.: Not known.

Sex.: No external distinguishing features.

Soc. B.: Very peaceful, active schooling fish.

M: As indicated for *Barbus apleurogramma,* but this species likes very soft, moderately acid water (2°–6° dGH and pH 5.5–6.0, respectively). Due to their diminutive size, caution must be observed when adding it to community tanks.

B: There is no information available concerning breeding this barb.

F: O; small live and frozen foods as well as freeze-dried and flake foods.

S: None.

T: 22°–25°C, L: 4 cm, A: 60 cm, R: m, b, D: 2–3

Barbus candens
Red three-spot barb

NICHOLS & GRISCOM, 1917

Syn.: None.

Hab.: Africa: Zaïre, in the central Zaïre River and the Lualaba River System.

F.I.: 1986.

Sex.: ♂♂ are slimmer, somewhat larger, and more intensely colored (especially the fins).

Soc. B.: An active, very amiable schooling fish.

M: As indicated for *Barbus amphigramma,* but a soft substrate should be offered (e.g., peat or fine sand). A species tank is optimal.

B: Reproductive behavior deviates from most *Barbus* species in that the eggs are laid on a soft substrate. To meet these needs, place several centimeters of peat along the bottom. The water should be very soft and acid (1°–2° dGH and pH 5.0–6.0, respectively). The pairs dig into the peat while spawning. At

25°C, the young hatch after about 6 days. Not a prolific species.

F: O; all kinds of very small live foods as well as frozen and flake foods.

S: See B.

T: 24°–26°C, L: barely 4 cm, A: 50 cm, R: b, m, D: 2–3

Barbus atakorensis

Barbus candens

Barbus caudovittatus
Striped tail barb

BOULENGER, 1902

Syn.: *Barbus chilotes sakaniae, B. euchilus, B. lestradei, B. miochilus, B. pojeri, Varicorhinus stappersii.*

Hab.: Africa: in the basins of the Zaïre and Luapula Rivers and some tributaries of Lake Tanganyika.

F.I.: Not known.

Sex.: No definite external differences known. ♀♀ are probably fuller during the spawning season.

Soc. B.: Active schooling fish. Older animals may become aggressive.

M: Offer *B. caudovittatus* a roomy tank with a sandy bottom and plenty of robust vegetation, but preserve ample swimming space. Water: hardness up to 15° dGH; pH around neutral (pH 6.5–7.5).

B: Has not been achieved in an aquarium. Probably impossible in normal aquaria because of its size.

F: O; all kinds of large live, frozen, freeze-dried, vegetable, flake, and tablet foods.

S: Without exception, *B. caudovittatus* has a pharyngeal dentition of 2.3.5–5.3.2. The species has a characteristic dark band on the upper and lower lobe of the tail fin (species name!).

T: 24°–27°C, **L:** 80 cm, **A:** from 120 cm, **R:** m, b, **D:** 2

Barbus chola
Cola barb

(HAMILTON, 1822)

Syn.: *Cyprinus chola, Capoeta chola, Puntius chola, P. perlee, Systomus chola, S. immaculatus.*

Hab.: Asia: India, from Malabar through Orissa, Punjab, Bengal to Assam; Bangladesh; Burma. Inhabits creeks, rivers, and static bodies of water.

F.I.: 1904 by H. STÜVE, Hamburg.

Sex.: ♂♂ are slimmer and have reddish fins at spawning time; ♀♀ are fuller, and their fins are yellowish during the spawning season.

Soc. B.: Peaceful, active schooling fish.

M: Needs a dark substrate, dense vegetation around the edges, floating plants to dim the light, and plenty of swimming space. Cover the tank well, since the animals are excellent jumpers. No particular demands are placed on water chemistry; however, regular water exchanges should be performed (every 2 weeks ¼ to ⅓ of the tank's volume). Excellent fish for a community tank.

B: 23°–25°C; reproduction is possible in tanks as small as 30 l. One ♂ and two ♀♀ is the best combination. Water: 8°–15° dGH; pH 6.0–6.5. Since all *Barbus* consider their eggs a delicacy, the substrate should consist of coarse gravel or a plastic grid should be placed over the substrate that allows the eggs to fall through and escape being devoured. Spawning is preceded by elaborate courtship. Several hundred eggs are adhered to water plants. It is best to remove the parents after they have spawned. Juveniles hatch in 30–48 hr, depending on water temperature.

F: O; live, frozen, freeze-dried, and vegetable foods.

S: In some regions of Burma, these fish are used as a source of oil while in spawning condition.

T: 20°–25°C, **L:** 15 cm, **A:** 90 cm, **R:** m, b, **D:** 1–2

Barbus caudovittatus, Kindu, Zaïre

Barbus chola

Barbus eburneensis

Barbus eburneensis

Fam.: Cyprinidae
Subfam.: Cyprininae

Barbus eburneensis

Barbus eburneensis

POLL, 1941

Syn.: *Barbus camptacanthus, B. flomoi, B. trispilus, B. trispilus* var. *quinquepunctata.*

Hab.: Africa: coastal rivers from Guinea to the western Ivory Coast.

F.I.: Unknown.

Sex.: No definite external differences are known to date.

Soc. B.: Agile, peaceful schooling fish.

M: As indicated for *Barbus amphigramma*, but water values vary slightly: 3°–8° dGH; pH ca. 5.5. Suitable for community tanks.

B: No known breeding successes.

F: O; live, frozen, freeze-dried, flake, and tablet foods.

S: *B. eburneensis* has three to five small black spots on each side of its body at about the height of the lateral line. Due to the variable design, the species has also been described as *B. trispilus*. It is sometimes still traded under that synonym.

T: 22°–25°C, **L:** 9 cm, **A:** 80 cm, **R:** m, b, **D:** 2–3

Barbus foerschi
Forsch's barb

KOTTELAT, 1982

Syn.: None.

Hab.: Southeast Asia: Indonesia (Kalimantan = Borneo), in the Mentaya Basin.

F.I.: 1978 by Edith KORTHAUS.

Sex.: No indisputable external differences are known. Usually ♀♀ are fuller and slightly deeper-bodied.

Soc. B.: Active, peaceful schooling fish. Always keep between 6–8 specimens. Individuals are shy and skittish.

M: Provide a dark substrate (Lavatit), dense vegetation around the edges, and plenty of swimming space. Offer some hiding places (e.g., roots). Water: hardness up to 10° dGH; pH 6.0–6.5.

B: No known breeding successes.

F: O; all types of live foods as well as frozen, freeze-dried, and flake foods.

S: *B. foerschi* has a complete lateral line with 24 perforated scales.

T: 24°–28°C, L: 6 cm, A: 60 cm, R: m, b, D: 2

Barbus guirali

THOMINOT, 1886

Syn.: *Barbus camptacanthus* var. *melanipterus, B. melanipterus.*

Hab.: Africa: southern Cameroon and Gabon.

F.I.: Unknown.

Sex.: No known distinguishing features.

Soc. B.: Active, nonaggressive schooling fish.

M: Similar to that of *Barbus amphigramma* or *Barbus apleurogramma*, but the water can be even softer and more acid (pH 5.5–6.0).

B: Has probably never been bred in an aquarium.

F: O; all types of live foods as well as frozen, tablet, and flake foods.

S: The tip of the dorsal fin is either black or dark (see photo).

T: 22°–26°C, L: 17 cm, A: 100 cm, R: m, b, D: 2–3

Barbus foerschi

Barbus guirali

Barbus kerstenii kerstenii
Kersten's barb

Syn.: *Barbus akeleyi, B. lumiensis, B. minchinii, B. mohasiensis* var. *paucisquamata, B. nigrolineata, B. zanzibaricus* var. *paucior.*

Hab.: Africa: Kenya, in rivers and lakes; Uganda, in the basins of Lakes Edward and Victoria; Tanzania, Lake Tanganyika; Rwanda, Lake Kivu.

F.I.: Probably in 1925 as *Barbus usambarae.*

Sex.: No definite differences are known. ♀♀ are fuller during the spawning season.

Soc. B.: Very agile, peaceful schooling fish.

M: As stated for *Barbus apleurogramma* (p. 182). Water hardness: up to 18° dGH; pH 6.5–7.5. Suitable fish for community aquaria.

B: To date, there are no reports concerning successfully spawning this species in an aquarium.

F: O; all kinds of live foods as well as frozen, freeze-dried, flake, and tablet foods.

S: Besides the nominate form presented here, the subspecies *B. k. luhondo* PAPPENHEIM & BOULENGER, 1914, known only from Lake Luhondo in northwestern Rwanda, has also been described.

T: 23°–26°C, **L:** 9 cm, **A:** 80 cm, **R:** m, b, **D:** 2

Barbus miolepis miolepis
Reticulated barb

Syn.: *Barbus decioi, B. nicholsi, B. squamosissimus, B. treadwelli.*

Hab.: Africa: in the Zaïre River basin, but not in the Luapula River or Lake Moero.

F.I.: In 1970 a few specimens were imported into former East Germany.

Sex.: Difficult to differentiate. ♀♀ are a lighter color. The first ray of the ♂♂'s dorsal fin seems to always be dark (see photo).

Soc. B.: Very agile, peaceful schooling fish.

M: Follow recommendations given for *Barbus apleurogramma.* Since the animals are accomplished jumpers, cover the tank. Shady, darkened areas, which should be provided, are eagerly sought by the animals.

B: ♂♂ strongly pursue ♀♀. Unripe ♀♀ escape the ♂♂'s intense courtship by jumping out of the water. *B. miolepis* does not seem to be very fertile. Feed juveniles newly hatched *Artemia* nauplii.

F: O; all types of live foods as well as frozen, tablet, and flake foods.

S: Besides this nominate form, there is also the subspecies *B. m. rubrostigma* POLL & LAMBERT, 1964. That subspecies inhabits coastal rivers of southern Cameroon to Zaïre and, with a total length of 83 mm, is somewhat smaller than the subspecies presented here.

T: 24°–28°C, **L:** 11 cm, **A:** 80 cm, **R:** m, b, **D:** 2

Barbus kerstenii kerstenii

Barbus miolepis miolepis

Fam.: Cyprinidae
Subfam.: Cyprininae

Barbus neumayeri
Neumayer's barb

FISCHER, 1884

Syn.: *Barbus carpio, B. luazomela, B. nairobiensis, B. percivali, B. percivali* var. *kitalensis, B. portali, B. serrifer.*

Hab.: Africa: widely distributed in the eastern African countries of Kenya and Uganda. Also found in Lakes Tanganyika and Basuto.

F.I.: Unknown.

Sex.: No definite sexual differences are known. During the spawning season, ♀♀ are fuller.

Soc. B.: Nonaggressive, active schooling fish.

M: As stated for *Barbus apleurogramma.*

B: No reported successes.

F: O; all types of live foods as well as frozen, freeze-dried, tablet, and flake foods.

S: None.

T: 23°–27°C, L: 12 cm, A: 80 cm, R: m, b, D: 2–3

Barbus partipentazona
Partially banded barb

FOWLER, 1934

Syn.: *Barbus sumatranus* (not BLEEKER), *Puntius partipentazona, P. sumatranus* (not BLEEKER).

Hab.: Asia: Thailand, Laos, Cambodia, Westmalaysia.

F.I.: 1933 by the company O. WINKELMANN, Altona, Germany.

Sex.: ♂♂ are slimmer, whereas ♀♀ are more compact and deeper-bodied.

Soc. B.: This schooling fish may occasionally turn aggressive towards small fishes. Peaceful towards equal- or larger-sized fishes. *B. partipentazona* may nip the tips of elongated fins.

M: Requires plenty of free swimming space as well as hiding places among roots and plants.

B: Has been successfully bred at 23°–25°C in medium-hard (12° dGH), neutral to slightly acid water. Does not seem to have a preference about what time of the day to spawn. Fine-leaved plants such as *Myriophyllum* and *Nitella* are an important part of the breeding tank's furnishings. ♂♂ strongly pursue ♀♀ and entice them into the plant thickets. The fish press against each other, and the ♀ releases several eggs which adhere to the plants. In total, up to 500 eggs are laid. The larvae hatch after about 30 hr and are free-swimming after 6 days. Feed them plankton. The parents have to be removed following spawning, before they eagerly consume the spawn.

F: O; all kinds of live and flake foods. Not a finicky eater.

S: Imported in 1933 as *B. "sumatranus,"* which today is the Sumatra barb, *Barbus tetrazona.* In 1935, after the "real" Sumatra barb was imported, the error was discovered.

T: 22°–25°C, L: 4.5 cm, A: 60 cm, R: all, D: 1–2

Barbus neumayeri

Barbus partipentazona

Barbus binotatus, spotted barb

Barbus sp. "Ethiopia"

Bandulla barb, *Barbus bandula* ♂

Bandulla barb, *Barbus bandula* ♀

Barbus plebejus tauricus
Crimea barb

KESSLER, 1877

Syn.: *Barbus tauricus.*

Hab.: Europe: former Soviet Union, in the freshwaters of the Crimea.

F.I.: Probably has not been imported into Germany.

Sex.: ♂♂ have nuptial tubercles during the spawning season; ♀♀ are fuller during the spawning season.

Soc. B.: Sedentary, twilight-active schooling fish. Peaceful.

M: *B. p. tauricus* should be given a substrate of sand or fine-grained gravel, a few refuges among rocks and/or roots, free swimming space, and coldwater plants along the tank's fringes. Water should be medium-hard (12°–15° dGH) and neutral to slightly alkaline (pH 7.0–7.5). Always keep several specimens.

B: To the best of our knowledge, the Crimea barb has not been bred in captivity. Spawning behavior in nature is similar to that of *Barbus barbus* (see Vol. 2, p. 364).

F: O; all types of live foods as well as frozen, freeze-dried, plant, flake, or tablet foods.

S: The nominate species, *B. p. plebejus* VALENCIENNES, 1842, is distributed in the Balkan region. There are several subspecies.

T: 10°–22°C (coldwater fish), **L:** 34 cm, **A:** 100 cm, **R:** b, **D:** 2

Oreichthys cosuatis

(HAMILTON, 1822)

Syn.: *Cyprinus cosuatis, Barbus cosuatis, Leuciscus cosuatis, Oreichthys parvus, Rohtee pangut, Systomus malacopterus.*

Hab.: Asia: Pakistan, India, Bangladesh, Burma, and Thailand.

F.I.: Unknown.

Sex.: No definite differences known. ♀♀ are fuller during the spawning season

Soc. B.: Peaceful schooling fish. Associate with nonaggressive fishes.

M: Caring for this fish is not difficult; even small aquaria are suitable. Use a dark substrate and plant the edges and background heavily. Always keep a small school. Water: pH 6.0–6.5; hardness up to 15° dGH; sometimes peat filtration is advisable.

B: Not very difficult. If possible, the water should be soft, not above 8°–10° (5°) dGH, with a slightly acid pH of around 6. Dense vegetation and a spawning screen on the bottom are needed because the breeders are sometimes predacious towards their eggs. Feed the parents well and remove them after spawning. The smallest plankton is needed to rear the fry.

F: O; all kinds of small live foods and flake, frozen, and freeze-dried foods.

T: 24°–28°C, **L:** 7.5 cm, **A:** 60 cm, **R:** all, **D:** 1–2

Barbus plebejus tauricus

Oreichthys cf. *cosuatis*

Discherodontus halei

Discherodontus halei
Somphong barb

(DUNCKER, 1904)

Syn.: *Barbus somphongsi, Puntius halei.*

Hab.: Asia: Thailand, in the Mekong River and its flood plains, including surrounding rice fields; Malay peninsula.

F.I.: 1958 by BENL through the Somphong Aquarium, Bangkok.

Sex.: ♀♀ are fuller during the spawning season.

Soc. B.: This peaceful schooling fish is hectic and often shy.

M: Aquarium with free swimming space and refuges among roots or dense vegetation.

B: There is no information available concerning successfully breeding this species in a captive environment.

F: O; all kinds of animal and plant fare as well as flake foods commiserate to its size.

T: 23°–26°C, L: 10.5 cm, A: 80 cm, R: all, D: 2

Fam.: Cyprinidae
Subfam.: Abraminae

Blicca bjoerkna

Blicca bjoerkna
Silver bream

(LINNAEUS, 1758)

Syn.: *Cyprinus bjoerkna, Abramis blicca, Blicca argyroleuca, B. laskyr, Cyprinus blicca, C. gibbosus, C. laskyr.*

Hab.: Central Europe to western Asia. Most successful when it colonizes small, shallow lakes, where it usually remains near the shore close to the bottom among plant growth. In rivers, it prefers the bream region to brackish water.

F.I.: European species.

Sex.: ♂♂ acquire nuptial tubercles; ♀♀ grow significantly larger.

Soc. B.: Peaceful, benthic schooling fish. Found in large schools during the spawning season. Winter months are spent hibernating singly.

M: Tall roomy tanks are best. Use fine sand as substrate and some bogwood and a few rocks as decoration. Keep in mind that dense vegetation is neces-

sary. Water chemistry is not of foremost importance.

B: In its native habitat, this species spawns from May to June. During the spawning season, these animals school. Amidst much splashing, the yellowish eggs are released at night along shallow, vegetated shores. The hatching larvae remain along the shores. This species grows slowly, attaining sexual maturity at a length of 10–12 cm (3 to 5 years of age).

F: O; all types of live foods such as plankton, small crustacea, insects and their larvae, and molluscs. Flake and tablet foods.

S: Silver bream are very similar to bream. They are unwanted by-catches in fishermen's nets, since their meat, as opposed to that of the bream, is not appreciated.

T: 4°–20°C, **L:** 25 (35) cm, **A:** 80 cm, **R:** all, **D:** 1

Capoeta damascina

(VALENCIENNES, 1842)

Syn.: *Scaphiodon fratercula, S. peregrinorum, S. socialis, Chondrostoma syriacum, Capoeta syrica.*

Hab.: Eastern Europe and western Asia: Levante and Mesopotamia.

F.I.: Unknown.

Sex.: Unknown.

Soc. B.: Peaceful schooling fish.

M: Needs a large tank with plenty of plants, yet sufficient free swimming space.

B: Has not been bred in an aquarium.

F: O; plant fare and flake foods.

S: Most common species found in the waters of the Levante and Mesopotamia regions. Morphologically variable.

T: 15°–26°C, **L:** 40 cm, **A:** from 150 cm, **R:** b, m, **D:** 3

Capoetobrama kuschakewitschi

(KESSLER, 1872)

Syn.: *Acanthobrama kuschakewitschi, A. bogdanovi.*

Hab.: Asia: former Soviet Union, rivers of the Aral Sea region (Syr-Darya, Amu-Darya), Lake Karakul, and the Zeravshan River.

F.I.: Has not been imported into Germany.

Sex.: None known (?); ♀ are more robust (note the photo).

Soc. B.: Peaceful schooling fish.

M: As for *Abramis brama. C. kuschakewitschi* can be housed with European species (*Abramis brama, Chondrostoma nasus, Vimba vimba*, etc.).

B: Information on breeding could not be found in western aquarium magazines. In nature, the species spawns from mid-April to the end of June. On average, a ♀ will lay 3,000–4,000 adhesive eggs in regions having a sluggish current.

F: O; in nature, this species feeds on detritus and mud and its associated microbes.

S: The primary difference between *Capoetobrama* and related genera lies in the strong unsegmented ray of the dorsal fin. *C. kuschakewitschi* has a very long (ca. 4x the body length) intestine. The genus *Capoetobrama* is monotypic—that is, it only contains one species which is further divided into 2 subspecies: the nominate form *C. k. kuschakewitschi* (KESSLER, 1872) and *C. k. orientalis* NIKOLSKI, 1934, from the river Chu.

T: 16°–20°C, **L:** 21 cm, **A:** 100 cm, **R:** m, † **D:** 2–3

Capoeta damascina

Capoetobrama kuschakewitschi

Carassius auratus gibelio

Carassius auratus gibelio
Prussian carp

(BLOCH, 1783)

Syn.: *Syprinus gibelio, Carassius gibelio, C. vulgaris* var. *kolenty.*

Hab.: Originally distributed from eastern Asia to Siberia. Today, this species is found in eastern, central, and northern Europe.

F.I.: Cannot be determined.

Sex.: No definite external differences are known. ♀♀ are fuller during the spawning season.

Soc. B.: Relatively sedate and peaceful cyprinids.

M: Provide a substrate of sand, and plant the tank with hardy coldwater species. Do not use fine-leaved plants. The fine sediments the fish constantly stir up will prove detrimental to these plants. Decorations should include roots, bamboo, reeds, and round rocks. The animals prefer clear, medium-hard, slightly alkaline water (hardness around 12° dGH and pH 7.1–7.5, respectively). Perform weekly water exchanges ($^1/_4$ of the tank's volume).

B: Though this would be an interesting fish to breed, it has not been bred in captivity. Once accomplished, we would then know whether or not this species needs ♂♂ of its own species to breed. According to observations in nature, ♀♀ of this species are part of spawning schools of related species and spawn with ♂♂ in this school. All offspring are said to be ♀♀.

F: O; all types of live foods as well as plant, flake, and tablet foods.

S: Parthenogenetic (asexual) reproduction is a unique (?) characteristic of this fish. ♂♂ of other species (*Cyprinus carpio, Carassius carassius*) are used as spawning partners for this species. Fertilization in the traditional sense does not take place. Egg "fertilization" merely triggers egg development.

T: 10°–20°C (coldwater fish), **L:** up to 45 cm, **A:** 100 cm, **R:** m, b, **D:** 1

Fam.: Cyprinidae
Subfam.: Abraminae

Chelaethiops rukwaensis ♀

Chelaethiops rukwaensis

(RICARDO, 1939)

Syn.: *Engraulicypris congicus rukwaensis.*

Hab.: Africa: Tanzania, endemic to Lake Rukwa.

F.I.: 1987 by KILIAN and SEEGERS.

Sex.: ♀♀ are significantly fuller during the spawning season.

Soc. B.: A peaceful schooling fish that prefers the upper water column.

M: No information is available concerning captive maintenance. The water of Lake Rukwa is very turbid and muddy with an average pH of 8.5 and a high concentration of sodium.

B: To the best of our knowledge, this fish has not been bred in an aquarium. There is no information available.

F: C; all kinds of small live foods, including floating insects.

S: Besides *C. rukwaensis*, there are five additional *Chelaethiops* species.

T: 24°–28°C, **L:** 8 cm, **A:** 80 cm, **R:** t, m, **D:** 2

Cyclocheilichthys janthochir

Cyclocheilichthys janthochir
Pretty-finned river barb

(BLEEKER, 1853)

Syn.: *Systomus janthochir, Barbus janthochir.*

Hab.: Southeast Asia: Indonesia, Kalimantan (Borneo).

F.I.: Unknown.

Sex.: Not certain; ♀♀ are probably larger and, at least during the spawning season, more rounded.

Soc. B.: Peaceful species.

M: *C. janthochir* is a relatively adaptive species which places no particular demands on water composition, yet soft, slightly acid water (hardness around 5° dGH and pH 6.0–6.5, respectively) should prove to be the most favorable, since these values correspond to those of its native habitat. Follow recommendations made for other *Cyclocheilichthys* species in regard to the aquarium's furnishings (see Vol. 1, p. 412).

B: Has not been accomplished in an aquarium.

F: O; all types of live foods as well as frozen, freeze-dried, and flake foods.

S: None.

T: 24°–26°C, **L:** over 20 cm, **A:** 80 cm, **R:** b, **D:** 1

Fam.: Cyprinidae
Subfam.: Leuciscinae

Erythroculter mongolicus

Erythroculter mongolicus (BASILOWSKI, 1855)

Syn.: *Culter mongolicus, C. rutilus.*

Hab.: Asia: Mongolia, former Soviet Union, and China; the Amur (to its mouth), Ussuri, and Sungari Rivers, Lakes Chanka and Hwangthe, the Yangtse Basin, and the Chientang River.

F.I.: Has not been imported into Germany.

Sex.: No definite external differentiating characteristics are known.

Soc. B.: This lively peaceful schooling fish should be housed with fishes that behave similarly.

M: Needs a roomy tank that has densely planted borders. Use sand or fine-grained gravel as substrate. Decorate with bogwood, reeds, and roots. Provide good aeration and filtration. Exchange up to ¹/₃ of the water weekly.

Water: hardness of 20° dGH; pH up to 7.0.

B: Has not been successful in an aquarium. The scant information available suggests that spawning occurs in June in Lake Chanka. The resulting eggs are pelagic.

F: C; floating foods (insects: caddisflies and mayflies), insect larvae, and zooplankton (small crustacea, etc.); full-grown animals chiefly feed on small fishes.

S: While *E. mongolicus* is not of great economic importance, its relative, *Erythroculter erythropterus,* is. In the years prior to WW II, the annual catch was 270 tons (NIKOLSKI 1957).

T: 10°–20°C, **L:** up to 60 cm, **A:** from 150 cm, **R:** m, b, **D:** 2–3

Esomus longimana
Longfin flying barb

Syn.: None.

Hab.: Asia: Thailand. A common fish, particularly in stagnant waters.

F.I.: Unknown.

Sex.: ♂♂ are slender, whereas ♀♀ are robust and full.

Soc. B.: Lively surface-oriented fish. Peaceful towards conspecifics as well as heterospecifics. Frequently shy and skittish. Good jumpers; therefore, cover the tank well.

M: Heavy vegetation, including floating plants, is favored. Do not house with excessively lively fishes, as this species fairs badly when forced to compete for food!

B: Probably similar to *Esomus malayensis*; see Vol. 2, p. 384.

F: C; primarily floating insects in nature. These should also be provided in captivity. Additionally, it consumes mosquito larvae, large *Artemia*, *Daphnia* and, sometimes, flake foods.

S: *E. longimana* is often confused with *Esomus danricus,* but according to H. M. SMITH, that species cannot be found east of the mountains of Burma.

T: 22°–26°C, **L**: 8.5 cm, **A**: 90 cm, **R**: t, m, **D**: 2

Esomus lineatus
Striped flying barb

AHL, 1925

Syn.: *Nuria daurica* var. *malabarica.*

Hab.: Asia: India, along the delta of the Ganges.

F.I.: 1911 by P. MATTE, Lankwitz, Germany

Sex.: No sexual dichromatism. Only the ♂♂'s slender body shape is indicative of sex.

Soc. B.: Active schooling fish if the aquarium permits. Other fishes are not bothered. Can be housed with much smaller species.

M: Provide plenty of free swimming space in the upper third of the aquarium. Refuge is sought under plant leaves when disturbed; therefore, there should be plenty of vegetation along the edges. Excellent jumpers. Cover the tank well!

B: Probably has been successfully bred in aquaria, but there is no information concerning such in the literature.

F: O. An undemanding omnivore.

S: Fluctuations of pH values are not always tolerated. Regular water exchanges are important. Avoid elevated nitrate concentrations.

T: 22°–25°C, **L**: ♂ 5 cm, ♀ 6 cm, **A**: 70 cm, **R**: t, **D**: 1–2

Esomus longimana (?) oder *E. metallicus*

Esomus lineatus

Esomus metallicus ♂

Esomus metallicus
Silvery flying barb, metallic flying barb

AHL, 1924

Syn.: *Nuria daurica.*

Hab.: Asia: Thailand and Laos. Common in its native habitat.

F.I.: Unknown.

Sex.: ♂♂ are more slender; ♀♀ are stouter and taller.

Soc. B.: Nonaggressive fish of the upper water column. Occasionally timid, especially in new environments. A good jumper, so cover the tank well.

M: A section of the tank should be densely planted; floating plants are also necessary. Do not associate with overly lively fishes, since this fish will be unable to successfully compete for food!

B: Probably like other *Esomus* species (Vol. 2, p. 384).

F: C; primarily feeds on floating insects in its natural biotope. These should be provided in captivity. Mosquito larvae, large crustacea, and water fleas as well as flake and frozen foods are also consumed.

T: 22°–26°C, **L:** 7.5 cm, **A:** 80 cm, **R:** t, **D:** 2

Fam.: Cyprinidae
Subfam.: Garrinae

Garra ceylonensis ceylonensis

Garra ceylonensis ceylonensis
Ceylon log sucker

BLEEKER, 1863

Syn.: *Crossochilus reba.*

Hab.: Asia: Sri Lanka (Ceylon), in both small and large rivers.

F.I.: Probably only after 1980.

Sex.: None known.

Soc. B.: Peaceful fish which constantly explores roots and glass panes in its search for food (suckermouth).

M: Spacious tank decorated with plants, roots, and rocks. Water: pH around 7; hardness up to 15° dGH, but lower values are better.

B: Has not been successfully bred in captivity.

F: O; any live or flake foods of appropriate size.

S: Besides the nominate form, there is also the subspecies *G. c. phillipsi* DE-RANIYAGALA, 1933, which has only been found in the Gammaduva region.

T: 24°–26°C, **L:** 15 cm, **A:** 100 cm, **R:** b, **D:** 2–3

211

Fam.: Cyprinidae
Subfam.: Garrinae

Carps

Garra congoensis
Congo log sucker

POLL, 1959

Syn.: None.

Hab.: Africa: Zaïre, in the lower Zaïre River.

F.I.: Unknown; the species has probably not been imported into Germany.

Sex.: No external differentiating characteristics are known.

Soc. B.: Nothing is known about the social behavior of *G. congoensis*.

M: The substrate should either be of sand or fine-grained gravel. Offer refuges among rocks or roots. The edges and back of the aquarium can be planted. Aerate the water well; perhaps water movement would be advantageous. The water should be medium-hard and slightly acid (hardness up to 15° dGH and pH 6.5, respectively).

B: Has not been bred in an aquarium.

F: O; all kinds of live foods as well as frozen, freeze-dried, flake, and vegetable foods.

S: *G. congoensis* is a typical inhabitant of the rapids of the lower Zaïre River (formerly the Congo River).

T: 23°–25°C, **L:** 10 cm, **A:** 80 cm, **R:** b, **D:** 2–3

Garra dembeensis
Cameroon log sucker

(RÜPPELL, 1836)

Syn.: *Chondrostoma dembeensis, Discognathus blanfordii, D. chiarinii, D. dembeensis, D. giarrabensis, D. hindii, D. johnstonii, D. quadrimaculatus, D. vinciguerrae, Garra giarrabensis, G. hindii, G. johnstonii, G. vinciguerrae.*

Hab.: Africa: from east Africa to Cameroon, in flowing waters.

F.I.: Not known.

Sex.: ♂♂ have orange-tipped fins.

Soc. B.: Most at ease when a group is kept. Other fishes are ignored.

M: Adaptable species. Although these fish are found in flowing, even turbulent, waters in their natural habitat, in the aquarium they can be seen resting on a leaf over long periods of time. They are much less restless than *Crossocheilus* (previously *Epalzeorhynchus*) species which live in similar habitats.

B: Has not been bred in an aquarium.

F: H, O; commercial dry foods are readily accepted. Algae are grazed. Insect larvae and similar foods are also eaten.

T: 22°–26°C, **L:** 11 cm, **A:** from 50 cm, **R:** b, m, **D:** 2–3

Garra congoensis

Garra dembeensis

Garra nasuta
Nose log sucker

(Mc CLALLAND, 1839)

Syn.: *Platycara nasuta.*

Hab.: South and southeast Asia: India (Assam), Burma, southern China, and Vietnam.

F.I.: After 1980 as by-catch.

Sex.: Unknown.

Soc. B.: Little is known about the social behavior of this species. Although they pass their time rasping algae from the glass and the decorations, they are not very effective cleaner fish.

M: This species seems to have a high oxygen requirement during its acclimation phase. Insure that the aquarium has strong filtration, current, and a moving water surface. Temperatures should be moderate. After acclimation, the animals are hardy and undemanding. Water: pH 6.5–7.5; hardness 10°–20° dGH.

B: Has not been bred. Pairs are scarce, since the animals have only been imported sporadically as by-catch.

F: O; flake and frozen foods.

S: Identification based on the head profile is relatively straightforward (note the species name and the photo).

T: 20°–25°C, **L:** 20 cm, **A:** 80 cm, **R:** b, m, **D:** 2–3

Garra ghorensis
Jordanian log sucker

KRUPP, 1982

Syn.: *Garratibanica ghorensis.*

Hab.: Asia: springs in the area around the southern Dead Sea.

F.I.: 1980.

Sex.: See *Garra rufa.*

Soc. B.: Peaceful schooling fish.

M: Unknown. Its habitat around the Dead Sea seems to indicate that this species, as opposed to the log suckers from Thailand and Africa, should be kept in hard saline water.

B: As for *G. rufa.*

F: H, O; plant fare and flake foods.

S: This relict species is found in very few springs around the Dead Sea.

T: 25°–28°C, **L:** 9 cm, **A:** from 80 cm, **R:** b, m, **D:** 2

Garra nasuta ♀

Garra ghorensis

Garra rufa
Reddish log sucker

(HECKEL, 1843)

Syn.: *Discognathus obtusus.*

Hab.: Asia: Levante and Mesopotamia.

F.I.: Unknown.

Sex.: ♂♂ have longer pectoral fins and more pronounced nuptial tubercles.

Soc. B.: Peaceful schooling fish.

M: Always keep a school. Appoint the tank with fine sand, hiding places, and robust vegetation. Though it will occasionally eat plants, it is otherwise undemanding.

B: Open spawners. Eggs are immediately eaten. Raising the fry with plankton is unproblematic. Dense vegetation is advantageous (e.g., with Java moss).

F: H, O; plant fare and flake foods.

T: 15°–28°C, **L:** 16 cm, **A:** from 100 cm, **R:** m, b, **D:** 2

Fam.: Cyprinidae
Subfam.: Gobioninae

Gobio gobio soldatovi
Soldatov's gudgeon

BERG, 1914

Syn.: *Gobio soldatovi.*

Hab.: Asia: former Soviet Union and China, in the Ussuri and Sungari Rivers and the Amur Basin upriver from Chabarowsk. Mainly lives in stagnate waters, but also found in slow-moving waters. It does not inhabit mountain streams.

F.I.: Has not been imported into Germany.

Sex.: Sexes are difficult to distinguish. At spawning time, ♂♂ have cranial nuptial tubercles.

Soc. B.: Peaceful, social schooling fish. Can be housed with European species that have similar requirements.

M: As for *Gobio gobio tungussicus.*

B: There is no information concerning successfully breeding this species in an aquarium. Although we are largely ignorant in regard to exact spawning data, it is known that the animals mature at a length of 46 mm and ♀♀ spawn 3 times per spawning season. Between 1,550 and 5,300 eggs are laid on a sandy or rocky bottom.

F: C; live foods, especially bloodworms.

S: In most Russian fish books, this subspecies is listed as an autonomous species. However, in the newest revision of the subfamily Gobioninae by BANARESCU and NALBANT (1973), this animal was classified as a subspecies.

T: 4°–18°C (coldwater fish), **L:** 12 cm, **A:** 80 cm, **R:** b, **D:** 2

217

Gobio gobio tungussicus

BORISOV, 1928

Syn.: *Gobio sodatovi tungussicus.*

Hab.: Asia: former Soviet Union, in the drainage of the Lena and Vitima Rivers (east Siberia) and the upper part of the Amur down to Chaborowsk.

F.I.: Has not yet been imported into Germany.

Sex.: Sexes are difficult to distinguish; during the spawning season, ♂♂ have nuptial tubercles.

Soc. B.: Peaceful, social schooling fish. Can be associated with European species that have similar requirements (e.g., *Gobio gobio, Nemacheilus barbatulus, Cobitis taenia*).

M: Provide a roomy aquarium with coarse sand or gravel as substrate, offer some hiding places among rocks,

and aerate the tank well. Clear, clean water with a hardness of up to 20° dGH and a pH of 7.0–7.5 is best.

B: Has probably not been accomplished in an aquarium. In nature, these animals spawn during the summer. Eggs are laid in shallow water over a sand substrate.

F: C; live foods. Primarily feeds on bloodworms in its natural habitat.

S: This subspecies almost exclusively lives in static waters. Of the four gudgeons of the genus *Gobio* found in this region, this is the most limnophilic. According to BANARESCU & NALBANT (1973), these animals have an average life expectancy of 4 years.

T: 10°–18°C, **L:** 11 cm, **A:** 80 cm, **R:** b, **D:** 2–3

Gobio tenuicorpus
White-finned Amur gudgeon

MORI, 1934

Syn.: *Gobio albipinnatus taenuicorpus, G. coriparoides tenuicorpus, G. gobio tenuicorpus.*

Hab.: Asia: China and the former Soviet Union, in the Amur and Huang Basins.

F.I.: Has not been imported into Germany.

Sex.: External differences between the sexes are very slight. ♂♂ probably have nuptial tubercles during the spawning season.

Soc. B.: This lively, peaceful schooling fish relishes current.

M: As for *Gobio gobio tungussicus.* However, a moderate to strong current should be provided, since *G. tenuicorpus* is one of the most rheophilic (current-loving) members of the genus *Gobio.*

B: Has probably not been bred in an aquarium. In nature, the animals reach

sexual maturity during their third summer. The reproductive biology of this fish is still unknown.

F: C; live foods. In nature, these fish primarily feed on black fly larvae (Simuliidae).

S: Most authors consider *G. tenuicorpus* a subspecies of *Gobio albipinnatus,* but a number of characteristics speak in favor of *G. tenuicorpus* being an autonomous species.

T: 12°–22°C, **L:** 10 cm, **A:** 60 cm, **R:** b, **D:** 2–3

Gobio gobio tungussicus

Gobio tenuicorpus

Hampala macrolepidota
Silver and red barb

van HASSELT, 1823
Subfam.: Cyprininae

Syn.: *Barbus hampal.*

Hab.: Southeast Asia: the Sunda Islands, Burma, and Thailand (widely distributed throughout the latter two).

F.I.: Unknown.

Sex.: Sexes cannot be distinguished based on external characteristics.

Soc. B.: Unknown. Though rare, single specimens are occasionally imported as "by-catch." Only juveniles are suitable because the animals grow too large for the average aquarium. Typical social behavior can hardly be displayed in the confines of an aquarium.

M: As for other large *Barbus* or *Osteochilus* species.

B: A home aquarium is an inappropriate breeding environment.

F: O; all typical foods, including plant-based foods.

S: Juveniles of *H. macrolepidota* and *Hampala dispar* are difficult to distinguish. However, adults can be differentiated, since *H. macrolepidota* has longer barbels.

T: 22°–25°C, **L:** 70 cm, **A:** 100 cm, **R:** m, b, **D:** 2–3

Hemibarbus maculatus
Spotted Amur barb

BLEEKER, 1871
Subfam.: Gobioninae

Syn.: *Acanthogobio maculatus, A. paltscheuskii, Barbus semibarbus, Gobiobarbus labeo* var. *maculatus, Hemibarbus joiteni, H. labeo maculatus, H. longibarbis.*

Hab.: Asia: former Soviet Union and China, throughout the Amur and Yangtze Basins to the eastern Sikang.

F.I.: Has not been imported to Germany.

Sex.: ♂♂ are slightly larger than ♀♀. Otherwise, there are no definite sexual differences.

Soc. B.: Very peaceful, active, rheophilic (current-loving) schooling fish.

M: Only roomy tanks with sand or fine-grained gravel substrates are appropriate. Secluded areas among rocks or roots should be provided. Coldwater vegetation can be planted densely along the edges of the tank. Water should be clear and neutral with a hardness of 20° dGH. Perhaps a slight current produced

with a powerhead would prove beneficial.

B: Has not been bred in Germany. In its natural habitat, these fish are sexually mature at 3 years of age. The spawning season extends from the middle of May to the end of June. During these months, the water temperature is 19° to 24°C. The 2 mm eggs are laid on aquatic plants and hatch after 4 days. The larvae lack adhesive organs and are pelagic for 6 days posthatching. Afterwards, they adopt a benthic lifestyle and actively feed.

F: C; in nature, these animals feed on benthic invertebrates such as insect larvae, small crustacea, and molluscs.

S: In some regions, *H. maculatus* is of slight economic importance.

T: 10°–24°C, **L:** 36 cm, **A:** from 120 cm, **R:** b, **D:** 3

Hampala macrolepidota

Hemibarbus maculatus

Hemigrammocypris lini
Garnet minnow

WEITZMAN & CHAN, 1966

Syn.: *Aphyocypris pooni.*

Hab.: Southern China: Kweiang System (mountains with white clouds, north of Hong Kong).

F.I.: Ca. 1953 to the USA.

Sex.: ♀♀ have a dark longitudinal band. ♂♂ are slightly more colorful. See photos.

Soc. B.: Peaceful schooling fish which can be kept in unheated community tanks with any nonpredatory species.

M: Few demands are placed on water composition. Vegetation can consist of *Vallisneria, Elodea, Sagittaria,* and other species capable of tolerating cooler waters. However, always keep enough free swimming space for these lively fish. When kept at temperatures above 22°C, good filtration and water circulation become important. If stones are used as decoration, place them so that there are no crevices where the fish can become stuck or abrade their scales.

B: Water with a temperature of 24°–26°C, a pH of 7.5–7.8, and a hardness of ca. 13° dGH is appropriate for reproduction. Filter the water through the finest filter materials, and insure that it is oxygen-rich. Separate the breeding pair before placing them together in the breeding tank. The tank can be as small as 40 x 25 x 25 cm. Since the parents will eat the eggs, a coarse plastic mesh or a coarse gravel substrate are recommended. Between 15 and 30 eggs are released daily for several days. They have an approximate diameter of 0.8 mm and are crystal clear. The 4 mm larvae hatch after about 60 hr. After 48 hr they are free-swimming and need small foods such as infusoria (e.g., squeeze the foam filter). Fine MicroMin, egg yolk, and liquifry can also be fed. However, feeding these foods makes it imperative that $^2/_3$ of the tank's volume is exchanged every 3–4 days (siphon the bottom). After 6 days, *Artemia* can be fed. At that time, the juveniles turn golden yellow and develop their characteristic black stripe.

After about 3 months the animals can be placed with other small species.

F: O, C; small flake foods and FD Menu. Offer Tetra Conditioning Food, *Artemia,* and small live foods, particularly bloodworms, for variety.

S: This species is often confused with *T. albonubes* when imported as by-catch (Vol. 1, p. 446). Both inhabit the same region. Source: TI 85 (1988).

T: 18°–22°C, **L:** 5 cm, **A:** 60 cm, **R:** m, t, **D:** 1–2

Hemigrammocypris lini ♂

Hemigrammocypris lini ♀, see page 257

Hemiculter leucisculus

(BASILEWSKY, 1855)

Syn.: *Culter leucisculus, Cultriculus kneri, Hemiculter dispar, H. kneri, H. schrenki, H. varpachovskii.*

Hab.: Asia: former Soviet Union (Amur Basin), western and southern Korea, and China south to Hong Kong, Annam, and Taiwan.

F.I.: Has not been imported into Germany.

Sex.: ♀♀ are fuller; see photo.

Soc. B.: This is a peaceful, surface-oriented schooling fish.

M: Needs a large tank with plenty of swimming space, vegetation along the back and edges, and water with a hardness of up to 15° dGH and a pH of ca. 7.0. Always keep a small group of at least 6 animals. Can be housed with other peaceful species that have similar requirements.

B: Probably has not been bred in an aquarium. In nature, the animals spawn during the summer.

F: O; all kinds of live foods. Juveniles consume zooplankton, whereas adults mainly eat insects.

S: In addition to the nominate form, *H. l. leucisculus* (BASILEWSKY, 1855), there is another subspecies, *H. l. lucidus* (DYBOWSKI, 1872) from the Ussuri River and Lake Khanka. *H. leucisculus* is an important part of the food chain for predacious fishes of the Amur.

T: 18°–22°C, **L:** 18 cm, **A:** 100 cm, **R:** m, t, **D:** 2

Horadandia atukorali
Ceylon dwarf barb

DERANIYAGALA, 1943

Syn.: None.

Hab.: Southeast Asia: Sri Lanka (Ceylon). Lives among aquatic plants in freshwater lakes of the coastal plains.

F.I.: Individually as by-catch. Probably only since 1985.

Sex.: None known.

Soc. B.: Very peaceful schooling fish. Maintain in a species tank or keep with small *Rasbora* species, e.g., *R. maculata*.

M: Even the smallest tanks suffice for *H. atukorali*. Use a dark substrate (e.g., Lavatit), dense vegetation, decorations riddled with hiding places, and a few floating plants to dim the illumination. Groups of more than eight fair better than individuals. Water: pH 6.0–6.5; hardness to 12° dGH.

B: No information could be found.

F: O; small live foods are preferred: *Artemia* nauplii, water fleas, cyclops, rotifers.

S: *H. atukorali* is the smallest cyprinid of Sri Lanka. This species was named after the person who first captured the animals, V. ATUKORALI.

T: 24°–26°C, **L:** 2.8 cm, **A:** 40 cm, **R:** m, t, **D:** 3

Hemiculter leucisculus ♀

Horadandia atukorali

Hypophthalmichthys molitrix
Silver carp

(VALENCIENNES, 1844)

Syn.: *Leuciscus molitrix, Hypophthalmichthys dabryi, H. dybowskii, Onychodon debryi.*

Hab.: Originally distributed in east Asia, but it has been introduced into many parts of Europe. Lives in eutrophic, shallow lakes and warm rivers.

Sex.: ♀♀ are significantly fuller.

Soc. B.: Peaceful fish that schools in the open water. Frequently cultured with carp and grass carp.

M: Only juveniles can be kept in aquaria. See *Cyprinus carpio* for further information.

B: Like grass carp, breeding is impossible without hormone treatments. Juveniles are imported or come from breeding stations. In their natural habitat, *H. molitrix* spawn in flood plain lakes during the summer at water temperatures

of 22° to 24°C. Up to 500,000 pelagic eggs are laid by each ♀. Juveniles migrate into rivers after their yolk sac is absorbed and feed on zooplankton found there. At a length of 5 to 10 cm, their dietary needs change and they begin feeding on phytoplankton. Their intestines grow to be 6–7 times their body length! Silver carp mature in 3 to 4 years in their native habitat, but sexual maturity is not attained in Hungarian waters until 5–6 years of age.

F: H; suspended algae. Normally plant-based foods are required. Feed flake foods as a dietary supplement.

S: Frequently stocked in large lakes to control algae blooms.
This species is very sensitive to chemical water pollutants. Insecticides and overfertilization are not tolerated.

T: 6°–24°C, **L:** 100 (80) cm, **A:** from 120 cm, **R:** m, **D:** 2

Hypophthalmichthys nobilis
Big head

(RICHARDSON, 1845) ·

Syn.: *Leuciscus nobilis, Aristichthys nobilis.*

Hab.: Asia: originally inhabited central and south Asia. However, it has been introduced into many parts of the world and can therefore now be found in the Mediterranean region and eastern Europe. Inhabits warm, deep, flowing waters.

Sex.: Difficult to distinguish. ♀♀ are stouter and usually larger.

Soc. B.: Peaceful schooling fish that does not bother other tankmates.

M: Only juveniles make suitable aquarium specimens. House in large, cold-water aquaria that have clear, oxygen-rich water. It remains timid and will refuse to feed when kept in confining environments.

B: See *Hypophthalmichthys molitrix*. Elevated temperatures exceeding 25°C over an extended period of time are

needed to stimulate this species to spawn.

F: H, O; juveniles primarily feed on zooplankton. As they grow, the fish begin to incorporate other items such as phytoplankton into their diet, becoming able to subsist entirely on it. Soft plants can be given as a supplementary food.

S: Big head carp feeds on phytoplankton throughout its life. But small animals such as worms, snails, insects, small crustacea, and fishes may be eaten at lower temperatures. Only at water temperatures above 19°C will it feed on phytoplankton like silver carp. The big head's intestine is 4–5 times its body length.
H. nobilis has been released to control phytoplankton in many parts of the world, including central Europe. The pictured animal is a juvenile. Older specimens, in contrast to *H. molitrix*, are mottled.

T: 10°–26°C, **L:** 100 (60) cm, **A:** form 120 cm, **R:** m, b, **D:** 2

Hypophthalmichthys molitrix

Hypophthalmichthys nobilis, silver coloration

lotichthys phlegethontis ♀

Iotichthys phlegethontis ♂

Iotichthys phlegethontis   (COPE, 1874)

Syn.: *Clinostomus phlegethontis, Gila phlegethontis, Leuciscus phlegethontis, Phoxinus phlegethontis.*

Hab.: North America: USA, in the Bonneville River Basin in Utah. Found in clear, shallow rivers, springs, lakes, and swamps with exuberant vegetation.

F.I.: 1988 to Holland.

Sex.: ♂ ♂ have a red abdomen during the spawning season.

Soc. B.: Robust schooling fish.

M: Provide a fine sand substrate, dense vegetation along the back and edges, a few hiding places among roots, and an open swimming area. No particular requirements are made on water composition or temperature.

B: Has probably not been bred in Europe. Sexual maturity is attained at a length of ca. 2.5 cm, which corresponds to approximately one year of age. In its native waters the spawning season extends from April to August with a peak in May.

F: O; all kinds of live foods, but also frozen, freeze-dried, and flake foods.

S: In some regions, this species has adapted to harsh environments of highly alkaline water, little dissolved oxygen, and temperature fluctuations of 15°C within a 24 hr period. Live expectancy in their natural biotope is 3 years.

T: 10°–26°C, **L:** 6.5 cm, **A:** 70 cm, **R:** b, m, **D:** 1–2

Labeo cylindricus
Cylindrical shark

PETERS, 1852

Syn.: *Labeo darlingi, L. kilossae, L. loveridgei, L. parvulus, Tylognathus cantini, T. montanus.*

Hab.: Africa: in the rivers of eastern and southern Africa from Ethiopia to the Sambesi, Limpopo, and Pongolo Rivers. Also present in Lakes Tanganyika and Malawi.

F.I.: Unknown.

Sex.: No known external differences.

Soc. B.: No information is available at this time, but probably very similar to other *Labeo* species (see *Labeo ruddi*). Animals from Lake Baringo (Kenya) have proven to be very predacious. Other fishes, including cichlids, are ambushed at night and their mucus layer is scraped off.

The pictured animal from Wami, Tanzania, in contrast, lived 4 harmonious years in a community aquarium.

M: As for *L. ruddi.*

B: Has not been bred in an aquarium.

F: O; all kinds of live foods and plant, flake, and tablet foods.

S: *L. cylindricus*'s closest relatives are *Labeo ansorgii* and *L. forskalii.* The latter species does not have a dark lateral band or a red iris.

T: 24°–28°C, **L**: up to 40 cm, **A**: from 120 cm, **R**: b, m, **D**: 3

Labeo forskalii
Plain shark

RÜPPELL, 1853

Syn.: None (?).

Hab.: Africa: in tributaries of both the Nile and the Blue Nile.

F.I.: 1935.

Sex.: In ♂♂, the first and last ray of the dorsal fin are elongated.

Soc. B.: While aggressive and quarrelsome among themselves, they are peaceful towards heterospecifics. Large individuals are territorial loners.

M: Requires a large tank with a fine sand substrate. Decorate with roots, flat rocks, and a plenitude of plants. Arrange the decor so that the animals can establish territories without having their neighbor in direct visual contact. Maintain free swimming space. The water should be medium-hard (12°–15° dGH) and around neutral (pH 7.0). Be wary of placing large specimens in community aquaria.

B: No information could be found. Breeding is probably only possible in large aquaria.

F: O; live, freeze-dried, flake, and frozen foods as well as plant fare (algae, lettuce, spinach).

S: ELIAS (1972) reported that *L. forskalii* "nibbles" on its tankmates at night, inflicting minor wounds (Aquarienmagazin 6, 14).

T: 18°–25°C, **L**: 35 (20) cm, **A**: 120 cm, **R**: b, m, **D**: 2

Labeo cylindricus

Labeo forskalii

Labeo ruddi
Limpopo shark

BOULENGER, 1907

Syn.: None.

Hab.: Africa: South Africa, Mozambique, and Zimbabwe, endemic to the Limpopo-Incomáti River system. Inhabits mud-bottomed bodies of water.

F.I.: Unknown.

Sex.: No definite external differences are known. During the spawning season, some ♂♂ supposedly have nuptial tubercles.

Soc. B.: May become aggressive and quarrelsome among themselves, but usually peaceful towards heterospecifics. It is unknown if large specimens are gregarious or solitary. If the latter is the case, do they claim territories like *Labeo forskalii*?

M: House in roomy tanks that have a fine sand substrate; provide hiding places among roots and pieces of slate; plant the sides and back densely; arrange the decor so that the animals, if they find the need, can establish territories out of direct visual contact with their neighbors; preserve an open area for swimming. Water: hardness of 10°–15° dGH; pH around 7.0. This fish can be kept with fishes which have similar requirements

B: No information could be found.

F: O; live foods (insects, insect larvae, small crustacea, worms), and plant fare (algae, lettuce, spinach) as well as frozen, tablet, and flake foods.

S: *L. ruddi* differs from other members of the *Labeo niloticus* group by, among other characteristics, the absence of a longitudinal stripe, a more ventral lateral line, and a short, blunt snout.

T: 23°–27°C, **L:** 26 cm, **A:** 120 cm, **R:** b, m, **D:** 2–3

Labiobarbus leptocheilus

(van HASSELT, 1823)

Syn.: *Dangila leptocheila, D. cuvieri.*

Hab.: Southeast Asia: Thailand, Malaysia, and Indonesia (Sumatra, Borneo, and Java).

F.I.: 1967 by the name *Osteochilus lini* FOWLER, 1935.

Sex.: No definite external characteristics are known. During the spawning season, ♀♀ are fuller (eggs).

Soc. B.: Active, peaceful schooling fish.

M: Give them a roomy tank with dense vegetation along the edges and back and refuges among roots and/or stones. Maintain ample swimming space. Good filtration and regular water exchanges are recommended. No major demands are placed on water composition. Only juveniles are suitable for normal home aquaria.

B: To the best of our knowledge, this species has never been bred in an aquarium. Breeding is probably similar to other large *Barbus* species and not too difficult. Typical home aquaria are likely to be too small for breeding.

F: O; vegetable matter (algae, lettuce, spinach) and all types of live foods as well as frozen, freeze-dried, and flake foods.

T: 24°–26°C, **L:** 25 cm, **A:** 120 cm, **R:** m, b, **D:** 2–3

Labeo ruddi

Labiobarbus leptocheilus

Ladislavia taczanowskii   DYBOWSKI, 1869

Syn.: None.

Hab.: Asia: former Soviet Union and China, around the upper and central Amur and the Yalu River; western Korea. They inhabit moving waters, especially mountain rivers and streams. Migration is limited.

F.I.: Has not been imported into Germany.

Sex.: Sexes are difficult to distinguish. During the spawning season, ♂♂ have nuptial tubercles on the head, sides, and in front of and below the eyes.

Soc. B. Very lively, peaceful schooling fish.

M: Aquarium with sand or gravel as substrate, some hiding places among rocks, and good aeration, since the animals have a high oxygen requirement. They

are especially fond of tanks which have a strong current. Clear, medium-hard (10°–20° dGH), clean water with a pH of 7.0–7.5 is best.

B: No information on breeding in captivity could be found. In nature, it spawns from June to July. Sexual maturity is obtained at 3 years of age and a length of 5 cm. The eggs have a diameter of 1.6–1.8 mm.

F: O; mainly vegetation (algae) from rocks, but benthic invertebrates are also consumed.

S: *Ladislavia* is a monotypic genus.

T: 4°–18°C (coldwater fish), **L:** 8 cm, **A:** 80 cm, **R:** b, **D:** 2–3

Leptocypris niloticus   (JOANNIS, 1835)

Syn.: *Leuciscus niloticus, Alburnus alexandrinus, A. niloticus, Barilius niloticus, B. niloticus occidentalis, B. niloticus voltae, B. thebensis, Leuciscus thebensis, Opsarius thebensis.*

Hab.: Africa: Nile, Omeo, Volta, and Senegal Rivers as well as the Lake Chad Basin.

F.I.: 1987 by Lothar SEEGERS.

Sex.: No definite external differentiating characteristics are known. During the spawning season, ♀♀ are significantly fuller.

Soc. B.: Active, peaceful schooling fish.

M: Offer a roomy aquarium that has plenty of free swimming space, dense vegetation along the edges, and a fine sand substrate. Use soft to medium-hard, neutral water (hardness of 8°–15° dGH and a pH of 7.0–7.8, respectively). Can be kept with fishes that have similar demands.

B: Though no breeding information is available, it should not be difficult. Probably similar to breeding African *Barbus* species.

F: O; small live foods as well as frozen, freeze-dried, flake, and supplemental plant foods.

S: *Leptocypris* contains two additional species: the type species, *L. modestus* BOULENGER, 1900, and *L. weynsii* (BOULENGER, 1899). These three species can easily be distinguished by the number of rays in the anal fin. *L. niloticus* has 11–12, whereas *L. modestus* has 8–9 and *L. weynsii* has 14–15.

T: 22°–27°C, **L:** 9.5 cm, **A:** 90 cm, **R:** m, t, **D:** 2

Ladislavia taczanowskii

Leptocypris niloticus

Leucalburnus satunini ♀

Upper course of the Kura River, Russia, biotope of *Leucalburnus satunini*.

Fam.: Cyprinidae
Subfam.: Leuciscinae

Leucalburnus satunini ♂

Leucalburnus satunini

(BERG, 1910)

Syn.: *Phoxinus satunini.*

Hab.: Asia: former Soviet Union, in the upper Kura in the District of Ardagan.

F.I.: Has not been imported into Germany.

Sex.: ♂♂ have nuptial tubercles during the spawning season.

Soc. B.: Amiable schooling fish. Can be housed with European species that have similar requirements, e.g., *Phoxinus phoxinus*, *Gobio gobio*, or *Nemacheilus barbatulus*.

M: Needs a long aquarium with plenty of swimming space and a relatively dark substrate with a few stones scattered about. Coldwater vegetation can be added around the edges. Water should be clear, medium-hard, and neutral to slightly alkaline (hardness of 10°–20°

dGH and a pH of 7.0–7.5, respectively). Aerate well. A current may prove beneficial.

B: Has not been successful in an aquarium.

F: C; live foods of all kinds such as small crustacea, worms, and insect larvae.

S: This genus is monotypic; therefore, this is the only species contained within the genus. Systematically, *Leucalburnus* is somewhere between *Leuciscus* and *Alburnus*.

T: 10°–20°C (coldwater fish), **L:** 17.5 cm, **A:** 80 cm, **R:** m, b, **D:** 2–3

237

Leuciscus cephalus cephalus
Chub

(LINNAEUS, 1758)

Syn.: *Cyprinus cephalus, Leuciscus dobula, L. latifrons, Squalius cephalus, S. dobula.*

Hab.: Throughout Europe with the exception of the most northern regions. Large, swift-current creeks and rivers are preferred. Rarely found in lakes or brackish water.

F.I.: European species.

Sex.: At spawning time, ♂♂ have small nuptial tubercles and ♀♀ have a noticeably extended abdomen.

Soc. B.: Juveniles are gregarious surface-oriented fish that live near the shore in static water. Large individuals are usually predatory loners that live in the open water.

M: The aquarium should be situated so that the water temperature, even during the summer, does not exceed 20°C.

Good aeration is essential at higher temperatures! Use sand or fine-grained gravel as substrate and roots, round stones, and reeds or bamboo to furnish the tank. While background vegetation is appreciated, it is not necessary. Exchange the water regularly. Only juveniles make suitable aquarium inhabitants.

B: This species spawns from April to June. Up to 200,000, 1.5 mm eggs are adhered to rocks and aquatic plants. Slow-growing: ♀♀ reach sexual maturity after 3 years, whereas ♂♂ need 4 years.

F: C, O; live foods and vegetable fare. Juveniles can be trained to accept fish meat, flake foods, and tablets.

S: *L. cephalus* is closely related to *L. leuciscus*. However, the two species can easily be distinguished by the different shape of their mouth and anal fin.

T: 4°–20°C, **L:** 45 (80) cm, **A:** 100 cm, **R:** all, **D:** 1

Leuciscus cephalus orientalis
Oriental chub

NORDMANN, 1840

Syn.: *Leuciscus orientalis, Squalius turcicus, Leuciscus cephalus orientalis* natio *aralychensis, L. c. orientalis* natio *ardebilicus, L. c. orientalis* natio *zangicus.*

Hab.: Asia: northern Caucasus Mountains, eastern and western Transcaucasia; headwaters of the Euphrates and Tigris Rivers, the Kuma River, and the drainage basin of the Kuban and Terek Rivers; in the rivers of the Iranian side of the Caspian Sea; in the basin of Lake Urmaia.

F.I.: Has probably not been imported.

Sex.: ♂♂ have nuptial tubercles, ♀♀ have a fuller ventral area.

Soc. B.: Juveniles are peaceful schooling fish, whereas older animals are predacious loners.

M: As for *Leuciscus cephalus cephalus*.

B: To the best of our knowledge, this species has not been successfully bred in an aquarium.

F: O; all kinds of live foods, including fishes. Frozen, flake, and tablet foods and, occasionally, plant fare are accepted as well.

S: The body of *L. c. orientalis* is longer than that of the nominate form.

T: 10°–20°C (coldwater fish), **L:** 45 cm, **A:** 100 cm, **R:** m, b, **D:** 1–2

Leuciscus cephalus cephalus

Leuciscus cephalus orientalis

Leuciscus leuciscus

(LINNAEUS, 1758)

Syn.: *Cyprinus leuciscus, Leuciscus grislagine, L. vulgaris, Squalius leuciscus.*

Hab.: All of Europe north of the Alps and the Pyrenees. Inhabits fast-flowing waters. Its distribution in lakes is limited to the lake's effluent and affluent waters.

F.I.: Native European species.

Sex.: Difficult to distinguish; ♂ ♂ are slimmer and have nuptial tubercles.

Soc. B.: A surface-oriented, peaceful schooling fish.

M: Keep a school of these very active fish in a large aquarium. Large, newly introduced individuals rarely overcome their timidness. Decorate the aquarium as for *Leuciscus idus.*

B: The spawning season is from March to June. Eggs are adhered to plants.

Successfully rearing the fry seems to be largely dependent on water quality. Breeding is probably only possible in a pond; see *L. idus* (Vol. 1, p. 424).

F: C, O; microorganisms, rarely plants. It quickly learns to accept flake foods.

S: Very similar to *Leuciscus cephalus. L. leuciscus* is smaller, has a black longitudinal stripe and a smaller mouth.

T: 6°–18°C, **L:** 30 cm, **A:** 100 cm, **R:** t, **D:** 2

Leuciscus souffia agassizi

VALENCIENNES, 1844

Syn.: *Leuciscus agassizi, Telestes agassizii.*

Hab.: Europe: in the headwaters of the Rhine and the middle course of the Danube as well as its tributaries (northwest Romania, Carpathian Ukrainia).

F.I.: Native European species.

Sex.: These animals, particularly ♂ ♂, have a dark violet longitudinal stripe immediately above the lateral line that runs from the eye to the caudal fin.

Soc. B.: Peaceful, inactive coldwater fish.

M: As for *Leuciscus cephalus cephalus.* This is a rarely kept coldwater fish. House with other European cyprinids.

B: No information on spawning these fish in captivity could be found. In nature, the species spawns from March to May over gravel substrates.

F: O; all types of live foods (plankton, worms, and other benthic organisms) as well as flake foods.

S: *L. s. agassizi* is a subspecies of *L. souffia* RISSO, 1826. The nominate form hails from the Rhône and Var Rivers in France. In Germany, this species is rapidly approaching extinction because of water pollution and man's manipulation of waterways.

T: 10°–20°C (coldwater fish), **L:** 25 cm, **A:** 80 cm, **R:** m, **D:** 2

Leuciscus leuciscus

Leuciscus souffia agassizi

Lobocheilus quadrilineatus

(FOWLER, 1935)
Subfam.: Cyprininae

Syn.: *Tylognathus quadrilineatus*.

Hab.: Asia: Thailand, relatively common in clear, fast-flowing waters.

F.I.: Ca. 1975 as by-catch.

Sex.: Unknown. ♀♀ are fuller at spawning time (?); ♂♂ have more pronounced tubercles around the mouth.

Soc. B.: Nonaggressive towards small fishes. But use caution when associating the two with larger species, since *L. quadrilineatus* may attack them, causing scale loss from the caudal region.

M: Undemanding charges which have no specific water chemistry requirements. According to conditions in their natural habitat, the water should be clear and oxygen-rich. House in a large aquarium offering plenty of swimming space.

B: Has not been successfully bred.

F: O; *Tubifex, Daphnia*, and commercial dry foods.

S: *Lobocheilus* species have a moveable dermal flap and a sharp horny-edged lower mandible, both of which help them graze algae from stones and roots. Though this behavior was observed in an aquarium, its effectiveness in algae control was deemed insignificant.

T: 20°–25°C, **L:** 26 cm, **A:** 150 cm, **R:** m, b, **D:** 1–2

Luciosoma spilopleura

BLEEKER, 1855
Subfam.: Rasborinae

Syn.: *Luciosoma pellegrini* is also called *"L. setigerum"* in the trade, even though the two are different species.

Hab.: Southeast Asia: Thailand, Malay Peninsula, Kalimantan (Borneo), and Sumatra.

F.I.: 1924 by Karl SCHULT, Hamburg.

Sex.: No definite external distinguishing characteristics are known.

Soc. B.: Very lively surface-oriented schooling fish.

M: Use a long, rather shallow tank with a good cover, since the animals are accomplished jumpers. Plant the tank's fringes densely. Roots make appropriate furnishings. Keep plenty of space open, allowing the fishes to swim. Soft, slightly acid water (hardness of 5°–8° dGH and pH of ca. 6.5, respectively). Exchange $^1/_4$ of the tank's volume each week. Suitable for community tanks.

B: Has not been bred in captivity.

F: O; all kinds of live foods (primarily insects), scraped meat, plant fare (lettuce, spinach), and flake and tablet foods.

S: In nature, *L. spilopleura* is a pronounced insectivore which hunts along the water surface.

T: 24°–27°C, **L:** 25 cm, **A:** 120 cm, **R:** t, m, **D:** 2

Lobocheilus quadrilineatus

Luciosoma spilopleura

Mesobola spinifer. See p. 246.

Microphysiogobio tungtingensis amurensis

Syn.: *Rostrogobio amurensis, Saurogobio amurensis, Saurogobius dabryi* (not BLEEKER!).

Hab.: Asia: former Soviet Union, Amur drainage basin; Mongolia; northern China, including the Ussuri and Sungari Rivers and Lake Chanka.

F.I.: Has not been imported into Germany.

Sex.: No external differentiating characteristics are known. ♂♂ lack nuptial tubercles.

Soc. B.: Very peaceful, agile schooling fish.

M: Use sand or fine gravel as substrate, stones for cover, and vegetation along the edges; keep plenty of free swimming space. Water: hardness up to 20° dGH; pH ca. 7.0. Either keep in a species tank or with fishes that have similar requirements.

B: Has not been bred in western aquaria. In nature, the fish reach sexual maturity at 2 years of age and a length of 5 cm. The spawning season extends from June to July. ♀♀ lay their pelagic, 2.8–3.1 mm eggs in several passes. The larvae hatch after 36 hr and are 3.5 mm long. They are unpigmented and have no larval respiratory organs. After $4^{1}/_{2}$ days, when the larvae have reached a length of 4 mm, they develop paired fins and adopt a benthic lifestyle.

F: C; mainly benthic invertebrates such as bloodworms and diatoms.

S: Besides the subspecies *M. t. amurensis*, four additional subspecies have been described: *M. t. anudarini* HOLCIK & PIUNICKA, 1967 from Lake Buir, Mongolia; *M. t. tungtingensis* (NICHOLS, 1926) in Lake Tungting of Hunan and Ningkwo, China; *M. t. suifuensis* (WU, 1930) of the upper Yang Tse and its tributaries, China; and *M. t. uchidai* BANARESCU & NALBANT, 1973, Korea.

T: 14°–22°C, **L:** 12 cm, **A:** 80 cm, **R:** b, **D:** 2–3

Mystacoleucus marginatus

Syn.: *Barbus marginatus.*

Hab.: Southeast Asia: Thailand, Laos, Malaysia, Sumatra, Java, Borneo.

F.I.: Ca. 1980 as by-catch.

Sex.: No definite external differentiating characteristics are known. Perhaps the ♂'s anal fin is concave, while the ♀'s anal fin is convex. It is also possible that the ♂'s upper mandible barbels are shorter than those of the ♀. Sexually mature from a length of 10 cm. Mature ♀♀ are clearly stouter.

Soc. B.: Peaceful schooling fish.

M: Undemanding, appreciative charges which do not place heavy demands on water chemistry. Soft, slightly acid water, however, is the most favorable environment for them. Regular water exchanges are beneficial. This species neither digs nor otherwise disturbs aquatic plants.

B: Has not been bred in captivity.

F: O; a peaceful omnivore which accepts such foods as water fleas, *Tubifex,* commercial flake foods, and supplementary foods like beef heart.

S: A rarely imported fish which apparently only reaches central Europe as an occasional by-catch. Regular imports would be desirable, since young animals are no less attractively colored than the popular Bala shark.

T: 22°–27°C, **L:** 20 cm, usually smaller, **A:** 150 cm, **R:** m, b, **D:** 1–2

Microphysiogobio tungtingensis amurensis

Mystacoleucus marginatus

245

Mesobola spinifer

(BAILEY & MATTHES, 1971)

Syn.: *Engraulicypris spinifer, Neobola spinifer.*

Hab.: Africa: Tanzania, only known from the Malagarasi and Rukwa drainage basins and the Great Ruaha River (Rufiji System).

F.I.: 1987 by KILIAN and SEEGERS.

Sex.: No definite distinguishing characteristics are known.

Soc. B.: Very peaceful, agile schooling fish. Skittish at times.

M: Substrate should either be of sand or gravel. Densely plant the tank, but maintain an open area for these active animals. Water should be around neutral and not overly hard (pH 6.5–7.5 and a hardness to 12° dGH, respectively). They can be kept with moderate-sized, peaceful fishes.

B: To the best of our knowledge, this fish has not been bred in an aquarium.

F: O; small live foods, frozen foods, and vegetable fare.

S: KILIAN and SEEGERS have discovered a *Mesobola* north of Lake Malawi which may be this species.

T: 22°–26°C, **L**: 4.5 cm, **A**: 60 cm, **R**: m, **D**: 2–3

Opsariichthys uncirostris amurensis

BERG, 1932
Subfam.: Cultrinae

Syn.: None.

Hab.: Asia: western Korea, northern China, former Soviet Union, in the southern tributaries of the Amur: Ussuri River and Lake Khanka, in the Rivers Sungari and Amur from the city of Blagoveshchensk.

F.I.: Has not been imported into Germany.

Sex.: Dorsal, ventral, pectoral, and anal fins of the ♂ are longer than those of the ♀. ♂♂ in spawning condition have nuptial tubercles on the head, caudal peduncle, and caudal and anal fins.

Soc. B.: Predatory animal that feeds on small fishes. Can only be associated with equal-sized fishes, since it also hunts in the aquarium.

M: Roomy tanks which have plenty of swimming space. Plant the aquarium with coldwater species. Substrate of sand or fine-grained gravel. There is no informa-

tion available concerning water values.

B: No information could be found concerning breeding these fish in captivity. The spawning season in its natural habitat extends from June to August. Eggs are laid on sand or gravel substrates.

F: C; live foods such as insects and small fishes.

S: The nominate form, *O. u. uncirostris* (TEMMINCK & SCHLEGEL, 1846), comes from Japan.

T: 10°–22°C (coldwater fish), **L**: 32.5 cm, **A**: 100 cm, **R**: m, t, **D**: 2–3

Mesobola spinifer

Opsariichthys uncirostris amurensis

A small river near Lake Baikal.

Oreoleuciscus potanini

Oreoleuciscus potanini

(KESSLER, 1879)

Syn.: *Chondrostoma potanini.*

Hab.: Asia: In lakes and rivers of north-western Mongolia and the headwaters of the Ob (former Soviet Union). Primarily found in waters of the Altai mountains and the region of the Katun and Bija Rivers.

F.I.: Has not been imported into Germany.

Sex.: ♂♂ in spawning condition have nuptial tubercles covering their heads.

Soc. B.: Amiable, lively schooling fish.

M: Needs a long tank with a sand or gravel bottom. Perhaps a powerhead-generated current should be provided. Cool, clear, oxygenated water is appreciated. There is no information concerning water hardness or pH preferences.

B: No information could be found concerning spawning these fish in captivity. In its native waters, spawning occurs from June to July. Sexual maturity is reached at a length of 15 cm. Between 21,000 and 32,000 eggs are laid.

F: C; live foods, chiefly invertebrates, e.g., bloodworms and *Daphnia*. Large individuals also consume fishes.

S: *O. potanini* is frequently found with *O. pewzovi* (HERZENSTEIN). They can hybridize.

T: 10°–20°C (coldwater fish), **L:** up to 60 cm, **A:** 100 cm, **R:** m, **D:** 2–3

Cirrhinus molitorella

(CUVIER & VALENCIENNES, 1831)

Syn.: ?

Hab.: Asia: China, Taiwan, Hong Kong. The species originated in China but has meanwhile been introduced into other countries (Thailand, Malaysia).

F.I.: Unknown.

Sex.: Unknown.

Soc. B.: Peaceful; suitable for cool community aquaria.

M: This fish needs a large tank with dense vegetation which, nevertheless, preserves sufficient swimming space. No particular demands are placed on water chemistry, but soft, slightly acid, oxygen-rich water is best. Since this fish is an accomplished jumper, the aquarium must be well-covered.

B: Has not been bred in captivity.

F: O; small live foods of all kinds such as protozoans, rotifers, nauplii, and *Daphnia*.

T: 18°–24°C, **L:** 15 cm (?), **A:** 100 cm, **R:** b, **D:** 1–2

Osteochilus microcephalus

(VALENCIENNES, 1842)

Syn.: *Rohita microcephalus, Osteochilus brachynotopterus, O. vittatus, Rohita brachynotopterus, R. vittata.*

Hab.: Asia: Indonesia (Sumatra, Borneo), Malay Peninsula, Cambodia, Laos, southern Vietnam, Thailand.

F.I.: 1954.

Sex.: Not precisely known. ♀♀ are fuller during the spawning season. Sexual maturity is reached at a relatively small size. SMITH (1945) found developed ovaries in ♀♀ less than 6 cm long.

Soc. B.: Sometimes aggressive towards other, particularly smaller, fishes. These animals establish territories as they mature, frequently expelling also conspecifics.

M: Roomy aquaria densely planted with tough vegetation (herbivore!). Provide numerous hiding possibilities such as roots. Limit tankmates to equal-sized individuals. Soft, slightly acid, oxygen-rich water. This animal spends little of its time rooting.

B: Has not been bred in an aquarium.

F: O, H; plenty of vegetable fare such as oats.

S: A relatively unattractive, rarely imported species.

T: 22°–26°C, **L:** 16 cm, **A:** 100 cm, **R:** m, b, **D:** 1–2

Cirrhinus molitorella

Osteochilus microcephalus

Pelecus cultratus (LINNAEUS, 1758)

Syn.: *Cyprinus cultratus.*

Hab.: Europe and Asia: Baltic, Black, Azov, and Caspian Seas and Lake Aral as well as their tributaries.

F.I.: Native to Europe.

Sex.: ♀♀ are fuller during the spawning season.

Soc. B.: Surface-oriented schooling fish which prefers brackish waters. Pelagic.

M: Large, long, but not necessarily tall tanks with plenty of free swimming space. Substrate of sand or fine gravel. Coldwater vegetation should be planted lightly along the edges and back of the aquarium. The water should be clear. Salt added to the water may be beneficial (brackish water). No particular water chemistry requirements (dGH, pH).

B: No information could be found concerning spawning these fish in captivity. In nature, the spawning season is from May to June, since the minimum spawning temperature is 12°C. The animals normally spawn in freshwater, occasionally in brackish, and reach sexual maturity at 3 years of age. On average, 33,000 planktonic eggs are laid. The large yolk helps keep the eggs suspended. Egg development is brief (3 days). The larvae's respiratory organs are poorly developed.

F: C; live foods such as planktonic crustacea, flying insects, insect larvae, and small fishes.

S: This species is characterized by an elongated, laterally compressed body, a superior mouth, and a naked keel that extends from the throat to the anus.

T: 10°–20°C (coldwater fish), **L:** up to 60 cm, **A:** from 100 cm, **R:** t, **D:** 2

Lagowskiella lagowskii (DYBOWSKI, 1869)
Amur dace

Syn.: *Phoxinus lagowskii lagowskii.*

Hab.: Asia: former Soviet Union and Korea. In the headwaters of the Lena and the Amur Rivers and their tributaries.

F.I.: Has not been imported into Germany.

Sex.: Difficult to determine. ♀♀ are larger and fuller, particularly during the spawning season.

Soc. B.: Active, peaceful schooling fish.

M: Needs a long tank with ample free swimming space. Substrate of sand or moderately coarse gravel. Plant the edges and back of the aquarium with appropriate coldwater species. Ensure that the water is clear, clean, and well-aerated. The water should be medium-hard to hard and neutral to slightly alkaline (hardness of 10° to 20° dGH and a pH of 7.0–7.5, respectively). Its tankmates should be organisms with similar require-

ments. Maintain a school of at least 6 specimens.

B: No information could be found in western aquarium magazines concerning spawning these fish in captivity. Breeding is probably similar to that of *Phoxinus phoxinus* and not overly difficult, see Vol. 1, p. 430. In its native waters, these fish spawn from mid-June to the beginning of August.

F: C; live foods such as insect larvae, water fleas, cyclops, *Gammarus*, *Asellus*, *Tubifex*, and Enchytraeidae.

S: Besides the nominate form *Lagowskiella lagowskii* DYBOWSKI, 1869, *P. l. oxycephalus* (SAUVAGE & DABRY, 1879) has been described. It is a very common fish found in the southern tributaries of the Amur: Ussuri, Sungari, the upper Kasu, and some rivers of Korea and China.

T: 16°–20°C, **L:** ♂ 11.5 cm, ♀ 15 cm, **A:** 100 cm, **R:** m, t, **D:** 2

Pelecus cultratus

Lagowskiella lagowskii

Pimephales promelas promelas
Fathead minnow

RAFINESQUE, 1820
Subfam.: Leuciscinae

Syn.: *Coliscus parietalis, Pimephales agassizi, P. fasciatus, P. milesi, Plargyrus melanocephalus.*

Hab.: Central North America: from Louisiana (United States) and Chihuahua (Mexico) to the drainage basin of the Great Slave Lake (Canada).

F.I.: Unknown.

Sex.: ♂♂ are larger. ♀♀ have a visible ovipositor when spawning, whereas ♂♂ have nuptial tubercles.

Soc. B.: Outside of the spawning season, *P. p. promelas* is a peaceful schooling fish. ♂♂ practice broodcare (paternal family).

M: Appoint the tank with a substrate of sand or fine-grained gravel and some stones and roots as hiding places and spawning substrates. Plant the edges of the tank with coldwater species (*Egeria, Myriophyllum*), yet preserve an open swimming area. While water chemistry is not of predominant importance, it should be clear and clean. An appropriate tankmate for other coldwater fishes.

B: 17°–25°C; there are no reports concerning breeding this species in European aquarium magazines. In nature, these fish spawn in the spring. Spawning activities begin when water temperature exceeds 17°C. ♂♂ are responsible for finding the spawning site, usually the underside of a branch or rock. There the ♀—the ovipositor is clearly visible at this time—lays her adhesive eggs. After the eggs are fertilized, the ♀ is chased away. The nest can contain the eggs of several ♀♀ and is intensely guarded and defended by the ♂. At 25°C, the eggs take about 5 days to develop. Newly hatched fry are about 5 mm long and white.

F: O; live foods of all kinds and frozen, freeze-dried, tablet, and flake foods.

S: This species does not have a long life span, rarely reaching more than 2 years of age in nature. Besides the nominate form, there are several subspecies.

T: 12°–20°C (coldwater fish), **L:** 9.5 cm, **A:** 80 cm, **R:** m, b, **D:** 2

Raiamas moorii

(BOULENGER, 1900)
Subfam.: Cyprininae

Syn.: *Barilius moorii.*

Hab.: Africa: endemic to Lakes Tanganyika, Rukwa, and Kivu.

F.I.: Unknown. At the latest, 1987 by KILIAN and SEEGERS.

Sex.: Difficult to distinguish outside of the spawning season.

Soc. B.: Active species that forms small schools.

M: Provide a roomy aquarium that has ample swimming space. A substrate of sand or gravel and dense vegetation along the edges is recommended. Cover the aquarium well, since the animals are accomplished jumpers. Regularly ex-

change part of the water ($^1/_4$ per week). The water should be up to medium-hard and about neutral (hardness up to 12° dGH and a pH of 6.5–7.5, respectively).

B: No successful aquarium spawns have been reported.

F: O; all kinds of live foods—floating insects are particularly relished. Flake and frozen foods are also consumed.

T: 24°–26°C, **L:** 19 cm, **A:** 120 cm, **R:** m, t, **D:** 2–3

Pimephales promelas promelas ♂; ♀ p. 273

Raiamas moorii from Lake Rukwa, Tanzania ♂

Raiamas senegalensis   (STEINDACHNER, 1870)
                                                       Subfam.: Cyprininae

Syn.: *Barilius senegalensis, B. senegalensis orientalis.*

Hab.: Africa: the Senegal, Gambia, Niger, Volta, and Comoe Rivers and the basin of Lake Chad.

F.I.: Unknown.

Sex.: No definite distinguishing characteristics are known. See previous species

Soc. B.: Lively, peaceful schooling fish.

M: As for *Raiamas moorii*. Due to their mature size, juveniles make better charges than adults in home aquaria.

B: Unknown.

F: O; live foods as well as frozen, freeze-dried, and flake foods.

T: 22°–26°C, **L**: 25 cm, **A**: from 120 cm, **R**: m, t, **D**: 2–3

Rasbora chrysotaenia (no photo)   AHL, 1937
                                                       Subfam.: Rasborinae

Syn.: None.

Hab.: Southeast Asia: Malay Archipelago and Sumatra (Thailand?).

F.I.: 1934.

Sex.: ♂♂ are slimmer; ♀♀ are deeper-bodied and fuller.

Soc. B.: This peaceful fish is considerably less active than zebra danios, passing the day either calmly swimming or hovering near the edge of planted areas.

M: Aquaria with sections of dense vegetation are best.

B: Like *Brachydanio rerio*, Vol. 1, page 408.

F: O; all kinds of live and flake foods.

T: 22°–24°C, **L**: ♂ 3 cm, ♀ 3.5 cm, **A**: 80 cm, **R**: m, **D**: 2

Raiamas senegalensis

Hemigrammocypris lini, see page 223

Rasbora sp. cf. *meinkeni*
Meinken's rasbora

De BEAUFORT, 1931

Syn.: None.

Hab.: Southeast Asia: Indonesia (Sumatra), southern Malaysia.

F.I.: Unknown.

Sex.: ♂♂ are slimmer and slightly more colorful. Both sexes may have nuptial tubercles on their head, snout, and lower mandible.

Soc. B.: Peaceful schooling fish. Shy when kept singly.

M: Keep in a long aquarium that has ample free swimming space. Plant the sides of the aquarium with fine-leaved plants and use a dark substrate. Slightly acid (pH 6.5), medium-hard (10° dGH) water is best.

B: Similar to *Brachydanio rerio*, Vol. 1, page 408. T: 24 - 25° C; more than 1000 eggs. Juvenils are fully grown with 1/2 year.

F: O; live, flake, and frozen foods.

S: *Rasbora* sp. cf. *meinkeni* is a member of the *Rasbora trifasciata*-group. *R. trifasciata* is its closest relative.

T: 24°–28°C, **L:** 5 cm, **A:** 70 cm, **R:** m, t, **D:** 1

Rasbora gracilis

KOTTELAT, 1991

Syn.: *Rasbora taeniata* (nicht AHL), *R. agilis* (nicht AHL).

Hab.: Southeast Asia: Indonesia, Malaysia, Sumatra, Kalimantan, both in flowing and static waters.

F.I.: Unknown.

Sex.: ♂♂ are more slender, and their ventral profile is virtually straight. ♀♀, particularly during the spawning season, are significantly plumper, having a convex ventral profile.

Soc. B.: Active, peaceful schooling fish.

M: Densely plant the aquarium, yet keep a large area free for swimming. Floating plants should be used to dim the light. Likewise, excess sunlight is detrimental. A soft substrate (sand with a layer of mulm) and roots are the suggested decor. The water should be slightly acid and not overly hard (pH 6.0–6.5 and a hardness of 10° dGH, respectively). Exchange the water regularly (¹/₄ each week). A good community fish.

B: See above.

F: O; live foods, plants (algae), and flake foods.

T: 22°–24°C, **L:** 12 cm, **A:** 80 cm, **R:** t, m, **D:** 1–2

Rasbora sp. cf. *meinkeni*

Rasbora gracilis

Rasbora somphongsi
Somphongs's rasbora

MEINKEN, 1958

Syn.: *Rasbora sompongsei.*

Hab.: Southeast Asia: Thailand, in the basin and flood region of the Menam River.

F.I.: 1957 by the WERNER Co., Munich.

Sex.: ♂♂ are slightly slimmer and more colorful; ♀♀ are stouter.

Soc. B.: This very peaceful fish lives in small groups. Due to its diminutive size and somewhat shy sensitive nature, aggressive species make inappropriate tankmates.

M: *R. somphongsi* is best kept individually in small tanks. Small bottom-dwelling fishes, e.g., armored catfishes or loaches, may make appropriate tankmates. Tanks with heavy vegetation and plenty of hiding places help overcome its shy nature.

B: Has been successfully bred. Up to 100 eggs are laid on plant leaves. Water: pH 6.0 to 6.5; hardness up to 8° dGH. At 25°C, the fry hatch after 24 hr and are free-swimming 4 days post-spawning. The young require the smallest planktonic organisms.

F: C, O; small live and FD foods.

S: One of the rarest fishes of Thailand. According to information from the Somphong Aquarium Co., which is where this fish got its name, during some years, only a few specimens are captured.

T: 22°–26°C, **L:** 3 cm, **A:** 50 cm, **R:** all, **D:** 2

Rasbora steineri
Steiner's rasbora

NICHOLS & POPE, 1927

Syn.: *Rasbora cephalotaenia steineri, R. allos, R. lateristriata-allos, R. pallopinna, R. volzi pallopinna.*

Hab.: East Asia: China, Canton, Haiman Island, and Hong Kong. Probably also found in Korea.

F.I.: Has probably not been imported into Germany.

Sex.: Difficult to distinguish. ♂♂ are more slender.

Soc. B.: Peaceful, active schooling fish.

M: Needs a long, low tank with about 20 cm of water, a sand substrate, plants around the edges, and free swimming space. Medium-hard (10° to 15° dGH), slightly acid (pH 6.0 to 6.5) water is best. Always keep a school of at least 6 animals.

B: No successful spawn has been reported.

F: O; live, freeze-dried, frozen, and flake foods.

S: According to BRITTAN, *R. steineri* is part of the *Rasbora lateristriata* group along with *R. lateristriata, R. rasbora, R. baliense,* and *R. aprotaenia. R. steineri* is the only member of the genus from southern China.

T: 22°–24°C, **L:** 6 cm, **A:** 70 cm, **R:** all, **D:** 2

Rasbora somphongsi

Rasbora sp. cf. *steineri*

Boraras brigittae
Mosquito rasbora

(VOGT, 1978)

Syn.: *Rasbora brigittae*.

Hab.: Asia: southern Borneo around Banjarmasin, in creeks and slow-flowing black and white waters. Chiefly found hovering around plants.

F.I.: 1976.

Sex.: ♂♂ are a more intense red with a bright red spot on each caudal fin tip. Dorsal and anal fin have a red edge. ♀♀ are clearly paler and do not have red dots on the caudal fin.

Soc. B.: Lively schooling fish.

M: Soft water and heavy vegetation along the back of the tank and floating plants are preferred. Animals kept in water filtered through peat tend to be darker red. An excellent inhabitant for small aquaria. Though best kept alone, they can be housed in community with other small *Boraras*-species such as *Boraras urophthalmoides* and *B. maculatus*.

B: Because of their diminutive size, prolific results cannot be expected. A continuous set-up yields the best results. Use soft, filtered water, dense vegetation, floating plants, and a 4 cm layer of peat as substrate. Every 2–3 weeks the parents should be placed in a new breeding tank. Watch the tank for fry over a period of 8 days. Feed infusoria.

F: C; small live foods, *Artemia*.

S: This very fragile fish is the smallest known cyprinid. Even the slightest pressure applied to its body is lethal; hence, capture and handling are particularly challenging.

T: 25°–28°C, **L**: 1.5–2 cm, **A**: 40 cm, **R**: m, t, **D**: 2–3

Rasboroides vaterifloris
Orange-finned rasbora

(DERANIYAGALA, 1930)

Syn.: *Rasbora vaterifloris*.

Hab.: Asia: Sri Lanka). Apparently there are several local varieties which differ primarily by their coloration. See **S**.

F.I.: 1936.

Sex.: ♂♂ are slimmer and more colorful.

Soc. B.: Absolutely peaceful fish, among themselves and heterospecifics. It forms loose schools; at least 6 animals must be kept together. Single animals wane.

M: Does not need a large aquarium. Provide dense vegetation and peaty water. See the red variant in Vol. 2, p. 422.

B: Difficult, but it has been done. A species tank is mandatory. *R. vaterifloris* is frequently the only species present in its native waters. For details, see Vol. 2, p. 422.

F: O; small insects such as ants, mosquitoes, flies, glassworms, and mosquito larvae (sieved). Flower pollen and plants are another part of its natural diet. Flake foods may be eaten, but do not make them its sole source of nutrition.

S: DERANIYAGALA defines 4 races of *R. vaterifloris*:
1. Average total length, 38.4 mm
   a) Body solid dark red; origin Meegahatenne to Valallavites ...*ruber*.
   b) Body greenish; origin Gilimale, Parakaduvz ...*typica*.
2. Average total length, 26.4 mm
   a) Upper edge of the eye socket is dark orange; origin Akurenz ...*rubrioculis*.
   b) Upper fringe of the eye socket is pale orange; origin Kottava ...*pallider*.

DERANIYAGALA suspects that *R. nigromarginata* MEINKEN, 1957 may be an additional race ("*R. v. nigromarginata*"). See Vol. 2, p. 422.

T: 25°–27°C, **L**: max. 4 cm, **A**: 60 cm, **R**: b, m, **D**: 3–4

Boraras brigittae ♂ and ♀

Rasboroides vaterifloris "blue"

Rhinichthys atratulus atratulus
Blacknose dace

(HERMANN, 1804)

Syn.: *Cyprinus atratulus, Argyreus atronasus, Cyprinus atronasus, Leuciscus atronasus, Rhinichthys atronasus.*

Hab.: North America: United States and Canada. Found in the United States from the Atlantic coast to the Great Lakes and North and South Dakota. In the southern regions, it is found on both sides of the Appalachians to Georgia, Alabama, and Mississippi; in Canada from Nova Scotia to Manitoba.

F.I.: 1896 by Paul MATTE, Lankwitz and Paul NITSCHE, Berlin.

Sex.: Ripe ♂♂ have pink-red sides, orange to red pectoral fins, and nuptial tubercles. ♀♀ have a well-developed anal papilla.

Soc. B.: ♂♂ are territorial during the spawning season. Throughout the rest of the year, the animals are peaceful schooling fish.

M: As for *Catostomus commersoni* or *Pimephales promelas* (pp. 165 and 254, respectively). Aerate the aquarium well.

B: 21°–26°C; has probably not been bred in European aquaria. In nature, the animals spawn in the spring (May and June) when the temperature reaches 21°C. Small (0.8 mm), transparent, amber eggs are laid above gravel substrates in shallow, fast-flowing water. There is no nest. Depending on temperature, the eggs need 3 to 5 days to develop. Newly hatched larvae are about 5 mm long.

F: O; live, frozen, freeze-dried, and flake foods.

S: *R. atratulus* is a highly variable species. There are several subspecies and numerous local races.

T: 12°–20°C (coldwater fish), **L:** 8 cm, **A:** 80 cm, **R:** m, b, **D:** 2

Rutilus rubilio rubilio
Southern European Roach

(BONAPARTE, 1837)

Syn.: *Leuciscus rubilio, Gardonus aula, Leuciscus aula, L. dobula, L. fucini, L. lascha, L. pagellus, L. pauperum, L. rubella, L. scardinus, L. trasimenicus, Leucos aula, Squalius elatus.*

Hab.: Europe: from Tagliamento, Etsch, and the Po in Italy to Calabria, Yugoslavia (Dalmatia to Aspropotamos).

F.I.: Unknown.

Sex.: ♂♂ have nuptial tubercles during the spawning season; ♀♀ are usually fuller at that time (eggs).

Soc. B.: Lively, amiable fish. Other cyprinids make suitable tankmates.

M: Do not allow the aquarium to become overly warm. Use a substrate of sand or fine gravel, coldwater plants along the edges and back of the tank, and rocks as decoration. Aerate and filter the aquarium well. Perform regular water exchanges (¹/₄ each week). Water: hardness to 20° dGH; pH around 7.

B: Normally, home aquaria are not spacious enough to allow these fish to breed. In nature, they spawn from March to June. The eggs have a diameter of 1 to 1.5 mm.

F: O; all kinds of live foods (e.g. small crustacea, insect larvae, worms, and floating insects), plants, detritus, flake foods, and tablet foods.

S: Besides the nominate form *R. r. rubilio*, two additional subspecies have been described: *R. r. ohridanus* (KARAMAN, 1924) from Lake Ochrid and *R. r. prespensis* (KARAMAN, 1924) from Lake Presper.

T: 10°–27°C, **L:** 25 cm, **A:** 100 cm, **R:** m, b, **D:** 1–2

Rhinichthys atratulus atratulus

Rutilus rubilio rubilio

Sarcocheilichthys nigripinnis czerskii

(BERG, 1914)

Syn.: *Chilogobio czerskii, C. soldatovi, Gobio czerskii, Sarcocheilichthys czerskii, S. soldatovi.*

Hab.: Asia: former Soviet Union, Mongolia, and China, in the Amur Basin, including the Ussuri and Sungari Rivers as well as Lakes Chanka and Buir. Probably also found in some Korean rivers.

F.I.: Has not been imported into Germany.

Sex.: ♀♀, unlike ♂♂, have black on their caudal peduncle. During the spawning season, ♂♂ have nuptial tubercles, while the ♀'s ovipositor grows up to 10 mm long.

Soc. B.: Active, peaceful schooling fish.

M: As for *Sarcocheilichthys sinensis.* Best kept in a species tank, but they can be associated with fishes that have similar requirements.

B: Has not been bred in western aquaria. In nature, the fish become sexually mature during their second summer. Exact information is missing, but this is not a fecund species. ♀♀ spawn several times during the spawning season. Some ichthyologists suspect that the eggs are released into the gill cavity of freshwater mussels. The eggs are oval and about 2 mm in diameter along their longitudinal axis.

F: C; in nature, benthic invertebrates are its main source of food: insect larvae, particularly bloodworms and mayfly larvae.

S: Besides this subspecies, an additional 5 subspecies of *S. nigripinnis* have been described.

T: 14°–22°C, L: 12.5 cm, A: 80 cm, R: b, D: 2–3

Sarcocheilichthys sinensis
Amur sucker

BLEEKER, 1871

Syn.: *Barbodon lacustris, Exoghossops geei, Georgichthys scaphignathus* (not NICHOLS), *Sarcocheilichthys geei, S. lacustris, S. sinensis lacustris, S. wakiyae* (not MORI).

Hab.: Asia: former Soviet Union, drainage basin of the Amur, including the Ussuri and Sangari Rivers and Lake Chanka; northwestern Korea; China, in the Yangtse, Chekiang, Minkiang, and Hsikiang drainage basins.

F.I.: Has not been imported into Germany.

Sex.: During the spawning season, ♂♂ have nuptial tubercles and ♀♀ display an ovipositor.

Soc. B.: This agile, peaceful schooling fish can be housed with native fishes that have similar requirements.

M: A roomy tank with a sand or gravel substrate and hiding places among rocks is suggested. Vegetation can be planted along the edges, but always keep in mind that these fish need free

swimming space. Provide clear, clean water with a hardness of about 20° dGH and a pH around 7.

B: Has not been accomplished in western aquaria. In nature, the animals reach sexual maturity at a length of 12 to 15 cm (3–4 years). From May to July each ♀ may spawn up to 3 times, laying 5,000–10,000 eggs. These have a diameter of 5 mm, which makes them the largest produced within this subfamily. During one spawning season, ♀♀ may spawn 3 times. Unlike other *Sarcocheilichthys, S. sinensis* lays pelagic (floating) eggs. The larvae, which hatch 4 days postspawning, are 7.5 mm long and pelagic.

F: C; primarily benthic invertebrates such as aquatic insect larvae, bloodworms, caddisfly larvae, and small crustacea.

S: During the winter, the animals stay in the main channel of large rivers and streams, but in the summer, they migrate upriver into rock-bottomed tributaries. In nature, *S. sinensis* has a life expectancy of 9 years.

T: 16°–22°C, L: 28 cm, A: 100 cm, R: b, m, D: 2–3

Sarcocheilichthys nigripinnis czerskii ♀

Sarcocheilichthys sinensis

Saurogobio dabryi

BLEEKER, 1871

Syn.: *Armatogobio dabryi, Gobiosoma amurensis, Pseudogobio amurensis, P. drakei, Saurogobio drakei, S. longirostris, S. productus, S. dabryi immaculatus.*

Hab.: Asia: from the Amur Basin and Korea throughout China to North Vietnam.

F.I.: Has not been imported into Germany.

Sex.: No external distinguishing features are known.

Soc. B.: Peaceful, bottom-dwelling schooling fish.

M: A spacious aquarium with a sand or gravel substrate, hiding places, loose side and background vegetation, and free swimming space. Water should be clear and clean and neutral with a hardness of up to 20° dGH.

B: Has not been bred in an aquarium. In nature, the animals reach sexual maturity at 3 years of age and a length of 13 cm. The spawning season extends from the end of May to the beginning of July when the water temperature is between 12° and 20°C. One ♀ can lay between 15,000 and 31,000 eggs during several spawning acts. Eggs are pelagic and have a diameter of 2.3–2.9 mm. The fry hatch after 3 days and are ca. 4 mm long at this time. They are unpigmented, pelagic, and lack special respiratory organs. After the pectoral fins are formed, they adopt their benthic lifestyle.

F: C; in nature, they primarily feed on benthic invertebrates such as insect larvae, crustacea, and molluscs.

S: Both sexes have nuptial tubercles during the spawning season.

T: 12°–22°C, **L:** 28 cm, **A:** 120 cm, **R:** b, **D:** 2–3

Squalidus chankaensis chankaensis

DYBOWSKI, 1872

Syn.: *Gnathopogon chankaensis, G. ussuriensis, Gobio chankaensis, G. ussuriensis, Leucogobio chankaensis.*

Hab.: Asia: former Soviet Union, Amur region, including Lakes Chanka and Buir.

F.I.: Has not been imported into Germany.

Sex.: None known.

Soc. B.: Lively, friendly schooling fish.

M: Needs a roomy tank with a sand or gravel substrate, some hiding places, a few coldwater plants along the tank's edges, and ample free swimming space. The water should be up to medium-hard (≤20° dGH) and around neutral (pH 7.0). Maintain in a species tank, or keep with fishes that have similar requirements.

B: Has not been bred in western aquaria. In nature, the animals reach sexual maturity after 3 years (corresponding to a length of 45–50 mm). The spawning season starts at the beginning of June, when water temperatures reach ca. 18°C, and ends in July. ♀♀ lay between 2,300 to 4,000, 1.2 mm eggs in several passes either on the bottom or on plants. At 12° to 20°C, the larvae hatch after 4 days and are 5 mm long.

F: C; virtually the entire diet is comprised of bloodworms.

S: According to BERG, *S. c. chankaensis* is a very rare species. The other 12 subspecies of *S. chankaensis* are distributed in Japan, Korea, China, and north Vietnam. See BANARESCU & NALBANT, 1973, *Das Tierreich*, ed. 93, p. 80–96.

T: 14°–22°C, **L:** 10 cm, **A:** 80 cm, **R:** b, **D:** 2–3

Saurogobio dabryi

Squalidus chankaensis chankaensis

Tor khudree
Giant barb

(SYKES, 1838)

Syn.: *Barbus mosal, Cyprinus mosal, Tor hamiltonii, Barbus khudree, B. megalepis, B. progeneius, B. (Labeobarbus) hamiltonii, Labeobarbus tor, Torkhudree longipinnis.*

Hab.: Asia: Sri Lanka.

F.I.: Unknown.

Sex.: Unknown.

Soc. B.: Though peaceful, it should not be kept with smaller fishes because of its size and robust body stature.

M: This aquatic "cow" needs a roomy tank and plenty of vegetation in its diet. Provide strong filtration because of its large food intake. The confining nature of an aquarium prevents it from reaching the gigantic proportions it does in nature.

B: Unknown.

F: O; flake foods and large quantities of plants.

S: In its native waters, this fish is an appreciated food fish. Only coincidentally imported.

T: 20°–30°C, **L**: up to 144 cm, **A**: at least 100 cm, **R**: all, **D**: 1 (4, S)

Varicorhinus capoeta capoeta

(GÜLDENSTÄDT, 1773)

Syn.: *Cyprinus capoeta, C. fundulus, Capoeta fundulus.*

Hab.: Former Soviet Union: eastern Transcaucasus and west Turkmenistan, in rivers and lakes.

F.I.: Has not been imported into Germany.

Sex.: The snout of ripe ♂♂ has 2–4 rows of conical, horny tubercles. Tubercles are also found on the scales and anal fin.

Soc. B.: Peaceful, bottom-oriented schooling fish.

M: Similar to *Barbus plebejus tauricus.*

B: There is no information concerning breeding this fish in the aquarium. In nature, the fish spawn from the end of May to July when the water temperature is 12°C or above. Spawning occurs over rock or sand substrates. The 10,000–74,000 eggs are either hidden among rocks or covered with sand. Generally one ♀ and several ♂♂ participate in the spawning act. At 17°C, the eggs need 6 days to develop.

F: H; lives almost exclusively off plant fare it finds growing on the substrate. The diet is chiefly composed of *Botryococcus braunii*, a green alga, and diatoms.

S: There are several subspecies of *V. capoeta. V. c. sevangi* (FILIPPI, 1865), which reaches a length of ca. 70 cm, is the most important economically.

T: 10°–22°C (coldwater fish), **L**: 41 cm, **A**: from 100 cm, **R**: b, m, **D**: 2–3

Tor khudree, juvenile

Varicorhinus capoeta capoeta

Abramis vimba
Vimba

(LINNAEUS, 1758)

Syn.: *Cyprinus vimba, Abramis vimba, A. melanops, Leucabramis vimba, Vimba vimba.*

Hab.: Europe: Ems, Elbe, Weichsel, eastern Baltic Sea, southern Sweden, southern Finland, Lakes Ladoga and Ilmen.

F.I.: Native European species.

Sex.: ♀♀ are thicker through the abdomen during the spawning season; otherwise, the sexes are difficult to distinguish. ♂♂ do not have nuptial tubercles.

Soc. B.: Nonmigratory, but partially anadromous. Gregarious (schooling fish).

M: As for *Barbus barbus,* Vol. 2, p. 364. *Chondrostoma nasus* and *Abramis brama* make appropriate tankmates.

B: Information about a successful spawn in captivity could not be found. In nature, it spawns from May to August in schools along shallow, rocky shores of the barb region (Epopotomon). More than 200,000 eggs may be laid. Though weakly adhesive, they fall among the rocks and develop there after being fertilized. The larvae hatch 3 days post-spawning.

F: C; all kinds of live foods, particularly benthic invertebrates (bloodworms, etc.).

S: This species chiefly differs from *C. nasus* by its greater number of anal fin rays (20–25 vs. 13–14) and its pharyngeal tooth configuration (5–5 vs. 7(6)–6) for *C. nasus*.

T: 10°–20°C (coldwater fish), **L:** 40 cm, **A:** 100 cm, **R:** b, **D:** 2

Pimephales promelas ♀, see p. 254

Rastineobola argentea, Lake Rukwa

Barbatula barbatula toni
Toni's stone loach

(DYBOWSKI, 1869)

Syn.: *Cobitis toni, Barbatula toni, B. toni-fowleri, B. toni posteroventralis, Nemacheilus compressirostris, N. sibiricus, Noemacheilus barbatulus toni, Oreias toni, Orthrias oreas.*

Hab.: Asia: former Soviet Union, in Siberia from the Ob to the Kolyma, all the Amur region; northern Japan, Hokkaido; throughout Korea and China, Shanshi.

F.I.: Has probably not been imported.

Sex.: ♂♂ are smaller and slimmer, and the second ray of their pectoral fins is thicker than the rest.

Soc. B.: No information is available concerning the social behavior of *B. b. toni,* but it probably does not differ much from that of *B. b. barbatula,* Vol. 1, p. 376.

M: House in a long tank that has a sand bottom and some large, flat stones, and clear, clean, moving, well-aerated water. Preferred water values are unknown but medium-hard, neutral water (hardness of 15° dGH, and a pH of 7, respectively) should suffice.

B: Has not been bred in an aquarium.

F: O; all types of live foods.

S: There are a number of varieties of *B. b. toni.* This loach rarely reaches 21 cm in length. The genus *Barbatula* was established in 1789 by LINCK. There are three subspecies: *B. b. barbatula* (LINNAEUS, 1758), *B. b. caucasica* (BERG, 1899), and *B. b. toni* (DYBOWSKI, 1869).

T: 18°–22°C, **L:** 16 (rarely 21) cm, **A:** 90 cm, **R:** b, **D:** 2–3

Nemacheilus binotatus
Two-spot loach

SMITH, 1933

Syn.: *Noemacheilus binotatus.*

Hab.: Southeast Asia: north and west Thailand, in the Mae Nam Chao Phraya and Mae Klong.

F.I.: Unknown.

Sex.: ♂♂ have an infraocular lobe, thicker forked rays in their dorsal fin (1–5), and small tubercles on their fin rays.

Soc. B.: KOTTELAT 1990 was able to observe the animals in nature. Groups of up to 20 animals swim about 20 cm above sandy bottoms around large rocks. The characteristic striation along the body seems to ease species recognition within the schools. This loach also associates with other cyprinids that have similar designs, such as *Garra cambodgensis.*

M: If possible, use a substrate of fine gravel to allow this species to root. Do not use sharp-edged materials on the bottom (e.g., lava), lest damage to the barbels ensues. Rock crevices or caves make appropriate shelters for these fish.

B: Has not been successful in an aquarium.

F: O; all kinds of live foods, particularly small worms (*Tubifex,* Enchytraeidae) and mosquito larvae. Dry commercial diets are accepted as well. Examined stomach contents have almost exclusively contained mayflies and their larvae (Ephemeroptera).

S: This species is a unique Thai *Nemacheilus,* since it is the only one that does not have crossbands.

T: 26°–28°C, **L:** 6 cm, **A:** 70 cm, **R:** b, **D:** 2

Barbatula barbatula toni

Nemacheilus binotatus

Yunnanilus brevis

(BOULENGER, 1893)

Syn.: *Noemacheilus brevis, Eonemacheilus brevis.*

Hab.: Southeast Asia: Burma, in Lake Inle.

F.I.: 1978 by Arthur WERNER, Munich.

Sex.: ♂♂ have a small fleshy lobe beneath the eye.

Soc. B.: No information concerning the social behavior of this species could be found.

M: Caring for this species is not difficult because it does not have any special requirements. Lake Inle is full of decaying plants, and its water is hard with a temperature of 22°C in mid-March.

B: Not known.

F: O; small benthic organisms such as worms, insect larvae, and small crustacea.

S: Extraordinarily tall for a loachlike fish. It may be more of a mid-water fish than other loaches. Its body shape and terminal mouth further reinforce this hypothesis.

T: 22°–24°C, **L:** 6 cm, **A:** 60 cm, **R:** b, m, **D:** 2

Acanthocobitis urophthalmus
Ocellated loach

(GÜNTHER, 1868)

Syn.: ?

Hab.: Asia: Burma and Bangladesh.

F.I.: 1987.

Sex.: No known external differences.

Soc. B.: In all likelihood, this species behaves like *Nemacheilus botia*.

M: House in a typical loach aquarium and ensure that each animal has at least one hiding place.

B: No information could be found.

F: O; like most loaches of the subfamily Nemacheilinae, these fish are omnivores.

S: This species was previously called *Acanthocobitis rubidipinnis*. It is a particularly suitable species for hobbyists with small aquaria.

T: 23°–25°C, **L:** 6 cm, **A:** 60 cm, **R:** b, m, **D:** 1–2

Yunnanilus brevis

Acanthocobitis urophthalmus

Schistura kessleri kessleri
Kessler's loach

(GÜNTHER, 1889)

Syn.: *Noemachilus kessleri, N. prashari, Nemacheilus kessleri kessleri.*

Hab.: Asia: eastern Iran, Afghanistan, Pakistan, former Soviet Union (Turkmenistan), and northern India (Punjab).

F.I.: 1988.

Sex.: ♂♂'s pectoral fins are more pointed, and they have a typical Canestrini scale.

Soc. B.: Peaceful, benthic fish that are frequently active during twilight hours.

M: MIRZA & AWAN (1976) provided water values from these fish's natural habitat in Punjab, India: 28° to 30°C, max. depth of 60 cm, rock and mud substrate. All the water in this region is hard. In captivity, the water temperature should be lower (24°C) than those measured in its natural habitat.

B: Has not been bred in an aquarium.

F: O; all kinds of live foods, particularly worms, *Daphnia, Asellus*, and aquatic insect larvae.

S: Other than the nominate form, *S. k. kessleri*, three additional subspecies have been described: *S. k. turcomanus* NICHOLSKI, 1947 from the Kushka River (Turkmenistan), *S. k. lepidocaulis* MIRZA & NALBANT, 1981, and *S. k. pardalis* TURDAKOV, 1941.

T: 22°–30°C, **L:** 8 cm, **A:** 80 cm, **R:** b, **D:** 2–3

Triplophysa kuschakewitschi

(HERZENSTEIN, 1890)

Syn.: *Nemacheilus kuschakewitschi.*

Hab.: Asia: former Soviet Union, in the Syr-Darya Drainage from Gergana to its mouth.

F.I.: Has not been imported into Germany.

Sex.: ♂♂ have a broader head.

Soc. B.: Inactive benthic animals.

M: As for *Barbatula angorae*.

B: No information is available concerning breeding this fish in captivity, and there is scant information concerning its reproductive biology in nature. In nature, its 100–200 eggs are laid through August, except in the Fergana. There the animals spawn in the spring.

F: C; all kinds of live foods. Chironomid larvae are their favorites.

S: This loach is a close relative of *Nemacheilus oxianus* KESSLER, 1877, which inhabits the drainage basin of the Amu Darya
An additional subspecies has been described: *T. k. badomensis* TURDAKOV, 1941.

T: 10°–20°C, **L:** 11 cm, **A:** 80 cm, **R:** b, **D:** 2–3

Schistura kessleri kessleri

Triplophysa kuschakewitschi

Barbatula labiata
Thick-lip loach

(KESSLER, 1874)

Syn.: *Diplophysia labiata, Nemacheilus labiatus.*

Hab.: Asia: former Soviet Union, in the drainage basin of Lakes Balkhash and Baikal.

F.I.: Has not been imported into Germany.

Sex.: There are no definite external distinguishing characteristics.

Soc. B.: Nothing is known about the social behavior of *B. labiata*.

M: Roomy tank with sand or fine-grained gravel as substrate. Provide refuges among stones and roots. Aerate the tank well; a slight current is not harmful. Specific water values could not be obtained; however, medium-hard, neutral water (hardness of about 15° dGH and a pH of ca. 7.0, respectively) should not be detrimental.

B: Has not been bred in the aquarium. In nature, the animals spawn from April to June, laying between 38,000 and 60,000 eggs.

F: O; all kinds of live foods such as *Daphnia*, *Asellus*, and insect larvae, but worms are particular favorites. Flake foods.

S: There are two subspecies of *B. labiata*: *B. l. conjugens* and *B. l. herzensteini*. According to BERG, it is possible that both subspecies are merely hybrids of *B. labiata* and *Triplophysa strauchii*, but in our opinion, this is highly unlikely.

T: 14°–20°C, **L:** 23 cm, **A:** 100 cm, **R:** b, **D:** 2–3

Barbatula angorae
Angora loach

(STEINDACHNER, 1897)

Syn.: *Nemachilus angorae, N. persa, N. bergianus, Cobitis persa, C. striata, C. taenia, Orthrias angorae angorae.*

Hab.: Asia: Turkey, in flowing waters of north and central Anatolia; former Soviet Union, in the drainage basin of the upper and middle Arak, Lake Urmia, and in the upper Kura.

F.I.: Has probably not been imported into Germany.

Sex.: The 2nd, 3rd and 4th rays on the ♂'s pectoral fins are ossified, enlarged, and broadened. Shortly before and during the spawning season, these fins, the head, and the body become densely covered by nuptial tubercles. Pectoral and ventral fins are somewhat larger in ♂♂ than they are in ♀♀.

Soc. B.: Inactive, usually diurnal, benthic fish.

M: Requires a sandy substrate, some large stones to act as hiding places,

and clean, clear water. Dense coldwater vegetation is advantageous. If possible, the tank should have a slight current. Water: hardness of 15° dGH; pH 7.0 to 7.5.

B: Apparently it has not been bred in captivity.

F: C; all types of live foods: small crustacea, insect larvae, worms.

S: There are several described subspecies of *B. angorae*: *B. a. angorae* (STEINDACHNER, 1897), *B. a. araxensis* (BANARESCU, NALBANT & BALIK, 1978), *B. a. lenkoraensis* (ABDURACHMANOV, 1962), *B. a. striata* (IKEDA, 1936), and *B. a. taenia* (IKEDA, 1936).

T: 14°–22°C, **L:** 8.5 cm, **A:** 80 cm, **R:** b, **D:** 2–3

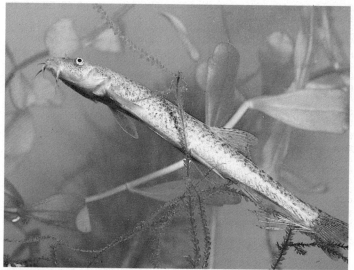

Barbatula labiata

Barbatula angorae

Barbatula brandti
Brandt's loach

(KESSLER, 1877)

Syn.: *Nemacheilus brandti, Noemacheilus brandti, Orthrias brandti brandti.*

Hab.: Asia: former Soviet Union, in the drainage basin of the Arak and the upper and middle Kura Rivers.

F.I.: Has not been imported into Germany.

Sex.: No definite external characteristics are known.

Soc. B.: Agile, but inactive benthic fish.

M: As for other members of the subfamily Nemacheilinae. Substrate of sand or fine-grained gravel; hiding places among rocks or roots; clear, well-aerated water; slight current; hardness up to 20° dGH; pH around 7.

B: There is no information concerning a successful aquarium spawn. Little is known about the reproductive biology of this species in its native habitat.

F: C; all kinds of live foods, particularly worms, small crustacea, and aquatic insect larvae.

S: *B. brandti* is a close relative of *Barbatula insignis* (HECKEL, 1843). The two can be differentiated based on *B. brandti*'s longer pectoral and ventral fins.

T: 10°–20°C (coldwater fish), **L:** 8.5 cm, **A:** 80 cm, **R:** b, **D:** 2

Barbatula insignis

(HECKEL, 1843)

Syn.: *Nemacheilus insignis, Noemacheilus insignis tortonesei, Orthrias insignis.*

Hab.: Middle East: Syria, Jordan, and Palestine, in the drainage grid of the Barada, Awaj, and Jordan Rivers.

F.I.: 1980.

Sex.: ♂♂ have longer fins. This is most noticeable on the pectoral fins, where the 1st to the 6th ray are broad and thick. Nuptial tubercles are present.

Soc. B.: See *Barbatula panthera.*

M: As for *B. panthera.*

B: Substrate spawner. Rear the fry with planktonic foods.

F: O; tablet, live, and plant foods.

T: 17°–24°C, **L:** 7 cm, **A:** 80 cm, **R:** b, **D:** 2

Barbatula brandti

Barbatula insignis

Barbatula panthera   (HECKEL, 1843)
Panther loach

Syn.: *"Cobitis leoparda,"* Cobitis panthera, Nemacheilus pantherus, Orthrias
panthera.

Hab.: Middle East: southwest Syria, in
the drainage basin of the Baranda and
Awaj Rivers.

F.l.: 1980.

Sex.: ♂♂ have longer pectoral fins and
more pronounced nuptial tubercles.

Soc. B.: Either lives alone or in loose
groups. Peaceful.

M: Fine substrate with dense vegetation
and an abundance of hiding places, e.g.,
among rocks. Bright illumination is not
appreciated.

B: Not known.

F: O; live, tablet, and plant foods.

T: 16°–24°C, **L:** 10 cm, **A:** from 80 cm, **R:** b, **D:** ∴

Barbatula namiri   (KRUPP & SCHNEIDER, 1991)

Syn.: None. The species was previously
considered to be *Nemacheilus tigris*.

Hab.: Asia: Asi River Basin, coastal rivers of Syria and Lebanon.

F.l.: 1979.

Sex.: The 2nd and 3rd ray of the ♂'s pectoral fins are broadened, and at spawning time, they have nuptial tubercles.

Soc. B.: Peaceful, solitary fish.

M: As for *B. panthera.*

B: Depressions are dug in the substrate
where they spawn. The eggs are guarded. Rearing is nonproblematic when the
fry are offered planktonic foods.

F: O; live, tablet, and plant foods.

S: *B. namiri* is very closely related to
Barbatula tigris. The former is characterized by 8 (7–9) divided dorsal fin rays,
19 caudal fin rays, and 35-37 vertebrae.
The length of the caudal fin is roughly
equivalent to its height.

T: 16°–22°C, **L:** 10 cm, **A:** 80 cm, **R:** b, **D:** 2

Barbatula panthera

Barbatula namiri

Paracobitis malapterura longicauda

Syn.: *Cobitis longicauda, Nemachilus malapterurus longicaudus.*

Hab.: Asia: former Soviet Union, in the Tedzhen and Mutgab Rivers of Turkmenistan. Also found in the drainage basin of the Amu-Dar'ya and the rivers Shirabad-Dar'ya, Surkhan, Kafirnigan, Dyushambinka, and Vakhsh; Kashka-Dar'ya, Zeravshan, and Sanzar.

F.I.: Has not been imported into Germany.

Sex.: No definite distinguishing characteristics are known.

Soc. B.: Lively, nonmigratory benthic fish.

M: As for *Barbatula angorae.*

B: Little is known about the reproductive biology of this species.

F: C; all kinds of live foods.

(KESSLER, 1872)
Subfam.: Nemacheilinae

S: In contrast to the nominate form, *P. m. malapterura* (VALENCIENNES, 1846) differs from the subspecies *P. m. longicauda* by its scales and larger size (20 cm). The nominate form is naked and only grows to 10 cm.

T: 10°–20°C (coldwater fish), **L:** 20 cm, **A:** 100 cm, **R:** b, **D:** 2

Homaloptera sp.
Chinese hillstream loach

Syn.: None.

Hab.: Asia: China, Kwangsi (Kiangsie) Province.

F.I.: Unknown.

Sex.: Unknown.

Soc. B.: Totally peaceful towards conspecifics as well as heterospecifics. Even smaller fishes are left alone.

M: Since these animals like a strong current, an overdimensioned pump or powerhead is recommended. Although *B. kwangsiensis* is a rheophile (current-loving), it can be kept in aquaria that do not have a current.

B: *Homaloptera* sp. has been bred in an aquarium. The spawn was laid beneath a piece of sandstone covered in *Anubias.* Before the ca. 30 eggs could be protected, the spawn was eaten by other fishes—*Nemacheilus* (*Acanthocobitis*) *botia.*

Subfam.: Homalopterinae

F: O; aufwuchs, but flake foods are readily accepted. Infusoria or *Vorticella* growing on rocks are especially relished.

S: Unfortunately, these fish are rarely imported. They often show up as by-catch.

T: 22°–24°C, **L:** 12 cm, **A:** 80 cm, **R:** b, m, **D:** 2

Paracobitis malapterura longicauda

Homaloptera sp.

Transamazonica, Brazil (1975). In 1975, when this photo was taken, sections of jungle were still left. Today, extended parts have been cleared by fire.

Corydoras araguaiaensis

Chrysichthys nigrodigitatus   (LACÉPÈDE, 1803)
Silver cat

Syn.: *Pimelodus nigrodigitatus, Arius acutivelis, Melanodactylus nigrodigitatus, Chrysichthys acutirostris, C. büttikoferi, C. ogowensis, C. macrops* (not GÜNTHER), *C. coriscanus, C. lagoensis.*

Hab.: West Africa: from Senegal to Cabinda, Liberia, and the Gold Coast, Ivory Coast, Gambia, Volta, Gabon, and Zaïre.

F.I.: Unknown. The pictured animals are from the Wilhelma Aquarium, Stuttgart.

Sex.: Genders can only be distinguished in full-grown animals. ♂♂ have a significantly broader head which they use to dig their nests.

Soc. B.: Juveniles are peaceful, even towards conspecifics. However, do not associate with small fishes.

M: Undemanding species. Since adults like to dig, place plants in pots.

B: Not possible in aquaria. In nature, the ♂ digs a nest using his mouth. Eggs are guarded by both parents.

F: O; undemanding omnivore. In nature mayflies and insect larva.

S: Its flesh is considered to be quite good, and they are frequently fished from Lake Togo using all types of capture methods, including nets and weirs.

T: 23°–26°C, **L:** 65 cm, **A:** 150 cm, **R:** b, **D:** 3–4 (S)

Continuation of *Amphilius atesuensis* (following page):

tance. This beige-brown marbled catfish changes color according to mood. Older specimens are generally darker. Catfishes from the family Amphiliidae are usually small, but rarely imported, unfortunately. Aquaria are probably very suitable environments for these catfish—both for maintenance and breeding. Populations in the wild are reputedly threatened because of introduced trout.

T: 18°–22°C, **L:** 6 cm, **A:** 60 cm, **R:** b, m, **D:** 2

Amphilius atesuensis

Amphilius atesuensis
Golden African kuhli

BOULENGER, 1904

Syn.: *Amphillius pictus, Amphilius platy-chir* (not GÜNTHER, 1869), *Anoplopte-rus atesuensis, Chimarrhoglanis atesu-ensis. Pimelodus atesuensis* is a commercial name, not a true synonym.

Hab.: West Africa: Ghana, in small fast-flowing creeks and rivers.

F.I.: Unknown

Sex.: No definite external differences are known. ♂♂ probably have a more intense design, whereas ♀♀ have a fuller ventral area.

Soc. B.: Peaceful small species which only occasionally pursues young. Can be housed with tranquil species.

M: Small aquaria of 80 l or more with a sand or fine-grained gravel substrate and dense vegetation are suitable. *Amphilius* are generally diurnal, but remain hidden among plants. Moderate water values: pH 6.5–7.7; hardness of 10°–

20° dGH; less than 15° dKH; temperature 18°–22°C. The temperature should not remain above 25° for long periods of time, since these fish chiefly inhabit flowing waters in nature. Regular partial water exchanges and well-filtered water are necessary. The latter two suggestions combined with good nutrition will ensure that these animals remain healthy charges.

B: There is no information available concerning breeding this species in an aquarium. Probably similar to *Phractura ansorgii*, where the key to success is good, bountiful food.

F: C, O; mosquito larvae, *Tubifex, Cyclops, Daphnia*, grindal worms, vegetables, lettuce, and tablet foods.

S: While searching for food or breeding, *Amphilius* species and their relatives frequently produce sounds audible to the human ear at several meters dis-

Continued on page 290.

Fam.: Amphiliidae

Amphilius sp. nov.

Syn.: None.

Hab.: East Africa: Tanzania.

F.I.: 1985 by L. SEEGERS into Germany.

Sex.: None known.

Soc. B.: Peaceful animals. Do not keep with very small fishes.

M: Dense vegetation and clean water with moderate values. See *Amphilius atesuensis* for additional data.

B: Unknown, but probably similar to *Phractura ansorgii*.

F: O.

T: 20°–25°C, **L:** 21 cm, **A:** 100 cm, **R:** b, m, **D:** 2

Amphilius uranoscopus (PFEFFER, 1889)

Syn.: *Amphilius grandis, A. hargeri, A. kreffti, A. oxyrhinus, A. brevidorsalis, A. transvaalensis, A. cubangoensis, A. jacksoni, Anoplopterus uranoscopus, Chimarrhoglanis leroyi.*

Hab.: Africa: Kenya, in flowing water. L. SEEGERS captured this species in the Athi River, Kenya.

F.I.: 1985 by SEEGERS to Germany.

Sex.: None known.

Soc. B.: This small peaceful fish makes a good addition to community aquaria.

M: Other than plenty of food and dense vegetation or other refuges, there are no particular requirements. See *Amphilius atesuensis.*

B: Unknown. Perhaps breeding is similar to that of *Phractura ansorgii.*

F: C, O; insect larvae and small crustacea are favorites, but vegetable, flake, and tablet foods are also accepted.

S: See *A. atesuensis* and *P. ansorgii* (pp. 291 and 294, respectively).

T: 20°–25°C, **L:** 7 cm, **A:** 70 cm, **R:** b, m, **D:** 2

Amphilius sp. nov.

Amphilius uranoscopus

Phractura ansorgii
African whiptailed catfish

BOULENGER, 1901

Syn.: *Phractura ansorgei, P. intermedia*. It is possible that *P. intermedia* is a valid species. The pictured fish would then be *P. intermedia*.

Hab.: West Africa: Nigeria and Zaïre. Inhabits fast-flowing, sunny coastal waters, never jungle creeks.

F.I.: 1954 by A. WERNER to Munich.

Sex.: ♂♂ are a very intense red-brown to red at spawning time. ♀♀ are larger, gray-black-red checkered, and significantly fuller when ripe.

Soc. B.: Relatively peaceful fish. Several specimens can be cared for and housed with equal-sized fishes. Only small fishes are considered food items. Usually brazen enough to emerge for food even if the lights are on.

M: House these fish in a relatively large shallow tank of at least 120 l. Algae are desired; solar illumination is not detrimental. Offer plenty of plants, wood, and hiding places close to the substrate; the latter are favored areas. Water values should be moderate: pH 6.3–7.2; hardness of 10°–18° dGH; carbonate hardness up to 12°dKH; temperature 20° to 24°C. These broad ranges of water values are not meant to encourage unnatural fluctuations. Clear water and good filtration are necessary for these rheophilic animals. When mosquito larvae, *Tubifex,* and other live foods are fed in addition to blanched lettuce, ♀♀ soon ripen.

B: Average water values suffice for breeding. FOERSCH successfully bred this fish in the late 50's. His set-up was a densely planted 30 l aquarium. ♂♂ produced 1.5 second chirping noises. These noises could be heard outside of the tank in the evening during courtship. Simultaneously, the ♂ circled around the ♀, who also turned restless after some time. For actual spawning, the ♂ curved his body into a U about the ♀'s ventral area and spread his anal fin. The ♂'s mouth rested on the ♀'s ventral fins. This position was maintained for several

seconds as the fish slowly sank towards the bottom. Several couplings produced at total of ca. 100 pelagic eggs. The eggs had a thick gelatinous cuticle and were similar in appearance to amphibian eggs. The fry hatched after 2–3 days and accepted food after an additional 5–6 days. FOERSCH was unable to determine what the fry were eating and, as a consequence, lost many of the young. They did not accept microworms, which limited his success to a few specimens. At a length of 12 mm, the body shape is similar to newt larvae.

F: O, C; prefers live foods such as chironomid larvae, grindal worms, *Tubifex,* small crustacea, and small insect larvae as well as algae, lettuce, or spinach.

S: The species name should not be confused with that of the American mudfish, *Phractolaemus ansorgei*. The noises these catfish produce as they search for food or engage in courtship are clearly audible outside of the aquarium.

T: 20°–24°C, **L**: 9.5 cm, **A**: 80 cm, **R**: b, **D**: 2

Phractura ansorgii ♂

Phractura ansorgii ♀

Waterfalls at the headwaters of a river in north Australia (Queensland)

Arius graeffei
Graeffe's salmon catfish

(KNER & STEINDACHNER, 1866)

Syn.: *Arius australis, Neoarius australis. Arius leptaspis* BLEEKER, 1862 is a different, autonomous species.

Hab.: New Guinea, Australia: coastal waters of Queensland, New South Wales, and the Northern Territory.

F.I.: Could not be determined.

Sex.: ♀♀ have longer and more rounded ventral fins than equal-sized ♂♂.

Soc. B.: Peaceful fishes which, at lengths of less than 20 cm, will not molest even the smallest tankmates, but this is not to say that you should tempt them with young fry.

M: Maintenance is easy in large tanks that have adequate filtration. Sparsely plant the tank with species such as giant vallisneria, protecting them with large pebbles around their base. Water; pH 7.0–8.5; hardness 15°–50° dGH.

B: Not very fecund. ♂♂ incubate the 25–70, 14 mm eggs buccally for 2–4 weeks at 32°C. Hatched young are relatively large. At 2 months of age, the fry are 6 cm long. Spawning occurs in mid-November to mid-December when the water temperature is 26°C.

F: O; large flakes, tablets, trout chow pellets, and live foods. Try plant foods.

S: Not really an aquarium fish; but these animals are an appreciated food fish in Australia. Dorsal and pectoral fin rays can produce painful injuries. Large animals are particularly sensitive to low temperatures and pHs.

T: 24°–32°C, **L:** 130 (30–40) cm, **A:** 200 cm, **R:** m, **D:** 1–4 (S)

297

Bunocephalus verrucosus scabriceps
Large-head banjo catfish

(EIGENMANN & EIGENMANN, 1889)

Syn.: *Agmus scabriceps, A. verrucosus, Bunocephalus scabriceps, Bunocephalichthys verrucosus scabriceps. Agmlus* is a typographical error.

Hab.: South America: in the central Amazon Basin, Rio Jutai.

F.I.: Unknown.

Sex.: None.

Soc. B.: This peaceful banjo cat can be housed with smaller species such as tetras or barbs. Though nocturnal, they do not bury themselves into the substrate during the day, making them better aquarium subjects than *Dysichthys* species. *B. v. scabriceps* is easily confused with *Dysichthys* species.

M: Nonproblematic when moderate values are used. Planted tanks probably suit these animals better than bare tanks, though differences in behavior could not

be discerned. It is important that extra foodstuffs are fed after the lights are turned off.

B: Unknown. Probably similar to *Dysichthys coracoideus*; see Vol. 1, p. 454.

F: C; live and frozen foods such as mosquito larvae, *Tubifex,* Enchytraeidae, and small crustacea. Flakes and tablets that have sunk to the bottom are also eagerly devoured.

S: *B. v. scabriceps* is easily confused with *Dysichthys knerii* and *D. coracoideus,* which are similarly colored. However, *Bunocephalus* species have a much rougher body surface than *Dysichthys* species. The type species, *B. v. verrucosus,* is described in Vol. 2, p. 436. In older literature, this fish can be found under the synonym *Agmus lyriformis.*

T: 21°–25°C, **L:** 10 cm, **A:** 90 cm, **R:** b, **D:** 2

Amaralia hypsiura
Two-rayed banjo catfish

KNER, 1855

Syn.: *Bunocephalus hypsiurus.*

Hab.: South America: northern Brazil, Rio Negro Basin.

F.I.: 1986 into Great Britain.

Sex.: Unknown.

Soc. B.: Sedentary fish. It prefers tranquil tanks that contain few fast swimming fishes. Unless they are hungry, they rarely swim.

M: As for the previous species.

B: Unknown.

F: O; small invertebrates such as chironomid larvae and *Tubifex* are the foods of choice.

S: This is the only species of the genus *Amaralia* that has a rudimentary, slender two-rayed dorsal fin. Rarely offered in stores. Most banjo cats were previously classified as *Bunocephalus.*

T: 22°–24°C, **L:** 7 cm, **A:** at least 75 cm, **R:** b, **D:** 2–3

Bunocephalus verrucosus scabriceps

Amaralia hypsiura

Entomocorus gameroi
Blue woodcat

MAGO-LECCIAF, 1983

Syn.: None.

Hab.: Southern Central America, northern South America, Bolivia.

F.I.: Unknown.

Sex.: First ray of the ♂'s pectoral fins is very thick and elongated, and the barbels on the upper lip are stiff and can only move up, back, and forward, not down. When resting, the maxillary barbels rest in channels behind the eyes. These barbels are probably used during spawning to help the ♂ cling to the ♀. ♀♀ are normally stouter.

Soc. B.: Small peaceful animals. Unfortunately, only incidental, single specimens are imported.

M: Small to medium aquaria with dense vegetation. This rare catfish should be kept in a species tank in order to at-tempt reproduction. A group or a pair is recommended. No particular demands are required of water chemistry, but moderate values should be maintained.

B: Unknown. AZUMA described a successful breeding attempt of *Parauchenipterus strialatus*, a similar species, in TFH, Aug. 1984. Internal fertilization can be assumed.

F: C, O; live foods, tablets, and flake foods are eaten off the bottom.

S: Besides *E. gameroi*, *Entomocorus benjamini* is the only other twilight- and night-active member of the genus that lies on its side and sleeps during the day on the substrate or among plants. Do not disturb, lest they heedlessly race around the aquarium. Also see *E. benjamini* in FRANKE, AM, p. 153, 1985.

T: 20°–24°C, **L:** 7 cm, **A:** 80 cm, **R:** b, m, **D:** 3

Tatia creutzbergi
Creutzberg's woodcat

(BOESEMAN, 1953)

Syn.: *Centromochlus creutzbergi, C. aulopygius. Centromochlus aulopygius* is a synonym of *Tatia creutzbergi* and *T. aulopygia.*

Hab.: South America: lowland creeks in Suriname and Cudajas, Brazil.

F.I.: Not known.

Sex.: In ♂♂, the rays of the anal fin form a copulatory organ, and the pectoral and dorsal fin rays are probably elongated during the spawning season. The ♀'s anal fin is fuller and undivided.

Soc. B.: Peaceful species that readily occupies secluded shelters. Young tankmates may become live food. Most at ease when kept in small groups.

M: Strong filtration and a moving surface are recommended to keep oxygen levels high. Water: pH 6.5 to 7.5; hardness to 15° dGH. Offer shelters and dense vegetation along the back of the tank.

B: Internal fertilization! The ♀ usually places the adhesive eggs on the underside of pieces of wood. Little broodcare. Rearing could not be observed. To the best of our knowledge, *Centromochlus* is the only genus in the family that does not have internal fertilization.

F: C; insect larvae, daphnia, *Tubifex*, and flake foods.

S: Juveniles are easily confused with *Parauchenipterus*; however, members of that genus have a significantly longer anal fin.

T: 21°–24°C, **L:** 4 cm, **A:** 60 cm, **R:** m, b, **D:** 1

Entomocorus gameroi

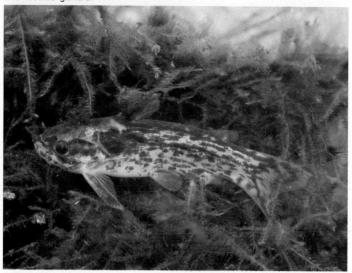

Tatia creutzbergi

Trachelyichthys exilis   GREENFIELD & GLODEK, 1977

Syn.: None.

Hab.: South America: Peru, Rio Mamón.

F.I.: 1978.

Sex.: The ♂'s genital pore can be easily seen in front of the anal fin. The pictured animal is a ♂.

Soc. B.: Keep in pairs or small groups. Slightly more diurnal than other catfishes, particularly when feeding.

M: House in well-planted tanks that have sufficient free swimming space; feed the animals in an open area. The water should be moderately soft with a pH of 6.5–7.0.

B: Well-fed fishes have been known to spawn in aquaria. The ♂ embraces the ♀ so that his genital papilla is very close to the anus of the ♀. Eggs are fertilized before they are laid among plants; Java moss makes an appropriate spawning substrate.

F: C; *Tubifex* and bloodworms should be used to ripen the ♀♀. However, commercial dry foods are also accepted.

S: Unfortunately, the picture at the top of the page does not show the attractive colors of this species. Irregular brown spots on the sides, which are normally present on these fish, are quite pretty. An improved diet may help rejuvenate the coloration. Variations in coloration may be seen in imported specimens.

T: 22°–24°C, **L:** 8 cm, **A:** 60 cm, **R:** m, b, **D:** 2–3

Auchenoglanis sp. cf. *biscutatus*
Yellow bagrid

(GEOFFREY, 1827)

Syn.: None, since this may still be an undescribed species.

Hab.: Africa: *A. biscutatus* has only been reported to inhabit the Nile. However, the pictured animal was caught off Kurilani in Lake Malawi.

F.I.: Unknown.

Sex.: Unknown.

Soc. B.: Like all members of the genus, this catfish searches for food in the upper substratum using its large mouth. Peaceful towards all fishes that are not overly small.

M: Large aquaria with potted plants. Do not use sharp-edged substrates, lest the catfish damages its barbels. Its digging activities make good filtration a must. Water: pH 7–8; hardness to 25° dGH.

B: Unknown.

F: O; despite its relatively large mouth, only small foods are eaten. Flake foods and tablets are accepted.

S: Lake Malawi was not previously known to contain *Auchenoglanis* catfishes. The pictured animal is an old specimen. Young animals surely have more contrasting mottling along their sides.

T: 24°– 26°C, **L:** 35 cm (or larger?), **A:** 120 cm, **R:** b, **D:** 2

Auchenoglanis ngamensis
Largemouth bagrid

BOULENGER, 1911

Syn.: *Auchenoglanis loennbergi, Parauchenoglanis loennbergi.*

Hab.: West Africa.

F.I.: Unknown.

Sex.: Unknown.

Soc. B.: Does not seem to be territorial. Relatively peaceful towards animals that are not too small.

M: A tank rich in hiding places is needed. Since these animals dig, the plants must be robust, e.g., *Vallisneria, Echinodorus, Anubias*, perhaps even potted. Floating plants fulfill the required prerequisite cover for these catfishes. Water: pH 6.2–7.5; hardness of 4°–25° dGH; carbonate hardness of 0°–14° dKH.

B: Unknown.

F: O; live and frozen foods commiserate to its size are accepted. Small fishes,

earthworms, and mealworms are also eaten. If sufficient live foods cannot be fed. Tablet foods and beef heart make appropriate supplements. This species spends almost all of its time searching for food.

S: The joints of the hard rays of the dorsal and pectoral fins can be locked, making nets an inappropriate capture technique. Be careful not to injure the animals. Often confused with *Parauchenoglanis guttatus*.

T: 22°–26°C, L: 25 cm, A: 120 cm, R: b, m, D: 2

Bagroides macracanthus
Humpbacked bagrid

(BLEEKER, 1852)

Syn.: *Pseudobagrichthys macracanthus.*

Hab.: Southeast Asia: according to BLEEKER, found in mountain streams of Sumatra, Musi, Kalimantan/Borneo, and Sintang. SANDS claims the species is also found in Thailand and Burma.

F.I.: Unknown. Probably imported into Holland in 1976.

Sex.: Have not been determined.

Soc. B.: Young specimens are totally peaceful, even towards much smaller fishes. The uncommon mouth of this family keeps even older specimens from being efficient predators.

M: Clear, well-filtered, oxygen-rich water is important. Water: pH 6.5–8.0; hardness up to 24° dGH. Besides open swimming space, parts of the aquarium should be heavily planted. These areas tend to be favored. Caves should also be provided. Rarely digs.

B: Unknown.

F: O; all kinds of small live and flake foods.

S: The pictured animal still has its attractive juvenile coloration; it will later become red-brown with broad, irregular crossbands. It is not sure that the species name is correct, since BLEEKER says the mature size is 80 cm for *B. hypselopterus*, a close relative. However, fish that reach the trade as *B. macracanthus* rarely reach lengths of more than 20 cm.

T: 20°–25°C, L: 40 cm, A: 150 cm, R: b, m, D: 3 (S)

Auchenoglanis ngamensis

Bagroides macracanthus

Pseudomystus poecilopterus (VALENCIENNES, 1839)

Syn.: *Leiocassis poecilopterus, Bagrus poecilopterus.*

Hab.: Asia.

F.I.: Unknown.

Sex.: Unknown.

Soc. B.: Nocturnal, peaceful bagrid. Probably not territorial, even towards conspecifics. Do not house with very small fishes.

M: Medium-large, well-planted aquarium with sufficient hiding places. Water: pH 6.0–7.5; hardness not over 20° dGH.

B: Breeding was accomplished in a 60 l breeding tank with the following water values: temperature 24°C, pH 7.2, 3.3° dKH. The 1000 eggs (Ø ca. 1 mm) were adhered individually, mainly to plant leaves. Two days after spawning, the 4 mm young hatched. Three days later the yolk sac was assimilated and foods such as *Paramecium caudatum, Brachionus, Anguilula silusiae*, and fine flakes were fed. Rearing the young proved difficult, probably because most did not feed until five days after the yolk sac was assimilated. The remaining 200 young (ca. 10 mm long) accepted newly hatched *Artemia* on the 6th day. (Breeding report from the Zoological Garden, Basel, Switzerland.)

F: C, O; small live and flake foods.

T: 23°–26°C, L: 20 cm, A: 100 cm, R: b, D: 2–3

Chrysichthys brevibarbis (BOULENGER, 1899)
Short-barbeled bagrid

Syn.: *Chrysobagrus brevibarbis, Clarotes brevibarbis, Pimelodus brevibarbis.*

Hab.: West Africa: Zaïre, Stanley Pool.

F.I.: Unknown.

Sex.: Unknown.

Soc. B.: Large predator. Only associate with large, robust species.

M: Active during twilight and night hours. Offer shelters where the animals can retreat during the day. Juveniles are active also during the day, so preserve sufficient swimming space. Plant the edges with such species as *Anubias, Echinodorus,* and *Vallisneria,* perhaps in pots. Use floating plants. A fine-grained gravel substrate is best, but sand will suffice. This will allow the animals to dig. Protect the plants with large stones. Insure that stones and rock edifications are firmly placed on the bottom pane to prevent the animals from undercutting the structure when they dig.

Clear, well-filtered water with a strong current is suggested. The water should be soft to moderately hard (4°–18° dGH; 10° dKH or less) with a pH of 6.3–7.5. As room temperature is sufficient for these fish—even 15°C is tolerated for short periods of time—an aquarium heater is not necessary. If you must use a regular aquarium heater, make sure it is protected with large, immovable decorations.

B: Information concerning captive breeding could not be found.

F: C; coarse live foods, tablets, and lean beef.

S: The protrusive eyes of juveniles become normal as the animal grows older.

T: 20°–25°C, L: 44 cm, A: 150 cm, R: b, m, D: 3 (S).

Pseudomystus poecilopterus

Chrysichthys brevibarbis

Chrysichthys nigrodigitatus. See p. 290.

Chrysichthys ornatus
Mottled catfish

Syn.: *Chrysichthys pictus.* Sometimes confused with *Goeldiella eques.*

Hab.: West Africa: Zaïre, Congo, Ubangi, Stanley Pool.

F.I.: Unknown.

Soc. B.: Large, nocturnal species. Young are rather gregarious and usually actively swim during the day. Do not house with very small animals. Predator.

M: Simple to care for. See *Chrysichthys brevibarbis.*

B: Unknown.

F: C; live and commercial foods.

S: Unfortunately, this attractive, relatively small species is rarely imported.

T: 20°–25°C, **L:** 19 cm, **A:** 100 cm, **R:** b, m, **D:** 2

Chrysichthys walkeri
Walker's bagrid

Syn.: *Chrysichthys macrops* (partially), *C. auratus* (partially), *C. persimilis, C. kingsleyae.*

Hab.: West Africa: Gold Coast, Ghana.

F.I.: Probably by L. SEEGERS in 1987.

Sex.: None.

Soc. B.: Adults are predators, but juveniles make good tankmates for robust fishes.

M: See *Chrysichthys brevibarbis.*

B: Unknown.

F: C; live and commercial foods.

S: It is suspected that the contrasting coloration pales and the body turns brown dorsally and silver ventrally as the fish ages.

T: 20°–25°C, **L:** 24 cm, **A:** 120 cm, **R:** b, m, **D:** 2

Chrysichthys ornatus

Chrysichthys walkeri

Clarotes laticeps   (RÜPPELL, 1829)
Flathead bagrid

Syn.: *Gonocephalus laticeps, Octone-matichthys laticeps, Pimelodus laticeps, Bagrus nigrita, B. laticeps, Clarotes heuglinii, Octonematichthys nigrita, Chrysichthys cranchii* not LOACH, *C. nigrita, C. macropogon, C. pitmani, C. laticeps.*

Hab.: Africa: Egypt, Chad, Niger, Senegal, and Sudan.

F.I.: Unknown.

Sex.: Not known.

Soc. B.: This large to colossal catfish is predacious towards small fishes. Prospective tankmates must be at least equal-sized. Since even slender fishes the same length as themselves are not exempt from being preyed upon at night, it has been known to suffocate on its prey. In case of doubt, it is best to forego keeping this species.

M: Large aquarium with robust plants and hiding places created with wood and rocks. Clear water and good filtration are necessary. Moderate water values.

B: Has not been successful in captivity.

F: C; live foods of all kinds as well as tablets. Feed beef heart sparingly.

S: According to BOULENGER, this species reaches 80 cm in length. However, "only" 57 cm has been confirmed.

T: 20°–26°C, **L:** 80 (20) cm, **A:** from 100 cm, **R:** b, m, **D:** 2

Gephyroglanis longipinnis   BOULENGER, 1899
Long-finned bagrid

Syn.: None.

Hab.: Africa: Zaïre, Congo, Stanley Pool.

F.I.: Unknown.

Sex.: ♂♂ are slender, while full-grown ♀♀ are stout.

Soc. B.: Even though *G. longipinnis* is a small, potentially very suitable tankmate, a breeding tank is suggested until more is known about this rare bagrid's reproductive biology.

M: House in large, densely planted aquaria. Clear, well-filtered water with moderate water values (i.e., pH 6.0–7.5 and hardness 4°–12° dGH) is best. Provide at least one hiding place for each animal!

B: Unknown.

F: C; all types of live foods of suitable size as well as flake and tablet foods. Freeze-dried and frozen foods can also be offered. Scraped beef heart and liver should only be used as a stopgap for times when live foods are in short supply.

S: Bagrids of the genus *Gephyroglanis* can be identified by their elongated, slightly laterally compressed body.

T: 20°–25°C, **L:** 14 cm, **A:** 100 cm, **R:** b, m, **D:** 2

Clarotes laticeps

Gephyroglanis longipinnis

Gephyroglanis sp.

Syn.: None.
Hab.: Tropical Africa: Zaïre.
F.I.: Unknown.
Sex.: ♂♂ are slender, whereas adult ♀♀ are clearly fuller.
Soc. B.: Large, nocturnal predator.
M: Appropriate inhabits for large, well-filtered tank. See *Gephyroglanis longipinnis*.
B: Unknown.
F: C; hardy live and commercial foods.
S: The pictured individual may be an undescribed species.

T: 20°–25°C, **L:** 48 cm, **A:** 150 cm, **R:** b, m, **D:** 3 (S)

Pelteobagrus brashnikowi
Brashnikow's bagrid, kosatok bagrid   BERG, 1907

Syn.: *Macrones brashnikowi, Liocassis brashnikowi, Leiocassis brashnikowi.* Often confused with *Mystus mica.*

Hab.: Asia: former Soviet Union, in the Amur, Ussuri, and Sungari Rivers and Lake Chanka.

F.I.: 1957.

Sex.: Unknown. ♀♀ are larger and probably have a bigger girth when full of eggs.

Soc. B.: Twilight- and night-active. Peaceful, good companion for heterospecifics as long as they are not overly small. If only a few specimens are kept, they claim territories and do not school.

M: *P. brashnikowi* easily adjusts to captivity. It does not have specific requirements in regard to water chemistry or aquarium decor. During the day, these catfish retire into plant groups or bogwood. Dense vegetation is both possible and advantageous, since these fish rarely dig. When kept in an aquarium, *P. brashnikowi* remains small, rarely growing more than 10 cm.

B: A. KOCHETOV claims that this catfish spawns in pairs, laying about 700 (2.0–2.3 mm) eggs. The young hatch in the aquarium after 3 days. Feed them small, chopped *Tubifex*, rotifers, and small crustacea. In nature, the adhesive eggs are laid among exposed roots of aquatic plants and are probably guarded by the ♂. Hatched larvae remain hidden for another 7 days along the substrate until their yolk sac is empty. At that time they are 8–9 mm long.

F: C; live foods such as mosquito larvae and *Daphnia* as well as frozen, flake, and tablet foods.

S: The name for this fish, *kosatok*, is derived from Russian and means "Kosa" or sickle. The name refers to the dorsal fin, which, when young, entangle the fish in fishermen's nets. Since incautious fishermen are often stabbed by its fins and its meat is not appreciated, it is considered a pest in its native habitat. Likewise, do not capture them with a net in the aquarium, lest its fin rays entangle it therein. In those cases the net generally has to be cut to free the fish. Glass containers make better tools for catching this species.

T: 12°–25°C, **L:** 17 (22) cm, **A:** 120 cm, **R:** b, m, **D:** 1

Gephyroglanis sp.

Pelteobagrus brashnikowi

Leiocassis stenomus   (VALENCIENNES, 1839)

Syn.: *Bagrus stenomus, Leiocassis ellenriederi, Liocassis stenomus, Pseudomystus stenomus.*

Hab.: Java, Sumatra, and Borneo. According to SANDS, this species can also be found in southern Thailand.

F.I.: Unknown.

Sex.: Ripe ♀♀ are probably thicker through the ventral area.

Soc. B.: Peaceful, twilight- and night-active fish.

M: *L. stenomus*, like many other catfishes, is photophobic and predominately nocturnal. Provide a large aquarium with plenty of hiding places: rocks, bogwood, and plants as well as coconut shells and flower pots. No particular water chemistry requirements are known.

Water: pH 6–8, hardness 4°–25° dGH; carbonate hardness 0°–16° dKH.

B: Unknown. Perhaps similar to that of *Pelteobagrus brashnikowi* and *Mystus* species.

F: C, O; live foods as well as flakes, tablets, freeze-dried, and frozen foods.

S: The fin rays are thorns to unwary fingers and nets. Beware! Bagrids can produce sounds which are audible outside of the aquarium. It belongs to the subgenus *Pseudomystus*, making its complete name *Leiocassis (Pseudomystus) stenomus*.

T: 20°–26°C, **L**: 15 cm, **A**: 100 cm, **R**: b, m, **D**: 2

Pelteobagrus ussuriensis   (DYBOWSKI, 1872)
Ussuri bagrid

Syn.: *Leiocassis ussuriensis, Rhinobagrus ussuriensis.*

Hab.: Former Soviet Union: the Amur, Ussuri, and Sungari Rivers.

F.I.: Unknown.

Sex.: ♀♀ are smaller and normally thicker through the ventral area.

Soc. B.: Nocturnal, peaceful schooling fish.

M: See *Pelteobagrus brashnikowi.*

B: Like some of its relatives, this species supposedly spawns among terrestrial plant roots that extend into the water.

F: C; live and frozen foods such as earthworms and insect larvae. Tablet foods.

S: Its fin rays can easily cause injuries.

T: 12°–25°C, **L**: 20 cm, **A**: 120 cm, **R**: b, m, **D**: 2

Leiocassis stenomus

Pelteobagrus ussuriensis

Leptoglanis sp. aff. *rotundiceps*   (HILGENDORF,1905)
Spotted mountain catfish

Syn.: *Gephyroglanis rotundiceps.*

Hab.: Africa: Tanzania, Lake Rukwa Basin.

F.I.: 1987 by KILIAN and SEEGERS.

Sex.: Unknown

Soc. B.: Small, active, peaceful fish. Best kept in groups.

M: Moderate-sized, well-planted aquaria rich in hiding places are suitable. Water should be clean, well-filtered, and not excessively hard (not over 20° dGH). Little is known about this species.

B: Unknown.

F: C; live foods such as *Cyclops, Daphnia,* Enchytraeidae, *Tubifex,* and mosquito larvae. During the winter, they can be fed frozen foods and *Artemia.*

S: This small, attractively designed *Leptoglanis* species would surely make a good aquarium fish if it were imported more frequently. Information is still lacking.

T: 22°–25°C, **L:** 7 (3.7) cm, **A:** 80 cm, **R:** b, m, **D:** 2

Liauchenoglanis maculatus   BOULENGER, 1916
Leopard-spotted bagrid

Syn.: None.

Hab.: Africa: Sierra Leone.

F.I.: Not known.

Sex.: Unknown.

Soc. B.: This rare, peaceful fish should be kept in a species tank.

M: Provide these animals with a densely-planted aquarium rich in hiding places. Keep the water clean. Water: pH 6.0–7.2; hardness 2°–14° dGH; carbonate hardness 0°–7° dKH.

B: Unknown.

F: C; small live and frozen foods.

S: *L. maculatus* has only been imported alive to Europe one time. W. FOERSCH (Munich) maintained the specimen.

T: 22°–25°C, **L:** 6 (8) cm, **A:** 80 cm, **R:** b, m, **D:** 2

Leptoglanis sp. aff. *rotundiceps*

Liauchenoglanis maculatus

Mystus armatus
Antenna bagrid

(DAY, 1865)

Syn.: *Hypselobagrus armatus, Macrones armatus.*

Hab.: Asia: India and Burma, perhaps throughout southeast Asia.

F.I.: Unknown.

Sex.: ♀♀ are smaller, yet usually fuller than ♂♂.

Soc. B.: Peaceful, but *M. armatus* may consider small fishes part of their diet. Good tankmates for larger fishes.

M: As for other *Mystus*; see Vol. 2, p. 452. Water: pH 6.2–7.5; hardness up to 20° dGH.

B: Has been repeatedly bred in Great Britain and former East Germany. Anywhere between several hundred to well over a thousand eggs are laid. Of these, frequently less than half hatch. Clean water is apparently vital to successfully rear the offspring; therefore, either perform water exchanges or transfer the fry into containers with fresh water. The very small young hatch after a mere 24 hr and must be fed planktonic food, particularly rotifers. The young grow rapidly.

F: C, O; insects and other arthropods! Additional foods, besides the aforementioned organisms, are also accepted.

S: Beware of the pointed pectoral fin spines! The picture to the right is of several juveniles and one adult. It is possible that dominant juveniles are almost totally black. *M. armatus* is best distinguished from similar *Mystus* species by the dark spot on the caudal peduncle.

T: 22°–25°C, **L**: 15 cm, **A**: 120 cm, **R**: b, **D**: 2–3

Mystus bleekeri
Bleeker's bagrid

(DAY, 1877)

Syn.: *Hypselobagrus bleekeri, Macrones bleekeri.*

Hab.: Asia: Pakistan, Nepal, Bangladesh, Burma.

F.I.: 1986.

Sex.: Unknown.

Soc. B.: Though a relatively social species, it will happily devour small fishes. Limit tankmates to larger species.

M: Large tanks with a multitude of hiding places are best. Due to its broad distribution, it probably tolerates a wide range of water values. Water: pH 5.8–8.0; hardness up to 30° dGH. Extreme water chemistry values and temperatures should be avoided.

B: Not known.

F: C; insects and other arthropods! Other live foods and tablets can be fed when the aforementioned animals are not available.

S: *Mystus vittatus* is a similar, but smaller species (see Vol. 1, pp. 456 and 451 [photo]). The small animal to the left is *M. vittatus*, while the larger animal on the right is *M. bleekeri.*
The adipose fin can be used to distinguish the two species, since it is twice as long on *M. bleekeri* than it is on *M. vittatus. Mystus tengara* is very similarly colored, but it does not achieve the mature size that the other two species attain (only 10 cm) and the barbels on its upper mandible are only long enough to reach the base of the ventral fins.

T: 18°–26°C, **L**: 30 (45) cm, **A**: 150 cm, **R**: all, **D**: 3

Mystus armatus

Mystus vittatus (left) and *Mystus bleekeri* (right)

Mystus mica
Dwarf bagrid

GROMOW, 1970

Syn.: None, but frequently confused with *Leiocassis brashnikowi.*

Hab.: Asia: Amur Basin.

F.I.: 1957.

Sex.: ♀♀ attain a larger mature size. The genital papilla of the ♂ is similar to other *Mystus* and *Leiocassis* species. ♂♂ have less rays in the anal fin, a thinner body, shorter maxillary barbels, and a more elongated tail fin than ♀♀.

Soc. B.: These peaceful animals can easily be kept in groups. Well suited for community tanks that contain moderate-sized fishes.

M: Medium-sized tank with vegetation around the edges. See *Leiocassis brashnikowi.*

B: Unknown; in nature, it spawns among roots of swamp plants. Fry hatch after 3 days and begin feeding ca. 1 week post-

hatching. In adult ♀♀, the 1 mm, greenish eggs can be seen through the anal periphery.

F: C; live foods such as *Daphnia, Cyclops,* and various types of mosquito larvae as well as flake and tablet foods. These catfish dig among detritus (mulm), as they search for food items.

S: According to STERBA, these catfish have special embryonic breathing organs. *M. mica* is occasionally confused with two other catfishes, *Leiocassis brashnikowi* and *Pelteobagrus fulvidraco. M. mica* is smaller than *L. brashnikowi* and has a white stripe below the lateral line. *M. mica* is likewise smaller than *P. fulvidraco,* and its dark central line extends from the posterior edge of the operculum to the caudal peduncle.

T: 16°–24°C, **L:** 6 cm, **A:** 60 cm, **R:** b, **D:** 2

Hemibagrus wyckii

(BLEEKER, 1858)

Syn.: *Bagrus wyckii, Macrones wykii, Mystus wikii, M. wykii.*

Hab.: Southeast Asia: Java, Sumatra, Borneo, and the Malay Archipelago as well as Sri Lanka, Burma, and Thailand. Inhabits lakes, creeks, and rivers.

F.I.: Unknown.

Sex.: Unknown; ♀♀ are probably smaller and fuller.

Soc. B.: *H. wyckii* is a social yet predacious species. Predominately nocturnal. Associate only with large fishes. Best kept in a species tank. According to SANDS, this species attacks anything near its own stature, making it one of the most aggressive catfishes.

M: Large, planted aquaria rich in hiding places are recommended. These catfish are found in a broad range of water chemistries in nature, but neutral to slightly acid, soft to medium-hard water is preferred.

B: Unknown. FRANKE bred one *Hemibagrus* species: The fish spawned in the open water, with the ♂ embracing the head and neck of the ♀ like a ring. During one pairing, 50 to 100 eggs were released. Approximately 8,000 to 10,000 eggs were laid by the time the animals had finished spawning. The adhesive eggs were about 1.2 mm in diameter. Young were fed finely chopped *Tubifex* at first; later the diet consisted of rotifers. While the specimens FRANKE bred were not *Hemibagrus wyckii,* they may have been *Hemibagrus malabaricus.*

F: C; all types of live and frozen foods commiserate to its size, including live fishes.

S: It is hard to differentiate the various *Hemibagrus* species. Various variants can be found in the extensive distribution area of *H. wyckii,* such that different species or subspecies may have been pooled. In nature, *H. wyckii* attains a total length of 50 cm, possibly even 80 cm.

T: 22°–25°C, **L:** 45 cm (possibly 80 cm in nature) cm, **A:** 150 cm, **R:** b, m, **D:** 2

Mystus mica

Hemibagrus wyckii

Pelteobagrus fulvidraco
Tawny dragon catfish

(RICHARDSON, 1846)

Syn.: *Pimelodus fulvidraco, Bagrus calvarius, Pseudobagrus fulvidraco, Fluvidraco fluvidraco, Silurus calvarius, Pseudobagrus changi.*

Hab.: Asia: in the Amur Basin.

F.I.: Unknown.

Sex.: ♀♀ are smaller and clearly fuller when ripe.

Soc. B.: Territorial species which is relatively peaceful towards conspecifics when kept in large groups, but unfortunately that demands a gigantic aquarium. Unlike *Leiocassis brashnikowi,* the tawny dragon catfish grows very rapidly in the aquarium, reaching lengths of about 20 cm. In its natural habitat, it grows up to 35 cm in length.

M: Create hiding places with rocks and bogwood in a large tank densely planted with robust vegetation. Floating plants should cover part of the surface. Water chemistry is of secondary importance, but moderate values are best. Water must be rich in oxygen.

B: Spawns in pairs along protected sites. After the up to 2,000, 2.5 mm eggs are laid, they are guarded by the ♂. The young hatch after 3 days and can be fed planktonic foods as well as finely grated *Tubifex.*

F: C; live foods such as worms, small fishes, and insect larvae. Flake foods and FD tablets are also accepted. While they prefer to take their food from the bottom, these catfish dig relatively little.

S: Of the 5 species of smaller catfish found in the Amur region, only *Mystus mica* and *P. fulvidraco* reach pet stores in significant numbers. The other three species are *Leiocassis brashnikowi, L. herzensteini,* and *L. ussuriensis.* All species have similar requirements, reach about 20 cm in size, and are difficult to bred. JAYARAM places this fish—for reasons not specifically explained—into the genus *Pelteobagrus* instead of *Pseudobagrus.*

T: 16°–25°C, **L:** 35 (20) cm, **A:** 150 cm, **R:** b, m, **D:** 2

Pelteobagrus ornatus
Ornate bagrid

(DUNCKER, 1904)

Syn.: *Pseudobagrus ornatus.*

Hab.: Southeast Asia: Malaysia and Indonesia, in the Muar River.

F.I.: 1982 into England.

Sex.: ♂♂ have a small genital papilla directly in front of the anal fin. ♀♀ are almost transparent, which allows their light green eggs to be seen in their abdominal cavity.

Soc. B.: This extremely congenial species prefers to be associated with conspecifics. Very similar to *Corydoras pygmaeus* in behavior. Unlike most catfishes, which prefer to sit quietly along the bottom, this catfish prefers to school in the water column.

M: A well-planted tank is best, but not necessary. Water: pH 6.6–7.2; hardness

up to 18° dGH. Slight filtration, plenty of light, and a dark substrate are recommended.

B: Has not been accomplished. The color of the eggs indicates that the animals spawn among plants. Sexual maturity is reached as the animals attain a length of 2.5 cm.

F: C; live and frozen foods commiserate to its size. Flake and freeze-dried foods are eaten, but must be fed in small, frequent portions (4–6 times per day).

S: In nature, there is a species of barb that mimics this catfish: *Crossocheilus pseudobagroides.* It seems that this barb seeks protection within schools of spiny catfish.

T: 21°–25°C, **L:** 4 cm, **A:** 50 cm, **R:** b, m, **D:** 1

Pelteobagrus fulvidraco

Pelteobagrus ornatus

Aspidoras fuscoguttatus
Spotted aspidoras

Syn.: None.

Hab.: South America: Brazil, Peru.

F.I.: 1988.

Sex.: Sexes are difficult to distinguish; ♀♀ have a slightly larger girth.

Soc. B.: Very peaceful species that is rarely active during diurnal hours. Keep in a school of at least 6 animals. *A. fuscoguttatus* makes an excellent tank-mate for small, peaceful, soft-water fishes.

M: Densely-planted, sand-bottomed aquaria are relished. A sand substrate allows the animals to root in their search for worms. Sensitive to abrupt changes in water conditions. Water: pH 5.5–6.8; hardness up to 12° dGH.

B: Not known, but probably similar to *Aspidoras pauciradiatus*.

T: 22°–25°C, **L:** 4 cm, **A:** 60 cm, **R:** b, **D:** 2

NIJSSEN & ISBRÜCKER, 1976

F: O; live foods such as *Tubifex* and mosquito larvae are its foods of choice. Flake and tablet foods will be eaten from the substrate.

S: This armored catfish likes a layer of floating plants to dim the light. Numerous new armored catfishes have been imported recently. Most, including this species, make excellent aquarium fishes.

Aspidoras rochai

v. IHERING, 1907

Syn.: None.

Hab.: South America: Brazil.

F.I.: Not known.

Sex.: ♀♀ are fuller during the spawning season.

Soc. B.: *A. rochai* is a peaceful schooling fish and an excellent addition for community tanks containing small characins and dwarf cichlids. Do not associate with large fishes.

M: House in tanks that are richly planted yet still have an open area in the foreground. That area should have a sand or fine-grained gravel substrate, allowing this armored catfish to dig for food. Water: pH 6.0–7.5; total hardness up to 14° dGH; carbonate hardness up to 6° dKH. *Aspidoras* species like oxygen-rich water. Strong filtration with surface movement is important.

B: No information concerning breeding this species was found, but it should be similar to other small *Corydoras* species.

F: C; small live, flake, FD, and tablet foods are readily eaten.

S: *A. rochai* is the type species for the genus *Aspidoras*. *Aspidoras* have two fontanelles, while *Corydoras* has but one. *A. menezesi*, a similar species, is usually sold under the name *A. rochai*. This species is occasionally confused with *A. fuscoguttatus* (see previous fish).

T: 21°–25°C, **L:** 4.5 cm, **A:** 60 cm, **R:** b, **D:** 2

Aspidoras fuscoguttatus

Aspidoras rochai

Brochis britskii   NIJSSEN & ISBRÜCKER, 1983
Giant brochis

Syn.: None.

Hab.: South America: Brazil, Paraguay, upper Rio Paraguay.

F.I.: 1984 by Heiko BLEHER, Frankfurt/Main.

Sex.: Have not been described.

Soc. B.: This peaceful, diurnal bottom-dweller likes to dig as it searches for food.

M: As for the following species. See also *B. splendens* in Vol. 1, p. 458.
Young *Brochis* often swim in mid-water, while adults are almost exclusively benthic.

B: Due to the limited number of imported specimens, this species has not been bred in captivity. The spawning behavior of *Brochis* species is said to be similar to that of large *Corydoras*. Brian

TODD, a British aquarist, has successfully bred *B. splendens*.

F: C; small worms, mosquito larvae, and *Tubifex* (well purged!) as well as flake and tablet foods (TetraTips, etc.).

S: Although *B. britskii* and *Brochis multiradiatus* are closely related, there are significant visible differences. Both have a large number of dorsal fin rays, but their coloration and head and mouth profiles deviate. *B. britskii* has a more convex head profile and a bony shield that covers the **entire** ventral side of the head.

T: 20°–24°C, **L:** 8 cm, **A:** 60 cm, **R:** b, m, **D:** 2

Brochis splendens   (CASTELNAU, 1855)
Common brochis

Syn.: *Brochis coeruleus, B. dipterus, Callichthys splendens, Chaenothorax bicarinatus, C. eigenmanni, C. semiscutatus, Callichthys taiosh, Corydoras semiscutatus.*

Hab.: Amazon Basin of South America: Peru, at Iquitos and in the Rio Tocantins; Ecuador, in the Rio Ambiyacu and Rio Napo.

F.I.: 1938 by the Münchener Tierpark AG, Hellabrunn, Germany.

Sex.: ♀♀ are larger and, when carrying eggs, fuller.

Soc. B.: Peaceful schooling fish that makes a suitable tankmate for all small to medium-sized fishes.

M: There are no particular requirements. See the species description in Vol. 1, p. 458.

B: As for *Corydoras*. However, many losses ensue, since the eggs and fry

are very sensitive to deteriorating water quality during the initial stages of life. Water: pH 6.0–6.5; hardness up to 4° dGH. Pairs separate from the school. The ♂ swims above the ♀. Pairing occurs slightly above the substrate. Eggs are collected by the ♀ in a cup formed by the pectoral fins as they leave her body. They are then adhered singly to plants and other items. In total, over 1000, 1.5 mm eggs may be laid. At 24°C the young hatch after 4 days. Feed them zooplankton and finely chopped *Tubifex*.

F: O; prefers live foods, but leftovers off the bottom will also be consumed (flake foods, tablets, and fresh live foods).

S: To differentiate between *Brochis* and *Corydoras*, see the previous species and the species description in Vol. 1, p. 458.

T: 22°–28°C, **L:** 7 (9) cm, **A:** 70 cm, **R:** b, **D:** 1

Brochis britskii

Brochis splendens, juvenile

Corydoras adolfoi
Adolfo's cory

BURGESS, 1982

Syn.: None.

Hab.: South America: Brazil, in the Rio Negro and Rio Uaupés.

F.I.: 1982 by Adolfo SCHWARTZ to the United States; described in his honor. Imported into Europe shortly thereafter.

Sex.: Unknown.

Soc. B.: Schooling fish. Keep at least 6 specimens.

M: As for all *Corydoras* species. Lives in schools and must be maintained as such in the aquarium. A sand bottom is preferred. Whichever substrate is used, it must have smooth edges. Plant the tank densely about the edges, leaving an open sandy surface in the foreground for the catfish to dig.

B: According to D. SANDS, breeding follows that of *Corydoras aeneus*. A group of ♂♂ and ♀♀ swims actively up and down the glass pane. Parts of the glass will be cleaned. Eggs are usually adhered to sites other than the glass panes, including water plants. Each ♀ lays about 25–30 eggs. Spawning generally occurs during the fall in their natu-

ral habitat and lasts about two weeks; then the fish spawn again. Reproduction is not very fecund, particularly when a small number of animals are bred. Fry can be raised using mashed *Tubifex*—only small pieces—and rotifers. After one week, they can handle small pieces of flake foods off the bottom. According to EVERS, Hamburg, who has bred this species, a low water level and a water hardness below 6° dGH are obligatory requisites to successfully rear the young.

F: O; small live foods are preferred. However, small flake and tablet foods are accepted.

S: In TFH, 9, May 1982, AXELROD gave an anecdote about the discovery of this species. *C. adolfoi* belongs to the *C. aeneus* group. Though *Corydoras imitator* is a very similar fish, it lacks the red-brown coloring in the dorsal region between the two black areas. If the two species are placed side by side (see photo on the back of book jacket), you can easily discern that *C. imitator* has a longer snout.

T: 22°–26°C, **L**: 6 cm, **A**: 60 cm, **R**: b, **D**: 2

Corydoras amapaensis
Amapa cory

NIJSSEN, 1972

Syn.: None.

Hab.: South America: Brazil, Amapari River; French Guyana, in the region of the Rio Oiapoque (Oyapok).

F.I.: Unknown.

Soc. B.: Schooling fish. Keep at least 6 animals.

M: Like most *Corydoras*. See *C. adolfoi* and Vol. 1, pp. 462 ff.

B: According to SANDS, this fish has been successfully bred several times in Great Britain, but detailed reports are not available. However, the coloration of the pictured specimen, which was bred by SANDS, does not coincide with the colors described within the original description.

F: O; small live foods are preferred.

S: One of the most variable *Corydoras*. The body design not only varies with geographical distribution, but within a single creek as well. For example, the dark wedge on the side can be very faint, while the upper half of the body may be totally dark. *Corydoras septentrionalis*, though very similar, never has a design on either the dorsal or caudal fin. *Corydoras ellisae*, another very similar species, does not have any spots in either the caudal or dorsal fin. It is possible that full-grown *Corydoras* of this group can be distinguished by their size, since the maximum length of *C. amapaensis* is 8 cm.

T: 22°–26°C, **L**: 6.5 cm, **A**: 60 cm, **R**: b, **D**: 2

Corydoras adolfoi

Corydoras amapaensis

Corydoras bondi coppenamensis
Bond's cory, Coppename cory

NIJSSEN, 1970

Syn.: None.

Hab.: South America: Suriname, Coppename River.

F.I.: Ca. 1970.

Sex.: Have not been described.

Soc. B.: Calm species that makes an appropriate addition to almost any community aquarium.

M: As for other *Corydoras* species.

B: According to SANDS, these animals have been bred in captivity.

F: C, O; does not have a selective appetite. Leftover flake, tablet, and frozen foods are all accepted.

S: A long-lived species.
C. b. coppenamensis mainly differs from *C. b. bondi* by the larger dots on its body and head. Similar differences exist between *C. julii* and *C. trilineatus.* NIJSSEN and others have discovered the existence of several natural hybrids of *C. b. coppenamensis* and *C. surinamensis,* which proves that these two species are closely akin.

T: 20°–24°C, **L:** 5 cm, **A:** 50 cm, **R:** b, **D:** 1–2

Corydoras copei
Cope's cory

NIJSSEN & ISBRÜCKER, 1986

Syn.: None.

Hab.: South America: Peru, Rio Huytoyacu.

F.I.: 1985.

Sex.: Unknown.

Soc. B.: Peaceful schooling fish. Keep at least 6 animals.

M: As for most *Corydoras*.

B: Unknown.

F: O.

T: 22°–25°C, **L:** 5 cm, **A:** 60 cm, **R:** b, **D:** 2

Corydoras bondi coppenamensis

Corydoras copei

Corydoras davidsandsi
Sand's cory

BLACK, 1987

Syn.: None. Occasionally confused with *Corydoras melini*.

Hab.: South America: Brazil, the Amazon and the Rio Unini, a white-water river in the Rio Negro Basin at Manaus.

Sex.: ♀♀ are stouter.

Soc. B.: Schooling fish. Keep at least 6 animals. *C. davidsandsi* are peaceful bottom-dwellers. Suitable for aquaria that have good water quality and peaceful inhabitants.

M: Use coarse sand or fine-grained gravel as the substrate. Plant the edges (any vegetation is appropriate). An open space in the foreground for digging is vital. Clean the filter material often. Water: pH 6.2–7.2; hardness to 20° dGH; carbonate hardness of 8° dKH.

B: P. MOYE successfully bred this species in Britain. Similar to other armored catfishes.

F: C, O; small live foods, tablets, and flake foods are eaten from the bottom. *C. davidsandsi* eats leftovers and likes to dig. Worms and mosquito larvae are particular favorites and should be fed frequently.

S: *C. davidsandsi* is supposedly part of the *C. aeneus* group, but this classification is questionable. With the exception of its shorter body and snout and the faint dots along its sides, *C. melini* is very similar to *C. davidsandi*. The longitudinal band is distinctive for *C. davidsandsi*, although *C. melini*'s band is almost identical. In the same habitat, a very similar species with similar coloration has been found: *Brachyrhamdia rambarani*. There are five pairs of *Corydoras/Brachyrhamdia* species with very similar designs. The reasons behind this mimicry are unknown.

T: 20°–25°C, **L:** 6.5 cm, **A:** 60 cm, **R:** b, **D:** 2

Corydoras delphax
Delphax cory

NIJSSEN & ISBRÜCKER, 1983

Syn.: None.

Hab.: South America: Colombia, in the Rio Inirida system.

F.I.: 1986.

Sex.: ♀♀ with eggs clearly have a larger girth. ♂♂ have a more pronounced design.

Soc. B.: Peaceful schooling fish. Keep at least 6 specimens.

M: Like most armored catfishes.

B: Unknown.

F: O.

S: This beautiful species with its notorious pointed head is presently being studied by ISBRÜCKER and NIJSSEN. It is probably a color morph of *C. delphax* (see Vol. 2, p. 462).

T: 20°–26°C, **L:** 7 cm, **A:** 80 cm, **R:** b, **D:** 3

Corydoras davidsandsi

Corydoras delphax

Corydoras fowleri
Fowler's cory

BÖHLKE, 1950

Syn.: None.

Hab.: South America: Peru, Caño del Chancho near Pebas.

F.I.: Unknown.

Sex.: ♀♀ are slightly stouter and have a larger girth.

Soc. B.: A very peaceful species which, like most bottom-dwelling catfishes, likes to live in groups.

M: As for other *Corydoras* species from fast-flowing waters.

B: Unknown, but probably like other *Corydoras* species. Feed breeders live foods.

F: C, O; tablets and leftover flake foods.

S: Redescribed by WEITZMAN, 1964 because the first description, which was published in an aquarium magazine, was incomplete and lacked a photo. Species identification is best done on preserved specimens. The thoracic and abdominal plates are species specific.

T: 21°–23°C, **L:** 8 cm, **A:** 70 cm, **R:** b, **D:** 2

Corydoras imitator
Imitator cory

NIJSSEN & ISBRÜCKER, 1983

Syn.: None. Very similar to *Corydoras adolfoi*.

Hab.: South America: Brazil.

F.I.: 1984.

Sex.: Full-grown ♀♀ are larger and fuller.

Soc. B.: Peaceful schooling fish. Keep at least 6 specimens.

M: As for all *Corydoras* species. See *C. adolfoi*.

B: Like *C. adolfoi,* but less fecund.

F: O.

S: The name "imitator" originated because of its great similarity to *C. adolfoi*. But *C. imitator* has a longer snout, is less common, and is usually found within schools of other *Corydoras*.

T: 22°–26°C, **L:** 6 cm, **A:** 60 cm, **R:** b, **D:** 2

Corydoras fowleri

Corydoras imitator

Corydoras loretoensis
Loreto cory

NIJSSEN & ISBRÜCKER, 1986

Syn.: None. Very similar to *Corydoras armatus*.

Hab.: South America: Peru.

F.I.: Unknown.

Sex.: Unknown.

Soc. B.: Peaceful schooling fish. Keep at least 6 animals.

M: As for most other *Corydoras*.

B: Unknown.

F: O.

S: Compare to *Corydoras armatus* in Vol. 1, p. 460. *C. armatus* is larger with striations on the posterior body and an unpigmented caudal fin.

T: 22°–25°C, **L:** 5 cm, **A:** 60 cm, **R:** b, **D:** 2

Corydoras loxozonus
Slant-bar cory

NIJSSEN & ISBRÜCKER, 1983

Syn.: *Corydoras "deckeri"* is a trade name. See Vol. 1, p. 462.

Hab.: South America: Colombia, in the Rio Meta and tributaries of the Rio Guaviare.

F.I.: 1980 into the United States as *"C. dekkeri."*

Sex.: Sexes cannot be distinguished from external features.

Soc. B.: This peaceful fish resides in groups. Easily maintained in community aquaria.

M: As for *Corydoras ornatus*.

B: Has not been bred?

F: O; small live foods, tablets, and left-over flake foods.

S: *C. loxonus* and *C. axelrodi* are similarly colored and hence often confused. However, *C. axelrodi* does not have a design on the fins or the ventral half of the body.

T: 21°–24°C, **L:** 6 cm, **A:** 60 cm, **R:** b, **D:** 1–2

Corydoras loretoensis

Corydoras loxozonus

Corydoras napoensis
Napo cory

NIJSSEN & ISBRÜCKER, 1986

Syn.: None. Previously considered a color morph of *Corydoras nanus*.

Hab.: South America: Ecuador and Peru, in the Rio Aguarico, Rio Napo, and Rio Nanay.

F.I.: Unknown.

Sex.: ♂♂ have a more distinct design. Full-grown ♀♀ are larger and usually fuller.

Soc. B.: Peaceful schooling fish. Keep at least 6 specimens.

M: As for most corys.

B: Although there is no information about successfully breeding this species, recommendations made for breeding *Corydoras nanus* may follow for *C. napoensis* as well. Otherwise, it can be expected that breeding *C. napoensis* is

very similar to the sympatrically occurring *Corydoras elegans*.

F: O.

S: A member of the *C. elegans* group. *C. elegans* and *C. nanus* are very similar.

T: 22°–26°C, **L:** 5 cm, **A:** 60 cm, **R:** b, **D:** 2

Corydoras orphnopterus
Spotfin cory

WEITZMAN & NIJSSEN, 1970

Syn.: *Corydoras orphanopterus*.

Hab.: South America: Ecuador and Brazil, in the Rio Bobonaza, Rio Pastaza system, and the Mato Grosso.

F.I.: 1984.

Sex.: ♀♀ are paler, generally fuller, and have smaller dots. ♀♀ can be easily confused with *Corydoras atropersonatus*.

Soc. B.: Peaceful schooling fish. Maintain at least 6 specimens.

M: As for other corys. See Vol. 2, p. 472.

B: Unknown, but it should be similar to other *Corydoras* of the *C. punctatus* group.

F: O.

S: In Vol. 2, p. 472, another color morph with fewer dots is described. Specimens with a lighter ocular band also occur. This species is easily distinguished from

C. atropersonatus, a very similar species, by its dark spot on the dorsal fin.

T: 20°–24°C, **L:** 5.5 cm, **A:** 60 cm, **R:** b, **D:** 1–2

Corydoras napoensis

Corydoras orphnopterus

Corydoras osteocarus
Pepper-spot cory

BÖHLKE, 1951

Syn.: None.

Hab.: South America: Venezuela and Suriname, in the Atabapo and Kabalobo Rivers.

F.I.: 1925 by TERNETZ.

Sex.: ♀♀ are larger and fuller.

Soc. B.: Peaceful schooling fish. Keep at least 6 specimens.

M: As for other *Corydoras*.

B: When breeding, the ♂ clamps the barbels of the ♀ to his body using his ventral fins. 2–5 eggs are immediately fertilized. These are carried within the ♀'s ventral fin pouch. Up to 300 eggs are laid and then adhered to a plant. At 24°C, the young hatch after 3–4 days and can be fed plankton and finely grated *Tubifex*.

F: O.

S: Despite its body design, *C. osteocarus* bears a certain similarity to *Corydoras aeneus*. *Corydoras bondi bondi* is another comparable species.

T: 22°–25°C, **L:** 5 cm, **A:** 60 cm, **R:** b, **D:** 2

Corydoras osteocarus ♂

Corydoras osteocarus, juvenile

Corydoras pastazensis
Pastaza cory

WEITZMAN & NIJSSEN, 1970

Syn.: None.

Hab.: South America: Ecuador and Peru, in the Rio Tigre system (Rio Conambo and Rio Pinto).

F.I.: Imported into England in 1983 as by-catch from Iquitos.

Sex.: ♀♀ are fuller through the anterior ventral area.

Soc. B.: Robust, peaceful fish. Well-suited for cool community tanks.

M: Inhabits the snow melt creeks along the eastern slope of the Andes. Clear, soft, cool water is preferred.

B: Attempts to date have proven unsuccessful. If you are lucky enough to acquire a pair, set them up in a 60–80 cm long species tank, add new water, and maybe filter over peat. A large potted

Echinodorus can serve as a spawning substrate.

F: C, O.

S: The name tiger cory has been suggested since the species comes from the Rio Tigre (= tiger river) system. Using a little imagination, you can see 5 tigerlike vertical dark bands on the fish's body.
C. pastazensis orcesi is one of the two described subspecies. However, due to the broad variability of the species, it has been withdrawn (NIJSSEN & IS-BRÜCKER, 1986).

T: 20°–24°C, **L:** 6.5 cm, **A:** 60 cm, **R:** b, **D:** 2

Corydoras polystictus
Many-spotted cory

REGAN, 1912

Syn.: *Corydoras virescens.*

Hab.: South America: Brazil, in the Rio Guaporé (Mato Grosso).

F.I.: Unknown.

Sex.: ♀♀ are slightly fuller and have a broader white ventral area.

Soc. B.: Peaceful schooling fish. Keep at least 6 animals.

M: As for other *Corydoras*. A young specimen is pictured in Vol. 2, p. 474.

B: See Vol. 2, p. 474.

F: O.

S: Very similar to *C. punctatus* and *C. concolor*. *C. punctatus* is spotted, whereas *C. concolor* hardly has any spots. The picture to the right is of an older specimen with extremely deviant coloration (see Vol. 2, p. 474).

T: 22°–28°C, **L:** 4 cm, **A:** 60 cm, **R:** b, **D:** 1–2

Corydoras pastazensis

Corydoras polystictus

Corydoras pulcher
White-fin cory

ISBRÜCKER & NIJSSEN, 1973

Syn.: None.

Hab.: South America: western Brazil, Rio Purus.

F.I.: Not known.

Sex.: No external differentiating characteristics have been described.

Soc. B.: Peaceful bottom-dwellers that do well in clear, well-filtered water. Associate with other amiable species.

M: Soft, brownish, slightly acid water is preferred (peat filtration). Include at least one corner of sand for the fish to root in.

B: Apparently this species has not been bred.

F: O; tablets (e.g., TetraTips) and leftover flake foods.

S: Very similar in color to *Corydoras ornatus* and *Corydoras schwartzi.* However, the cream-colored dorsal and pectoral fin rays can be used to distinguish this species from other corys. Note that the light coloring of these fin rays bleeds into the first soft fin rays.

T: 21°–24°C, **L:** 6 cm, **A:** 50 cm, **R:** b, **D:** 1

Corydoras sodalis
Netted cory

NIJSSEN & ISBRÜCKER, 1986

Syn.: None.

Hab.: South America: Peru to the border of Brazil, in the Rio Yavari and Rio Solimoes.

F.I.: 1971.

Sex.: Unknown.

Soc. B.: Peaceful schooling fish. Keep a group of at least 6 animals.

M: As for other *Corydoras.*

B: Unknown; probably like *Corydoras reticulatus.*

F: O.

S: Differentiating *C. sodalis* and *C. reticulatus* is difficult. There are differences in the median longitudinal line and the base of the dorsal fin. The body design is variable and is not considered a dependable criterion to differentiate species.

T: 22°–27°C, **L:** 5 cm, **A:** 60 cm, **R:** b, **D:** 2

Corydoras pulcher

Corydoras sodalis

Corydoras surinamensis
Surinam cory

NIJSSEN, 1979

Syn.: *Corydoras schwartzi surinamensis.*

Hab.: South America: Suriname.

F.I.: Unknown.

Sex.: No distinguishing external characteristics are known.

Soc. B.: A peaceful species that likes to reside in groups.

M: As for other *Corydoras.* However, this species is sensitive to nitrates. Keep nitrate levels low by performing water exchanges every 2–3 weeks ($^1/_3$ to $^1/_2$ of the tank's volume). Use a good water conditioner. Water: pH 6.0–7.2; hardness up to 15° dGH.

B: Probably like other *Corydoras* species.

F: C, O; small live foods such as *Daphnia* and well-purged *Tubifex.* Frozen mosquito larvae, tablet foods, and left- over flake foods are also eaten.

S: The pictured animal may be a color morph of *Corydoras melanistius brevirostris.* Its barbels are particularly sensitive.

T: 22°–25°C, **L:** 6 cm, **A:** 60 cm, **R:** b, **D:** 1–2

Corydoras treitlii
Long-nosed cory

STEINDACHNER, 1906

Syn.: None.

Hab.: South America: Brazil, in the Rio Parnaiba and Rio Maranhao.

F.I.: 1958.

Sex.: Unknown.

Soc. B.: Peaceful schooling fish. Keep a group of at least 6 animals.

M: As for other *Corydoras.*

B: Unknown; has been successfully bred in Scotland.

F: O.

S: Similar to *Corydoras barbatus,* but morphologically closer to *C. acutus* and *C. semiaquilus* (see Vol. 1, p. 460). Rarely imported.

T: 20°–25°C, **L:** 7 cm, **A:** 60 cm, **R:** b, **D:** 2

Corydoras surinamensis

Corydoras treitlii

Corydoras prionotus

NIJSSEN & ISBRÜCKER, 1980

Syn.: Corydoras "triseriatus" (an invalid species).

Hab.: South America: southern Brazil.

F.I.: 1986 to England.

Sex.: Ripe ♀♀ are clearly fuller.

Soc. B.: Peaceful schooling fish. Keep a group of at least 6 animals.

M: As for other Corydoras species.

B: Unknown.

F: O.

S: Though described in 1980, it was not imported alive into England until 1987. Hopefully C. prionotus will be imported into Germany promptly. C. prionotus and Corydoras nattereri are two very similar species which were previously considered synonymous, but the former has a slimmer, lighter-colored body, a more pointed head, and lacks the dark spot anterior to the dorsal fin found in C. nattereri. Compare the photo to the right with the one of C. badei, another similar species, in Vol. 1, p. 471. This species is considered to be part of the Corydoras barbatus group.

T: 20°–26°C, **L:** 8 cm, **A:** 80 cm, **R:** b, m, **D:** 3

Corydoras zygatus
Zygatus cory

EIGENMANN & ALLEN, 1942

Syn.: None.

Hab.: South America: Peru, Rio Huallaga in the Loreto region.

F.I.: Unknown, because C. zygatus has been continuously confused with C. rabauti.

Sex.: ♀♀ are larger and notably fuller.

Soc. B.: Peaceful, gregarious fish which constantly searches for food items.

M: Not particular. Conditions demanded by cardinal tetras seem to suit this catfish well, including filtering over peat. Water: pH 6.0–7.0; hardness up to 20° dGH, but 10° dGH is better. Use a dark, fine-grained substrate and floating plants to subdue light.

B: Has been bred in England. Spawning transpires in a typical Corydoras fashion. See C. melanotaenia (Vol. 2, p. 470).

F: C, O.

S: Although adult C. zygatus and C. rabauti are very difficult to distinguish, juveniles can easily be differentiated by coloration.

T: 22°–25°C, **L:** 5.5 cm, **A:** 60 cm, **R:** b, **D:** 1

Corydoras prionotus

Corydoras zygatus

A sluggish jungle creek during the dry season (Amazon, Brazil). During the rainy season, the water level rises several meters. Such black-water tributaries of the Amazon are home to many catfishes such as *Corydoras* and *Hoplosternum*.

Continuation of *Hoplosternum thoracantum* var. *niger* (facing page):

Black fry tend to grow slower; hence, the two color morphs are best reared separately. Brooding ♂♂ must be left undisturbed, since they will eat the spawn at the slightest provocation.

F: O; aufwuchs and live, flake, and tablet foods.

S: The mottled nominate form was presented in Vol. 1, p. 478.

T: 18°–28°C, L: 16 cm, A: 70 cm, R: all, D: 1

Fam.: Callichthyidae
Subfam.: Callichthyinae

Hoplosternum thoracatum var. *niger*
Black port hoplo

(VALENCIENNES, 1840)

Syn.: *Callichthys thoracatus, C. longifilis, C. personatus, C. exaratus, Hoplosternum thorae, H. longifilis, H. magdalenae, H. thoracatum surinamensis, H. thoracatum dailly, H. punctatum.*

Hab.: South America: usually found in static waters. Hordes of this catfish can be found in waters near human settlements, living off the trash thrown into the creeks.

F.I.: 1911.

Sex.: ♂♂ have a significantly thicker spiny ray on their pectoral fins.

Soc. B.: Peaceful species. The ♂'s territorial behavior is limited to the spawning season.

M: The black form tends to be more sensitive; nevertheless, this species is quite easy to care for. Offer hiding places and feed during the evening hours. Water: pH 5.5–8.3; hardness to 30° dGH, although extreme values should be avoided.

B: ♂♂ build a bubble nest beneath large floating leaves. Styrofoam plates can be offered as a substitute. Spawning is triggered by a drop in barometric pressure. Courtship is frequently elaborate, often extending into the following day. The ♂ guides a ripe ♀ to the nest and clamps her barbels with his ventral fins for the actual spawning act. The ♀♀'s ventral fins form a pouch into which the eggs are laid. Later the ♀ places the up to 500 eggs into the bubble nest. Remove the ♀ after spawning is completed to save her from further pursuit. Young hatch after 4–6 days. Stabilize the water temperature between 26°–28°C. Even though the ♂ guards the eggs, he cannot be trusted with the newly hatched young. Remove him after the eggs hatch. The young immediately accept newly hatched *Artemia* nauplii. With frequent water exchanges and hardy meals, they grow well. Even if both parents are black, only up to 50% of the young will be black.

Continued on page 350.

Fam.: Chacidae
Subfam.: Chacinae

Chaca bankanensis
Chocolate frogmouth catfish

BLEEKER, 1852

Syn.: *Chaca bancanensis.*

Hab.: Indonesia and the southern Malay Peninsula, in rain forest creeks and rivers.

F.I.: Not known.

Sex.: Not known.

Soc. B.: Though it appears to be a peaceful and calm species, it is predacious. Like angler fishes, smaller fishes (less than $1/2$ *C. bankanensis*'s length) are ambushed by *Chaca* and sucked into its jowls.

M: *C. bankanensis* needs hiding places, a soft peaty substrate (perhaps leaves), and a darkened water surface. Water: pH 6.0–7.2; hardness up to 10° dGH.

B: Has not been bred.

F: C; fishes, tadpoles, earthworms, and large aquatic insects and their larvae. After acclimation, tablet food is accepted (found by smell).

S: *C. bankanensis* can barely be differentiated from *Chaca chaca,* impossible from photographs. The following are anatomical and geographical differences:

C. chaca
Pectoral rays: I/5
Habitat: India (Ganges and Bramaputra). Virtually always found in large sunny rivers.
Lower lip: Normally has numerous hooklets or teethlets.
Hooklets on the body: One row above and sometimes also below the lateral line.

C. bankanensis
Pectoral rays: I/4
Habitat: Shady waters in the rain forest of Malaysia and Indonesia.
Lower lip: Either has very few or no hooklets.
Hooklets on the body: None.

C. burmensis BROWN & FERRARIS, 1988 is a third species. It is only known from Burma. See DATZ 6/89, pp. 327 f.

T: 24°–28°C, **L:** 15 cm, **A:** 80 cm, **R:** b, **D:** 3–4 (C)

Chaca chaca
Frogmouth catfish

(HAMILTON, 1822)

Syn.: *Platystacus chaca.*

Hab.: Borneo (presently Kalimantan), India, Sumatra.

F.I.: 1938.

Sex.: Unknown.

Soc. B.: Sometimes predacious. Not suitable for community aquaria.

M: These nocturnal animals are only active while feeding. Resting fishes as large as 6 cm are not respected. Hardly any demands are placed on water composition. Water: pH 6–8; hardness 4°–25° dGH. Provide hiding places among large rock edifications. Plants are not damaged.

B: Not known.

F: C; FD tablets are accepted after acclimation. The large mouth leads one to suspect a predatory lifestyle. According to MEINKEN, the broad mouth serves as a weir for plankton. Generally acknowledged as a predator.

S: Only for aquarists who like the weird and unusual.
Chaca was considered to be monotypic until a second species, *Chaca bancanensis*, was described in 1983. A third species was described in DATZ 6/89 (see above).

T: 22°–24°C, **L:** 20 cm, **A:** 100 cm, **R:** b, **D:** 3

Chaca bankanensis

Chaca chaca

Heterobranchus longifilis
Long-fin walking catfish

VALENCIENNES, 1840

Syn.: *Heterobranchus laticeps*.

Hab.: Widely distributed in central and western Africa.

F.I.: Unknown.

Sex.: There may be a slight difference at the anus, but it is not easily noticed without a thorough examination.

Soc. B.: Both adults and juveniles are greedy predators. Even large fishes are not exempt from being attacked. Best kept alone.

M: Not recommended for home aquaria because of its fast growth and predatory behavior.

B: Unknown.

F: C; fishes and substitute foods.

S: Easily differentiated from other Clariidae by its shorter dorsal fin and long adipose fin.

T: 22°–23°C, L: over 70 cm, A: 2 m, R: b, D: 4 (S, C)

Hassar wilderi   KINDLE, 1894

Syn.: None.

Hab.: South America: Brazil, Rio Tocantins.

F.I.: 1983 to Great Britain.

Sex.: Unknown.

Soc. B.: Timid, retiring fish which is sometimes active during the day. Easily frightened. Peaceful towards smaller fishes.

M: Clean, oxygen-rich water is a necessity. Prone to infections; wounds should be treated fast and prophylactically.

B: Unknown.

F: O, C; likes to search the bottom for worms, particularly *Tubifex*.

S: None.

T: 22°–25°C, **L:** 20 cm, **A:** 120 cm, **R:** b, **D:** 3–4

Megalodoras irwini

EIGENMANN, 1925

Syn.: None.

Hab.: South America: Brazil, in the Amazon and Marañón; Guianas.

F.I.: Usually these infrequently imported catfish arrive as single specimens; 1975 to Great Britain.

Sex.: Unknown.

Soc. B.: Even colossal full-grown specimens are quite docile, but the restrictive environment of most home aquaria is unsuitable for such large fish.

M: Only juveniles are suitable for the home aquarium, which is a pity since large, well-colored specimens are very attractive.

B: Unknown.

F: O; mainly snails, but palm fruits, etc., are also eaten.

T: 22°–25°C, **L**: 60 cm, **A**: 2 m, **R**: b, **D**: 4 (S)

S: One of the largest Doradidae. Its dark brown plates, strong "spines," and olive and brown spots make it easy to identify. Only suitable for large show aquaria.

Platydoras dentatus

(KNER, 1855)

Syn.: *Doras detantus, D. dentatus.*

Hab.: South America: Suriname.

F.I.: In 1978 a single specimen reached Great Britain as by-catch.

Sex.: Unknown.

Soc. B.: Not an active predator, but it will devour small fishes. It only emerges from secluded hiding places during the night.

M: Adaptable in regard to water chemistry. Nevertheless, alkaline water should be avoided. Dim hiding places out of direct light are preferred.

B: Unknown.

F: O, C; a plenitude of live foods such as *Tubifex*.

S: Primarily reaches the trade as single specimens among shipments of *Platydoras costatus* (LINNAEUS, 1766). *P. dentatus* is very similar to *P. costatus*, but lacks the white lateral stripe of the latter (see *P. costatus* in Vol. 1, p. 484).

T: 22°–25°C, **L**: 13 cm, **A**: 120 cm, **R**: b, **D**: 3

Megalodoras irwini

Platydoras dentatus

Helogenes marmoratus   GÜNTHER, 1863

Syn.: *Helogenes unidorsalis.*

Hab.: South America: common from the upper Amazon (Rio Ucayali) in Peru to the mouth of the Amazon; Guyana, Rio Essequibo.

F.I.: 1913.

Sex.: Unknown.

Soc. B.: Almost exclusively nocturnal. Food may entice the fish to emerge during daylight hours. Peaceful among conspecifics and other fishes that cannot be considered bite-size.

M: Medium-sized tank with plenty of hiding places and plants. It remains hidden among plants during the day. There their coloration provides excellent camouflage. Filter the water, but minimize water movement, since this catfish prefers tranquil zones. Water: pH 6–7; hardness up to 15° dGH.

B: Unknown.

F: C; small live foods, particularly insect larvae and small worms; rumors claim that ants are also eaten. Flake foods can be fed occasionally. Feed just prior to turning off the illumination.

S: Despite its wide distribution, this catfish is rarely imported because of its nocturnal lifestyle.
SCHRAMM wrote an interesting report in "Das Aquarium," **2**/93.

T: 22°–26°C, L: 12 cm, A: 80 cm, R: b, D: 2–3

Ameiurus melas
Black bullhead

(RAFINESQUE, 1820)

Syn.: *Ictalurus melas, Silurus melas.*

Hab.: North America: United States from Lake Ontario to Wyoming and the Gulf of Mexico. Rio Grande, Sonora, and Kentucky Rivers.

F.I.: Uncertain, since this species is often confused with *A. nebulosus.*

Sex.: Cannot be distinguished from external characteristics outside of the spawning season. At that time, ♀♀ are significantly fuller.

Soc. B.: Either lives alone or in schools. Peaceful among conspecifics. Limit tankmates to those either equal to or larger than *A. melas.* Twilight-active. Predator!

M: Keep in a pond or large aquarium. Use a limited number of plants, each of which must be well-rooted in pots then further protected with flat stones. Water conditions are not important. Water: pH 6.5–8.0 (7.0); hardness 4°–25° (10°) dGH. Subdued illumination, a cave of roots and rocks, and a substrate of gravel or coarse sand are suggested. Use a dimmer to observe the fish.

B: Only possible in ponds. A cave is created among shoreline vegetation. The eggs form a ball on the substrate. Depending on temperature (8°–15°C), the young hatch in 10–16 days. Feed them small live foods.

F: C, O; omnivores that predominately feed on live foods such as earthworms and fishes. Juveniles can easily be trained to accept tablet foods. Fresh meat, canned dog food, and carp pellets are also eaten.

S: *A. nebulosus* can easily be distinguished from *A. melas* by its coloration: *A. melas* is virtually black, whereas *A. nebulosus* is brown, dark brown and, depending on the light, iridescent green. Sometimes eaten in the United States, but the flavor is poor.

T: 8°–30°C, **L:** 35 cm, **A:** 200 cm, **R:** b, **D:** 1–4, depending on size (C)

Ameiurus nebulosus
Brown bullhead

(LESEUR, 1819)

Syn.: *Pimelodus nebulosus, Silurus coenosus, S. nigrescens, Pimelodus vulgaris, P. felis, P. catus, P. atrarius, Amiurus nebulosus, A. vulgaris, A. catus, Ameiurus lacustris, A. vulgaris, Ictalurus nebulosus, I. n. nebulosus, I. n. marmoratus.*

Hab.: Eastern and central North America and coastal provinces of Canada. Although it normally inhabits freshwater, it was found in the Miramichi River (Canada) in 1959 at a salinity of 8–15%.

F.I.: Before 1900.

Sex.: At spawning time, ♀♀ are fuller through the stomach region. Sexes cannot be distinguished during the rest of the year.

Soc. B.: Only territorial during the spawning season. Nevertheless, aggressions are sometimes displayed without apparent reason. Only associate with equalsized fishes. Predator!

M: At the end of the previous century, this species was one of the few aquarium fishes that could easily be maintained, which explains its popularity and why it was bred by many aquaculture enterprises. Aquarium specimens should be limited to those smaller than 20 cm. Feeding and filtration becomes too complicated with larger fish. Even caring for these animals in a garden pond is not simple. No demands are placed on water composition.

B: Spawns at 21°–23°C from March to May. The 500 eggs are laid along shallow shores or under overhanging shore vegetation in depressions that the fish excavate by fanning their fins. ♀♀ fan the eggs, and ♂♂ guard the spawn. After 5–8 days, the fry hatch and are guided by the parents for an additional 10 days.

F: C, O; tablet foods, carp pellets, or any live foods, including small fishes.

S: This species hybridizes with *A. melas* where they occur together in their natural habitat. It is unknown whether or not the offspring are fertile.

T: 4°–30°C (coldwater fish), **L:** 40 cm, **A:** 250 cm, **R:** b, **D:** 1–4 (S, C)

Fam.: Loricariidae
Subfam.: Ancistrinae

Acanthicus adonis   ISBRÜCKER & NIJSSEN, 1988

Syn.: None.

Hab.: South America: Brazil and Peru, in the Amazon Basin, Rio Branco, Rio Huallaga, Rio Purus, and Rio Tocantins.

F.I.: By A. WERNER in 1983.

Sex.: ♂ ♂ grow larger; ♀ ♀ are frequently fuller. See **S**.

Soc. B.: This peaceful species makes an appropriate tankmate for medium-sized, soft water fishes such as cichlids and characins.

M: Very resilient species that does not have any particular demands other than a large aquarium. The presence of bogwood seems to curtail damage to aquatic plants, since *A. adonis* rasps the bogwood in lieu of the plants. Clear, fast-flowing water that is soft and slightly acid provides a healthy environment for this fish.

B: Unknown.

F: H, O; an omnivore which primarily subsists on aufwuchs. In the aquarium, they can be fed with tablet foods. Carrots, peas, spinach, and a variety of other vegetables should be tried.

S: *A. adonis* was originally sold as a spotted form of *A. hystrix*. The attractive juvenile coloration turns solid brown as the fish ages. Additional species or color morphs of *Acanthicus* are known, but not yet described. There are *A. adonis* specimens with and without a spotted head; see Vol. 2, pp. 432 and 503. The type specimen of *A. hystrix* in Munich was unfortunately lost during the war. This makes species descriptions within the genus *Acanthicus* problematic.

T: 22°–27°C, **L:** 70 (100) cm, **A:** 200 cm, **R:** b, **D:** 4 (S)

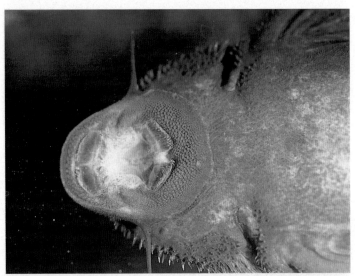

Acanthicus adonis, ventral view

Acanthicus hystrix, ventral view

Fam.: Loricariidae
Subfam.: Ancistrinae

Acanthicus hystrix   SPIX, 1829

Syn.: None.

Hab.: South America: Brazil, Peru, and Guyana, in the Amazon Basin and the Rio Tocantins.

F.I.: 1987 by A. WERNER.

Sex.: ♂♂ are larger; ♀♀ are fuller.

Soc. B.: Peaceful species which can be associated with larger fishes as long as they are not too restless.

M: Young do not have specific requirements. Large specimens have to be kept in large tanks. Prior to acquiring *A. hystrix*, the hobbyist should know where the fish will be housed in years to come (perhaps arrangements can be made with a public aquarium). Bogwood for rasping is a necessity, though its inclusion in the decor will not diminish damage to plants. Create hiding places among rocks and wood. Water values can be moderate, but soft water will surely be appreciated. Frequent water exchanges and strong filtration are important. See Vol. 2, p. 502.

B: Unknown. Its mature size makes breeding in an aquarium dubious.

F: H, O; vegetable components in its diet are important.

S: On pages 432 and 503 of Vol. 2, an as yet undescribed species of the genus *Acanthicus* or *Pseudacanthicus* was erroneously presented by the name *A. hystrix*. Two color morphs of *A. hystrix* have been introduced to the trade, a brown and a black form. The black form has a heavy "beard."
The attractive white-spotted species has been described by ISBRÜCKER & NIJSSEN, 1988 as *Acanthicus adonis*. *Acanthicus* have two characteristic bladders in the roof of their skull that are similar to diving tanks.

T: 22°–27°C, **L:** 70 (106) cm, **A:** ca. 120 cm, **R:** b, **D:** 2–4 (S)

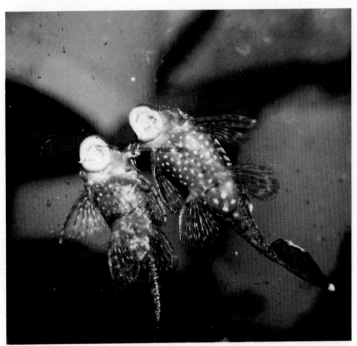

Unique photos of *Ancistrus dolichopterus* spawning. Both sexes (♀ right, ♂ left) hold fast to each other for extended periods of time with interopercular hooks. This was interpreted by FRANKE (1985) as minor quarreling.

Ancistrus sp. aff. *leucostictus* ♂
A bristlenose

Fam.: Loricariidae
Subfam.: Ancistrinae

Ancistrus dolichopterus
Big-fin bristlenose

KNER, 1854

Syn.: *Xenocara dolichoptera, Chaetostomus dolichopterus.*

Hab.: South America: Brazil, Rio Negro Basin.

F.I.: Unknown.

Sex.: ♂♂ have branched bristles on and along the edge of their head (the pictured animal is a full-grown ♂). ♀♀ do not have bristles on the head itself, and those along its edge are less developed.

Soc. B.: Although peaceful towards small fishes such as neons, tetras, etc., sexually active ♂♂ may be aggressive towards conspecifics, particularly as they begin to spawn. Territorial.

M: Water: pH 6.7–7.0; variable hardness. Prefers slight water movement. Large pieces of bogwood make ideal decorations.

B: Forms pairs. Live foods are needed to ripen the breeders. Eggs are usually laid in caves and depressions. Water hardness is not important, but the ideal pH is between 6.5 and 7.0. ♀♀ guard the eggs and care for them by fanning oxygen-rich water over them. Juveniles should be fed ground lettuce leaves and peas.

F: O; primarily omnivores. Small quantities of crustacea such as *Daphnia* and *Cyclops* can be added to the diet. Lettuce leaves and peas can provide part of the required vegetable fare.

S: Often confused with *Ancistrus hoplogenys* (GÜNTHER, 1864), but the two are differently colored. *A. dolichopterus* is chiefly brown, while *A. hoplogenys* is blue-black.

T: 22°–25°C, **L:** 10 cm, **A:** 100 cm (max. 2 pairs), **R:** m, b, **D:** 1

Ancistrus sp. cf. *temminckii*
Temminck's bristlenose

(VALENCIENNES, 1840)

Syn.: *Hypostomus temminckii, Plecostomus aculeatus, Hypostomus schneideri, Xenocara temminckii.*

Hab.: South America: Guyana.

F.I.: Unknown.

Sex.: ♀♀ have small, unbranched tentacles along the edge of the head. The pictured animal is a ♂.

Soc. B.: Peaceful towards all heterospecifics, including much smaller species. ♂♂ are territorial and demand a very large tank if they are to be housed with other territorial catfishes to prevent serious confrontations.

M: Small aquaria are inappropriate. Provide hiding places among roots, stones, flower pots, or coconut shells. Avoid extreme water values.

B: This species, like other *Ancistrus*, is relatively easy to breed.

F: O; to ripen the breeding pairs, foods of animal origin should be added to the diet.

S: Identifying *Ancistrus* species without detailed morphological studies is very difficult. Hence the tentative identification of the pictured specimen.

T: 22°–25°C, **L:** 10 cm, **A:** 100 cm, **R:** b, **D:** 1

Fam.: Loricariidae
Subfam.: Ancistrinae

Dekeyseria scaphirhyncha
Flathead suckermouth

(KNER, 1854)

Syn.: *Ancistrus scaphirhynchus, Hemiancistrus scaphirhynchus, Peckoltia scaphirhyncha, Peckoltia scaphyrhynchus.*

Hab.: South America: Brazil, Amazon Basin, Rio Negro.

F.I.: Unknown.

Sex.: Sexes cannot be distinguished from external characteristics.

Soc. B.: This peaceful species rarely exhibits territorial behavior or participates in intraspecific quarrels. Appropriate tankmates for peaceful fishes.

M: Medium-sized aquarium with well-filtered water. Provide this twilight- and night-active species with hiding places it can retire to during the day, such as below or within wood, rocks, or pipes. Avoid housing it with food competitors, e.g., algivorous species. Plants are not damaged. Water: pH 5.0–7.0; hardness up to 16° dGH.

B: Unknown. Probably similar to *Peckoltia brevis*; see Vol. 2, p. 512.

F: H, O; algae! Plant fare such as lettuce, spinach, peas, and carrots as well as tablets and sunken vegetable flakes.

S: These fish can be enticed from their hiding place during the day with food if the aquarium is peaceful and dim. Floating plants can be used to minimize light penetration. Since members of the *Peckoltia* group do not grow very large, they are better suited for small aquaria than large *Hypostomus* and *Pterygoplichthys* species. Because of their inability to successfully compete for food, special attention must be given to ensure their nutritional needs are met if they are not kept in a species tank. Feed during the evening hours so they do not wane! This species has a notoriously compressed body. See the picture on the bottom of p. 373.

T: 22°–26°C, **L:** 20 cm, **A:** 80 cm, **R:** b, **D:** 2–3

Hemiancistrus annectens (REGAN, 1904)

Syn.: *Ancistrus annectens.*

Hab.: South America: northwest Ecuador, San Javier and Rio Durango.

F.I.: Into England in 1986.

Sex.: Unknown; external differences are probably absent.

Soc. B.: Relatively peaceful; aggressions only develop between ♂♂ in very small aquaria where territories cannot be defended. Peaceful towards heterospecifics.

M: See *Hemiancistrus landoni.*

B: Unknown.

F: H, O; aufwuchs and algae.

S: *Hemiancictrus* are closely related to *Peckoltia.*

T: 22°–28°C, L: 18 cm, A: 100 cm, R: b, D: 2

Fam.: Loricariidae
Subfam.: Ancistrinae

Hemiancistrus landoni   EIGENMANN, 1916

Syn.: None.

Hab.: South America: western Ecuador, in tributaries of the Rio Guayas at Naranjito and Babahoyo.

F.I.: In 1985 by U. WERNER and R. STAWIKOWSKI.

Sex.: Unknown.

Soc. B.: Like other medium-sized Loricariidae. Occasional intraspecific quarrels of tail beatings and lateral threat behavior occur. Otherwise, these fish are peaceful and totally harmless. Well-suited for community tanks.

M: *H. landoni* hails from clear, clean flowing waters which are soft and almost neutral. Their colors pale, and they become lethargic when housed in "old" or medicated water. Include wood and, more importantly, many large, smooth stones in the decor.

B: Unknown.

F: H, O; though *H. landoni* is a specialized algivore and aufwuchs feeder, other foodstuffs, both vegetable and animal based, are not refused.

S: *H. landoni* can easily be thought of as a *Hypostomus* species; but *Hypostomus* do not have hook-shaped spines on the interoperculum.

T: 24°–28°C, **L:** at least 25 cm, **A:** 100 cm, **R:** b, **D:** 2

Hypoptopoma carinatum

STEINDACHNER, 1879
Subfam.: Hypoptopomatinae

Syn.: None.

Hab.: South America: in a tributary of the Amazon River at the Peruvian border.

F.I.: 1974.

Sex.: Adult ♀♀ are larger and fuller than ♂♂.

Soc. B.: Peaceful animals; keep a group.

M: See *Otocinclus leucofrenatus,* p. 376.

B: Unknown; see *Otocinclus flexilis,* Vol. 2, p. 508.

F: H; feeds on aufwuchs (algae and their accompanying microorganisms). Tablet and sunken flake foods are also accepted.

S: Similar to *Otocinclus notatus*; see Vol. 2, p. 508. Repeatedly confused with

Otocinclus paulinus REGAN, 1908. The primary difference between *Hypoptopoma* and *Otocinclus* are the ventrally positioned eyes of the former. The presence or absence of an adipose fin does not identify these fishes to genus level.

T: 20°–25°C, **L:** 5 cm, **A:** 60 cm, **R:** b, all, **D:** 3

Hypostomus regani
Regan's hypostomus

(v. IHERING, 1905)
Subfam.: Hypostominae

Syn.: *Plecostomus regani.*

Hab.: South America: Brazil, Rio Piracicaba, Sao Paulo.

F.I.: Unknown.

Sex.: Unknown.

Soc. B.: Peaceful towards other fishes, even if smaller. Since most Loricariidae are territorial, only keep single specimens in average-sized tanks.

M: Decorate the aquarium with tough plants and bogwood. Soft plants are eaten when the diet does not contain enough vegetable matter. Water: pH 6–7; hardness up to 15° dGH.

B: Unknown.

F: H, O; besides algae, vegetable fare and plant based flake foods (Tetra Conditioning Food) should be offered. Feed live foods such as *Tubifex* and frozen mosquito larvae occasionally.

T: 22°–25°C, **L:** 30 cm, perhaps larger, **A:** 2 m, **R:** b, **D:** 4 (S)

Hypoptopoma carinatum

Hypostomus regani

Isorineloricaria spinosissima
Spiny suckermouth catfish

(STEINDACHNER, 1880)
Subfam.: Hypostominae

Syn.: *Isorineloricaria festae, Plecostomus spinosissimus, P. festae.*

Hab.: South America: Ecuador, west of the Andes in the Guayas Basin, Rio Daule and Rio Peripa.

F.I.: In 1985 by U. WERNER and R. STAWIKOWSKI.

Sex.: ♂♂ have long needlelike odontodes and long spines on the hard fin rays.

Soc. B.: This species is sedate, peaceful, and shy, only emerging for food after becoming acclimated to its environment, chiefly during evening hours. Limit tankmates to peaceful species.

M: Undemanding and adapting. Water: pH around 7; hardness up to 15° dGH. Use plenty of wood and rocks as decoration. These items should be arranged to form secluded areas. Clear, well-filtered, oxygen-rich water is required.

B: Unknown.

F: H, O; though a specialized algivore and aufwuchs feeder, other foods of vegetable or animal origin are accepted.

S: In nature, this species grows up to 60 cm in length. At that size, ♂♂ are so spiny they cannot be captured with an unprotected hand or a net. The pictured animal is a juvenile with as yet invisible spines.

T: 24°–30°C, **L:** 60 (30) cm, **A:** 150 cm, **R:** b, **D:** 2–3

Lasiancistrus carnegiei (no photo)
Carnegie's suckermouth

(EIGENMANN, 1916)
Subfam.: Ancistrinae

Syn.: *Pseudancistrus carnegiei.*

Hab.: South America: Colombia, in the Rio Magdalena Basin at Santander.

F.I.: Unknown.

Sex.: ♂♂ have longer pectoral fin rays; the interopercular spines typically found in this subfamily are longer on ♀♀.

Soc. B.: Peaceful towards all other fishes. Adult ♂♂, however, will defend a territory against conspecifics and possibly congeners as well.

M: Well-planted aquaria with bogwood and hiding places. When fed an adequate diet, plants are left undisturbed. Water: pH 6–7; hardness up to 20° dGH. Large ♂♂ can only be housed together in large tanks.

B: Unknown; however, it should be similar to representatives of the genus *Ancistrus* (see Vol. 2, p. 502).

F: O; plant based foods, including blanched lettuce and vegetable flakes. Feed live or frozen foods such as *Tubifex* and frozen mosquito larvae once a week.

S: The genus *Lasiancistrus* differs from most other similar genera by the greater number of dorsal fin rays (10, rarely 9) and hence its notoriously broader dorsal fin. The thick odontodes along the pectoral spines of *Lasiancistrus* are a valid characteristic to distinguish members of that genus from the virtually identical *Dolichancistrus*.

T: 22°–26°C, **L:** 14 cm, **A:** 80 cm, **R:** b, **D:** 2–3

Isorineloricaria spinosissima

Dekeyseria scaphirhyncha, see p. 367

Leporacanthicus galaxias. See p. 386.

Lithoxus lithoides
Rock suckermouth

EIGENMANN, 1910
Subfam.: Ancistrinae

Syn.: None.

Hab.: South America: Suriname and Guyana, in the Sand Creek and Rupununi River. Lives in fast-flowing waters near waterfalls.

F.I.: Unknown.

Sex.: The ♂♂'s first pectoral fin ray is enlarged and covered with odontodes (see photos).

Soc. B.: Peaceful, but territorial when spawning.

M: Requires large aquaria, a current, and cool, oxygen-rich water. Provide vegetation and plenty of hiding places among rocks, bogwood, and coconut shells. Similar to *Ancistrus* in other regards.

B: Unknown.

T: 18°–22°C, **L:** 9 cm, **A:** 80 cm, **R:** b, **D:** 2–3

F: H, O; aufwuchs feeder. Algae, peas, carrots, tablet foods, and blanched lettuce and spinach leaves are accepted. Animal fare must also be offered.

S: Sadly, this interesting rheophilic fish is rarely imported. *Lithoxus bovalli* (REGAN, 1906) is very similar. BOESEMANN described three additional new *Lithoxus* species in 1983.

Lithoxus lithoides, ♀

Loricaria nickeriensis
Nickerie suckermouth

ISBRÜCKER, 1979
Subfam.: Loricariinae

Syn.: None.

Hab.: South America: Suriname, Nickerie River and Tjawassi Creek, a tributary of the Nickerie below the Lombok waterfalls. Lives in fast-flowing waters over sand and stone substrates.

F.I.: Unknown.

Sex.: ♂♂ have an enlarged lower lip.

Soc. B.: Like other members of this family, *L. nickeriensis* is an amiable species.

M: Do not keep in densely populated aquaria. High oxygen levels, frequent water exchanges, and strong filtration are necessary. Water: pH 6.2–7.2; hardness up to 14° dGH. This nocturnal creature needs plethoric plants and bogwood to retire to during the day.

B: Has not been successful. ♀♀ prob-

ably lay their eggs in one cluster which is sucked up and guarded by the ♂ until the young hatch.

F: O; aufwuchs feeder.

S: Few specimens of this interesting species have been imported to date.

T: 20°–24°C, **L:** 15 cm, **A:** 80 cm, **R:** b, **D:** 2

Loricaria nickeriensis, ventral view

Lithoxus lithoides

Loricaria nickeriensis

Monistiancistrus carachama
Black suckermouth catfish, carachama

FOWLER, 1940
Subfam.: Hypostominae

Syn.: *Pogonopomoides parahybae, Rhinelepis carachama.*

Hab.: South America: east Peru, Contamana and the Rio Ucayali Basin.

F.I.: Unknown.

Sex.: Unknown.

Soc. B.: Peaceful. Adults are loners (see *Ancistrus*, Vol. 1, p. 486).

M: Requires oxygen-rich, fast-flowing, clean water. While moderate water values are suitable, soft water corresponds the closest to values found in its native habitat. Twilight- and night-active. Hiding places are needed for daylight hours. Clean water is important, since this catfish is susceptible to bacterial infections. The presence of bogwood seems to curb its appetite for aquatic plants. Feed in the evening just prior to turning the lights off.

B: Unknown.

F: H, O; algae, blanched lettuce, and spinach leaves. Flake foods and tablets will be eaten from the bottom. Animal based foods must be offered occasionally.

S: *Monistiancistrus* is a monotypic genus; that is, it only contains one species, *M. carachama. Monistiancistrus, Rhinelepis,* and *Pseudorinelepis* all have a round iris, unlike most of their loricariid brothers which have an omega-shaped iris! However, due to its taxonomic position, *M. carachama* should not have this deviant feature. It is now known that the iris lobe disappears in the dark, but reappears under intense illumination.

T: 20°–24°C, **L:** 11 cm, **A:** 80 cm, **R:** b, **D:** 1–2

Otocinclus leucofrenatus

MIRANDA-RIBEIRO, 1908
Subfam.: Hypoptopomatinae

Syn.: None.

Hab.: South America: Brazil.

F.I.: Unknown.

Sex.: ♀♀ are fuller and larger.

Soc. B.: Adult ♂♂ are solitary abiding animals. Younger animals do best, however, when kept in a small group. An apt companion for small, peaceful fishes.

M: This small, peaceful *Otocinclus* needs a well-planted aquarium with plenty of algae. The water should be strongly filtered and clear. Filtering over peat or adding peat extracts is advantageous. Water: pH 5.0–7.0; hardness up to 16° dGH; carbonate hardness to 6° dKH.

B: Unknown. Probably similar to *Otocinclus flexilis;* see Vol. 2, p. 508. Compare this species to *O. affinis,* Vol. 1, p. 492.

F: H; aufwuchs (algae and the microorganisms contained therein). Tablet foods as well as flake foods will be eaten from the substrate.

S: Mature yet clean aquaria are demanded by this sensitive *Otocinclus* species. New acquisitions have to be handled with particular care.

T: 20°–25°C, **L:** 7 cm, **A:** 60 cm, **R:** b, all, **D:** 3

Monistiancistrus carachama

Otocinclus leucofrenatus

Otocinclus vittatus

REGAN, 1904
Subfam.: Hypoptopomatinae

Syn.: *Otocinclus macrospilus, O. mariae.*

Hab.: South America: Paraguay, in the Rio Paraguay; Peru, in the Amazon River; Bolivia, in the Rio Chimore; Brazil, in the Descalvados, Mato Grosso region. Often inhabits heavily vegetated sections of clear, fast-flowing creeks.

F.I.: Ca. 1921.

Sex.: ♀♀ are notably fuller than ♂♂.

Soc. B.: Peaceful. Often found with related species in numerous small schools in localized areas. Well-suited for community tanks containing small fishes.

M: Plant the tank densely. The substrate should be dark and partially shaded by roots and rocks. Requires clear, oxygen-rich water and current. Water: pH 6.0–7.5; hardness of 2°–18° dGH. If adequate quantities of algae are not offered, young fish may damage delicate plant leaves.

B: Possible. Eggs are adhered to plants and the glass. The fry hatch after 2–3 days and can be reared on hard-boiled egg yolk, infusoria, rock-encrusting algae, and *Artemia*.

F: O; algae, tablets, and small flake and live foods (*Artemia*).

S: This cute fish is inactive during diurnal hours, only becoming active during the evening. Unlike *Otocinclus affinis*, *O. vittatus* does not have a large black spot on the caudal peduncle. See Vol. 1, p. 492.

T: 20°–25°C, **L:** 5.5 cm, **A:** 60 cm, **R:** m, b, **D:** 2

Parancistrus aurantiacus
Gold-fin suckermouth

(CASTELNAU, 1855)
Subfam.: Ancistrinae

Syn.: *Acanthodermus aurantiacus, Ancistrus aurantiacus, A. nigricans, Hypostomus aurantiacus, Parancistrus nigricans, Peckoltia aurantiaca.*

Hab.: South America: Peru, Rio Ucayali.

F.I.: Unknown.

Sex.: Sexes are difficult to distinguish. ♂♂ have thick spines on the first hard ray of the pectoral fins. ♀♀ also have spines.

Soc. B.: *P. aurantiacus*'s amiable nature makes it an appropriate addition to community aquaria. ♂♂ may become aggressive towards each other and other Loricariidae in confining spaces.

M: Clean, well-filtered, oxygen-rich water is important. Offer bogwood as a rasping medium, but do not expect this to curb its tendency to chew on tender plants and rasp large leaves. Only use hard-leaved plants such as *Anubias* or *Cryptocoryne* or extremely fast-growing vegetation. Provide a layer of floating plants. The water should be moderately hard and slightly acid. Homemade feeding substrates can be made by encrusting rocks with a paste of vegetables, plant flake foods, etc., and allowing it to dry before introducing it to the aquarium. Feed in the evenings.

B: Unknown.

F: H, O; algae! Tablets and animal fare should also be offered every 2–3 days. Any vegetable can be tried (parboiled). Try as many types of food as possible! *P. aurantiacus*, like most Loricariidae, readily eats peeled cucumbers.

T: 22°–27°C, **L:** 18 cm, **A:** 100 cm, **R:** b, **D:** 2–3

Otocinclus vittatus

Parancistrus aurantiacus

Baryancistrus niveatus
Snowflake bristlenose

(CASTELNAU, 1855)

Syn.: *Hypostomus niveatus, Ancistrus niveatus, Cheatostomus niveatus, "Hypostomus margaretifer", Parancistrus niveatus.*

Hab.: South America: Brazil, Rio Araguay, in the Goyaz Province.

F.I.: 1981 into Great Britain.

Sex.: Unknown.

Soc. B.: Shy reclusive fish.

M: Oxygen-rich water is recommended. Limiting the number of plants will reduce the chance of *P. niveatus* either eating or uprooting them. Water: pH 6.5–7.0; hardness of 8°–10° dGH.

B: Unknown.

F: H.

S: The presence of interopercular spines precludes this fish from being a *Hypostomus*.

T: 22°–24°C, **L:** 20 cm, **A:** 150 cm, **R:** b, **D:** 2–3

Pseudacanthicus spinosus

(CASTELNAU, 1855)

Syn.: *Hypostomus spinosus, Chaetostomus spinosus, Hemiancistrus spinosus.*

Hab.: South America: Rio Torbes, Orinoco system in Venezuela.

F.I.: By A. WERNER in 1984.

Sex.: ♂♂ have odontodes on the pectoral fins and elevated eye sockets.

Soc. B.: Peaceful community fish. Adult ♂♂ may sometimes claim small territories and aggressively defend them against conspecifics. Largely similar to *Chaetostomus*.

M: House in spacious aquaria that have clear, oxygen-rich water. Hiding places, robust vegetation along the tank's sides, and floating plants induce a feeling of security for these animals. This catfish, though predominately twilight- and night-active, will approach food items during the day.

B: Breeding successes have been coincidental. Rearing the young is said to be simple.

F: O, H; primarily algae, but plant fare such as blanched lettuce or spinach is also consumed. Tablet and flake foods are eaten from the substrate. Feed animal based foods often.

S: Members of this genus are difficult to impossible to identify to species level by photograph. The type specimen of the genus is *P. histrix*, which VALENCIENNES described from a drawing he received.

T: 20°–24°C, **L:** 12 cm, **A:** 120 cm, **R:** b, **D:** 3–4

Baryancistrus niveatus

Pseudacanthicus spinosus

Pterygoplichthys in Hawaii

In 1989 the journal of the Catfish Association of Great Britain contained an interesting article about *Pterygoplichthys* (probably *multiradiatus*). In 1986, *Pterygoplichthys* were discovered in reservoirs in Hawaii, probably having been released by Hawaiian aquarists. Initial attention was drawn to them when anglers caught a 31 cm long specimen in January of 1986 in the Wahiawa Reservoir on Oahu, the largest island of Hawaii. Later, as additional specimens were captured, they were found to be widely distributed. In fact, the young suckermouth cats covered almost all submersed wood and other hard substrates. A light shone into the water at night easily pinpointed the location of the numerous catfish, since their irises reflected red. Their eyes looked like countless underwater lasers.

The fish excavate tunnels where they live and spawn. Heiko Bleher took photographs of one such tunnel (Vol. 2, p. 515). The tunnel's dimensions is indicative of the animal's size.

Spawning occurs at depths of up to 60 cm (2 ft) between the months of June and October on Hawaii. The eggs are laid and fertilized within the tunnel which is constructed by the ♂. Here he guards the eggs and hatched fry until they are free-swimming and abandon the tunnel. One clutch can contain anywhere between 400 and 1000 yellow to orange eggs. The egg's coloration depends on the stage of development. It is said that these eggs are very tasty when salted and prepared according to a Chinese recipe. Most of the animals in the reservoir were 25 to 45 cm long, the longest being 65 cm.

Additional catfish species such as *Ancistrus* and *Hypostomus* have now been discovered in Hawaiian reservoirs as well. The fish are not appreciated, even though they do not disturb the native population, since they fill a previously unoccupied niche. Despite their tasty meat (bake in foil and carefully break the tail section open), they have absolutely no appeal to sports fishermen.

Photos have shown that the larvae of *Pterygoplichthys* form a sphere inside the cave. We are confident that those of you who wish to read the original article will be able to receive a copy through the British Catfish Association, Gian Sandford, 5 Sparrow's Mead, Gb-Redhill, Surrey RH1 2EJ (include return postage).

Perhaps some readers would like to try breeding *Pterygoplichthys* in an aquarium. I would suggest a large tank of at least 500–1000 l and a lateral wall with 30 cm of unfired clay (brick-making industry). Drill a cave into the clay that corresponds to the size of your captive *Pterygoplichthys*. Of course, it will be difficult to find a suitable breeding pair, but it should be possible to achieve either through the British Catfish Association or your local catfish association.

The water chemistry is probably not overly important. A pH of between 6 and 7 and a hardness of 6° to 12° dGH should be within the tolerance values of these Loricariidae. I offer my *Pterygoplichthys* sections of drainage pipes which are available in various diameters. One of my *Pterygoplichthys* has a 30 cm long clay pipe with an inner diameter of 10 cm. The fish itself is about the same length. The clay will increase the water's turbidity, so I do not consider peat-filtered water a necessity. The animals do not seem to be shy in front of bright illumination. My animals emerge during the day for food, even though there are two 125 W mercury lights illuminating the 500 l tank. The high intensity is great for growing algae. In the aforementioned aquarium, I also keep *Sturisoma aureum*. However, despite the high light intensity, I do not have any algae growth in this tank. The catfish must be grazing everything.

I have fed my Loricariidae exclusively on frozen peas and TetraTips for years, but they also accept mosquito larvae and leftover flake foods. For information concerning rearing the young, see the breeding report given under *Sturisoma aureum* in Vol. 2, p. 520.

Pterygoplichthys etentaculatus   (SPIX, 1829)

Syn.: *Hypostoma etentaculatum, Hypostomus duodecimalis, Ancistrus longimanus.*

Hab.: South America: Brazil, in the Rio Sao Francisco.

F.I.: Unknown.

Sex.: Unknown.

Soc. B.: There is no information available, but it should be similar to most other *Pterygoplichthys* species.

M: House in spacious, well-filtered aquaria that have a current, vegetation around the edges, and a cave, e.g., a section of drainage pipe.

B: Unknown.

F: H; vegetable foods such as lettuce and peas and small amounts of animal based foods.

S: Not all have an adipose fin, as was demonstrated by a 40 mm juvenile. Precise identification of this species is difficult because the holotype that was stored in Munich was destroyed during WWII.

T: 22°–25°C, L: 40 cm, A: 150 cm, R: b, D: 2–3

Glyptoperichthys sp. cf. *lituratus*
Spotted sailfin sucker catfish

Syn.: None.

Hab.: Southamerica, Peru, Cocha Supay and Trueno Cocha, Caño Supay near Jenaro Herrera at Rio Ucajali.

F.I.: This new, undescribed species has not been imported.

S: Juveniles and adults are differently colored. Juveniles have red or orange-fringed black spots and bands. In contrast, the upper ray of the caudal fin, the first ray of the dorsal fin, and the first ray of the ventral fins are intense red-orange on adult specimens (♂?). See DATZ *Sonderheft Harnischwelse*, Sept. 92; Ulmer Verlag.

Apparently, *Glyptoperichthys* do not have much longevity. Six to eight years seems to be their maximum age in an aquarium. They have been successfully bred in an aquarium.
The photo was taken at Cocha Supay, Peru.

B: Unknown.

F: O.

T: 24°–28°C, L: 40 cm and more, A: 100 cm and more, R: b, D: 3–4

Pterygoplichthys etentaculatus

Glyptoperichthys sp. cf. *lituratus*

Leporacanthicus galaxias
Galactical suckermouth

Syn.: None.

Hab.: South America: Brazil, in the Amazon Basin and Rio Tocantins. Lives in roaring rapids.

F.I.: 1987 by A. WERNER.

Sex.: Unknown.

Soc. B.: Peaceful.

M: The aquarium has to be at least 120 cm long. Use rocks or, better, bogwood to create hiding niches. Medium-hard to soft water with a pH of 6.2–7.2 is best. According to conditions in their natural habitat, oxygen-rich, well- filtered water is necessary. See STAWIKOWSKI, DATZ, 1/1988, p. 44.

B: Unknown.

F: H; feeds on aufwuchs, algae, vegetable fare, and tablets.

T: 22°–25°C, **L:** 40 cm (?), **A:** 120 cm, **R:** b, **D:** 3

ISBRÜCKER & NIJSSEN, 1989
Subfam.: Ancistrinae

S: *L. galaxias* is capable of extending its upper mandible until it looks like a trunk. This suckermouth cat has uncommon dentition: 10 long teeth in the lower mandible and 2 in the upper. Its attractive coloration is reminiscent of *Acanthicus hystrix*.

Ricola macrops

Syn.: *Loricaria macrops*.

Hab.: South America: Uruguay and Argentina, in the lower Rio Paraná and the Rio de la Plata.

F.I.: Unknown.

Sex.: The ♂'s dorsal fin spine is slightly thicker than its consort's. Unlike *Rineloricaria*, ♂♂ do not have a beard.

Soc. B.: This peaceful species is a good companion for similarly-natured fishes, regardless of size. Sexually mature ♂♂ do not claim territories; confrontations between ♂♂ are rather harmless.

M: Well-filtered, oxygen-rich water is the most important aspect for successful care. Plants can be included in the decor. Place flat stones on a fine-grained gravel substrate. Hiding places are not necessary. Water: pH 6–7; hardness 5°–15° dGH.

B: Has been repeatedly bred in captivity. These fish spawn like other open

(REGAN, 1904)
Subfam.: Loricariinae

spawners of this subfamily (see *Sturisoma*), either on stone plates or large plant leaves. The yellowish eggs form an elongated clump which the ♂ picks up with his mouth and carries until they hatch.

F: O; besides vegetable fare (algae and blanched spinach), animal based foods are readily accepted.

S: ISBRÜCKER and NIJSSEN established the genus *Ricola* in 1978. *Ricola* can be distinguished from *Loricaria* by morphological aspects. *Ricola* have heavily bifurcated barbels (even more than *Loricaria nickeriensis*) and larger fins. Its uncommon reproductive behavior combined with its rarity in pet stores makes breeding attempts doubly worthwhile.

T: 20°–24°C, **L:** 27 cm, **A:** 100 cm, **R:** b, m, **D:** 2–3

Leporacanthicus galaxias

Ricola macrops

Rineloricaria castroi
Castro's whiptail catfish

ISBRÜCKER & NIJSSEN, 1985

Syn.: None.

Hab.: South America.

F.I.: Unknown.

Sex.: ♂♂ have a "beard."

Soc. B.: Peaceful.

M: As for other Loricariinae; see *Rineloricaria heteroptera* for specific information.

B: Has been successfully bred in captivity. Pipes or bamboo are preferentially chosen as spawning sites. The approximately 100 eggs are guarded by the ♂. After about 7 days, the fry hatch and are free-swimming after an additional 3 to 5 days. Feed the young live plankton, algae, and mashed peas. See *S. aureum*, Vol. 2, p. 520, for details on how to rear the young.

F: H, O; aufwuchs.

S: Similar species or forms have been repeatedly imported.

T: 20°–24°C, **L:** 14 cm, **A:** 80 cm, **R:** b, m; **D:** 2

Rineloricaria heteroptera

ISBRÜCKER & NIJSSEN, 1976

Syn.: None.

Hab.: South America: Brazil, in waters near Manaus.

F.I.: Unknown.

Sex.: Older, full-grown ♂♂ have a "beard" of bristles (odontodes) along the edge of their head and the anterior edge of their pectoral fins. ♀♀ never have a "beard."

Soc. B.: Peaceful, but several ♂♂ can only be kept for extended periods of time in large aquaria. Each catfish requires its own hiding place! Only associate with tranquil fishes.

M: Though a species tank is ideal, it can be maintained in sparsely populated community aquaria. A strong water current and a high capacity filter help meet this fish's oxygen demand. Water: pH 6.2–7.2; hardness up to 14° dGH; carbonate hardness up to 6° dKH. Dense vegetation and hiding places among rocks and bogwood should be included in the tank's decor.

B: Unknown, but probably similar to that of *Sturisoma aureum*. See Vol. 2, p. 518.

F: H, O; aufwuchs.

S: Very similar to *R. lanceolata*. See Vol. 2, p. 518.

T: 20°–25°C, **L:** 26 cm, **A:** 80 cm, **R:** b, m; **D:** 2–3

Rineloricaria castroi

Rineloricaria heteroptera

Rineloricaria morrowi
Yellow suckermouth catfish

FOWLER, 1940

Syn.: None.

Hab.: South America: Peru, Sira Mountains. See FOERSCH and HANRIEDER, Aquarien-Magazin 12/1980, pp. 686 ff.

F.I.: 1980 by FOERSCH and HANRIEDER.

Sex.: So far, only "bearded" ♂♂ have been imported.

Soc. B.: Peaceful.

M: As for all Loricariinae. See *Rineloricaria heteroptera* for details.

B: Unknown.

F: H, O; aufwuchs.

S: Unfortunately, this attractive species has only been imported once (♂♂).

T: 20°–24°C, **L:** 12 cm, **A:** 80 cm, **R:** b, **D:** 2–3

Rineloricaria teffeana
Tefe suckermouth catfish

(STEINDACHNER, 1879)

Syn.: *Loricaria teffeana, L. valenciennesii, L. typus.*

Hab.: South America: Peru, in fast flowing waters. The type locality is the Amazon River at Tefé.

F.I.: Unknown.

Sex.: The ♂'s head is broader. Sexing *R. teffeana* is a difficult task, but only because additional differentiating characteristics are still unknown.

Soc. B.: A peaceful species. Keep in a species tank when attempting to breed them. *R. teffeana* is eminently suitable for community tanks containing small fishes as long as appropriate water conditions are maintained.

M: *R. teffeana* requires hiding places of wood, rocks, bamboo, or plastic tubes (only use the nontoxic gray plastic!), clean oxygen-rich water, and current. When the water is low in oxygen, these animals fasten themselves to the glass pane just below the water surface. If corrective measures are not taken, they soon perish. At least one meal per day must be given during the evening to guarantee that *R. teffeana* receives sufficient food. Thin, undernourished fish often go undetected because of the armored body. The aquarium can be well-planted, since plants are not bothered. Unfortunately for tank maintenance, not even algae are proficiently eaten. A soft, perhaps sandy, substrate permits the catfish to dig. Water: pH 5.6–7.0; hardness up to 16° dGH; carbonate hardness of 7° dKH.

B: Unknown. Probably similar to *Rineloricaria fallax* (see Vol. 1, p. 498).

F: H, O; plant fare, algae, tablet foods, small live foods, and sunken flakes.

S: Although the black-edged reddish fins are quite appealing to aquarists, these animals are rarely seen in pet stores.

T: 20°–25°C, **L:** 16 cm, **A:** 80 cm, **R:** b, **D:** 3

Rineloricaria morrowi

Rineloricaria teffeana

Rineloricaria teffeana

Sturisomatichthys leightoni ♀

Fam.: Loricariidae
Subfam.: Loricariinae

Sturisomatichthys leightoni ♂ guarding a spawn

Sturisomatichthys leightoni   (REGAN, 1912)

Syn.: *Sturisoma leightoni, Loricaria leightoni, Oxyloricaria leightoni.*

Hab.: South America: Colombia, Rio Magdalena at Honda. In fast-flowing waters.

F.I.: Unknown.

Sex.: The ♂'s first dorsal fin ray as well as its upper and lower caudal fin rays are very elongated. ♂♂ have facial odontodes, whereas ♀♀ do not (see photo).

Soc. B.: Peaceful.

M: Dedicated hiding places are not required. Average water chemistry values.

B: W. FOERSCH has successfully bred this species. It spawns on open surfaces, never in secluded locals. A maximum of 65, 2 mm, yellow-brown eggs are laid by the ♀, but guarded by the ♂.

The eggs darken over time. At 24°C, the young hatch after about one week. Juveniles are dark brown with spotted fins and light stripes along their dorsum. Rear the young with blanched spinach, *Artemia* nauplii, and pieces of tablet food. After 8 months, the young exceed 8 cm in length and are sexually mature.

F: H; aufwuchs, spinach, peas, tablet foods, and sunken flake foods.

S: Unfortunately, this beautiful and interesting species has disappeared from the hobby. When imports are renewed, breeders should do their best to assure that the hobby has a steady source of this lovely fish.

T: 20°–24°C, **L:** 15 cm, **A:** 80 cm, **R:** b, **D:** 2

Malapterurus microstoma
Small electric catfish

POLL & GOSSE, 1969

Syn.: None.

Hab.: Tropical Africa: Zaïre Basin.

F.I.: Unknown.

Sex.: There are no distinguishing external characteristics.

Soc. B.: Solitary, nocturnal, predatory fish. Limit care to one individual, since neither conspecifics nor heterospecifics can be housed with *M. microstoma*.

M: Only suitable for show aquaria with a volume of at least 500 l. Juveniles should not be purchased unless you know beforehand what you will do with the colossal fish it turns into. A zoo might be able to help you. Strong filtration is important because of their large dietary intake.

B: Unknown.

F: C; live foods such as fishes, insects, and worms. Lean meat and commercial foods can be fed. Juveniles also accept flakes and tablets.

S: Although this species does not grow as large as *Malapterurus electricus* (see Vol. 1, p. 500), it can only be appropriately housed in show aquaria. Impulses of up to 450 volts are produced by this catfish as either a defense mechanism or to stun or kill prey. Caution is advised when handling this catfish. Do not startle the fish!

T: 23°–28°C, **L:** 70 cm, **A:** 120 cm, **R:** b, **D:** 3 (S)

Chiloglanis cameronensis

Chiloglanis deckenii, ventral view

Chiloglanis deckenii

PETERS, 1868

Syn.: *Synodontis eurystomus*

Hab.: East Africa: Kenya and Tanzania, usually in fast-flowing waters.

F.I.: Unknown; definitely by 1985 by SEEGERS.

Sex.: Sexually mature ♀♀ are fuller.

Soc. B.: Peaceful, social fish.

M: Provide good filtration, vegetation, and some bogwood. Water: pH 6.0–7.2; hardness up to 15° dGH.

B: Unknown.

F: H, O; algae and aufwuchs as well as flake, live, and frozen foods.

S: Species identification of the pictured animal is not definite. There is still significant taxonomic confusion within this genus.

T: 20°–26°C, **L:** 7 cm, **A:** 60 cm, **R:** m, **D:** 2–3

Chiloglanis cf. neumanni

BOULENGER, 1911

Syn.: None, since it may as yet be an undescribed species.

Hab.: East Africa: Tanzania, mostly in fast-flowing waters.

F.I.: Unknown. However, this form was imported in 1987 by SEEGERS.

Sex.: Adult ♀♀ are fuller.

Soc. B.: Amiable social fish. Even the smallest heterospecific fishes are not molested.

M: Although most *Chiloglanis* species prefer fast-flowing waters, SEEGERS discovered that this species also inhabited almost static waters and even swamps, meaning they are very adaptive fish. However, good filtration and a current are recommended. Bogwood, plants, and a dark substrate should be the basis of the decor. Water: pH 6.0–7.5; hardness to 15° dGH.

B: Not known.

F: H, O; aufwuchs (algae), insect larvae, flake foods, and tablets.

S: Identification of the pictured animal as *C. neumanni* is still unsure, since exact studies are still missing. Certain features of this animal do not correspond to the original description by BOULENGER, namely the shape of the fins (pointed according to BOULENGER, but clearly rounded in this fish) and the coloration.
Not even the number of species within the genus *Chiloglanis* is known. The number fluctuates between 13 (SANDS) and 34 (GOSSE, Checklist of Freshwater Fishes of Africa), whereby the latter probably includes all mentioned "species" without further consideration. However, the existence of additional species beyond those described to date is not out of the realm of possibilities.

T: 20°–26°C, **L:** 5 cm, **A:** 60 cm, **R:** m, **D:** 2–3

Chiloglanis deckenii, Athi River, Kenya

Chiloglanis cf. *neumanni*

Synodontis caudovittatus
White-finned synodontis

BOULENGER, 1901

Syn.: None.

Hab.: Africa: upper Nile, Sudan, and Uganda. Inhabits large bodies of water.

F.I.: Unknown.

Sex.: Unknown.

Soc. B.: Though peaceful, do not house with small fishes, since they could be considered food items.

M: Maintenance is nonproblematic. A dark gravel substrate is best. The vegetation along the back of the tank should be dense, perhaps potted, and composed of tough plants. Water: pH 6.5–7.5; hardness to 18° dGH.

B: Unknown.

F: C, O; primarily worms and insect larvae, but tablets and frozen foods are also accepted in captivity.

T: 21°–24°C, **L:** 25 cm, **A:** 120 cm, **R:** b, m, **D:** 2

Synodontis granulosus
Granular synodontis

BOULENGER, 1900

Syn.: None, but the name is sometimes erroneously written *S. granilosus*.

Hab.: Africa: endemic to Lake Tanganyika. This underwater photograph was taken at Kigoma.

F.I.: 1983 into England.

Sex.: Unknown.

Soc. B.: Peaceful, but generally resides alone in nature.

M: See *Synodontis multipunctatus*.

B: Unknown.

F: O.

S: One of the world's most uncommon catfishes. Rarely encountered in its natural habitat.

T: 22°–26°C, **L:** 27 cm, **A:** 150 cm, **R:** b, m, **D:** 3

Synodontis caudovittatus

Synodontis granulosus in its natural habitat

Synodontis cf. *khartoumensis*   ABU GIDEIRI, 1967

Syn.: None.

Hab.: Africa: White Nile.

F.I.: Has not been imported into central Europe.

Sex.: Unknown.

Soc. B.: Though peaceful, small fishes may be considered prey.

M: No particular demands, but each fish should have at least one hiding place.

B: Unknown.

F: O.

S: The pictured specimen is a 6 cm long juvenile. Since coloration and fin shape may change as the fish matures, species identification is tentative.

T: 23°–26°C, **L:** 30 cm, **A:** 150 cm, **R:** b, m, **D:** 2

Synodontis cf. *koensis*   PELLEGRIN, 1933

Syn.: *Synodontis tourei.*

Hab.: West Africa: Guinea and the Ivory Coast, in the Nzo and Ko Rivers.

F.I.: Unknown.

Sex.: While sexes normally cannot be distinguished, ♀♀ surely have a larger girth during the spawning season.

Soc. B.: Peaceful towards heterospecific tankmates. Conspecifics frequently quarrel.

M: Found over mud substrates in its natural biotope. Of course, mud makes an unsuitable substrate in the aquarium, so another loose medium must be used. Provide good filtration. Plants should be potted. Water: soft to medium-hard (up to 18° dGH); pH 6.5 to 7.2.

B: Has not been bred in captivity.

F: C, O; benthic insect larvae (frozen bloodworms are voraciously eaten) and leftover flake foods. This species has a highly developed ability to locate foodstuffs.

S: While the pictured animal was identified by POLL as being *S. koensis*, its design differs somewhat from others of that species. Furthermore, there are differences in the cephalic armor and nuchal shield morphology between *S.* cf. *koensis* and *S. koensis*, although they seem to be closely related.

T: 22°–25°C, **L:** 15 cm, **A:** 120 cm, **R:** b, **D:** 2

Synodontis cf. khartoumensis

Synodontis cf. koensis

Synodontis macrops
Large-eyed synodontis

GREENWOOD, 1963

Syn.: None.

Hab.: Africa: Uganda, in the upper Nile Basin.

F.I.: Not known.

Sex.: Sexes cannot be distinguished by external characteristics.

Soc. B.: Peaceful, yet housing this fish with fishes less than 3 cm long is inadvisable.

M: As for other *Synodontis* species. Water: pH 6.5–7.5; hardness to 18° dGH.

B: Not known.

F: C, O; insect larvae, flake foods, and tablets.

S: *S. macrops* is incredibly similar to *Synodontis schall*. Their similarities aside, *S. macrops* is lighter colored with small dark dots and a shorter body. These differences are enough to make it a species in its own right.

T: 20°–24°C, **L:** 18 cm, **A:** 120 cm, **R:** b, **D:** 2

Synodontis marmoratus
Marble synodontis

LÖNNBERG, 1895

Syn.: None.

Hab.: Africa: Cameroon.

F.I.: 1988 as *Synodontis schoutedeni*.

Sex.: None known.

Soc. B.: Aggressive fishes are unsuitable tankmates for this peaceful catfish.

M: Needs at least one corner of fine sand to root in and subdued illumination. Floating plants can fulfill the latter condition. Water should be soft, slightly acid, and filtered over peat. Moderate filtration.

B: Has not been successfully accomplished.

F: C, O; small foods of animal origin: mosquito larvae, *Daphnia*, and *Artemia* (even frozen). Flake foods.

S: This is one of the smallest *Synodontis*.

T: 22°–25°C, **L:** 6 cm, **A:** 70 cm, **R:** b, m, **D:** 2–3

Synodontis macrops

Synodontis marmoratus

Synodontis nigromaculatus
Leopard synodontis

BOULENGER, 1905

Syn.: *Synodontis colyeri, S. melanostictus.* Often confused with *S. zambesensis.*

Hab.: Africa: found in many southern tributaries of the Zaïre River, Lake Tanganyika and its tributaries, the Okavango and Limpopo Rivers, and all of the upper Zambezi Basin.

F.I.: Unknown; surely it has been frequently imported but under incorrect nomenclature.

Sex.: Unknown.

Soc. B.: Predominately peaceful, twilight-active fish. As for many *Synodontis*, this fish is slightly territorial, so be sure to include hiding places in the decor. Do not associate with small fishes.

M: The aquarium should not be cramped. Vegetation can be included, but the plants should be well-rooted before *S. nigromaculatus* is introduced into the tank. Clear, oxygen-rich, well-filtered water is a necessity. Water: pH 6.0–7.5; hardness up to 20° dGH.

B: Unknown. Is it possible it has been bred in captivity, but under a different name? Hiding places large enough for two animal should be offered.

F: C, O; any food suitable to its size. Chiefly live foods should be fed when trying to ripen the animals.

S: Its broad distribution undoubtedly allows for variations in design. In comparison to the pictured animal which is a juvenile, adults have a slightly less pronounced design (smaller dots) and a longer dorsal fin spine (slightly larger than the body height).

T: 22°–26°C, **L:** 40 cm, **A:** 120 cm, **R:** b, **D:** 2

Synodontis obesus
Obese synodontis

BOULENGER, 1898

Syn.: *Synodontis hollyi, S. loppei.*

Hab.: Africa: western Africa, coastal waters of the Gulf of Guinea.

F.I.: Unknown.

Sex.: Unknown.

Soc. B.: Like many *Synodontis*, somewhat territorial. Twilight-active.

M: Twilight- and night-active fish. They have been known to eat very small fishes on occasion. Sometimes quarrelsome towards other territorial fishes, predominately congeners. Numerous hiding places will curb aggressions. Fast-rooting plants can be used. Water: pH 6.0–7.5; hardness of 25° dGH or less. This species can probably tolerate low salinities.

B: Not known.

F: C, O; though an omnivore, a certain proportion of live foods is required; nevertheless, it can be maintained on flake and tablet foods awhile.

S: The contrasting coloration fades slightly as the fish ages.

T: 24°–28°C, **L:** 40 cm, **A:** 120 cm, **R:** b, **D:** 2

Synodontis nigromaculatus, Zaïre, Shaba

Synodontis obesus

Synodontis petricola
Even-spotted synodontis

MATTHES, 1959

Syn.: *Synodontis multimaculatus.*

Hab.: Africa: endemic to the northern sector of Lake Tanganyika. This photo was taken at Kigoma.

F.I.: Ca. 1975.

Sex.: Unknown.

Soc. B.: Although this species is expressly peaceful, only associate with larger species. Very small fishes may be considered prey. An appropriate addition to a Lake Tanganyika cichlid aquaria.

M: See Vol. 2, p. 546.

B: Like cuckoos, these fish introduce their eggs into the clutch of other species (mouthbrooding cichlids) which unwittingly assume responsibility for them.

F: C, O; an omnivore that prefers live foods.

S: *S. petricola* is similar to *S. multipunctatus* and *S. polli* (**Syn.**: *S. eurystomus*). *S. petricola* is presented again in this volume because of this rare photo taken in its natural biotope.

T: 22°–25°C, **L**: 11 cm, **A**: 100 cm, **R**: b, m, **D**: 2

Synodontis polli
Poll's upside-down catfish

GOSSE, 1982

Syn.: *Synodontis eurystoma, S. eurystomus.*

Hab.: Africa: endemic to Lake Tanganyika.

F.I.: Unknown; it probably has not been imported into Germany. Imported into England ca. 1986.

Sex.: Unknown.

Soc. B.: Peaceful, but likes its solitude.

M: See *Synodontis multipunctatus.*

B: Unknown; probably like cuckoos, introducing their eggs into the clutch of other species which unwittingly brood them.

F: O.

S: Previously known as *S. eurystomus.* The new name, *S. polli,* was assigned when it was discovered that *S. eurystomus* was used in a description by MATTHES, 1959. Hence, *S. eurystomus* was a homonym and, as dictated by nomenclature rules, required a *"nomen novum"* (new name).

T: 22°–26°C, **L**: 15 cm, **A**: 120 cm, **R**: b, m, **D**: 3

Synodontis petricola in its natural biotope at Kigoma

Synodontis polli

Synodontis polli in its natural biotope at Karilani

Synodontis multipunctatus in its natural biotope at Kigoma

Synodontis soloni
Scissortail synodontis

BOULENGER, 1899

Syn.: None.

Hab.: Africa: the Zaïre Basin, in Stanley Pool and rapids of Libenge.

F.I.: To Great Britain in 1975.

Sex.: Unknown.

Soc. B.: Solitary abiding animals; do not house with small fishes.

M: Clear, slightly acid water.

B: Unknown.

F: C, O; small live foods such as *Daphnia* and *Tubifex* are readily accepted.

S: None.

T: 23°–25°C, L: 16 cm, A: 120 cm, R: b, D: 3

Synodontis rebeli
Cameroon synodontis

HOLLY, 1926

Syn.: *Synodontis hollyi*, *S. "velifer"*.

Hab.: Africa: Cameroon, in the Sanaga River.

F.I.: Unknown.

Sex.: There are no external distinguishing characteristics. At spawning time, the ♂'s genital papilla protrudes. ♀♀ are stouter.

Soc. B.: Though generally peaceful, small fishes may be eaten. Associate with fishes at least $1/2$ its length.

M: Needs a large, well-filtered tank, a large cave, a dark substrate, and peat-filtered water. Water: pH 6.2–7.5; hardness up to 20° dGH. At least one corner should have a sand substrate to allow the fish to root.

B: Not known.

F: C, O; insect larvae, earthworms, and large frozen foods. Large flakes and tablets are readily accepted.

S: *S. rebeli* is easily confused with *Synodontis velifer*. However, the latter has larger spots on the body and, as adults, a dorsal fin that is mare than 2x the height of *S. rebeli*'s dorsal fin.

T: 22°–25°C, **L:** 27 cm, **A:** 150 cm, **R:** b, m, **D:** 2–3

Synodontis waterloti
Waterlot's synodontis

DAGET, 1962

Syn.: None.

Hab.: Africa: Ghana, Ivory Coast, Liberia, Sierra Leone.

F.I.: Not known.

Sex.: Have not been described.

Soc. B.: Overall, this is a peaceful species. But once it has attained a respectable size, small fishes might "accidentally" be consumed.

M: A contrasting design appears on animals housed in tanks having light-colored substrates. Though dark substrates are more appropriate, the animals turn a dull black-brown, making them less appealing to aquarists. Strong filtration is necessary. Create caves within rock and root edifications. Water: pH 6.8–7.8; hardness up to 20° dGH.

B: Not known.

F: C, O; flake foods, frozen mosquito larvae, large live foods, and earthworms.

S: The heavily serrated pectoral fin rays are a good distinguishing characteristic for this species.

T: 22°–25°C, **L:** 18 cm, **A:** 150 cm, **R:** b, **D:** 2–3

Synodontis rebeli

Synodontis waterloti

Pangasius pangasius   (HAMILTON, 1822)
Black-finned shark

Syn.: *Pimelodus pangasius.*

Hab.: Asia: from Pakistan through India, Bangladesh, Burma, Thailand, Malaysia, and Vietnam to Indonesia.

F.I.: Unknown.

Sex.: Unknown.

Soc. B.: Despite its size, this is a relatively peaceful catfish, yet it often panics in cramped quarters. Diurnal.

M: Good filtration and aeration and a very large aquarium are requisites for successful care. Plants should be waived. Hiding places are not necessary. Water: pH 6–7.5; hardness up to 25° dGH.

B: Not known.

F: O; everything from small fishes to plants, fruits, and worms. Predator!

S: A commonly eaten food fish in its native land. Only juveniles are imported.

T: 23°–28°C, **L:** 130 (70) cm, **A:** 300 cm, **R:** m, **D:** 4 (S!)

Fam.: Pimelodidae
Subfam.: Pimelodinae

Brachyrhamdia marthae
Blue imitator catfish

SANDS & BLACK, 1985

Syn.: None; however, it has not been definitely decided if *Brachyrhamdia* is a genus or subgenus. If the latter is the case, then this fish's name would be *Pimelodella marthae*.

Hab.: South America: Peru. The exact habitat is unknown. The species description is based on imported specimens.

F.I.: Unknown; surely it has been repeatedly imported.

Sex.: Not known.

Soc. B.: Territorial towards congeners and other related species. Usually peaceful towards heterogeners. Only very small fishes are eaten. Their territorial behavior can be countered by keeping at least 6 specimens (aggressions are then diluted) and providing numerous hiding places using roots as territorial boundaries.

M· House in moderate-sized aquaria. Include plenty of vegetation and hiding

places in the decor. Water: pH 6–7; hardness up to 15° dGH.

B: Not known.

F: C, O; voracious omnivores. Live or frozen foods are occasionally required.

S: SANDS discovered that *B. marthae* is mainly imported with shipments of *Corydoras pygmaeus*. Juvenile *B. marthae* and *C. pygmaeus* are very similar exteriorly. But the exaggerated size difference between these two species precludes it from the degree of success *Brachyrhamdia imitator* has achieved in its "mimicry" (see Vol. 2, p. 552).
B. marthae mainly differs from *B. meesi*, a similar species, by its lack of a "mask," the clear blue sheen on its body, and the dorsal spot, which is limited to the upper anterior part of the dorsal fin in *B. meesi*.

T: 24°–26°C, **L:** 9 cm, **A:** 80 cm, **R:** b, **D:** 2

Brachyrhamdia meesi
Mees' pimelodid

Syn.: None; however it has not yet been determined if *Brachyrhamdia* is a genus or subgenus. If the latter is the case, then this fish's name would be *Pimelodella meesi*.

Hab.: According to information given by the original describer, this catfish was first noticed in a shipment of aquarium fishes that came from Belem at the mouth of the Amazon. However, as has been repeatedly determined, such a habitat description is dubious, since Belem is an export station. Fishes supposedly caught at Belem are often collected in more remote locals and shipped there. Little information can be extracted from the fact that this species has been imported together with *Pimelodella lateristriga* because exporters are apt to combine their catches, especially similar looking fishes.

F.I.: 1985 by GLASER, Frankfurt. Probably imported earlier, just not properly identified.

T: 24°–26°C, **L:** 8 cm, **A:** 60 cm, **R:** b, **D:** 2

SANDS & BLACK, 1985
Subfam.: Pimelodinae

Sex.: Not known.

Soc. B.: Like *B. marthae* (previous page).

M: As for *B. marthae*.

B: Not known.

F: C, O; large live foods are particular favorites, but tablets and leftover flake foods are also accepted.

S: See *B. marthae* for species differences.

The probability that this species mimics *Pimelodella lateristriga* is small despite SANDS' suspicions. Unlike *B. imitator* (see Vol. 2, p. 552), there does not seem to be an advantage to mimicry in this case. As mentioned above, simultaneous imports can be coincidental. Behavioral studies have apparently not been made in its natural habitat. This is a prime example of the problems encountered in making first descriptions from aquarium imports and why they should be limited to exceptional cases (when the habitat can be indisputably determined).

Duopalatinus malarmo
Malarmo catfish

Syn.: *Platysilurus malarmo.*

Hab.: South America: Venezuela, in the Rio Negro and the area around Maracaibo.

F.I.: 1988.

Sex.: Unknown.

Soc. B.: Peaceful towards equal-sized conspecifics and heterospecifics. Significantly smaller fishes (less than $1/3$ of its body length), however, are considered food. Primarily twilight- and night-active.

M: Only large tanks with several spacious hiding places (e.g., bogwood) are appropriate. The substrate in its captive environment should be of sand, reflecting that found in its natural biotope. Even delicate plants are left unharmed. Long-leaved plants provide hiding places,

(SCHULTZ, 1944)
Subfam.: Sorubiminae

contributing to this catfish's well-being. Water: pH 6–7; hardness up to 20° dGH.

B: Unknown.

F: C; mainly live fishes, but large live foods such as earthworms, wax moth larvae, and meal worms are also accepted.

S: *D. malarmo* has a very distinctive pair of maxillary barbels. They are up to 2x the length of the body and generally held posteriorly. Surely their extreme length is an adaptation to its biotope and lifestyle—lurking in profound holes for prey.

T: 24°–28°C, **L:** 65 (40) cm, **A:** 150 cm, **R:** m, b, **D:** 2–3

Brachyrhamdia meesi

Duopalatinus malarmo

Imparfinis longicauda
Long-tail antenna catfish

(BOULENGER, 1887)

Syn.: *Pimelodus longicauda, Rhamdia longicauda, Nannorhamdia longicauda, Imparfinis longicaudus.*

Hab.: South America: Ecuador and Peru, in the upper Amazon and its tributaries.

F.I.: Unknown.

Sex.: Unknown.

Soc. B.: This is a relatively peaceful twilight- and night-active catfish.

M: Hiding places must be included in the decor. The water should be well-filtered, slightly acid (pH 6–7), and moderately hard (to 10° dGH).

B: Unknown.

F: C, O; all kinds of small live foods. Flakes and tablets are occasionally accepted.

T: 20°–24°C, **L:** 15 cm, **A:** 80 cm, **R:** b, **D:** 2

S: BORODIN described another member of this genus as *I. longicauda* in 1927. Since the same name cannot be used twice within the same genus, the more recent name is a homonym and must be replaced with a new name (*nomen novum*). G. F. MEES, a Dutch scientist, is presently engaged in this task. MEES' report confirms the preliminary classification by SAUL 1975, which placed this species into the genus *Imparfinis*.

Imparfinis minutus

(LÜTKEN, 1874)

Syn.: *Cetopsorhamdia hasemani, C. pijpersi, Imparfinis hasemani, Rhamdella minuta, Rhamdia minuta.*

Hab.: South America: western Brazil and the Guianas.

F.I.: Unknown.

Sex.: Unknown.

Soc. B.: Peaceful towards conspecifics as long as they are not overly small. Territorial in front of congeners. However, if a small school is maintained, aggressions are not as pronounced. Primarily twilight- and night-active.

M: Moderate-sized aquarium containing plants, bogwood and rock edifications, and hiding places, which are primarily used during the day. Because it lives in rapids in its natural habitat, good filtration and aeration are mandatory. Water: pH 6.0–7.0 (slightly acid); hardness of 15° dGH or less.

B: Not known.

F: C, O; live and flake foods commiserate to its size. This voracious fish can be acclimated to substitute foods relatively easily.

T: 24°–28°C, **L:** 12 cm, **A:** 80 cm, **R:** b, **D:** 2

Imparfinis longicauda

Imparfinis minutus

Microglanis parahybae (STEINDACHNER, 1880)

Syn.: *Pseudopimelodus parahybae, P. charus, P. cottoides, Batrachoglanis parahybae, Microglanis cottoides.*

Hab.: South America: southeast Brazil, Argentina, Paraguay, and probably Uruguay.

F.I.: 1926.

Sex.: Have not been described.

Soc. B.: Nocturnal and predatory. Do not house with small characins.

M: A sandy substrate is best because of *M. parahybae*'s penchant to bury itself. Undemanding. Water: pH 6.2–7.8 (7.0); hardness up to 25° (12°) dGH. Provide hiding places among bogwood.

B: Has not been bred in captivity.

F: C, O; tablet, flake, and frozen foods as well as mosquito larvae and *Gammarus.*

S: None.

T: 21°–26°C, **L:** 9 cm, **A:** 70 cm, **R:** b, **D:** 1–2

Pimelodella rambarrani
Masked imitator catfish

AXELROD & BURGESS, 1987

Syn.: *Brachyrhamdia rambarrani* (this name has to be considered a synonym until it has been established whether *Brachyrhamdia* is a subgenus of *Pimelodella* or a genus).

Hab.: South America: Brazil, in the Rio Unini, a tributary of the Rio Negro.

F.I.: To England in 1987. Into Germany in 1988 by HIERONIMUS.

Sex.: ♀♀ are fuller through the ventral area.

Soc. B.: Peaceful towards heterofamilials. Territorial towards conspecifics and other catfishes of similar stature and design. If the tank lacks hiding places, fatal confrontations may ensue.

M: Planted medium-sized aquarium with good filtration and aeration. Perform regular water exchanges and provide sufficient secluded areas among roots. Water: pH 5.5–7.0; hardness up to 15° dGH.

B: Unknown; it is surely difficult to acquire sufficient animals to attempt breeding since, to date, only single specimens have been found mixed among imported *Corydoras davidsandsi* (see **S**). Lack of specimens aside, endeavors to breed these animals are probably most likely to succeed if the attempt is made to breed them in the presence of *C. davidsandsi*, as British aquarists have shown with *Brachyrhamdia imitator* and *Corydoras melanistius melanistius.*

F: C, O; leftovers, TetraTips, FD foods, and frozen mosquito larvae.

S: Not only does this species live within groups of *Corydoras davidsandsi* BLACK, 1987, albeit in small numbers, it has an almost identical design.

T: 24°–26°C, **L:** 7 cm, **A:** 80 cm, **R:** b, **D:** 2

Microglanis parahybae

Pimelodella rambarrani

Pinirampus pirinampu
Long-finned catfish

(SPIX, 1829)

Syn.: *Pimelodus pirinampu, Pirinampus typus, Pinirampus typus.*

Hab.: South America: from Paraguay through the Tocantins region to Venezuela.

F.I.: Unknown.

Sex.: Unknown.

Soc. B.: This night- and twilight-active predator is territorial towards conspecifics and similar fishes. It should only be associated with very large tankmates.

M: Only large aquaria with stable rock or root edifications are appropriate. Limit vegetation to very robust specimens. The filter must be capable of handling the high nitrogenous load these animals produce. Water: pH 6–8; hardness up to 25° dGH.

B: Unknown.

F: C; live foods. Young animals accept insect larvae, while older specimens need coarser foods such as earthworms. Tablets are occasionally consumed.

S: The long-finned catfish has only been included in this text to warn prospective buyers, since it grows too large and is not attractive enough to be of interest to normal aquarists.

T: 22°–28°C, **L:** 120 (50) cm, **A:** 200 cm, **R:** b, **D:** 4 (S!)

Rhamdia laticauda laticauda

(HECKEL, 1858)

Syn.: *Pimelodus brachypterus, P. hypselurus, P. laticaudus, P. motaguensis.*

Hab.: South and Central America.

F.I.: 1984 by K. and M. K. MEYER.

Sex.: Not one species of the genus *Rhamdia* has secondary sexual characteristics.

Soc. B.: Relatively shy, enduring "benthic" fish. Peaceful.

M: Needs hiding places, a dark substrate, floating plants to diminish light penetration, and an open area for swimming. The water in its natural habitat has a pH of 7.5 and a hardness of 14° dGH.

B: Unknown

F: O; live foods, FD Menu, and flake and tablet foods.

S: *Rhamdia laticauda typhla* GREENFIELD, GREENS & WOODS, 1982 has also been described.

T: 24°–28°C, **L:** 12 cm, **A:** 100 cm, **R:** b, **D:** 1

Pinirampus pirinampu

Rhamdia laticauda laticauda

Schilbe marmoratus
African shoulder-spot catfish

BOULENGER, 1911

Syn.: None.

Hab.: Africa: Zaïre, in large bodies of water.

F.I.: Unknown.

Sex.: Mature ♀♀ are much fuller than ♂♂.

Soc. B.: This active diurnal fish is peaceful towards all fishes except those that are significantly smaller.

M: Large aquarium with sufficient free swimming space and vegetation around the edges. Hiding places are not needed, but shelter among roots or rocks is occasionally sought. Water must be well-filtered, aerated, and regularly exchanged. Water: pH 6.0–7.5; hardness up to 20° dGH.

B: Not known.

F: C, O; all foods that can be swallowed, including small fishes. Flake foods will be eaten for extended periods of time.

S: Rare, coincidentally imported species.

T: 24°–26°C, **L:** 15 cm, perhaps longer, **A:** 100 cm, **R:** m, **D:** 2–3

Fam.: Siluridae
Subfam.: Silurinae

Silurus glanis
Wels

LINNAEUS, 1758

Syn.: None.

Hab.: Europe: from the upper Rhine to Lake Aral in Russia. Not found in England or Italy.

F.I.: Native to Europe.

Sex.: ♀♀ are fuller through the ventral area during the spawning season.

Soc. B.: Juveniles live in schools. Its gregariousness changes into a predacious solitary nature as it ages. Only suitable for large show aquaria. Limit tankmates to fishes larger than itself.

M: Species tank with hiding places (large caves), subdued illumination, and a few potted robust plants is best. Nocturnal. At twilight, this fish becomes restless and begins its quest for food. A light dimmer allows better observation. Other than a large filter, there are no special water quality demands.

B: Spawns from May to June, but apparently only in large rivers and lakes. Sexual maturity is reached two to three years of age; at that time the fish weighs 1–2 kg. The ♂ guards the nest (depression) and the spawn.

F: C; all types of animal based foods. Tablets and trout/carp pellets are accepted by juveniles. Fishes, particularly cyprinids, are also readily consumed. Animals kept in ponds do not feed during the winter.

S: This long-lived species (up to 80 years) happens to be the largest European fish. Considered to be good tasting, 10,000 tons are captured and consumed each year in Russia!

T: 4°–20°C (coldwater fish), **L.** said to reach 2.5 m usually up to 1 m, **A:** 200 cm, **R:** b, **D:** 4 (S)

Conta conta　　　　　　　　　　　　　　　(HAMILTON, 1822)

Syn.: *Pimelodus conta, Hara filamentosa, Hara conta.*

Hab.: Asia: India, north Bengal and Assam; Bangladesh.

F.I.: Unknown.

Sex.: The photos on the facing page clearly show the ♂'s elongated caudal fin ray and the difference in coloration between ♂♂ and ♀♀—the ♂ is dark brown with light brown mottling, while the ♀ is a solid clay color.

Soc. B.: This is a peaceful, nocturnal schooling fish.

M: Can be maintained in small, heavily vegetated aquaria. Include hiding places. Water: pH 6.0–7.5; hardness up to 20° dGH.

B: Unknown.

F: O; small live foods and flake foods.

T: 18°–28°C, **L:** 12 cm, **A:** 60 cm, **R:** b, **D:** 2

Silurus glanis, yellow morph bred in Poland

Conta conta ♂

Conta conta ♀

Gagata cenia   (HAMILTON, 1822)

Syn.: *Pimelodus cenia.*

Hab.: Asia: Pakistan, northern India, Bangladesh, Burma, and Nepal. The pictured animal was captured in Assam.

F.l.: Ca. 1985.

Sex.: Unknown.

Soc. B.: Peaceful, lively, diurnal catfish. Keep at least 6 specimens.

M: *G. cenia* requires good filtration and aeration, a smooth-edged substrate, and plenty of swimming space. Plants are left undisturbed, but mulm may be whirled up as it searches for food. Hiding places are only occasionally sought. Water: pH 6.0–7.2; hardness up to 15° dGH.

B: Not known.

F: C; all types of live and frozen foods. In nature, these fish primarily feed on insects floating on the water surface.

S: According to SANDS, some specimens may reach a length of 30 cm (ca. 12 in.). However, a maximum length of 12 cm seems more realistic, since HAMILTON reports a maximum length of ca. 8 cm (3 in.). Perhaps we are dealing with a communication problem. The latter measurement will probably not be surpassed in the aquarium.
Unlike this species, all of *G. gagata*'s fins with the exception of the caudal fin have black tips.

T: 20°–24°C, **L:** 8 (12 cm), **A:** 80 cm, **R:** b, m, **D:** 2–3

Glyptosternum reticulatum   McCLELLAND, 1842

Syn.: *Glyptosternum stoliczkae.*

Hab.: Asia: northwestern Indian states, Afghanistan, Pakistan, China, and the southern republics of the former Soviet Union.

F.l.: Unknown.

Sex.: Unknown.

Soc. B.: Peaceful towards heterospecifics. Slight territorial behavior may be displayed towards conspecifics.

M: Needs a large, unheated aquarium with strong filtration and illumination. The aquarium should have plants especially chosen to tolerate the low temperatures that will reign in the tank. Water: pH around 7; hardness up to 20° dGH.

B: Unknown.

F: O; flake foods and FD tablets will probably be accepted.

S: In contrast to its relatives in the genus *Glyptothorax*, *Glyptosternum* species do not have a suckermouth.
Species identification using this photo is not unequivocal, since the anal fin cannot be clearly seen. JAYARAM indicates that *G. reticulatum* has a membrane connecting the anal and caudal fins.

T: 12°–24°C, **L:** 15 cm, **A:** 100 cm, **R:** b, **D:** 3

Gagata cenia from Assam

Glyptosternum reticulatum

Glyptothorax platypogon
Brown hillstream catfish

(VALENCIENNES, 1840)

Syn.: *Pimelodus platypogon, P. cyano-chlorus, Glyptosternum platypogon, G. kükenthali.*

Hab.: Asia: Java, Sumatra, Borneo, Malaysia.

F.I.: Unknown.

Sex.: Unknown.

Soc. B.: This peaceful catfish neither disturbs plants nor other fishes.

M: Because *G. platypogon* inhabits mountain creeks in its natural habitat, a good filtration system complete with aeration must be provided and high temperatures will have to be avoided. A moderate-sized aquarium is sufficient. Water: pH 6.0–7.0; hardness up to 15° dGH.

B: Unknown.

F: O; small live foods, algae, and flake foods.

T: 18°–22°C, **L:** 10 cm, **A:** 80 cm, **R:** m, b, **D:** 2–3

Glyptothorax trilineatus
Three-striped hillstream catfish

BLYTH, 1860

Syn.: *Glyptothorax laosensis.*

Hab.: Asia: Thailand, Burma, northern India, eastern Himalayas, Pakistan, Bangladesh.

F.I.: Unknown.

Sex.: Unknown.

Soc. B.: Though little is known, it is probably a peaceful, diurnal catfish. Cover is occasionally sought.

M: House in large, well-filtered, oxygen-rich aquaria. Specimens imported to date have proven to be very sensitive to high temperatures, so keep the water cool. Little free swimming space is needed. Water: pH 6.0–7.2; hardness up to 10° dGH.

B: Not known.

F: O; unfortunately, more exact information is not available. Probably an omnivore that also feeds on aufwuchs. Try good flake foods.

S: These catfish are rarely imported because their delicacy in front of elevated temperatures makes them difficult to transport.

T: 10°–20°C, **L:** 30 cm, usually smaller, **A:** 100 cm, **R:** b, **D:** 4 (T)

Glyptothorax platypogon

Glyptothorax trilineatus

Hara hara   (HAMILTON, 1822)

Syn.: *Pimelodus hara.*

Hab.: Asia: in the northern and north-eastern Indian states. Also found in Nepal and Bangladesh.

F.I.: Unknown.

Sex.: Unknown.

Soc. B.: Peaceful, nocturnal schooling fish. Hiding places are sought during the day. Its behavior is similar to that of South American armored catfishes.

M: *H. hara*'s captive environment must be well-filtered and aerated, heavily planted, and riddled with hiding places. Water: pH 6.0–7.5; hardness up to 20° dGH. Its temperature requirement varies according to origin.

B: Unknown.

F: O; primarily small live foods, but flake foods can occasionally be offered.

T: 12°–28°C (depending on origin), **L:** 7 cm, **A:** 60 cm, **R:** b, **D:** 2–3

Fam.: Trichomycteridae
Subfam.: Pygidiinae

Bullockia maldonadoi
Chilenian parasitic catfish

(EIGENMANN, 1927)

Syn.: *Hatcheria maldonadoi.*

Hab.: South America: in the Pacific Andean rivers of central Chile.

F.I.: Unknown.

Sex.: Unknown.

Soc. B.: Peaceful inhabitant of the lower water strata. When danger threatens, it may bury itself in the substrate.

M: Small, temperate, well-planted tanks with a fine-grained substrate and a few hiding places make appropriate habitats for these animals. Do not house with significantly larger fishes. Good filtration is recommended, but current is not appreciated. *B. maldonadoi* can be maintained in unheated aquaria. Water: pH 6–7; hardness up to 15° dGH.

B: Unknown.

F: O; detritus (mulm) is readily searched. Best to alternate small live foods and flake foods.

S: In the course of her ecological study, Gloria ARRATIA discovered that both juveniles and adults prefer shallow standing water zones of large rivers and bodies of water.

T: 16°–26°C, **L:** 5 cm, **A:** 60 cm, **R:** b, **D:** 2–3

Pygidium cf. *stellatum*

EIGENMANN, 1918

Syn.: None.

Hab.: South America: Brazil, Puerto Barrios.

F.I.: Not exactly known.

Sex.: Unknown.

Soc. B.: Peaceful, small catfish that generally remains hidden in the sandy substrate during the day, they are therefore frequently overlooked.

M: Even the smallest aquaria are appropriate. Substrate should be of fine sand. Plants are left unharmed. Limit *P.* cf. *stellatum*'s tankmates to other small, peaceful fishes. Water: pH 6.0–7.5; hardness below 20° dGH.

B: Unknown.

F: C, O; the tiniest live and flake foods.

S: This species is very difficult to identify without exact information on its origin, since over 30, often very similar looking species have been described.

T: 22°–24°C, **L:** 4 cm, **A:** 40 cm, **R:** b, **D:** 2–3

Aphyosemion [Diapteron] georgiae, see page 496

Order: Cyprinodontiformes

Order: Cyprinodontiformes   BERG, 1940

The scheme is based on PARENTI (1981) and NELSON (1984) as well as our own classifications. The number of species in each taxon is indicated in parenthesis.

FAMILY:
  Subfamily:
    Genera:

ADRIANICHTHYIDAE   WEBER, 1913 (3)
  Adrianichthys   WEBER, 1913 (1)
  Xenopoecilus   REGAN, 1911 (2)

HORAICHTHYIDAE   KULKARNI, 1940 (1)
  Horaichthys   KULKARNI, 1940 (1)

ORYZIIDAE (=ORYZIATIDAE ROSEN, 1964)(11)
  Oryzias JORDAN & SNYDER, 1906 (11)

APLOCHEILICHTHYIDAE   (66)
  Aplocheilichthyinae MYERS, 1928 (65)
    Aplocheilichthys BLEEKER, 1863 (43)
    Congopanchax POLL, 1971 (2)
    Hylopanchax POLL & LAMBERT, 1965(1)
    Hypsopanchax MYERS, 1924 (6)
    Laciris HUBER, 1981 (1)
    Lamprichthys REGAN, 1911 (1)
    Pantanodon MYERS, 1955 (2)
    Plataplochilus AHL, 1928 (6)
    Procatopus BOULENGER, 1904 (3)
  Fluviphylacinae ROBERTS, 1970 (1)
    Fluviphylax WHITLEY, 1965 (1)

POECILIIDAE   GARMAN, 1895 (164)
see page 582

CYPRINODONTIDAE   GILL, 1865 (100+
        5 to 43 *Orestias*)

Aphaniinae SCHEEL, 1968 (12)
  Aphanius NARDO, 1827 (12)
Cyprinodontinae GILL, 1865 (35)
  Cualac MILLER, 1956 (1)
  Cyprinodon LACÉPÈDE, 1803 (29)
  Floridichthys HUBBS, 1926 (2)
  Garmanella HUBBS, 1936 (1)
  Jordanella GOODE & BEAN, 1879 (1)
  Megupsilon MILLER & WALTERS, 1972(1)
Fundulinae JORDAN & GILBERT, 1882(42)
  Adinia GIRARD, 1859 (1)
  Chriopeoides FOWLER, 1939 (1)
  Cubanichthys HUBBS, 1926 (1)
  Fundulus LACÉPÈDE, 1803 (35)
  Leptolucania MYERS, 1924 (1)
  Lucania GIRARD, 1859 (3)
Valenciinae (2)
  Valencia MYERS, 1928 (2)
Profundulinae, (5)
  Profundulus HUBBS, 1924 (5)

Orestiinae GILL, 1893 (5 to 43)
  Orestias VALENCIENNES, 1839 (5–43)
Empetrichthyinae JORDAN, EVERMANN
             & CLARK, 1930 (4)
  Crenichthys HUBBS, 1932 (2)
  Empetrichthys GILBERT, 1893 (2)

GOODEIDAE   JORDAN, 1923 (35)
see page 582

APLOCHEILIDAE   BLEEKER, 1860, (308)
  Aplocheilinae   (182)
    Adamas HUBER, 1979 (1)
    Aphyoplatys CLAUSEN, 1976 (1)
    Aphyosemion MYERS, 1924 (102)
    Aplocheilus McCLELLAND, 1839 (4)
    Diapteron HUBER & SEEGERS, 1977 (5)
    Epiplatys GILL, 1862 (32)
    Foerschichthys SCHELL & ROMAND,
               1981 (1)
    Fundulosoma AHL, 1924 (1)
    Nothobranchius PETERS, 1868 (31)
    Pachypanchax MYERS, 1933 (2–3)
    Paranothobranchius SEEGERS,1985(1)
    Pronothobranchius RADDA, 1969 (1)
  Rivulinae HOEDEMANN, 1962 (new
               usage) (126)
    Austrofundulus MYERS, 1932 (2)
    Campellolebias VAZ-FERREIRA &
      SIERRA, 1974 (3) (= *Cynopoecilus*?)
    Cynolebias STEINDACHNER, 1876 (28)
    Cynopoecilus REGAN, 1912 (9)
    Neofundulus MYERS, 1924 (4)
    Pterolebias GARMAN, 1895 (8)
    Rachovia MYERS, 1927 (5)
    Rivulus POEY, 1860 (62)
    Terranatos TAPHORN & THOMERSON,
        1978 (1) (= *Cynolebias*?)
    Trigonectes MYERS, 1925 (4)

ANABLEPIDAE   GARMAN, 1895 (5)
  Anablepinae GARMAN, 1895 (3)
    Anableps (GRONOW) SCOPOLI, 1777(3)
  Jenynsiinae GÜNTHER, 1866 (1)
    Jenynsia GÜNTHER, 1866 (1)
  Oxyzygonectinae PARENTI, 1981 (1)
    Oxyzygonectes FOWLER, 1916 (1)

Fam.: Anablepidae
Subfam.: Oxyzygonectinae

Oxyzygonectes dovii ♂

Oxyzygonectes dovii ♀

Oxyzygonectes dovii   (GÜNTHER, 1866)

Syn.: *Haplochilus dovii, Zygonectes dovii, Fundulus dovii, Aplocheilus dovii, Oxyzygonectes dowi.*

Hab.: Central America: Pacific Coast of Panama and Costa Rica, possibly further north as well. From the sea to freshwater, but preferably brackish water lagoons.

F.I.: 1979 by D. FROMM from Golfito, Costa Rica, to the United States. Exported from the United States in 1983 by G. ZURLO to Germany.

Sex.: See photos. ♂♂ are yellow-brown, turning lighter ventrally, and have more elongated yellowish fins. ♀♀ are fuller through the ventral area and have small, rounded, transparent fins.

Soc. B.: Peaceful and somewhat shy. Can be housed with equal-sized fishes that tolerate salt in the water. In nature, these fish swim in large schools; this behavior is not exhibited in captivity.

M: According to FROMM (J. AKA, **15** (5); 201–210, 1982) and ZURLO (DATZ, **38** (12): 547– 550, 1985), caring for this species is unproblematic as long as it is kept in a very large tank and salt is added to the water. Cover the tank well, since the animals jump.

B: Refer to the above mentioned articles by FROMM and ZURLO. FROMM is the most explicit. He bred the fish at 24°–29.5°C. Typical for killifishes, *O. dovii* spawned on an artificial fiber mop. A ♀ with a total length of 17 cm released 41 eggs in one day. The young were easily reared on *Artemia* nauplii.

F: C; live foods and all kinds of commercial diets.

S: The systematics of this species is controversial. While numerous authors place this monotypic genus into the subfamily Fundulinae, PARENTI considers it more closely related to *Anableps* species.

T: 22°–28°C, **L:** 15–35 cm, **A:** 200 cm, **R:** t, m, **D:** 2–3

Fam.: Poeciliidae
Subfam.: Aplocheilichthyinae

Aplocheilichthys camerunensis RADDA, 1971
Cameroon lampeye

Syn.: None.

Hab.: West Africa: southern Cameroon and northern Gabon, in creeks and rivers of the rain forests of the inland plateau.

F.I.: 1971 by RADDA and fellow travelers.

Sex.: The ♂'s fins, most notably the dorsal fin, are yellowish, whereas its flanks are metallic blue. ♀♀ have a transparent and rounded, not elongated, dorsal and anal fins and an anteriorly fuller body.

Soc. B.: Peaceful but shy schooling fish.

M: Not an easy fish to care for, since it demands exceptional water quality. Very

soft, slightly acid water is best. Despite its small size, the aquarium must be comparatively large with many plants, including floating species. Do not illuminate the tank excessively.

B: Difficult. Though the animals spawn on plants such as Java moss or filters or similar items, they prefer a wool mop. The breeding tank has to be set up so that the eggs can be removed one by one. The fry hatch after 10–14 days and must be fed infusoria at first. Add *Artemia* to the diet later. Frequent cautious water exchanges (drip method) are important to maintain the excellent water quality demanded by this species.

F: C; small live foods.

T: 20°–24°C, L: 3 cm, A: 60 cm, R: t, m, D: 4

Aplocheilichthys kongoranensis (AHL, 1924)

Syn.: *Haplochilichthys kongoranensis, Haplochilus atripinnis* (not PFEFFER, 1896), *Aplocheilichthys johnstoni* (not GÜNTHER, 1893).

Hab.: Africa: coastal plains of east Tanzania, including the Rufiji and Ruvu Basins.

F.I.: January 1981 by EGGERS, KASSELMANN, and SEEGERS from Kibiti, Tanzania.

Sex.: Not always easy to distinguish. ♂♂ are generally more intensely colored and bigger with slightly elongated fins. The coloration and morphology of ♂♂ of different populations may vary. The ♀♀ have transparent fins and a more slender caudal peduncle.

Soc. B.: Like most *Aplocheilichthys* species, *A. kongoranensis* lives in groups, though there does not seem to be an intense cohesion between the animals as is found in some schooling fishes. Every fish within the school maintains its individual space. The animals tend to be shy and peaceful in aquaria.

M: Place in well-planted aquaria that have peaceful inhabitants, possibly small barbs or characins would make suitable tankmates. The water should be soft and neutral to slightly acid. Cover the aquarium, since the animals are accomplished jumpers.

B: For unknown reasons, this species is problematic to breed. Perhaps it is because upon hatching the fry are extremely tiny, demanding correspondingly small foodstuffs. In general, this species is an adhesive spawner which lays its eggs among plants. A species tank with plenty of Java moss is best for breeding. Remove the juveniles, or place a pair or 1 to 2 ♂♂ and several ♀♀ in a tank by themselves and pick the eggs from the spawning substrate. Put the eggs in a rearing container until they develop. After about 14–20 days, the young hatch. Feed them small *Artemia* nauplii and infusoria.

F: C; all kinds of small live foods. Flakes can be fed occasionally.

T: 22°–26°C, L: 4 cm, A: 60 cm, R: t, m, D: 3–4

Aplocheilichthys camerunensis

Aplocheilichthys kongoranensis, WC, Rufiji River Camp, Tanzania

Fam.: Poeciliidae
Subfam.: Aplocheilichthyinae

Aplocheilichthys lacustris   SEEGERS, 1984

Syn.: *Aplocheilichthys maculatus lacustris.*

Hab.: Africa: Tanzanian coastal basin south of Dar es Salaam in the Mbezi Basin and at Kibiti.

F.I.: January 1981 by EGGERS, KASSELMANN, and SEEGERS.

Sex.: ♂♂ are slightly larger, have a deeper caudal peduncle, a golden brown body, and brightly colored fins. ♀♀ are generally paler with a stout anterior body and rather transparent fins.

Soc. B.: Like *A. maculatus*; in their natural biotope, *A. lacustris* can be found swimming along the water surface in small groups, though each preserves its "personal space," even while swimming.

M: As for *A. kongoranensis.*

B: As for *A. kongoranensis,* but this species is easier to breed.

F: C; small live foods. Flakes can be fed occasionally.

S: *A. lacustris* was initially described as a subspecies of *A. maculatus*, but an additional population was found outside the type locality in a large lake at Kibiti, and since the two populations correspond both in color and meristic values, yet deviate from the two like populations of *A. maculatus* of Lake Baringo and north of Dar es Salaam, *A. lacustris* deserves species status. Morphological characteristics further confirm this taxonomic classification.

T: 22°–26°C, **L**: 3.5 cm, **A**: 60 cm, **R**: t, m, **D**: 2–3

Aplocheilichthys maculatus   KLAUSEWITZ, 1957
Spotted lampeye

Syn.: None.

Hab.: Africa: Lake Baringo, Kenya, and Tanzanian coastal regions north of Dar es Salaam.

F.I.: 1956 by Tropicarium Frankfurt, Co.

Sex.: ♂♂ have brighter colors and larger fins. ♀♀ have virtually transparent fins, a more slender caudal peduncle, and a fuller anterior body.

Soc. B.: In nature, these fish are usually found in small groups, rarely singly. Peaceful animals that only resort to biting if placed in limited confines. They do not school.

M: Keep in a small, well-planted aquarium containing either conspecifics or small heterospecifics. Water chemistry does not seem to be particularly important; populations from the coastal region of Tanzania are found in neutral to slightly acid and soft water, while those from Lake Baringo live in hard, alkaline water.

B: The animals are adhesive spawners. Eggs are laid on plants, peat fibers, or similar materials. After 2–3 weeks—depending on temperature—the young hatch and can immediately be fed *Artemia* nauplii.

F: C; small live foods and flakes.

S: This species has a notoriously disjointed distribution. The relation between the populations of Lake Baringo in Kenya and those of the coastal regions of Tanzania is not clear; the fish look identical.

T: 22°–26°C, **L**: 3.5 cm, **A**: 60 cm, **R**: t, m, **D**: 2–3

Aplocheilichthys lacustris, WC, Kibiti, Tanzania

Aplocheilichthys maculatus, WC, S Bagamoyo, Tanzania

Fam.: Poeciliidae
Subfam.: Aplocheilichthyinae

Aplocheilichthys moeruensis
Moeru lampeye

(BOULENGER, 1914)

Syn.: *Haplochilus moeruensis, Haplochilichthys moeruensis, Micropanchax moeruensis.*

Hab.: Africa: south Zaïre (Shaba) and north Zambia in Lakes Moero and Mweru Wantipa as well as their respective drainages and headwaters, e.g., Luapula River.

F.I.: 1986 by SEEGERS and co-travelers from Lake Mweru Wantipa, Zambia.

Sex.: Sometimes differences are very slight. ♂♂ are comparatively more slender and brighter blue with yellowish gray fins. The ♀♀ are often larger with a rounder anterior body. Their colors are less intense, and the fins are almost transparent.

Soc. B.: Retiring, almost shy species. Although the fish seek the company of conspecifics in a community aquarium, each animal requires individual space. They are not true schooling fish.

M: Can be kept in small to medium-sized aquaria. Aquatic vegetation should be arranged to form hiding places. *A. moeruensis* is nearly always found among plants close to the shore, rarely in the open water. Only calm, small fishes are suitable tankmates. The water should be soft to medium-hard with an acidic to neutral pH.

B: Not very difficult in a species tank. As long as the tank is choked with plants, fry can be left in the tank, since they will find shelter among the vegetation. Breeding these fish in a more efficient manner requires a small tank with fine-leaved plants (peat or synthetic fibers) and either pairs or a group made-up of more ♀♀ than ♂♂. Remove the parents after one week. Young hatch after about 2 weeks and are collected or left in the same tank and fed infusoria and *Artemia salina*. Growth is slow.

F: C; small live foods, particularly *Artemia salina* nauplii.

S: This very unpretentious species has possibly been confused in the literature with other species. Its relationship to *A. myaposae* (BOULENGER, 1908) is undefined.

T: 20°–26°C, **L:** 4 cm, **A:** 60 cm, **R:** t, m, **D:** 3

Aplocheilichthys myaposae

(BOULENGER, 1908)

Syn.: *Haplochilus myaposae, Haplochilichthys myaposae, Micropanchax myaposae.*

Hab.: South Africa: small bodies of water and swampy regions of the basins of the Cuianzu and Ciulo Rivers in Angola to the Okavango Basin in Botswana, the Zambezi Basin in Zambia, Zimbabwe, Mozambique, and northern South Africa (Natal, Transvaal).

F.I.: Unknown.

Sex.: ♂♂ are a brighter blue and have larger fins. ♀♀ are fuller anteriorly.

Soc. B.: Peaceful, small fish. Like most *Aplocheilichthys* species, these animals form loose schools.

M: As for *A. kongoranensis.*

B: Refer to *A. kongoranensis* and *A. maculatus.*

F: C; small live foods and flake foods.

T: 20°–26°C, **L:** 4 cm, **A:** 60 cm, **R:** t, m, **D:** 3

Aplocheilichthys moeruensis, WC, Lake Mweru Wantipa, Zambia

Aplocheilichthys myaposae, WC, South Africa

Fam.: Poeciliidae
Subfam.: Aplocheilichthyinae

Aplocheilichthys normani
Norman's lampeye
AHL, 1928

Syn.: *Aplocheilichthys gambiensis, Micropanchax macrurus manni, Aplocheilichthys manni, Poropanchax manni, P. normani.*

Hab.: Africa: savanna regions south of the Sahel from Senegal through the Chad Basin to the White Nile in Sudan and the Niger and Benue Basins in Nigeria.

F.I.: Unknown.

Sex.: ♂♂ are brighter colored, particularly in regard to the blue marking on the top of the iris, and have elongated fins. ♀♀ are more matte and have transparent, rounded fins, a rounded anterior body, and a more elongated caudal peduncle.

Soc. B.: Peaceful, shy species. It requires less personal space within its loose group than other *Aplocheilichthys* species.

M: Do not associate with large aggressive fishes. Subdued light (floating plants) will emphasize its bright eye color. Cover the aquarium well, and leave free swimming space. The water should be acid to slightly alkaline and soft. Frequent water exchanges are recommended.

B: Spawns among plants, etc. Place a group in a moderate-sized tank containing fine-leaved plants. If a high yield is desired, remove the parents when the first young appear, remove the young as they hatch, or collect the eggs. When efficiency is not an issue, parents and young can be kept together in large tanks, since well-fed breeders are not cannibalistic towards their young. Infusoria and *Artemia* nauplii make appropriate starter foods.

F: C; small live foods such as water fleas and *Artemia* nauplii. Offer flake foods to add variety.

T: 22°–26°C, **L:** 4 cm, **A:** 60 cm, **R:** t, m, **D:** 3

442

Aplocheilichthys normani, WC ♂

This creek in Uganda is inhabited by labyrinth fishes, cichlids, barbs, and *Aplocheilichthyidae*.

Fam.: Poeciliidae
Subfam.: Aplocheilichthyinae

Aplocheilichthys omoculatus

WILDEKAMP, 1977

Syn.: None.

Hab.: Africa: Tanzania, in the Little Ruaha Basin of central Tanzania.

F.I.: 1976 by WILDEKAMP and company.

Sex.: ♂♂ are somewhat larger and have a metallic blue body with yellow dorsal and anal fins. ♀♀ are more matte and have transparent unpaired fins.

Soc. B.: Peaceful and shy species. Not a marked schooling fish, even though they live in loose groups. Only found singly or in small groups in their natural habitat.

M: Although best kept in a plant-choked aquarium, an area must be kept open to allow the fish to swim. In nature, the fish were found along swampy creek edges (Little Ruaha, southwest Sao Hill, Tanzania). Data from this biotope on June 24,

1985, at about 2 p.m. were as follows: air temperature 17.8°C, water temperature 15.2°C, pH 6.3, dGH and dKH less than 1°, conductivity 13.5 µS. Barbs and one *Amphilius* were by-catches. Similar water values should prevail in aquaria containing these animals. Note the cool water temperature.

B: Water values should be very close to those found in its natural habitat; however, the temperature should be slightly higher. These animals are adhesive spawners, so add Java moss, peat fibers, or synthetic fibers to the tank to act as a spawning substrate. Juveniles hatch after about 14 days and immediately accept *Artemia salina* nauplii.

F: C; live foods commiserate to its size.

T: 16°–22°C, **L:** 3.5 cm, **A:** 60 cm, **R:** t, m, b, **D:** 3

Aplocheilichthys pfaffi
Pfaff's lampeye

DAGET, 1954

Syn.: *Micropanchax pfaffi, Aplocheilichthys kingi* (not BOULENGER, 1913), *A. longicauda.*

Hab.: Africa: savanna regions south of the Sahel belt from Guinea through Mali, the northern Ivory Coast, north Ghana, Burkina Faso, north Nigeria, Niger, north Cameroon, Chad, and Sudan.

F.I.: To Holland in February of 1980 by K. ZISDERVELD from Ouagadougou, Burkina Faso.

Sex.: Sometimes differences are very slight. ♂♂ tend to be a more pronounced blue-silver, and their fins are larger and slightly silver-blue. ♀♀ are an inconspicuous hue with rounder and more transparent fins. Their anterior body is rounder, and their caudal peduncle is somewhat narrower.

Soc. B.: See *Aplocheilichthys omoculatus.*

M: As for *A. omoculatus;* however, it should be kept at higher temperatures, i.e., 23°–26°C. *A. pfaffi* likes moving water.

B: As for *A. omoculatus* and *A. usanguensis,* though when breeding, the temperature must be elevated.

F: C; small live foods as well as flakes.

S: The pictured fish's identification is not absolutely sure. *A. pfaffi* may be a synonym of a previously described species.

T: 22°–26°C, **L:** 3 cm, **A:** 60 cm, **R:** t, m, **D:** 3–4

Aplocheilichthys omoculatus, WC, Kibaha, Tanzania

Aplocheilichthys pfaffi, Ovagadougou, Burkina Faso

Fam.: Poeciliidae
Subfam.: Aplocheilichthyinae

Aplocheilichthys rancureli
Filamentous lampeye

DAGET, 1964

Syn.: *Poropanchax rancureli, Micropanchax rancureli, Aplocheilichthys macrophthalmus* MEINKEN, 1932.

Hab.: Africa: rivers and creeks of the coastal plains of southwestern Ghana and the southern Ivory Coast.

F.I.: 1954 by SHELJUZHKO from the Ivory Coast to Munich.

Sex.: Sexes are not always easy to distinguish. ♂♂ are slimmer and have elongated unpaired fins. Their body is blue-green and, depending on the light, strongly iridescent with a faint longitudinal stripe running along its center. The fins are yellow; some populations have red-fringed fins (see photo). ♀♀ have a stouter, anteriorly fuller body and small, rounded, transparent fins.

Soc. B.: See *Aplocheilichthys kongoranensis*.

M: As for *Aplocheilichthys camerunensis*. Clean water and good filtration are necessary to maintain this somewhat sensitive species.

B: As for *A. camerunensis*. Not very prolific.

F: C; small live foods and *Artemia* nauplii.

S: *A. rancureli* is repeatedly confused with *A. macrophthalmus*, its closest relative. The latter has a more southern distribution.

T: 24°–26°C, **L:** 3.5 cm, **A:** 40 cm, **R:** t, m, **D:** 4

Aplocheilichthys usanguensis
Usangu lampeye

WILDEKAMP, 1977

Syn.: *Aplocheilichthys* sp. "Mbeya."

Hab.: Africa: southeast Tanzania, at Usangu Flats and the upper basin of the Great Ruaha.

F.I.: 1976 by WILDEKAMP and co-travelers.

Sex.: Both sexes have a bluish silver body. ♂♂ have a black line along the upper edge of the operculum and yellow dorsal, ventral, and anal fins. Dominant specimens occasionally have a yellow caudal peduncle as well. ♀♀ have a fuller anterior body, a slimmer caudal peduncle, and transparent fins.

Soc. B.: As for *Aplocheilichthys omoculatus*. Not a pronounced schooling fish. Gregarious, yet they require individual space.

M: See *A. omoculatus*. Maintain under moderate temperatures.

B: See *A. omoculatus*. Fry can be reared in the breeding tank if sufficient shelter

is present, e.g., Java moss. Newly hatched fry must be fed infusoria, since *Artemia* nauplii are too large.

F: C; small live foods. Flake foods are occasionally accepted.

S: Like *A. maculatus*, *A. usanguensis* is also a member of the subgenus *Lacustricola*. The black spot on the upper edge of the operculum is one characteristic of the subgenus.

T: 17°–22°C, **L:** 3 cm, **A:** 40 cm, **R:** t, m, **D:** 3–4

Aplocheilichthys rancureli

Aplocheilichthys usanguensis

Fam.: Poeciliidae

Fluviphylax pygmaeus
South American lampeye, pygmy lampeye

(MYERS & CARVALHOI in MYERS, 1955)
Subfam.: Fluviphylacinae

Syn.: *Potamophylax pygmaeus.*

Hab.: South America: the Amazon and its tributaries.

F.I.: In July of 1985, E. FRECH and A. WERNER imported three specimens from Santarem.

Sex.: ♂♂ have yellowish fins and a yellow-brown to bluish body that has several vertical gray stripes that fade posteriorly. The gray-blue ♀♀ (see photo) do not have vertical stripes, the fins are smaller and, for the most part, transparent.

Soc. B.: This schooling fish is probably similar to *Aplocheilichthys* species, where each animal, despite living in a group, requires a certain distance from other members of the school.

M: Information is sparse because FOERSCH (DATZ, **40** (2): 65–66, 1987)

is the only person to date that has ever maintained this fish. It will live in captivity, but its diminutive size complicates its maintenance. A species tank is definitely required. However, the most difficult part of caring for these animals is acquiring them in the first place.

B: A lack of imported animals has precluded this endeavor. Breeding is probably similar to other small *Aplocheilichthys*. Whether or not the smallest foods are administered the first days posthatch is probably decisive for success or failure.

F: C; smallest live foods, including *Artemia* nauplii.

S: This very small sensitive Aplocheilichthyidae is the only family member found in the Americas.

T: 24°–26°C, **L:** 2 cm, **A:** 30 cm, **R:** t, **D:** 4

Hypsopanchax catenatus
Chain lampeye

RADDA, 1981
Subfam.: Aplocheilichthyinae

Syn.: None.

Hab.: Africa: southeast Gabon, 61 km south of Franceville on the road to Boumango between Madziba and Mboki.

F.I.: July 1980 by HOFMANN and PÜRZL to Vienna.

Sex.: ♂♂ have brighter colors and a broader anal fin base; ♀♀, in contrast, are smaller and have a more rounded anterior body.

Soc. B.: Peaceful fish. Keep a group.

M: As for *Plataplochilus ngaensis. H. catenatus* also requires clean, excellent water.

B: This species was not further distributed after its import (only ♂♂?). Consequently, nothing is known about its breeding behavior, but it should be similar to *P. ngaensis.*

F: C; moderate-sized live foods. Try to avoid worms.

S: Closely related to *Hypsopanchax zebra.*

T: 22°–26°C, **L:** 6 cm, **A:** 80 cm, **R:** t, m, **D:** 4

Fluviphylax pygmaeus

Hypsopanchax catenatus, WC from the type locality

Fam.: Poeciliidae
Subfam.: Aplocheilichthyinae

Pantanodon podoxys MYERS, 1955

Syn.: None.

Hab.: Africa: narrow coastal regions of east Africa from Kenya to Tanzania, perhaps also in Mozambique, near mangroves and brackish water swamps. To date it has been found at three sites: Malindi, Tanga, and Dar es Salaam.

F.I.: 1978 by WILDEKAMP and co-travelers from Dar es Salaam.

Sex.: ♂♂ are commonly larger and brighter blue with bigger dorsal and anal fins; the dorsal fin may be yellowish. ♀♀ hardly have any color in their fins, and their anterior body is rounder.

Soc. B.: Not a schooling fish in the true sense of the word, though the animals live in groups. Rarely found alone. Peaceful towards both conspecifics and heterospecifics.

M: Little information is available, but the species seems to be easier to keep than initially thought. Successful breeding and long-term care have failed because of lack of imports. Following water values in its natural habitat, the aquarium water should be saline and not overly soft or acid. The fish require plenty of free swimming space.

B: Little information is available, but the fish seem to breed like *Aplocheilichthys* species (substrate spawners).

F: C; all kinds of live foods and, occasionally, flake foods.

S: Due to research on preserved specimens by WHITEHEAD (1962), it was initially supposed that *P. podoxys* subsisted solely on planktonic foods. But live imported animals have proven this false. There are no special dietary requirements.

T: 24°–28°C, **L:** 5 cm, **A:** 80 cm, **R:** t, m, **D:** 4

Plataplochilus chalcopyrus LAMBERT, 1963

Syn.: None.

Hab.: West Africa: Gabon, in the Diala River 50 km south of Lambarene towards Mouila. The pictured strain comes from Fougamou, south of Lambarene towards Mouila (not far from the type locality).

F.I.: 1976 by BOCHTLER and HERZOG.

Sex.: ♂♂ have a blue body and transparent yellow fins with a reddish fringe. Although all fins are elongated, the caudal fin is notably so. The lighter colored ♀♀ are smaller without elongated fins.

Soc. B.: See *Plataplochilus ngaensis*.

M: As for *P. ngaensis*.

B: As for *P. ngaensis*.

F: C; live foods and, occasionally, flake foods.

S: HUBER (1981) considers *P. chalcopyrus* and *P. ngaensis* synonymous, but the type specimens would have to be examined and compared to make this decision. The pictured animal seems to have much in common with the type specimen of *P. chalcopyrus* and is definitely not identical to the fish now imported as *P. ngaensis* (LANDSBERG and NUMRICH have made new collections which can be used as a reference). Specimens imported in 1976 by BOCHTLER and HERZOG and distributed as *P. chalcopyrus* are slimmer fish that have a longer snout and a more posteriorly situated dorsal fin.

T: 22°–26°C, **L:** 5 cm, **A:** 80 cm, **R:** t, m, **D:** 3

Pantanodon podoxys, WC, TZ 83/1, Dar es Salaam, Tanzania

Plataplochilus chalcopyrus, Fougamou, south of Lambarene, Gabon

Fam.: Poeciliidae
Subfam.: Aplocheilichthyinae

Plataplochilus loemensis   (PELLEGRIN, 1924)

Syn.: *Haplochilus loemensis, Aplochei-lichthys loemensis, Procatopus loemensis, P. cabindae* (not BOULENGER, 1911).

Hab.: West Africa: coastal plains of Zaïre, Angola, Congo (country of type locality), and southwest Gabon.

F.I.: 1986 by Max AMMER, Wapenfeld, Holland.

Sex.: Full-grown ♂♂ are more colorful, but less so in bred specimens. The ♂'s anal fin is rectangular. ♀♀ have an almost triangular anal fin.

Soc. B.: Very lively, active schooling fish. Shy and skittish, particularly if only one or two specimens are kept.

M: *P. loemensis* can be associated with small barbs and/or characins, etc. The tank should contain plenty of free swimming space, but still have roots and vegetation around the edges. Provide diffused lighting and some sun. Water should be soft to medium-hard and slightly acid. Very sensitive to suboptimal water conditions. Good filtration,

regular water exchanges, and aeration are necessary. Avoid high temperatures; 22°–24°C are sufficient. Since this species is susceptible to *Oodinium*, salt added to the water is recommended.

B: Quite difficult, even for specialists. The animals are adhesive spawners which place their eggs on plants or a perlon mop. If the water is not exceptionally clean, many of the eggs will fungus. The eggs should be stored in water containing acriflavine (but very little and not during the days just prior to hatching). After 12–14 days, the fry hatch from the relatively large eggs and immediately eat *Artemia salina* nauplii. Growth is not fast.

F: All types of live foods such as *Daphnia, Cyclops,* glassworms, mosquito larvae, and *Artemia;* cautiously feed bloodworms and *Tubifex!*

S: *P. loemensis* is a lively swimmer that demands a roomy tank. To date, only individual specimens have been imported from Gabon by dedicated aquarists.

T: 22°–24°C, **L**: 6 cm, **A**: 60 cm, **R**: m, t, **D**: 3–4

Plataplochilus miltotaenia   LAMBERT, 1963

Syn.: *Procatopus miltotaenia, Plataplochilus pulcher.*

Hab.: West Africa: Gabon. The type locality of *P. miltotaenia* is on the road from Libreville to Kango in northwest Gabon at PK 40. The pictured specimen was captured 20 km south of Lambarene, that is, south of Ogowe.

F.I.: 1976 by BOCHTLER and HERZOG.

Sex.: Similar to other species of *Plataplochilus.* ♂♂ are larger with elongated fins, a red stripe that extends from their eye into the caudal fin, and a blue body, the intensity of which depends on the amount of light. ♀♀ are inconspicuously colored and lack elongated fins. Though present, the red lateral stripe is almost invisible.

Soc. B.: Like *P. ngaensis.*

M: As for *P. ngaensis.*

B: As for *P. ngaensis.*

F: C; live foods and, occasionally, flake foods.

S: The pictured population was sold as *Plataplochilus pulcher.* HUBER (1981) considers *P. pulcher* to be a synonym of *P. miltotaenia.* This book follows the latter opinion. It is possible that *P. pulcher* is a synonym of *P. ngaensis,* which may also be the case for *P. miltotaenia.* Although the red line is less accented in *P. ngaensis,* it is present. Comparing the type specimens is the only way to resolve these questions.

T: 22°–26°C, **L**: 5 cm, **A**: 80 cm, **R**: t, m, **D**: 3

Plataplochilus loemensis

Plataplochilus miltotaenia, south of Lambarene, Gabon

Syn.: *Haplochilichthys ngaensis, Procatopus ngaensis, Aplocheilichthys ngaensis, Plataplochilus mimus,* ? *P. pulcher.*

Hab.: West Africa: northwest Gabon and southwestern Equatorial Guinea.

F.I.: 1986 by LANDSBERG & NUMRICH?

Sex.: ♂♂ are blue, becoming more iridescent towards the caudal fin, with a faint stripe running along its side. The fins are transparent and yellowish and partially elongated, particularly the upper lobe of the caudal fin. In contrast, ♀♀ are smaller, have rounded instead of elongated fins, and a more matte coloration.

Soc. B.: Although *P. ngaensis* is a social fish, it does not school. Each specimen requires its own free space lest hostilities and injuries occur.

M: Requires very clean, well-filtered water. The aquarium cannot be overly small. Plant the edges with a free hand, and partially cover the surface with floating plants. The water should be soft with a neutral or slightly acid pH. Frequent water exchanges are a necessity.

B: While Java moss or similar materials may be used as a spawning substrate, they are just as likely to press their eggs into crevices and cracks, for example, filter intake slits or large-pored sponges. For efficient reproduction, each ♂ requires his own spawning substrate. Sometimes the fish spawn in a group. After the fish spawn, remove the substrate and transfer it into a small aquarium until the young hatch. While it is possible to collect the eggs, those laid deep in the substrate may be damaged as they are removed. The young, depending on temperature, need about 2 weeks to hatch. Infusoria and *Artemia* nauplii are suitable initial foods. Growth is slow.

F: C; live foods, particularly planktonic items.

S: The type specimens hail from the Noja River south of the border between Gabon and Equatorial Guinea. It is possible that nga = ngaensis originated from a typographical error (nga vs. noja).

T: 20°–26°C, **L:** 5 cm, **A:** 80 cm, **R:** t, m, **D:** 3

Plataplochilus miltotaenia

Plataplochilus ngaensis, WC, northern Cristal Mountains, Gabon

Lake George, Uganda. The reed or papyrus shore may best be crossed at a hippopotamus pass, but beware ...

Fam.: Aplocheilidae
Subfam.: Aplocheilinae

Epiplatys [*Aphyoplatys*] *duboisi* (POLL, 1952)
Congo killie

Syn.: *Aplocheilus duboisi.*

Hab.: Africa: eastern Congo and western Zaïre, in drainage basins of the lower Kasai and central Zaïre as well as the western Zaïre tributaries.

F.I.: 1953 (?) by P. BRICHARD.

Sex.: ♂♂ are blue to blue-green with red dots arranged in 5–6 longitudinal rows. The fins are usually blue with red dots and elongated. Depending on the population, the fins will either have a yellow or blue fringe with submarginal red stripes. ♀♀ are paler and do not have elongated fins.

Soc. B.: Small, peaceful, shy species.

M: In accordance with their origin of rain forest biotopes, use soft, slightly acid water. Though the aquarium does not need to be large, it should offer hiding places, for example, within dense vegetation.

B: Set the tank up as if breeding adhesive-spawning *Epiplatys* species, one spawning mop or peat fibers as its sole decoration and perhaps a small filter. One pair per breeding tank is optimal. The parents are removed after one week, or the eggs can be collected from the spawning substrate. The young, which hatch after 1–2 additional weeks, have to be fed infusoria, since *Artemia* nauplii are too large.

F: C; small live foods. *Artemia* nauplii can also be fed to adults.

S: A very small, relatively sensitive species.

T: 22°–26°C, L: 3.5 cm, A: 60 cm, R: t, m, D: 4

Continuation of *Aphyosemion bualanum kekemense* (p. 462):

This species can also be bred like a substrate spawner; hydrate the peat (peat fibers are better than just peat) after 3 weeks. Raise the newly hatched young with *Artemia* nauplii and infusoria.

F: C; live foods.

S: *A. b. kekemense* is one of numerous geographic strains found from Cameroon to the Central African Republic. Almost every creek within its distribution area (savanna zones) has a different strain. Each of the various strains should be kept separate to avoid crossbreeding. Pass each strain on with corresponding habitat information to maintain pure strains and prevent chaotic crosses.

T: 20°–24°C, L: 5 cm, A: 60 cm, R: m, b, D: 3–4

Epiplatys [Aphyoplatys] duboisi

Aphyoplatys duboisi

Aphyosemion amieti
Amiet's killie

RADDA, 1976

Syn.: None.

Hab.: Africa: western Cameroon, in a small area near the lower Sanaga and neighboring systems in the rain forest.

F.I.: In 1974 by RADDA to Vienna, but the animals died. A new import was made in February of 1975 by PÜRZL to Vienna.

Sex.: See photos. ♂♂ are brown dorsally and dark orange ventrally. There are horizontal rows of dots running above the pectoral fins to the caudal fin which frequently coalesce into pronounced lines, outlining the orange zone. The outer edge of the anal fin and the lower caudal fin are blue with a dark red stripe proximally. The dorsal and upper tail fin are red and blue-green patterned with a blue fringe. ♀♀ are brown with rows of small, light red dots which may extend into the fins.

Soc. B.: A robust and usually peaceful species. Behaves like *Aphyosemion gardneri*.

M: Not difficult to care for. Recommendations made for *A. gardneri* largely hold true for this species.

B: See *A. gardneri*. *A. amieti* should be treated as a substrate spawner.

F: C; hardy live foods. After the fish are acclimated, frozen foods and various commercial foods can be fed occasionally.

S: This species is related to *A. puerzli*, the *A. gardneri* group, and *A. fallax*.

T: 22°–28°C, **L:** 7 cm, **A:** 80 cm, **R:** m, b, t, **D:** 2–3

Aphyosemion banforense, see p. 460

Aphyosemion amieti ♂

Aphyosemion amieti ♀

Fam.: Aplocheilidae
Subfam.: Aplocheilinae

Aphyosemion amoenum   RADDA & PÜRZL, 1976

Syn.: None.

Hab.: West Africa: Cameroon, the Nyong system, in a creek close to Sonbo.

F.I.: December 1975 by PÜRZL and RADDA.

Sex.: ♂♂ are a colorful blue to blue-green, becoming orange posteriorly. Of the four longitudinal rows of red dots, the dots of the top two often merge into lines. *A. cameronense* forms—which includes this species—typically have a red stripe along their ventral side that extends into the caudal fin. The unpaired fins have numerous close red stripes running along the fin rays. These stripes are less pronounced along the edge of its tail fin, being replaced by blue-white and orange areas. The dorsal and anal fins are orange. ♀♀ are a solid brown with red spots or lines and round, brown transparent fins.

Soc. B.: Peaceful and rather shy. ♂♂ are hostile towards ♂ conspecifics and congeners.

M: Like all representatives of the *A. cameronense* group, this species is somewhat problematic to maintain. The aquarium should contain soft to medium-hard, slightly acid water. The substrate should be dark, and vegetation should be included to provide hiding places. A species tank is recommended, but they can be kept with small, peaceful fishes.

B: Not simple. Treat them as adhesive spawners. Collect the eggs regularly from the spawning substrate (wool mop) and place them in another container to hatch. After 12–14 days, the fry hatch and require infusoria and *Artemia* nauplii for the first few days.

F: C; live foods of all kinds. Feed worms sparingly.

S: *A. amoenum* belongs to the subgenus *Mesoaphyosemion* in the *A. cameronense* group.

T: 20°–24°C, **L:** 5 cm, **A:** 60 cm, **R:** b, m, **D:** 3–4

Aphyosemion [Roloffia] banforense   (SEEGERS, 1982)

Syn.: *Aphyosemion liberiensis* (not BOULENGER, 1908), *A. nigrifluvi.*

Hab.: West Africa: central Guinea near Mamou, southern Burkina Faso around Banfora and the Comoé Basin, and possibly south of the Sahel zone in Guinea, Mali, and the Ivory Coast.

F.I.: July 1979 by ROMAND, SCHMITT, and GUIGNARD from Guinea to France. October 1980 by B. BAUER from Burkina Faso to Germany.

Sex.: ♂♂ are green with red-brown dots. Both the top and the bottom of the caudal fin have a submarginal red-brown longitudinal stripe. The dorsum and dorsal fin are bronze. The pectoral, ventral, and anal fins have a smoky black edge. ♀♀ are solid brown with dark red-brown

dots. Their fins are round and translucent.

Soc. B.: The fish live singly and are relatively shy, though to what extent depends on the individual.

M: As for all other *Aphyosemion* species—a dark substrate (peat?), dim light, and plants that tolerate these conditions such as Java moss, Java fern, and *Anubias*. The water should be soft and neutral.

B: Set up either as an adhesive or substrate spawner. Similar to most other small *Aphyosemion* species. See *A. punctatum.*

F: C; live foods commiserate to its size, particularly mosquito larvae.

T: 22°–26°C, **L:** 5 cm, **A:** 60 cm, **R:** t, m, b, **D:** 3

Aphyosemion amoenum

Aphyosemion [Roloffia] banforense ♂, WC, Banfora, Burkina Faso

461

Fam.: Aplocheilidae
Subfam.: Aplocheilinae

Aphyosemion batesii

(BOULENGER, 1911)

Syn.: *Fundulus batesii, Fundulopanchax batesii, Raddaella batesii, Aphyosemion spectabile, Fundulus gustavi, Fundulus splendidus?, Aphyosemion (Fundulopanchax) schreineri, Aphyosemion kunzi?*

Hab.: Africa: from the Dja and Sanaga Basins in southeast Cameroon through northern Gabon and the Ivindo Basin to the Congo region of northern Zaïre.

F.I.: 1971 by HERZOG, RADDA, and co-travelers.

Sex.: ♂♂ are usually larger and, depending on population, quite colorful with elongated fins. ♀♀ are brown to gray with round fins.

Soc. B.: ♂♂ are usually peaceful towards heterospecifics, particularly in large tanks. However, they tend to be aggressive towards conspecific ♂♂. Even unripe ♀♀ are not spared from enmities when housed in small tanks. ♀♀ are generally peaceful.

M: Never keep two ♂♂. Either keep singly or a group in a medium-sized aquarium with several ♀♀. Hiding places must be provided for nondominant fish. The water should be acidic to neutral and soft to medium-hard water.

B: Most successful when bred as a substrate spawner. Offer a peat substrate. Place one ♂ with several ♀♀ and feed sparingly. After one week, the breeders should be removed and the peat lightly pressed and stored warm in a plastic bag for about 6 weeks (label). The peat is then rehydrated in an aquarium with cool water, and the hatching young are immediately fed *Artemia* nauplii. Growth is rapid. The peat can be dried and rehydrated in 14 days; this can be repeated several times.

F: C; all types of live foods as well as larger food items, including beef heart.

S: It has not been unquestionably decided if the nominate species *A. splendidum* (PELLEGRIN, 1930) and *A. kunzi* RADDA, 1975 are autonomous species. They are probably merely populations within one large distribution area. *A. batesii* has been placed within the subgenus *Raddaella* by HUBER (1977).

T: 22°–26°C, **L**: 7.5 cm, **A**: 80 cm, **R**: m, b, **D**: 3

Aphyosemion bualanum kekemense

RADDA & SCHEEL, 1975

Syn.: None.

Hab.: Africa: west Cameroon, near the town of Kekem, 35 km north northeast of N'kongsamba on the road to Bafoussam.

F.I.: 1973 by RADDA and SCHEEL.

Sex.: ♂♂ have elongated fins and numerous red vertical striations along their blue to blue-green body, resulting in a bright, colorful animal. ♀♀ are brownish with red spots that form short vertical stripes on the body. Their fins are largely transparent and round.

Soc. B.: Peaceful, rather shy subspecies.

M: As for most small *Aphyosemion* species. See *A. punctatum*. The red colors are displayed the best under moderate lighting. The water in their natural habitat was soft and slightly acid (pH 6) and between 21° and 23°C. The water in its captive environment should mirror these values.

B: *A. bualanum* should be bred as an adhesive spawner. Either use a continuous set-up or remove the parents after one week. Collect the eggs regularly from the spawning material (Java moss, wool mop, peat fibers). Egg development in a rearing dish containing aquarium water requires about 16–18 days.

Continued on p. 456.

Aphyosemion batesii ♂, WC, Bumba, Zaïre, Z 86/9

Aphyosemion bualanum kekemense

Fam.: Aplocheilidae
Subfam.: Aplocheilinae

Aphyosemion buytaerti
Buytaert's killie

RADDA & HUBER, 1978

Syn.: None.

Hab.: Africa: southwest Congo, in the Ekouma Creek near Ogooué between Zanaga and Voula II. Only known from the type locality (collection code RPC 28).

F.I.: July 1978 by BUYTAERT and WACHTERS to Belgium.

Sex.: ♂ ♂ are more colorful. They are green along their anterior dorsum, but yellow ventrally. Within the green area are longitudinal rows of red dots. The dorsal fin and upper caudal fin are finely outlined in blue. The lower fins, including the lower lobe of the caudal fin, have a yellow fringe. ♀ ♀ are brown with red dots that are also present in their colorless, transparent fins.

Soc. B.: Thoroughly peaceful.

M: This form is difficult to maintain and especially troublesome to breed. It requires meticulously clean water. Other-

wise, follow recommendations made for *A. punctatum*. The water temperature should be temperate. Water in its natural biotope was as follows: 18°C, pH 7.2, conductivity 40 μS, and a high iron concentration.

B: See *A. punctatum*. Breeding has proven to be extraordinarily difficult. Captive populations are extinct once again.

F: C; live foods commiserate to its size.

S: *A. buytaerti* is probably not a true species, but a strain of *A. wachtersi*. The photos in the Aquarium Atlas bear witness to this. Bred specimens of nominate *A. buytaerti* are even more similar to *A. wachtersi*. Both *A. buytaerti* and *A. wachtersi mikeae* are probably just regional strains of *A. wachtersi*. Only new collections can prove whether or not they have stable characteristics and can be recognized as subspecies.

T: 17°–21°C, **L:** 5 cm, **A:** 80 cm, **R:** m, b, **D:** 4

Aphyosemion celiae
Margined killie

SCHEEL, 1971

Syn.: None.

Hab.: Africa: west Cameroon, springs and small rain forest creeks in the basin of the Mungo River.

F.I.: 1971 by SCHEEL.

Sex.: ♂ ♂ are red-brown, but blue-green anteriorly. The fins have a yellow or white edge followed proximally by a red band. ♀ ♀ are a uniform brown. Red-brown dots are only faintly visible.

Soc. B.: Peaceful, rather shy species. Since it has been known to leap from the water when disturbed, a cover is necessary.

M: Like all small *Aphyosemion* species, it should be maintained in soft and slightly acid to neutral water. See *A. punctatum*.

B: As for *A. bualanum*, but this is a more pronounced substrate spawner. The fry

can be fed *Artemia* nauplii from the beginning.

F: C; live foods.

S: *A. celiae* is an extemely variable species that has very different geographical morphs. There are a number of transitional strains that are very similar in appearance to *A. calliurum* which confounds groupings. This includes very colorful forms with broad yellow fin fringes, one of which has been described as *A. celiae winifredae*. All of these morphs should be kept pure and passed along with a description of their origin—if available—as mentioned under *A. bualanum*.

T: 22°–26°C, **L:** 4.5 cm, **A:** 60 cm, **R:** m, b, **D:** 3

Aphyosemion buytaerti

Aphyosemion celiae, F₁ Loc. 26, Cameroon

Fam.: Aplocheilidae
Subfam.: Aplocheilinae

Aphyosemion citrineipinnis
Lemon-fin killie

HUBER & RADDA, 1977

Syn.: None.

Hab.: West Africa: central Gabon, in the Ngounié system on the western slope of the Du-Chaillu Massif.

F.I.: 1976 by HUBER and RADDA.

Sex.: The ♂♂ have blue sides, a brown dorsum, and yellow fins. ♀♀ are predominantly brown, and their fins are mostly transparent.

Soc. B.: This small, peaceful, shy species leads a reclusive life in large aquaria, hardly ever emerging.

M: As for all small *Aphyosemion* species; refer to *A. punctatum*. Due to its delicate nature, this fish should not be kept in a community aquarium. Water should be soft to medium-hard, slightly acid, and temperate.

B: See *A. punctatum*. Either breed as an adhesive or substrate spawner. Correspondingly, the eggs can be collected and hatched in water or dried. This species is not very prolific. At high temperatures (above 22°C), breeding frequently terminates.

F: C; live foods, especially mosquito larvae.

S: It is questionable if *A. citrineipinnis* is truly an autonomous species, as it may be just a population of *A. ocellatum*.

T: 18°–22°C, **L:** 5 cm, **A:** 50 cm, **R:** m, b, **D:** 4

Aphyosemion fallax
Swallow-tail killie

AHL, 1935

Syn.: *Fundulopanchax spurrelli* (not BOULENGER, 1913), *Aphyosemion gulare schwoiseri, A. kribianum.*

Hab.: Africa: coastal basin of west Cameroon, from Malende-Nyoke N Muyuka to Kribi.

F.I.: 1930 or 1931 by Aquarium Hamburg.

Sex.: See Vol. 2, p. 602. ♂♂ are quite colorful, being green-yellow to green-blue with red spots. These spots, depending on the population (Malende strain), can coalesce into longitudinal bands, particularly above the lateral line. The fins are elongated. The tail fin is forked and both the topmost and bottommost rays are elongated. Particularly beautiful specimens have an elongated anal fin. ♀♀ are brown and can be distinguished from other *Aphyosemion* species by their dark spot on the caudal peduncle.

Soc. B.: Normally peaceful towards heterospecifics. ♂♂ can be aggressive among themselves. Immature ♀♀ may be bitten to death. As a precaution, transport singly.

M: See Vol. 2, p. 602. Compare this species to *A. sjoestedti*.

B: See Vol. 2, p. 602.

F: C; large live foods.

S: The northern strain from Malende which was described as *Aphyosemion gulare schwoiseri* has reached Germany in recent years. It is therefore presented here as a comparison to the southern form from Kribi that was introduced in Vol. 2, p. 602. *A. fallax* has different geographic populations in the coastal regions of Cameroon. That these populations are in fact *A. fallax* has only recently become apparent (SEEGERS: DATZ, **39** (8): 347–351, 1986). The fish maintained from the '60's to prior to 1986 (some perhaps even today) as *A. fallax* are really a strain of *Aphyosemion gulare* (see in Vol. 1, p. 533). *A. fallax* is the closest relative of *A. sjoestedti* and continues its distribution south. Its body morphology and design are similar (see Vol. 1, p. 539 and Vol. 2, p. 603).

T: 22°–26°C, **L:** 9 cm, **A:** 100 cm, **R:** b, m, **D:** 3–4

Aphyosemion citrineipinnis

Aphyosemion fallax ♂, Malende, Cameroon

Aphyosemion fallax ♀, Malende, Cameroon

Aphyosemion fallax, Movanke, Cameroon

Aphyosemion franzwerneri ♂, WC, Cameroon, type locality

Aphyosemion franzwerneri
Werner's roundtail killie

SCHEEL, 1971

Syn.: None.

Hab.: West Africa: Cameroon, basin of the lower Sanaga and Wuri. Few habitats are known; the type locality is a small spring pool 15 km north of the fork in the road of Douala-Edea-Yabassi towards Yabassi.

F.I.: To Denmark in January 1969 by J. J. SCHEEL.

Sex.: Not always as clearly defined as other *Aphyosemion* species. ♂♂ have a design of red-brown dots and spots on a yellowish to greenish brown background. The caudal fin has a yellow fringe. The ♀♀'s fins are more rounded, and the caudal fin hardly has a yellow fringe. Their body is not quite as colorful, and their anterior body is fuller.

Soc. B.: Peaceful, shy species.

M: In nature the fish live in tiny bodies of water among fallen leaves, plants, and similar items. The water was acidic (pH 6) with a hardness of less than 1° dGH. Provide shallow, similarly composed water in its captive environment. The shallow water is to accommodate its poor swimming ability and benthic lifestyle.

B: Difficult and not very productive; best attempted in a separate breeding tank with peat fibers, wool mops, etc., from which the eggs can be collected and transferred into a hatching dish. After 14–16 days, the young hatch and should be fed infusoria at first; from the second to third day, *Artemia* nauplii can be added to their diet. Growth is slow.

F: C; live foods.

S: Do not confuse their unusual hopping locomotion with ill health.

T: 22°–26°C, **L:** 5 cm, **A:** 60 cm, **R:** b, **D:** 4

Fam.: Aplocheilidae
Subfam.: Aplocheilinae

Aphyosemion gardneri gardneri
Clausen's steel-blue killie

(BOULENGER, 1911)

Syn.: Haplochilus brucii, Fundulus gardneri, Fundulopanchax gardneri.

Hab.: West Africa: Nigeria. The type locality is Okwoga (70°N, 7°45'E), Cross River Basin, southeastern Nigeria

F.I.: The nominate form was probably imported for the first time in 1974 by PÜRZL and RADDA.

Sex.: ♂♂ are a colorful blue-green with red dots. ♀♀ are brown to gray-brown with red-brown dots.

Soc. B.: This robust species is a suggested beginner fish. To minimize aggressions among ♂♂, keep either one or a group of the gender, never only two. A group of ♀♀ should be kept as well, since the ♂♂ tend to be aggressive towards unripe ♀♀.

M: Odds for successfully maintaining this species are enhanced in tanks supporting heavy plant growth, particularly "Dutch" aquaria. Hiding places should be available. Water values are not critical, though the water should not be overly hard or alkaline.

B: A. gardneri and all its subspecies can be bred as either substrate spawners or adhesive spawners. In the first case, a trio (1 ♂ and 2 ♀♀) is introduced into a 20 l tank containing a peat substrate and medium-hard water with a temperature of 24°–26°C. Provide hiding places among peat fibers and plants for the ♀♀. Leave the breeders in the tank for one week. During that time, feed the breeders light meals of live foods. Remove the water after the parents are transferred and keep the peat slightly moist for 3 weeks in a plastic bag. Afterwards, rehydrate the substrate and eggs with fresh water. The young can be raised with Artemia nauplii. Growth is rapid. When breeding as an adhesive spawner, use a spawning mop, synthetic fibers, or peat fibers instead of peat and regularly collect the eggs and place them in a separate container (2–3 weeks).

F: C; live foods. After acclimation, beef heart and flakes are also accepted.

S: Several subspecies of A. gardneri have been described. Moving from northwest to southeast within the distribution area allows several trends to be followed. The fringes of the fins become less and less yellow and, at the same time, its annual nature diminishes somewhat. The latter development is probably a consequence of the fish adapting to its surroundings. In the north, the fish live in savannas, but in the south, its distribution includes rain forests.

T: 22°–26°C, **L:** 6 cm, **A:** 60 cm, **R:** t, m, **D:** 2

Aphyosemion gardneri gardneri, Nsukka, Nigeria

Aphyosemion gardneri lacustre

Fam.: Aplocheilidae
Subfam.: Aplocheilinae

Aphyosemion gardneri lacustre RADDA, 1974

Syn.: None.

Hab.: West Africa: Nigeria, basin of Lake Ejagham; west Cameroon.

F.I.: 1970 by HAEFELIN and RADDA.

Sex.: It is difficult to distinguish ♀♀ of this subspecies from those of other subspecies. ♂♂, in comparison, are more colorful, with a greenish brown and orange body. The anal fin is orange. The intensity of the red spots varies from specimen to specimen, but as a whole, they are generally duller in this subspecies than in the others.

Soc. B.: Like the nominate form.

M: As for the nominate form.

B: Experience has shown that this strain is best bred as a substrate spawner. Therefore, use peat as the spawning medium and dry it afterwards.

F: C; like the nominate form.

T: 22°–26°C, L: 6 cm, A: 60 cm, R: t, m, D: 2–3

Aphyosemion gardneri mamfense RADDA, 1974
Mamfe killie

Syn.: None.

Hab.: West Africa: western Cameroon, drainage of the upper Cross River around Mamfe.

F.I.: 1966 by SCHEEL to Denmark.

Sex.: ♀♀ are brownish with red-brown dots, while ♂♂ are very colorful. This subspecies varies greatly in coloration. Hardly one ♂ is similar to another, particularly when comparing various populations. In contrast to other subspecies, *A. g. mamfense* are generally more greenish. *A. g. gardneri*, particularly *A. g. nigerianum*, tends to be more blue. Instead of a broad yellow fringe on the unpaired fins, blues predominate.

Soc. B.: Like the nominate form.

M: As for the nominate form.

B: Principally like *A. gardneri gardneri*. In concordance to its rain forest habitat, this subspecies is easier to breed as an adhesive spawner than the nominate form.

F: C; like the nominate form.

S: *A. g. mamfense* is found in the western region of *A. gardneri*'s distribution.

T: 22° 24°C, L: 6 cm, A: 60 cm, R: t, m, D: 2–3

Aphyosemion gardneri nigerianum CLAUSEN, 1963
Nigeria killie

Syn.: *Aphyosemion gardneri obuduense*.

Hab.: West Africa: Nigeria and western Cameroon. Type locality is the Arum at the southern edge of Jos Plateau in central Nigeria.

F.I.: In 1913 by BRANDT, Leipzig, Germany.

Sex.: Similar to the nominate form. However, *A. g. nigerianum* ♂♂ generally have intense yellow borders on the fins followed proximally by a red stripe. The "blue" morph has white- or blue-bordered fins and a dull red-brown stripe instead of the bright red stripe of the previously described morph.

Soc. B.: Like the nominate form, but this form may be even more aggressive.

M: Like the nominate form.

B: In comparison to other *A. gardneri* subspecies, *A. g. nigerianum* is a more pronounced substrate spawner. Use peat as the spawning substrate.

F: C; like the nominate form.

S: The subspecies *A. g. nigerianum* lives in southern and central Nigeria, predominately in the lower Niger and Benoué Basins. It inhabits the majority of the species' distribution area. See Vol. 1, p. 532.

T: 22°–26°C, L: 6 cm, A: 60 cm, R: t, m, D: 2

Aphyosemion gardneri lacustre, Lake Ejagham, Cameroon

Aphyosemion gardneri mamfense, WC, 2 km E Mamfe, Cameroon

Aphyosemion gardneri nigerianum, Akure, Nigeria

Fam.: Aplocheilidae
Subfam.: Aplocheilinae

Aphyosemion hanneloreae
Hannelore's killie

RADDA & PÜRZL, 1985

Syn.: None.

Hab.: Africa: tributaries of the Nyanga in the central Du Chaillu-Massif in Gabon and possibly Congo.

F.I.: To Vienna, in June of 1985 from the locality GHP 85/11 at Malinga, Gabon.

Sex.: As for almost all *Aphyosemion* species, ♂♂ are more colorful and have elongated unpaired fins. They are yellow-green to brown-green with rows of red dots which often coalesce, forming interrupted longitudinal stripes. The unpaired fins have a yellow fringe followed proximally by a red band. The area between the body and the red band is blue-green with red dots. ♀♀ are brown with colorless, transparent, round fins.

Soc. B.: Peaceful, small killifish.

M: As indicated for *A. punctatum*.

T: 19°–21°C, L: 4 cm, A: 60 cm, R: m, b, D: 4

B: As for *A. punctatum*. Unfortunately, due to the inconsistency of breeding successes, supply does not always keep up with demand.

F: C; small- to moderate-sized live foods.

S: RADDA & PÜRZL, 1985 described *A. h. wuendschi* as a subspecies of *A. hanneloreae*. *A. hofmanni* RADDA, 1980 is one of its relatives.

Aphyosemion hofmanni
Hoffmann's killie

RADDA, 1980

Syn.: None.

Hab.: Africa: southwest Gabon, in the drainage of the Mbomi River of the Du Chaillu-Massif.

F.I.: In June of 1980, one ♂ was imported to Vienna from the type locality GHP 12/80.

Sex.: ♂♂ have a red-brown body with dark red longitudinal striations, even along the ventral area. The fins are yellow-brown and have red lines running along the fin rays. ♀♀ are gray-brown with transparent and colorless fins. The longitudinal stripes, while also present, are very faint.

Soc. B.: Probably peaceful.

M: Information is sparse, since only one ♂ has been imported alive. It can be supposed that its needs are very similar to those of *Aphyosemion punctatum*.

B: Probably similar to *A. punctatum*.

T: 19°–22°C, L: 4 cm, A: 60 cm, R: m, b, D: 3–4?

F: C; live foods.

S: This species is a close relative of *A. hanneloreae* RADDA & PÜRZL, 1985. More specific information has to wait until further collections can be made.

Aphyosemion hanneloreae, WC from the type locality, Gabon

Aphyosemion hofmanni, WC from the type locality, Gabon

Fam.: Aplocheilidae
Subfam.: Aplocheilinae

Aphyosemion joergenscheeli HUBER & RADDA, 1977

Syn.: None.

Hab.: Africa: Gabon, Du Chaillu-Massif.

F.I.: 1977.

Sex.: While ♂♂ have red and blue designs on their blue-green body, ♀♀ are brown and do not have a colorful design.

Soc. B.: Peaceful, shy species with a solitary lifestyle.

M: Care should be similar to that of all other small *Aphyosemion* species (see *A. punctatum*). Depending on the origin of the specimens, moderate temperatures and/or perfect water may be important maintenance conditions. Hence, provide good filtration.

B: Breeding is apparently difficult, since it has not been successful despite repeated imports. In principle, follow recommendations under *A. punctatum*.

F: C; live foods.

S: *A. joergenscheeli* has a stouter body than other *Aphyosemion* species. In addition, its dorsal and anal fins are almost exactly opposite to each other. It has some rather primitive characteristics which leads us to believe this species is a relict.

T: 18°–20°C, **L:** 5 cm, **A:** 60 cm, **R:** m, b, **D:** 4

Aphyosemion lefiniense WOELTJES, 1984
Lefini killie

Syn.: *Aphyosemion cognatum* (not MEINKEN, 1951).

Hab.: Africa: southern Congo, in the Lefini Basin north of Brazzaville.

F.I.: The exact date is unknown. Probably by P. BRICHARD in the '60's.

Sex.: ♂♂ are blue to brown with numerous red dots which extend into the fins. The fins have submarginal red bands. *A. lefiniense* differs from related forms by its yellow-edged fins (occasionally white-edged). ♀♀ are brown with very defined red-brown dots. Their fins are round.

Soc. B.: Shy and peaceful. ♂♂ may engage in hierarchical fights.

M: Requires a rather small tank, preferably one housing conspecifics, small characins, or other peaceful fishes. Decorate the aquarium as a jungle biotope with plants such as Java moss and *Anubias* tied to bogwood. Use soft, acid water (about 10° dGH and pH 6.0–6.5, respectively). The illumination should be moderate. Do not forget to cover the tank.

B: Use normal protocol for small *Aphyosemion* species. They can be bred as either adhesive or substrate spawners. If the eggs are collected, they will need 14–16 days in water to hatch. When using peat, rehydrate after 3 weeks.

F: C; all types of live foods commiserate to its size.

S: *A. lefiniense* belongs to the *A. christy* group, that is, the *A. elegans* species group.

T: 22°–26°C, **L:** 4.5 cm, **A:** 50 cm, **R:** m, b, **D:** 3

Aphyosemion joergenscheeli

Aphyosemion lefiniense

Fam.: Aplocheilidae
Subfam.: Aplocheilinae

Aphyosemion loennbergii
Loennberg's killie

(BOULENGER, 1903)

Syn.: *Fundulus loennbergii, F. pappenheimi, Fundulopanchax loennbergii, Aphyosemion bivittatum* (not LÖNNBERG, 1895), *A. (Fundulopanchax) unistrigatus.*

Hab.: Africa: southwest Cameroon, in the basins of the Nyong, Loikundje, and Kienke Rivers.

F.I.: Unknown because this species has been repeatedly confused with related species from the subgenus *Chromaphyosemion.*

Sex.: ♂♂ have red dots distributed over their body, a bluish caudal fin, and elongated fins. They are very colorful. ♀♀, like all *Aphyosemion* ♀♀, are a nondescript brown with round fins.

Soc. B.: Chiefly peaceful and shy. Displays and occasional confrontations are limited to the ♂ gender.

M: Maintenance is fairly easy as long as they are kept in a dark tank with an appropriate substrate and good vegetation. Decorate the tank with bogwood, Java moss, and Java fern. The fish often leap vertically from the water when frightened, so cover the aquarium. Water chemistry is of little importance as long as extreme values are avoided.

B: Though it can be bred as a substrate spawner, *A. loennbergii* prefers to adhere its eggs on plants or artificial substrates. The eggs can be collected or stored in peat and rehydrated after about 3 weeks. This is the most difficult *Chromaphyosemion* species to breed.

F: C; live foods. Flakes may occasionally be accepted.

S: *A. bivittatum, A. bitaeniatum* (synonym *A. multicolor*), *A. splendopleure,* and *A. volcanum* as well as this species all belong to the subgenus *Chromaphyosemion.*

T: 22°–26°C, **L**: 7 cm, **A**: 60 cm, **R**: m, b, **D**: 3

Aphyosemion mirabile traudeae

RADDA, 1971

Syn.: None.

Hab.: West Africa: west Cameroon, near Manyemen.

F.I.: 1970 by RADDA and co-travelers.

Sex.: ♂♂ are brown anteriorly, turning blue-green towards the caudal fin. They are covered with red dots that tend to unite on the anterior half of the body, forming longitudinal stripes. The caudal fin has a yellow stripe along the dorsal and ventral edge which is followed proximally by a red stripe. ♀♀ are comparatively dull, being brown with transparent fins.

Soc. B.: Generally peaceful; ♂♂ may occasionally be aggressive among themselves.

M: This species is easy to maintain, even in community tanks, as long as there is an abundance of vegetation. Its colors are enhanced with subdued lighting and a dark substrate. The water should be slightly acid and not too hard.

B: As for *A. gardneri.* Best bred as a substrate spawner. Store the peat for about 3 weeks before adding water.

F: C; live foods, particularly mosquito larvae.

S: Experimental crosses seem to indicate that *A. mirabile mirabile* is independent, while its subspecies—*moense, traudeae,* and *intermittens*—seem to be much more closely related among themselves than to the nominate form.

T: 22°–26°C, **L**: 5 cm, **A**: 50 cm, **R**: m, b, **D**: 2–3

Aphyosemion loennbergii, CCMP 85/12, Soca Palm, Cameroon

Aphyosemion mirabile traudeae

Fam.: Aplocheilidae
Subfam.: Aplocheilinae

Fundulopanchax [*Callopanchax*] *monroviae*   (ROLOFF & LADIGES, 1972)
Monrovia killie

Syn.: *Aphyosemion monroviae*, *"Roloffia"* *monroviae*.

Hab.: Africa: southern Liberia, in swamps and swampy remnants of flowing waters in tropical rain forests between the St. Paul and the Mano Basins.

F.I.: 1971 by ROLOFF.

Sex.: ♂♂ have a very colorful bright red design. ♀♀ are a simple brown without much red. Their fins are smaller and transparent.

Soc. B.: Lively. Aggressive among themselves. Do not associate with very small fishes and always keep in large aquaria.

M: Arrange the tank's furnishings such that the animals are not in constant contact with each other. Include ample vegetation. Water should be soft and slightly acid to neutral. Keep either one ♂ or several ♂♂ with a group of ♀♀ to prevent hostilities from becoming focused.

B: Breed as substrate spawners. Place one ♂ with 2–3 ♀♀ for one week in a moderate-sized tank with a peat bottom and peat fibers. Check the fish regularly and feed sparingly. Afterwards, remove the peat, press lightly, and allow to dry briefly. The peat should be stored in a plastic bag and kept warm. After 6–8 weeks, add cool fresh water. The young immediately accept *Artemia salina* nauplii upon hatching. While growth is rapid, it may be irregular. You may want to redry the peat and add water again after 2–3 weeks.

F: C; live foods, even some large items. Frozen foods and beef heart can also be fed.

T: 22°–26°C, **L:** 9 cm, **A:** 80 cm, **R:** m, b, **D:** 3

Biotope where *Fundulopanchax* [*Callopanchax*] *monroviae* can be found

Fundulopanchax [*Callopanchax*] *monroviae* "blue"

Fundulopanchax [*Callopanchax*] *monroviae* "red"

Fam.: Aplocheilidae
Subfam.: Aplocheilinae

Aphyosemion ndianum
Red-tail killie

SCHEEL, 1968

Syn.: None.

Hab.: West Africa: Ndian Basin at Osomba, the border of southeast Nigeria and southwest Cameroon.

F.I.: 1959 by H. S. CLAUSEN to Denmark. However, these imported specimens did not become distributed. In 1975 the species was again imported by W. WACHTERS to Belgium.

Sex.: ♂♂, depending on the population, are green to blue and covered with red dots and lines. A red stripe runs along the ventral posterior body into the tail. Even the green to blue-green fins have red dots or stripes (tail fin). The throat is white. ♀♀ are brownish with small red-brown spots on the body and fins.

Soc. B.: Although *A. ndianum* looks like a robust species, it is usually very shy and skittish. It may overcome its timidity to a certain degree if housed with larger *Aphyosemion* species (*A. gardneri, A. sjoestedti*, and related species), though this should only be attempted in large show tanks that are at least 1.20 m long. Avoid hybrids.

M: As for *A. gardneri*. Due to its bashful nature, the species is problematic and not appropriate for beginners.

B: As for *A. gardneri*. Either breed as an adhesive or a substrate spawner. In the latter case, the peat is stored for about two months and then rehydrated with fresh water. The young immediately accept *Artemia* nauplii.

F: C; live foods, beef heart and, occasionally, flake foods.

T: 22°–25°C, **L:** 7 cm, **A:** 80 cm, **R:** t, m, b, **D:** 3–4

Aphyosemion oeseri
Oeser's killie

(SCHMIDT, 1928)

Syn.: *Panchax oeseri, P. pictus, Aphyosemion meinkeni, A. santaisabellae*.

Hab.: West Africa: Equatorial Guinea, Fernando Poo Island.

F.I.: 1928 by R. OESER.

Sex.: ♀♀, like those of most *Aphyosemion* species, are brownish with transparent, round fins. *A. oeseri* has longitudinal rows of red-brown dots on the body. In ♂♂, these rows of dots are more pronounced, and the body is yellow-green to bluish. The tail fin has a white to yellow fringe which is followed proximally by a red stripe. The dorsal and anal fins may have the same pattern.

Soc. B.: Amiable as a whole, but ♂♂ may be aggressive towards conspecific or congener ♂♂.

M: *A. oeseri*'s robust nature allows it to be kept in community aquaria. The water should not be too hard or alkaline. Part of the aquarium should have a dense plant thicket; a dark substrate and moderate illumination serve to enhance its colors.

B: As for *A. gardneri*. Best bred as an adhesive spawner, collecting the eggs from the spawning substrate. Breeding the fish as a substrate spawner is also possible. If bred in this manner, rehydrate the peat after four weeks.

F: C; live foods. Beef heart and flake foods are occasionally accepted after the fish become acclimated.

T: 22°–26°C, **L:** 7 cm, **A:** 80 cm, **R:** m, b, **D:** 3

Aphyosemion ndianum

Aphyosemion oeseri

Fam.: Aplocheilidae
Subfam.: Aplocheilinae

Aphyosemion punctatum
Spotted killie

RADDA & PÜRZL, 1977

Syn.: *Aphyosemion striatum ogoense* (not PELLEGRIN, 1930), *A* aff. *wildekampi.*

Hab.: Africa: northeast Gabon to Congo, in rain forest creeks of the Ivindo and Ogowe Basins.

F.I.: 1974 by BOCHTLER and co-travelers.

Sex.: ♂ *A. punctatum* have a blue-green body overlaid with red dots and longitudinal stripes. Their yellow fins have a red fringe. The ♀♀ are light brown with greenish yellow, slightly transparent fins.

Soc. B.: Peaceful species with a solitary lifestyle.

M: Best kept in a species tank. This species can be cared for in a community tank containing small, retiring fishes such as characins. Subdued illumination enhances its colors. Java moss is the spawning substrate of choice. Water should be soft and acid with a moderate temperature.

B: In show tanks where the parents receive good nutrition, young survive. The fish spawn on fine-leaved plants, peat fibers, and similar materials. For more efficient breeding, a pair or one ♂ and two ♀♀ should be placed in a small tank (about 10 l). The breeders are either left for an extended continuous set-up or removed after a few days. In the former case, collect the eggs regularly and transfer them into a rearing container where they will hatch after about 14–16 days. When peat fibers are used, they can be removed and stored moist in a plastic bag then rehydrated as for substrate spawners. Newly hatched young immediately accept *Artemia* nauplii.

F: C; small live foods of all kinds.

S: Some authors feel that *A. punctatum* is at most a subspecies of *A. wildekampi,* merely extending its northern distribution. *A. aureum* is another close relative.

T: 20°–22°C, **L:** 4.5 cm, **A:** 60 cm, **R:** m, b, **D:** 3–4

Aphyosemion raddai
Radda's killie

SCHEEL, 1975

Syn.: *Aphyosemion meinkeni* (not MYERS, 1933).

Hab.: Africa: southern Cameroon, in rain forest creeks of the upper Kellé-Nyong system at the western edge of the inland plateau.

F.I.: 1971 by RADDA and co-travelers.

Sex.: ♂♂ have an intense red design on a blue-green background. The colors tend to vary according to the animal's origin. ♀♀, in contrast, are an inconspicuous brown with round fins.

Soc. B.: Predominately peaceful and shy. Hiding places should be furnished, even though they are so appreciated the fish rarely emerge. ♂♂ will occasionally fight among themselves.

M: These animals can be kept in community with smaller, nonaggressive fishes such as characins. Plant the tank well. Intense illumination is not appreciated. Water should be soft and slightly acid. Vary its diet.

B: Adhesive spawners which either adhere their eggs to plants and other substrates or bury them in a peat substrate. The eggs can be collected (only possible in breeding tanks with few spawning possibilities) or removed with the spawning substrate each week and incubated separately. This species is somewhat sensitive and not very fecund.

F: C; live foods of corresponding size. Limit the amount of worms fed.

T: 22°–26°C, **L:** 5 cm, **A:** 50 cm, **R:** t, m, b, **D:** 3–4

Aphyosemion punctatum, WC, Mekambo, Gabon

Aphyosemion raddai, WC at Pouma, 25 km from Yaounde, Cameroon

Fam.: Aplocheilidae
Subfam.: Aplocheilinae

Aphyosemion scheeli
Orange-fringed killie

RADDA, 1970

Syn.: *Aphyosemion* "burundi," *A. akamk-paense.*

Hab.: Africa: southeast Nigeria, in rain forest and gallery forest creeks of the lower Cross River system.

F.I.: 1968 by SCHEEL, perhaps already in 1964 as the undescribed species *A. "burundi."*

Sex.: ♂♂ are more colorful. They are green to blue-green with red dots that can merge to form horizontal stripes. Unpaired fins are green to blue-green proximally with a red stripe distally and yellow, rarely yellow-orange, fringes. The dorsal fin is generally free of striations. ♀♀ are brown with—at the most—a faint rendition of the ♂♂'s coloration.

Soc. B.: A robust, but generally peaceful species.

M: Not particularly sensitive. They can be kept in a community aquarium. Like all *Aphyosemion* species, subdued lighting and a dark substrate enhance their colors. A moderate water hardness is not detrimental, although water in its natural biotope is soft. The pH should be around neutral.

B: *A. scheeli* can either be bred as a substrate or an adhesive spawner. Egg development in a rearing container takes about 16–21 days. If the animals are treated like substrate spawners (see *Nothobranchius eggersi*), then water can be added to the peat after 3–4 weeks. Newly hatched fry can be fed *Artemia salina* nauplii. Growth is quite rapid when the young are fed a good diet.

F: C; all types of live foods. After acclimation, frozen foods are accepted. Flake foods may be eaten.

T: 22°–26°C, **L:** 5 cm, **A:** 60 cm, **R:** m, b, **D:** 2–3

Aphyosemion splendopleure
Splendid killie

(BRÜNING, 1929)

Syn.: *Fundulopanchax splendopleuris, Aphyosemion bivittatum* (not LÖNNBERG, 1895).

Hab.: West Africa: coastal regions of southeastern Nigeria through Cameroon and Equatorial Guinea to northwestern Gabon.

F.I.: To Germany during the first half of 1929 by GRIEM from Tiko, Cameroon.

Sex.: ♀♀ are simply brownish with—depending on their mood—two dark longitudinal stripes and transparent, rounded fins. ♂♂ are a colorful iridescent blue-green with very elongated fins. There are a number of differently colored local populations.

Soc. B.: Peaceful towards nonrelated species. Hostilities may break out between conspecific ♂♂ and some congeners.

M: As for *A. punctatum*, though this species is slightly more suitable for community tanks as long as they are not densely stocked and the population consists of small species such as characins. Some specimens—each individual is different—are very shy and remain hidden. Others have a more robust nature and patrol their territory to expel rivals.

B: Breed as an adhesive spawner as described under *A. bualanum.*

F: C; live foods. Some animals will accept flakes once in a while.

S: *Aphyosemion bitaeniatum, A. bivittatum, A. loennbergii, A. volcanum,* and this species belong to the subgenus *Chromaphyosemion* RADDA, 1971.

T: 22°–26°C, **L:** 6 cm, **A:** 80 cm, **R:** t, m, b, **D:** 3

Aphyosemion scheeli

Aphyosemion splendopleure ♂, WC, Meme River, Cameroon

Fam.: Aplocheilidae
Subfam.: Aplocheilinae

Aphyosemion wachtersi wachtersi
Wachter's killie

RADDA & HUBER, 1978

Syn.: None.

Hab.: Africa: southern Congo, surroundings of Zanaga in the upper basin of the Ogowe River.

F.I.: July/August 1978 by BUYTAERT and WACHTERS.

Sex.: ♂♂ are more colorful and have larger fins. They are yellow ventrally and even have a yellow stripe on the lower edge of the anal and caudal fins. The dorsal half of the body has red spots which merge into longitudinal bands and transgress into the dorsal and caudal fins. Both of these fins have blue spots and a superior white-blue edge of variable width. ♀♀ are solid brown with round fins. A shadow of the ♂♂'s colors is represented in ♀♀.

Soc. B.: Generally considered to be a peaceful species. Only ♂♂ fight to establish a social hierarchy.

M: As for most small *Aphyosemion* species, for example, *A. bualanum kekemense*. At the type locality on July 24,

1978, at 8:30 the following values were measured: air temperature 19°C, water temperature 17°C, pH 5.5. *Gymnallabes alvarezi* was found in the same biotope. Never keep at overly warm temperatures.

B: As for *A. bualanum kekemense*. However, lower temperatures are important. WACHTERS (DKG Journal 11 [8/9], 1979) left the juveniles in the breeding tank with the parents until the young were about 8 weeks old. But this is probably only possible when the parents are well fed. WACHTERS mentions that some juveniles have xanthic (yellow) coloration which disappears as the fish age. This has also been observed in other *Aphyosemion* and *Rivulus* species and seems to be in response to prevailing water conditions.

F: C; all types of live foods.

S: *A. wachtersi* has one described subspecies other than the nominate form: *A. wachtersi mikeae*.

T: 17°–22°C, L: 5 cm, A: 80 cm, R: m, b, D: 3–4

Aphyosemion wildekampi
Wildekamp's killie

BERKENKAMP, 1973

Syn.: *Aphyosemion* "K 4."

Hab.: Africa: southeast Cameroon and southwestern Central African Republic.

F.I.: Imported into the Netherlands during the summer of 1972 by P. J. VLAMINCK from Diang, 40 km west of Bertoua, Cameroon.

Sex.: ♂♂ are yellowish brown with 4–6 rows of dots which sometimes coalesce into lines. The dots may form a herringbone design over the posterior body. Unpaired fins are yellow with small red dots and lines and a red edge. ♀♀ have a solid brown body with small red dots and colorless fins.

Soc. B.: Peaceful, small *Aphyosemion* species.

M: As for *A. punctatum*.

B: As for *A. punctatum*.

F: C; medium-sized live foods.

S: *A. wildekampi* is a close relative of *A. punctatum* RADDA & PÜRZL, 1977. Some authors consider the latter synonymous to *A. wildekampi*. Other references claim *A. wildekampi* is more closely tied to *A. striatum* (BOULENGER, 1911) and *A. escherichi* (AHL, 1924).

T: 20°–24°C, L: 4.5 cm, A: 60 cm, R: m, b, D: 3–4

Aphyosemion wachtersi wachtersi, RPC 78/30, Voula II, Congo

Aphyosemion wildekampi

Aphyosemion zygaima, WC, "Mindouli"

Aphyosemion zygaima
Mindouli killie

HUBER. 1981

Syn.: *Aphyosemion louessense* (not PELLEGRIN, 1931).

Hab.: West Africa: Congo, near the town of Mindouli in the basin of the upper Niari.

F.I.: 1964 by P. BRICHARD and T. ROBERTS.

Sex.: ♂♂ are more colorful, having red spots on a green body. The fins are likewise green. The spots on the fins, particularly the tail fin, merge into longitudinal stripes. ♀♀ have a similar red-brown spotted design, but on a solid brown body.

Soc. B.: Generally peaceful to the point of extreme shyness. Virtually always hidden.

M: As for all small *Aphyosemion* species (see *A. punctatum*). *A. zygaima* is rarely seen when housed in a commu-nity tank. Even maintaining the animals in a species tank does little to overcome its reclusive nature. If several ♂♂ are kept in a moderate-sized tank, they will chase each other out of their hiding places.

B: As for *A. punctatum*. *A. zygaima* is not very fecund, and the young are slow growing.

F: C; live foods, particularly mosquito larvae.

S: *A. zygaima* is closely related to *A. louessense.*

T: 18°–22°C, **L:** 5 cm, **A:** 60 cm, **R:** m, b, **D:** 3–4

Fam.: Aplocheilidae
Subfam.: Rivulinae

Cynolebias elongatus ♂

Cynolebias elongatus
Blue pearl fish

STEINDACHNER, 1881

Syn.: *Cynolebias holmbergi, C. spinifer, C. robustus* (in part).

Hab.: South America: southern Uruguay and Argentina, pampas region in the lower basin of the Rio de la Plata.

F.I.: 1912 by A. HAASE.

Sex.: ♂♂ are somewhat larger, blue-gray to gray-brown, and have more fin rays. ♀♀ have dark brown spots and a fuller ventral area.

Soc. B.: Generally peaceful, but due to their size, they should not be housed with small fishes. Spent ♀♀ are often unduly molested; therefore, provide hiding places.

M: This species is often kept in overly warm water. In nature, water temperatures range from a few degrees (southern winter) to above 30°C (southern summer). A large aquarium is necessary.

B: Substrate spawner. Breeding can only be accomplished in a separate tank containing a deep layer of peat. The animals dive into the peat to spawn. After one week, decant the water and store the peat in a plastic bag for 3–4 months. Then add cool water, as is normally done for substrate spawners. See *Pterolebias staecki* for details. Raise the fry on *Artemia* nauplii. Larger foods can quickly be added to the diet. Growth is rapid.

F: C; all types of large live foods.

S: There are two species which have been imported under the name *C. elongatus*. The species bred by FOERSCH (Aquarienmagazin **12** (2): 86–93, 1978) is probably not *C. elongatus*, but *C. robustus*.

T: 16°–25°C, **L:** to 14 cm, **A:** 100 cm, **R:** m, b, **D:** 3

Fam.: Aplocheilidae
Subfam.: Aplocheilinae

Aplocheilus werneri
Werner's panchax

MEINKEN, 1966

Syn.: *Aplocheilus dayi werneri.*

Hab.: Asia: relictlike presence in the Kottawa Forest of southern Sri Lanka (Ceylon).

F.I.: 1964 by WERNER Co, Munich.

Sex.: ♂♂ are usually larger and have elongated dorsal, anal, and caudal fins. They are generally more colorful, primarily having more red. ♀♀ are shorter and stouter with rounder and more transparent unpaired fins. The degree of color in the longitudinal band that extends from the base of the pectoral fins to the caudal peduncle depends on their mood.

Soc. B.: Peaceful. Small fishes may be considered prey. When several ♂♂ are kept in one aquarium, they display until a social hierarchy is established.

M: Can be placed in almost any standard aquarium. Under these conditions, it is easily cared for. It appreciates plants that reach the water surface and those that float. The water should be soft and neutral to slightly acid. However, water chemistry is not important for captive-bred specimens. Cover the aquarium.

B: Continuous adhesive spawner. Well-conditioned ♀♀ daily lay eggs among plants. For directed reproduction, it is best to use one ♂ and two ♀♀ in a moderate-sized spawning tank. Regularly collect the eggs from the spawning substrate. They hatch in the brooding container after about two weeks.

F: C; live and flake foods.

T: 22°–26°C, L: 9 cm, A: 80 cm, R: t, D: 2

Aplocheilus werneri ♂, Kottawa Forest, Sri Lanka

Aplocheilus werneri ♀, WC, Kottawa Forest, Sri Lanka

Aplocheilus werneri, WC, Kottawa Forest, Sri Lanka

Fam.: Aplocheilidae
Subfam.: Rivulinae

Cynolebias elongatus. See p. 491.

Cynolebias nonoiuliensis
Giant pearl fish

TABERNER, SANTOS & CASTELLI, 1975

Syn.: None.

Hab.: South America: Argentina, 15 km north of the town of 9 de Julio, province of Buenos Aires.

F.I.: 1980 by Dr. K. H. LÜLING.

Sex.: ♂♂ are larger with more pronounced fins. Like most ♂ *Cynolebias*, the dorsal and anal fins have more fin rays. They are reddish brown, turning lighter ventrally, with bluish fins. ♀♀ are light brown with dark brown mottling.

Soc. B.: Peaceful, but its size allows it to tackle relatively large fishes, which excludes small fishes from being suitable tankmates.

M: As is customary with *Cynolebias* species. House in a species tank. A peat substrate is recommended. Java moss, *Anubias*, or Java fern growing on bog-

wood can be distributed around the edges. Conditions in its natural habitat were as follows (LÜLING, Das Aquarium, 14 [134]: 394–396): ambient temperature 26°C, water temperature 18°C at the surface, 14°C at $1/2$ m depth, pH 6.8, and a total hardness of 1.7° dGH. Maintain these fish at cool temperatures.

B: Substrate diver. A large container of peat placed into the maintenance tank will quickly be accepted as a spawning substrate. After one week, the peat is treated as described for *Pterolebias staecki* and *P. wischmanni*, that is, pressed, briefly dried, and stored in a plastic bag for 4–5 months. The fry immediately eat *Artemia* nauplii upon hatching and grow very quickly.

F: C; large live foods.

T: 15°–25°C, **L:** 10 cm, **A:** 80 cm, **R:** m, b, **D:** 3–4

Cynopoecilus melanotaenia
Black-banded pearl fish

(REGAN, 1912)

Syn.: *Cynolebias melanotaenia.*

Hab.: South America: southeastern Brazil and northern Uruguay, usually in shallow, stationary waters. Often found with *Cynolebias adloffi* and *C. wolterstorffi.*

F.I.: 1912 by A. MAYER from the area around Paranagua, southeast Brazil.

Sex.: ♂♂ are more colorful and larger with elongated dorsal and anal fins. The throat is white, and the body is red-brown with a dark brown band running from the mouth through the eye to the tail. A second band lays over the stomach. Both are framed by light green-gold scales. The red-brown unpaired fins frequently have a dark edge. ♀♀ are light brown with less pronounced lateral stripes. Fins are more rounded.

Soc. B.: These animals are relatively aggressive among themselves; thus sufficient refuges should be offered. Peaceful towards characins, catfishes, etc.

M: As for *Rachovia hummelincki.* A thin layer of peat or peat fibers makes an

adequate substrate. Use peat fibers, roots, and plants (i.e., Java moss and Java fern) to provide secluded areas. Soft to medium-hard and slightly acid to neutral water with moderate temperatures is recommended.

B: Best when bred as a substrate spawner. See *R. hummelincki.* The animals rarely dive into the substrate. Instead, they normally spawn on top of the substrate, or even in the open water or on plants. Treat the substrate as you would for any substrate spawner. Rehydration can be attempted after 2–3 months, depending at what temperature the substrate was stored. The large fry immediately accept *Artemia* nauplii.

F: C; hardy live foods.

S: *C. aureoguttatus* CRUZ, 1974 is probably its closest relative. The newly described *Campellolebias* species from southeastern Brazil is presumably related to this species as well.

T: 18°–24°C, **L:** 5.5 cm, **A:** 60 cm, **R:** t, m, b, **D:** 3–4

Cynolebias nonoiuliensis ♂, WC, 9 de Julio, Argentina

Cynopoecilus melanotaenia

Fam.: Aplocheilidae
Subfam.: Aplocheilinae

Aphyosemion [*Diapteron*] fulgens (RADDA, 1975)

Syn.: *Aphyosemion georgiae fulgens, Diapteron fulgens.*

Hab.: Africa: northeastern Gabon, in the Ivindo Basin.

F.I.: 1972 by HERZOG and BOCHTLER.

Sex.: ♂♂ are blue, turning red-brown posteriorly. The fins are very colorful. The caudal and anal fins have a broad orange stripe along the edge which is followed proximally by a narrow blue-white stripe. The dorsal fin is orange to red-brown with a reticulated light blue to light orange design and a narrow light blue to whitish fringe. ♀♀ are small and brown with almost colorless fins.

Soc. B.: This tiny species is peaceful towards heterospecific fishes. ♂♂ are frequently involved in intense hierarchical fights.

M: Can be kept with small fishes such as characins. The aquarium should have a dark substrate and plenty of vegetation, e.g., *Anubias barteri nana,* Java fern, Java moss, and *Bolbitis,* to enhance the animal's colors. The plants can be fastened to bogwood. Water should be slightly acid to neutral, medium-hard, and temperate.

B: Breed in a small aquarium that has plenty of Java moss or peat fibers. The eggs can be collected and allowed to develop in a separate receptacle, though finding them is problematic. It is best to leave the eggs in the tank and remove the fry after 2–3 week. More fry result when the parents are removed at that time as well. The young should be fed infusoria and *Artemia* nauplii. Rearing the offspring in the breeding tank has the added advantage that the young can find additional microfoods among the plants during the first days.

F: C; small live foods.

T: 18°–22°C, L: 3.5 cm, A: 60 cm, R: t, m, b, D: 4

Aphyosemion [*Diapteron*] georgiae (LAMBERT & GERY, 1967)

Syn.: *Aphyosemion georgiae, Diapteron georgiae.*

Hab.: West Africa: central Gabon, basins of the Ivindo and the central Ogowe between Booué and Mékambo.

F.I.: 1972 by HERZOG and BOCHTLER.

Sex.: ♂♂ are red-brown with blue dots. These dots are distributed differently in distinct populations. The lower tail fin as well as the dorsal, anal, and ventral fins are dark orange. Blue dots cover the dorsal fin and, to a lesser degree, the red-brown upper lobe of the tail fin. ♀♀ are smaller and totally light brown with translucent, round fins.

Soc. B.: As for *A. fulgens.*

M: See *A. fulgens.*

B: As for *A. fulgens.* This species will also spawn in peat fibers. The peat can then be left "dry" for about 3–4 weeks. After this time lapse, add water.

F: C; the diminutive size of the animals limits its menu to those live foods small enough for the fish to consume.

T: 18°–22°C, L: 3.5 cm, A: 60 cm, R: t, m, b, D: 4

Aphyosemion fulgens

Aphyosemion georgiae

Fam.: Aplocheilidae
Subfam.: Aplocheilinae

Epiplatys coccinatus

BERKENKAMP & ETZEL, 1982

Syn.: None.

Hab.: Africa: Wadalna, central Liberia.

F.I.: December of 1978 by Dr. V. ETZEL.

Sex.: ♂♂ have blue to blue-green sides and a bronze dorsum. Depending on its mood, 8–11 oblique dark crossbands are visible. The fins have a light blue edge followed proximally by a red-brown then a blue-green stripe. ♀♀ are a simple red-brown with round, transparent fins.

Soc. B.: Like *E. f. fasciolatus*; however, *E. coccinatus* is generally shyer and more retiring.

M: See *E. f. fasciolatus*. The collection site was a forest creek with brown, soft, slightly acid (pH 6.2) water. Captive-bred specimens can be maintained in subop-timal water and even bred therein as long as the water chemistry values are not extreme. The aquarium should contain opportunities for concealment in the form of dense plant stands, etc.

B: As for *E. f. fasciolatus*.

F: C; all types of live foods, including aquatic insects.

S: This species belongs to the *E. fasciolatus* group. Based on coloration and meristic values, *E. coccinatus* could be a subspecies (?) of *E. ruhkopfi*.

T: 22°–26°C, **L:** 7 cm, **A:** 80 cm, **R:** t, m, **D:** 2–3

Epiplatys esekanus
Eseka panchax

SCHEEL, 1968

Syn.: None.

Hab.: West Africa: Cameroon, in a small creek in the basin of the lower Sanaga and Nyong Rivers near the Edea-Yaounde-Eseka crossroad.

F.I.: 1966 (?) by SCHEEL to Denmark.

Sex.: ♂♂ are more colorful. They have a number of red-brown to black-brown dots arranged in longitudinal rows on their gray-green body. The semielongated fins are blue (dorsal, upper caudal) or yellow-brown (anal, lower caudal). ♀♀ are smaller and browner with less intense dots and smaller, less colorful fins.

Soc. B.: Generally a peaceful, rather shy species.

M: Due to their somewhat delicate nature, *E. esekanus* is best kept in a species tank with soft, slightly acid water. Floating plants will serve to dim the illu-mination, which in turn tends to enhance the ♂♂'s colors.

B: Breeding is difficult and not prolific. Best bred as an adhesive spawner. Follow suggestions for *E. sexfasciatus rathkei*, however, the fry of *E. esekanus* grow slower.

F: C; all types of live foods commiserate to its size, particularly flying insects (*Drosophila*, wax moths).

T: 22°–26°C, **L:** 7 cm, **A:** 60 cm, **R:** t, m, **D:** 4

Epiplatys coccinatus, WC, RL 46, Wadalna, Liberia

Epiplatys esekanus

Fam.: Aplocheilidae
Subfam.: Aplocheilinae

Epiplatys fasciolatus puetzi

Syn.: None.

Hab.: Africa: Liberia, 20 km north of Buchanan.

F.I.: 1982 by Dr. V. ETZEL and W. PÜTZ.

Sex.: ♂♂ are larger and have elongated fins. They are shiny blue to violet with a copper brown dorsum. The caudal, anal, and ventral fins have yellow to orange fringes. ♀♀ are smaller with a brownish body and colorless fins.

Soc. B.: See *E. f. fasciolatus*.

M: As described for *E. f. fasciolatus*. According to the first describers, the animals were fished from a 80 cm wide, 20–50 cm deep, clear water creek that had the following characteristics on November 11, 1982 at 16:30: ambient temperature 27°C, pH 5.8, conductivity 0.68 μS. The water was acid and poor in

BERKENKAMP & ETZEL, 1985

ions. *E. f. puetzi* will tolerate values outside those of its natural habitat as long as extremes are avoided.

B: As for *E. f. fasciolatus*.

F: C; all kinds of live foods, even larger ones. See *E. f. fasciolatus*.

S: Although *E. f. puetzi* definitely belongs within the *E. fasciolatus* group, it should be more closely related to *E. olbrechtsi* (= *E. fasciolatus olbrechtsi*?), mediating between *olbrechtsi* and *fasciolatus*.

T: 22°–28°C, **L:** 8 cm, **A:** 80 cm, **R:** t, m, **D:** 2–3

Epiplatys fasciolatus tototaensis
Totota panchax

ROMAND, 1978

Syn.: *Epiplatys fasciolatus huwaldi*.

Hab.: Africa: southwest Liberia, near Monrovia and Totota.

F.I.: 1964 by BRASCH and a co-worker; perhaps imported earlier under a different name.

Sex.: ♂♂ are blue with a brown dorsum. The posterior body has oblique stripes which may darken or virtually disappear, depending on their mood. The anal and tail fins are blue distally with a red-brown to black edge. ♀♀ are smaller with round fins and inconspicuous colors.

Soc. B.: See *E. f. fasciolatus*.

M: This subspecies is robust and easy to maintain. Instructions concerning care can be found under *E. f. fasciolatus*. *E. f. tototaensis* undergoes pronounced mood-related color changes. Oblique stripes and sometimes a dark longitudinal band appear when the fish becomes frightened.

B: As for *E. f. fasciolatus*.

F: C; live foods.

T: 22°–28°C, **L:** 8 cm, **A:** 80 cm, **R:** t, m, **D:** 2–3

Epiplatys fasciolatus puetzi, F₁, 20 km north of Buchanan, Liberia

Epiplatys fasciolatus tototaensis

Fam.: Aplocheilidae
Subfam.: Aplocheilinae

Epiplatys nigricans
Black panchax

BOULENGER, 1913

Syn.: None.

Hab.: The type specimens of *E. nigricans* hail from Dungu along the upper Uele River in northeast Zaïre. If the specimens which nowadays are considered *E. nigricans* are indeed this species, then *E. nigricans* is broadly distributed throughout the entire Congo Basin to Kasai.

F.I.: Probably in the '50's by P. BRICHARD.

Sex.: The ♂♂'s fins are larger, more elongated, and yellowish, frequently with a black edge. The body is yellowish-brown and often has a reticulated red-brown design. When excited, a black band appears along its side from the snout to the caudal peduncle, but it almost totally disappears as the fish calms. ♀♀ have a fuller anterior body, a more slender caudal peduncle, and more transparent, rounded fins. It is not always easy to distinguish genders.

Soc. B.: Peaceful. Conspecific ♂♂ may display among themselves.

M: Heavy vegetation, including a section of natant or floating plants, and soft to medium-hard and neutral to slightly acid water are required. Moderate-sized fishes can be housed in the same tank.

B: Use a separate breeding tank and follow suggestions made under *Aphyosemion punctatum*. The eggs can be stored in a plastic bag for about 2–3 weeks in peat fibers then rehydrated. However, the more common method is to collect the eggs from the spawning substrate (wool mop, spawning fibers, peat fibers) or to transfer all of the spawning substrate into a separate tank after one week. When the fry hatch, feed them *Artemia* during the first days, graduating slowly to larger live foods.

F: C; live foods. Mosquito larvae are ideal.

S: It is very questionable whether this species is indeed *E. nigricans*. Numerous authors consider this taxon a synonym of *E. chevalieri*, while others consider it a subspecies. All these hypotheses remain conjecture until more live specimens from *E. nigricans*'s type locality are imported.

T: 20°–26°C, **L:** 5.5 cm, **A:** 60 cm, **R:** t, m, **D:** 3

Epiplatys njalaensis
Red-spotted panchax

NEUMANN, 1976

Syn.: None.

Hab.: Africa: in flowing waters of the rain forests of southwest Sierra Leone to neighboring Guinea.

F.I.: 1975 by E. ROLOFF from Njala, Sierra Leone.

Sex.: ♂♂ are larger and have a pale blue to brownish body with a few rows of red dots along their sides that extend into the caudal peduncle. The caudal fin is yellow superiorly and blue inferiorly with a red line running along both the superior and inferior edges. The dorsal fin, the central section of the caudal fin, and frequently the anal fin have red lines running along the fin rays. The dorsal fin is yellow, whereas the anal fin is light blue to yellowish. The ♀♀ have a brown-yellow body and transparent fins. The posterior body has 10–12 slanted bands that vary in intensity depending on mood.

Soc. B.: See *E. fasciolatus*, though this species is considered more peaceful and shy.

M: As for *E. fasciolatus*.

B: As for *E. fasciolatus*.

F: C; live foods, including larger ones.

S: A member of the *E. fasciolatus* group. This species has a broader distribution than presently thought, as BLEHER found this species in Guinea as well.

T: 22°–28°C, **L:** 6 cm, **A:** 80 cm, **R:** t, m, **D:** 3

Epiplatys nigricans

Epiplatys njalaensis

Fam.: Aplocheilidae
Subfam.: Aplocheilinae

Epiplatys sexfasciatus baroi
Red six-barred panchax

BERKENKAMP, 1975

Syn.: None.

Hab.: Africa: southwestern Cameroon, the area around Kumba and the Kiende Basin.

F.I.: 1970.

Sex.: As the picture shows, ♂♂ are an intense red-brown, becoming metallic green to blue anteriorly. The scales have a red center which form longitudinal rows of red dots along its sides. There are 5–7 vertical dark stripes on the posterior body. All fins are orange-red except the clear pectoral fins. ♀♀ have less intense colors, and their fins are round.

Soc. B.: See *E. s. rathkei,* though this subspecies is more bashful.

M: As for *E. s. rathkei.*

B: See *E. s. rathkei.*

F: C; as for *E. s. rathkei.*

T: 22°–26°C, **L:** 7 cm, **A:** 80 cm, **R:** t, m, **D:** 2–3

Epiplatys sexfasciatus rathkei
Rathke's six-barred panchax

RADDA, 1970

Syn.: *Panchax sexfasciatus, Aplocheilus sexfasciatus, Haplochilus infrafasciatus.*

Hab.: Africa: west Cameroon, in the drainage basins of the Mungo, Sanaga, and Nyong Rivers.

F.I.: Unknown.

Sex.: ♂♂ are larger and more intensely colored with 6–9 slightly oblique crossbands on their yellowish brown body. The elongated fins are red-brown distally, yellow proximally. The ♀♀ are browner, smaller, and have round, almost colorless fins. They also have crossbands.

Soc. B.: Usually peaceful, but larger specimens have been known to turn predacious towards small fishes. Hence, small species make inappropriate tankmates.

M: Not difficult. Suitable for community aquaria. Although the water values should be soft and slightly acid, *E. sexfasciatus* tolerates medium-hard, slightly alkaline water as well. Vegetation is advantageous. The fish like to hover beneath leaves of floating plants such as water sprite (*Cerotopteris*).

B: Adhesive spawners. Place one ♂ and several ♀♀ into a moderate-sized tank containing a spawning mop of artificial or peat fibers, Java moss, or similar. Methodically collect the eggs and transfer them into a separate container, perhaps one containing acriflavine as a fungal prophylactic. Depending on temperature, the eggs will need between 14 and 16 days to hatch. Juveniles immediately accept *Artemia salina*. With a good diet and regular water exchanges, the fry grow rapidly.

F: C; live foods, including small water beetles, etc. After acclimation, flake foods are also accepted.

S: *E. sexfasciatus rathkei* is one of four subspecies. The others are the nominate form *E. s. sexfasciatus* (see Vol. 1, p. 562), *E. s. togolensis,* and *E. s. baroi.*

T: 22°–26°C, **L:** 8 cm, **A:** 80 cm, **R:** t, m, **D:** 2–3

Epiplatys sexfasciatus baroi

Epiplatys sexfasciatus rathkei, WC, Kumba, Cameroon

Fam.: Aplocheilidae
Subfam.: Aplocheilinae

Nothobranchius eggersi
Eggers' notho

SEEGERS, 1982

Syn.: *Nothobranchius* sp. "Ruhoi."

Hab.: Africa: east Tanzania, in the lower Rufiji Basin.

F.I.: January 1981 by EGGERS, KASSEL-MANN, and SEEGERS.

Sex.: ♂♂ are large, colorful fish with gorgeous fins. ♀♀ are light brown with gray overtones and brownish transparent fins.

Soc. B.: Peaceful towards heterospecific fishes. ♂♂ are aggressive among themselves, particularly in small aquaria. Congener ♂♂ will also fight. Individual ♀♀ will be chased to death as soon as they are spent.

M: Their colors are brightest when kept in a species tank with a dark substrate (peat). Never keep 2 ♂♂ together. It is always best to keep either one ♂ or a group of ♂♂. Without exception, keep several ♀♀. The fish are not very demanding in regard to water values, but neutral to slightly acid, soft water is the most favorable. A good diet of live foods is important.

B: Substrate spawner. Place one ♂ and 2–3 ♀♀ into a 20 l spawning tank that has a layer of peat or peat fibers and feed sparingly. After one week, the animals and the water are removed and the peat lightly pressed, slightly dried, then stored in a plastic bag for 6 weeks at moderate temperatures. Afterwards, water is added to the peat in a small aquarium. The fry immediately accept *Artemia* nauplii. If the eggs do not hatch, redry the peat and add water again after 14 days. The process may need to be repeated several times.

F: C; all types of live foods; beef heart is less appreciated than worms.

S: Three color morphs have been found: *N. eggersi* "blue," which the type belongs to (see photo); *N. eggersi* "red head," and *N. eggersi* "red." Only one ♂ of the latter has been imported (see photo on p. 509). All animals offered as "red" are a cross of the pictured animal with the blue form or its descendants. The "red head" morph is probably totally diluted by crosses.

T: 24°–28°C, **L:** 5 cm, **A:** 60 cm, **R:** b, m, **D:** 3

Spawning sequence of *Nothobranchius eggersi*

Fam.: Aplocheilidae
Subfam.: Aplocheilinae

Nothobranchius eggersi "blue"

Nothobranchius eggersi, "red" x "blue" hybrid

Habitat of *Nothobranchius eggersi*

Nothobranchius eggersi, WC, red morph, Selous Game Reserve, Tanzania

Fam.: Aplocheilidae
Subfam.: Aplocheilinae

Nothobranchius elongatus
Slender notho

WILDEKAMP, 1982

Syn.: *Nothobranchius guentheri* (not PFEFFER, 1893), *N. palmqvisti* "elongate," *N.* sp. "Munyenze," *N.* sp. "Kaloleni," *N.* sp. "Mariakani," *N.* sp. "Uganda," *N.* sp. "U 11."

Hab.: Africa: southeast Kenya, in seasonal pools and flood plains about 20–30 km northwest of Mombasa around the towns of Kaloleni and Mariakani.

F.I.: 1962 by J. H. E. LEAKY to the United States; from there it was exported to Great Britain and Germany.

T: 24°–28°C, **L:** 6 cm, **A:** 60 cm, **R:** m, b, **D:** 3

Sex.: ♂♂ are blue-green with a bright red caudal peduncle and tail fin. All their fins are larger. ♀♀ are smaller and gray-brown with almost colorless fins.

Soc. B.: Peaceful. Comparable to *N. eggersi.*

M: See *N. eggersi.*

B: As for *N. eggersi.*

F: C; live foods of all kinds, particularly worms and mosquito larva. Beef heart is accepted after the fish are acclimated.

A small water remnant in the jungle; habitat of *Roloffia liberiensis.*

Nothobranchius elongatus, WC, Kalaleni, Kenya

Nothobranchius elongatus

Fam.: Aplocheilidae
Subfam.: Aplocheilinae

Nothobranchius foerschi
Foersch's notho

WILDEKAMP & BERKENKAMP, 1979

Syn.: *Nothobranchius palmquisti* (not LÖNNBERG, 1907), *N.* sp. "Dar es Salaam," *N.* "Vivoplani."

Hab.: Africa: coastal lowlands of eastern Tanzania, probably the drainages of the Rufiji and Ruvu Rivers. Its precise distribution is unknown.

F.I.: 1956 by Tropicarium Co., Frankfurt.

Sex.: ♂♂ are more colorful, having a carmine caudal fin and reddish dorsal and anal fins. ♀♀ are smaller and brown. Their fins are brownish and transparent.

Soc. B.: Peaceful towards heterospecifics. Conspecific ♂♂ may engage in fights. Immature or spent ♀♀ may be treated rough. It is best to transport these fish singly.

M: Of all the *Nothobranchius*, this is one of the most undemanding. The animals frequently wane when housed with lively tankmates. An ideal fish either for a species tank or tranquil community tanks that have a dark substrate (peat), bogwood, Java moss, and Java fern. The water should be soft with a pH of 6.5 to 7.5. Copious quantities of live foods are important.

B: *N. foerschi* is an annual fish and a substrate spawner. Breeding is similar to that of *N. eggersi*. Like said species, *N. foerschi* is usually kept at temperatures that are too low. Higher temperatures (up to 30°C) stimulate the spawn to hatch sooner.

F: C; live foods of all kinds. Although the animals relish worms, these foodstuffs should be fed in a controlled manner lest diseases and fatty degeneration result.

T: 22°–26°C, **L:** 5 cm, **A:** 60 cm, **R:** m, b, **D:** 3

Nothobranchius interruptus
Kikambala notho

WILDEKAMP & BERKENKAMP, 1979

Syn.: *Nothobranchius* "U 6," *N. jubbi interruptus*.

Hab.: East Africa: southeast Kenya, coastal regions around the Mwatsuma River, particularly the surroundings of Kikambala.

F.I.: August 1978 by E. HOLLER.

Sex.: ♂♂ have a gray-blue body with a reticulate design formed by the red-brown edges of their scales. The caudal fin is blunt and dark red with a dark to transparent edge. The anal fin is yellowish green; the dorsal fin is bronze with brown spots. ♀♀ are smaller and solid gray-brown with round, transparent fins.

Soc. B.: Peaceful towards heterospecifics. ♂♂ are aggressive among themselves. Occasionally, aggressions may be directed towards immature ♀♀ as well.

M: See *N. eggersi*.

B: As for *N. eggersi*.

F: C; all types of live foods, especially worms.

S: *N. interruptus* is closely related to *N. melanospilus* and continues its distribution roughly towards the north.

T: 22°–26°C, **L:** 6.5 cm, **A:** 60 cm, **R:** m, b, **D:** 3

Nothobranchius foerschi

Nothobranchius interruptus, WC, Kikambala, Kenya

Fam.: Aplocheilidae
Subfam.: Aplocheilinae

Nothobranchius kafuensis. See p. 522.

Nothobranchius lourensi
Green notho

WILDEKAMP, 1977

Syn.: None.

Hab.: Africa: Tanzania, in the Ruvu Basin. So far only known from the type locality, a puddle along the Morogoro-Dar es Salaam road between the Ruvu Bridge and Kwaraza.

F.I.: 1976 by WILDEKAMP and companions.

Sex.: ♀♀ are gray-brown, and their fins are mostly transparent. Larger ♂♂ have a gray-blue to greenish body. The scales are distinctly edged in red-brown, creating a reticulate pattern. Unpaired fins have red-brown stripes running parallel to the fin's edges which frequently disintegrate into dots.

Soc. B.: Peaceful. ♂♂ occasionally fight to establish hierarchy. A shy species when compared to other members of the genus.

M: As for *N. eggersi*. However, *N. lourensi* is more sensitive.

B: As for *N. eggersi*. Usually not as fecund.

F: C; moderate-sized live foods.

S: *N. lourensi* is similar in color and pattern to *N. korthausae*, a species from the island of Mafia in Tanzania. *N. korthausae* is probably *N. lourensi*'s closest relative.

T: 24°–28°C, **L:** 5 cm, **A:** 60 cm, **R:** m, b, **D:** 3

Nothobranchius luekei
Lüke's notho

SEEGERS, 1984

Syn.: None.

Hab.: Africa: Tanzania, east Atlantic coastal lowlands, Mbezi Basin, ca. 40 km south of Dar es Salaam.

F.I.: January 1983 by SEEGERS and WISCHMANN.

Sex.: The ♂♂'s unpaired fins have a red fringe. The body is blue-gray. ♀♀ are uniformly brown with transparent fins.

Soc. B.: Peaceful, shy species.

M: As for *N. eggersi*, though the diminutive size of the fish has to be taken into account. A species tank is recommended. This species was found with *Nothobranchius melanospilus, N. rubripinnis, Ctenopoma muriei, Clarias gariepinus,* and various barbs and characins, though they were all juveniles. The water temperature was around 30°C at 18:00. The pH was 7.3.

B: As for *N. eggersi*. Fry are very small when they hatch and must be fed infusoria and microfoods until they can handle *Artemia*. Growth is relatively slow. Judging from prevailing temperatures found in their natural habitat, this species is normally maintained and bred at suboptimal temperatures.

F: C; all types of small live foods. *Artemia* nauplii are suitable for full-grown specimens.

S: *N. luekei* is the smallest known *Nothobranchius* species. It and *N. janpapi* belong to the subgenus *Aphyobranchius*.

T: 24°–30°C, **L:** 4 cm, **A:** 60 cm, **R:** t, m, b, **D:** 4

Nothobranchius lourensi

Nothobranchius luekei, WC, Mbezi River type, Tanzania

Fam.: Aplocheilidae
Subfam.: Aplocheilinae

Nothobranchius melanospilus
Beira notho

(PFEFFER, 1896)

Syn.: *Fundulus melanospilus, F. orthonotus* (not PETERS, 1844), *Nothobranchius guentheri* (not PFEFFER, 1893), *N. emini, N. eimincki, N. seychellensis.*

Hab.: Africa: southeast Kenya and east Tanzania, coastal lowlands from the basin of the Umba River (Kenya) to the Lukuledi (Tanzania). This is the most common *Nothobranchius* species within its distribution area. Inhabits seasonal puddles and flood areas.

F.I.: Unknown.

Sex.: ♂♂ are colorful. The red edges on their blue scales form a reticulate pattern. The caudal fin is carmine red; the dorsal and anal fins have red spots. ♀♀ are brown with black spots and transparent fins.

Soc. B.: Generally peaceful towards heterospecifics. ♂♂ are aggressive towards each other. Occasionally, ♂♂ may direct their hostilities towards ♀♀ as well. Pack singly when anticipating a lengthy transport.

M: As for *N. eggersi*. However, because of its larger stature, this species needs a bigger tank.

B: Substrate spawner. As for *N. eggersi*.

F: C; live foods, particularly worms. Beef heart is accepted once the fish are acclimated.

T: 22°–28°C, **L:** 7 cm, **A:** 80 cm, **R:** m, b, **D:** 2–3

Nothobranchius neumanni
Neumann's notho

HILGENDORF, 1905

Syn.: *Fundulus neumanni.*

Hab.: Africa: central Tanzania, basins of the Bubu River and Lakes Manyara and Ruaka.

F.I.: January of 1982 by CLASSEN and SEEGERS from Chipogola, Tanzania.

Sex.: ♀♀ are a drab gray-brown with fins that are virtually always transparent. ♂♂, in contrast, normally have a bright red caudal fin and a blue-gray body. The anal fin has red-brown, yellow, white, and black stripes, depending on the population. These stripes are frequently incomplete.

Soc. B.: Normally peaceful towards heterospecifics. ♂♂ are frequently aggressive towards conspecific ♂♂ and immature or spent ♀♀. Aggressions are more pronounced in wild caught specimens than in captive-bred specimens.

M: As for *N. eggersi*. However, while *N. neumanni* is generally considered more robust, it is more delicate in many regards. For example, rapid environmental changes and food shortages are to its detriment, as it quickly becomes emaciated and wanes. Likewise, a negative response is quickly displayed when the water quality or temperature become suboptimal. It seems that these animals have a shorter life span than species from coastal lowlands.

B: Principally like *N. eggersi*. If possible, place several ♀♀ in the breeding tank. A group set-up consisting of several ♂♂ and a number of ♀♀ in a large aquarium *sans* decoration other than a dish of peat for oviposition has proven effective. Feed the breeders well. Frequent water exchanges are required. *N. neumanni* fry must be "swimming in food" after they hatch. Lack of food causes growth defects which are hard to compensate for.

F: C; all types of hardy live foods, including worms.

S: Its closest relative, whose distribution partially overlaps that of *N. neumanni*, is *N. taeniopygus*.

T: 24°–28°C, **L:** 6 cm, **A:** 80 cm, **R:** m, b, **D:** 3

Nothobranchius melanospilus, WC, Mtanza, Tanzania

Nothobranchius neumanni, WC, Bahi Swamps, ca. 70 km from Dodoma towards Singida, Tanzania

Fam.: Aplocheilidae
Subfam.: Aplocheilinae

Nothobranchius polli
Poll's notho

WILDEKAMP, 1978

Syn.: *Nothobranchius brieni* (not POLL, 1938), *N. taeniopygus* (not HILGEN-DORF, 1981).

Hab.: Africa: southeast Zaïre and perhaps Zambia, in seasonal puddles, swamps, and ditches in the upper Lufira Basin in the province of Shaba.

F.I.: 1960 by E. GRAINDORGE to the Netherlands.

Sex.: Like all *Nothobranchius* species, ♂♂ are very colorful. The photo, due to its age, is too red and does not show the true colors of the species (see DATZ, **15** (8): 225, 1962). In reality the ♂♂'s body is reddish to dark brown. Every scale along the fish's side has a bright blue center. Though the upper edge of the dorsal fin and the stripe on the tail fin appear white in the photo, they are really light blue. The distal half of the anal fin is orange with a red-brown design, while the proximal half has a blue design. ♀♀ are light brown with transparent fins.

Soc. B.: Aggressive towards congener ♂♂ and immature or spent ♀♀. Otherwise, this is considered a peaceful species.

M: As for *N. eggersi*.

B: As for *N. eggersi*.

F: C; hardy live foods.

S: *N. polli* is one of a group of similar species that comes from southern central Africa, inhabiting southern Zaïre, Zambia, eastern Namibia, and northern Zimbabwe. Of this group, *Nothobranchius* sp. "Kayuni State Farm," *N.* sp. "Chunga," and "Nega Nega" from Zambia have been recently described as *N. kafuensis* (see pp. 522–523).

T: 22°–28°C, **L:** 5 cm, **A:** 60 cm, **R:** m, b, **D:** 3

Nothobranchius robustus
Robust notho

AHL, 1935

Syn.: *Nothobranchius* sp. "K 86/13, Sio River."

Hab.: Africa: Tanzania, Kenya, and Uganda, in the Lake Victoria Basin. Found in swamps and dead river arms.

F.I.: To Switzerland in 1985 by DE RHAM from the area around Ahero, Kenya, though they probably died out. Imported into Germany in 1986 by EGGERS and SEEGERS from the Sio River, Kenya. Imported to the Netherlands and Great Britain from Uganda in 1988 by WILDEKAMP and companions.

Sex.: Only ♂♂ have large, bright red unpaired fins and ventral fins that are blue anteriorly. ♀♀ are a solid brownish-gray, and their fins are more rounded.

Soc. B.: See *N. eggersi*. Although this species is generally considered shyer than its congeners, it is possible that its ♂♂ are more aggressive among themselves. *N. robustus* frequently hide in the bottom.

M: As for *N. eggersi*.

B: Substrate spawner. See *N. eggersi* for details.

F: C; like all *Nothobranchius* species, it prefers live foods. Flake foods are only exceptionally accepted.

S: The type specimens of *N. robustus* were collected south of Lake Victoria in northern Tanzania. Nevertheless, no live specimens matching the pictured fish have been collected from that local, so its identity is not entirely definite. But the description by AHL (somewhat skimpy) fits the presented fish.

T: 24°–28°C, **L:** 5.5 cm, **A:** 60 cm, **R:** b, m, **D:** 3

Nothobranchius polli

Nothobranchius robustus, WC, K 86/13 Sio River, Kenya

Fam.: Aplocheilidae
Subfam.: Aplocheilinae

Nothobranchius rubripinnis
Red-finned notho

SEEGERS, 1986

Syn.: *Nothobranchius* sp. "TZ 83/5," *N.* sp. "KTZ 85/28."

Hab.: Africa: Tanzania, along coastal lowlands, Mbezi (TZ 83/5) and Mbemkuru Basins (KTZ 85/28).

F.I.: January 1983 by SEEGERS and WISCHMANN.

Sex.: ♂♂ are colorful fish with red fins. Only the dorsal fin is yellowish to bronze with red-brown dots and stripes. The snout and throat are red, while the flanks are blue-green. ♀♀ are smaller and brownish with transparent, round fins.

Soc. B.: Peaceful. ♂♂, especially those of the small southern form from Mbemkuru, become very aggressive among themselves when kept in a limited space. Their shy nature and tendency to zigzag through the aquarium as they search out new hiding places among the substrate is quite deviant from the norm.

M: Generally, suggestions given for *N. eggersi* hold true. Animals from Mbemkuru, however, should be kept in a species tank with a peat bottom. In nature, both forms live together with *N. melanospilus*, though this should not be carried over to the aquarium lest the smaller *N. rubripinnis* proves inferior.

B: As for *N. eggersi*. The offspring of the Mbemkuru form (KTZ 85/28) are very small, requiring infusoria as their initial food.

F: C; live foods.

S: Now that the southern form from Mbemkuru has been kept in captivity for several generations and there is more information, it is questionable whether it and the Mbezi population are indeed the same species. Corresponding research has not been concluded.

T: 22°–28°C, **L:** 5 cm, **A:** 80 cm, **R:** m, b, **D:** 3–4

Nothobranchius rubripinnis, WC, KTZ 85/28 Mbemkuru River, Tanzania

Nothobranchius rubripinnis, WC, TZ 83/5 Mbezi River, Tanzania

Fam.: Aplocheilidae
Subfam.: Aplocheilinae

Nothobranchius taeniopygus
Stripe-finned notho

HILGENDORF, 1891

Syn.: *Fundulus taeniopygus, F. (Nothobranchius) orthonotus* (not PETERS, 1844)

Hab.: East Africa: central Tanzania, in the Bubu and Wembere River Basins.

F.I.: One ♂ in 1978 by R. WILDEKAMP and companions; several specimens were imported in 1985 from various locals by ROTH, SEEGERS, WILDEKAMP, and companions.

Sex.: ♂♂ have a yellowish to light gray body overlaid by a gray or brown reticulate design created by the edges of the scales. The fins are medium gray and yellow mottled, while the anal and caudal fins have a black edge and a yellow or white stripe proximally. This stripe may be followed by other stripes, some complete, others broken, on the anal fin. ♀♀ are smaller and brown with round transparent fins.

Soc. B.: Like most *Nothobranchius* species, this fish is usually peaceful towards heterospecifics. Conspecific ♂♂ or related species may be attacked.

M: As for *N. eggersi*. The values at the collection site at the upper Wembere Basin close to the type locality 37 km west of Itigi at the train tracks to Tabora (KTZ 85/9) on the June 22, 1985, at about 9:00 were the following: ambient temperature 20.5°C, water temperature 17.2°C, pH 8.2, 6° dGH, 5° dKH, conductivity 210 μS. Other localities likewise had rather low temperatures and a neutral to alkaline pH.

B: See *N. eggersi*, but the temperature does not need to be as high.

F: C; hardy live foods, including worms. Beef heart is accepted after the animals are acclimated.

T: 18°–24°C, **L:** 6 cm, **A:** 60 cm, **R:** m, b, **D:** 3

Nothobranchius kafuensis

WILDEKAMP & ROSENSTOCK, 1989

Syn.: None.

Hab.: Africa: Zambia, in the Kafue Basin southwest of Lusaka. The pictured wild caught specimens represent a population from the area around the town of Chunga. A similar population was found at the town of Nega Nega.

F.I.: 1979 by the Dane ROSENSTOCK from the Kayuni State Farm, Monze, Zambia.

Sex.: ♂♂ have colorful orange-edged blue scales and orange fins. ♀♀ are a simple gray-brown with transparent fins.

Soc. B.: Peaceful. ♂♂ are aggressive towards other ♂♂ and immature or spent ♀♀. Best if transported singly, particularly over long distances.

M: As for *N. eggersi*. Although this species can be cared for in a community tank, it is not recommended. These animals require tropical temperatures and good foods (live).

B: As indicated for *N. eggersi*. Fecund species.

F: C; live foods; worms are readily accepted. After acclimation, beef heart is eaten.

T: 22°–28°C, **L:** 5 cm, **A:** 60 cm, **R:** m, b, **D:** 3

Nothobranchius taeniopygus, WC, KTZ 85/9 Kazi Kazi, east Lake Chaya, Tanzania

Nothobranchius kafuensis, WC, Chunga, Zambia

Fam.: Aplocheilidae
Subfam.: Aplocheilinae

Pachypanchax omalonotus (DUMERIL, 1861)
Powder-blue panchax

Syn.: *Poecilia omalonota, Epiplatys homalonotus, Aplocheilus omalonotus, Haplochilus omalonotus, Pachypanchax homalonotus, Poecilia nuchimaculata, Pachypanchax nuchimaculatus, Panchax sakaramyi* (?).

Hab.: Western and northern Madagascar and the islands of Nossi Bé. Found in rivers and creeks.

F.I.: To France at the end of 1953 by J. ARNOULT.

Sex.: ♂♂ have elongated fins and more intense colors. The ♀♀'s fins are round, and they have a larger girth.

Soc. B.: Generally peaceful. Single specimens, however, may be quarrelsome.

M: Simple. A suitable species for community aquaria. Water values are of secondary importance. The aquarium should

contain opportunities for concealment among plants, since ♀♀ may be intensely pursued by ♂♂.

B: Not very difficult. As for *Epiplatys fasciolatus*. However, the large eggs can frequently be collected from the maintenance aquarium if the fish have a preferred spawning site. Juveniles frequently survive in a species tank or lightly stocked community aquarium without further ado.

F: C; all types of live foods as well as commercial diets.

S: This species was widely distributed in the '50's and '60's. Unfortunately, it has since disappeared from the hobby. In 1975 a new group was imported into France, but all the ♂♂ died, leaving only ♀♀ until the captive population was once again extinct.

T: 22°–28°C, **L:** 8 cm, **A:** 80 cm, **R:** t, m, **D:** 2

Nothobranchius [Paranothobranchius] ocellatus (SEEGERS, 1985)

Syn.: *Paranothobranchius ocellatus.*

Hab.: Africa: east Tanzania, in the Rufiji Basin at Mtanza and the Ruvu Basin.

F.I.: One ♀ was imported in 1981 by G. EGGERS, C. KASSELMANN, and L. SEEGERS.

Sex.: The sexes are not always easy to distinguish. The only captured ♂ was larger than the ♀. The body was blue-gray, turning whitish ventrally, and the fins were yellowish to blue-gray. There were two black ocelli on the tail fin which had a yellow ring around them (sex determining characteristic?). The ♀ only had one ocellus. Her fins were transparent, and her body was gray-brown.

Soc. B.: While nothing is known about its social behavior, it is probably similar to other *Nothobranchius* species.

M: The ♀ was easily cared for using suggested maintenance conditions listed

under *N. eggersi*. *N. eggersi* and *P. ocellatus* are found together in nature.

B: Has proven impossible, since ♂♂ have not been imported. But it is suspected that breeding is similar to that of *N. eggersi* and *N. melanospilus*.

F: C; live foods. In contrast to its appearance, this species does not seem to be particularly predacious.

S: *N. ocellatus* was found in a flood pool with *N. melanospilus* and *N. janpapi*, but despite several attempts throughout the year and many seasons, it proved impossible to capture more specimens. In contrast to the two other species found in the same pool, this species seems to be rare.

T: 22°–26°C, **L:** 6 cm, **A:** 80 cm, **R:** m, b, **D:** 3?

Pachypanchax omalonotus

Nothobranchius ocellatus ♀, WC, Mtanza, Tanzania

Nothobranchius [*Pronothobranchius*] *kiyawensis* "Accra Hills, Ghana"

Nothobranchius [*Pronothobranchius*] *kiyawensis*   (AHL, 1928)

Syn.: *Nothobranchius kiyawensis, Aphyosemion kiyawense, Fundulus gambiensis, Nothobranchius gambiensis, Aphyosemion seymouri, Pronothobranchius kiyawensis.*.

Hab.: West Africa: Gambia, Ghana, northern Nigeria, in savannas. So far only very disjunct distributions are known.

F.I.: To Great Britain in 1968.

Sex.: ♂♂ have larger fins and a light body with numerous variable longitudinal rows of red dots. The unpaired fins have a red edge followed by a distinct (caudal fin) or faint (dorsal, anal) yellow to orange zone. From the caudal peduncle, a flamelike red-brown zone extends posteriorly into the caudal fin. ♀♀ are more brown, even though their colors are basically the same as those found in ♂♂, particularly the red dots. Their anterior body is rounder, and their fins are small and transparent.

Soc. B.: Peaceful, but ♂♂ can be very aggressive among themselves.

M: Corresponds to most *Nothobranchius* species. See *N. eggersi.*

B: Similar to many *Nothobranchius* species, but considered more difficult. See *N. eggersi.* For unknown reasons, some set-ups incur high losses during storage.

F: C; all types of live foods, particularly worms.

S: So far, only the form from Ghana (Accra Plains) has been imported alive. It has been described as *Aphyosemion seymouri.* An additional form from Gambia has been imported under the name *Fundulus gambiensis.* It is strange that no additional populations have been found in this large distribution area.

T: 22°–26°C, **L:** 6 cm, **A:** 80 cm, **R:** m, b, **D:** 4

Fam.: Aplocheilidae
Subfam.: Rivulinae

Pterolebias staecki ♂, WC, type local "Lago Janavacá, Manaus, Brazil"

Pterolebias staecki
Staeck's longfin killie

SEEGERS, 1987

Syn.: None.

Hab.: South America: only known from the type locality: Lago Janauacá, south of the Amazon just above the confluence of the Rio Negro, south-southwest of Manaus, Brazil.

F.I.: March of 1986 by Dr. W. STAECK.

Sex.: ♂♂ are larger, more slender, and have elongated fins. They are generally more colorful and have an intense design. The smaller, stouter ♀♀ commonly have transparent fins.

Soc. B.: Comparatively shy and retiring. Peaceful. Conspecifics are largely ignored. They spend extensive amounts of time alone, hidden.

M: Keep this sensitive delicate fish in a species tank. Decorate as instructed for *P. wischmanni*. Water values from the collection site on March 20, 1986, at 14:00 hr were as follows: ambient tem-perature 30°C, water temperature 27°C, dGH and dKH less than 1°, pH 7.2, conductivity 52 µS.

B: This annual toothcarp is a substrate diver. Decorate the breeding tank as described for *P. wischmanni*. The peat containing the eggs is pressed lightly and slightly dried, e.g., with some newspaper, then placed into a labeled plastic bag. Apparently, *P. staecki* demands a relatively long storage time (6 months), even at high temperatures. Place the peat into a small aquarium and add water. After one day, the peat is again dried then rehydrated. *P. staecki* frequently only hatch after this process has been repeated several times. Rearing the young is nonproblematic as long as *Artemia salina* nauplii are fed and regular water exchanges are performed.

F: C; live foods.

T: 24°–28°C, **L:** 10 cm, **A:** 80 cm, **R:** t, m, b, **D:** 4

Fam.: Aplocheilidae
Subfam.: Rivulinae

Pterolebias wischmanni
Spangled longfin killie

SEEGERS, 1983

Syn.: None.

Hab.: South America: so far only known from the type locality, a small creek between the Rio Chipiria and Rio Amaquiria about 120 km south of Pucallpa, Peru.

F.l.: July of 1981 by H. J. WISCHMANN.

Sex.: ♂♂ are larger with elongated fins and a brightly colored body. ♀♀ are red-brown with round, transparent fins.

Soc. B.: Peaceful and rather shy. ♂♂ may be aggressive among themselves.

M: Either a species tank or a community aquarium containing tranquil, not overly small fishes is appropriate. Provide hiding places and filter the tank's illumination through floating plants. Choose a dark substrate (peat), and decorate the tank with bogwood, Java moss, and Java fern. The substrate in its natural habitat was covered by a thick layer of leaves, branches, etc. The water should be slightly acid to slightly alkaline and soft.

B: *P. wischmanni* is an annual and a substrate diver. Place a dish containing at least 10 cm of boiled peat, which is usually an acceptable spawning substrate, in a separate breeding tank. This relatively large species demands a roomy breeding tank of corresponding proportions. Treat the peat as described for *P. staecki*.

F: C; all types of live foods. Frozen foods and beef heart are accepted after acclimation.

T: 24°–26°C, **L:** 14 cm, **A:** 80 cm, **R:** t, m, b, **D:** 3–4

Rachovia hummelincki
Coastal spot-finned killie

DE BEAUFORT, 1940

Syn.: None.

Hab.: South America: Colombia and Venezuela, mouth of the Rio Magdalena to the Paraguana Peninsula east of Lake Maracaibo, immediate coastal regions.

F.l.: 1968 or 1969. A more exact date could not be determined.

Sex.: ♂♂ are gray-brown with individual light gray scales distributed over the body. Dorsal and anal fins are gray-brown to green with dark brown spots that sometimes join to form short lines. The inferior caudal fin has a white, yellow, or orange stripe. ♀♀ are smaller, more uniformly brown, and have small, round, almost colorless fins.

Soc. B.: Peaceful. ♂♂ may be aggressive towards conspecific ♂♂ and immature or spent ♀♀.

M: This annual species is a substrate divers. Maintain in a species tank. A dark substrate is recommended. Decorate the tank with bogwood adorned with plants such as Java moss, Java fern, water sprite, and *Anubias*. Use peat instead of sand as the substrate.

B: The breeding tank can be decorated as described above, or the peat can be placed in a container. Each week, or after the fish have utilized the peat for spawning, remove it, blot and dry it briefly on a newspaper, and store it in a plastic bag. Diapause is about 6 months, depending on temperature. The fry immediately accept *Artemia* nauplii upon hatching.

F: C; live foods.

T: 22°–26°C, **L:** 6 cm, **A:** 60 cm, **R:** m, b, **D:** 3–4

Pterolebias wischmanni, WC, Amaquira, Peru

Rachovia hummelincki

Fam.: Aplocheilidae
Subfam.: Rivulinae

Rachovia pyropunctata
Red-spotted spot-finned killie

TAPHORN & THOMERSON, 1978

Syn.: *Rachovia hummelincki* (not DE BEAUFORT, 1940).

Hab.: South America: Venezuela, in the Lake Maracaibo Basin.

F.I.: Since this species was considered to be a population of *R. hummelincki* until its scientific description, the date it was first imported cannot be exactly determined. However, it was imported prior to 1973.

Sex.: While ♂♂ have numerous orange spots on their brown body (scientific name) and large fins, ♀♀ are smaller, virtually solid brown with small fins.

Soc. B.: Usually peaceful.

M: As for *R. hummelincki.*

B: As for *R. hummelincki.*

F: C; all types of live foods, including worms.

T: 22°-26°C, **L:** 6 cm, **A:** 60 cm, **R:** m, b, **D:** 4

Rivulus atratus
Butterfly rivulus

GARMAN, 1895

Syn.: None.

Hab.: South America: Peru, in the lower Rio Ucayali and upper Amazon Basin.

F.I.: 1981 by P. DE RHAM.

Sex.: Sexes are usually difficult to distinguish. ♂♂ sometimes have a longer caudal fin, but not always. ♀♀ are slightly fuller through their anterior body.

Soc. B.: Very peaceful and shy. This solitary living species tends to jump from the water when threatened (cover the tank!).

M: Keep in densely planted, shallow aquaria. They are frequently found above the water surface on aquatic plants or stuck to the glass panes. Generally surface oriented. Use soft, slightly acid to neutral water.

B: Very difficult and rarely successful. The few breeding successes have been unable to span several generations, and unfortunately, they can probably be attributed more to chance than skill. The eggs are laid on fine-leaved plants.

F: C; small live foods, preferably those that move in the open water or along the surface.

T: 22°–26°C, **L:** up to 5 cm, **A:** 60 cm, **R:** t, **D:** 4

Rachovia pyropunctata

Rivulus atratus ♂, WC, Peru

Fam.: Aplocheilidae
Subfam.: Rivulinae

Rivulus cf. *brunneus*   MEEK & HILDEBRAND, 1913

Syn.: None.

Hab.: Central America: Panama, Costa Rica.

F.I.: The exact date is unknown. D. FROMM probably collected this fish in 1981 in Panama and imported it into Europe at the beginning of the '80's.

Sex.: ♂♂ are often larger and always more colorful. The brown to greenish body has longitudinal rows of red-brown dots which frequently coalesce into broad striations. The caudal fin has a dark brown subjacent band and a variable yellow edge. The dorsal and anal fins are greenish to yellowish brown with longitudinal rows of red-brown dots which may either merge, forming longitudinal stripes, or be randomly distributed. Generally, the various populations have very patent designs and colors.

With fewer red-brown dots on their brown body and little color on their unpaired fins, ♀♀ have little of note to distinguish themselves.

Soc. B.: Usually peaceful. Single ♂♂ may be waspish, particularly towards conspecific ♂♂. Individuals may be extraordinarily shy.

M: As for *R. hartii* and *R. rubrolineatus*. A close fitting cover is important.

B: As for *R. rubrolineatus*.

F: C; all types of live foods commiserate to its size, preferably those that swim or float along the water surface.

S: The relationship between the morph presented and *R. fuscolineatus* BUSSING, 1980 has not been resolved. It is not unlikely that *R. fuscolineatus* is a synonym of *R. brunneus*.

T: 20°–26°C, **L:** up to 7 cm, **A:** 60 cm, **R:** t, m, **D:** 3

Rivulus chucunaque   BREDER, 1925

Syn.: None.

Hab.: Central America: Panama.

F.I.: 1984.

Sex.: ♂♂ are more colorful. They have a silver-blue body with 7–8 vertical blue-gray stripes or, more probable, spots. The two anterior longitudinal stripes are also blue-gray. The dorsum is gray-brown, the fins are yellowish, and the caudal fin is transversed by two longitudinal stripes, one above and one below the caudal peduncle. ♀♀ have a brownish body, a very faint rendition of the ♂'s design, and a *Rivulus*-spot on the upper caudal peduncle.

Soc. B.: Peaceful. Unfortunately, these animals are often very shy.

M: A shallow, moderate-sized, densely planted species tank is best, since this corresponds the best to conditions in its natural habitat. Due to the fish's timid nature, few animals will ever be visible.

B: As for *R. rubrolineatus*.

F: C; all types of live foods, particularly mosquito larvae.

S: BREDER described two forms in 1925: *Rivulus chucunaque chucunaque*, the nominate form, and *R. c. sucubti* from the lower Rio Sucubte Basin. It is possible that the pictured animal is not the species described by BREDER.

T: 22°–26°C, **L:** 7 cm, **A:** 60 cm, **R:** t, m, **D:** 3

Rivulus cf. *brunneus*

Rivulus chucunaque

Fam.: Aplocheilidae
Subfam.: Rivulinae

Rivulus derhami

FELS & HUBER, 1985

Syn.: *Rivulus beniensis* (not MYERS, 1927).

Hab.: South America: Peru, in the Rio Huallaga system at Tingo María.

F.I.: 1966 by K. H. LÜLING, Bonn.

Sex.: ♂♂ are brown laterally, becoming blue-green posteriorly. There are red-brown spots on the body which sometimes merge. The unpaired fins also have red-brown dots, though they are predominantly blue-green, particularly distally. ♀♀ have a *Rivulus*-spot on the upper caudal peduncle, a corporal pattern similar to that found on the ♂♂, but duller colors.

Soc. B.: Peaceful. Usually shy. ♂♂ may occasionally be quarrelsome among themselves.

M: No major demands are placed on water chemistry, but overly hard water should be avoided. They can be housed with equal-sized fishes, but ensure that there are hiding places among Java moss, etc., so that ♂♂ can avoid each other.

B: As for *R. magdalenae*. The water should be soft with a neutral pH. Some of the very large eggs are laid just below the water surface, occasionally even above the water.

F: C; all types of live foods; worms are readily consumed.

S: Much of the information about this fish has been conveyed under the name *Rivulus beniensis*. But *R. beniensis* comes from Bolivia and has never been imported.

T: 22°–26°C, **L:** 5 cm, **A:** 60 cm, **R:** t, m, **D:** 3

Rivulus dibaphus

MYERS, 1927

Syn.: None.

Hab.: South America: northeast Brazil.

F.I.: To Vienna at the beginning of the '80's by A. RADDA.

Sex.: ♂♂ have larger fins and more color. They are a medium brown with dark gray to yellow-green sides overlaid with red-brown crossbands. Their stomach and throat are white, the dorsal and caudal fins are striated, and the anal fin is blue-green. ♀♀ are smaller with round fins and medium to dark brown spots on the body.

Soc. B.: Normally peaceful. ♂♂ are sometimes aggressive towards conspecific ♂♂ and immature or spent ♀♀.

M: As for *R. speciosus*. The aquarium does not necessarily have to be large, but it ought to have sections with dense vegetation (Java moss). The water should be soft to medium-hard and neutral to slightly acid. The illumination should be subdued. Excellent jumper, cover the tank well!

B: As for *R. speciosus*.

F: C; moderate-sized live foods.

S: The pictured species is related to *R. geayi* and *R. agilae*. While this species is probably *R. dibaphus*, it is not conclusive.

T: 24°–28°C, **L:** 5 cm, **A:** 50 cm, **R:** t, m, b, **D:** 4

Rivulus derhami

Rivulus dibaphus

Fam.: Aplocheilidae
Subfam.: Rivulinae

Rivulus fuscolineatus

BUSSING, 1980

Syn.: None.

Hab.: Central America: northwestern Costa Rica, in the Lake Arenal and Rio Bebedero Basins.

F.I.: To the United Sates in 1979 (?) by D. FROMM; imported to Europe from there during the early '80's.

Sex.: Very similar to those of *R.* cf. *brunneus* (refer to text there). The dark design of the ♂♂, however, is brighter red. ♀♀ have more intense markings, a *Rivulus*-spot on the caudal peduncle, and frequently a dark shoulder spot.

Soc. B.: Like comparable *Rivulus* species (see *R.* cf. *brunneus*). Often very shy.

M: As for *R. hartii* and *R. rubrolineatus*.

B: See *R. rubrolineatus*.

F: C; all live foods small enough to be consumed.

S: The relationship between the forms from Costa Rica described by BUSSING (1980) and the priorly described animals from Panama is largely unclear. *R. fuscolineatus* may be a synonym of a previously described taxon. While there are readily apparent similarities to *R.* cf. *brunneus*, there are also divergent characteristics.

T: 20°–26°C, **L:** 7 cm, **A:** 60 cm, **R:** t, m, **D:** 3

Rivulus hartii
Giant rivulus

(BOULENGER, 1890)

Syn.: *Haplochilus hartii, Rivulus holmiae* (not EIGENMANN, 1909).

Hab.: South America: Trinidad and Tobago, perhaps also along the northern coast of Venezuela.

F.I.: February/March of 1926 through Amsterdam to Hamburg.

Sex.: ♂♂ are greenish and have longitudinal rows of dark round dots which can also be found in the dorsal and anal fins. The caudal fin has an inferior and superior dirty yellow fringe and an unpronounced dark fringe posteriorly. The solid brown ♀♀ are usually smaller with rounder fins.

Soc. B.: Robust fish which may predate upon small fishes (characins, etc.). Otherwise, generally peaceful.

M: Care is easy as long as water values are not extreme. Not an animal for the community aquarium. When disturbed, they leap vertically from the water, dart around the aquarium, attempt to hide, or dive into a soft substrate. In well-planted aquaria they are hardly visible. Their behavior is highly individual. Some specimens may never overcome their shyness, while others may become relatively tame after acclimation. The tank's cover must be tight fitting.

B: As for *Rivulus magdalenae*.

F: C; live foods, including larger items.

T: 22°–26°C, **L:** 9 cm, **A:** 60 cm, **R:** t, m, b, **D:** 3

Rivulus fuscolineatus

Rivulus hartii, Arima, Trinidad

Fam.: Aplocheilidae
Subfam.: Rivulinae

Rivulus hildebrandi
Panama rivulus

MYERS, 1927

Syn.: *Rivulus volcanus*.

Hab.: Central America: western Panama.

F.I.: Unknown; maybe imported into the United States in the early '80's by D. FROMM and exported from there to Europe.

Sex.: ♀♀ have the typical *Rivulus*-spot on the upper edge of the caudal peduncle; however, it may be obscure in older specimens. Their fins tend to be smaller and mostly transparent. ♂♂ have slightly brighter colors. Sexual differences are little pronounced in young specimens.

Soc. B.: Very shy animals. They immediately try to hide or jump out of the water when disturbed, making housing this species with other fishes problematic.

M: As indicated for *R. peruanus*, though *R. hildebrandi* is not quite as quarrelsome.

B: See *R. rubrolineatus*. *R. hildebrandi*, however, has proven to be less fecund.

F: C; all types of live foods, particularly those found at the water surface (e.g., wax moths). Feed flakes as the exception, not the rule.

S: *R. hildebrandi*'s long body is not particularly attractive. The species might have had an ephemeral presence in the hobby.

T: 20°–22°C, **L:** 8 cm, **A:** 60 cm, **R:** m, t, **D:** 3

Rivulus iridescens
Iridescent rivulus

FELS & DE RHAM, 1981

Syn.: None.

Hab.: South America: Peru, area around Jenaro Herrera, lower Ucayali Basin.

F.I.: 1979 by P. DE RHAM.

Sex.: ♂♂ are greenish brown and covered with longitudinal rows of red dots. The anal fin is yellow distally, whereas the upper lobe of the tail fin and upper dorsal fin are reddish-bronze color. ♀♀ are gray-brown and have a *Rivulus*-spot.

Soc. B.: This solitary fish is peaceful towards other fishes.

M: As for *R. rubrolineatus*.

B: As for *R. rubrolineatus*.

F: C; all types of live foods, preferably those floating on the water surface. Flakes are occasionally accepted.

S: *R. iridescens* belongs to the *R. rubrolineatus* or *R. limoncochae* complex. The relationship of these populations is confounded at this time due to new discoveries. It is possible that several of these nominate species are merely strains of *R. rubrolineatus* or *R. limoncochae*.

T: 22°–26°C, **L:** 7 cm, **A:** 60 cm, **R:** t, m, **D:** 3

Rivulus hildebrandi, western Panama

Rivulus iridescens, Jenaro Herrera, Peru

Fam.: Aplocheilidae
Subfam.: Rivulinae

Rivulus luelingi
Lüling's rivulus

SEEGERS, 1984

Syn.: None.

Hab.: South America: southern Brazil, near Joinville.

F.I.: October of 1982 by LÜLING.

Sex.: ♂♂ are stouter and more colorful. They are iridescent green with red-brown spots and bands on the posterior body. The caudal fin has a red semicircle near the caudal peduncle which is followed distally by yellow-green and red-brown stripes. ♀♀ have little to recommend them as far as coloration, being solid brown with traces of darker spots and lines. The *Rivulus*-spot is present on the upper caudal peduncle.

Soc. B.: Peaceful and rather shy animals.

M: Keep these animals in a species tank, though it does not necessarily have to be large. Densely planted sections should be present. The water should be soft and slightly acid.

B: Principally similar to that of *Rivulus magdalenae*. Difficult and rather unproductive. The origin of the difficulties, and hence, corrective measures, are obscure at this time. The species has been maintained in captivity, but it is not considered to be an easy feat.

F: C; all kinds of moderate-sized live foods.

T: 18°–24°C, **L:** 4.5 cm, **A:** 50 cm, **R:** t, m, **D:** 4

Continuation of *Rivulus rubrolineatus* (p. 544):

F: C; all types of live foods, preferably those that float such as insects and their larvae (*Drosophila,* wax moths). Flake foods are also occasionally accepted.

S: The relationship of *R. limoncochae* and *R. rubrolineatus* and their relatives is confounded at this time due to numerous intermediate populations being discovered.

T: 22°–28°C, **L:** 7 cm, **A:** 60 cm, **R:** t, m, **D:** 3

Rivulus luelingi ♂, WC, Joinville type, southern Brazil

Rivulus luelingi ♀, WC, Joinville type, southern Brazil

Fam.: Aplocheilidae
Subfam.: Rivulinae

Rivulus peruanus
Perimparoo rivulus

(REGAN, 1903)

Syn.: *Haplochilus peruanus, Aplocheilus peruanus.*

Hab.: South America: Peru, Rio Ucayali and Huallaga Basins on the eastern slope of the Andes.

F.I.: 1963 to the United States.

Sex.: Sometimes difficult to distinguish. ♀♀ do not have a *Rivulus*-spot. ♂♂ are blue-green with irregularly distributed red dots that extend into their fins. ♀♀ are similarly colored, but generally more matte.

Soc. B.: Downright brutal among themselves. Peaceful towards equal-sized heterospecifics when housed in roomy aquaria.

M: These fish are very robust and have few requirements. The main prerequisite is an ample tank containing sections of heavy vegetation. Unfortunately, hostilities are such that the strongest animal may lynch all others until either one pair remains or only the ♂.

B: The bellicosity of this species tends to make reproduction difficult, but it principally follows that of *R. magdalenae*. The breeding tank should be plenty large and contain hiding places for the ♀. One pair or one ♂ and 2 ♀♀ should be set up for a limited time (usually a few days). The fish need to be observed—in regard to their behavior. Eggs should be collected, since some animals will eat their spawns. Not fecund.

F: C; hardy live foods of all kinds.

T: 22°–26°C, **L:** 7 cm, **A:** 80–100 cm, **R:** t, m, **D:** 3

Rivulus punctatus
Spotted rivulus

BOULENGER, 1895

Syn.: None.

Hab.: South America: northeast Argentina, Paraguay, southwestern Brazil to the basin of the Rio Paraná.

F.I.: 1960 to the United States. The date the species first entered Germany is unknown.

Sex.: Sexes are sometimes difficult to distinguish. Usually ♂♂ are somewhat larger with brighter colors. ♀♀ are fuller through the anterior ventral area.

Soc. B.: Peaceful, shy species.

M: Uncomplicated. A moderate-sized aquarium with areas of heavy vegetation is appropriate. Water should be soft and neutral. These animals are accomplished jumpers. Cover the tank well.

B: Significantly more difficult than maintenance. Follow suggestions given for *R. speciosus*. These adhesive spawners are not prolific.

F: C; small live foods, preferably those that float on the water surface, e.g., *Drosophila*.

S: Due to its extensive area of distribution, this species exists in a variety of colors. Specimens from its eastern population are particularly easy to confuse with *Rivulus zygonectes*, a close relative.

T: 22°–26°C, **L:** 6 cm, **A:** 60 cm, **R:** t, m, b, **D:** 3–4

Rivulus peruanus, WC, Peru

Rivulus punctatus, WC, Brasilia, Brazil

Fam.: Aplocheilidae
Subfam.: Rivulinae

Rivulus rectocaudatus
Straight-tail rivulus

FELS & DE RHAM, 1981

Syn.: *Rivulus beniensis* (not MYERS, 1927).

Hab.: South America: Peru, in tributaries of the upper Amazon (Solimoes) in the extended area around Iquitos.

F.I.: 1963 as *R. beniensis* to the United States; September of 1979 by DE RHAM to France.

Sex.: Sexes are often very difficult to distinguish. Beautiful full-grown ♂♂ have an intense orange body and fins and a spatula-shaped tail fin. The ♀♀'s colors are more matte, and their fins more rounded. ♀♀ usually have a *Rivulus*-spot on their upper caudal peduncle, though adult ♂♂ may also have one.

Soc. B.: Peaceful and usually shy. They frequently spend their time secluded. ♂♂ tend to be very aggressive among themselves.

M: A densely planted species tank makes the best captive habitat for this species. Upper water strata are preferred. Cover the tank. The water should be neutral to slightly acid and, at the most, medium-hard. Tank dimensions must correspond to the stature of the animals.

B: A normal species tank can serve as the breeding tank as well if the eggs can be collected from the plants. A separate tank may be needed to separate the genders and allow the ♀♀ to enter spawning condition. Java moss, peat fibers, wool mops, etc., can serve as spawning substrates. These should be fastened under the cover so that the fibers hang into the water. Collect the very large eggs, store them in moist peat, and then add water. *Artemia* nauplii are an appropriate initial food. Larger live foods can be fed later.

F: C; live foods, even larger ones.

T: 22°–25°C, **L:** 8 cm, **A:** 80 cm, **R:** t, m, **D:** 3–4

Rivulus rubrolineatus
Red-line rivulus

FELS & DE RHAM, 1981

Syn.: None.

Hab.: South America: Peru, lower Ucayali Basin and the Amazon and its tributaries on the eastern slope of the Andes.

F.I.: 1961 by E. ROLOFF.

Sex.: These fish are reddish violet, fading to green then brown dorsally. ♂♂ have longitudinal rows of red dots which extend from the head to the caudal peduncle. The unpaired fins and the ventral fins are orange to bronze with a red-brown pattern. The posterior edge of the caudal fin may be light blue. ♀♀ are brownish with dark brown mottling dorsally. They have a typical *Rivulus*-spot on the upper caudal peduncle.

Soc. B.: Generally peaceful. They live a rather solitary existence.

M: Not difficult. A shallow species tank with dense vegetation and floating plants suits this fish's needs very well. Cover the tank, as this fish tends to jump from the water, often sticking to the glass above the water surface. Characins and *Corydoras* might make appropriate tankmates. The fish's colors are more pronounced under subdued illumination.

B: These are adhesive spawners that prefer to lay their eggs on fine-leaved plants such as Java moss or artificial spawning materials and peat. For focused reproduction, one pair is placed in a 15–20 l tank containing one of the above mentioned spawning substrates. Under favorable conditions, the fish lay eggs almost daily. Collect the eggs. The fry hatch 2–3 weeks later and can easily be reared with *Artemia* nauplii. *R. rubrolineatus* can also be bred as a substrate spawner when peat fibers are used. If this is the method of choice, the peat should be removed after one week and stored for an additional 3 weeks slightly moist in a plastic bag prior to water being added.

Continued on p. 540.

Rivulus rectocaudatus

Rivulus rubrolineatus

Fam.: Aplocheilidae
Subfam.: Rivulinae

Rivulus urophthalmus, WC, 1981/20 SW Matoury, Guyana

Rivulus urophthalmus
Golden rivulus

GÜNTHER, 1866

Syn.: *Rivulus urophthalmus* var. *aurata*, *R. poeyi*, *R. lungi*, *R. xanthonotus* (?).

Hab.: South America: coastal plains from Guyana to Brazil.

F.I.: October of 1905 by J. HEINRICH, Darmstadt, Germany.

Sex.: ♂♂ are gray-blue to brownish with red and golden dots. The fins have a yellowish to bronze margin. The ♀♀ are gray-brown with mostly transparent fins. Some populations have a *Rivulus*-spot on the upper part of the caudal peduncle.

Soc. B.: Solitary living species. Generally peaceful.

M: Not difficult. *R. urophthalmus* usually remains hidden in community tanks, occasionally hanging from the humid glass pane above the water surface (the cover must be tight fitting!). A shallow species

tank or a bog aquarium best meets its needs. The water should be slightly acid and soft to moderately hard. Fry repeatedly appear without further ado under the above mentioned conditions.

B: Breeding is unproblematic. Place one pair in a small tank with Java moss, a wool mop, peat fibers, etc. The eggs should be collected daily. If stored in water, the eggs hatch after 2–3 weeks. If peat is used, the eggs can also be stored "dry," as for substrate spawners. That is, the moist peat is stored for 3–4 weeks in a plastic bag then cool water is added. Rear the young with *Artemia* nauplii.

F: C; all types of live foods. Insects are relished to such an extent that the fish may even jump from the water after them.

T: 22°–26°C, **L:** 6 cm, **A:** 60 cm, **R:** t, m, **D:** 3

Fam.: Cyprinodontidae
Subfam.: Cyprinodontinae

Aphanius anatoliae, WC, Aksaray, Turkey

Aphanius anatoliae
Anatolian killifish

(LEIDENFROST, 1912)

Syn.: *Cyprinodon anatoliae, C. lykaoniensis, Aphanius chantrei venustus, A. c. meandricus, A. c. obrukensis, A. c. flavianalis, A. c. aksaranus, A. burduricus iconii.*

Hab.: Central Asia Minor.

F.I.: Unknown.

Sex.: ♂♂ are light gray with dark gray vertical stripes. ♀♀ are frequently larger and gray-brown with dark gray to blackish dots. Unpaired fins are mostly transparent.

Soc. B.: Peaceful, active fish.

M: The tank should have plenty of swimming space as well as regions of dense vegetation. The water should be hard and alkaline with a temperature of 10°–25°C; lower or higher values are tolerated for short periods of time.

B: Substrate spawner. Eggs are laid on substrates such as fine-leaved plants (i.e., Java moss), synthetic fibers, or spawning mops. Sometimes breeders consume their spawn, so collect and place the eggs into a separate container. After about one week, depending on temperature, the fry hatch. *Artemia* nauplii are an acceptable initial food. Growth is slow.

F: C; all types of live foods as well as flakes and filamentous algae.

T: 10°–25°C, **L:** up to 5 cm, **A:** 80 cm, **R:** m, b, **D:** 3

Aphanius anatoliae ♂ (text on previous page)

Aphanius (Tellia) apodus   (GERVAIS, 1853)

Syn.: *Tellia apoda.*

Hab.: North Africa: northwestern Algeria, highlands south of Constantine.

F.I.: 1968 by VILLWOCK.

Sex.: ♂♂ are gray-brown anteriorly and metallic blue to blue-black posteriorly. Broad vertical dark crossbands cover the sides. The fins are metallic blue with a broad dark fringe. ♀♀, in contrast, are solid brown with narrow vertical bands and transparent fins.

Soc. B.: Generally peaceful, but ♂♂ establish and energetically defend territories.

M: Due to *A. apodus*'s delicate nature, keep in a spacious species tank. Parts of the tank should be densely planted. The water should be alkaline and medium-hard. Sea salt is recommended (1 teaspoon per 10 l).

B: ♂♂ have territories in which conspecifics and ♀♀ not in spawning condition are *persona non grata*. *A. apodus* spawn within these territories on filamentous algae and similar materials. The eggs should be collected and hatched in separate containers for optimal results. The young hatch after about 2 weeks and immediately accept *Artemia salina* nauplii.

F: O; all types of live foods as well as flake foods and algae.

T: 18°–28°C, L: 4.5 cm, A: 80 cm, R: m, b, D: 4

Fam.: Cyprinodontidae
Subfam.: Cyprinodontinae

Aphanius sirhani
Sirhanian killifish

VILLWOCK, SCHOLL & KRUPP, 1983

Syn.: *Aphanius dispar* (not RÜPPELL, 1828).

Hab.: Asia: Jordan, Azraq Oasis, Wadi Sirhan.

F.I.: 1979 by HÖLZER.

Sex.: ♂♂ have dark gray vertical stripes on their whitish silver body; the more compact ♀♀ are gray-brown with dark brown spots and basically colorless fins.

Soc. B.: Like all *Aphanius*, this lively species is peaceful towards heterospecifics.

M: As for *Aphanius anatoliae*. The original describer listed the following water values from the type locality (creek at Qasr al-Azraq): temperature 25°C, salinity 0.8%, conductivity 900 µS, 10° dGH, pH 8.0. Adding magnesium sulfate seems to be called for, since a concentration of 25 mg/l Mg^{++} was measured at the type locality.

B: As for *A. anatoliae.*

F: O; various live foods as well as flake foods and algae.

T: 20°–25°C, **L:** 4.5 cm, **A:** 80 cm, **R:** m, t, **D:** 3

Azraq Oasis in Jordan, habitat of *Aphanius sirhani*

Aphanius sirhani ♂

Aphanius sirhani ♀

Fam.: Goodeidae
Subfam.: Empetrichthyinae

Crenichthys baileyi albivallis   WILLIAMS & WILDE, 1981

Syn.: None.

Hab.: North America: springs around Preston and Lund, White Pine County, Nevada.

F.I.: First imported into Europe (Netherlands) in 1987 by the American Killifish Association. *Crenichthys* populations of unknown origin, however, were imported in the mid seventies into Germany by SCHREIBER.

Sex.: At spawning time ♂♂ darken and two dark longitudinal bands appear, one along the dorsum and the other from the eye to the caudal peduncle. A golden band runs between these two dark stripes from the mouth through the eye to the upper caudal peduncle. At most, ♀♀ have a faint rendition of this pattern.

Soc. B.: Peaceful and rather shy. Occasionally territorial.

M: There are limited experiences to derive information from, but it seems the animals are not very demanding. Keep them in freshwater like *Fundulus* species (see *F. olivaceus*).

B: They have been bred using peat. The specific nature of the substrate appeared to be rather unimportant as long as it was soft. Hence, Java moss or synthetic fibers can both be used. Great numbers of this subspecies have been bred in the United States, but probably not in Europe.

F: O; live, frozen, and flake foods.

T: 20°–25°C, **L**: 5.5 cm, **A**: 60 cm, **R**: m, b, **D**: 3

S: Various morphologically divergent relict populations of *Crenichthys baileyi* inhabit the water remnants and springs along the White River in southeastern Nevada. WILLIAMS and WILDE, 1981 described the following subspecies of the nominate form *C. b. baileyi* GILBERT, 1893: *C. b. albivallis, C. b. thermophilus, C. b. grandis,* and *C. b. moapae.*

Crenichthys baileyi albivallis

Crenichthys baileyi baileyi

Fam.: Cyprinodontidae
Subfam.: Cyprinodontinae

Cualac tessellatus
Checkered pupfish

MILLER, 1956

Syn.: None.

Hab.: Central America: exists in relictlike populations in several thermal springs around Rio Verde, San Luis Potosí, Mexico, primarily the Laguna Media Luna and Laguna Los Anteojitos.

F.I.: To Switzerland in 1982 by E. HNILICKA. In 1983 it was imported into Germany by SEEGERS and STAECK.

Sex.: ♀♀ have pale, transparent fins and a dark longitudinal stripe down the center of the body which is occasionally framed by light scales. ♂♂ are more intensely colored. They have a yellow anal fin, a yellow and gray marbled dorsal fin, a dark black caudal fin that takes on a velvety green sheen during courtship, and 2–4, usually 3, black spots along their sides.

Soc. B.: In nature, ♂♂ establish territories which ♀♀ enter to spawn. Other ♂♂ and, occasionally, heterospecifics are expelled from these territories. Otherwise peaceful.

M: Very hard, alkaline water is required for breeding, though perhaps more moderate values will be acceptable for maintenance. Water values in their natural habitat (Laguna Media Luna) on March 24, 1983, at about 15:30 were as follows: ambient temperature 26°C, water temperature 30.5°C, 53° dGH, 11° dKH, pH 7.9, 1680 μS. Use moderately coarse sand as the substrate. Plant individual bundles of vegetation and be sure to include filamentous algae.

B: Has not been successfully bred in captivity. Although eggs were laid and even began to develop, the embryos died before hatching. Lack of proper hardness probably arrested development ("only" 22° dGH).

F: O; all live foods are consumed, but vegetable fare (algae) needs to be included in the diet as well.

S: This species is close to extinction in its natural habitat for various reasons. See SEEGERS and STAECK in DATZ, **37** (4): 128–131 and (5): 164–168, 1984.

T: 28°–30°C, **L:** 5.5 cm, **A:** 80 cm, **R:** m, b, **D:** 4

Laguna Media Luna, Mexico

Cualac tessellatus ♂, WC, Laguna Los Anteojitos, Rio Verde, Mexico

Cualac tessellatus ♀, WC, Laguna Media Luna, Rio Verde, Mexico

Fam.: Cyprinodontidae
Subfam.: Cyprinodontinae

Cyprinodon atrorus   MILLER, 1968

Syn.: None.

Hab.: Central America: Mexico, in the Cuatro Cienegas Basin, Coahuila. Shallow, silty, swampy waters with substrates covered with a rich layer of algae are choice biotopes.

F.I.: 1973 by Dr. Alfred RADDA, Vienna, Austria.

Sex.: ♂♂ have a courtship coloration. Iridescent blue colors predominate and the fins are milky yellow. The ♀♀ have simple colors and 5–9 irregular spots along their sides. All their fins are colorless.

M: Use a fine sand substrate, plants tolerant of brackish water, a shallow tank (20–30 cm), and medium-hard (12°–15° dGH), alkaline (pH 7.5–8.0) water. Sea salt can be added (1–2 teaspoons per 10 l). The animals are especially attractive in a species tank, but they can be housed with other fishes that have similar requirements.

B: Not very difficult. Beware—these fish will voraciously consume their spawn. BÖHM successfully bred these fish and published his methods in the DKG-Journal **9**: 4–8, 1977. The animals were kept in tap water (12°–15° dGH) with one heaping teaspoon of salt (without iodine) per 10 l. ♂♂ and ♀♀ were separated for 3 to 4 days then placed together for a maximum of 40–60 min, which is enough time for the ♀♀ to lay all of her eggs. A clump of fiber as the spawning substrate makes the eggs more difficult for the parents to find and consume. Remove the breeders after spawning. The eggs hatch after about 10 days and are raised with *Artemia* nauplii. Rearing is comparatively easy.

F: H; the majority of the diet consists of algae, but small crustacea, mosquito larvae, *Tubifex*, and flake foods are accepted as well.

S: Breeding this species by the methods described under **B** is unnatural, yet it produces a better yield. In planted community tanks, ♂♂ claim shallow self-excavated depressions in the sand as their territories. Other ♂♂ are chased away, and only ♀♀ are allowed within these 8–10 cm territories.

T: 25°–35°C, L: 5 cm, A: 50 cm, R: t, m, D: 3

Cyprinodon macrolepis   MILLER, 1976
Dolores pupfish

Syn.: None.

Hab.: Central America: Mexico, el Ojo de la Hacienda Dolores, 12.5 km south-southwest of Jiménez, Chihuahua. Only known to inhabit one warmwater spring.

F.I.: 1984 by WIRTH, ALLSPACH, MEYER, and MEYER.

Sex.: ♂♂ are identical to ♀♀ (see photos), but have brighter colors, a yellow dorsal fin, and a deeper body.

Soc. B.: ♂♂ are territorial and vigorously pursue ♀♀. Generally peaceful towards heterospecifics.

M: Temperature between 28° and 30°C, dense vegetation, and a dark substrate are best. The native waters of this species have a salinity of 0.5 ppt. Use intense illumination to encourage algae to coat rocks and the aquarium panes.

B: Breeding has proven unproblematic at 23°–25°C. Wool mops make the best spawning substrate, and the eggs can be collected from there. At 25°C, the eggs hatch after 7 days.

F: H, O; algae and flake foods are the foods of choice. Mosquito larvae, water fleas, *Tubifex*, and frozen foods are also readily accepted.

S: A severely endangered species!!! *Gambusia gaigei* (previously *G. alvarezi*) lives with *C. macrolepis* in its natural habitat.

T: 26°–32°C, L: 5 cm, A: 50 cm, R: m, D: 3

Cyprinodon atrorus

Cyprinodon macrolepis ♂, ♀ pictured on p. 562

Fam.: Cyprinodontidae
Subfam.: Cyprinodontinae

Cyprinodon variegatus dearborni   MEEK, 1909

Syn.: None.

Hab.: Southern Antilles and the northern coast of South America: Venezuela, Bonaire, Aruba, Curaçao.

F.I.: ? Maybe in the mid sixties or previously by KRISTENSEN. At the very latest, it was imported in 1986 by JOCHEMS to the Netherlands.

Sex.: Similar to *C. v. variegatus*. ♂♂ are bluer, particularly through the fins, and frequently have a red or orange throat. ♀♀ have a black spot on the dorsal fin, but since immature ♂♂ may also have this spot, it cannot be considered a sure differentiating characteristic.

Soc. B.: See the nominate form, *C. v. variegatus*.

M: As for *C. v. variegatus*, but maintain at higher temperatures.

B: Unfortunately, the first "pair" imported to Germany was two ♂♂. Needless to say, these fish could not be bred. Follow suggestions given under the nominate form.

F: O; as indicated for *C. v. variegatus*. Primarily live foods, but algae, other vegetable fare, and flake foods are also greatly appreciated.

S: *C. v. dearborni* has been described as an autonomous species and is still considered such by many authors today.

T: 20°–27°C, **L:** 4.5 cm, **A:** 60 cm, **R:** m, b, **D:** 3

Cyprinodon variegatus variegatus   LACÉPÈDE, 1803
Sheepshead minnow

Syn.: *Lebias rhomboidalis, L. ellipsoidea, Cyprinodon gibbosus, Trifarcius felicianus*.

Hab.: North and Central America: eastern coast of the USA from Carolina to northern Mexico (south of Tampico).

F.I.: 1905 by Paul MATTE.

Sex.: ♂♂ undergo color changes according to mood. When participating in courtship or spawning, the anterior dorsum is steel blue, the areas next to it are dark to blackish, and the ventral area is light orange. In contrast, ♀♀ are less colorful, tending to be silver-gray with mostly colorless fins and a dark spot on the dorsal fin.

Soc. B.: Territorial. The dominant ♂ will chase all conspecific ♂♂, sometimes even heterospecifics, out of his territory. Only ♀♀ in spawning condition are allowed within the territorial boundaries.

M: Because salt added to the water seems to be advantageous (about 1 teaspoon per 10 l, more may be borne), a species tank is probably best. In nature, these animals live at salinities ranging from 0 ppt (freshwater) to more than 35 ppt (average salinity found in the sea). The pictured animal comes from a channel with isolated pools south of Panuco, southwest of Tampico. The water there was very polluted with a temperature of 26°C and a conductivity of 10,000 μS (out of range). The fish survived water changes during transit despite variable values, and were easily maintained in captivity.

B: Collect the eggs from the spawning substrate and incubate them in a separate container. Fry are free-swimming after 6–8 days and immediately feed on *Artemia salina* nauplii.

F: O; live foods and flakes as well as vegetable fare such as algae and blanched lettuce.

S: Several subspecies of *C. variegatus*, namely *C. v. ovinus, C. v. hubbsi, C. v. artifrons, C. v. baconi,* and *C. v. riverendi,* are distributed along the entire eastern coast of the United States to northern Mexico and around the Yucatan Peninsula as well as the West Indies in the southern Caribbean. Strangely, this species cannot be found between Tampico and the Yucatán Peninsula.

T: 15°–25°C, **L:** 6 cm, **A:** 80 cm, **R:** m, b, **D:** 3

Cyprinodon variegatus dearborni, WC, Soroton, Bonaire

Cyprinodon variegatus variegatus ♂, WC, Panuco Canal, southern Tampico, Mexico

Fam.: Fundulidae
Subfam.: Fundulinae

Floridichthys polyommus. See p. 574.

Fundulus catenatus
Chain topminnow

(STOBER, 1846)

Syn.: *Poecilia catenata, Hydrargyra catenata, Zygonectes catenatus, Xenisma catenata.*

Hab.: North America: United States, in Kentucky, Tennessee, Virginia, Alabama, Kansas, Arkansas, Indiana, and Mississippi. In streams with a moderate current.

F.I.: 1905.

Sex.: ♂♂ are a particularly beautiful blue-green color during the spawning season. Their longitudinal rows of red dots can form a chain design (name!). The fins are yellow-green with red dots and abbreviated lines. The ♀♀ are less ornate, being brownish with fine brown dots.

Soc. B.: Peaceful. Can be kept in cool water community tanks.

M: Not a tropical fish, so maintain at room temperature. Keep cool during the winter; perhaps an unheated basement would be suitable. The tank's dimensions should be commiserate to the size of the fish. While no particular demands are placed on water chemistry, the water must be clean and unpolluted.

B: Summer temperatures (24°–25°C) stimulate the fish to spawn on plants and roots, though a spawning mop is best. Collect the eggs from the spawning mop. After about 2 weeks, the fry hatch and immediately accept *Artemia* nauplii. Keeping these fish at tropical temperatures constrains gamete development or maturity, complicating breeding. High temperatures prove detrimental to the young as well.

F: C; live foods.

T: 15°–25°C, **L:** up to 20 cm, **A:** 120 cm, **R:** t, m, **D:** 3–4

Fundulus confluentus
Marsh killifish

GOODE & BEAN, 1879

Syn.: *Fundulus ocellaris, F. chaplini, F. bartrami.*

Hab.: North America: United States, southeastern coastal basin of Chesapeake Bay, Maryland, to a few miles west of Pensacola Bay, Alabama.

F.I.: ? The summer of 1971 by O. BÖHM, Vienna, Austria.

Sex.: ♂♂ are olive-brown superiorly and yellowish to bronze inferiorly with 15 dark crossbands covering the flanks. The yellowish fins frequently have golden spots and lines that may also cover the entire body. A black spot is frequently, but not always, present on the dorsal fin. ♀♀ are more drab, being brown with transparent, round fins.

Soc. B.: Easily associated with tankmates that have similar requirements.

M: Unproblematic. In nature the animals are found in fresh and brackish waters. Hence, adding salt to the water is recommended. Otherwise, water chemistry is of secondary importance. Since these animals are nimble swimmers, provide plenty of open space in the aquarium as well as densely planted areas.

B: As indicated for *F. olivaceus.* According to BÖHM (DATZ, **26** [10]: 333, 1973), ♂♂ energetically chase the ♀♀. Collect the eggs, since these fish are said to consume their spawns. Young hatch after 10 days. Lower the temperature during the winter to bring breeders into spawning condition.

F: C; live foods as well as flake foods.

T: 15°–26°C, **L:** 6 cm, **A:** 80 cm, **R:** t, m, b, **D:** 3

Fundulus catenatus

Fundulus confluentus

Fundulus dispar
Thin-stripe topminnow

(AGASSIZ, 1854)

Syn.: *Zygonectes dispar, Z. melanops, Z. inurus, Fundulus notti dispar.*

Hab.: North America: mid-West United States, Mississippi Basin in the states of Arkansas, Illinois, Louisiana, Michigan, and Tennessee.

F.I.: Unknown.

Sex.: ♂♂ have vertical stripes on their body. Adult ♀♀ have smaller, more transparent fins, a larger girth, and a notable absence of vertical stripes on their body

Soc. B.: Peaceful. Fishes with similar requirements make suitable tankmates.

M: Plant the edges with a liberal hand. Although water chemistry is not very important, extreme values should be avoided. Allow the water temperature to fall to ca. 15°C during the winter.

B: As for *F. olivaceus.*

F: C; all types of live foods. Flake foods can be fed occasionally.

S: *Fundulus dispar* belongs to the *F. nottii* group (subgenus *Zygonectes*) and is not always easy to distinguish from its relatives, *F. nottii, F. lineolatus,* and *F. blairae.*

T: 15°–25°C, **L:** 7 cm, **A:** 60 cm, **R:** m, t, **D:** 3–4

Cyprinodon macrolepis ♀, see p. 556

Fundulus dispar

Fundulus dispar, WC, Ohio River, United States

Fam.: Fundulidae
Subfam.: Fundulinae

Fundulus jenkinsi
Jenkins' topminnow

(EVERMANN, 1892)

Syn.: *Zygonectes jenkinsi.*

Hab.: North America: southeastern United States, brackish waters and salt marshes from Galveston Bay, Texas, east to the mouth of the Escambia River as well as the states of Texas, Louisiana, Mississippi, Alabama, and Florida.

F.I.: Unknown. The pictured animal may have been the first imported specimen (1986).

Sex.: Unknown, since only a single specimen (♂) was imported. ♀♀ of this species, like those of all *Fundulus* species, probably have an unremarkable design and a dermal fold around the anterior anal fin region.

Soc. B.: Tends to be retiring and peaceful. Easily maintained with fishes that have similar requirements.

M: As per conditions in its natural habitat, one would assume that brackish or saline water would be required. Yet the pictured specimen was successfully maintained for an extended amount of time in soft, neutral, slightly saline water (1 teaspoon per 10 l) with congeners and heterogeners.

B: Has not been bred. But *F. jenkinsi* should be bred as an adhesive spawner, like other *Fundulus* species. Equip the breeding aquarium with filamentous algae or synthetic fibers as the spawning medium, and collect and raise the eggs in a separate container.

F: C; all types of live foods. Filamentous algae should be offered.

T: 18°–25°C, **L:** 7 cm, **A:** 80 cm, **R:** t, m, b, **D:** 4

Fundulus julisiae

WILLIAMS & ETNIER, 1982

Syn.: *Fundulus albolineatus* (not GILBERT, 1891).

Hab.: North America: United States, the Barrens Plateau area, Coffee County, Tennessee.

F.I.: To the Netherlands in 1987 by D. KORAN (American Killifish Association).

Sex.: ♂♂ are more colorful. Their body is blue to blue-green laterally, yellow to green-yellow anteriorly, and brown dorsally. They have numerous orange or red-brown spots. All fins are yellowish. The dorsal and caudal fins have a white stripe which is followed distally by a black edge. ♀♀ are a dull gray-brown with a scattering of dark brown spots.

Soc. B.: Peaceful to shy in front of heterospecifics.

M: Difficult. The few specimens imported to date have proven to be sensitive, even under conditions favorable to other *Fundulus* species. The reasons are unknown.

B: These fish have been successfully and repeatedly bred in the United States. According to WILLIAMS and ETNIER, at 20°–22°C the fish laid about 25 eggs a day on floating vegetation and a nylon spawning mop. Specific protocol for rearing the fry is unknown, but assumed to be fairly easy with *Artemia* nauplii. *F. julisiae* has not been bred in Europe.

F: O; live and flake foods. Even though imported animals were offered and consumed various foods, they became progressively thinner until they died. It is doubtful that the cause of death was the diet, however. WILLIAMS and ETNIER kept the fish at room temperature and fed them frozen shrimp and TetraMin.

S: *F. julisiae* has a very reduced population and is probably the *Fundulus* species closest to extinction in the United States at the present time. It is on the endangered species list.

T: 10°–25°C, **L:** 9 cm, **A:** 80 cm, **R:** t, m, b, **D:** 4

Fundulus jenkinsi

Fundulus julisiae

Fam.: Fundulidae
Subfam.: Fundulinae

Fundulus luciae (BAIRD, 1855)

Syn.: *Hydrargyra luciae, Haplochilus luciae, Zygonectes luciae.*

Hab.: North America: United States, in fresh and brackish waters of the east coast from Long Island to Georgia.

F.I.: Unknown.

Sex.: ♀♀ are solid brown with faint slender crossbands. Apparently ♂♂ are frequently smaller than ♀♀.

Soc. B.: Peaceful. Usually very shy.

M: Uncomplicated in a species tank that offers opportunities for concealment among dense vegetation. *F. luciae* is so timid, it only emerges after an extended period of acclimation. Hard, slightly alkaline water is advantageous. Saline water is recommended.

B: Probably has not been bred in captivity. Most likely similar to that of *Fundulus olivaceus.*

F: C; live foods of all kinds.

T: 10°–25°C, L: 4.5 cm, A: 60 cm, R: t, m, b, D: 4

Fundulus majalis (WALBAUM, 1792)

Syn.: *Cobitis majalis, Esox flavulus, E. zonatus, Cyprinodon flavulus, Fundulus fasciatus, F. insularis, F. similis, Hydrargyra trifasciata, H. vernalis, H. majalis, Micristius zonatus.*

Hab.: North America: eastern coastal regions from New Hampshire to northeast Mexico. Usually inhabits brackish water, but occasionally found in the sea or bodies of freshwater.

F.I.: 1897.

Sex.: ♂♂ have a silver-green, sometimes yellowish to reddish, body and a dark dorsum. ♀♀ are clearly larger and—depending on the population—usually only have vertical stripes on the posterior section of the body; the anterior body has horizontal stripes. The design is very variable.

Soc. B.: Very active and restless. Generally amiable towards tankmates.

M: Not easy to maintain for extended periods of time. Unsuitable for community aquaria. A large tank with plenty of swimming space and perfect water is required. Sea salt should be added to the water. Allow the water temperature to fall during the winter months. The fish usually wane quickly under normal aquarium conditions. They seem to fair better when kept in a garden pond.

B: Hardly possible. Seasonal temperature changes are probably important—at least for the northern populations—to bring breeders into spawning condition. Even though sporadic ovipositions have occurred, the species has never been bred over several generations.

F: C; live and flake foods.

S: *F. similis* was previously considered to be an autonomous species and is still considered such today by some authors.

T: 10°–25°C, L: 14 cm, A: 100 cm, R: m, b, D: 4

Fundulus luciae

Fundulus majalis, ♀ bottom

Fam.: Fundulidae
Subfam.: Fundulinae

Fundulus notatus

(RAFINESQUE, 1820)

Syn.: *Haplochilus aureus, Fundulus aureus, F. tenellus, Hydrargyra notata, Semotilus notatus, Zygonectes notatus, Z. tenellus.*

Hab.: North America: mid-West United States, drainage of the Mississippi. Its area of distribution largely coincides with that of *Fundulus olivaceus.*

F.I.: 1911 by F. MAYER and A. RACHOW.

Sex.: ♂♂ are brown-olive with a light gray to whitish ventral area. A dark longitudinal band runs along is side from the tip of its snout to the caudal peduncle. Unlike *F. olivaceus*, the edges of the band tend to be jagged. ♀♀ have rounder fins and less intense colors.

Soc. B.: Peaceful. They prefer to live in small groups. In nature, they seek open regions of the water, particularly close to the surface.

M: As indicated for *F. olivaceus.*

B: See *F. olivaceus.*

F: C; live foods. Flake foods are occasionally accepted.

S: This species is frequently confused with *F. olivaceus. Fundulus euryzonus* SUTTKUS & CASHNER, 1981 is another similar species.

T: 15°–25°C, L: 7.5 cm, A: 100 cm, R: t, m, D: 3–4

Fundulus olivaceus
Olive topminnow

(STORER, 1846)

Syn.: *Poecilia olivacea, Fundulus balboae, Haplochilus pulchellus, Oxyzygonectes balboae, Zygonectes lateralis, Z. olivaceus, Z. pulchellus.*

Hab.: Central North America: from the Mississippi Basin to southern Illinois, east Texas, and west Florida.

F.I.: Unknown; perhaps first imported as *F. notatus* in 1911.

Sex.: ♂♂ have elongated fins. ♀♀ have a larger anterior girth.

Soc. B.: Peaceful. In nature, these animals live in small groups close to the water surface where they search for food.

M: Keep several specimens in a large tank. Good water quality is important, but its chemistry is of less consequence. Provide good filtration, aeration, and regular water exchanges.

B: Like many fishes of temperate zones, it is problematic to bred *F. olivaceus* over several generations. Allow the temperatures to drop during the winter months—but not so much that the tank freezes. All *Fundulus* species can be kept outdoors during the summer. The eggs are laid on plants and similar items and should be collected , since the parents have a tendency to prey on their offspring. A plastic container is an appropriate receptacle to brood the eggs. The hatched young immediately accept *Artemia* nauplii.

F: C; all live foods commiserate to its size.

S: Unlike this species, *Fundulus notatus* has a dentate longitudinal band. This characteristic aside, the two are easily confused. Both are members of the subgenus *Zygonectes.*

T: 15°–25°C, L: 8 cm, A: 100 cm, R: t, m, D: 3–4

Fundulus notatus, WC, Indiana, United States

Fundulus olivaceus

Fundulus olivaceus ♀, see previous page

Fundulus pulvereus
Powder topminnow

(EVERMANN, 1892)

Syn.: *Fundulus spilotus, F. limbatus, Zygonectes pulvereus, Z. funduloides.*

Hab.: North America: United States, Alabama to Corpus Christi, Texas.

F.I.: Imported to Germany in 1986 by ALLEN.

Sex.: ♂♂ have 13–15 vertical silver-gray stripes on their yellow-brown to gray body. At spawning time, they are orange ventrally. The posterior body and the fins in particular have numerous small silver dots which may coalesce into larger spots on the posterior dorsal fin and sometimes the anal fin as well. The ♀♀ are drab yellow-brown with many dark dots and spots along their sides.

Soc. B.: Peaceful. Sometimes even shy.

M: See *Fundulus confluentus*. Inhabits true freshwaters as well as brackish water.

B: As for *Fundulus confluentus*.

F: C; live and flake foods.

S: *F. pulvereus* is frequently thought of as a subspecies of *Fundulus confluentus*, but as of yet, there is no definite opinion. The two have been known to crossbred

T: 15°–26°C, **L:** 7 cm, **A:** 80 cm, **R:** t, m, b, **D:** 3

Fam.: Fundulidae
Subfam.: Fundulinae

Leptolucania ommata
Pygmy killifish

(JORDAN, 1884)

Syn.: *Heterandria ommata, Lucania ommata, Rivulus ommatus, Zygonectes manni.*

Hab.: North America: United States, in swamps and waters of northern Florida and southern Georgia.

F.I.: 1924 by A. RACHOW.

Sex.: ♂♂ have a clay-yellow to light brown body which, in some populations, can have blue hues, particularly along the posterior body. The fins are elongated and yellow. The caudal peduncle has a dark spot. The smaller ♀♀ have less elongated fins, drabber corporal colors, and more transparent fins. The second spot about midway along their side usually has a white circle around it.

Soc. B.: Peaceful and rather shy. Best kept in a species tank, since they are generally subjugated by tankmates.

M: A small aquarium is sufficient. Dense vegetation and moderate illumination will bring out the fish's colors. The water must be slightly acid and soft. They can not be maintained in hard, alkaline water. Filtering over peat is best. If possible, lower the temperature to less than 20°C for a few weeks.

B: A small aquarium, soft, slightly acid water, and a spawning substrate of perlon, peat fibers, or Java moss meets the prerequisites well. Regularly collect the eggs and transfer them to a separate container with a low concentration of acriflavine. The eggs need almost 2 weeks to hatch. Another option is to transfer the breeders after a week, leaving the eggs in the aquarium. Infusoria must be fed at first. The young are rather sensitive, especially to water exchanges; add fresh water by drops.

F: C; only small live foods.

T: 18°–24°C, **L:** 4 cm, **A:** 40 cm, **R:** t, m, b, **D:** 4

Leptolucania ommata ♂, WC, Lake Brandford, Florida, United States

Leptolucania ommata ♀

Fam.: Cyprinodontidae (top) / Fam.: Fundulidae (bottom)

Floridichthys polyommus

HUBBS, 1936
Subfam.: Cyprinodontinae

Syn.: *Floridichthys carpio barbouri.*

Hab.: Central America: Mexico, Yucatán Peninsula and coastal regions of the states of Campeche and Yucatán.

F.I.: One ♂ was imported in March of 1983 by SEEGERS and STAECK. It was captured by E. HNILICKA in Cancún.

Sex.: The ♂♂ are brightly colored with a distinct pattern; ♀♀ are smaller and have rounded, less colorful fins.

Soc. B.: Similar to that of *Garmanella pulchra*, which is found in the same habitat (see Vol. 2, p. 660).

M: As for *Garmanella pulchra*. Because the fish are found in brackish water and seawater in nature, salt should be added to their water (about 6–7 gm/l).

B: Due to a lack of specimens, attempts to breed this species have not been suc-

cessful. Follow recommendations made for *Garmanella pulchra*, but because *F. polyommus* is larger and more robust, use a bigger aquarium.

F: O; all types of live foods as well as flake foods and vegetable fare such as algae.

S: *F. polyommus* was described as *F. carpio barbouri*, a subspecies of *F. carpio* that inhabits the coastal regions of Florida and Texas. However, new data have shown that *F. carpio* and *F. polyommus* are autonomous species and *barbouri* a synonym of the latter.

T: 22°–28°C, **L:** 9 cm, **A:** 100 cm, **R:** t, m, b, **D:** 4

Lucania parva

(BAIRD, 1855)
Subfam.: Fundulinae

Syn.: *Cyprinodon parvus, Limia poecilioides, L. venusta, Lucania affinis, L. parva venusta, L. venusta.*

Hab.: North America: drainage of the east coast of the United States. Introduced into several biotopes of the west coast as well as some sites in the interior of the country. Inhabits all waters regardless of salinity (0-35 ppt).

F.I.: Unknown.

Sex.: The ♂'s dorsal fin is black anteriorly and may have a red posterior edge. Both the anal and caudal fins are yellowish. ♀♀ have more matte colors, and their fins are normally transparent.

Soc. B.: Peaceful and active, but occasionally shy.

M: Nonproblematic; suitable tankmates for other North American fishes of comparable size. Water chemistry is of secondary importance, but the water should

be alkaline. Add salt (1 teaspoon per 100 l).

B: Fine-leaved plants are utilized as spawning substrates, although filamentous algae or synthetic materials are preferable. The eggs should be collected and placed in a separate container. There they hatch after 14 days. Raise the young with *Artemia*.

F: C, O; live foods are the sustenance of choice, though flake foods and filamentous algae may be accepted, depending on the individual.

S: *L. parva* is broadly distributed and greatly variable in regard to coloration and morphology. The populations range in color from gray to brighter colors reminiscent of those seen in *Lucania goodei*, demonstrating the close relationship of these two species. Some forms are quite stout, while others are very slender and elongated.

T: 10°–25°C, **L:** 5 cm, **A:** 60 cm, **R:** m, b, **D:** 2–3

Floridichthys polyommus ♂, WC, Cancún, Mexico

Lucania parva ♂

Fam.: Cyprinodontidae
Subfam.: Cyprinodontinae

Megupsilon aporus ♂, WC, El Potosí, San Luis Potosí, Mexico

Megupsilon aporus
Black-blotch pupfish

MILLER & WALTERS, 1972

Syn.: None.

Hab.: Central America: Mexico, Nuevo León, at the town of El Potosí and southern Monterrey.

F.I.: ? April of 1983 by SEEGERS and STAECK.

Sex.: ♂♂ have a white throat and stomach and a blue body that turns black posteriorly. Particularly well marked specimens have an orange caudal peduncle during courtship. The smaller ♀♀ are gray-brown.

Soc. B.: Peaceful. Spacious tanks are needed, since the animals are territorial.

M: Not difficult. Part of the aquarium should have dense vegetation, as found in their natural habitat. At the collection site on March 26, 1983, at 16:30 the following values were measured: ambient temperature 24.5°C, water temperature 20°C, 10.5° dGH, 8.5° dKH, pH 7.45, conductivity 3150 μS. The species, as indicated from these values, should be kept in medium-hard, slightly alkaline, temperate water.

B: Breeding has not been possible because the only ♀ imported was weakened by the trip and never recovered. It should be similar to *Cyprinodon alvarezi*, which coexists with this species in nature. *C. alvarezi* is territorial and spawns on algae, synthetic fibers, or similar. The newly hatched fry immediately eat *Artemia* nauplii.

F: O; live foods as well as algae and flake foods.

S: *M. aporus* is closely related to the genus *Cyprinodon*. As a relict form, it has some peculiarities. For example, it lacks ventral fins.

T: 18°–22°C, **L:** 4.5 cm, **A:** 80 cm, **R:** m, b, **D:** 3–4

Killifishes, Egg-Laying Toothcarps

Profundulus labialis, Rio de las Flores, Chiapas, Mexico

Profundulus labialis

(GÜNTHER, 1866)

Syn.: *Fundulus labialis, Zoogoneticus labialis, Tlaloc mexicanus.*

Hab.: Central America: southeast Mexico and western Guatemala, in mountain waters of the Atlantic and Pacific slopes of the Andes.

F.I.: 1983 by SEEGERS and STAECK from Rio de las Flores, Paso Chiapa, Rio de la Venta Basin, Chiapas, Mexico.

Sex.: ♂♂ are intensely colored. They have orange-yellow fringed dorsal and anal fins. ♀♀ are rounder, fuller-bodied, and have less notable colors in their fins.

Soc. B.: Peaceful, though ♂♂ may be quarrelsome among each other. Their behavior and size calls for a spacious tank. Found singly and in small groups in their natural habitat.

M: Totally unproblematic. Neutral to slightly alkaline and medium-hard to hard water is recommended. Corresponding to their high altitude habitats, tropical temperatures are not necessary.

B: Detailed information is not available because only ♂♂ have been successfully imported. However, it should not deviate much from that of *Profundulus punctatus* (see Vol. 2, p. 670). It will be interesting to discover if *P. labialis* has courtship coloration like *P. punctatus*.

F: C. O; all types of live foods as well as frozen and flake foods.

T: 18°–26°C, **L:** up to 10 cm, **A:** 80 cm, **R:** all, **D:** 2

Fam.: Valenciidae
Subfam.: Valenciinae

Valencia hispanica (VALENCIENNES, 1846)

Syn.: *Fundulus hispanicus, Hydrargyra hispanica.*

Hab.: Europe: drainage of the Mediterranean coast of east Spain.

F.I.: 1881.

Sex.: ♂ ♂ are gray-green to gray-brown with slender vertical striations on the posterior body. The posterior body and the fins, which are mostly yellow, are peppered with dark brown dots. ♀ ♀ are solid brown with colorless fins.

Soc. B.: Keep singly or in small groups. Large ♂ ♂ are particularly prone to contentious behavior. Otherwise the animals are peaceful.

M: *V. hispanica* is easy to keep. A well-planted aquarium or, better, a small garden pond or an outdoor tank is best. They can remain outside throughout the summer, but they should spend the winter months in the house, protected from freezing temperatures. Water chemistry is not important, but algae seem to be crucial to the animals' well-being.

B: Algae are the spawning substrate of choice. Collect the very large eggs and brood them in a separate container for best yields. The fry hatch after 2 weeks, somewhat later at cool temperatures. In plant-choked outdoor tanks, some young always escape predation without further ado, but periodically check the brood, making sure there are both ♂ ♂ and ♀ ♀.

F: C, O; live foods, but also frozen and flake foods as well as algae.

S: To the best of our knowledge, this species is on the verge of extinction.

T: 10°–28°C, **L:** 8 cm, **A:** 100 cm, **R:** t, m, b, **D:** 2–3

Oryzias minutillus ♂, WC, Satul, Thailand

Oryzias minutillus
Minute rice fish

SMITH, 1945
Subfam.: Oryziinae

Syn.: None.

Hab.: Southeast Asia: coastal regions of southeast Thailand from Bangkok to the Malay border. Probably beyond as well.

F.I.: Into Denmark in 1968 by L. CHRIS-TENSEN; to Germany in 1984 by SCHAL-LER.

Sex.: Often difficult to distinguish. While both sexes have a stripe along their side, it is generally more lustrous in ♂♂. ♀♀ have a somewhat larger anterior girth and slightly smaller fins.

Soc. B.: Peaceful. They form loose groups along the water surface, but are not true schooling fish.

M: Caring for *O. minutillus* has proven relatively easy. They were kept in a species tank void of decorations with only a sponge filter and soft, neutral water that had salt added to it. Undoubtedly the fish can be kept in an aquarium with a substrate (sand) and plants. In nature, the species coexists with *Brachygobius* sp. The two species can be kept together in captivity as well.

B: Successfully reproduced under the specified maintenance conditions without further encouragement. The fish laid their eggs on plants and similar substrates. SCHEEL reported that the first imported fish were carrying eggs (frequently visible in larger species of the genus). We could not confirm this. Newly hatched fry received infusoria. Later a diet of *Artemia* nauplii and fine pond plankton was administered.

F: C; small live foods commiserate to its diminutive size, i.e., *Artemia* nauplii, freshwater plankton.

T: 22°–26°C, **L:** 2 cm, **A:** 60 cm, **R:** t, m, **D:** 4

The Pangani is one of the rivers that originates at the Kilimandjaro. Many aquarium fishes inhabit its waters.

Xiphophorus variatus, captive-bred ♂, Hawaii, brush-highfin

Livebearing Toothcarps

We have separated the killifishes (Group 5) from the livebearers (Group 6) for practical, aquaristic reasons. Based on the listing on page 434 and the one presented below, the species presented in Volumes 1 and 2 of the Aquarium Atlas can be classified into a modern taxonomic scheme.

Family:

Genera:

Allodontichthys	HUBBS & TURNER, 1939 (4)
Alloophorus	HUBBS & TURNER, 1937 (2)
Allotoca	HUBBS & TURNER, 1937 (6)
Ameca	MILLER & FITZSIMONS, 1971 (1)
Ataeniobius	HUBBS & TURNER, 1939 (1)
Chapalichthys	MEEK, 1902 (3)
Characodo	GÜNTHER, 1866 (2)
Girardinichthys	BLEEKER, 1860 (2)

Goodeidae (Goodeids)

Genera:

Goodea	JORDAN, 1880
Hubbsina	DE BUEN, 1941 (1)
Ilyodon	EIGENMANN, 1907 (4)
Skiffia	MEEK, 1902 (4)
Xenoophorus	HUBBS & TURNER, 1937 (1)
Xenotaenia	TURNER, 1946 (1)
Xenotoca	HUBBS & TURNER, 1937 (3)
Zoogoneticus	MEEK, 1902 (1)

Family:

Genera:

Alfaro	MEEK, 1912 (2)
Belonesox	KNER, 1860 (1)
Brachyraphis	REGAN, 1913 (8)
Carlhubbsia	WHITLEY, 1951 (2)
Cnesterodon	GARMAN, 1895 (2)
Flexipenis	TURNER, 1940 (1) (= *Gambusia*?)
Gambusia	POEY, 1854 (ca. 31)
Girardinus	POEY, 1854 (8)
Heterandria	AGASSIZ, 1853 (1)
Heterophallus	REGAN, 1914 (3)
Limia	POEY, 1854 (ca. 18) (= *Poecilia*?)
Neoheterandria	HENN, 1916 (3)
Phallichthys	HUBBS, 1924 (4)
Phalloceros	EIGENMANN, 1907 (1)

Poeciliidae (Livebearing Toothcarps)

Genera:

Phalloptychus	EIGENMANN, 1907 (2)
Phallotorynus	HENN, 1916 (3)
Poecilia BLOCH & SCHNEIDER, 1801 (ca.26)	
Poeciliopsis	REGAN, 1913 (20)
Priapella	REGAN, 1913 (3)
Priapichthys	REGAN, 1913 (7)
Pseudoxiphophorus	BLEEKER, 1860 (8)
Quintana	HUBBS, 1934 (1)
Scolichthys	ROSEN, 1967 (2)
Tomeurus	EIGENMANN, 1909 (1)
Xenodexia	HUBBS, 1950 (1)
Xenophallus	HUBBS, 1924 (1) (= *Neoheterandria*?)
Xiphophorus	HECKEL, 1848 (17)

Continuation of *Anableps dowi* (p. 583):

The eyes are divided by a constriction of the conjunctiva, making each eye look like two (four-eyes). The inferior half of the eyes serves for underwater vision, while the superior half projects above the water surface, enabling foes or food to be seen.

*Not all Anablepidae are livebearers. See subfamily under Anablepidae on p. 434.

T: 24°–28°C, L: ♂ 22 cm, ♀ 34 cm, A: 100 cm, R: t, D: 3

Anableps dowi
Dow's four-eye

Syn.: None, but frequently written incorrectly, e.g., *dowii*, *dovii*, or *dowei*.

Hab.: Central America: along the western coast. Can also be found in pure seawater!

F.I.: Cannot be determined, since this fish has often been confused with *Anableps anableps*.

Sex.: The ♂'s anal fin is modified into a gonopodium, a copulatory organ. ♀♀ are noticeably larger.

Soc. B.: *A. dowi* is a surface-oriented fish that lives in large schools. Peaceful. A nice tankmate for congenial fishes that have similar requirements (brackish water).

M: A large, shallow shore aquarium with a sand substrate and hard, saline water is best. The pH should be around 8. Aquatic plants should be omitted because of the saline water, but bog plants should be planted along the shore. Open spaces along the water surface should be preserved for swimming. When kept in a freshwater aquarium, *A. dowi* wanes and the eyes become cloudy. Cover the aquarium well, since this fish is an accomplished jumper. Four-eyes are mature from a length of 15 cm, half their full-grown size.

B: Pregnant ♀♀ should be placed in their own shallow tank (15–20 cm of water). The gestation period is 20 weeks. Young immediately consume large foods (insects). A temperature of 26°C is appropriate for both breeding and maintenance.

F: C; floating insects and other live foods. Surely they can be accustomed to flakes and beef heart.

S: Copulation and fertilization are only possible from one side of the body; for successful propagation, partners with corresponding lateral orientation must be present.

Continued on p. 582.

Fam.: Goodeidae
Subfam.: Goodeinae

Ataeniobius toweri
Tower's goodeid

(MEEK, 1904)

Syn.: *Goodea toweri.*

Hab.: Central America: Mexico, in the Rio Verde Basin near the cities of Rio Verde and San Luis Potosí, particularly the lagoons of Los Anteojitos and La Media Luna.

F.I.: By HINZ and MEYER in 1979.

Sex.: Both sexes have similar colors. ♂♂ are a slightly brighter green bronze, while ♀♀ tend to be more matte brown. However, it is easy to differentiate them based on the anal fin, the first rays of which are shorter in ♂♂, forming a gonopodium.

Soc. B.: Peaceful, shy fish which can be housed with delicate species. Keep either schools or pairs. Cichlids, catfishes, and characins coexist with this fish in its natural habitat.

M: Not difficult. The aquarium should be spacious with sections of dense vegetation. Water chemistry is probably not very important, though the water should be hard and alkaline and rather warm. SEEGERS and STAECK measured the following values at the collection site of La Media Luna on March 24, 1983, at 15:30: ambient temperature 26°C, water temperature 30.5°C, 53° dGH, 11° dKH, pH 7.9, conductivity 1680 μS. The sulfurous odor which is repeatedly mentioned in descriptions of the collection site, the result of sulfur-containing springs, was not detected. *A. toweri* prefers to live among vegetated side ditches. Wild specimens are capable of leaping 20 cm out of the water. Cover the tank well! Place large rocks in the tank to provide additional hiding places.

B: Livebearers. Only 10 to 15, 10–15 mm long young are born. It is best to keep the fish in a species tank with densely vegetated sections and collect and raise the offspring in a separate tank. The young can flee into the vegetation to avoid predation. Despite their slow growth, one should try and propagate the species! They may be becoming extinct in nature, since food competitors (*Gambusia* and *Tilapia*) have been released in their habitat.

F: C, O; all types of live foods as well as flake and frozen foods. It is not sure whether or not algae are eaten.

S: This is the only known species among the Goodeidae not born with an "umbilical cord."
Although *A. toweri* has a very relictlike distribution area limited to the Rio Verde, Mexico, SEEGERS and STAECK (1983) found it was fairly common there and did not seem to be threatened like other species, some of which are found exclusively in that habitat. Indications that the species is close to extinction could not be confirmed by SEEGERS and STAECK. See MILLER (1956): A new genus and species of cyprinodont fish from S. L. Potosí, Mexico, Occ. Pap. Mus Zool. Michigan, 581.

T: 22°–30°C, **L:** ♂ 7 cm, ♀ 10 cm, **A:** 80 cm, **R:** all, **D:** 3

Ataeniobius toweri ♂, Laguna los Anteojitos, Rio Verde, Mexico

Ataeniobius toweri ♀

Lake Zirahuen, Michoacán, Mexico.
Habitat of *Allotoca dugesi, Allotoca meeki*, and *Chirostoma* sp.

Fam.: Goodeidae
Subfam.: Goodeinae

Chapalichthys pardalis ♂

Chapalichthys pardalis   ALVAREZ, 1963

Syn.: None.

Hab.: Central America: Mexico, Tocumbo, Michoacán.

F.I.: To England in 1981 by DIBBLE.

Sex.: ♂♂ have a modified anal fin and a yellow-fringed caudal fin. ♀♀ do not have colored fins.

Soc. B.: Peaceful towards equal-sized fishes, making it an appropriate addition for community tanks containing large, peaceful species.

M: *C. pardalis* likes clean, clear water. They need good filtration, but little circulation. Therefore, wash the filter medium frequently and use a large, slow flow filter. Decorate the tank with a dark substrate and plenty of plants. Cover part of the surface with floating plants. Water: hardness up to 25° dGH; pH 7.2–8.0.

B: Reproduction is no more difficult for this species than for other goodeids. Breeding pairs are brought into spawning condition with live or frozen foods. The few young, rarely more than 12, are 15 mm long at birth. They are unmolested by the parents if the tank has dense vegetation.

F: C, O; flake and live foods.

S: A very slow-growing species.

T: 18°–24°C, **L:** ♂ 6 cm, ♀ 7 cm, **A:** 70 cm, **R:** m, **D:** 3

Fam.: Goodeidae
Subfam.: Goodeinae

Goodea atripinnis atripinnis
Black-finned goodeid

JORDAN, 1880

Syn.: *Characodon atripinnis* and *C. variatus* as well as many additional subspecies. *Xenendum caliente, Goodea caliente, G. calientis.*

Hab.: Central America: Mexico, León, Guanajuato, Rio Lerma, Lake Patzcuaro.

F.I.: To Hamburg by F. MAYER in 1937.

Sex.: The ♀♀'s yellow fins turn black under favorable maintenance conditions. ♂♂ are smaller and have a gonopodium, which can be seen as a lobe-shaped appendage on the anal fin itself. The ♀♀ have a round anal fin.

Soc. B.: Quite peaceful considering its size. When not breeding, *G. a. atripinnis* can easily be housed with other large livebearers, peaceful cichlids, and characins.

M: Relatively undemanding. Leave the entire length of the foreground open for swimming, and provide a section of heavy vegetation. Water: pH 7.5–8.0; hardness 5°–25° dGH. Their voracious appetite and the resulting dissolved metabolites calls for good filtration and regular water exchanges ($\frac{1}{3}$ of the tank's volume every 2 to 3 weeks).

B: 20°–24°C. Use a species tank for breeding. Feed the breeders hardy live foods. Depending on the size of the ♀, between 15 and 60, 2 cm long young are born. After 40 to 55 days, the ♀ gives birth again. The offspring are sexually mature in about four months when fed a good diet.

F: O; good flake foods, live foods, earthworms, and frozen foods.

S: *G. a. luitpoldi* (T. v. BAYERN & STEINDACHNER, 1895) and *G. a. martini* DE BUEN, 1947 are two described subspecies. The ♀♀ of the latter species (according to MEEK) reportedly only grow to a length of 9 cm, which is somewhat smaller than the nominate form. *G. a. gracilis* HUBBS & TURNER, 1939 and *G. a. xaliscone* (JORDAN & SNYDER, 1900) are probably synonyms of *G. a. atripinnis*.

T: 18°–24°C, **L:** ♂ 8 cm, ♀ 12 cm, **A:** 100 cm, **R:** b, m, **D:** 2

Goodea atripinnis atripinnis ♀

Goodea atripinnis atripinnis ♂

Fam.: Goodeidae
Subfam.: Goodeinae

Ilyodon furcidens

(JORDAN & GILBERT, 1882)

Syn.: *Characodon furcidens, Ilyodon paraguayense, I. xantusi.*

Hab.: Central America: Mexico, in the Rio Colima and Jalisco. Found in coastal lowland rivers.

F.I.: To England in 1981 by I. DIBBLE. Bred specimens soon reached Germany and Austria from the aforementioned country.

Sex.: The ♂'s anal fin is concave; gonopodium.

Soc. B.: Though peaceful, it should be kept in a species tank.

M: Almost any tank is acceptable. The substrate should be of dark, coarse gravel. Vegetation is not necessary, but it may be advantageous for breeding. The tank should have a filtration system, either weak or strong. Predominantly found in clearwater biotopes. Water: pH 7–8; hardness up to 20° dGH.

B: *I. furcidens* is sexually mature at 4 to 5 months of age. About every 2 weeks, 15–40, 10 mm young are born. The parents do not eat their young. Use *Artemia* nauplii and other small live foods to rear the fry. However, since the young require 6 feedings per day, finely sieved flake foods (FD Menu, etc.) will greatly ease meeting its dietary needs.

F: O; flake foods, algae, all types of live foods, frozen mosquito larvae, and brine shrimp.

T: 24°–27°C, **L:** ♂ 7 cm, ♀ 9 cm, **A:** 80 cm, **R:** all, **D:** 2

Terra typica of *Ilyodon furcidens*

Ilyodon furcidens ♂

Ilyodon furcidens ♀

Fam.: Goodeidae
Subfam.: Goodeinae

Skiffia bilineata   (BEAN, 1888)

Syn.: *Characodon bilineata, Goodea bilineata, Neotoca bilineata.*

Hab.: Central America: Mexico, Rio Grande de Santiago, Jalisco, Michoacán, Guanajuato.

F.I.: By F. MAYER in 1935 to Germany. Imported anew in 1982 by RADDA, GEORG, and DAUL.

Sex.: The ♂'s posterior ventral region is steel blue as long as the fish is content in its surroundings. Dominant ♂♂ have dark anal and dorsal fins, while ♀♀ have light fins. ♂♂ can also be recognized by their gonopodium.

Soc. B.: Restless. Good tankmates for robust species.

M: *S. bilineata* prefers stable water conditions. Water changes and filter maintenance, therefore, should be performed every 8 to 14 days. Correspondingly, exchange only $1/8$ of the tank's volume. Water: pH 7.0–7.5; hardness up to 20° dGH. Decorate the tank with a dark gravel substrate, a few rock edifications, and sparse vegetation along the back and edges. Use floating plants when rearing young.

B: Under favorable conditions, ♀♀ will bear 7 to 20, 10 mm long young every 55 days. Under good conditions, the fry reach sexual maturity within 3 months. Juveniles are particularly sensitive to water changes; so feed them sparingly to minimize the need for water exchanges. The breeding tank should be equipped with a large foam filter. Insure that the filter is biologically active. Young can be fed microworms, *Artemia* nauplii, and MicroMin. An airstone can provide the necessary movement for nonliving foodstuffs. In sufficiently large tanks, the young are left unmolested by their parents.

F: O; flake foods, FD Menu, and live foods such as *Artemia, Daphnia, Cyclops*, and mosquito larvae. Algae and other plant fare are important.

S: Like many Goodeids, an annual "winter" helps keep this species large and robust, even after two or three generations.

T: (18°) 22°–28°C, **L:** ♂ 4 cm, ♀ 6 cm, **A:** 60 cm, **R:** m, t, **D:** 2

Skiffia bilineata ♂

Skiffia bilineata ♀

Fam.: Goodeidae
Subfam.: Goodeinae

Skiffia multipunctata (PELLEGRIN, 1901)

Syn.: *Xenendum multipunctatum, Goodea multipunctata, Ollentodon multipunctatus.*

Hab.: Central America: Mexico, in the states of Michoacán and Jalisco.

F.I.: By F. WAITZE in 1939 (?).

Sex.: ♂♂ are slightly smaller and have a yellow-fringed dorsal fin and a gonopodium.

Soc. B.: This somewhat aggressive, rare species should not be associated with other species.

M: Most *Skiffia* species are very sensitive to ectoparasites and often difficult to maintain. Adding salt to the aquarium water is not recommended.

B: These animals are sexually mature at 2 months of age. Breeding is easier at cooler temperatures. Up to 20, 7–12 mm long fry are released. Gestation takes between 35 and 60 days. See *Skiffia bilineata.*

F: O; flake foods, algae, water fleas, *Cyclops* as well as freeze-dried and frozen foods.

T: 20°–25°C, **L:** ♂ 5 cm, ♀ 6 cm, **A:** 70 cm, **R:** all, **D:** 3

Fam.: Poeciliidae
Subfam.: Poeciliinae

Brachyrhaphis parismina ♂, see ♀ on following page

Brachyrhaphis parismina (MEEK, 1912)

Syn.: *Gambusia parismina, Priapichthys parismina.*

Hab.: Central America: only found on the Atlantic side of Costa Rica. The pictured specimen is from the Rio Barbilla.

F.I.: Unknown; probably first imported by T. SCHULZ in 1982.

Sex.: ♂♂ have a gonopodium. Full-grown ♀♀ are clearly larger than their counterparts.

Soc. B.: Peaceful. Nevertheless, it is best maintained in a species tank. Parents are very cannibalistic towards their young.

M: Needs a densely planted tank with a minimum volume of 80 l and access to numerous hiding places. Rocks and bogwood can be used to create secluded areas. Good filtration and frequent water changes are necessary. The water should be slightly alkaline and moderately hard (pH 7–8.2 and a hardness of 4°–10° dGH, respectively). Help protect these rare, sensitive animals by carefully guarding against introducing diseases into the aquarium.

B: Reproduction is difficult, though exact information could not be found. Pregnant ♀♀ should be placed in a separate tank that has a volume of at least 30 l). The ♀ gestates the 10–20 young for about 6 weeks. At birth the fry are 6 to 7 mm long. The young are very delicate and require small *Artemia* nauplii and a variety of other small live foods. Small plant foods should also be tried!

F: C; offer a variety of live foods as well as flake and freeze-dried foods.

T: 25°–28°C, **L:** ♂ 4 cm, ♀ 5 cm, **A:** 60 cm, **R:** all, **D:** 3–4

Fam.: Poeciliidae
Subfam.: Poeciliinae

Brachyrhaphis roseni

BUSSING, 1988

Syn.: None.

Hab.: Central America: Pacific side of southern Costa Rica.

F.I.: Imported into Germany from England in 1975.

Sex.: ♂♂ are slender and have a gonopodium. ♀♀ are larger and appear stouter. Compare the photos.

Soc. B.: These toothcarps can be aggressive towards small fishes. Conversely, they should be kept in a species tank, since they are frequently subjugated by larger fishes.

M: Clear water with a pH of 7.2–8.0 and a hardness of up to 10° dGH.

B: Like *B. rhabdophora*, this fish is a voracious cannibal that pursues its young. A roomy, densely planted aquarium is needed to successfully breed this species. Gestation requires 7 weeks.

F: C, O; all kinds of live and flake foods.

T: 25°–28°C, **L:** ♂ 4 cm, ♀ 6 cm, **A:** 60 cm, **R:** all, **D:** 2

Brachyrhaphis parisminia ♀ (see p. 595 for text)

Brachyrhaphis roseni ♂

Brachyrhaphis roseni ♀

Fam.: Poeciliidae
Subfam.: Poeciliinae

Brachyrhaphis terrabensis
Terraba mosquitofish

(REGAN , 1907)

Syn.: *Gambusia terrabensis, Pseudoxiphophorus terrabensis.*

Hab.: Western Central America: Pacific side of southern Costa Rica and western Panama, in ditches and creeks.

F.I.: Imported to Vienna in 1980 by RADDA and FRITSCHER.

Sex.: ♂♂ have a gonopodium. ♀♀ are larger than ♂♂.

Soc. B.: A species tank is needed for these peaceful but sensitive animals. Parents pursue their young.

M: Keep in a spacious, densely planted species tank. The water should be neutral and soft (pH 7.0–7.5 and a hardness of 5° dGH or less, respectively). Stimulate healthy plant growth with strong illumination. Frequent water exchanges and a well-filtered aquarium as well as the previous suggestions are necessary to successfully care for any *Brachyrhaphis* species. Provide many hiding places so that socially inferior animals and unwilling ♀♀ can escape.

B: The gestation period lasts about 6 weeks. ♀♀ give birth to 10–30 young that are about 8 to 9 mm long. The young are very sensitive, requiring a variable diet. With good care, young are sexually mature at 6 months of age. See *B. parismina* for instructions on rearing.

F: C; all types of live and flake foods.

S: The numbers of rays in the dorsal fin varies from population to population. The different morphs should be kept strictly separate to preserve pure strains.
The species *B. terrabensis* is named after its natural habitat: Rio Grande de Térraba.

T: 23°–26°C, **L:** ♂ 5 cm, ♀ 6 cm, **A:** 60 cm, **R:** all, **D:** 3

Gambusia atrora
Black-fin mosquitofish

ROSEN & BAILEY, 1963

Syn.: None.

Hab.: Central America: Mexico, San Luis de Potosí, in the Rio Axtla and the Rio Matlapa. It prefers to live among rubble along steep riverine banks.

F.I.: 1978 by RADDA to Vienna.

Sex.: ♂♂ are more colorful, smaller, and have a gonopodium (see photos).

Soc. B.: *G. atrora* is aggressive towards heterospecifics. A species tank is suggested.

M: Occupies fluvial biotopes in nature. A powerful filtration system will produce the clear water and current this species desires. Frequent partial water exchanges are necessary. Neutral to slightly alkaline water with a hardness of 10°–20° dGH should prove adequate. Plants are not necessary, but the tank should be well furnished with rocks and bogwood to provide hiding places for pursued animals.

B: *G. atrora* is very sensitive and rarely bred. Separate and provide a high quality diet for pregnant ♀♀. Hold the temperature steady between 25° and 26°C. Ten to twenty young are born after 5 weeks. Feed with *Artemia* nauplii and small flakes.

F: O; a diet consisting of both animal and vegetable fare is mandatory. Flakes are readily accepted.

S: The name *G. atrora* means "black fringe."

T: 24°–28°C, **L:** ♂ 3 cm, ♀ 4 cm, **A:** 50 cm, **R:** b, m, **D:** 3–4

Brachyrhaphis terrabensis

Gambusia atrora ♀ top, ♂ bottom

Fam.: Poeciliidae
Subfam.: Poeciliinae

Gambusia lemaitrei   FOWLER, 1950

Syn.: *Gambusia meadi.*

Hab.: South America: Colombia, in lake Totuma.

F.I.: Imported into Vienna in 1984 by MÖRTH.

Sex.: ♂ ♂ are smaller, more colorful, and easily identified by their gonopodium (see photos).

Soc. B.: Species tank. See previous species

M: See *Gambusia atrora.*

B: Probably similar to that of *G. atrora*, though *G. lemaitrei* has a shorter gestation period (25 to 28 days). Exact information is not available. According to the species description, they live in brackish waters of coastal regions. This has not been confirmed.

F: O.

T: 24°–28°C, **L:** ♂ 3 cm, ♀ 4 cm, **A:** 50 cm, **R:** all, **D:** 3

Gambusia lemaitrei ♂

Gambusia lemaitrei ♀

Fam.: Poeciliidae
Subfam.: Poeciliinae

Gambusia panuco
Rio Panuco mosquitofish

HUBBS, 1926

Syn.: None.

Hab.: Central America: Mexico, in the Panuco Basin. Released into the Laguna Media Luna, San Luis Potosí. This livebearer colonizes slow-flowing waters and neighboring pond regions.

F.I.: Imported into Vienna in 1978 by RADDA.

Sex.: ♂♂ are clearly smaller and easily recognized by their modified anal fin, the gonopodium.

Soc. B.: Aggressive. Since *G. panuco* attacks heterospecifics, it should be kept in a species tank. Parents are predacious towards their fry.

M: With the exception that the water should not be overly soft, the Rio Panuco mosquitofish does not place particular demands on water chemistry. Include many hiding places in the decor because this species sometimes becomes intraspecifically aggressive, pursuing smaller congeners. Dense vegetation helps. Good filtration and regular partial water exchanges are beneficial.

B: When breeding, try to cross-in different lines to keep the offspring strong. The captive population is endangered, as *G. panuco* tends to degenerate in captivity. *G. panuco* is not difficult to propagate. Gestation takes 5–6 weeks, and the 10 to 40 young are 6 to 7 mm long at birth. They can be fed with *Artemia* nauplii and very small flakes. Mulm has to be removed, since it consumes oxygen. Hold the temperature in the spawning tank steady between 23° and 24°C.

F: O; mosquito larvae, *Daphnia*, and vegetable fare such as algae and flake foods.

S: *G. panuco* is very similar to *Gambusia affinis*, but is corporally stouter. Both sexes have essentially identical coloration.

T: 22°–28°C, **L:** ♂ 3.5 cm, ♀ 5.5 cm, **A:** 60 cm, **R:** all, **D:** 3

Gambusia rhizophorae
Mangrove mosquitofish

RIVAS, 1969

Syn.: *Gambusia punctata* (not POEY, 1954).

Hab.: Cuba and southern Florida. Found exclusively in brackish and salt water of coastal regions.

F.I.: 1983; possibly imported previously by the BAUNs to Germany as *G. punctata*.

Sex.: ♂♂ have a gonopodium. ♀♀ are larger.

Soc. B.: Like most *Gambusia*, this species is slightly aggressive. Keep in a species tank.

M: Easily maintained in hard water that has salt added to it. Due to the salt, plants have to be omitted. Use rocks to create the many required hiding places. The water should be well-filtered and frequently exchanged.

B: Pregnant ♀♀ have to be separated, since these animals prey on their offspring. Gestation takes about 6 weeks. The approximately 30 young can immediately feed on *Artemia* nauplii and small flakes. Rearing is easy, and the offspring reach sexual maturity at 6 months of age.

F: O; flakes with a compliment of live foods and plant fare should be offered.

S: *G. rhizophorae* is a close relative of *G. punctata*. Both species were once considered to be one and the same.

T: 22°–28°C, **L:** ♂ 3.5 cm, ♀ 5 cm, **A:** 60 cm, **R:** all, **D:** 3

Gambusia panuco

Gambusia rhizophorae

Girardinus creolus

GARMAN, 1895

Syn.: *Toxus creolus.*

Hab.: Cuba: in highland rivers at an altitude of about 100 m. Tranquil zones are sought in fast-flowing waters.

F.I.: 1986 by MEYER and RADDA.

Sex.: ♂♂ are slender and have a gonopodium. Full-grown ♀♀ are larger and stouter (compare photos).

Soc. B.: Its amiable nature makes this fish an appropriate tankmate for peaceful smaller fishes. Due to its rarity, however, a species tank is recommended.

M: Clear, slightly alkaline, medium-hard water with a slight current is preferred. The tank should have dense vegetation, yet free swimming space as well. Part of the surface should be covered by floating plants.

B: In warm water with temperatures between 24° and 26°C, a ♀ will give birth monthly. Because the parents prey upon their offspring, provide copious amounts of floating plants and transfer the young from the breeding tank. The young can be raised with *Artemia* nauplii, Liquifry Green, MicroMin, and/or algae.

F: C, O; algae and live foods commiserate to its size as well as flake and tablet foods.

S: This attractive species has just recently been imported alive. Hopefully it will soon be broadly distributed.

T: 22°–26°C, **L:** ♂ 4 cm, ♀ 7 cm, **A:** 60 cm, **R:** m, **D:** 2

Highland of Cuba, home of *Girardinus creolus*

Girardinus creolus ♂

Girardinus creolus ♀

Fam.: Poeciliidae
Subfam.: Poeciliinae

Girardinus microdactylus
Finger girardinus

RIVAS, 1944

Syn.: None.

Hab.: Cuba, Isle of Pines. Colonizes fast-flowing waters of highlands.

F.I.: In 1986 by MEYER and RADDA.

Sex.: ♂♂ have a gonopodium. ♀♀ are larger.

Soc. B.: This lively, peaceful fish makes a good addition to community tanks. Due to its rarity, separate pregnant ♀♀ to help maintain captive populations.

M: As typical fluvial fish, strong filtration and frequent water exchanges are needed to provide the clear, moving water conditional for successful maintenance. Water: pH 7; hardness 10°–25° dGH. Dense vegetation, including floating plants, makes *G. microdactylus* at ease in its environment. Only remove the algae from the front pane of the aquarium.

B: Pregnant ♀♀ should be kept singly in 30 l or larger, densely planted spawning tanks. At a stable temperature between 24° and 25°C, 10 to 50 young are born after about 4 weeks. The 6–9 mm long young do not need to be separated from the mother. After a recuperation period of 3–5 days, the ♀ can be reintroduced into the breeding tank. A heavy layer of floating plants offers the young places to hide. Use live and plant foods to raise the offspring. Under good conditions, sexual maturity is achieved at 4 months of age.

F: O; flake foods, tablets, algae, blanched lettuce or spinach, and live foods of suitable size such as *Artemia* and *Cyclops*.

S: Though very similar to *G. metallicus*, there are behavioral and morphological (gonopodium) differences.

T: 22°–26°C, **L:** ♂ 3.5 cm, ♀ 6 cm, **A:** 60 cm, **R:** all, **D:** 3

Girardinus uninotatus
Single-spot girardinus

POEY, 1860

Syn.: *Glaridodon uninotatus, Glaridichthys uninotatus, G. torralbasi.*

Hab.: Cuba: in the highlands at Sierra de los Organos, Pinar del Rio.

F.I.: Captive-bred specimens were imported into Germany from New York by STÜVE in 1900.

Sex.: ♂♂ are smaller and easily recognized by their gonopodium. ♂♂ have a black spot on their side (see photo).

Soc. B.: Peaceful. Appropriate tankmates for other peaceful, small species. Pregnant ♀♀ of this rare species should be separated.

M: Relatively undemanding. Plenty of free swimming space and dense vegetation are greatly appreciated. A gravel substrate and good filtration meet its requirements.

B: Breeding *G. uninotatus* is easy in heavily planted species tanks. Gestation takes about 4 weeks, and the 10 to 40 young are 8 mm in length at birth. Rear with *Artemia* nauplii, small flake foods, and plant fare. Under good conditions, the fry reach sexual maturity in 6 months.

F: O; flakes, algae, frozen foods, and all other foodstuffs of suitable size.

T: 24°–28°C, **L:** ♂ 5 cm, ♀ 8 cm, **A:** 60 cm, **R:** m, **D:** 2

Girardinus microdactylus

Girardinus uninotatus, pair

Fam.: Poeciliidae
Subfam.: Poeciliinae

Heterandria jonesi
Puebla mosquitofish

(GÜNTHER, 1874)

Syn.: *Mollienesia jonesii, Gambusia jonesii, Pseudoxiphophorus jonesii, P. bimaculatus jonesii, P. reticulatus, P. pauciradiatus, P. bimaculatus, Heterandria bimaculata.*

Hab.: Central America: Mexico, from the Rio Guayalejo in southern Tamaulipas to the Rio Tehuacán, Puebla. Lives in ponds as well as swift- and slow-flowing rivers in both highlands and lowlands.

F.I.: Unknown; repeatedly imported under other names.

Sex.: ♂♂ are easily recognized by their long gonopodium; ♀♀ are slightly larger.

Soc. B.: Tranquil, peaceful species which can be housed with equal-sized fishes. Small fishes and juveniles are pursued and preyed upon, though *H. jonesi* is more peaceful than *Gambusia* or *H. bimaculata.*

M: Good vegetation and strong filtration foster the well-being of these livebearers. The pH should be neutral, and the hardness between 10° and 15° dGH. Limit vegetation to the edges of the tank and floating plants, since *H. jonesi* is a very active swimmer.

B: Pregnant ♀♀ should be separated. In comparison to *H. bimaculata*, fewer offspring are born. The parents usually only pursue their young under deficient dietary conditions. About 20 to 50 relatively large (11–14 mm) fry are born every 2 weeks. Siphon mulm from the bottom every 2–3 days to help maintain the excellent water conditions the offspring require. Good feedings of *Artemia* and flake foods encourage uniform growth. Java moss and floating plants offer hiding places for the young and harbor additional foods.

F: C; flake and live foods.

S: Optimal temperature and current depends on the population's origin. The size and degree of yellow varies from population to population.

T: 20°–28°C, **L:** ♂ 7 cm, ♀ 9 cm, **A:** 70 cm, **R:** all, **D:** 2

Gambusia rachowi
Rachow's mosquitofish

(REGAN, 1914)

Syn.: *Gambusia atzi, Heterophallus rachowi.*

Hab.: Central America: Mexico, at Veracruz. Found along the shore regions of the Laguna de la Sapote and the neighboring Rio Jaltepec.

F.I.: To Germany in 1913 by HOPP.

Sex.: ♂♂ are slightly smaller and have a gonopodium.

Soc. B.: Peaceful. Easily associated with other small, peaceful fishes.

M: Maintain in a species tank. Normally the parents ignore their offspring. Nevertheless, the aquarium should have good vegetation, including floating plants. Moderate water values are appropriate, since the animals do not have any special demands.

B: ♀♀ give birth to 5–20 young every 5 weeks. The fry are about 6–7 mm long at birth and ignored by congeners. Feed *Artemia* nauplii and very small flake foods. Keep dissolved metabolite concentrations low.

F: C, O; flake foods. Foods must be commiserate to this diminutive fish's size.

S: The blue dorsal fin distinguishes this fish from *Heterophallus echeagarayi* and *H. milleri* from the Rio Teapa (see photo).

T: 22°–26°C, **L:** ♂ 2.5 cm, ♀ 3.5 cm, **A:** 50 cm, **R:** m, t, **D:** 2

Heterandria jonesi

Gambusia rachowi

Fam.: Poeciliidae
Subfam.: Poeciliinae

Phalloceros caudimaculatus
a) Spotted caudo
b) Unspotted caudo

(HENSEL, 1868)

Syn.: *Girardinus caudimaculatus, G. reticulatus, Poecilia caudimaculata, Glaridichthys caudimaculatus, Phalloceros caudomaculatus.*

Hab.: South America: southern Brazil, Paraguay and Uruguay, usually found in flowing waters.

F.I.: To Berlin in 1898 by MATTE.

Sex.: ♂♂ are smaller and have a gonopodium. The gold morph of this species was introduced in Vol. 1, p. 594. Like the gold morph, ♂♂ of this form have a black-fringed dorsal fin and a more colorful operculum when compared to ♀♀.

Soc. B.: Peaceful. Even fry are rarely pursued. However, its demand for cooler temperatures makes it an inappropriate addition to most community tanks.

M: Like most livebearers, this fish does best in hard water, and the pH should be neutral to slightly alkaline (pH 7.5–8.0 and a hardness of 14°–30° dGH, respectively). Respect this fish's inability to adapt to changing water conditions by avoiding large additions of fresh water. Frequent minimal water exchanges, good filtration, and good plant growth are more advantageous. Tanks with a volume of 30 l or more are large enough for one pair and a few young.

B: Simple. Use the water values mentioned under **M** and a temperature of 20°–22°C. After about 24 days, 10 to 50 fry with a length of 5 to 6 mm are born. As long as conspecific tankmates have received an adequate diet, they will not prey on the young. Frequently the young sink to the bottom when born, only becoming free-swimming after an hour. For this reason, the bottom must be kept free of oxygen-consuming mulm. Feed the fry *Artemia* nauplii and small vegetable-based flake foods.

F: O; flake foods, freeze-dried foods, and all kinds of small live foods.

S: Adding about 1 teaspoon of salt per 10 l of water helps keep these fish healthy. The gold form of the spotted caudo was introduced in Vol. 1, p. 594.

T: 18°–24°C, **L:** ♂ 3.5 cm, ♀ 4.5, **A:** 50 cm, **R:** m, t, **D:** 1

Phalloceros caudimaculatus ♂, unspotted

Phalloceros caudimaculatus ♀, spotted

Fam.: Poeciliidae
Subfam.: Poeciliinae

Poecilia branneri
Ocellated micromolly

EIGENMANN, 1894

Syn.: *Micropoecilia branneri, Poecilia heteristia.* Sometimes erroneously written *P. brauneri.*

Hab.: South America: Brazil, at Pará, Santarém.

F.I.: Into Germany in 1905 by KITTLER.

Sex.: ♂♂ have a gonopodium, a distinctly patterned caudal fin (see photo), and a black-edged, elongated dorsal fin which is clearly larger than that of the ♀♀.

Soc. B.: Peaceful but delicate. Courtship is an elaborate spectacle, a true pleasure to behold.

M: Due to the delicate nature of this small fish, a species tank is recommended. An almost zero tolerance level for sudden changes in water conditions make actions such as large water exchanges fatal. Adding vitamin D_3 to the aquarium water helps prevent illnesses and miscarriages. Soft water may be better than brackish water.

B: Reproduction is not considered easy. From 3 to 5 young are born every few days, but unfortunately, they are often born with a defective swimbladder. Hormones and vitamins added to the water during the gestation period may help. *Poecilia parae* has similar problems (see p. 618).

F: C; small live foods are preferred. Freeze-dried foods and FD tablets are readily accepted.

S: The unusual fin design and shape makes us hope that the few aquarium strains will soon stabilize, making it more available. Rare livebearers are sometimes available at the DGLZ (ALA in the United States). See the news section of aquarium magazines for an address. ♂♂ have an unusual, elaborate courtship.

T: 26°–28°C, **L:** ♂ 3 cm, ♀ 4 cm, **A:** 50 cm, **R:** all, **D:** 3

Poecilia butleri
Pacific Mexican molly

JORDAN, 1889

Syn.: *Platypoecilus nelsoni.* Often confused with *Poecilia sphenops* (see Vol. 1, p. 602).

Hab.: Central America: Mexico to Panama, in tributaries flowing to the Pacific.

F.I.: Unknown, since it was surely imported as *P. sphenops.*

Sex.: ♂♂ have a gonopodium, whereas ♀♀ have a pregnancy spot.

Soc. B.: This peaceful species is suitable for community tanks. Because it is so infrequently imported, a species tank is recommended. Adults usually do not pursue young.

M: Stimulate algae growth with abundant illumination! Moderate filtration. Water: pH 7.0–7.8; hardness from 6° to 20° dGH. Water in its natural habitat according to SCHREIBER had a hardness of 8° dGH.

B: These fish should be bred in tanks with a minimum capacity of 200 l. Sexual maturity is attained at 5 to 6 months of age. ♀♀ give birth to 20–60, 8 mm long offspring every 4 weeks. Raise with green algae, infusoria, *Artemia* nauplii, and finely ground flake foods.

F: H; algae! Vegetable flakes. *Daphnia* and other live foods can be used to add variety to the diet. If only flake foods are fed, abstain from feeding one day per week.

S: This molly is closely related to *Poecilia sphenops.*

T: 23°–27°C, **L:** ♂ 7 cm, ♀ 8 cm, **A:** 100 cm, **R:** all, **D:** 2

Poecilia branneri

Poecilia butleri

Fam.: Poeciliidae
Subfam.: Poeciliinae

Poecilia catemaconis
Lemon molly

MILLER, 1975

Syn.: *Mollienesia sphenops* (partially).

Hab.: Central America: endemic to Lake Catemaco, Veracruz, Mexico.

F.I.: 1979 by MEYER to Germany.

Sex.: ♂♂ are smaller and have a gonopodium.

Soc. B.: Relatively peaceful. If kept in a community tank, make sure they receive sufficient food. A species tank is recommended for this rare species.

M: House these fish in tanks with a volume of at least 200 l. Dense vegetation and a partial cover of floating plants should be included. A section of the tank, preferably in the foreground, should have an open swimming area. It is not necessary to add salt. Water: pH 7.2–8.2; hardness 6°–30° dGH.

B: The breeding aquarium needs to have a volume of at least 200 l. Pregnant ♀♀ are placed into large aquaria early to avoid miscarriages. Rearing is relatively easy, similar to that of *Poecilia sphenops.*

F: H, O; algae, plant fare, small live foods, and flake and tablet foods.

S: This uncommon species has a restricted distribution. It is rarely offered in the trade.

T: 24°–28°C, **L:** ♂ 8 cm, ♀ 10.5 cm, **A:** 100 cm, **R:** all, **D:** 2–3

Poecilia caucana
Cauca molly

(STEINDACHNER, 1880)

Syn.: *Girardinus caucanus, Mollienesia caucana, Allopoecilia caucana.*

Hab.: Central and South America: Panama, Colombia, and Venezuela.

F.I.: Imported in 1906 by STÜVE to Germany.

Sex.: ♂♂ are more colorful and have a gonopodium.

Soc. B.: Peaceful. Appropriate for small aquaria containing other delicate species.

M: Like many small Poeciliidae, *Poecilia caucana* demands temperatures of 27° to 29°C. Salt helps keep specimens healthy (1 teaspoon per 10 l). Vegetable foodstuffs such as algae are preferred. Water: pH 7.0–7.5; hardness 10° to 20° dGH. Water changes and good filtration are necessary, since plant growth is normally aborted or suppressed in saline water.

B: Breeding has been accomplished in aquaria with algae blooms. One ♀ gives birth about every 4 weeks to 8–25 young that are 7 mm long. The fry are sexually mature at 4 to 5 months of age if well fed. The parents do not pursue the newborns as long as they receive an adequate diet and the tank offers ample vegetation (floating plants). The young must swim in food. If enough algae are not available, MicroMin, Liquifry Green, or Preis Microplan have to be fed. These foods are kept in suspension longer if the tank is well aerated. Snails help maintain water quality when commercial diets are fed, but they also eat the available algae.

F: H, O; algae, vegetable flakes, tablets, and small live foods such as *Artemia* nauplii and *Cyclops.*

S: The colorful fins make the cauca molly very appealing, which is why this species has always had at least a limited distribution among hobbyists.

T: 26°–30°C, **L:** ♂ 4 cm, ♀ 6 cm, **A:** 60 cm, **R:** all, **D:** 2

Poecilia catemaconis ♂, ♀ pictured on p. 616

Poecilia caucana ♂

Poecilia catemaconis ♀

Poecilia latipunctata ♀, population from Mante, Mexico

Fam.: Poeciliidae
Subfam.: Poeciliinae

Poecilia latipunctata, WC, Laguna Media Luna, Rio Verde, Mexico (photo on p. 554)

Poecilia latipunctata
Porthole molly

MEEK, 1904

Syn.: *Mollienesia latipunctata.*

Hab.: Central America: Mexico, in muddy ditches and slow-flowing creeks of the Rio Panuco Basin, Tamaulipas.

F.I.: Imported as early as 1934. Imported again into Austria in 1978 by RADDA.

Sex.: ♂♂ have a darker design and a gonopodium.

Soc. B.: Its delicate, sickly nature makes it difficult to keep with tankmates.

M: *P. latipunctata* is susceptible to diseases, particularly piscine tuberculosis. Large, heavily planted tanks are conditional to successfully care for this species. Especially avoid housing this species with potential tuberculosis carriers such as guppies. Floating plants give these animals a feeling of security and provides additional food.

B: After about 4 weeks of gestation, 10–30 young with a length of 7 mm are released. The parents leave their young in peace if they are receiving an adequate diet. Fry are sexually mature at 5 months of age.

F: H, O; algae mats represent a good source of food. Small live foods and *Artemia* nauplii are valuable supplements. Flake foods are also readily accepted.

T: 25°–29°C, L: ♂ 5 cm, ♀ 6 cm, A: 80 cm, R: all, D: 3

Fam.: Poeciliidae
Subfam.: Poeciliinae

Micropoecilia parae
Para molly

(EIGENMANN, 1894)

Syn.: *Poecilia vivipara parae, Poecilia parae, Lebistes parae, Acanthophacelus bifurcus, Micropoecilia bifurca, M. melanzona, Poecilia melanzona.*

Hab.: South America: Brazil and British Guyana, along the coast to the Amazon.

F.I.: 1910 by F. MAYER.

Sex.: ♂♂ are smaller, more colorful, and have a gonopodium.

Soc. B.: Though extremely peaceful, a species tank is suggested because of its tendency to hybridize and its water requirements. It may be possible to associate this species with *P. branneri* or *P. picta.*

M: Despite the fact that it lives in brackish water in nature, this species is best maintained and bred in soft water. Saline water is not necessary. Strongly illuminate the tank to encourage plant growth, particularly algae. Use a dark substrate, floating plants, good filtration,

and perform small weekly water exchanges. These animals show a remarkable lack of ability to adapt to abrupt changes in water quality. *P. parae* transferred into different water without slow acclimation are death candidates!

B: Bring the breeders into spawning condition with small mosquito larvae, *Drosophila*, and algae. ♂♂ need 8 months to reach sexual maturity. Only 5 to 16 young are born. Vitamin D_3 and hormones are needed for successful reproduction. Young are even more sensitive to suboptimal water quality than adults.

F: O, C; small live foods and algae as well as flake and freeze-dried foods.

S: Some strains are much more colorful and have a more interesting design than the pictured animals. *P. parae*'s care and breeding parallel that of *P. picta* in many ways (see Vol. 2, p. 740).

T: 26°–28°C, **L:** ♂ 3 cm, ♀ 5 cm, **A:** 50 cm, **R:** all, **D:** 3

Poecilia petenensis
Petén molly, swordtail molly

(GÜNTHER, 1866)

Syn.: *Mollienesia petenensis.*

Hab.: Central America: Guatemala, Mexico, Belize, in creeks, ditches, and lakes (Lake Petén).

F.I.: 1938 by THUMM.

Sex.: ♂♂ can be distinguished from an early age from their thick-bellied consorts by their gonopodium. Adult ♂♂ are larger and have beautiful fins and a small sword. Pregnant ♀♀ have a spot on the ventral area above the anal fin.

Soc. B.: Peaceful. A good addition to hard water community aquaria containing fishes that are roughly the same size. Their offspring and those of other livebearers are rarely pursued.

M: 1%–2% salt can be added to the water. Hard or prolific plants such as

Java fern, water sprite, sagittaria, vallisneria, and *Anubias* are wise choices, since they will not be nibbled on. The fish's propensity for nibbling on the plants diminishes when algae and vegetable flakes are fed. Because these animals are hardy eaters, good filtration and frequent partial water exchanges are necessary.

B: If the aquarium has a heavy cover of floating plants, some offspring are generally able to escape predation. Pregnant ♀♀ need to be placed into large separate tanks (60 cm or longer) full of algae or other vegetation. Every 6 to 8 weeks, 10–60 young are born. These 8–12 mm long fry should be fed plant fare and small live foods. *P. petenensis* has been known to crossbreed with *P. latipinna* and *P. velifera.*

Continued on p. 626.

Micropoecilia parae

Poecilia petenensis

Fam.: Poeciliidae
Subfam.: Poeciliinae

Poeciliopsis catemaco
Catemaco poeciliid

MILLER, 1975

Syn.: None.

Hab.: Central America: Mexico, endemic to Lake Catemaco.

F.I.: 1980 by MEYER (2 ♀♀).

Sex.: ♂♂ have a gonopodium. ♀♀ are larger.

Soc. B.: Similar to *Poeciliopsis gracilis*.

M: Water: pH 7.0–7.8; hardness from 10° to 25° dGH. See *P. gracilis,* Vol. 2, p. 746, for additional information.

B: There is no available information. As with other representatives of the genus (with the exception of *P. gracilis*), it may be very difficult to successfully breed this species over several generations. A nutrient may be missing from the food or water.

F: O.

S: Virtually only ♂♂ are found in its natural habitat (at a ratio of 100:1).

T: 24°–28°C, **L:** ♂ 4 cm, ♀ 8 cm, **A:** 80 cm, **R:** all, **D:** 2

Poeciliopsis fasciata
Cross-striped poeciliid

(MEEK, 1904)

Syn.: *Gambusia fasciata, Heterandria fasciata.*

Hab.: Central America: Mexico. Inhabits shallow, swift-flowing freshwater or brackish water.

F.I.: Imported into Austria in 1976 by E. SCHLOSSER.

Sex.: ♂♂ are smaller and have a gonopodium.

Soc. B.: This peaceful species makes a good community fish when housed with small, not overly rough fishes.

M: Protection is sought among floating plants or plants with large leaves near the surface. *P. fasciata* is a simple charge without particular water chemistry requirements. Water: pH of 7–8; hardness of 25° dGH or less. Good filtration and regular water exchanges are necessary. Some mulm can be allowed to settle on the possibly dark substrate.

These livebearers can find nourishment among algae.

B: Sexual maturity is attained at 4 months of age. About every month, 15–30, 8 mm long young are released. Breeding is easier in large algae-laden tanks. Well-fed adults seldom pursue their offspring. With algae, *Artemia* nauplii, and other small foods, the fry grow rapidly. Like with many livebearers, reproduction over 4 consecutive generations has failed.

F: O; flake and freeze-dried foods, *Artemia* nauplii, etc. Provide a varied diet.

S: *P. fasciata* can easily be confused with *P. latidens* and some forms of *P. gracilis*. Maintenance is largely identical for the three.

T: 24°–28°C, **L:** ♂ 3 cm, ♀ 5 cm, **A:** 70 cm, **R:** all, **D:** 3

Poeciliopsis catemaco

Poeciliopsis fasciata ♀

Fam.: Poeciliidae
Subfam.: Poeciliinae

Poeciliopsis occidentalis
Arizona poeciliid

(BAIRD & GIRARD, 1853)

Syn.: *Heterandria occidentalis, Girardinus occidentalis, G. sonoriensis, Poecilia occidentalis, Mollienesia occidentalis.*

Hab.: North America: United States and northern Mexico, at Bylas Springs, Arizona.

F.I.: Imported into Germany from Mexico in 1984 by MEYER and in 1987 by SCHARTL from Arizona.

Sex.: ♂♂ are smaller and have a gonopodium.

Soc. B.: Unknown.

M: Occasional dramatic drops in temperature are tolerated, making it suitable for unheated aquaria.

B: No information could be found.

F: C, O.

S: *P. occidentalis* is one of the most beautiful species of the genus. Unfortunately, this slender dark species is on the verge of extinction. It can no longer be found at the type localities of Rio Santa Cruz and Rio Gila.
P. occidentalis was erroneously identified as *P. monacha* in *Lebendgebärende Zierfische*, MERGUS VERLAG, Melle, Germany.
MINCKLEY (1973) claims that *P. occidentalis* has two subspecies, *P. o. occidentalis* from Arizona and *P. o. sonoriensis* (GIRARD, 1895) from Mexico. As per MINCKLEY, the pictured animals are *P. o. sonoriensis.*

T: 25°–28°C, **L:** ♂ 3 cm, ♀ 5 cm, **A:** 60 cm, **R:** t, m, **D:** 3

Poeciliopsis prolifica

MILLER, 1960

Syn.: None.

Hab.: Central America: Mexico, in fresh and brackish waters of coastal regions.

F.I.: Imported into Europe in 1984 by ALLSPACH, MEYER, MEYER, and WIRTH.

Sex.: ♂♂ are smaller and have a gonopodium.

Soc. B.: Keep with small peaceful fishes.

M: Two teaspoons of salt per 10 l of water are recommended. Plant and algae growth are desired. Water: pH 7–8; hardness of 2° to 10° dGH.

B: Like *Heterandria formosa*, young are normally born over several weeks time. Breeding is not overly difficult, but the great majority of successful breeding endeavors have taken place in a species tank. This species has been bred over more than 4 generations, an exceptional feat for this genus. See *Poeciliopsis fasciata* or *P. latidens*, Vol. 2, p. 749. According to its scientific name, it should be "very prolific."

F: H, O; algae, flake foods, and small live foods such as *Cyclops* and *Artemia* nauplii.

S: This rare, small species is bright yellow along its midbody and ventral region when healthy and content.

T: 24°–28°C, **L:** ♂ 2 cm, ♀ 3.5 cm, **A:** 40 cm, **R:** all, **D:** 2

Poeciliopsis occidentalis sonoriensis, Mexico

Poeciliopsis prolifica

Fam.: Poeciliidae
Subfam.: Poeciliinae

Poeciliopsis retropinna

(REGAN, 1908)

Syn.: *Poecilia retropinna.*

Hab.: Central America: Costa Rica and western Panama.

F.I.: 1985 by MEYER to Germany.

Sex.: ♂♂ are smaller and have a gonopodium.

Soc. B.: Though normally peaceful, this small species often devours its offspring. Good tankmates for equal-size fishes.

M: Clear, well-filtered water with a slight current best meets its needs. Frequent water exchanges and filter maintenance are necessary. Water: pH 7.0–7.5; hardness of 3°–15° dGH. The addition of salt may prove beneficial. An abundance of plants, including floating plants, helps keep the water quality high and provides cover for the fry. *P. retropinna* is disease prone.

B: After about 5 weeks gestation, 5–15, 7 mm long young are born. They should be separated from the parents and raised in aquaria that have plenty of plants and algae. Feed the young with *Artemia* nauplii and small flakes (vegetable-based). The captive population died out after a few generations.

F: O; small live foods are preferred, but flake and freeze-dried foods are readily accepted.

T: 25°–28°C, **L:** ♂ 5 cm, ♀ 8 cm, **A:** 70 cm, **R:** all, **D:** 3

Poeciliopsis scarlli
Scarll's poeciliid

MEYER, RIEHL, DAWES & DIBBLE, 1985

Syn.: None.

Hab.: Central America: Mexico, in Guerrero and Michoacán.

F.I.: Imported into Germany in 1984 by ALLSPACH, MEYER, MEYER, and WIRTH.

Sex.: ♂♂ are smaller and have a gonopodium.

Soc. B.: This is a small peaceful species.

M: Though found in freshwater, the addition of salt (1 teaspoon per 10 l) seems to be beneficial. The water should be oxygen-rich. Frequent water exchanges are recommended.

B: Difficult. ♀♀ normally give birth to fewer than 10 young every 4 to 6 weeks. However, in compensation, the young are quite large at birth, capable of consuming *Artemia*.

F: O, C; small live foods and flake foods.

S: The little known *P. scarlli* is very similar to *P. turrubarensis,* but has a totally different distribution.

T: 23°–30°C, **L:** ca. 4 cm, **A:** 60 cm, **R:** all, **D:** 2–3

Poeciliopsis retropinna

Poeciliopsis scarlli ♂

Fam.: Poeciliidae
Subfam.: Poeciliinae

Poeciliopsis turrubarensis (MEEK, 1912)
Turrubarés poeciliid

Syn.: *Gambusia fasciata, G. turrubarensis, Heterandria colombianus, Poeciliopsis colombianus, P. maldonadoi, Priapichthys fosteri, P. turrubarensis.*

Hab.: Central America: Turrubarés, Costa Rica, as well as Guatemala and Mexico. Lives in fresh, brackish, and salt water.

F.I.: Imported into Austria in 1977 by SCHLOSSER.

Sex.: ♂♂ are usually smaller and have a gonopodium. Dominant ♂♂ develop an enlarged dorsal fin.

Soc. B.: Relatively peaceful, but due to the required salinity, only conditionally suitable for community tanks. In nature, this species is sometimes found sympatrically (together) with *Anableps dowi.*

M: Use a large aquarium and make sure respectable oxygen concentrations are maintained. A powerhead with air injection is advantageous, since salinity suppresses or aborts most plant growth, curtailing oxygen production from that source. Add about 1 teaspoon of salt per liter. Since plants are absent, use rockwork to provide hiding places. Do not include wood in the decor, as it frequently lowers the pH and colors the water, both of which are detrimental to this species.

B: Difficult to bred. Gestation takes about one month. The 10–60 young are about 8 mm long at birth. With plenty of food and regular water exchanges, the young may be sexually mature as early as 4 months after birth.

F: H, O; vegetable based foods are preferred and should never be omitted from their diet.

S: This species, which loves saline water, has rarely been bred in aquaria. Several essential nutrients are probably either missing from the water or the diet. Marine salt will probably come closer to supplying necessary trace elements than table salt.

T: 23°–28°C, **L:** ♂ 4 cm, ♀ 8 cm, **A:** 100 cm, **R:** all, **D:** 3

Continuation of *Poecilia petenensis* (p. 618):

F: H, O; algae and other tender plants are the foods of choice. Small live foods and flake foods are also accepted.

S: *P. latipinna* (Vol. 2, p. 738) and *P. velifera* (Vol. 1, p. 604) are very similar species whose hybrids are also fertile. To avoid such crosses and maintain pure strains, the species have to be kept separate!

Dominant ♂♂ have extensive, distinctly yellow fins and yellow along the body's edges. The attractive large dorsal fin only develops in spacious aquaria.

T: 22°–28°C, **L:** ♂ 8 cm, ♀ 12 cm, **A:** 120 cm, **R:** all, **D:** 2

Poeciliopsis turrubarensis ♂

Poeciliopsis turrubarensis ♀

Fam.: Poeciliidae
Subfam.: Poeciliinae

Priapichthys chocoensis
Colombian diamond-scale

(HENN, 1916)

Syn.: *Diphyacantha chocoensis.*

Hab.: South America: Colombia, in the Rio Calima and Rio San Juan, Chocó.

F.I.: Imported into Vienna in 1984 by RADDA.

Sex.: ♂♂ are smaller and have a gonopodium. ♀♀ have a yellow anal fin.

Soc. B.: Peaceful. Even fry are rarely pursued, but to ensure offspring survival in light of its rarity, separate pregnant ♀♀. A good tankmate for many fishes.

M: Relatively hard water (15°–35° dGH) facilitates maintenance. Adding salt seems to be beneficial. Small but regular water exchanges and good filter maintenance are required. The hard, saline water greatly limits the number of appropriate plant species and suppresses their growth. Hence, rocks are by far the best way to provide hiding places. The pH should lie between 7.2 and 8.5.

B: A 30 l aquarium is suitable as a breeding tank and is easier to handle than larger tanks. Use a dense layer of floating plants. When fed a good diet, the ♀ will ignore her offspring. In two week intervals, 3 to 15, 5–7 mm long young are born. Feed them *Artemia* nauplii and other small live foods. Breeding and rearing are not easy. Adding salt (about 1 teaspoon per 10 l) promotes healthy offspring.

F: C; small live foods such as *Artemia* nauplii, small *Daphnia*, and *Cyclops* as well as freeze-dried foods. Only feed flake foods when the above mentioned foods are unavailable.

S: Care and breeding of *P. chocoensis* has proven to be just as problematic as that of *P. festae.* See Vol. 2, p. 752.

T: 23°–28°C, **L:** ♂ 3.5 cm, ♀ 4.5 cm, **A:** 50 cm, **R:** all, **D:** 3

Pseudopoecilia nigroventralis ♀, text on p. 630

Priapichthys chocoensis ♂

Priapichthys chocoensis ♀

Pseudopoecilia nigroventralis ♂, ♀ on p. 628

Pseudopoecilia nigroventralis
Black-finned poeciliid

(EIGENMANN & HENN, 1912)

Syn.: *Gambusia caudovittata, G. nigroventralis, Alloheterandria nigroventralis, Priapichthys nigroventralis.*

Hab.: South America: Colombia, Rio Atrato and Rio San Juan.

F.I.: 1984 by RADDA and companions.

Sex.: ♂♂ are smaller and have a gonopodium (see photos).

Soc. B.: Peaceful.

M: As for *Priapichthys chocoensis* (previous page).

B: See *P. chocoensis.*

F: C; small live foods.

S: In "Lebendgebärende Zierfische" by MEYER, WISCHNATH, and FOERSTER, the ♀ of *P. chocoensis* was erroneously labeled as *P. nigroventralis* (♀). Compare the photos here.

T: 23°–28°C, **L:** 3 cm, **A:** 50 cm, **R:** all, **D:** 2–3

Fam.: Poeciliidae
Subfam.: Poeciliinae

Xiphophorus helleri from Lake Catemaco

Xiphophorus helleri
Swordtail

HECKEL, 1848

Syn.: *Mollienesia helleri, Xiphophorus jalapae, X. rachovi, X. brevis, X. guentheri.*

Hab.: Central America: Mexico, Veracruz, Lake Catemaco.

F.I.: 1978.

Sex.: The ♂'s inferior caudal fin rays are elongated into a sword; they have a gonopodium. ♀♀ are larger and fuller.

Soc. B.: Peaceful, but frequently cannibalistic towards juveniles. A good community fish.

M: Plant the edges of the tank heavily, and maintain plenty of free swimming space. Water: pH 7.0–8.3; hardness 10° to 30° dGH.

B: As for all races of *X. helleri*, the morph from Lake Catemaco is easily bred. Normally 20–60, 8 mm long young are born every 25–28 days. Tanks with a volume of 100–200 l offer ample room for several ♂♂ to be kept together, which allows impressive displays between the animals. A rubble zone (walnut-sized pebbles) provides hiding places for the young.

F: O.

S: A very beautiful *helleri* population. A similar, less attractive color morph was presented in Vol. 2, p. 765.

T: 24°–28°C, **L:** 8 (12) cm, **A:** 80 cm, **R:** all, **D:** 3

Xiphophorus birchmanni ♂

Fam.: Poeciliidae
Subfam.: Poeciliinae

Xiphophorus birchmanni
Swordless swordtail

LECHNER & RADDA, 1987

Syn.: *Xiphophorus montezumae birchmanni.*

Hab.: Mexico: Rio La Candelaria, Rio Axtla, Pexco Drainage, Rio Santa María, Rio Tuxpan System, Rio Los Hules System, Rio Panuco Basin, Rio Calabozo Drainage, Hidalgo, Veracruz.

F.I.: 1990.

Sex.: ♂♂ do not have a sword! They have a very high, rounded dorsal fin, intense, regularly spaced vertical bands, and a gonopodium. The ♀♀ have a smaller dorsal fin.

Soc. B.: Peaceful; however, ♂♂ are aggressive among themselves. They can be kept with any livebearers with the exception of *Xiphophorus* (hybrids may result!). Small, peaceful species make appropriate companions (catfishes, etc.).

M: *X. birchmanni* requires high oxygen levels, water movement, and a fine-grained gravel or rock fragment substrate. Plants should be limited to the background. Water: pH 7.0–8.0 (7.5); hardness of 15°–25° dGH.

B: About every 28 days, 15 to 35 young are born.

F: O; small live and frozen foods. High quality flakes are also appreciated. Feed plant fare occasionally.

S: This is the only species within the group that does not have a sword, hence the common name.

T: 24°–28°C, **L:** ♂ 6 cm, ♀ 7 cm, **A:** from 50 cm, **R:** m, b, **D:** 3

Xiphophorus birchmanni ♀

Xiphophorus nezahualcoyotl RAUCHENBERGER, KALLMANN & MORIZOT, 1990
Neza swordtail

Syn.: *Xiphophorus montezumae, "X. montezumae* Hamburg 64."

Hab.: Central America: Mexico, in the Rio Tamesi System, Tamaulipas (tributary of the Rio Tampaon), San Luis Potosí.

F.I.: 1964 by the Zoological State Institute of Hamburg.

Sex.: Sexes can clearly be distinguished on the photo; ♂♂ have a gonopodium.

Soc. B.: Peaceful. Suitable for some community tanks.

M: Since raising pure strains is important, a species tank is recommended. A well-planted tank with plenty of swimming space and hiding places for the ♀ or ♀♀ is necessary. Water: pH 6.8–7.5; hardness around 15° dGH. A floating cover of water ferns is advantageous—particularly when breeding the animals. Use a sand or fine-grained gravel substrate.

B: As for *Xiphophorus birchmanni.*

F: C, O; mosquito larvae are best. However, flake foods are readily accepted. TetraTips and other FD foodstuffs can replace live foods.

S: This species was presented in Vol. 1 and Vol. 2 as *X. montezumae.* The original describers corrected the error.

T: 24°–28°C, **L:** 6 cm, **A:** from 50 cm, **R:** all, **D:** 3

Betta coccina breeding

Macropodus chinensis ✕ *M. opercularis*
Red macropodus*

Syn.: None, this is a hybrid.

Hab.: Not applicable.

F.I.: Not applicable.

Sex.: ♂♂ are larger and have marvelous finnage. They turn dark during courtship, while ♀♀ turn lighter.

Soc. B.: Peaceful. ♂♂ in spawning condition may turn aggressive in small tanks.

M: Requires a large tank, an open area for swimming, and vegetation around the edges. Hiding places for the ♂ are particularly important. No special demands are placed on water chemistry.

B: These hybrids are usually sterile. Breeding the offspring should not be attempted!

F: O.

S: It is incomprehensible why such crosses repeatedly appear in the hobby, since the parent species are much more attractive. But because it is being sold as a new "species," it is introduced here.

Avoid Hybrids!

T: 18°–28°C, **L:** 10 cm, **A:** 70 cm, **R:** m, t, **D:** 1

*The other red macropodus is not a cross, but a mutant called the albino macropodus. See photo on p. 638.

636

Fam.: Anabantidae
Subfam.: Anabantinae

Anabas oligolepis   BLEEKER, 1855

Syn.: *Anabas macrocephalus*; perhaps additional synonyms of *Anabas testudineus* apply to *A. oligolepis*.

Hab.: Asia: Bangladesh and northeastern India. Found in rivers and brackish water, but shallow, plant-rich, static waters are preferred.

F.I.: Probably has not been imported alive.

Sex.: Difficult to distinguish. The ♂ has a longer anal fin. Mature ♀♀ are fuller.

Soc. B.: Aggressive towards conspecifics and heterospecifics. Nevertheless, they are frequently shy. Keep in a species tank or with similar climbing perches.

M: Easily cared for in large tanks. *A. oligolepis* does not have any special requirements in regard to tank decoration or water chemistry.

B: Has not been bred in an aquarium. Probably similar to that of *Anabas testudineus*.

F: O; plant fare, live foods, earthworms, small fishes, and many commercial foods such as tablets and flake foods.

S: *A. oligolepis* and *A. testudineus* are difficult to distinguish. *A. oligolepis* is smaller and has a characteristically deep body, fewer scales along the lateral line, and fewer hard spines and more soft rays in the dorsal fin. In nature the species is said to distinguish itself with its beautiful dark green to copper colored body (Horst Linke, *Labyrinthfische—Farbe im Aquarium*, Tetra Verlag, 1987).

T: 22°–28°C, **L:** to 18 cm, **A:** 80 cm, **R:** all, **D:** 1

Fam.: Anabantidae

Ctenopoma multispinis
Many-spined ctenopoma

(PETERS, 1844)

Syn.: *Anabas multispinis, A. scandens, Ctenopoma multispine, C. multispinnis, C. machadoi, Spirobranchus smithii, S. multispines.*

Hab.: Southern Africa: Zaïre, Zambia, Mozambique, Zimbabwe, Botswana, and Angola. Lives in rivers and lakes.

F.I.: One specimen was imported in 1935. In 1973, D. SCHALLER imported animals into Munich.

Sex.: Difficult to distinguish. ♂♂ have spiny areas on their operculum and caudal peduncle (see photo). ♀♀ are sometimes fuller.

Soc. B.: This robust, active species is often aggressive. Though it is possible to associate it with other stalwart fishes, species maintenance is better.

M: *C. multispinis* needs a large tank with a volume of at least 200 l, plenty of free swimming space, and numerous hiding places. Plant *Echinodorus* and *Vallisneria* around the edges. No particular requirements are placed on water chemistry.

B: Open spawners that do not practice brood care. FOERSCH successfully bred the species in 1975 after bringing the breeders into spawning condition with a heavy diet of insects given for several days.

F: C; earthworms and other large live or frozen foods. Whole tablets are eaten, but flakes are not particularly relished.

S: Previously thought to be a mouth-brooder, but it was discovered that the "eggs" were actually parasitic cysts.
C. multispinis was introduced in Vol. 2, p. 790. However, the opportunity to present better photos could not be ignored.

T: 22°–27°C, **L:** 16 cm, **A:** 80 cm, **R:** all, **D:** 3

Macropodus opercularis, albino macropodus; see page 636

Ctenopoma multispinis

Ctenopoma multispinis ♂

Fam.: Anabantidae

Ctenopoma pellegrini
Pellegrin's ctenopoma

(BOULENGER, 1902)

Syn.: *Anabas pellegrini*.
Perhaps this fish is identical to *Ctenopoma nigropannosum*. If that is the case, the older name, *C. nigropannosum*, would be valid and *Ctenopoma ashbysmithii* would be a synonym.

Hab.: Tropical Africa: northern Zaïre, Ubangi system.

F.I.: 1987.

Sex.: The ♂ has spiny areas on the opercula. The ♀ is sometimes fuller.

Soc. B.: *C. pellegrini* is a quarrelsome species that can defend itself against bellicose tankmates. Best maintained in a species tank. These animals can be housed with large cichlids, catfishes, and labyrinth fishes, including other climbing perches.

M: A large tank with many hiding places and robust vegetation around the edges is required. Good filtration is a necessity, but *C. pellegrini* adapts to a wide range of water chemistries.

B: Open spawners that do not practice brood care. See SEEGERS, DATZ **41** (8): 291–295, 1988.

F: C, O.

S: *C. pellegrini* is very similar to *Anabas testudineus*. Hopefully more information will come to light about these peculiar, slender climbing perches as more specimens are imported.

T: 22°–27°C, **L:** 15 cm, **A:** 80 cm, **R:** m, t, **D:** 3

Ctenopoma petherici
Blunt-headed ctenopoma

GÜNTHER, 1864

Syn.: *Ctenopoma breviventralis, C. brunneum, C. caudomaculatum, C. davidae, C. garuanum, C. machadoi, C. pekkolai, C. riggenbachi, C. vermayi, Anabas petherici*. This fish may be synonymous to *Ctenopoma argentoventer* and *C. kingsleyae*; in that case, the older name, *C. petherici*, would be correct.

Hab.: Central Africa: Lake Chad and the White Nile, Bahr el Djebel.

F.I.: Unknown.

Sex.: ♂♂ have spiny areas on the opercula and caudal peduncle that help to hold the ♀ while pairing. These spines entangle in netting material, identifying the fish's gender even though the spines are often invisible to the naked eye. Ripe ♀♀ are clearly fuller than ♂♂.

Soc. B.: Do not keep this robust species in community with delicate fishes. Suitable for community tanks containing large, hardy fishes such as large cichlids, catfishes, and other climbing perches. Since it has not been bred in captivity, a species tank is suggested.

M: Use a roomy aquarium and decorate with numerous hiding places and some floating plants. Strong filtration is important, since large climbing perches have a voracious appetite. Moderate water values can be used, though soft, slightly acid water is best.

B: Open spawner. It has not been successfully bred in captivity.

F: C; hardy live foods such as earthworms, small fishes, and insects and their larvae. It also accepts beef heart and fish flesh as well as tablets and flakes.

S: *C. petherici* has less serration on its gill cover than *C. kingsleyae*. Aquarists can differentiate the two species by comparing profiles (see Vol. 1, p. 622, for *C. kingsleyae*).

T: 22°–26°C, **L:** 16 cm, **A:** 100 cm, **R:** m, **D:** 3

Ctenopoma pellegrini

Ctenopoma petherici

Fam.: Belontiidae
Subfam.: Macropodinae

Betta bellica
Slender betta

SAUVAGE, 1884

Syn.: *Betta fasciata, B. bleekeri.*

Hab.: Southeast Asia: Thailand, Malaysia, and Sumatra. Lives among plants in ditches and inundated grasslands.

F.I.: 1905 by REICHELT to Berlin.

Sex.: Full-grown ♂♂ are larger, more colorful, and have longer fins. ♀♀ are fuller through the ventral area and have crossbands during courtship.

Soc. B.: Generally peaceful. Only ♂♂ in the process of building a bubble nest or caring for offspring will inflict deadly wounds if housed in overly small aquaria. Hiding places must be included for ♀♀ and subdominant animals. *B. bellica* makes a good tankmate for equal-sized fishes.

M: Undemanding. It can be kept in soft to medium-hard, acid to slightly alkaline water. Create hiding places among either bogwood or dense vegetation. Reproduction is more difficult than maintenance.

B: Breeding is similar to that of *Betta splendens.* A bubble nest is constructed and the fish embrace to mate. The eggs are typically held between the ♀'s stomach and ventral fins while she lays motionless and belly-up after the mating embrace. From there the ♂ gathers the eggs and places them into the bubble nest. The larvae hatch the following day. They need an additional 3 days to absorb their yolk sac and become free-swimming. Rearing the offspring is simple using pond plankton. After 3 days, the diet can be supplemented with *Artemia* nauplii.

The water in the breeding tank should have a pH below 6 and a hardness of less than 6° dGH. Carbonate hardness is particularly detrimental to the egg's developmental process. Water filtered over peat seems to heighten the fish's willingness to spawn. See Das Aquarium, 203, 5-1986 for more information.

Breeding aquarium-bred specimens is easier.

F: C; all types of foods. Occasionally offer live insects. The fish will choke on overly large earthworms.

S: Every now and then these fish can be seen resting on leaves above the water surface. *B. bellica* are able to jump high and precisely; cover the aquarium well.

T: 24°–30°C, L: ♂ 13 cm, ♀ 10 cm, A: 60 cm, R: m, t, D: 2

Continuation of *Betta akarensis* (p. 644):

ting them out. The eggs may deteriorate in the mouth when water conditions are suboptimal. The ♂ probably mouthbroods the eggs for 14 days. The fry can immediately be fed *Artemia* and *Cyclops* nauplii when released.

F: C; all types of live foods as well as flake foods and halved tablet foods.

S: The taxonomy and nomenclature of bettas is still largely in flux, as has been illustrated by this species. Unfortunately, further changes are expected.

B. akarensis is very difficult to distinguish from *Betta fusca* and *B. pugnax.*

Only the natural habitat is a sure way for aquarists to distinguish species: *B. akarensis* hails from Borneo, *B. fusca* comes from Sumatra, and *B. pugnax* from the Malay Peninsula and Thailand. *B. akarensis* predominantly has ocher yellow to brown hues, while the latter two species are more red-brown to gray-black in color and design. The ladderlike design on the tail fin cannot be used as a distinguishing characteristic, since it is present on all three of the named species, among others.

T: 21°–27°C, L: 14 cm, A: 80 cm, R: all, D: 3

Betta bellica ♂

Betta bellica ♀ from Sumatra

Fam.: Belontiidae
Subfam.: Macropodinae

Betta brederi
Breder's betta
MYERS, 1935

Syn.: Frequently confused with *Betta pugnax* and *Betta taeniata*.

Hab.: Southeast Asia: Indonesia, Sumatra, Java (?).

F.I.: 1935.

Sex.: The ♂ has larger, more elongated fins and metallic, iridescent colors during courtship.

Soc. B.: Peaceful; keep pairs when breeding. *B. brederi* can be housed with fishes that are roughly the same size. Do not keep with *B. pugnax* or similar species, lest the two species hybridize.

M: Use slightly acid to neutral, soft to medium-hard water for maintenance, but lower both values for breeding.

B: Similar to *Betta picta* and *B. pugnax*, only here both parents gather the eggs and the ♀ spits the eggs it gathers at the ♂. The ♂ mouthbroods the eggs for about 12 to 14 days. The young are approximately 7 mm long when they emerge and can be raised with *Artemia* nauplii and plankton.

F: C; all types of foods. Earthworms are particular favorites.

S: *B. pugnax* was erroneously identified and imported as *B. brederi*. Even after the mistake was discovered (LADIGES, 1972), *B. brederi* was considered a synonym of *B. pugnax* for a long time. Extremely rare. Attempts to maintain these animals in captivity for extended periods of time have proven unsuccessful.

T: 23°–28°C, **L:** 11 cm, **A:** 60 cm, **R:** all, **D:** 2–3

Betta akarensis
Ladder-fined betta
REGAN, 1910

Syn.: *Betta climacura*, *Betta taeniata* (not REGAN, 1910). This species has been confused with *B. anabatoides*.

Hab.: Southeast Asia: widely distributed in the western and northern part of Borneo. Usually lives in small shaded creeks that have a strong current. There they are often found beneath overhanging shore vegetation. However, the species can also survive in relatively polluted waters, such as stagnant puddles in dry creek beds.

F.I.: 1984.

Sex.: ♂♂ are larger and have slightly more elongated fins and, occasionally, metallic, iridescent dots and spots on the scales. The ♀ is markedly fuller and longitudinally striated at spawning time. The ladder design on the caudal fin is only clearly visible on ♂♂.

Soc. B.: This peaceful betta can be housed with similar-sized fishes as long as the tank has ample space. Small quarrels, usually seen during feeding and breeding, normally only result in fin damage as long as subdominant animals have a place to retreat.

M: *B. akarensis*, like all mouthbrooding bettas, relishes clear, clean water with a good current. These conditions can be met using a powerhead. Cover part of the water surface with floating plants to provide the shaded areas they prefer. In nature, the species is usually found in extremely soft, acid water, though they are quite adaptable. Water: pH 5.5–6.8; hardness up to 12° dGH; carbonate hardness to 5° dKH.

B: It seems that soft, acid water is necessary to breed this species. Spawning is largely similar to that of *Betta pugnax*. A mature ♂ courts a ♀ and, after an extended courtship and some pseudo-pairings, mating soon occurs. The ♀ is embraced, and the resulting eggs fall onto the ♂'s anal fin. After the ♀ recovers from her spawning paralysis, she takes the eggs into her mouth and spits them towards the ♂. He, in turn, accepts the eggs and incubates them in his mouth. Endeavors to breed this species in captivity have always ended in the ♂ either swallowing the eggs or spit-

Continued on p. 642.

Betta brederi

Betta akarensis

Betta akarensis "pointed head"

Betta akarensis "Matang"

Betta akarensis "pointed head"

Fam.: Belontiidae
Subfam.: Macropodinae

Betta coccina
Wine-red betta

VIERKE, 1979

Syn.: None. Easily confused with the very similar *Betta tussyae*. There are several strains which may actually be autonomous species.

Hab.: Southeast Asia: Sumatra and the southern part of the Malay Peninsula. B. and A. BROWN found a form very similar to *B. coccina* on Borneo. All slender, red bettas live in small, shallow bodies of water that are either stagnant or have a sluggish current. Some collection sites could be described as swampy grasslands.

F.I.: 1979. Though imported in 1956, it was not recognized as a species.

Sex.: ♂♂ have larger fins and sometimes a blue or green spot on their side. Apparently this spot is limited to ♂♂. Older ♂♂ have a pointed caudal fin. Mature ♀♀ have an ovate genital papilla.

Soc. B.: Like *B. splendens*, ♂♂ are territorial, and only one ♂ can be kept in small tanks for any length of time. Do not keep these sensitive fish with heterospecifics. Very shy and retiring when not maintained adequately.

M: A 20 l aquarium is sufficient for one pair. Many hiding places, particularly for the ♀, are necessary. A dense cover of floating plants foments a feeling of security and serves as a supporting structure for the bubble nest the ♂ builds. *B. coccina* requires clear clean water slightly filtered with a sponge filter. Filtering through peat may be beneficial. Water: pH 4.5–6.0; hardness up to 6° dGH; carbonate hardness not more that 2° dKH. Susceptible to diseases in hard water, especially *Oodinium*. Use salt to treat *Oodinium* (1 teaspoon per 10 l).

B: The water should be as soft and acid as possible. Use floating plants. Feed live mosquito larvae, particularly glassworms, to bring the animals into spawning condition. The ♂ builds a small bubble nest under floating vegetation or in a cave. When mating, the ♂ embraces the ♀ in a U around her ventral region.

A total of 20 to 60 eggs are laid. The young hatch after 1 to 2 days and are free-swimming after an additional 3 days at 24°C. Initially, the young require planktonic foods. After 3 days they are large enough for newly hatched *Artemia* nauplii. Neither this species nor *Betta persephone* consume their young, and if fed well, older brothers and sisters leave younger siblings in peace, allowing several spawns to live side by side in larger aquaria. Of course, you have to insure that the smaller animals receive sufficient food. Young that are reared with their parents have a significantly better growth rate than fry that have been separated from their parents. The young are very sensitive to deteriorating water quality and *Oodinium,* and unfortunately, they are also sensitive in front of some copper containing medications, making salt a better medication for that disease.

F: C, O; small live foods such as *Artemia* (important during the winter) are preferred. Frozen or freeze-dried mosquito larvae are accepted as well.

S: Easily confused with *Betta tussyae*; however, *B. coccina* generally has smaller fins and never has white-tipped ventral fins, and *B. tussyae* never has a spot on its side.

T: 22°–28°C, L: 6 cm, A: 40 cm, R: b, m, D: 3

Betta coccina ♂, Malaysia

Betta coccina ♀

Fam.: Belontiidae
Subfam.: Macropodinae

Betta fusca
Dark betta

REGAN, 1910

Syn.: *Betta picta, Betta pugnax, Betta trifasciata,* each only in part.

Hab.: Southeast Asia: Sumatra and the southern tip of the Malay Peninsula. Primarily inhabits small flowing waters.

F.I.: Imported into Germany in 1971 by ETZEL from western Sumatra. Imported again 1980 by LIEM.

Sex.: ♂♂ have larger, more elongated fins; ♀♀ have a fuller stomach. Difficult to distinguish (see photos).

Soc. B.: Peaceful, social fish. They can readily be kept with other medium-sized species. At spawning time, small territories are established. Very small fishes may be considered food.

M: *B. fusca* needs heavy vegetation around the sides of the aquarium, strong filtration, and water movement with a few calm sites, as found in its natural biotope. The water should be slightly acid (pH 5.5–7.0) and soft (to 12° dGH). Either use subdued illumination or cover the surface with floating plants. The fish are very skittish in well-lit environments.

B: Breeding *B. fusca* is probably very similar to breeding *Betta pugnax.* Mouthbrooder.

F: C; all kinds of live foods and commercial diets (may have to move to attract the fish). Mosquito larvae, *Daphnia,* insect larvae, earthworms, fish meat, beef heart, halved tablet foods, flakes, and FD foods are all accepted.

S: It is still undetermined whether or not *B. fusca* actually merits species status. Originally confused with *Betta picta,* but it is much more similar to *Betta pugnax. B. fusca* has fewer fin rays in the dorsal and anal fins and more scales along the lateral line than *B. pugnax.*

T: 22°–26°C, **L:** 8 (12) cm, **A:** 80 cm, **R:** m, b, **D:** 3

Betta fusca ♂, Sumatra

Betta fusca ♂

Betta fusca ♀, Sumatra

Fam.: Belontiidae
Subfam.: Macropodinae

Betta imbellis
Peaceful betta, Pinang strain

LADIGES, 1975

Syn.: *Macropodus pugnax* var., *Betta splendens* (partially).

Hab.: Southeast Asia: Malay Peninsula, Pinang Island.

F.I.: Unknown.

Sex.: ♂♂ are more colorful and have larger fins (compare photos). Normally, ♀♀ have longitudinal stripes, but crossbands develop during courtship.

Soc. B.: Several ♂♂ can only be kept together in large aquaria where each can establish his own territory. Prior to fighting, these bettas have an elaborate display. Nevertheless, ♂♂ will kill each other when placed together in small tanks, similar to *Betta splendens*. With the exception of similar bettas such as *B. persephone*, *B. smaragdina*, or *B. splendens*, *Betta imbellis* is markedly peaceful. A good tankmate for other small species.

M: A tank with a volume of 20 l or more can house one pair. But plenty of hiding places must be available for the ♀. Water: pH 6.0–7.0; hardness up to 10° dGH; carbonate hardness (dKH) should be less than 10°.

B: The ♂ builds a bubble nest under floating leaves or in a corner of the aquarium. A gravid ♀ seeks out the ♂

under the bubble nest and nudges his side. After a few pseudopairings, the ♂ embraces the ♀ and turns her upside-down. Eggs are fertilized as they emerge and fall onto the anal fin and stomach of the ♀. The ♂, the first to recover from the spawning paralysis, collects the sinking eggs and spits them into the bubble nest. The ♀ helps him gather the eggs as soon as she recovers from the spawning paralysis. However, the ♀ is not permitted to introduce the eggs directly into the bubble nest, so she releases them with a few air bubbles slightly beneath. The fry hatch after about 24 hr and are free-swimming after another 2 to 3 days. At that time they must be fed plankton. Three days later they are large enough to handle *Artemia* nauplii. Some *B. imbellis* can ingest very small *Artemia* from the first day. Young breeders are important, since older animals frequently refuse to bred.

F: C; all kinds of live foods and flake, frozen, and freeze-dried foods.

S: The clay-yellow body color is notorious for the *B. imbellis* population of Pinang Island. ♂♂ frequently have color-deficiency mutations, and the otherwise red areas on the fins are orange or yellow.

T: 22°–26°C, **L:** 5 cm, **A:** 40 cm, **R:** t, m, **D:** 2

Betta imbellis
Peaceful betta, Phuket strain

LADIGES, 1975

Syn.: *Macropodus pugnax* var., *Betta phuket*, *Betta splendens* (partially).

Hab.: Southeast Asia: Phuket Island and the western coast of the Malay Peninsula.

F.I.: Ca. 1981.

Sex.: ♂♂ are larger and more colorful. Gravid ♀♀ are fuller and have a visible oval papilla.

Soc. B.: Peaceful; refer to previous strain.

M: More sensitive than other forms of *B. imbellis*! Water: pH 5.5–6.5; hardness up to 8° dGH. See *B. imbellis* "Pinang"

(above) for maintenance recommendations, but keep at warmer temperatures!

B: Breeding is only possible in soft water; otherwise, the process parallels that of *B. imbellis* "Pinang."

F: C; all types of live foods as well as flake, frozen, and freeze-dried foods.

S: *B. imbellis* was previously discussed in Vol. 1, p. 630, but this strain is clearly slimmer and longer than the nominate form. It is NICOLAS's opinion that this population should be taxonomically separated from *B. imbellis*, although the differences are slight.

T: 25°–30°C, **L:** 5 cm, **A:** 40 cm, **R:** t, m, **D:** 3

Betta imbellis ♀, Pinang

Betta imbellis, Phuket

Biotope of *Betta macrostoma*, Vol. 2, p. 796

Continuation of *Betta macrophthalma* (facing page):

S: *B. macrophthalma* has been repeatedly imported as "*Betta pugnax*," but it differs from all other bettas by its size and characteristic vertical facial stripes. Populations from other geographical areas have longitudinal stripes that are arranged differently.

One form from the Pinang Island of Malaysia, is more intensely colored, while another form imported from Pekan Nenas, Malay Peninsula by the BROWNs has entire caudal fin rays, even in full-grown specimens. These different characteristics lead us to believe that these populations may in fact be autonomous species or subspecies, in which case, offspring of the crosses might be sterile.

T: 20°–26°C, L: 14 cm, A: 80 cm, R: all, D: 2–3

Fam.: Belontiidae
Subfam.: Macropodinae

Betta macrophthalma
Giant betta

REGAN, 1910

Syn.: *Betta waseri*.

Hab.: Southeast Asia: Malay Peninsula, including Pinang and Sumatra.

F.I.: By NAGY in 1976 and SCHALLER in 1983.

Sex.: ♂♂ have larger, more elongated fins; ripe ♀♀ are fuller through the ventral area. Genders are difficult to distinguish.

Soc. B.: Peaceful. House with calm species or, because of its rarity, keep in a large species tank.

M: Though a labyrinth fish, *B. macrophthalma* needs clear, clean, well-filtered, oxygen-rich water. Plant the edges of the tank heavily and use floating plants. The plants offer hiding places. A flat stone or a piece of slate is readily accepted as a spawning substrate. Soft, slightly acid water is preferred: pH 5.5–6.8; hardness up to 12° dGH; carbonate hardness less than 5° dKH.

B: *B. macrophthalma* is a mouthbrooder. By and large, breeding is similar to that of *Beta pugnax*. However, the ♂ incubates the eggs for up to 4 weeks. Few eggs are laid (about 70) but each has a very large diameter of over 2 mm. Spawning occurs just beneath the water surface; both mating and the embrace are of a very short duration. The eggs lie on the ♂'s anal fin after pairing. From there the ♀ takes them into her mouth and spits them towards the ♂. He collects them in his mouth to incubate. Unfortunately, the ♂♂ swallow the eggs or the hatched larvae or development of the eggs or fry is arrested. This is why breeding is considered problematic. There is no information available concerning artificially incubating the eggs.

F: C; all kinds of live and frozen foods as well as flake and halved tablet foods.

Continued on previous page.

Betta patoti
Black betta

WEBER & DE BEAUFORT, 1992

Syn.: None; previously considered synonymous to *Betta unimaculata.*

Hab.: Southeast Asia: western and northwestern Borneo and Pulau Laut Island.

F.I.: 1988 by KETTNER, KRUMMENACHER, and WITTE.

Sex.: ♂♂ have slightly larger fins and more intense colors. Gravid ♀♀ are fuller.

Soc. B.: Though slight intraspecific aggressions are displayed, serious injuries do not result. Peaceful towards heterospecifics, and a good tankmate for all but small "bite-sized" fishes.

M: Keep in large, densely planted aquaria that have a partial cover of floating plants. The tank must have tranquil water zones and sections with strong current. A powerhead is recommended. Water: pH 5.5–6.8; hardness up to 10° dGH; carbonate hardness of 4° dKH.

This species has been collected in typical black waters, but it readily adapts to less extreme conditions. Hiding places for inferior animals have to be provided.

B: Unknown; reproduction is probably similar to that of *Betta unimaculata,* which means *B. patoti* is very likely a mouthbrooder.

F: C; all kinds of live foods as well as flake and tablet foods.

S: Father STROH was the first to capture this species, but he could only sent preserved specimens to Germany. The group of animals imported in 1988 from the same habitat included both specimens with and without ventral fins. Very similar to *Betta unimaculata,* though smaller and darker. Specimens preserved in formaldehyde are black; hence, the German common name, black betta.

T: 23°–28°C, **L:** 9 cm, **A:** 80 cm, **R:** all, **D:** 2

Betta patoti

654

Betta sp. cf. *patoti*, adult ♂ with ventral fins

Betta sp. cf. *patoti* without ventral fins

Betta persephone
Dwarf betta

SCHALLER, 1986

Syn.: None.

Hab.: Southeast Asia: southern Malaysia, close to Ayer Hitam. *B. persephone* lives in saturated "aquaphillic" forests, retiring among moist leaves during the dry season.

F.I.: 1985 by D. SCHALLER, Munich.

Sex.: Difficult to distinguish. ♂♂ are larger and have slightly larger fins.

Soc. B.: Very aggressive. Even large aquaria can only support a pair of adults over extended periods of time. Parents and juveniles leave larvae and young unmolested, so several generations can be housed in the same tank until the oldest offspring are almost full-grown. See *B. coccina*.

M: At 3.2 cm, this is the smallest known betta. Limit maintenance to pairs or pairs and their respective offspring in a species tank. Reproduction is greatly encouraged by soft, peat-acid water. For maintenance, a hardness of 10° dGH and a pH of 7.0 should not be exceeded. The fish are comfortable at 25°C.

B: Breeds like *B. splendens*, building a bubble nest. Use clean, brown water and raise the young with plankton and *Artemia* nauplii. Breed in pairs!

F: C, O; small freshwater plankton and *Artemia*. Small flake foods can be fed for short periods of time during emergencies.

S: Its defense behavior of hiding among leaves (SCHALLER, DATZ 7/86), their extreme intraspecific aggressions (like *B. splendens*), and its familial relationships during reproduction make *B. persephone* an interesting subject for dedicated aquarists despite its brownish, less than beautiful coloration.

T: 23°–28°C, L: 3.2 cm, A: 40 cm, R: all, D: 3

Betta persephone ♂

Betta persephone, nuptial coloration of the ♂

Betta persephone, normal-colored ♂

Fam.: Belontiidae
Subfam.: Macropodinae

Betta tussyae   SCHALLER, 1985

Syn.: None. Very similar to *B. coccina.*

Hab.: Southeast Asia: Malaysia, springs in very humid meadows under shore vegetation and between terrestrial plants in water puddles.

F.I.: Imported into Salzburg in 1983 by NAGY. Introduced to the aquarium hobby in 1985 by SCHALLER, Munich.

Sex.: ♂♂ have larger fins, most notably the dorsal and anal fins. ♀♀ have vertical stripes and a visible oval genital papilla during courtship.

Soc. B.: ♂♂ in possession of a spawning territory are very aggressive, limiting one pair to a 40 cm tank despite their small size. Maybe several ♀♀ can be housed in one tank, but a multitude of hiding places have to be included in the decor. Due to its timid nature in front of heterospecifics, tankmates should be restricted to small, peaceful fishes, but a species tank is preferable.

M: ♂♂ may engage in intense battles, necessitating hiding places if losses are to be avoided. While average water chemistry values are sufficient for maintenance as long as the water is free of metabolites, successful breeding demands extreme values. Floating plants are preferred hiding locals. At temperatures above 24°C, inexplicable deaths occur.

B: Difficult but possible in water that has a very low hardness, a pH of 4–5, and a temperature of 24°C. Place a layer of oak leaves along the substrate. The eggs are gathered and placed into a tiny bubble nest by the ♂, which then chases the ♀ away. The young are free-swimming after 4 to 5 days and can be reared with plankton and, after an additional 3 days, *Artemia* nauplii. The young demand small but continuous meals, making their care time-consuming and tedious.

F: C, O; live foods. Small flakes are rarely accepted.

S: This beautiful burgundy red betta spends most of its time hidden; nevertheless, it deserves the interest of hobbyists. Note the differences between *B. tussyae* and *B. coccina.* The former has larger scales and fins, a different coloration, and white-tipped ventral fins.

T: 21°–24°C, **L:** 5.5 cm, **A:** 40 cm, **R:** all, **D:** 3

Betta tussyae ♂♂

Betta tussyae ♀

Fam.: Belontiidae
Subfam.: Macropodinae

Ctenops nobilis McCLELLAND, 1845

Syn.: None.

Hab.: Asia: India, Bangladesh in Bramaputra.

F.I.: Imported into Germany by KROPAC in 1912 and EIMEKE in 1924.

Sex.: While ♂♂ have a narrow red rim around the anal and tail fins, ♀♀ have a faint fringe and a fuller ventral area. Difficult to distinguish (see photos).

Soc. B.: Very aggressive towards conspecifics. Dominant animals are capable of killing inferior animals if maintained incorrectly. A large aquarium, multitudes of hiding places, and a large group of *C. nobilis* are basic conditions for successful care. Fishes unwilling to abandon their secluded locals should be fed individually.

M: Keep at cooler temperatures. Medium-hard, neutral water is adequate for maintenance, but soft, acid water may be necessary to reproduce the species. Salt helps keep the animals healthy, perhaps because it helps check disease organisms, conceivably even killing them. Use a maximum of 1 heaping teaspoon per 20 l.

B: Mouthbrooders.

F: C; ambush predator, similar to leaf fishes. Live, frozen, and occasionally flake foods. Large foods cannot be eaten.

S: This brown fish is not very attractive. Interest stems from its intriguing shape and hunting behavior, which is similar to leaf fishes. *C. nobilis* is a fairly recent aquarium fish and considered to be very sensitive. This was further supported when specimens imported in 1986 proved to be disease-prone and difficult to maintain because of intraspecific aggressions. In principle, all wild caught animals are infested with metacercariae (= larval digenians). Luckily these parasites cannot infect tankmates, as intermediate hosts are normally absent in captive environments. Its body shape leads one to believe this is a rheophile fish, while in reality, this gourami avoids currents and expresses its displeasure when placed in such surroundings by clamping its fins.

T: 20°–24°C, **L:** 10 cm, **A:** 100 cm, **R:** all, **D:** 2 (–4; diseases)

Ctenops nobilis ♂

Ctenops nobilis ♀

Fam.: Belontiidae

Parasphaerichthys ocellatus
Burmese chocolate gourami

PRASHAD & MUKERJI, 1929
Subfam.: Trichogasterinae

Syn.: None.

Hab.: Southeast Asia: Burma, in the surroundings of Lakes Indawggyi and Inle.

F.I.: 1978 by A. WERNER, Munich.

Sex.: Unknown.

Soc. B.: Peaceful, but sometimes aggressive towards conspecifics. Small catfishes and small, slow-moving species may make appropriate tankmates and help *P. ocellatus* overcome its shyness, but because of its scarcity and sensitive nature, a species tank is recommended.

M: Like the chocolate gourami, house in tanks that have a large surface area and an abundance of hiding places. Water should be neutral to acid and soft to medium-hard with a temperature around 25°C.

B: Unknown; possibly like the chocolate gourami, *Sphaerichthys osphromenoides*.

F: C; frozen foods and small live foods such as *Artemia*.

S: This rare gourami from remote Burma was only imported once by WERNER. See Das Aquarium, 177, **3**-1984, for details.

T: 24°–26°C, **L:** 4 cm, **A:** 50 cm, **R:** m, t, **D:** 3–4

Parosphromenus alleni
Allen's gourami

BROWN, 1987
Subfam.: Macropodinae

Syn.: None.

Hab.: Southeast Asia: in the Sarawak region of Malaysia on the island of Borneo. Found in stagnant black water.

F.I.: Imported into England in 1986 by B. and A. BROWN. Imported to Germany and Switzerland in 1988 by KETTNER, KRUMMENACHER, and WITTE.

Sex.: ♂♂ have colorful blue- and red-fringed fins. ♀♀ are pale gray to beige during courtship.

Soc. B.: Peaceful and very sensitive animals. Keep in a species tank. Avoid housing with similar gouramis, since most ♀ gouramis are indistinguishable.

M: A pair can be kept in 10 l or larger tanks, and a tank with a volume exceeding 50 l is sufficient for a group. *P. alleni* requires at least one cavelike hiding place for each fish, clean water (partial water exchanges at least every 2 weeks, though once a week is better, and remove leftover food regularly), a sponge filter, and only a slight current if any.

Water movement at the surface is not bothersome. A bare substrate to facilitate tank cleaning and floating plants are beneficial. Water: pH 4.5–6.2; hardness up to 5° dGH; carbonate hardness should be immeasurably low. Higher values are tolerated for short periods of time, but breeding will not occur under less than optimal conditions.

B: While these fish have not been bred in captivity, it should be similar to *Parosphromenus deissneri* and *P. nagyi*.

F: C; small live foods. Full-grown fish can handle small mosquito larvae and water fleas. *Cyclops* are favorites. In the winter, *Artemia* nauplii and microworms are good dietary supplements. MicroMin can be offered sparingly.

S: This species is very similar to *P. deissneri*, but the black spot at the base of the caudal fin of *P. alleni* is triangular. *P. alleni* comes from Borneo, while *P. deissneri* is found on the Malay Peninsula. *P. nagyi* and *P. harveyi* are two other close relatives.

T: 20°–24°C, **L:** 3.5 cm, **A:** 40 cm, **R:** m, b, **D:** 4

Parasphaerichthys ocellatus

Parosphromenus alleni

Fam.: Belontiidae
Subfam.: Macropodinae

Parosphromenus harveyi
Harvey's gourami

BROWN, 1987

Syn.: None.

Hab.: Southeast Asia: Malay Peninsula, in the province of Selangor near Batu Arang.

F.I.: 1984 by B. and A. BROWN to England. Imported into central Europe later.

Sex.: The splendidly colored ♂ has blue and black-fringed fins. The ♀ is paler and differently colored. See photos.

Soc. B.: In nature, many specimens live together. Keep a pair or a group in captivity. Each fish needs at least one hiding place to minimize stress. Individuals defend a small territory around the cave, but do not inflict injuries.

M: As for *Parosphromenus nagyi*.

B: Has been successfully bred in captivity. Breeding is similar to that of *P. nagyi*; refer to the page after the next.

F: C; small live foods.

S: *P. harveyi* is a close relative of *P. nagyi* and *P. deissneri*. The three species can only be distinguished under dominant coloration. At that time, the ♀ is more colorful (compare photos) and the ♂ keeps its longitudinal stripes. Batu Arang, the habitat of *P. harveyi*, is along the western side of the Malay Peninsula, in the Selangor Province. The habitat of *P. nagyi* is along the eastern coast of the Malay Peninsula at Kuantan.

T: 20°–24°C, **L:** 3.5 cm, **A:** 40 cm, **R:** m, b, **D:** 4

Parosphromenus harveyi ♂

Parosphromenus harveyi ♀

Fam.: Belontiidae
Subfam.: Macropodinae

Parosphromenus nagyi   SCHALLER, 1985
Nagy's licorice gourami

Syn.: None; this species is easily confused with *P. deissneri.*

Hab.: Southeast Asia: eastern Malaysia,
Kuantan. In lowland creeks.

F.I.: To Salzburg in 1979 by NAGY. To
Munich in 1985 by D. SCHALLER.

Sex.: ♂♂ are colorful. During courtship
they are black with neon blue fin edges.
♀♀ normally have two black longitudinal bands, but during courtship they are
solid beige-yellow.

Soc. B.: Lives in groups in its natural
habitat. In captivity, each ♂ must have
at least one cave. ♀♀ also seek hiding
places. Injuries are not inflicted between
conspecifics during fights.

M: Easily maintained in clear, soft, acid
water at slightly cooler temperatures.
Keeping *P. nagyi* with other species presents the problems of possible starva-
tion and, if kept with congeners, hybridization and the inability to distinguish the
♀♀. Subdue the illumination with floating plants, and offer abundant hiding
places. The substrate should be kept
open and leftovers siphoned away for
hygienic reasons.

B: Water needs a pH of 4.5–5.0, a very
low hardness (never above 5° dGH),
and a temperature of 25°C or below. *P.
nagyi* are cave spawners. The ♀ takes
the eggs from the ♂'s anal fin and adheres them onto the ceiling of the cave.
After the ♂ recovers from the spawning
paralysis, he helps by bringing air bubbles from the surface. The 10–40 larvae
hatch after 3 to 4 days and are free-
swimming after an additional 4 to 6 days.
They can immediately feed on *Artemia*
nauplii and very small freshwater plankton. Rearing is laborious and demands
good water quality. See Das Aquarium,
Vol. 2/88.

F: C; small live foods. Small flakes should
only occasionally be fed. A good additional food is *Artemia.*

S: This new labyrinth fish is a living jewel.
Unfortunately, it will always remain rare

because of its low fecundity and difficult
care. Specialists should take precautions
to prevent the captive population from
becoming extinct.
As for all members of this genus, *P. nagyi*
does not breathe air from the surface.
Only ♂♂ take air from the surface to
build their bubble nest.

T: 20°–24°C, **L:** 4 cm, **A:** 40 cm, **R:** m, b, **D:** 3–4

Parosphromenus nagyi ♂

Parosphromenus nagyi ♀

Fam.: Belontiidae

Trichogaster trichopterus sumatranus
Blue gourami

LADIGES, 1933
Subfam.: Trichogasterinae

Syn.: Refer to the nominate form *T. t. trichopterus* in Vol. 1, p. 648.

Hab.: Southeast Asia: Sumatra.

F.I.: 1933 to Hamburg.

Sex.: ♂♂ have longer and more pointed dorsal and anal fins.

Soc. B.: Peaceful when kept in spacious aquaria. In confined areas, it transforms into a "tyrant." ♂♂ will fight, often inflicting serious injuries. Both ♂♂ and ♀♀ must have sufficient hiding places at their disposal. A good community fish.

M: This robust species fits into most communities regardless of decor and water chemistry, yet it may be bashful in front of stalwart tankmates.

B: For reproduction, the water should be soft and slightly acid (ca. 10° dGH and pH 6.5–7.0, respectively) with a temperature of about 28°C. *T. t. sumatranus*

embraces to spawn. The eggs rise to the surface and are gathered and placed into the nest by the ♂. The ♀ is treated very harshly, and sufficient hiding places must be at her disposal. Several hundred young hatch after 1 to 2 days and are free-swimming after about 4 days. Feed them plankton, rotifers, and infusoria. After one week, *Artemia* nauplii and small live foods can be added to their diet. Raising the young is easy as long as they receive sufficient foodstuffs. The young must be later sorted by size.

F: O; flake foods. Live mosquito larvae are recommended to ripen the breeders. When there is not enough food, the animals will consume planaria!

S: These animals are appealing, recommendable aquarium fish. This blue form as well as various bred forms should be considered color deficiency mutations of the nominate form.

T: 22°–28°C, **L:** 12 cm, **A:** 50 cm, **R:** t, m, **D:** 1

Trichopsis schalleri
Three-striped croaking gourami

LADIGES, 1962
Subfam.: Macropodinae

Syn.: *Trichopsis vittatus, Trichopsis vittatus harrisi*, each only partially.

Hab.: Southeast Asia: Thailand, at Korat.

F.I.: 1961 by D. SCHALLER.

Sex.: The ♂ has slightly longer fins. When the ♀ is placed in a jar and held against a strong light, the cuneiform ovaries are clearly visible under the posterior spinal column; do not confuse them with the elongated, brighter swimbladder!

Soc. B.: Actually peaceful, only becoming aggressive in small aquaria. Growling during aggression and courtship is clearly audible outside the aquarium. Good tankmates for similar-sized fishes with comparable requirements.

M: *T. schalleri* needs a planted tank with moderate water values and a temperature of 25°C. Though more sensitive than *T. pumilus* and *T. vittatus*, it is still not considered a difficult fish to keep. Small tanks generally suffice for maintenance. Water: pH 6–7; hardness up to 12° dGH.

B: The fish embrace each other in the manner of labyrinth fishes, but breeding takes place in the midwater column instead of at the water surface. The ♂ grabs the egg bundle and deposits it in a small bubble nest at the surface, usually under a leaf. Up to 300 young hatch after one day and are free-swimming after an additional 3 days. They must be fed plankton and rotifers at first. After another 3 days, *Artemia* nauplii can be fed. Once this point is reached, rearing follows that of other labyrinth fishes and is considered easy. To bring the breeders into spawning condition, fed generously and raise the temperature to 28°C; live mosquito larvae are advantageous.

F: C, O; any foods of suitable size and quality.

S: These gouramis produce audible grating noises. *T. schalleri* was previously considered to be a subspecies of *T. vittatus* and given the invalid name *T. v. harrisi*. Even though *T. schalleri* can be crossed with *T. pumilus* and *T. vittatus*, it is considered an autonomous species.

T: 22°–28°C, **L:** 6 cm, **A:** 40 cm, **R:** m, **D:** 2–3

Trichogaster trichopterus sumatranus

Trichopsis schalleri

Osphronemus gorami
Giant gourami, edible gourami

(LACÉPÈDE, 1802)

Syn.: *Osphronemus olfax, O. notatus, O. satyrus, O. gourami, Osphromenus gorami.*

Hab.: Widely distributed in southeast Asia as a food fish.

F.I.: 1895.

Sex.: Difficult to distinguish. The ♂'s dorsal and anal fins are slightly pointed. Adult ♀♀ are usually fuller.

Soc. B.: Loner. Juveniles are very aggressive. Adults are normally more peaceful.

M: House in very large aquaria. Actually only suitable for public aquaria. See Vol. 1, p. 652, for details.
If adults are kept, plants should be omitted from the tank, since the water must be changed almost daily. Decorate the tank with bamboo and wood.

B: This species has been successfully bred during the summer in covered garden ponds. Due to its mature size, breeding in an aquarium is problematic but not impossible, because some animals supposedly mature at 6 months of age. A spherical bubble nest containing plant fragments is build at the water surface. The large buoyant eggs (Ø 2.7–2.9 mm) are placed into the nest and guarded until the fry leave the nest after 2$^{1}/_{2}$ weeks.

F: O; omnivores in every sense of the word.

S: Juveniles of this appreciated food fish are sometimes sold as aquarium fish. The fish pictured above is an adult and complements the photo of a juvenile in Vol. 1, p. 653.

T: 20°–30°C, **L:** 70 cm, **A:** from 120 cm, **R:** m, t, **D:** 4 (S)

Channa asiatica
Northern green snakehead

(LINNAEUS, 1758)

Syn.: *Ophicephalus asiaticus, Ophicephalus asiaticus.*

Hab.: Asia: southern China and southeast Asia.

F.I.: Probably in 1958.

Sex.: Cannot be determined by external characteristics.

Soc. B.: Predator! If housed with large fishes, they are usually peaceful.

M: Needs a large aquarium with secluded areas as well as free swimming space. Water chemistry is not particularly important, but filtration should be sufficiently strong.

B: Snakeheads begin their courtship several days prior to the actual spawning act. Courtship behavior is similar to its threat behavior, consisting of open mouths, jaw locking, and spread fins. The actual spawning act is preceded by several pseudopairings. To mate, the ♂ embraces the ♀ and turns her onto her back. The gametes are then released.

The 1500 to 3000 buoyant eggs are immediately fertilized and gathered into one area by the ♂ which attentively guards the spawn. The larvae hatch after 2 days. The large yolk sac is assimilated after 3–4 days, and at that time the young must be fed. They can be fed *Artemia* nauplii and microworms. Larger foods can be offered after one week. The 1500 to 2000 young decimate each other; their cannibalistic slant can be curtailed by offering abundant foodstuffs. The body begins to develop pigmentation after 6–8 weeks. The young grow very quickly and are guarded for an extended period of time by the parents. After about 2 months, the offspring must be separated from their parents, since the parents are ready to spawn again and turn cannibalistic towards their offspring. A 160 l aquarium is large enough to bred one pair, though there must be enough places where the ♀ can hide, since the ♂ occasionally turns very antagonistic. The pair's relationship is enhanced when

Continued on p. 672.

Continuation of *Channa asiatica* (p. 671):

another aquarium with "opponents" is within view.

F: C; coarse live foods, including fishes and substitute foods. Vegetable fare is invariably ignored.

S: Like *Channa orientalis*, *C. asiatica* lacks ventral fins. Though growth is rapid when plenty of food is offered, its maximum length of 35 cm will not be reached in an aquarium.

T: 22°–28°C, **L:** 30 (35) cm, **A:** 100 cm, **R:** all, **D:** 2

Continuation of *Channa punctata* (p. 676):

S: *C. punctata* has a thicker, differently patterned head and an irregular dot design when compared to *Channa lucia*. These are appreciated food fish in their natural habitat. *C. punctata* can be confused with *Channa africana* because of its corporal design. However, *C. punctata* is much stouter and has noticeably fewer rays in its dorsal and anal fins.

T: 22°–28°C, **L:** 35 cm, **A:** 100 cm, **R:** all, **D:** 1 (–4; C)

Channa gachua
Ceylonese green snakehead

HAMILTON, 1822

Syn.: *Ophicephalus gachua, Channa orientalis.*

Hab.: Southeast Asia: from Pakistan, India, and Burma to Vietnam, Thailand, Malaysia, and the Greater Sunda Islands.

F.I.: 1929.

Sex.: Difficult to distinguish. The ♀ has a fuller stomach.

Soc. B.: Only pairwise maintenance is possible during the spawning season, as they become very aggressive. Normally it should be kept in groups and associated with robust fishes approximately equal to or larger in size. Allow pairs to develop from a group of about 6 juveniles.

M: Needs an aquarium with plants and hiding places for inferior fishes. Floating plants are suggested. Water: pH 6–7; hardness ca. 4° to 15° dGH; carbonate hardness to 5° dKH; temperature ca. 25°C.

B: The animals reach sexual maturity at a length of about 15 cm. Like labyrinth fishes, *C. gachua* embraces to spawn. The buoyant eggs are collected by the ♂, and after about 14 days, 50 to 80 young are released behind the opercula; they are readmitted into the mouth when threatened. Raise with small live foods, starting with *Artemia* and following later with larger foodstuffs. Due to the active parental care, do not separate the young too soon from the parents!

F: C; all kinds of live foods and earthworms. As a substitute food, offer whole tablets. Hungry animals also consume small snails, shell and all!

S: Although it was a shock that this species is a mouthbrooder, it is not unusual for fishes that inhabit fluvial waters. *C. gachua* is closely related to *C. orientalis*; however, the former has ventral fins and produces more, but initially smaller, young. See ETTRICH, DATZ, Vol. 7-1986. All snakeheads have an additional respiratory organ, the labyrinth, which has developed independently from that of the Anabantoidei. In Vol. 1, p. 828, *C. orientalis* was introduced, but older editions merely refer to strains with and without ventral fins instead of acknowledging *C. gachua* and *C. orientalis*

T: 22°–26°C, **L:** 25 cm, **A:** 80 cm, **R:** all, **D:** 2–3

Channa gachua

Channa gachua

Channa insignis
Square-spotted African snakehead

(SAUVAGE, 1884)

Syn.: *Ophicephalus insignis, Parachanna insignis, Ophiocephalus obscurus, Parophiocephalus obscurus, Channa obscura.*

Hab.: Tropical Africa: Congo Basin.

F.I.: Probably 1984.

Sex.: The ♂ is larger; the ♀ is slightly fuller during spawning season. The two sexes are difficult to distinguish.

Soc. B.: This is a predator which may attack and overpower almost equal-sized fishes. It can be associated with larger, hardy fishes if adequate food is available. An insufficient diet often leads to cannibalism.

M: Requires a large aquarium with robust plants (perhaps in pots). Bogwood and rocks should form hiding places. Preserve plenty of swimming area, preferably in the foreground. The water chemistry is not particularly important, though the water should be slightly acid and not overly hard. Good filtration and some water movement is desired.

B: This species has been successfully bred in captivity using a pair or a pair housed with other snakeheads in a large aquarium. During the embrace, 1,000 to 3,000 buoyant eggs are laid then guarded by the ♂ while the ♀ defends the territory around the nest. If bred in a small aquarium, the ♀ must be removed after spawning. The young hatch after 2 days and are free-swimming after another 4 days. *Artemia* nauplii are a suitable initial food with *Daphnia* and mosquito larvae becoming appropriate as the young grow. The young are very cannibalistic among each other, though the initial brood size is so large, survival is adequate. The ♂ defends the young for 1 to 2 weeks, even though the young do not have strong ties to the father and quickly develop their independence. With a good diet, the snakeheads grow rapidly. After one year and a length of 25 cm, they are sexually mature. For successful reproduction, breeders need an adequate diet, particularly live fishes.

F: C; fishes are favored. Earthworms, beef heart, and fish meat jiggled on a string will be accepted after training. In an emergency, whole tablets and large insect larvae will be accepted.

S: The African snakeheads were separated from the other snakeheads by TEUGELS and DAGET and placed in their own genus, *Parachanna*. Since this division is still under discussion and not accepted by many scientists, we kept the genus *Channa*. *C. insignis* is very similar to *Channa obscura*; see Vol. 1, pp. 827 and 828.

T: 22°–28°C, **L:** 40 cm, **A:** 100 cm, **R:** all, **D:** 2 (–4; C)

Channa lucius
Shiny snakehead

(CUVIER & VALENCIENNES, 1831)

Syn.: *Channa lucia, Ophicephalus lucius, Ophiocephalus lucius.*

Hab.: Southeast Asia: Burma, Thailand, Cambodia, Vietnam, Malaysia, and Indonesia. Mainly found in rivers, but also found in pools and ponds.

F.I.: Ca. 1974.

Sex.: Difficult to distinguish.

Soc. B.: Predators. Limit tankmates to large, robust fishes.

M: Use large tanks containing hiding places and robust plants such as giant *Vallisneria*, large *Echinodorus, Anubias,* and *Cryptocoryne* species.

B: Has not been bred successfully.

F: C; prefers fishes, but it can also be trained to accept substitute foods.

S: *C. lucius* has a slow growth rate in captive environments, even with sufficient foodstuffs. It is an appreciated food fish in southeast Asia.

T: 22°–26°C, **L:** 50 (25) cm, **A:** from 100 cm, **R:** all, **D:** 2 (–4; C, S)

Channa insignis

Channa lucius, juvenil

Channa punctata
Spotted snakehead

(BLOCH, 1793)

Syn.: *Ophicephalus punctatus, Ophiocephalus punctatus.*

Hab.: Asia: India, Sri Lanka, and China, in the Yunnan Province. This relatively common species is found in all types of water, but fluvial biotopes are preferred.

F.I.: Ca. 1958.

Sex.: There are no known distinguishing characteristics.

Soc. B.: GÜNTHER describes *C. punctata* as being relatively peaceful (Das Aquarium 224, 2-1988). But experiences with specimens from Sri Lanka have shown these animals to be very aggressive, especially towards conspecifics. Over long periods of time, single maintenance is recommended, although the animals are often shy when kept alone. A voracious predator which can only be housed with larger fishes.

M: A robust, easily maintained charge. House singly in large aquaria. Caves and secluded areas are readily used. Vegetation around the edges and other hiding places among plants are advantageous, especially if several specimens are kept. Snakeheads are proficient jumpers; therefore, the tank needs a snug cover. No particular demands are placed on water chemistry.

B: Has not been bred in captivity. According to VIERKE (1978): *Labyrinthfische*, p. 209, in nature, the gold-striped juveniles are particularly numerous in the months of May and June. The fish probably spawn several times a year. There is no nest, and the amber 1.2 mm eggs are laid in densely vegetated tranquil waters where they float along the water surface. The eggs hatch after 24 hr, and the emerging fry are colorless and about 3 mm long. Four days later, they have grown to a length of 5 mm and have attained their chocolate-brown juvenile coloration.

F: C; prefers fishes, but it is very easily trained to various substitute foods.

Continued on p. 672.

Microgeophagus altispinosus, p. 802

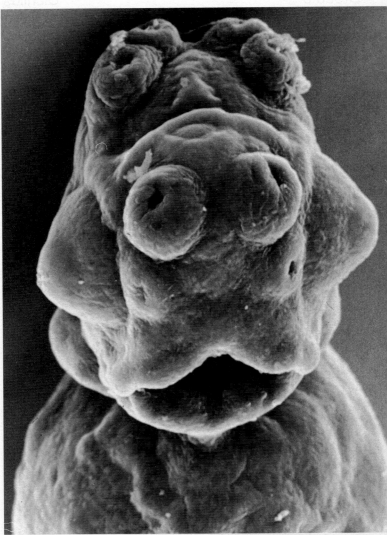

An electronmicrograph of a newly hatched discus larrva (*Symphysodon aequifasciatus*). The toothless mouth, the nasal orifices, and the lateral eyes are clearly distinguishable. There are three pairs of larval adhesive glands, one on the forehead and two on the head (x350).

Pterophyllum scalare

Fam.: Cichlidae

Aequidens metae
Twin-spot flag cichlid

EIGENMANN, 1922

Syn.: None.

Hab.: South America: Colombia. Endemic to the upper Rio Meta at Barrigón, Caño Carnicería, and Cumaral.

F.I.: Not known.

Sex.: Clear secondary sexual characteristics are lacking; there is neither dimorphism nor dichromatism. At the most, ♂ ♂ grow slightly larger and somewhat stouter, while mature ♀ ♀ appear to be slightly more rounded in the ventral region.

Soc. B.: Tranquil and peaceful even among themselves. Since the fish neither dig nor eat plants, vegetation makes a suitable decoration.

M: *A. metae* can be housed in a community of tranquil fishes as long as a few hiding places and cover are included. Care is nonproblematic, even if the fish is not considered easy to breed.

B: Open spawner; horizontal substrates are chosen for spawning. They have a conspicuous contrasting coloration during brood care: the lateral spot is separated by two light vertical bands, the eye is a luminescent yellow-orange, and the rest of the body, primarily the opercula, chest, and throat, is dark.

F: Any normal cichlid foods.

S: *A. metae* is recognized by its dark brown, green-framed vertical stripe which extends downward from the eye (along the anterior edge of the operculum). In contrast to *Aequidens diadema*, *A. metae* lacks bands across the forehead.

T: 24°–28°C, **L:** to 20 cm, **A:** from 100 cm, **R:** b, m. **D:** 1–2

Aequidens tetramerus
Blue-scale flag cichlid

HECKEL, 1840

Syn.: *Acaronia trimaculata.* The pictured fish is also considered to be *Aequidens stollei, A. uniocellatus. Acara tetramerus, Acaronia trimaculata, Chromis punctata, C. uniocellata.*

Hab.: South America: Peru, in Yarina Cocha at the Rio Ucayali.

F.I.: Unknown.

Sex.: ♂ ♂ are larger, and their dorsal fin is elongated into a tip. Juveniles are hard to sex.

Soc. B.: Forms pairs. Aggressive during brood care.

M: Water values do not play a predominant role. Only use robust and well-rooted plants (perhaps potted). Even though *A. tetramerus* does not dig much, delicate plants are destroyed if they are considered a disruptive presence in the pair's territory. They can be housed with large characins or other fishes.

B: Open spawner; the up to 500 eggs are laid on rocks, wood, or directly on the substrate. The larvae hatch after 48 hr and are free-swimming after an additional 4 days. Both ♂ ♂ and ♀ ♀ care for the brood. Rearing the fry is simple.

F: C, O.

S: Previously, *A. tetramerus* was often confused with *Cichlasoma portalegrense* (known as *Aequidens portalegrensis* to hobbyists) and *C.* cf. *amazonarum.* In contrast to *Cichlasoma, ♀ A. tetramerus* have a vertical, silver stripe both in front of and behind the lateral body spot during brood care.

T: 25°C, **L:** ♂ 15 cm, ♀ 8 cm, **A:** from 80 cm, **R:** b, m, **D:** 2

Aequidens metae

Aequidens sp. (*tetramerus* group)

Apistogramma borelli
Umbrella dwarf cichlid, borelli

(REGAN, 1906)

The yellow morph of this species was previously known as *"A. reitzigi"* and was presented in Vol. 1, p. 676. Now, the blue morph from the Rio Paraguay Basin presented here is the more sought after. These two strains should not be cross-bred!

Apistogramma cruzi

KULLANDER, 1986

Syn.: None.

Hab.: South America: lower Amazon Basin, in the triangle formed by Brazil, Colombia, and Peru.

F.I.: 1982 by the Discus-Center-Royal, Witten, Germany.

Sex.: ♂♂ are significantly larger, the ends of the dorsal and anal fins are elongated, and there are three parallel rows of dots under the longitudinal band on the body. ♀♀ are yellow and have a submarginal golden band on the dorsal fin.

Soc. B.: ♂♂ tend toward polygamy. ♀♀ are very aggressive among themselves during brood care.

M: One ♂ and three or more ♀♀ can be housed in an aquarium 1 m or more in length. Plant the tank heavily and decorate with rocks and wood to establish breeding territories for the ♀♀. Water values for care and breeding: hardness around 6° dGH; pH 6.0; temperature 26°C.

Characins make good tankmates.

B: These fish spawn on the ceiling of cavelike structures. The larvae hatch after 3 days and are free-swimming after an additional 6 days. The ♀ tends to the brood alone and remains at the spawning site during the egg and larval phases, keeping largely hidden. ♂♂ can breed consecutively with several ♀♀. While ♂♂ do not participate in direct brood care, they energetically defend the superterritory against predators.

F: O.

S: Some ♂♂ have a threadlike elongation at the superior posterior edge of the tail fin.

T: 26°C, **L:** ♂ 8 cm, ♀ 5 cm, **A:** from 80 cm, **R:** b, **D:** 3

Apistogramma borelli ♂

Apistogramma cruzi ♂

Color Variations of *Apistogramma cacatuoides*

Apistogramma cacatuoides ♂. Another color morph is pictured in Vol. 1, p. 676.

Apistogramma cacatuoides ♂. Another color morph is pictured in Vol. 1, p. 676.

Apistogramma inconspicua ♂

Apistogramma inconspicua
Undistinguished dwarf cichlid

KULLANDER, 1983

Syn.: *Heterogramma corumbae, H. taeniatum.*

Hab.: South America: Bolivia, Brazil, and Paraguay, in the headwaters of the Rio Guapore and the Rio Paraguay.

F.I.: Probably imported in 1906 by the SIGGELKOW Co., Hamburg.

Sex.: Slight sexual dimorphism. ♂ ♂ have pointed fin tips, while ♀ ♀ have rounded fin tips, rounded sections in the soft-rayed part of the dorsal and anal fins, and a more pronounced dark fringe on the upper edge of the anal fin.

Soc. B.: Territorial but peaceful dwarf cichlid. Digging activities are minimal. Plants are not molested. The species can be kept in pairs, even though ♂ ♂ tend towards polygamy. Cave spawner with patriarch-maternal family.

M: Requires plants, many hiding places, and a fine-grained, dark substrate. Create hiding places among rocks and roots close to the bottom. These areas will be used by ♀ ♀ as breeding caves. Keep an area open for swimming. Peaceful, surface-oriented fishes make good tankmates. Water: pH 6.5–7.0; hardness to 10° dGH.

B: 25° to 28°C; maintenance water values are also appropriate for breeding. Cave spawners. The ♀ cares for the eggs, while the ♂ defends the superterritory against tankmates. Each superterritory can contain the breeding territories of several ♀ ♀.

F: C; small live foods such as mosquito larvae, *Daphnia, Cyclops, Artemia* and, occasionally, Enchytraeidae.

S: *A. inconspicua* is part of the *A. regani* group.

T: 23°–28°C, **L:** 8 cm, **A:** 60 cm, **R:** b, **D:** 3

Fam.: Cichlidae

Apistogramma linkei
Linke's dwarf cichlid

KOSLOWSKI, 1985

Syn.: None.

Hab.: South America: Bolivia, near Santa Cruz in lagoons, creeks, and water agglomerations.

F.I.: 1983 by LINKE and STAECK.

Sex.: ♂♂ are larger. The ends of their dorsal and anal fins are pointed, and the chest and ventral areas are yellow-orange.

Soc. B.: ♂♂ tend to be polygamous.

M: Medium-hard, neutral to slightly alkaline water with a temperature of about 26°C is best. Decorate the aquarium with many plants, and provide hiding places among rocks and wood. Keep one ♂ with two or more ♀♀, depending on the size of the aquarium.

B: Spawning occurs in cavelike hiding places or beneath plant leaves. The ♀ cares for the brood, while the ♂ defends

the superterritory. Each spawn consists of about 100 eggs, which hatch about 3 days postspawning. Fry are free-swimming after another 5 days. The ♀ guides the young. Raise with *Artemia* and MicroMin.

F: O.

S: The spot on the caudal peduncle and the caudal band form a "double spot," typically found in species closely related to *A. commbrae*.

T: 24°–26°C, **L:** ♂ 6 cm, ♀ 4 cm, **A:** from 60 cm, **R:** b, **D:** 2

Apistogramma luelingi
Golden apisto

KULLANDER, 1976

Syn.: *Apistogramma borelli* (not REGAN, 1906).

Hab.: South America: Bolivia, in the area around Todos Santos and the drainage basins of the Rio Chapore and Rio Chipirei.

F.I.: 1985 by H. LINKE and Dr. W. STAECK.

Sex.: ♂♂ are larger, have elongated membranes in the dorsal fin, and elongated superior and inferior extensions on the caudal fin.

Soc. B.: Relatively peaceful. ♂♂ tend to be polygamous.

M: Medium-hard, neutral water with a temperature around 24°C is best. Offer plenty of vegetation and many hiding places. One ♂ should always be in the company of several ♀♀.

B: The species breeds in cavelike hiding places; the spawn consists of about 60

eggs. The ♀ tends the brood, while the ♂ defends the territory. Three days are required for the eggs to hatch. After an additional 4 days the larvae are free-swimming under the mother's guidance and capable of feeding on *Artemia* nauplii.

F: O.

S: Closely related to *Apistogramma cacatuoides*, although *A. luelingi* lacks the zigzag stripe beneath the longitudinal band.

T: 22°–26°C, **L:** ♂ 7 cm, ♀ 4 cm, **A:** 80 cm, **R:** b, **D:** 2

Apistogramma linkei ♂

Apistogramma luelingi ♂

Fam.: Cichlidae

Apistogramma resticulosa
Reticulated apistogramma

KULLANDER, 1980

Syn.: None.

Hab.: South America: Brazil, in the area around Humaitá at the Rio Madeira.

F.I.: Probably 1977.

Sex.: ♂♂ have pointed ends on the dorsal and anal fins, rust-red spots on the opercula, and a bluish sheen on the body. ♀♀ are yellow, particularly when caring for eggs or young.

Soc. B.: ♂♂ are not very polygamous, usually dedicating themselves to one ♀. Not very aggressive.

M: For extended care, use medium-hard (≤10° dGH), slightly acid (pH ≤6.5) water with a temperature of about 25°C. Dense vegetation around the edges and wood and rocks riddled with hiding places heighten their well-being. Use sand or a fine-grained gravel substrate. Suitable for community tanks.

B: The water values mentioned above are sufficient to successfully reproduce this species. Eggs are laid on the ceiling of a cavelike retreat. Fry and juveniles are the exclusive responsibility of the ♀; however, the ♂ defends the territory against predators. The fry hatch after 3 days and are free-swimming after an additional 6 days. About 100 young result from each spawn. Artemia nauplii are an appropriate initial food.

F: O.

S: Sometimes ♀♀ spawn as soon as one week after their previous brood is free-swimming. To avoid a conflicting situation for the ♀, remove the young and raise them separately.

T: 26°C, **L:** ♂ 5 cm, ♀ 3 cm, **A:** 50 cm, **R:** b, **D:** 2

Apistogramma staecki
Staeck's apistogramma

KOSLOWSKI, 1985

Syn.: None.

Hab.: South America: northern Bolivia near Trinidad.

F.I.: 1983 by H. LINKE and Dr. W. STAECK.

Sex.: ♂♂ are larger, and their superior and inferior caudal fin rays are elongated.

Soc. B.: Peaceful; ♂♂ tend to be monogamous.

M: Use soft, neutral to slightly acid water with a temperature of ca. 26°C. Decorate the tank with plenty of plants and create many hiding places among rocks and wood. Several pairs can be kept in large tanks.

B: A. staecki lays about 80 eggs on the ceiling of a cavelike hiding place. The ♀ cares for the brood alone, while the ♂ defends the spawning territory. The eggs hatch after 2½ to 3 days, and the fry are free-swimming 5 days later. Artemia nauplii are an appropriate initial food.

F: O.

S: The relationship of this species to other members of the genus is difficult to classify; it is similar to species within the Apistogramma steindachneri group.

T: 24°–28°C, **L:** ♂ 5 cm, ♀ 3 cm, **A:** from 60 cm, **R:** b, **D:** 2–3

Apistogramma resticulosa

Apistogramma staecki

Fam.: Cichlidae

Asprotilapia leptura

BOULENGER, 1901

Syn.: None.

Hab.: Africa: Lake Tanganyika (endemic). Very common in the southern rocky zones of the lake.

F.I.: 1986 by Walter EYSEL and companions.

Sex.: No definite external distinguishing characteristics are known.

Soc. B.: Outside of the spawning season, the animals form small schools, but during the spawning season, they swim in pairs and are territorial. Mouthbrooder. Intense brood care is practiced by both parents (see B).

M: Provide rock edifications with a multitude of crevices, niches, and caves. The animals spend most of their time along steep slabs of rock. These rocks and vertical algae-covered glass panes are grazed by the animals. Use a sandy substrate. Water should be medium-hard and slightly alkaline (hardness of ca. 15° dGH and a pH of 7.5–8.5, respectively).

B: A successful spawning endeavor was reported by EYSEL (1988) in DATZ **40**, 355–357. He observed that the animals spawned above a sandy substrate without first digging a depression. When completed, the ♀ took the eggs into her mouth, and the pair defended a small territory together. The ♂ was particularly active. After 6 days, the roles reversed: the ♂ took the larvae, and the ♀ aggressively defended the territory. The young were released about 13 days afterwards, which is an extremely short incubation time for a Lake Tanganyikan cichlid. However, this did not signify the end of brood care. The fry continued to be intensely guarded by both parents. Even significantly stronger fishes were attacked and driven away. Growth was very rapid. During danger, the fry were admitted once again into the ♂'s mouth. When not all of the young fit, the ♀ also participated. The young also spent the night in the parents' mouth.

F: O; in nature, the animals graze algae lawns. In the aquarium, they can be fed any live, frozen, or freeze-dried foods as well as algae.

Continued on p. 692.

Astatoreochromis alluaudi
Allaundi cichlid

PELLEGRIN, 1903

Syn.: *Astatore alluaudi, Astatoreochromis alluaudi occidentalis, Haplochromis alluaudi.*

Hab.: Africa: in the basins of Lakes Victoria, Edward, and George and Lakes Nakavali and Kachira.

F.I.: Probably not until after 1980. If imported earlier, it entered as a "*Haplochromis.*"

Sex.: Slight sexual dichromatism is present. Sexually mature ♂♂ have numerous egg spots on the anal fin and black ventral fins. ♀♀ and immature ♂♂ have bright yellow or transparent ventral fins.

Soc. B.: Territorial and relatively aggressive during the spawning season, especially ♂♂. Ovophile mouthbrooder, maternal family.

M: *A. alluaudi* prefers its habitat to have dense edge and background vegetation, hiding places among rocks and roots, a substrate of sand or fine-grained gravel, and an open area to allow swimming. The water should be medium-hard and slightly to moderately alkaline (hardness of ca. 15° dGH and a pH of 7.5–8.5, respectively). An appropriate species for large community tanks.

B: Occasionally successful. Similar to that of *Astatotilapia* species (see *A. brownae*).

F: C, O; all kinds of live, frozen, freeze-dried, and flake foods.

S: The dentition of the genus *Astatoreochromis* is typical for nonpiscivorous haplochromines.

T: 24°–28°C, **L:** 15 cm, **A:** 100 cm, **R:** m, b, **D:** 2–3

Asprotilapia leptura

Astatoreochromis alluaudi, WC, Nairobi, Kenya

Fam.: Cichlidae

Continuation of *Asprotilapia leptura* (p. 690):

S: *A. leptura* exhibits surprisingly well-developed brood care, particularly in relation to cooperation between the parents. It would be difficult to improve.

T: 24°–26°C, L: 11 cm, A: 80 cm, R: b, D: 2–3

Astatoreochromis straeleni
Yellow-bellied cichlid

(POLL, 1944)

Syn.: *Haplochromis straeleni*.

Hab.: Africa: in the estuaries of two tributaries of Lake Tanganyika, Lukuga and Rusizi, and their bordering swamp regions. Sometimes found in the lake proper.

F.I.: Probably after 1980.

Sex.: Slight sexual dichromatism. Mature ♂♂ have richer colors and egg spots on the anal fin. ♀♀ have plainer colors and fewer, less defined egg spots on the anal fin.

Soc. B.: Like *Astatoreochromis alluaudi*.

M: As for *A. alluaudi*.

B: Has probably been bred successfully in captivity, even though there is no information in the literature.

F: C, O; all types of live, frozen, freeze-dried, and flake foods.

S: The genus *Astatoreochromis*, unlike members of the former megagenus *Haplochromis*, has four or more hard rays in the anal fin.

T: 24°–28°C, L: 12 cm, A: 90 cm, R: m, b, D: 2–3

Astatotilapia bloyeti
Bloyet's mouthbrooder

(SAUVAGE, 1883)

Syn.: *Hemichromis bloyeti, Haplochromis bloyetii, H. sparsidens, Paratilapia kilossana, Tilapia sparsidens*.

Hab.: Africa: Tanzania. Described from the Wami River System.

F.I.: 1980.

Sex.: Clear sexual dichromatism. ♂♂ are more colorful and have defined egg spots on the anal fin.

Soc. B.: Territorial and aggressive at spawnig time, especially towards conspecific ♂♂. Ovophile mouthbrooder, maternal family.

M: As for *Astatotilapia brownae*.

B: Has probably been bred in captivity.

F: C, O; all kinds of live, frozen, freeze-dried, and flake foods.

S: There are a number of strains of *A. bloyeti*. Since this species has not been revised, it is better to speak of the

Astatotilapia bloyeti group (see GREENWOOD, 1979: Bull. Br. Mus. nat. Hist. (Zool.) **35**, p. 283).

T: 24°–28°C, L: 14 cm, A: 100 cm, R: m, b, D: 2

Astatoreochromis straeleni

Astatotilapia bloyeti, TZ 87/2, north Mikumi, Wami Basin

Fam.: Cichlidae

Astatotilapia brownae
Brown's mouthbrooder

(GREENWOOD, 1962)

Syn.: *Haplochromis brownae.*

Hab.: Africa: Lake Victoria (endemic). The holotype was captured in Uganda at Entebbe.

F.I.: 1985 (?).

Sex.: Clear sexual dichromatism. ♂ ♂ are brighter and more colorful with black ventral fins and defined egg spots on the anal fin. With the exception of their lemon yellow ventral fins, ♀ ♀ are less intensely colored.

Soc. B.: Territorial while spawning. During this time they are very aggressive towards conspecifics and, occasionally, heterospecifics. The ♂ is polygamous; always keep one ♂ with several ♀ ♀. Ovophile mouthbrooder, maternal family.

M: Set the tank up with dense vegetation around the edges, many hiding places among rocks and roots, an open area for swimming, and a gravel or sand substrate.

Medium-hard (12°–18° dGH), alkaline (pH 8–9) water is suggested.

B: Use the above mentioned water values. Keep one ♂ with several ♀ ♀ (3–5). Up to 40 eggs are laid in depressions and then taken into the ♀'s mouth. Eggs are fertilized via the egg spot method and hatch after 14 days at 25°C. Newly released young are quite robust and capable of immediately tackling newly hatched *Artemia* nauplii. Once released, the fry are guarded for an additional week by the ♀.

F: C, O; all kinds of live foods (predominately insects), frozen foods, freeze-dried foods as well as vegetables (lettuce, algae) and flake foods.

S: According to GREENWOOD, *A. brownae* is a typical representative of lacustrine haplochromines.

T: 22°–28°C, **L:** 12 cm, **A:** 100 cm, **R:** m, b, **D:** 2

Astatotilapia calliptera
Callipterus hap

(GÜNTHER, 1893)

Syn.: *Chromis callipterus, Ctenochromis callipterus, Haplochromis callipterus, H. centropristoides, Neochromis simotes nyassae, Tilapia calliptera.*

Hab.: Africa: Malawi, Mozambique, Zimbabwe, in Lakes Malawi and Chilwa and coastal rivers to the Samer, Busi, and the lower Sabi-Lundi Rivers as well as the lower Zambezi and Pungwe systems.

F.I.: 1985 (?).

Sex.: Clear sexual dichromatism; ♂ ♂ are more colorful and have pronounced egg spots on the anal fin.

Soc. B.: Only territorial at spawning time. At that time, ♂ ♂ are particularly aggressive. Ovophile mouthbrooder, maternal family.

M: As for *Astatotilapia brownae*.

B: There is no in-depth information available, but it should not differ much from other *Astatotilapia* species (e.g., *A. brownae*).

F: C, O; all types of live, frozen, and freeze-dried foods. Sometimes vegetable supplements are accepted.

S: JUBB (1967) considers *Astatotilapia swynnertoni* synonymous to *A. calliptera*, but does not justify his opinion. GREENWOOD claims both species are autonomous.

T: 24°–28°C, **L:** 14 cm, **A:** 100 cm, **R:** m, b, **D:** 2–3

Astatotilapia brownae ♂

Astatotilapia calliptera ♂

Fam.: Cichlidae

Astatotilapia nubila (BOULENGER, 1906)

Syn.: *Tilapia nubila, Haplochromis centropristoides victorianus, H. nubilus.*

Hab.: Africa: in Lakes Victoria, Kioga, Edward, George, Nabugabo, Kachira, Nakeavali, and Kijanebalola and their effluent and affluent systems.

F.I.: Single specimens were imported as early as 1980.

Sex.: Pronounced sexual dichromatism. ♂♂ are black during the spawning season with red-fringed anal and dorsal fins and pronounced egg spots on the anal fin. ♀♀ are nondescript.

Soc. B.: Territorial when spawning; dominant ♂♂ are extremely aggressive and intolerant of conspecific ♂♂ and other ♂ haplochromines. Ovophile mouthbrooder, maternal family.

M: The tank can be densely planted around the edges. The animals should be offered many hiding places among rocks, rock edifications, and roots; at the same time, preserve sufficient open swimming space. The substrate should be of sand or fine-grained gravel. Cover the tank well, since the animals are accomplished jumpers. Water: hardness of 10°–15° dGH; pH ca. 8.0. Sensitive to excessive nitrate concentrations, making a 50%–75% water exchange every 7–10 days recommendable.

B: To minimize the risk that the dominant ♂ injures or even kills a ♀, at least 4–5 ♀♀ should be kept. The more ♀♀, the more the ♂'s aggressions are distributed. The animals spawn like mouthbrooders, whereby the eggs are inseminated by the egg spot method. One ♀ can lay up to 60 eggs, but 20–40 eggs are more common. At 25°C, the young are released from the ♀'s mouth after about 2 weeks. They are 8–10 mm long at that time. Feed them *Artemia* nauplii.

F: C, O; all kinds of live foods, particularly small crustacea and insect larvae. Juveniles and ♀♀ also feed on algae and detritus.

S: The presence of a dominant ♂ precludes inferior ♂♂ from acquiring their intense coloration.

T: 21°–30°C, **L:** ♂ 9 (13) cm, ♀ 6 (13) cm, **A:** 80 cm, **R:** m, b, **D:** 2–3

Continuation of *"Cichlasoma" centrarchus* (p. 722):

"remnant stripe." Antagonistic encounters are usually settled without jaw locking. The numerous, small eggs are laid on vertical substrates and the underside of roots, which is the extent of its cave-spawning tendencies. Even small ♀♀ with a length of 7–8 cm lay 300 to 500 eggs. At a hardness of 7° dGH, a pH of 7, and a temperature of 27°C, the young hatch after 3 days. The larvae, which are still unable to swim, are "hung" on exposed plant roots or algae-covered rocks. When free-swimming, the fry are less bottom-oriented than other cichlid young. The ♂ maintains his dark coloration while tending the fry.

F: O; all normal fish foods are accepted.

T: 25°–27°C, **L:** 15 cm, **A:** 80 cm, **R:** m, **D:** 1–2

Astatotilapia nubila ♂, F₁ K 86/12 Nzaiu River, west Siaya

Astatotilapia sp., Wembere River, Tanzania

Fam.: Cichlidae

Aulonocara ethelwynnae MEYER, RIEHL & ZETZSCHE, 1987
Northern aulonocara

Syn.: None.

Hab.: Africa: endemic to Lake Malawi around Chitendi Island. Found at depths greater than 3 m.

F.I.: 1980 by A. GRESHAKE.

Sex.: Adult ♂♂ have bright blue-black unpaired fins; ♀♀ are a plain brown.

Soc. B.: There are intraspecific aggressions among ♂♂. Territorial. This species can be housed with similar-sized haplochromines.

M: Requires rock edifications, caves, sand surfaces, and open swimming areas. Medium-hard to hard, alkaline (pH 7.4–8.0) water is best.

B: Reproduction is considered unproblematic; mouthbrooder. At 3 weeks of age and an average length of 1 cm, the fry leave the mother's mouth. Raise the young with *Artemia* and flake foods.

F: C, O; mosquito larvae, small crustacea, commercial diets (tablets).

S: The back rows of teeth are tricuspids.

T: 22°–26°C, **L:** 8 cm, **A:** 80 cm, **R:** m, b, **D:** 3

Aulonocara ethelwynnae, photo taken at Chitendi Island

Aulonocara hansbaenschi
"Red flush" aulonocara

MEYER, RIEHL & ZETZSCHE, 1987

Syn.: None. Usually called *Aulonocara nyassae*, see Vol. 1, p. 682. However, *A. nyassae* has never been imported, meaning *A. hansbaenschi* was sold for years under an erroneous name.

Hab.: Africa: endemic to the eastern coast of Lake Malawi near Masinje. Found at depths of 4–6 m. Released at Thumbi Island.

F.I.: Not precisely known, but imported prior to 1980 as "peacock blue." Peter DAVIES exported the first specimens to the United States.

Sex.: Adult ♂♂ have brilliant blue colors and an intense orange or red throat. ♀♀ are solid gray-brown.

Soc. B.: Like *A. ethelwynnae. A. hansbaenschi*, in comparison, is more cave oriented. Likes to dig.

M: As for *A. ethelwynnae. A. hansbaenschi* is very susceptible to hole-in-the-head and worms; they are often in-fected in their natural habitat. Offer caves. Plants must be strongly anchored. Water: pH 7.5–8.0; hardness 15°–25° dGH; carbonate hardness 10°–20° dKH.

B: Each ♂ should have 2 or more ♀♀. The ♀ buccally incubates the eggs and fry for up to 3 weeks. After they emerge, feed them *Artemia* nauplii and small live foods and flake foods.

F: C, O; mosquito larvae, small crusta-cea, dry commercial diets (tablets).

S: Even today this species is frequently confused with *A. nyassae* which, accord-ing to the original description by REGAN (1922) and available material, also have reddish ventral fins and, occasionally, a red throat. Despite this common charac-teristic, the two species can be distin-guished by their overall coloration and morphological and meristic characteris-tics.

T: 23°–27°C, **L:** 10 cm, **A:** 80 cm, **R:** b, m, **D:** 2–3

Aulonocara hansbaenschi "Thumbi"

Aulonocara hansbaenschi ♂, Makanjila Point

Aulonocara hansbaenschi ♀

Aulonocara hueseri
White top

MEYER, RIEHL & ZETZSCHE, 1987

Syn.: None.

Hab.: Africa: endemic to Lake Malawi around Likoma Island. Found at depths greater than 12 m.

F.I.: 1980 by A. GRESHAKE.

Sex.: Adult ♂♂ are notoriously blue and yellow. ♀♀ are gray.

Soc. B.: Like *A. ethelwynnae*.

M: As for *A. ethelwynnae*.

B: As for *A. ethelwynnae*.

F: C, O; mosquito larvae, small crustacea, and dry commercial diets (tablets).

S: In comparison to its close relative, *A. korneliae*, *A. hueseri* has fewer vertical stripes and a black and white fringe on the dorsal fin.

T: 24°–26°C, **L:** 9.5 cm, **A:** 80 cm, **R:** m, b, **D:** 2–3

Chisumulu Island

Aulonocara hueseri

Aulonocara hueseri

Fam.: Cichlidae

Aulonocara korneliae
Blue-gold aulonocara

MEYER, RIEHL & ZETZSCHE, 1987

Syn.: None.

Hab.: Africa: endemic to Lake Malawi around Chisumulu Island. Found at depths of 9–12 m.

F.I.: Cannot be determined.

Sex.: Adult ♂♂ are predominately blue-gold. ♀♀ are a dull gray-brown.

Soc. B.: Like *Aulonocara ethelwynnae.*

M: As for *A. ethelwynnae.*

B: As for *A. ethelwynnae.*

F: C, O; mosquito larvae, small crustacea, dry commercial diets (tablets).

S: See *Aulonocara hueseri.*

T: 23°–27°C, **L:** 9 cm, **A:** 80 cm, **R:** b, m, **D:** 2–3

Aulonocara saulosi

MEYER, RIEHL & ZETZSCHE, 1987

Syn.: None.

Hab.: Africa: endemic to the eastern coast of Lake Malawi near Masinje. Found at depths of 6–15 m.

F.I.: 1986 by H. W. DIECKHOFF.

Sex.: Adult ♂♂ are a dark brown with red ventral fins and a blue head. ♀♀ are a plain brown.

Soc. B.: Like *Aulonocara ethelwynnae.*

M: As for *A. ethelwynnae.* Susceptible to hole-in-the-head.

B: As for *A. ethelwynnae.*

F: C, O; mosquito larvae, small crustacea, and dry commercial diets (tablets).

S: ♂♂ and ♀♀ are found singly or in pairs in their natural habitat; trios are rarely encountered. ♀♀ of all other *Aulonocara* species live in groups.

T: 22°–26°C, **L:** 11 cm, **A:** 100 cm, **R:** b, m, **D:** 2–3

Aulonocara korneliae

Aulonocara saulosi

Aulonocara korneliae in its natural habitat

Continuation of *"Cichlasoma" guttulatum* (p. 728):

S: *"Cichlasoma" guttulatum* has been described from the Pacific Coast of Guatemala. However, cichlids matching its description have never been captured in that area. Various reports from the Atlantic tributaries of Guatemala seem to have confused *"C." microphthalmus* with *"C."* *guttulatum*. The fish pictured here is generally considered to be *"C." guttulatum*. It hails from the rivers of the Atlantic side of Mexico. Collections need to be made in Guatemala to confirm identification, because we may be dealing with several similar species.

T: 25°–28°C, **L:** 30 cm, **A:** 120 cm, **R:** b, **D:** 1

Aulonocranus dewindti
Gold-striped aulonocranus

(BOULENGER, 1899)

Syn.: *Paratilapia dewindti, Paratilapia lukugae.*

Hab.: Africa: widely distributed in Lake Tanganyika (found in all four countries). Inhabits the transition area between the sand and the rubble littoral zone.

F.I.: Unknown.

Sex.: ♀♀ are silver-gray and have rounded fins. ♂♂ are also silver-gray, but have a number of blue and yellow scales arranged in horizontal rows along their sides, and their fins are elongated.

Soc. B.: *A. dewindti* seems to be a social species which can be housed with a large number of sand and rubble inhabitants in the aquarium. Because of its conspicuously large mouth, some authors consider this fish a carnivore.

M: *A. dewindti* requires a spacious tank, a fine sand substrate to allow digging, and rock edifications, but only along the back wall. While plants are not necessary, a few can be included in the decoration as long as they are placed so that they do not disturb the animals.

B: Has not been successfully bred in captivity. HERRMANN has observed ♂♂ making small depressions in the sand in shallow waters of Lake Tanganyika and defending them energetically against intruders. ♀♀ and young ♂♂ swim in groups in the open water. There the former are courted by territorial ♂♂. Spawning occurs in the depressions. ♀♀ are mouthbrooders.

F: C; in contrast to similar looking mouthbrooders, this species may be a carnivore, as suggested by its large mouth. Its diet should reflect its possible carnivorous bent. Chopped shrimp are a particularly appropriate food item.

T: 24°–26°C, **L:** 11 cm, **A:** 150 cm, **R:** b, m, **D:** 3–4

707

Fam.: Cichlidae

Biotodoma cupido
Cupid cichlid

(HECKEL, 1840)

Syn.: *Geophagus cupido, Acara subocularis, Mesops cupido.*

Hab.: South America: central Amazon, from Peru to southeastern Brazil. Information claiming *B. cupido* is found in the Guianas or the Orinoco region is probably erroneous, referring to another, as yet undescribed *Biotodoma* species.

F.I.: 1935 by the HÄRTEL Co., Dresden. After a long absence, wild-caught specimens were again imported into Germany towards the end of 1987 thanks to A. WERNER; these animals came from the Tapajos system, a southern Amazon tributary close to Santarém, Brazil.

Sex.: ♂♂ are larger, much more colorful, and have prettier fins. Some animals have a pronounced black and white design in the dorsal and caudal fins. The caudal fin has threadlike extensions along the top and bottom. Adult ♂♂ often have a prominent black and white design along the edge of the tail and two parallel shiny blue streaks underneath the eye that extend toward the mouth. ♀♀ have single, shiny dots.

Soc. B.: Territorial, pair-forming fish (monogamous). When spawning, the species is aggressive and very territorial. At this time the animals dig extensively to make their deep crater-shaped nests, which is where they spawn. Nuclear family.

M: Decorate the back pane of the tank with rockwork and roots, creating hiding places; plant robust vegetation around the edges; use a sand-gravel substrate and place a few stones in the foreground.

B: 24°–27°C. Though water values are of secondary importance, the eggs need medium-hard (up to 20° dGH), neutral to slightly alkaline (pH 7.5–8) water. *B. cupido* is an open spawner that lays up to 400 "p" eggs. Defending them is largely the ♀'s responsibility, whereas guarding the territory is the ♂'s duty. Nuclear family.

F: C; all kinds of live foods such as *Daphnia, Tubifex,* mosquito larvae, earthworms, and *Mysis* as well as flake and frozen foods.

S: Similar fish often arrive from Guyana under the name *B. cupido,* but these fish are probably still undescribed. According to observations in their natural habitat (CICHOCKI), the animals from Guyana are likewise open spawners that lay their eggs in depressions. KUHLMANN, who has bred this *Biotodoma* in captivity, confirmed CICHOCKI's report.

T: 22°–25°C, **L:** 12 cm (?), **A:** 60 cm, **R:** m, b, **D:** 3

Biotodoma wavrini
Wavrin's cichlid

(GOSSE, 1963)

Syn.: *Geophagus wavrini.*

Hab.: South America: upper Orinoco, Rio Negro, and the Rio Preto da Eva (northern tributary of the Amazon).

F.I.: Sporadically imported, only reaching the hobby as by-catch.

Sex.: ♂♂ have very elongated, white-fringed tail and ventral fins and a more pronounced glistening blue design along their sides. This design often forms parallel bands.

Soc. B.: Tranquil, peaceful, shy animals.

M: The water should be very soft, slightly acid, and low in metabolic wastes. Use a sandy substrate. Decorate with roots, rocks, and plants.

B: Reports on how to breed *Biotodoma* are contradictory. *B. wavrini* has probably never been bred in captivity.

F: C; small live, frozen, and flake foods.

S: Unlike *Biotodoma cupido,* this species lacks facial striations, has fewer dorsal fin rays, a different scale arrangement, and is more shallow-bodied through the dorsal region. Note that the lateral spot is beneath the lateral line rather than above it.

T: 26°–30°C, **L:** 15 cm, **A:** 120 cm, **R:** b, m, **D:** 4

Biotodoma cupido

Biotodoma wavrini

Fam.: Cichlidae

Boulengerochromis microlepis
Giant Tanganyika cichlid

(BOULENGER, 1899)

Syn.: *Tilapia microlepis, Paratilapia microlepis.*

Hab.: Africa: endemic to Lake Tanganyika. Found throughout the lake.

F.I.: Since 1980 (?).

Sex.: ♂♂ are usually larger, their coloration, at least when sexually mature, is more intense, and the 2nd and 3rd soft anal fin rays are longer. The ♀ has a pronounced genital papilla.

Soc. B.: Predatory. Territorial during the spawning season. Juveniles hunt in schools of 100–500 specimens. Adults over 25 cm long are usually found in groups of 5–20. Open spawners, nuclear family.

M: *B. microlepis* requires a spacious tank with a sand or gravel substrate, plenty of free swimming space, rock edifications, and clear alkaline (up to pH 9), hard (10° dGH and above), well-oxygenated water. The last is particularly important, since these animals seem to be very sensitive to low oxygen concentrations. Due to their predatory nature, a species tank is suggested.

B: Their respectable size probably precludes aquarium breeding. Substrate spawner. Territories are located in the rocky littoral zone at depths of 2 to 6 m and guarded by both parents. More than 10,000 eggs can be laid, depending on the size of the ♀. All of the round, 1.6–2.0 mm, olive eggs are laid at one time. One parent hovers above the spawn and fans fresh water over the eggs using its fins, while the other partner keeps vigil some distance away.

F: C; adults are pronounced piscivores. In nature, they primarily feed on herring-like fishes and cichlids. Fry and juveniles feed on algae, crustacea, snails, aquatic insects, and worms.

S: *B. microlepis* is the largest recent cichlid species. Large specimens can reach a weight of 3.5 kg and are appreciated food fish in their natural habitat.

T: 24°–26°C, **L:** 80 cm, **A:** from 150 cm, **R:** all, **D:** 3 (C)

Boulengerochromis microlepis fry, Kigoma

Boulengerochromis microlepis from Tanzania

Boulengerochromis microlepis from Kigoma

Fam.: Cichlidae

Callochromis macrops
Large-eyed mouthbrooder

(BOULENGER, 1898)

Syn.: *Paratilapia macrops, Tylochromis macrophthalmus, Pelmatochromis xenotilapiaformis.*

Hab.: Africa: in the southern regions of Lake Tanganyika. Primarily in shallow waters over sand-rock substrates.

F.I.: Unknown.

Sex.: ♂ ♂ grow somewhat larger and have an attractive courtship dress. ♀ ♀ remain pale and lack the red-yellow spot on the anal fin.

Soc. B.: Belligerence among conspecifics is so pronounced, that normally only one ♂ can be kept with several ♀ ♀. Hardly aggressive towards heterospecific cichlids.

M: Subdivide the tank in such a manner that the fish are out of direct visual contact with each other. A sandy substrate is important. Plants are left unmolested.

B: Agamic maternal mouthbrooders. The ♂ excavates small depressions in the sand at spawning time then lures ♀ ♀ within with his quivering body. Eggs are laid and fertilized in the depression. The ♀ cares for the brood for about 20 days. Polygamous.

F: O; live, frozen, and flake foods are accepted.

S: Until 1986 and POLL's revision, *C. melanostigma* was classified as a subspecies of *C. macrops.* Now the two are autonomous species. *C. macrops* has several geographic color races. The pictured animal comes from Ndole Bay, Zambia.

T: 24°–26°C, **L:** 15 cm, **A:** 150 cm, **R:** b, m, **D:** 2–3

Callochromis melanostigma
Blackspot callochromis

(BOULENGER, 1906)

Syn.: *Pelmatochromis melanostigma, Callochromis macrops melanostigma.*

Hab.: Africa: only in the northernmost part of Lake Tanganyika.

F.I.: Unknown.

Sex.: Only ♂ ♂ are brightly colored. ♀ ♀ are gray.

Soc. B.: ♂ ♂ are very quarrelsome among each other. If housed with other fishes, aggressions are visibly diminished. Tankmates can include very different cichlids from Lake Tanganyika, even other sand dwellers. In fact, this allows the tank to be more densely populated.

M: Use a large tank, a fine sand substrate, and rock edifications along the back of the aquarium. Vegetation is usually not bothered, but do not infringe into the space required by the fish. If possible, include several ♀ ♀ for each ♂.

B: According to HERRMANN, ♂ ♂ excavate depressions in the sand when they start courting, often making several side by side in one territory. ♀ ♀ are drawn to the depressions by the ♂'s shivering body. Maternal mouthbrooders. Eggs are incubated for 19 days.

F: O; food is taken from the bottom. Frequently, sand is chewed as they search for edibles. Thawed frozen foods and flakes are accepted.

S: The subspecies *C. macrops macrops* inhabits the southern part of the lake and apparently has several color morphs. The form from around Kigoma is particularly similar to *C. m. melanostigma.* The primary differentiating characteristic is the black design exclusively found on *C. m. melanostigma.*

T: 24°–26°C, **L:** 15 cm, **A:** 150 cm, **R:** b, **D:** 3

Callochromis macrops ♂

Callochromis melanostigma ♂

Fam.: Cichlidae

Callochromis pleurospilus
Redspot callochromis

(BOULENGER, 1906)

Syn.: *Pelmatochromis pleurospilus, P. rhodostigma, P. stappersii, Callochromis rhodostigma, C. stappersii.*

Hab.: Africa: endemic to Lake Tanganyika. Primarily encountered in sand littoral zones and in the sand-rock littoral transition zone.

F.I.: Unknown.

Sex.: ♂♂ grow 1–2 cm larger and have a colorful fringe on the anal fin. ♀♀ are solid silver gray.

Soc. B.: Strong intraspecific aggressions. Several ♀♀ should be present for each ♂. Agamic mouthbrooder.

M: Needs free sand substrates. It sifts through the sand searching for food! Hiding places in the form of rock edifications must be offered for subdominant animals.

C. pleurospilus does not molest plants.

B: 25° to 28°C. The water should be medium-hard and neutral to slightly alkaline (hardness of 10°–15° dGH and a of pH 7.0–8.5, respectively). Agamic mouthbrooder. At spawning time, the ♂ excavates small craters in the sand and spawns therein with the ♀. The ♀ incubates the 20–30 eggs for about 3 weeks.

F: O; large and small *Artemia*, mosquito larvae (frozen), and flake foods. Voracious omnivore.

S: Occasionally sold as *Callochromis* sp. "*greshakei,*" which is a color morph from the central east coast.

T: 23°–28°C, **L:** 15 cm, **A:** 120 cm, **R:** b, m, **D:** 2–3

Caquetaia spectabilis

(STEINDACHNER, 1875)

Syn.: *Cichlasoma spectabile, Acara spectabilis, Petenia spectabilis, Astronotus spectabilis, Heros spectabilis.*

Hab.: South America: central and lower Amazon.

F.I.: Unknown.

Sex.: Although the ♀♀ remain somewhat smaller, there is neither dimorphism nor dichromatism.

Soc. B.: This is a tranquil cichlid which can nevertheless hold its own. They are subdued, yet have a stately elegance which is fostered by territorial animals, since they always swim with spread fins.

M: The deep body of this cichlid indicates that it is a mid-water fish, not a bottom dweller. It stands among vertical plants, uses large plant leaves as cover, or peeks out of rock edifications or crevices. Water values seem to play a subordinate role.

B: Sexual maturity is reached at an ap-proximate length of 15 cm. Pair bonding is gradual but strong once established. Conflict situations resulting in aggressive behavior are rare. *C. spectabilis* is an open spawner that lays its numerous small eggs on vertical and horizontal surfaces. Under the following conditions the fry hatch on the 4th day: temperature 27°C, 7° dGH, 6° dKH, pH 7. The larvae are usually hidden in narrow crevices among rocks. The ♀ is somewhat more active during brood care.

F: C; its premaxilla and maxilla allow the mouth to be very protrusive. The large anterior teeth attest to its being a specialized, very precise predator. Even enormous animals are not exempt from becoming prey. Beef heart, strips of fish, shrimp, *Gammarus*, and even large flakes are voraciously consumed.

T: 26°–27°C, **L:** ♂ up to 25 cm, **A:** 120 cm, **R:** m, **D:** 1–2

Callochromis pleurospilus

Caquetaia spectabilis

Fam.: Cichlidae

Chalinochromis sp. "bifrenatus"

Syn.: None, because "bifrenatus" is a trade name.

Hab.: Africa: the rocky littoral zone of Lake Tanganyika (endemic).

F.I.: 1975.

Sex.: ♂ ♂ are larger than ♀ ♀ and have a more or less pronounced frontal hump.

Soc. B.: Territorial, yet tranquil and plant friendly. They can be very aggressive when spawning. Pairs form a close bond. Cave spawner with nuclear family.

M: Provide rock edifications with many crevices, niches, and caves; if vegetation is desired, use species that have tough leaves. Nice additions for communities of other cichlids from the rubble and rocky zone (e.g., *Julidochromis, Neolamprologus,* or *Telmatochromis* species).

Water: hardness 8°–18° dGH; pH 7.5–9.0.

B: JACH (1982) described breeding in "Das Aquarium" **17**, 525–527. A spawn is generally comprised of 40–50 eggs. Rearing the fry was easily accomplished with crumbled flake foods.

F: C; live foods of all kinds such as small crustacea, mosquito larvae, and worms. Acclimating this fish to flake foods can be accomplished.

S: *C.* sp. "bifrenatus" lacks the upper black line on the head (see photo). There are two black-brown longitudinal bands running the length of the body with the lower line extending from the operculum to the caudal peduncle.

T: 24°–28°C, **L:** 11 cm, **A:** 80 cm, **R:** m, b, **D:** 2–3

Cichlasoma amazonarum
Amazon cichlid

KULLANDER, 1983

Syn.: None.

Hab.: South America: Ucayali-Solimoes-Amazon system.

F.I.: Cannot be determined, since it is possible that this species has been repeatedly imported, but under a different name (for example, *"Aequidens" portalegrensis*).

Sex.: ♂ ♂ are larger, more colorful, and have very long threadlike extensions on the dorsal and anal fins. ♀ ♀ are fuller, especially when ready to spawn.

Soc. B.: Calm, peaceful cichlids which respect plants. Only territorial when spawning. During that time, it is particularly aggressive towards conspecifics. Nuclear family with intense brood care.

M: Substrate of sand and/or gravel; some hiding places among rocks and bogwood; robust plants (e.g., *Sagittaria, Echinodorus, Vallisneria,* or *Microsorium*) surrounded by pebbles to protect them from being uprooted (after spawning, the fish occasionally create deep pits for their larvae, frequently directly among plant roots); optical boundaries for the territories. Several pairs can be kept in large aquaria, where they will establish and defend territories and spawn.

B: 23°–27°C. Breeding requires soft to medium-hard, acid to neutral water (hardness up to 15° dGH and a pH of 6–7, respectively). Open spawner. Hard substrates (e.g., rocks, roots, plant leaves) are chosen and meticulously cleaned before the 100–300 eggs are laid. Larvae are placed in previously dug pits. Pairs can raise numerous broods each year.

F: C, O; all kinds of live foods, freeze-dried foods, tablets, and flake foods. This is a nonselective, nonproblematic omnivore.

S: Since the revision by KULLANDER in 1983, *Cichlasoma* contains 12 species.

Continued on p. 718.

Chalinochromis sp. "bifrenatus" from Ikola

Cichlasoma amazonarum

"Cichlasoma" bartoni
Barton's cichlid

(BEAN, 1892)

Syn.: *Acara bartoni, Cichlosoma bartoni.*

Hab.: Central America: northern Mexico, endemic to the Rio Panuco system.

F.I.: 1983 by W. STAECK and L. SEEGERS.

Sex.: ♂♂ are larger. As they grow older, they develop a nuchal hump.

Soc. B.: Normally temperamental, but totally intolerant of conspecifics when breeding. Even heterospecifics are not totally exempt from aggressions at that time. Plants may be uprooted as they dig their pits for their larvae. Nuclear family with very intense brood care.

M: *"C." bartoni* needs a sand-gravel substrate, secluded areas among rocks and roots, and robust plants such as *Sagittaria, Echinodorus, Vallisneria, Microsorium*, or *Cryptocoryne*. Protect the vegetation from being uprooted with a few stones around each plant. Free swimming space is not as important as clearly delimited territories. Six to eight young and half-grown specimens can be kept in groups until two animals pair off. At this time it is best to remove the rest of the group unless the tank is very large.

B: 22°–27°C; medium-hard to hard and neutral to slightly alkaline water (hardness ≥8° dGH and a pH of 7.0–8.5, respectively). Open spawner. Secluded rocks or roots are cleaned in preparation for the 100–300 eggs. Depressions are excavated to receive the larvae when they hatch. ♀♀ are sexually mature from a length of 6 cm. Several broods can be raised each year in an aquarium.

F: C, O; all kinds of live, freeze-dried, tablet, and flake foods. Cautiously feed beef heart and *Tubifex*!

S: In 1983 STAECK and SEEGERS reported that *"C." bartoni* populations were endangered in some habitats by released tilapia. For this reason, caring for and breeding this species in the aquarium is encouraged. The coloration of *"C." bartoni* assumes during courtship and maintains throughout brood care is notable: their white speckled gray body is replaced by dark black sides and a highly contrasting white-yellow forehead, upper head, dorsum, and dorsal fin (see photos).

T: 21°–27°C, **L:** 18 cm, **A:** 80 cm, **R:** m, b, **D:** 2

Continuation of *Cichlasoma amazonarum* (p. 716):

Species identification within this genus based on live specimens is not always simple, particularly without exact habitat information. Some species have been known to aquarists for a long time, but were repeatedly imported and cared for under erroneous names (e.g., *Cichlasoma dimerus* as *"Aequidens" portalegrensis*).

Other species have probably never been imported as aquarium fishes (for example, *Cichlasoma sanctifranciscense* or *C. araguaiense*). Most *Cichlasoma* species will probably never be popular aquarium fishes, since their colors are often less than spectacular and typically digress with age.

T: 22°–27°C, **L:** 14 cm, **A:** 60 cm, **R:** m, b, **D:** 1

"Cichlasoma" bartoni ♂

"Cichlasoma" bartoni ♀

Fam.: Cichlidae

"Cichlasoma" beani
Bean's cichlid

(JORDAN, 1888)

Syn.: *Heros beani, Astronotus beani, Cichlasoma beani, Parapetenia beani.*

Hab.: Central America: Pacific seaboard of northern Mexico. Lowland rivers of the states of Sinaloa and Jalisco, in the Rio Grande de Santiago and the Rio Presidio Basins.

F.I.: Only a few specimens have reached Germany alive.

Sex.: Not known; probably lacking sexual dimorphism and dichromatism.

Soc. B.: Since we are dealing with a moderately specialized predator, it can be assumed that *"Cichlasoma" beani* can stand its ground in front of other cichlids and is particularly aggressive towards conspecifics.

M: Decorate a spacious tank with several securely-based rock edifications and hiding places. Plants can probably be included. Avoid high temperatures and extreme acidity. A pH of 7.5 and a hardness of 10° dGH or less are suitable values.

B: Open spawner with intense brood care. Courtship dress consists of contrasting black vertical lines and a light dorsum. Juveniles should be easy to raise.

F: O; hardy fare is needed, but no particular demands have to be met.

T: 23°–25°C, **L:** 30 cm, **A:** 120 cm, **R:** b, **D:** 1–2

Cichlasoma boliviense
Bolivian cichlasoma

KULLANDER, 1983

Syn.: None.

Hab.: South America: Bolivian Amazon Basin. Found in the Mamoré, Guaporé, San Miguel, Beni, and Madre de Dios River systems.

F.I.: 1985 by W. STAECK and co-travelers.

Sex.: Sexes are difficult to distinguish. ♂♂ are larger with a stouter head profile and more elongated fins. Sometimes behavior is a better distinguishing characteristic than physical features.

Soc. B.: Tranquil retiring species which is not even particularly aggressive towards similar cichlids

M: Small aquaria are adequate owing to its inactive demeanor. Use stones, roots, and plants to provide ample hiding opportunities. Water chemistry is secondary. A pH around 7 and a hardness of 15° dGH or less will prove suitable.

B: Open spawner. Eggs are small, but numerous. Fry are free-swimming six or seven days postspawning. Raising the fry with *Artemia* nauplii is unproblematic. Parents remain relatively congenial towards tankmates through spawning and brood care, yet are trustworthy parents.

F: O; all normal foods will be placidly accepted.

S: Even after KULLANDER's revision of the genus, *C. boliviense* maintained its taxonomic place within *Cichlasoma*. The irregular spots on the caudal peduncle are a distinctive feature of this species.

T: 23°–27°C, **L:** 17 cm, **A:** from 80 cm, **R:** b, **D:** 1–2

"Cichlasoma" beani

Cichlasoma boliviense

Fam.: Cichlidae

"Cichlasoma" calobrense
Red-spotted cichlid

MEEK & HILDEBRAND, 1913

Syn.: *Cichlaurus calobrensis.*

Hab.: Central America: Panama, on both the Pacific and Atlantic seaboard. Inhabits, among others, the Bayano and Tuyra Basins, Rio Maye, Rio Sucubti, Rio Cricamola, Rio San Juan, Rio Zepeque, and the Rio Guarumo. Named after the Rio Calobre, an additional habitat.

F.I.: 1984 by the "Diskus Center Royal" Co., Witten, Germany.

Sex.: ♂♂ are larger and more colorful with more luminescent red dots. Older ♂♂ develop a cephalic hump. ♀♀ are generally paler, and those animals in spawning condition are fuller through the ventral area. They have a relatively large, blunt ovipositor while spawning.

Soc. B.: Territorial, pair-forming species. The animals are very unsociable and bellicose, particularly at spawning time. Pits are excavated for hatched larvae. Nuclear family (or patriarch-maternal family). Parents conscientiously tend the brood.

M: The substrate should be a sand-gravel mixture. Construct caves and hiding places among rocks and roots. Aquatic plants are occasionally uprooted at spawning time, making floating aquatic plants in lieu of rooted specimens more advisable.

B: 24° to 27°C; water should be medium-hard and neutral (hardness up to 15° dGH and pH 6.5–7.5, respectively). This open spawner spawns on previously cleaned hard substrates such as rocks or roots. When the approximately 500 eggs hatch, they are placed in pits and carefully guarded and tended by the parents (primarily by the ♀).

F: O; all kinds of hardy live foods. Occasionally plant fare in the form of algae, aquatic plants, lettuce, or spinach and mixtures (beef heart, marine salmon filets) can be offered.

S: EIGENMANN (1922) placed the species into the "*atromaculatum-ornatum* group." MILLER (1966) listed it as "*incerta sedis*," that is, having an uncertain taxonomic position. BUSSING (1973) claims the Pacific Coast species "*C.*" *calobrense* and "*C.*" *altifrons* developed from the same ancestor in the middle Tertiary Period; "*C.*" *calobrense* occupies the same niche in the Atlantic tributaries, e.g., the Rio Cricamola, that its sister species "*C.*" *altifrons* occupies on the Pacific seaboard.

T: 22°–27°C, **L:** up to 25 cm, **A:** 100 cm, **R:** m, b, **D:** 2

"Cichlasoma" centrarchus
Flier cichlid

(GILL & BRANSFORD, 1877)

Syn.: *Astronotus centrarchus, Cichlasoma centrarchus, C. (Archocentrus) centrarchus, Heros centrarchus.*

Hab.: Atlantic side of Central America: from the Great Lakes in Nicaragua to the drainage basin of the Rio San Juan in Costa Rica. Tranquil or stationary water with vegetation is preferred.

F.I.: Unknown.

Sex.: There is neither sexual dimorphism nor dichromatism. ♂♂ have a slightly stouter head profile. Both sexes have elongated fins. ♀♀ remain pronouncedly smaller than ♂♂, yet still grow to a length of 15 cm.

Soc. B.: Peaceful and calm when not spawning; only aggressive towards conspecifics.

M: Keep in aquaria with vertical rock surfaces. The tank should contain a multitude of hiding places, planted sections, and areas shaded with floating plants.

B: Well-conditioned, mature ♀♀ acquire a dark coloration, whereby the entire lower body to the caudal peduncle is dark black and the dorsum has a metallic silver

Continued on p. 696.

"Cichlasoma" calobrense

"Cichlasoma" centrarchus

Fam.: Cichlidae

Cichlasoma dimerus (HECKEL, 1840)
Dimerus cichlid

Syn.: *Acara centralis, A. dimerus, Aequidens centralis, A. dimerus.*

Hab.: South America: the Rio Paraguay and the Rio Paraná systems down to Santa Fé, possibly even to Buenos Aires.

F.I.: Unknown.

Sex.: Unfortunately there are no clear sexual differences. However, ♀♀ remain smaller and their fins are not as elongated. Older ♂♂ may have a more convex forehead.

Soc. B.: Peaceful and tranquil, not even very aggressive towards conspecifics. Juveniles are more lively than adults.

M: Adaptive, robust fish which are easily cared for using moderate water values (pH ca. 7, hardness up to 20° dGH). The aquarium does not need to be large, and plants can be part of the decor. The animals quickly become tame.

B: Open spawners with a strong instinct to procreate. Frequently the animals spawn within an already present juvenile school. The juveniles will attack the eggs and larvae. The choice of partners is not crucial, and courtship is normally short. The larvae hatch after 48 hr, and the young are free-swimming after an additional 4 days. Both parents participate almost equally towards tending the eggs and young.

F: O; any usual fish food as long as it is not too small.

S: Deep-bodied fish which can only be distinguished from *Cichlasoma portalegrense* by its dentition.

T: 23°–27°C, **L:** 17 cm, **A:** from 80 cm, **R:** b, **D:** 1

"Cichlasoma" diquis BUSSING, 1974

Syn.: None.

Hab.: Central America: Costa Rica, southern slopes of the Pacific Coast, from Punta Mala to the Rio Coto Basin in the southeastern part of the country.

F.I.: 1987 by W. IHLENFELDT and H. and B. WEBER.

Sex.: The ♀ has dark regions on the dorsal fin. The intensity of these areas varies with mood, meaning they are not always prevalent.

Soc. B.: In nature it "stands" alone or in small groups of 4 to 7 fish under overhanging shore vegetation. They are highly aggressive among themselves in the aquarium. Peaceful in front of strong tankmates.

M: "C." diquis needs a large, well-subdivided aquarium with rubble, many caves, and roots. A good diet and clear, fast-flowing water produced by a strong filter are advised.

B: Has not been bred in captivity, but breeding probably follows that of *C. alfari,* a sister species from the Caribbean side of Costa Rica.

F: O; hardy foods are preferred.

S: When at ease in its environment, this species has a turquoise iridescent eye, a pink-edged operculum, and a black band that extends from eye to eye over the head to the lateral spot.

T: 25°–28°C, **L:** 20 cm, **A:** from 150 cm, **R:** b, **D:** 2–3

Cichlasoma dimerus

"Cichlasoma" diquis

Fam.: Cichlidae

"Cichlasoma" fenestratum (GÜNTHER, 1860)

Syn.: *Chromis fenestrata, Heros parma, Cichlasoma gadovii, C. sexfasciatum.*

Hab.: Central America: on the Atlantic side of southern Mexico from Veracruz to the Rio Coatzacoalcos. Found in coastal regions and inland.

F.I.: 1983 by H. G. BREIDOHR, R. STAWIKOWSKI, and U. WERNER.

Sex.: Adult ♀♀ are darker with pronounced banding and a dark area on the dorsal fin.

Soc. B.: Temperamental and energetic when young. Later, they become more sedate. A spacious environment minimizes aggressions.

M: Adaptive and robust. Water: pH ca. 7.5; hardness of 10°–20° dGH. Maintenance poses no problem when *"C."*

fenestratum is kept in a roomy aquarium that has numerous hiding places.

B: ♀♀ are sexually mature at a length of 12 cm, but ♂♂ are not sexually mature until they are 14 cm long. It likes to dig and usually spawns on oblique surfaces. Large pairs raise over 1,000 young. In comparison to fry of other open spawners, *"C." fenestratum*'s offspring are very large and robust. They can be fed sieved pond organisms a few days after becoming free-swimming.

F: O; voracious omnivores. Vegetable fare must be part of the diet. Plants in the aquarium are conditionally possible.

S: Supposedly this species was imported in 1912, but it apparently disappeared from the hobby again around 1920.

T: 25°–28°C, **L:** 30 cm, **A:** 150 cm, **R:** b, **D:** 1–2

"Cichlasoma" godmani (GÜNTHER, 1862)
Godman's cichlid

Syn.: *Astronotus godmani, Cichlaurus godmani, Cichlasoma godmani, Cichlosoma godmani, Heros godmani.*

Hab.: Central America: Belize and Guatemala, in the Moho River, Rio Cahabon, Rio Polochic, and tributaries of Lake Izabel.

F.I.: 1985 by H. G. BREIDOHR and U. WERNER.

Sex.: ♂♂ are bright red through the throat and shoulder region and iridescent blue along the posterior body. ♀♀ have more contrasting colors and a darker throat.

Soc. B.: Slightly aggressive. Young specimens prefer to school.

M: These elegant swimmers colonize clear, fast-flowing water where they either swim in the current or in deep, open waters. Behavioral parallels between *"Cichlasoma" intermedium* and this species are irrefutable. Keep in a large aquarium with plenty of free swimming space, open

hiding places, and perhaps robust plants, even though they may be eaten. A frequent water turnover and partial water changes are recommended. Water values are not particularly important. However, the pH should be above 7.5, and the hardness should be high, 10° to 20° dGH.

B: Although this species has yet to be bred in captivity, it can be assumed that it is an open spawner with reproductive behavior similar to that of *"C." intermedium*.

F: O; hardy foods and plant fare.

S: *"C." godmani* seems to be a close relative of *"C." intermedium* and *"C." microphthalmus*. Both of the latter species have a geographic distribution that adjuncts *"C." godmani*'s.

T: 26°C, **L:** ♂ ca. 25 cm, **A:** 150 cm, **R:** b, m, **D:** 1–2

"Cichlasoma" fenestratum

"Cichlasoma" godmani

"Cichlasoma" grammodes
Many-pointed cichlid

TAYLOR & MILLER, 1980

Syn.: None.

Hab.: Central America: highlands of Chiapas in southern Mexico, endemic to the Rio Grande de Chiapa Basin from Villa Flores to the Rio Lagartero in the province Huehuetenango of western Guatemala. Usually found sympatrically (in the same area) with *Paratheraps hartwegi* and *Paratheraps breidohri*.

F.I.: 1983 by H. G. BREIDOHR, R. STAWIKOWSKI, and U. WERNER.

Sex.: At 25 cm, ♂♂ are larger than ♀♀. They are also lighter, more golden, and frequently lack dark elements. Red-brown dotted scales create regular longitudinal rows. Adult ♀♀ have a uniform reticulated design formed by rust-red scale edges. The courtship coloration of ♀♀ is brown-black, interrupted by a few turquoise to green iridescent spots and a greenish area between the eyes and the mouth.

Soc. B.: Territorial and well able to defend its area. Only one pair can be kept for long periods of time.

M: In nature, this adaptive species colonizes fast-flowing waters, yet calm zones are sought for breeding. It is a benthic, shore-oriented fish that lives above hard substrates and seeks prey from its hiding place. Corresponding to large rivers, creeks, and reservoirs (Angostura Reservoir) within its natural distribution area, temperatures between 20° and 29°C are suitable. The water should be hard to very hard and alkaline (hardness of 10°–33° dGH and pH 7–9, respectively). Carbonate hardness frequently exceeds total hardness. Plants can be used.

B: ♀♀ are sexually active at a length of about 9 cm, while ♂♂ obtain maturity at a length of ca. 12 cm. Despite intense spawning activity, both sexes keep away from each other until spawning finally occurs. The species prefers to spawn on oblique substrates either under an overhang or in other secluded locals. The eggs are large for an open spawner and transparent. At 26°C, 10° dGH, and a pH of 7, the eggs need 5 days to hatch. Another 6 days and the fry become free-swimming. Until this time, the parents care for the spawn, each fulfilling its own role. The ♂ secures the territory, while the ♀ tends to the fry's immediate needs. While tending her offspring, the ♀ has a broad longitudinal stripe, a tail spot, and dark ventral fins it uses to signal and guide the young.

F: O; all normal large cichlid foods are accepted.

S: *"C."* *grammodes* hails from almost pristine fast-flowing water. In captivity it demands regular water exchanges and a frequent water turnover.

T: 25°C, **L:** up to 25 cm, **A:** 120 cm, **R:** b, **D:** 2

"Cichlasoma" guttulatum
Gold-cheeked cichlid

(GÜNTHER, 1864)

Syn.: *Heros guttulatus.*

Hab.: Central America: Mexico and Guatemala (see **S**).

F.I.: 1983 by H. G. BREIDOHR, R. STAWIKOWSKI, and U. WERNER.

Sex.: Adult ♀♀ develop a washed-out dark zone on the dorsal fin.

Soc. B.: Temperamental; aggressive behavior is indirectly proportional to the amount of living space provided.

M: Adaptive. Use moderate water values: pH over 7; hardness 10° to 20° dGH. Requires ample room and numerous hiding places.

B: Young fish 12–15 cm long readily spawn. Coloration diminishes and all light/dark contrasts become more pronounced. Open spawner. Large adults are capable of laying over 1,000 eggs!

F: O; all hardy cichlid foods; supplemental vegetable fare must be offered!

Continued on page 706.

"Cichlasoma" grammodes

"Cichlasoma" cf. *guttulatum*

"Cichlasoma" heterospilum
Candelaria cichlid

HUBBS, 1936

Syn.: None.

Hab.: Central America: Mexico, in the Rio Candelaria in the south and the Usumacinta Basin in Mexico and Guatemala. Also found in the Rio de la Pasión, its tributaries, and other habitats in Guatemala.

F.I.: 1985 by BREIDOHR and WERNER. Possibly imported before then.

Sex.: ♀♀ have an undefined spot on their dorsal fin, darker coloration and, during brood care, more contrasting colors.

Soc. B.: Deep-bodied, relatively calm and social cichlids.

M: Undemanding and adaptive. Medium-hard water suffices for both maintenance and reproduction.

B: Open spawner. Oblique or vertical surfaces are generally chosen for spawning. The eggs and resulting robust young are comparatively large. Growth is rapid.

F: O; vegetable fare. Aquatic plants are normally consumed.

S: *"C." heterospilum* was probably previously considered to be *"C." maculicauda*. However, that species has a completely different distribution area!

T: 25°–30°C, **L:** up to 25 cm, **A:** 120 cm, **R:** b, **D:** 2

"Cichlasoma" hogaboomorum
Hogaboom cichlid

CARR & GIOVANNOLI, 1950

Syn.: None.

Hab.: Central America: Honduras, in the lower Rio Choluteca.

F.I.: 1986 by BREIDOHR and WERNER.

Sex.: ♀♀ are smaller, darker, and have a highly variable spot on the dorsal fin.

Soc. B.: Temperamental, somewhat rude cichlids which are capable of confronting large fishes in an uncompromising manner.

M: Undemanding and adaptive. They can be cared for in medium-hard water under normal aquarium temperatures, even though the water values from the Rio Choluteca during the dry season are quite extreme: 5° dGH, 8° dKH, pH 8.5, temperature 30°–34°C. The aquarium should be rich in hiding places, but *sans* plants.

B: Prolific open spawners. Eggs and fry are zealously guarded.

F: O; all hardy foods are eagerly taken.

S: *"C." hogaboomorum* is not as closely related to *"C." urophthalma* as the original describer suspected. Instead, it seems to be a link between *"C." trimaculatum,* which lives further north, and the more southern *"C." labiatum/"C." citrinellum.*
"C." hogaboomorum is called "Guapotillo" in Honduras.

T: 25°–30°C, **L:** 30 cm, **A:** 150 cm, **R:** b, **D:** 2

"Cichlasoma" heterospilum

"Cichlasoma" hogaboomorum

Fam.: Cichlidae

"Cichlasoma" intermedium
Jordan's cichlid

(GÜNTHER, 1862)

Syn.: *Acara rectangularis, Astronotus intermedius, A. angulifer, A. rectangularis, Astatheros rectangularis, Cichlasoma anguliferum, C. rectangure, Cichlosoma anguliferum, C. intermedium, Cichlaurus intermedius, Heros angulifer, H. intermedius.*

Hab.: Central America: from the Rio Pichucalco/Blanco, Rio Grijalwa, and Rio Tulija Basins and the Rio Usumacinta in southern Mexico to the Rio de la Pasión Basin in Petén, Guatemala.

F.I.: 1983 by W. STAECK, L. SEEGERS, H. G. BREIDOHR, R. STAWIKOWSKI, and U. WERNER.

Sex.: Sexes are difficult to distinguish, though ♂♂ grow larger and have brighter colors. ♂ specimens from the Rio de la Pasión system in Guatemala have a reddish chest. ♀♀ can be recognized by their dark throat.

Soc. B.: Only slightly aggressive. Young and juvenile specimens tend to school.

M: These cichlids are normally found in fast-flowing clear waters over rubble or rock substrates. In contrast to other cichlids, they do not flee into hiding places, but into open or deep water instead. Suggested maintenance includes a spacious environment, strong current, frequent partial water exchanges, and a few open hiding places. While tall plants are either rare or absent in its natural habitat, they can be part of the aquarium's decor. If the diet contains sufficient vegetable fare and the plants are tough enough, these animals may leave them alone.

B: Very shy open spawners. Their timid nature means they are easily distracted from tending their brood. The ♀ plays a dominant role in caring for the eggs and newly hatched larvae; later, the ♂ joins her in guiding and defending the free-swimming young. Sexual maturity is reached at a length of 14 cm for ♀♀ and 16 cm for ♂♂. Water values are of secondary importance, though the pH should exceed 7.5 and the hardness should be between 10° and 30° dGH.

F: O; vegetable fare must be part of the diet.

S: *"C." intermedium* seems to be closely related to *"C." godmani* and *"C." microphthalmus.* Their areas of distribution abut those of *"C." intermedium.*

T: 25°–27°C, **L:** ♂ up to ca. 30 cm, **A:** 120 cm, **R:** b, m, **D:** 1–2

"Cichlasoma" intermedium, Rio Chamata

"Cichlasoma" intermedium, Rio Nototun, southern Mexico

Fam.: Cichlidae

"Cichlasoma" istlanum
Papagallo cichlid

(JORDAN & SNYDER, 1899)

Syn.: *Heros istlanus, Cichlosoma istlanum, Cichlasoma istlarius.*

Hab.: Central America: southern Mexico, in the Rio Balsas Basin and Pacific coastal rivers from Rio Armería in the state of Jalisco to the Rio Papagallo in the state of Guerrero.

F.I.: After 1980.

Sex.: ♀♀ are smaller and have pronounced contrasting colors: the body is yellowish, but the stomach is red, and the dark crossbands along the dorsum coalesce until the upper half of the body is almost totally black. ♂♂ are lighter, lack strong contrasts, and have more pronounced light blue iridescent scales.

Soc. B.: A typical representative of the *Parapetenia*. A robust, domineering fish.

M: Needs a roomy tank with many hiding places, roots, and stones. Tough plants can be used. The water should be warm, 28° to 30°C, with a pH of about 8 and a dGH and dKH of around 5°. At a length of about 7 cm, ♀♀ are sexually mature. ♂♂ are not sexually mature until they are approximately 10 cm long.

B: Courtship is initiated by the ♀. Open spawners that produce large eggs. The young are rapid growing.

F: C; hardy live, frozen, and flake foods.

S: Particularly 3–4 cm long juveniles are sensitive to intestinal parasites. Massive losses often result!

T: 27°–30°C, **L:** 20 cm, **A:** from 100 cm, **R:** b, m, **D:** 2

"Cichlasoma" labridens
Curve-bar cichlid

(PELLEGRIN, 1903)

Syn.: *Heros labridens, Cichlosoma labridens, Parapetenia labridens.*

Hab.: Central America: northern Mexico, in the entire Rio Panuco Basin.

F.I.: Probably in 1980 by Austrian aquarists.

Sex.: ♂♂ grow larger than ♀♀ and acquire more elongated dorsal and anal fins. Additionally, adult ♂♂ tend to develop a slight frontal hump, resulting in a steeper forehead.

Soc. B.: Territorial, pair-forming animals. Large specimens can be very asocial and waspish—particularly during brood care. Occasionally the animals dig extensively (pits for hatched brood). During this time plants may be uprooted.

M: Substrate of sand or gravel; caves or hiding places among rocks or roots; plants (floating plants are best).

B: 24° to 27°C; water should be medium-hard to hard (over 30° dGH) and neutral to slightly alkaline (pH 7.0–8.5). This open spawner spawns on hard, previously cleaned substrates. The 300–600 eggs and the resulting young are placed in pits where they are guarded and cared for by the ♀. The ♂ rarely directs his attention towards the eggs or the larvae Once the fry are free-swimming—approximately 8 days postspawning (27°C)—they are guarded by both parents.

F: O; all kinds of hardy live, frozen, flake, and tablet foods.

S: *"C."* *labridens* exists in a number of different color morphs. However, all forms share the contrasting checkerboardlike brood care coloration.

T: 22°–26°C, **L:** up to 25 cm, **A:** 100 cm, but larger is better, **R:** m, b, **D:** 2

"Cichlasoma" istlanum

"Cichlasoma" labridens from Tamasopo, two additional photos on the following page.

"Cichlasoma" labridens ♀

"Cichlasoma" labridens

"Cichlasoma" lyonsi   GOSSE, 1966

Syn.: None.

Hab.: Central America: southeastern Costa Rica. Supposedly inhabits the Rio Coto system and the Rio Lagarto. However, the few specimens IHLENFELDT and WEBER found in March of 1987 were exclusively from the Rio Coloradito, just north of the border of Panama.

F.I.: One animal was imported ca. 1983 by H. J. MAYLAND and P. SIEGFRIED. Seven fish were imported in 1987 by W. IHLENFELDT and H. and B. WEBER.

Sex.: ♂♂ are larger and more slender. ♀♀ have a dark zone in the anterior part of the dorsal fin.

M: In its natural biotope, it is found over sand-mud substrates that are covered in leaf litter. Hence, a sand substrate, moderate illumination, rocks, cover, and roots lend the aquarium environment a familiar and welcome air. A good current and clean water further contribute to its well-being. Excessive illumination makes *"C." lyonsi*'s colors look washed-out.

B: Open substrate spawner. Sexually mature from a length of ca. 14 cm. A pronounced stripe design appears after spawning and remains as they tend their free-swimming offspring (normally, they have a row of blue-framed black spots from the operculum to the caudal peduncle). A good diet increases the amount of red on the fins and ventral-chest area.

F: O; likes to root.

S: Very aggressive towards conspecifics in aquaria smaller than 1.20 m.

T: 25°–28°C, **L:** 30 cm, **A:** from 120 cm, **R:** b, **D:** 2–3

"Cichlasoma" macracanthum
High-spine cichlid

(GÜNTHER, 1864)

Syn.: *Cichlasoma evermanni, C. guija, C. guiza, C. meeki* (see S), *Heros heterodontus, H. macracanthus.*

Hab.: Central America: Pacific side of southern Mexico (Oaxaca, Chiapas), Guatemala, El Salvador, northwestern Honduras.

F.I.: 1983 by H. G. BREIDOHR, R. STAWIKOWSKI, and U. WERNER.

Sex.: ♂♂ grow larger and have longer fins and a more convex forehead. ♀♀ are darker, especially ventrally, and have darker crossbands.

Soc. B.: Lively, but not particularly aggressive. Although the fish often chase each other, injuries are rare.

M: A tank with a large area is particularly appropriate for these bottom-oriented fish. Numerous open but secluded hiding places are suggested. Robust plants are optional.

B: Open spawner. Offspring of this remarkably fecund species are resilient and unproblematic to raise. Due to their great capacity to adapt, they can be maintained and bred under a wide range of different water conditions. Water in its natural habitat is generally soft to medium-hard (2°–10° dGH) with a pH greater than 7.5.

F: O; prefers to feed off the bottom.

S: In 1925 HILDEBRAND gave *"C." macracanthum* the invalid name *C. meeki,* the scientific nomen for the firemouth. The present day scientific name for the firemouth is *Thorichthys meeki.*

T: 25°–28°C, **L:** 25 cm, **A:** 120 cm, **R:** b, **D:** 1–2

"Cichlasoma" microphthalmus

(GÜNTHER, 1862)

Syn.: *Heros microphthalmus, H. oblongus, Cichlasoma guentheri, C. milleri, C. coeruleogula, Astronotus microphthalmus, Cichlaurus microphthalmus, Astatheros oblongus, Chuco milleri.*

Hab.: Central America: Guatemala, in the Rio Motagua Basin, Lake Amatitlan, and small Atlantic seaboard rivers; Honduras, in tributaries of the Motagua River.

F.I.: Spring of 1985 by BREIDOHR and WERNER.

Sex.: ♂♂ are larger, more colorful, and develop a convex forehead as they age. ♀♀ have a more contrasting design.

Soc. B.: These temperamental, active fish are not particularly aggressive, which allows a group of adult specimens to be kept in spacious tanks.

M: *"Cichlasoma" microphthalmus* hails from clear, alkaline (pH ca. 8), fast-flowing water of moderate hardness (ca. 10° dGH). Besides hiding places and territorial delimiters in the form of bogwood and rocks, the fish need plenty of free swimming space. Since these cichlids relish tender plants, greenery is best avoided.

B: Open spawner. It seems that this species requires 2 years to attain sexual maturity. The large eggs hatch after 4–5 days (depending on water temperature), and the fry are free-swimming nine to ten days later. *Artemia* nauplii make an appropriate first food.

F: O; omnivore. Easily handles larger foods.

S: FOWLER (1935) seems to have confused the species with *"Cichlasoma" guttulatum.*

T: 22°–28°C, **L:** 25 cm, **A:** 120–140 cm, **R:** b, m, **D:** 2

"Cichlasoma" macracanthum ♂

"Cichlasoma" microphthalmus

Fam.: Cichlidae

"Cichlasoma" motaguense (GÜNTHER, 1869)
Motaguense

Syn.: *Heros motaguensis, Astronotus motaguensis, Cichlosoma motaguense, Parapetenia motaguensis.*

Hab.: Central America: Guatemala, Rio Motagua and its tributaries; Honduras and El Salvador, in rivers of the Atlantic seaboard.

F.I.: 1986 by BREIDOHR and WERNER.

Sex.: Clear sexual dichromatism: ♂♂ are lighter and greener with spots on the opercula. ♀♀ are generally redder with solid orange-red opercula.

Soc. B.: This peaceful but forceful "Guapote" stands its ground without compromise. It establishes a large territory. Paired specimens generally stay together exemplarily in the aquarium, even outside times of sexual activity.

M: Undemanding and adapting. Maintain in large roomy aquaria that have rocks and roots. Since the animals frequently dig, omit vegetation from the tank's decor.

B: Open spawner. ♀♀ play the dominant role in tending the more than 2,000 eggs. The offspring are guarded in a pit until they are free-swimming. At that time both parents guide the school of young.

F: O; voracious omnivores. Large foods are required.

S: *"C." motaguense* is the most beautiful "Guapote."

T: 25°–30°C, **L:** 30 cm and more, **A:** 150 cm, **R:** b, **D:** 3

"Cichlasoma" ornatum (REGAN, 1905)
Esmeraldas cichlid

Syn.: *Cichlosoma ornatum, Cichlaurus ornatum.*

Hab.: South America. Described from the Rio Durango (Esmeraldas system) at the town of San Javier in northwestern Ecuador, but probably also found in the southwest Colombian tributaries of the Rio Esmeraldas.

F.I.: 1987 by aquarists from the Netherlands.

Sex.: Unknown.

Soc. B.: Comparatively tranquil, peaceful cichlids which neither dig extensively nor eat plants. (This information is based on young specimens with a maximum length of 14 cm on the verge of sexual maturity.)

M: Keep in roomy tanks that have hiding places and a good water turnover. Water values are of secondary importance as long as the pH is 7 or slightly above and extreme hardness is avoided.

B: There is no information concerning successfully breeding this fish in captivity, though it can be assumed that it is an open spawner with a nuclear family structure.

F: Commonly accepts any cichlid food.

S: EIGENMANN described the subspecies *"C." ornatum gephyrum* in 1924, which reputedly comes from the Rio San Juan and the Rio Dagua in western Colombia. It may be a hybrid of *"C." ornatum* and *"C." atromaculatum.*

T: 24°–27°C, **L:** unknown, probably 20 cm and more, **A:** from 120 cm, **R:** b, m, **D:** 2

"*Cichlasoma*" *motaguense*

"*Cichlasoma*" *ornatum*

Fam.: Cichlidae

"Cichlasoma" panamense
Panama cichlid

(MEEK & HILDEBRAND, 1913)

Syn.: *Neetroplus panamensis.*

Hab.: Central America: Panama. Two different populations have been imported, a reddish Atlantic population and a brownish form from the Pacific seaboard. The former is found in the Rio Chagres system and other systems, while the latter inhabits the Rio Chepo and the Rio Tuira systems.

F.I.: Both populations were first imported in the '80's.

Sex.: Adult ♀♀ are smaller than ♂♂ and have a dark area on their dorsal fin.

Soc. B.: Despite its moderate size and relatively peaceful nature as a juvenile, mature *"C". panamense* turn feisty when defending their brood.

M: Due to tidal influences in its natural habitat, "C." panamense must be capable of adapting to rapid changes in water parameters; pH 6.8–7.7; 4°–18° dGH; 4°–26° dKH. All types of plants are a welcome part of the decoration.

B: Sexually mature at a length of 5–6 cm. A large number of animals converge in colonylike fashion along the shores of rocky rivers to spawn. There the eggs are laid in caves. The ♀ plays a dominant role in brood care until the fry are free-swimming. At that time the ♂ shares the responsibility for the offspring by helping to guide them. When either parent—or the two—is tending the brood, contrasting brood care coloration is adopted.

F: C; small live, frozen, and flake foods.

S: The 6 to 9 largest teeth of the Panama cichlid are incisor-shaped, a distinctive feature of this species.
Juveniles seem to be particularly delicate.

T: 23°–26°C, **L:** 15 cm, **A:** 80 cm, **R:** b, **D:** 3–4

"Cichlasoma" panamense, red morph

"Cichlasoma" panamense, brownish morph, nuptial coloration.

Fam.: Cichlidae

"Cichlasoma" pantostictum　　　TAYLOR & MILLER, 1983

Syn.: None.

Hab.: Central America: northern Mexico on the Atlantic seaboard in the Rio Panuco Basin. It is said to primarily inhabit brackish coastal lagoons south to the Laguna de Tamiahua.

F.I.: Has not been imported alive.

Sex.: Unknown.

Soc. B.: Behavior should be similar to its sister species *"C." labridens.* It can be assumed that *"C." pantostictum* is particularly hostile towards conspecifics.

M: Large tanks with plenty of hiding places facilitate maintenance. The water should be hard and alkaline (pH ≥7.5). Add sea salt.

B: That *"C." pantostictum* is an open spawner with highly contrasting brood care coloration is a reasonable conjecture.

F: C; feed hardy foods of animal origin.

T: 23°–26°C, **L:** possibly 20 cm and more, **A:** 120–150 cm, **R:** b, m, **D:** 2

Vieja regani
Regan's cichlid　　　(MILLER, 1974)

Syn.: *"Cichlasoma" regani.*

Hab.: Central America: southern Mexico, endemic to the upper region of the Coatzcoalcos (Rio Almoloya, Rio Malatengo, Rio de Sarabia).

F.I.: Probably in 1985 by J. ENDRES.

Sex.: ♀♀ are smaller. ♂♂ are probably more colorful (lighter, more golden).

Soc. B.: Relatively peaceful cichlids, though prone to mercurial movements and intraspecific pursuits without express aggressiveness. (This information is based on specimens with a maximum length of 14 cm.)

M: Proper nitrogen cycle management must be observed in sight of its riverine environment in nature. Water quality aside, requirements are minimal. Moderate water conditions are appropriate. Ample space and hiding places are appreciated.

B: Open spawner. According to observations in nature, the ♀ plays a dominant role in caring for the offspring. Very fertile animals.

F: O; voracious omnivore. When the diet lacks the required plant fare, tender plant shoots are eaten.

S: Even within its limited distribution area, this cichlid is far from common.

T: 24°–27°C, **L:** ♂ up to 25 cm (?), ♀ somewhat smaller, **A:** 150 cm, **R:** b, m, **D:** 1–2

"Cichlasoma" pantostictum ♂

Vieja regani

Fam.: Cichlidae

"Cichlasoma" robertsoni
Robertson's cichlid

(REGAN, 1905)

Syn.: *Cichlosoma robertsoni, Astatheros robertsoni, Heros robertsoni, Cichlasoma acutum, Chuco acutum.*

Hab.: Central America: southern Mexico, in the Rio Pichucalco; Honduras, in the Departamento de Colóu and along the lowlands of the Atlantic seaboard.

F.I.: 1983 by BREIDOHR, STAWI-KOWSKI, and WERNER.

Sex.: ♂♂ grow larger and have more iridescent dots. ♀♀ have extensive dark zones on the dorsal fin; however, they are not always discernible.

Soc. B.: Territorial. Robust fish that are occasionally aggressive. Nuclear family with extensive brood care. Like *Geophagus*, this species roots in the substrate, sometimes damaging plants.

M: Good water quality, an open swimming area combined with secluded areas among rocks, roots, and robust plants, and a fine-grained gravel substrate meet its requirements.

B: 24° to 28°C. Open spawners that lay up to 400 eggs. Larvae are placed in pre-dug pits. Classified as exemplary parents which is further demonstrated by their bellicose behavior towards tankmates while engaged in custodial duties.

F: C; large live foods and flake and frozen foods. They masticate the substrate, searching for edible detritus.

S: Especially attractive when sexually active. At that time it has pronounced vertical crossbands and intense iridescent blue tones that contrast nicely with its golden body.

T: 22°–26°C, **L:** 20 cm, **A:** from 120 cm, **R:** b, **D:** 2–3

"Cichlasoma" rostratum

(GILL & BRANSFORD, 1877)

Syn.: *Heros rostratus, Astatheros rostratum, Astronotus rostratum, Cichlosoma rostratum.*

Hab.: Central America: Atlantic seaboard from Nicaragua to northern Costa Rica, in Lakes Managua, Nicaragua, Masaya and their effluent and affluent waters as well as the Rio Matina system and coastal tributaries of the Rio San Juan. Not very numerous in any of its habitats.

F.I.: Probably imported for the first time in 1987 by Willem HEIJNS (Holland) through the United States to Germany.

Sex.: There are no pronounced secondary sexual characteristics. ♂♂ grow larger than ♀♀, and their fins have brighter dots.

Soc. B.: Acclimated specimens appear tame and tranquil; alarmed specimens are quick to flee. Largely retiring and peaceful. Even intraspecific quarrels normally do not result in injuries.

M: The aquarium should have a large surface area, a few secluded sites, and many open areas with loose, smooth-edged gravel or sand. Like *Geophagus*, sieving the substrate in search of edibles is part of their natural behavior.

B: "*C.*" *rostratum* is an open spawner. Small, numerous eggs are laid. Nuclear family.

F: C, O; detritus and aquatic insect larvae are consumed in its natural habitat. They will accept all normal cichlid foods in the aquarium, chiefly worms and meat (beef heart).

S: Its shape, bottom-oriented life, and feeding behavior are similar to South American *Geophagus*.

T: 25°–28°C, **L:** ♂ up to 24 cm, ♀ somewhat smaller, **A:** from 120 cm, **R:** b, **D:** 2

"Cichlasoma" robertsoni ♂

"Cichlasoma" rostratum

Lake Edward harbors numerous aquaristically suitable and colorful *Haplochromis* species. They support much of the bird life. Note the mountains of Zaïre in the background.

Top photo on facing page:
A swiftly flowing river from the Ruwenzori Mountains in Uganda, home of *Hypsopanchax modestus* and barbs.

The Ruaha is one of the largest rivers in Tanzania.

"Cichlasoma" sp. "Usumacinta"

Syn.: None, since it is an undescribed species.

Hab.: Central America: southern Mexico and Guatemala, from the western Grijalva drainage (at the town of Pichucalco) to the eastern Usumacinta Basin (Rio Subin).

F.I.: Two or three specimens reached Germany at the end of 1985 through a Belgian importer.

Sex.: The sexes seem to be difficult to distinguish. ♂ ♂ grow larger and develop a conspicuous cephalic hump with age. Sexually active ♀ ♀ may have black areas on the dorsal fin.

Soc. B.: The only observations available are based on a single ♂ specimen which proved to be very peaceful towards heterospecific fishes (cichlids).

M: *"C."* sp. "Usumacinta" lives in slightly alkaline, medium-hard waters of riverine habitats in Mexico and Guatemala. In captivity, it adapts to various water conditions (pH over 7.5, 15° to 20° dGH). Maintain at temperatures of 24° to 28°C. Offer an open area for swimming as well as some cover (roots). While other Central American cichlids make good tankmates, choose those that are different in regard to body shape and coloration. Large catfishes such as loricariids can be included in the community.

B: While there is no direct information available concerning captive breeding, it is assumed to be similar to its close relatives (e.g., *"Cichlasoma" synspilus,* *"Cichlasoma" maculicauda,* and *"Cichlasoma" bifasciatum*).

F: O; include vegetable fare in its diet.

S: This undescribed species seems to be a very close relative of *"Cichlasoma" regani,* as implied by its coloration and design. *"Cichlasoma" regani* is endemic to the Coatzacoalcos drainage, a region that abuts the western edge of *"C."* sp. "Usumacinta"'s distribution.

T: 24°–28°C, **L:** ca. 25 cm, **A:** 150 cm, **R:** b, m, **D:** 2

"Cichlasoma" sp. "Usumacinta"

"Cichlasoma" sp., green cichlid from panama

Fam.: Cichlidae

"Cichlasoma" steindachneri

JORDAN & SNYDER, 1899

Syn.: *Cichlosoma steindachneri, Parapetenia steindachneri.*

Hab.: Central America: northern Mexico, in certain rivers of the Panuco drainage of the Atlantic seaboard (Rio Tamasopo, Rio Gallinas, and Rio Ojo Frío).

F.I.: Has not been imported alive.

Sex.: Unknown.

Soc. B.: Unknown, but probably similar to *"C." labridens* and *"C." bartoni*; that is, they are aggressive, particularly towards conspecifics.

M: Keep in roomy aquaria that have many hiding places. Hard water with a pH above 7.5 is suggested. Since the animals live in flowing water, a frequent water turnover and regular partial water exchanges are necessary.

B: It can be assumed that *"C." steindachneri* is an open spawner with distinctive brood care coloration.

F: Hardy animal-based foods should be fed, e.g., beef heart, mosquito larvae, shrimp, and *Mysis*.

S: Note the long, pointed head and the protruding lower mandible.

T: 23°–26°C, **L:** ♂ 20 cm, perhaps somewhat more, **A:** 120–150 cm, **R:** b, m, **D:** 2

Cichlasoma taenia

(BENNET, 1830)

Syn.: *Chromis taenia, Acara taenia, Cychlasoma taenia.*

Hab.: Northern South America: Trinidad Island (on the eastern and western side) and Venezuela, in the Rio Guarapiche in the Orinoco Basin.

F.I.: Unknown; it may have been imported previously as *"Aequidens."* Animals with reliable habitat information reached Germany in 1987.

Sex.: There is neither sexual dimorphism nor dichromatism.

Soc. B.: Tranquil and peaceful. Very tame and often sexually active.

M: Even small aquaria with vegetation are suitable. Besides a few secluded areas (roots and rocks), provide an open space with a flat stone in the center as a spawning substrate.

B: Considered easy to breed. They are very adaptable and spawn in moderately hard, neutral water without further ado. Open spawners. Reliable parenting can be expected throughout all phases of brood care.

F: All normal cichlid foods are accepted.

S: *C. taenia* is a particularly elongated species with a short head, four anal fin rays, and a pronounced longitudinal line along its body.

T: 24°–27°C, **L:** ♂ max. 14 cm, ♀ somewhat smaller, **A:** from 70 cm, **R:** b, m, **D:** 2

"Cichlasoma" steindachneri, WC, Tamasopo, Mexico

Cichlasoma taenia, Trinidad

Fam.: Cichlidae

"Cichlasoma" tuba

MEEK, 1912

Syn.: *Heros tuba, Tomocichla underwoodi*.

Hab.: Central America: Atlantic seaboard of Costa Rica, e.g., Rio Barbilla, Rio Sucio.

F.I.: 1982 by T. SCHULZ (see DATZ).

Sex.: The ♂ grows larger, whereas the ♀ has a dark zone on the dorsal fin and a slightly more compact body.

Soc. B.: This very active, swift, and elegant fish lives either singly or in loose groups. At spawning time, pairs form and leave the group. Juveniles can be found during the dry season from January to April.

M: The tank must be at least 1.80 m long to comfortably house these large active animals. Strong filtration and crystal clear water are required. Water values in nature are as follows: 2°–4° dGH, up to 7° dKH, 24°–30°C. Feeds on aufwuchs, small crustacea, plants, and fruits. Avoid difficult to digest foods such as beef heart, bloodworms, or *Tubifex*.

B: Open, substrate spawner. Keep a group until two specimens pair off. Offer pebbles as spawning substrates. Parents develop a beautiful mask after spawning and which persists until brood care is terminated.

F: O; *Daphnia*, aufwuchs, vegetable fare, shrimp, *Gammarus*, fruit, glassworms, krill, and tablet foods.

S: Sensitive to dissolved metabolites.

T: 24°–30°C, **L**: 35 cm, **A**: 180 cm, **R**: all, **D**: 3

"Cichlasoma" tuyrense
Tuyre cichlid

MEEK & HILDEBRAND, 1913

Syn.: *Astatheros tuyrensis, Heros margaritifer* var. STEINDACHNER, 1879.

Hab.: Central America: Panama, endemic to the Rio Bayano and the Rio Tuyra Basin.

F.I.: After 1980.

Sex.: ♀♀ are generally darker, smaller, with an undefined spot or a dark zone on the dorsal fin. ♂♂ have a nuchal hump.

Soc. B.: Confident, yet comparatively peaceful and retiring.

M: *"C."* tuyrense requires warm, medium-hard water, a sandy substrate, and opportunities for concealment. Plants will be eaten.

B: Open spawner. In captivity, two years are needed to reach sexual maturity. Not trustworthy parents. During brood care, ♀♀ display a contrasting stripe design.

F: O; the diet must include vegetable components.

S: None.

T: 25°–30°C, **L**: up to 25 cm, **A**: 150 cm, **R**: b, m, **D**: 4

"Cichlasoma" tuba

"Cichlasoma" tuyrense

Crenicichla anthurus

COPE, 1872

Syn.: *Crenicichla lucius.*

Hab.: South America: Ecuador and Peru, on the eastern side of the Andes in the Rio Aguarico, Rio Ucayali, Huallaga, Putumayo, and the Amazon and its tributaries.

F.I.: 1985 by MINDE, KRANZ, STAWIKOWSKI, and WERNER.

Sex.: ♀♀ have a red ventral area and an evident fringe on the dorsal fin. They do not have iridescent spots on their sides and fins. Those markings are exclusively found on ♂♂.

M: Requires a spacious tank, plants, shelters in the form of flat rock edifications and roots, and soft to medium-hard water.

B: Cave spawner. As for other pike cichlids from this group, courtship is initiated by the ♀. Their numerous whitish eggs are attached by their pole. Brood care—guarding and fanning—is mainly the responsibility of the ♀. Rearing the young is easy.

F: C; hardy live and frozen foods.

S: *C. anthurus* was considered to be a synonym of *C. lucius* COPE, 1870 until KULLANDER (1986) classified it as an autonomous species. *C. anthurus*'s shoulder spot is framed in a light color, whereas *C. lucius*'s shoulder spot is not outlined.

T: 25°–27°C, **L:** up to 25 cm, **A:** from 120 cm, **R:** b, m, **D:** 3

Crenicichla saxatilis
White-spotted pike cichlid

(LINNAEUS, 1758)

Syn.: *Sparus saxatilis, Scarus rufescens, S. pavonius, Cychla rutilans, Crenicichla vaillanti.*

Hab.: South America: Suriname. According to the latest information by PLOEG, it is only found in Carolina Creek, a tributary of the Para River in the Suriname River Basin.

F.I.: Not known.

Sex.: ♂♂ are larger with many silver spots along the flanks. The caudal and shoulder spots are delineated in silver. While ♀♀ have several conspicuous ocelli on the dorsal fin and a small caudal spot, they do not have any silver spots.

Soc. B.: Hostile towards conspecifics. In the long run, only one harmonizing pair can be kept in the tank. Fishes too large to swallow are not molested.

M: The aquarium should be as large as possible with various hiding places among rocks and roots incorporated into the decor. Vegetation is ignored. Roomy caves are eagerly used. The water should have moderate values: pH around 7.0; hardness of 10° dGH.

B: The ♀ curves her body into an "S" to entice the ♂ to breed. The large, whitish eggs are attached by their poles to the ceiling of a cave. After 4–6 days the eggs hatch. In another 5 days the fry are free-swimming. During this time the ♀ tends to direct brood care, while the ♂ defends the territory. After the fry are mobile, direct brood care is shared.

F: C; hardy live and frozen foods. With some patience, these animals can also be trained to accept tablets.

S: The lunar-shaped shoulder spot is a good identifying mark.

T: 25°–30°C, **L:** around 25 cm, **A:** 150 cm, **R:** b, **D:** 3

Crenicichla anthurus

Crenicichla saxatilis

Ctenochromis horei (GÜNTHER, 1893)
Red-spotted mouthbrooder, spothead hap

Syn.: *Chromis horei, Haplochromis horei, Tilapia rubropunctata, Tilapia horei.*

Hab.: Africa: Lake Tanganyika in shallow water above sandy substrates and vegetation.

F.I.: Unknown.

Sex.: ♂♂ are much more colorful than the gray ♀♀.

Soc. B.: Their extremely bellicose nature is matched by few species. Whether it can be housed with other species depends upon tank size, the number of shelters, and the size of the intended tankmates (the larger the better).

M: In sight of the highly aggressive personality of ♂♂, several ♀♀, numerous territories with visual delimiters, and shelters are vital. A sandy substrate is recommended, since the animals like to search for food therein.

B: Probably not overly difficult. Maternal mouthbrooders.

F: O; due to its size, only large foods are suitable for adults. Large crustacea, which can be chopped for smaller specimens, are an appropriate food.

S: Their constant movement, contrasting coloration, and yellow hues make them an eye catcher in large aquaria. Small or delicate fishes would be totally inappropriate tankmates.

T: 24°–26°C, L: 18 cm, A: 150 cm, R: m, b, D: 3–4 (aggressive)

Ctenochromis polli (THYS, 1964)

Syn.: *Haplochromis polli.*

Hab.: Africa: Zaïre, in the lower courses of the Congo around Kinshasa.

F.I.: Unknown.

Sex.: ♂♂ are larger than ♀♀ and usually have a steeper cranial profile. Unlike ♀♀, ♂♂ have a single egg spot on the anal fin and dark carmine scales between the ventral fins and the operculum.

Soc. B.: ♂♂ are very aggressive towards ♀♀ and subdominant ♂♂. They can be kept in community with other fishes as long as the tank is heavily decorated and includes shelters. Heterospecific fishes are rarely bothered.

M: The shallow pits they excavate for breeding do not disturb plants. They are not particular in regard to water composition, even breeding in normal tap water. The size of their captive habitat should be in accordance to the number of specimens.

B: Mouthbrooder, maternal family. The ♂♂ make shallow depressions and entice the ♀♀ to spawn therein. After about 30 days at a temperature of 26°C, the young are released from the mouth for the first time. Care is not terminated at this point, however. The offspring continue to be readmitted to the buccal cavity during danger. Offspring are sexually mature at a length of 3 to 4 cm.

F: C; live foods are preferred, but dry commercial foods are not refused.

S: *C. polli* is not very colorful.

T: 24°–26°C, L: 11.5 cm, A: from 50 cm, R: b, m, D: 2

Ctenochromis horei ♂

Ctenochromis polli

Fam.: Cichlidae

Cyathopharynx furcifer
Furcifer

(BOULENGER, 1898)

Syn.: *Paratilapia furcifer, Ectodus foae, Ophthalmotilapia foae, Tilapia grandoculis, Cyathopharynx grandoculis.*

Hab.: Africa: Tanzania, in Lake Tanganyika. While *C. furcifer* is endemic throughout the lake, this particular morph is from Karilani.

F.I.: 1984 by H. W. DIECKHOFF.

Sex.: ♂ ♂ are metallic gold with very long ventral fins; ♀ ♀ are silver with abbreviated ventral fins.

Soc. B.: ♂ ♂ form breeding colonies of so-called sand nests (50–60 cm diameter). ♀ ♀ live in groups.

M: Needs a spacious tank with a sand substrate and rock edifications. The water should be medium-hard to hard and alkaline (hardness 10°–20° dGH and a pH of 7.8–8.5, respectively).

B: Maternal mouthbrooder. Young are released from the ♀'s buccal cavity after about 3 weeks (see Vol. 2, p. 888).

F: C, O; acclimated fish accept live foods such as mosquito larvae and small crustacea as well as dry foods.

S: These animals are very sensitive to helminthic and bacterial diseases. ♀ ♀ of the various color morphs are difficult to distinguish. See Vol. 2, p. 888.

T: 24°–26°C, **L:** 20 cm, **A:** 120 cm, **R:** b, m, **D:** 3

Cyprichromis microlepidotus
Smallscale slender cichlid

(POLL, 1956)

Syn.: *Limnochromis microlepidotus.*

Hab.: Africa: endemic to Lake Tanganyika. Found in the open water of the rocky littoral zone.

F.I.: Unknown.

Sex.: ♂ ♂ are typically larger with dark dorsal and anal fins and a black-blue or yellow caudal fin.

Soc. B.: Occasional intraspecific aggressions and fights occur, though they do not result in injuries. Agamic mouthbrooder. They live in large aggregations.

M: Sufficient swimming space must be offered. If possible, maintain a group of 10 or more fish. Plants are ignored. Cover the aquarium well, since the species is a precise jumper.

B: Water for breeding should be temperate, medium-hard, and neutral to slightly alkaline (25°–28°C, 10°–15° dGH, and pH 7–8.5, respectively). Agamic, open spawning mouthbrooder. The ♀ releases the eggs into the open water. They are immediately fertilized and then taken into the ♀'s buccal cavity. Not a prolific species—only 5 to 10 fry are produced. Brood care lasts for about 3 weeks.

F: C; large and small live and frozen *Artemia* as well as flake foods. Zooplanktivores feeder.

S: The species occurs in two color morphs, a yellow-tailed population—pictured here—and a blue-tailed population. *Cyprichromis* species occasionally loose their sight in aquaria, probably as a result of a dietary and/or water problem. See Vol. 2, p. 890.

T: 23°–28°C, **L:** 11 cm, **A:** 120 cm, **R:** t, **D:** 4

Cyathopharynx furcifer, "Karilani," see p. 781

Cyprichromis microlepidotus

Fam.: Cichlidae

Ectodus descampsi
Descamp's strange-tooth

BOULENGER, 1898

Syn.: *Pelmatochromis stappersii, Callochromis stappersii.*

Hab.: Africa: endemic to Lake Tanganyika. Primarily found in open waters of the sandy littoral zone.

F.I.: 1985 by C. J. Aquarium.

Sex.: The ♀'s blue and black oval spot on the dorsal fin is said to be smaller than the ♂'s.

Soc. B.: This peaceful schooling fish is an uncommon aquarium fish. Like most other fish from the open water or sand zone, they are apt tankmates for fishes with comparable requirements, e.g., cichlids. Gregarious—even in large aquaria they try to huddle close to similar species.

M: Its social nature demands a group of at least 10 specimens of this or a similar

species. The need for a large group of animals and their active mode of swimming make a large aquarium a necessity. Use a sand substrate and place rock edifications along the fringes. Plants are optional and of subordinate importance.

B: Only scattered observations have been made on its reproductive biology. Maternal mouthbrooders. The ♀ bears full responsibility for the eggs and fry. Spawning occurs in small sand craters that are dug by sexually active ♂♂.

F: O; their small mouth limits their diet to small and moderate-sized foods. Insect larvae, *Daphnia*, and small frozen foods as well as flake foods are eaten.

T: 24°–26°C, **L:** 10 cm, **A:** 100 cm, **R:** all, **D:** 2

Enantiopus melanogenys
Black-chinned xenotilapia

(BOULENGER, 1898)

Syn.: *Ectodus longianalis, E. melanogenys, Enantiopus longianalis.*

Hab.: Africa: colonizes sandy littoral zones of Lake Tanganyika to a depth of 40 m.

F.I.: 1985 by C. J. Aquarium, Schnathorst, Germany.

Sex.: ♂♂ are colorful with pointed dorsal and anal fins, while ♀♀ are a drab beige-gray with rounded dorsal and anal fins.

Soc. B.: ♂♂ establish and defend spawning territories, though there are no strong hostilities against conspecifics. Agamic mouthbrooder, maternal family.

M: The two most important factors for successful maintenance are a roomy aquarium and a substrate of fine river sand. By decorating the aquarium with rock, several spawning territories can be established. Other cichlids from the

sandy littoral zone make appropriate tankmates. Prone to transport injures. Water: pH 7.5–8.5; hardness up to 20° dGH.

B: At spawning time, ♂♂ dig large, shallow depressions in the sand. The ♀ is enticed to join him, and they swim in circles above the depression. Before the ♀ takes the eggs in her mouth, the ♂ fertilizes the spawn. The 20 days of brood care are the sole responsibility of the ♀.

F: O; voracious omnivore which particularly appreciates foods it finds on the substrate.

S: In contrast to *Xenotilapia* species, this species only has two lateral lines. Avoid housing with nocturnal catfishes. Easily startled by sudden movements outside the aquarium.

T: 28°C. **L:** 16 cm, **A:** 150 cm, **R:** b, m, **D:** 4

Ectodus descampsi

Enantiopus melanogenys

Vallisneria spiralis var. *denseserrulata* grows along the substrate of the sandy littoral zone of Lake Malawi (comparable to seaweed in the ocean).

Enantiopus ochrogenys
Red-striped xenotilapia

BOULENGER, 1914

Syn.: *Xenotilapia achrogenys, Stappersetta singularis, Stappersia singularis.*

Hab.: Africa: endemic to Lake Tanganyika. Found in small groups along the sandy littoral zones.

F.I.: Around 1984.

Sex.: ♂♂ generally have an elongated dorsal fin and brighter colors.

Soc. B.: Only slightly aggressive. Kept in groups. Territorial at spawning time. Mouthbrooder, maternal family.

M: Nonproblematic when the tank exceeds 1 m in length. A sandy substrate is necessary, as it allows the fish to root. The water should be clear and clean with a pH above 7 and a hardness over 10° dGH .

B: *E. ochrogenys* has been successfully spawned in captivity. The animals excavate large, shallow craters in the sandy substrate. The ♂ then entices the

♀ to the depression with his shivering body. The ♀ lays the eggs and immediately takes them into her mouth. It is unknown whether the eggs are fertilized before or after they are taken into her mouth.

F: O; all kinds of live foods. These hardy eaters readily accept flake foods.

S: *E. ochrygenys bathyphilus* POLL, 1956 was described, but today it is acknowledged as being an independent species (*E. bathyphilus*).

T: 24°–26°C, **L:** 11 cm, **A:** from 100 cm, **R:** b, **D:** 3–4

Fam.: Cichlidae

Geophagus sp.

Hab.: South America: Venezuela, so far only found in two locals, both of which are in the Orinoco Basin: the Rio Catanapo near Raudales of Atures at Puerto Ayacucho in the Territorio Federal Amazonas and in the Rio Caroni at Caruachi near the city of Guayana in the state of Bolivar.

F.I.: The first specimens appeared at the end of the '70's in import shipments of unknown origin from South America.

Sex.: Unknown. ♂♂ probably grow larger and have longer ventral and unpaired fins than their consorts.

Soc. B.: Vivacious in captive environments. Aggressive among themselves; ♂♂ are especially inclined to display and participate in frontal threat actions which eventually end in jaw locking.

M: According to the limited available information, this Geophagus prefers clear, oxygen-rich water. Moderate temperatures suffice. Slightly acid to neutral water (pH 6–7) is probably more appreciated than alkaline water; hardness should be less than 20° dGH. The aquarium should have both free swimming space and concealed private areas (bogwood, plants). Other Geophagus, triangle cichlids (Uaru), catfishes, characins, and other peaceful species are judged appropriate tankmates.

B: Unsuccessful to date. Probably mouthbrooders like all Geophagus species that have been bred. Whether it is an ovophile or a larvophile mouthbrooder has yet to be determined.

F: O; undemanding, but large foodstuffs are unacceptable.

S: A few years ago, specimens of an additional undescribed Geophagus of unknown origin were imported. They were very similar to this fish—probably a close relative.

T: 22°–26°C, **L:** ca. 20 cm, **A:** 100 cm, **R:** b, m, **D:** 3

"Geophagus" crassilabris
Thick-lipped eartheater

STEINDACHNER, 1877

Syn.: Satanoperca crassilabris.

Hab.: Central America: Panama.

F.I.: Unknown.

Sex.: Sexual dichromatism and dimorphism, as ♂♂ clearly grow larger than ♀♀.

Soc. B.: A relatively social species without particularly pronounced territorial demands. Even several ♂♂ can be kept in one tank.

M: Depending on the number of species to be maintained, a large aquarium should be chosen. Bogwood, plants, and rocks can be used as decorations. Use a sand substrate to allow the fish to root as it searches for edibles.

B: As for "Geophagus" steindachneri.

F: O; vegetable fare and all normal cichlid foods.

S: Half-grown animals are very similar to "Geophagus" steindachneri. Only full-grown ♂♂ have enlarged lips, a primary difference between the two species.

♀

T: 25°–30°C, **L:** 15 cm, **A:** from 80 cm, **R:** m, b, **D:** 2–3

Geophagus sp.

"Geophagus" crassilabris ♂

Gnathochromis pfefferi
Tanganyika hap

(BOULENGER, 1898)

Syn.: *Paratilapia pfefferi, Haplochromis pfefferi, Limnochromis pfefferi.*

Hab.: Africa: endemic to Lake Tanganyika.

F.I.: Not known.

Sex.: Unlike ♀♀, ♂♂ have several orange dots on the opercula, egg spots on the anal fin, and black-rayed caudal and ventral fins.

Soc. B.: Similar to *Astatotilapia* or *Limnochromis* species. Territorial and aggressive when spawning. Ovophile mouthbrooder, maternal family.

M: As for *Astatotilapia brownae*. Like other fishes from Lake Tanganyika, this cichlid needs hard, alkaline water (10°–18° dGH, pH 7.5–8.5).

B: Has been successfully bred in captivity. Its reproductive biology is similar

to that of *Astatotilapia* species. Buccal incubation takes about 3 weeks. When released, the fry are about 1 cm long and can feed on any food of suitable size.

F: C, O; live, frozen, and freeze-dried fare. They can be trained to flake foods.

S: Two species are classified under the genus *Gnathochromis*, which was established by POLL in 1981. *Gnathochromis* and *Limnochromis* are close relatives. There are two anatomical differences, however, that distinguish the two: *Gnathochromis* has a longer snout, and its maxillary bone extends below the eye.

T: 24°–26°C, **L:** 12 cm, **A:** 80 cm, **R:** m, b, **D:** 2–3

"Haplochromis" ahli = *Sciaenochromis ahli*
Electric blue hap

(TREWAVAS, 1935)

Syn.: *Haplochromis serranoides* AHL, 1927. While not a synonym of *"H." ahli,* there was initial confusion between *Haplochromis jacksoni* and this species.

Hab.: Africa: various rocky coastal regions of Lake Malawi.

F.I.: Around 1979.

Sex.: Pronounced sexual dichromatism in mature animals. Sexual differentiation is more confounding in half-grown specimens because immature ♂♂ are the same color as ♀♀.

Soc. B.: Not considered particularly aggressive in front of other Lake Malawi cichlids. However, that does not signify that *S. ahli* is a suitable tankmate for smaller fishes. In nature, its diet is largely based on fry.

M: If possible, with other Lake Malawi cichlids in a roomy aquarium with many rock edifications. Ambivalent towards

plants—they are neither molested nor appreciated. A sandy substrate is recommended to ease waste removal and prevent food from rotting between crevices.

B: Since the eggs are fertilized in the ♀'s mouth, this species is deemed a highly specialized mouthbrooder. After the young are released, they are independent and do not return to the mother's mouth.

F: C; frozen foods seem to be best in captivity. Shrimp (chopped to a commiserate size), krill, fish and similar items can be fed.

S: These fish were initially imported as *Haplochromis jacksoni*—clearly an identification error, since the two species are very dissimilar.

T: 24°–26°C, **L:** 20 cm, **A:** from 100 cm, **R:** m, **D:** 3

Gnathochromis pfefferi, WC, Ndole Bay, Zambia

"Haplochromis" ahli

Fam.: Cichlidae

Copadichromis "Kadango" (Commercial name!)

Syn.: "*Haplochromis* Kadango." Also known as "Hap. red fin" in the trade.

Hab.: Africa: exclusively found in Lake Malawi. Even there, *C.* "Kadango" seems to have a restricted distribution on the southeast coast of the lake. Specimens caught for export predominately come from the town of Kadango. It colonizes rocky shores at depths of 2–10 m.

F.I.: Probably at the beginning of '80's.

Sex.: Clear sexual dichromatism in mature specimens (compare photos). Immature, half-grown ♂♂ have a white-fringed dorsal fin and a reddish body.

Soc. B.: Agamic maternal mouthbrooder. Sexually active ♂♂ claim territories. ♀♀ and ♂♂ bereft of a territory usually live together in small groups.

M: To successfully maintain adult specimens of this splendid species demands a tank at least 1.5 m long. Hiding places are of subordinate importance, but include a few for brooding ♀♀ or inferior animals. Plants are ignored. Provide plenty of open areas for swimming and spawning. The best results were obtained when one or two ♂♂ were kept with several ♀♀ and other similar-sized Malawian *Copadichromis* species. Water: pH 7.8–8.3; hardness 10°–20° dGH. Nitrite concentrations above 0.1 mg/l cause the skin of *C.* "Kadango" to turn milky. Regular partial water exchanges (about 20%–30% every 10 days) and an exemplary filtration system are required.

B: Relatively simple with the maintenance indications given above and a good diet. Eggs are fertilized via the egg spot method. Since this is a maternal mouthbrooder, ♀♀ can be transferred to a separate aquarium after they spawn to optimize survival of the offspring. The number of eggs depends on the size of the ♀, usually fluctuating between 20 and 60. After about 3 weeks, the young are released; they are often readmitted into the ♀'s mouth for a few additional days. The young show the reddish fins of ♀♀ and immature ♂♂ after a few weeks. Sexual maturity and the ♂'s associated color transformation occurs after about one year posthatching.

F: O; unproblematic to feed in captivity, since flake foods, most frozen foods, and all live foods are readily accepted. To maintain the red color composition, carotenoid-containing foods (red *Daphnia, Cyclops*) should be fed. Caution—it is easy to overfeed wild caught specimens with fiber-poor foods (e.g., fish, beef heart, earthworms).

S: A related fish—probably a geographical variant of *C.* "Kadango"—frequently appears in pet stores; however, in contrast to *C.* "Kadango," ♂♂ are more yellowish with a small proportion of blue on the body and, overall, ♀♀ are paler. Captive specimens are often difficult to differentiate into their respective populations, since a poor diet often results in less dynamic colors. While both come from the east coast of Lake Malawi, "*H.* gold fin" comes from further north, around Makanjila Point and south thereof.

T: 24°–26°C, **L:** 12–15 cm, **A:** from 120 cm, **R:** b, m, **D:** 2–3

Copadichromis "Kádango" ♂

Copadichromis "Kadango" ♀

Fam.: Cichlidae

Buccochromis lepturus
Slender-tail hap, green lepturus

(REGAN, 1922)

Syn.: *Haplochromis lepturus, H. gigas, Cyrtocara lepturus.*

Hab.: Africa: endemic to Lake Malawi. Widely distributed above sandy bottoms.

F.I.: Unknown.

Sex.: Dominant ♂♂ can be recognized by their spotted anal fin and blue-green body. ♀♀ and young, inferior ♂♂ are not easy to distinguish.

Soc. B.: Dominant ♂♂ are territorial. Agamic mouthbrooder, maternal family.

M: Similar to other haplochromines from Lake Malawi. Free swimming space is particularly important. Hiding places among rocks and similar items should be provided for inferior animals. Robust plants can be used, even though plants are largely absent in their natural habitat. Only associate with similar species.

B: Ovophile mouthbrooder, maternal family. Carefully transfer the brooding ♀♀ into a separate aquarium to raise the young.

F: O; voracious omnivore. Hardy live foods as well as frozen and substitute foods are immediately accepted. Dry foods in the form of sticks or tablets are also recommended.

S: This species is sold as "green lepturus." A second, very closely related species, probably "*H.*" *rhoadesii,* is sold as "yellow lepturus."

T: 24°–26°C, **L:** up to 40 cm, **A:** 150 cm, **R:** b, m, **D:** 2–3

"Haplochromis" cf. lobochilus

Syn.: None.

Hab.: Africa: endemic to Lake Malawi. Specimens captured for the pet trade mostly hail from the eastern coast of Lake Malawi near Makanjila. Additional known habitats are Chilumba, Nkhata Bay, and the Maleri Islands. Mainly found in shallow waters at depths of 2–10 m over sand-rock substrates.

F.I.: Unknown.

Sex.: Full-grown specimens are easy to sex, since ♀♀ are usually light silver with dark crossbands (see picture of ♂). Juveniles are difficult to sex. They, like ♀♀, are light silver, though they usually have a broken longitudinal band or rows of dots along their side with a row of dots above it and a row of dots on the base of the dorsal fin. With age, the individual spots fuse into vertical arrangements, forming a crossband pattern.

Soc. B.: Agamic ovophile mouthbrooder, maternal family. ♂♂ are territorial and aggressive towards tankmates during courtship. Nevertheless, considered to be a relatively peaceful cichlid. Keep one ♂ with 2–3 ♀♀.

M: A spacious tank is an important condition for successful and prolonged care of this beautiful species. Use coarse sand or a fine-grained gravel substrate. Otherwise, maintenance requirements parallel those of "*Haplochromis*" species of Lake Malawi.

B: As for *Copadichromis* "Kadango."

F: C, O.

S: This species is well-known aquaristically, but for a long time it was known erroneously as "*H. flavimanus.*" Unfortunately there is only one type specimen of "*H.*" *lobochilus.* It was collected at Chilumba. Careful research is needed to show if the cichlid pictured here is identical to "*H.*" *lobochilus.* An additional species with similarly colored ♂♂ is known as "*H. hertae,*" but it has not been scientifically described.

T: 24°–26°C, **L:** 20 cm, **A:** 150 cm, **R:** b, m, **D:** 2-3

Buccochromis lepturus ♂

"Haplochromis" cf. *lobochilus* ♂

Fam.: Cichlidae

"Haplochromis" melanonotus = Platygnathochromis melanonotus (REGAN, 1922)
Black-line hap

Syn.: *Cyrtocara melanonotus.*

Hab.: Africa: widely distributed in Lake Malawi.

F.I.: Unknown.

Sex.: Adults have distinctive sexual dichromatism. ♂♂ are more colorful.

Soc. B.: Their behavior does not significantly differ from that of other *"Haplochromis"* species from Lake Malawi. Moderately aggressive. ♀♀ are not overly molested.

M: Include a rock edification full of niches, yet arranged in such a manner that all the hiding places cannot be monitored from one point in the aquarium. Limit plants to robust species. Use a sand substrate. Frequent water exchanges and good filtration are impor-

tant contributions towards successful maintenance.

B: Probably has not been bred in captivity. Only occasionally imported. Inappropriate for all but the largest tanks. Surely *P. melanonotus*, like all other cichlids from this group, is a mouthbrooder.

F: C; only hardy foods are suitable for adult animals. When feeding frozen beef heart, etc., include vitamin supplements to avoid deficiencies.

S: The scant information available suggests that this species is a feeding specialist because of its dentition. They will probably be separated into another genus when the Malawi *"Haplochromis"* group is revised.

T: 24°–26°C, **L:** 26 cm, **A:** from 120 cm, **R:** b, m, **D:** 3

"Haplochromis" mola = Maravichromis mola (TREWAVAS, 1935)

Syn.: *Cyrtocara mola.*

Hab.: Africa: endemic to Lake Malawi. Widely distributed, primarily over sand or mixed substrates in shallow waters.

F.I.: Unknown.

Sex.: Adult specimens have pronounced sexual dichromatism (see photos).

Soc. B.: Social fish which can be housed with a number of similar species. To the best of our knowledge, robust plants will be left alone.

M: Requires rock edifications, stands of *Vallisneria*, and a sandy substrate to prevent food remains from falling into crevices and rotting. Frequent water exchanges and good filtration are of visible benefit.

B: Has not been observed. However, it can be assumed that the fish are mouthbrooders and that the ♀, as for most

similar species, has sole responsibility of the brood.

F: O; in nature the fish are specialized snail eaters. Yet all normal substitute foods are accepted in the aquarium.

T: 24°–26°C, **L:** 17 cm, **A:** from 100 cm, **R:** b, m, **D:** 2–3

"Haplochromis" melanonotus ♀

"Haplochromis" mola ♂, ♀ on following page

Platygnathochromis melanotus ♂

Maravichromis mola ♀

Maravichromis formosus

(TREWAVAS, 1935)

Syn.: *Haplochromis formosus, Cyrtocara formosa.*

Hab.: Africa: endemic to Lake Malawi, in the rocky littoral zone. Rare.

F.I.: 1978.

Sex.: ♂♂ are golden to bluish dorsally; ♀♀ are silver.

Soc. B.: Unknown.

M: As for *Cyrtocara mola.*

B: There is no information available. However, it should not be significantly different from that of other *"Cyrtocara"* species from Lake Malawi.

F: C, O; live, freeze-dried, frozen, and flake foods and vegetable supplements (algae).

T: 24°–26°C, **L:** 12.5 cm, **A:** 90 cm, **R:** m. b, **D:** 2

Maravichromis formosus ♀

Fam.: Cichlidae

Copadichromis azureus

KONINGS, 1990

Syn.: See S.

Hab.: Africa: endemic to Lake Malawi, around the islands of Mbenji and Maleri and at the Nkhomo and Eccles Reefs. At depths of 0–20 m.

F.I.: Ca. 1980 under various names.

Sex.: In all of the several color morphs, ♂♂ are more colorful. Some animals are pink, but it is unknown what gender these animals represent.

Soc. B.: Peaceful for an utaka species. ♀♀ and immature ♂♂ live gregariously. Sexually active ♂♂ are bellicose.

M: Needs hiding places among stones and rocks, dense vegetation around the edges, and free swimming space. Water: hardness 10°–15° dGH; pH 8.0–8.5.

B: *C. azureus* spawns within small caves it constructs under stones lying on sandy substrates. Maternal mouthbrooders. The ♂ defends the cave. Brooding ♀♀ commonly live together. Rear the offspring with *Artemia* and small flakes.

F: C, O; planktivores in their natural biotope. Flake and freeze-dried foods and frozen mosquito larvae are accepted in the aquarium.

S: The fish pictured on the opposite page has been misidentified as "*H.*" *ovatus* and "*H.*" *quadrimaculatus*. *Haplochromis chrysonotus* has been used as a trade name.

T: 22°–28°C, **L:** 16 cm, **A:** 80 cm, but larger is better, **R:** m, **D:** 2

Fossorochromis rostratus
Rostratus

(BOULENGER, 1899)

Syn.: *Tilapia rostrata, Haplochromis macrorhynchus, H. rostratus, Cyrtocara rostrata.*

Hab.: Africa: endemic to Lake Malawi. Widely distributed within the lake. Lives above sandy substrates either with or without interspersed rocks. Breeding and incubation are carried out in rocky regions. ♀♀ have been observed defending newly released young in the rocky littoral zone.

F.I.: Unknown.

Sex.: Fully colored ♂♂ are easy to recognize (see photos). Juveniles, ♀♀, and subdominant ♂♂, however, are silver with a longitudinal row of 5 large black dots along their side. An additional 5 black spots are located under the base of the dorsal fin. This pattern can vary from individual to individual. A stripe may result if the dots fuse.

Soc. B.: *F. rostratus* lives singly or in small groups in its natural habitat. Sexually active ♂♂ are always found alone.

Nevertheless, *F. rostratus* is by far less territorial than many other "*Haplochromis*" species from Lake Malawi. Intraspecific aggressions are minimal. Maternal ovophile mouthbrooder, like almost all Malawi cichlids. After spawning, the ♀ has the sole responsibility of the eggs.

M: A large aquarium is a significant factor for successful, long term maintenance. Use a thick layer of coarse sand as substrate. Though the need for rock structures is less pronounced in this species in comparison to other Malawi cichlids, they are still considered necessary for subdominant animals and brooding ♀♀. An alkaline pH of 7.8–8.3 is important, while hardness does not seem to be as crucial (between 10° and 20° dGH). In view of its respectable appetite, use a strong filter and perform regular water exchanges (30% every 10–14 days). Based on the lack of intense intraspecific aggressiveness, a small groups of 3–5 specimens can be kept.

Continued on p. 780.

Copadichromis sp. aff. azureus, Tanzania

Fossorochromis rostratus

Fam.: Cichlidae

Protomelas similis
Gorgeous hap

(REGAN, 1922)

Syn.: *Cyrtocara similis, Haplochromis similis.* Sometimes sold as "*H.* rainbow."

Hab.: Africa: endemic to Lake Malawi. Broadly distributed. Colonizes the littoral zone over vegetated sandy substrates to a depth of about 10 m. The pictured specimen, like most sold in pet stores, was captured at Likoma Island.

F.I.: Unknown.

Sex.: Clear sexual dichromatism between sexually active adults. ♂♂ are a brilliant blue-green (see photo). ♀♀, fry, and juveniles are light silver with a black longitudinal stripe.

Soc. B.: Maternal agamic mouthbrooder. ♂♂ are territorial while spawning. Outside times of sexual activity, they are frequently found in small groups.

M: Keep a small group of this comparatively peaceful cichlid. Associate with behaviorally compatible "*Haplochromis*" species from Lake Malawi. Otherwise, follow suggestions for *Copadichromis* "Kadango."

B: Maternal agamic ovophile mouthbrooder. The egg spot method of fertilization is followed as the fish move in a circular pattern. In captivity it is best to transfer the ♀ into a separate aquarium until she releases the fry. Beware—vigorous chasing or rough handling may result in the eggs being expelled. The chances of this coming to pass are diminished if she is left alone for 18 days postspawning. At this point there is a great chance of successfully raising the offspring even if she does spit them out. Once the yolk sac has been absorbed, feed *Artemia* nauplii or small flake foods.

F: O; various frozen, live, or flake foods.

S: This broadly distributed species is represented by several color morphs. A detailed taxonomic study is still pending. Several species may be encompassed within these populations, all of which are traded as *P. similis* and "*Hap.* rainbow."

T: 24°–26°C, **L:** ca. 12 cm, **A:** from 120 cm, **R:** b, m, **D:** 2–3

Continuation of *Fossorochromis rostratus* (p. 778):

B: With a good diet and the described maintenance conditions, *F. rostratus* is easy to breed. When offspring are desired, it is recommended that brooding ♀♀ be carefully transferred into a separate tank a few days after spawning. About 3 weeks postspawning, depending on the size of the ♀, between 50 and 100 fully developed young are released from her mouth. The ♀ continues to re-admit the young for a few more days in the face of perceived danger. Afterwards, brood care is terminated and the ♀ can be removed. *Artemia* nauplii and flake foods are an appropriate starter diet; later, larger foods can be added. Easily reared with this regime. With good care and feeding, the young are 5–6 cm long after 2 months.

F: O; ravenous omnivores. Large foods are preferred. All kinds of live, frozen, or prepared foods such as flakes, sticks, or tablets.

S: When confronted with danger, *F. rostratus* can quickly and totally bury itself in a fine substrate. Minutes later the fish reappear. Unfortunately, they do not modify their behavior in captive environments with coarse gravel substrates. Hence, injuries may result when you try to catch them. Use a sand or fine-grained gravel substrate.

T: 24°–26°C, **L:** 20–25 cm, **A:** from 150 cm, **R:** b, m, **D:** 2

Protomelas similis

Cyathopharynx furcifer ♂, brood care coloration, see p. 760

Fam.: Cichlidae

"Haplochromis" taeniolata = Protomelas taeniolatus (TREWAVAS, 1935)
Spindle hap

Syn.: *Cyrtocara taeniolata, Haplochromis cancellus.*

Hab.: Africa: endemic to Lake Malawi. Widely distributed over rocky substrates.

F.I.: Unknown.

Sex.: Clear sexual dichromatism in adults. Distinguishing genders is significantly more difficult in juveniles and half-grown animals.

Soc. B.: Dominant ♂ ♂ are territorial, particularly during courtship. ♀ ♀ and young are commonly found swimming alone or in small groups. This relatively peaceful cichlid is usually only aggressive towards heterospecifics when spawning.

M: As for other *"Haplochromis"* species from Lake Malawi. *P. taeniolatus* requires an aquarium with a minimum length of 1.5 m and a large surface area, preferably with a coarse sand or fine-grained gravel substrate, rock structures, and plants. Keep one ♂ with 2 or more ♀ ♀. Use water values listed under *Copadichromis* "Kadango."

B: Simple. Maternal agamic ovophile mouthbrooder. After spawning, the brooding ♀ should be carefully transferred into a separate aquarium. The ♀ incubates the brood for 3 weeks. Depending on her size, 20–40 young are produced. They are easily raised with newly hatched *Artemia salina* and small flake foods.

F: In its natural habitat, *"H." taeniolatus* normally feeds off aufwuchs on rocks and the microorganisms contained therein as well as planktonic foods. In the aquarium, *"H." taeniolatus* has proven to be an omnivore. Various live, frozen, and commercial dry foods are accepted. Fiber-poor foods such as beef heart are detrimental to wild caught specimens, inviting infirmities of the digestive tract.

S: Some populations show geographic variations in regard to coloration. In addition, wild caught specimens from Likoma are generally larger than animals from Mbenji. Different names have been used commercially for this cichlid, e.g., "fire blue" for the Likoma population or, among others, "Steveni Mbenji" for animals from the Mbenji Islands.

"H." taeniolatus is a very close relative of *"H." fenestratus*. The latter species also has several color morphs, further confounding species differentiation (particularly ♀ ♀). A detailed taxonomic study of the various populations of both species is still pending (see *"Haplochromis steveni* eastern").

T: 24°–26°C, **L:** 12 cm, **A:** from 150 cm, **R:** b, m, **D:** 2–3

"*Haplochromis*" *taeniolatus* ♂

"*Haplochromis*" *taeniolata* ♀

"*Haplochromis steveni* eastern"   (Commercial name!)

Syn.: None; the addition "eastern" is in reference to this species' distribution along the eastern coast of Lake Malawi.

Hab.: Africa: endemic to Lake Malawi. Most specimens in pet stores come from the east coast of Lake Malawi around Makanjila.

F.I.: Unknown.

Sex.: Clear sexual dichromatism. ♂♂ are intense blue with a reddish ventral area. ♀♀ are silver with numerous irregular crossbands.

Soc. B.: Ovophile mouthbrooder, maternal family. ♂♂ are territorial when sexually active. ♂♂ and ♀♀ are solitary abiding animals when not spawning.

M: As for most cichlids from Lake Malawi, this beautiful species requires a spacious tank with rock edifications to protect subdominant animals and sufficient free swimming space. The substrate should be of coarse sand. Although plants are not found in its natural habitat, they can be included in the decor, since they are usually left alone. Use the water values suggested for *Copadichromis* "Kadango". It is best to keep one ♂ with several ♀♀. Large, relatively peaceful Malawi cichlids, other haplochromines, and peacocks of the genus *Aulonocara* make suitable tankmates, mbunas less so.

B: Easy. After spawning, the brooding ♀ should be very carefully transferred to another aquarium. After about 3 weeks, the young are released from the mother's mouth. They immediately start to search for food. Follow suggestions given under *C.* "Kadango" for rearing. The number of eggs per spawn fluctuates between 20 and 40, depending on the size of the ♀.

F: Unselective omnivore. Water fleas, insect larvae, shrimp, or full-grown *Artemia* are readily accepted. Small quantities of small earthworms, fish, and mussel meat can be fed. Frozen foods and various dry commercial foods are also accepted.

S: A detailed taxonomic study of this species has not been attempted. So far, only the provisional commercial name is listed. "*Haplochromis steveni* eastern" is obviously very closely related to "*Haplochromis*" *fenestratus* and may even be the same species.

In the '80's, several species characterized by habitats or colors reached the trade which were also known as "*H. steveni.*" The best known cichlids of this group are "*Haplochromis steveni* Maleri" from the Maleri Islands, "*Haplochromis steveni* tiger" from the Island of Likoma, and "*Haplochromis steveni* Mbenji" from the Mbenji Islands. All of these species are very closely related to each other and probably to "*H.*" *taeniolatus* and "*H.*" *fenestratus* as well.

T: 24°–26°C, **L:** 12 cm (ca. 15 cm), **A:** from 150 cm, **R:** b, m, **D:** 3

"*Haplochromis steveni* eastern"

"*Haplochromis steveni* Maleri"

Haplotaxodon microlepis
Bulldog cichlid

BOULENGER, 1906

Syn.: *Haplotaxodon microlepis.*

Hab.: Africa: endemic to Lake Tanganyika. Lives in rocky littoral zones.

F.I.: Unknown.

Sex.: ♂♂ grow larger and have elongated fin tips.

Soc. B.: Generally found in large schools.

M: An ample open area for this large cichlid is an absolute necessity. Keep a group if possible. Plants are not disturbed.

B: Use temperate, medium-hard, neutral to slightly alkaline water (25°–28°C, 10°–15° dGH, and pH 7.0–8.5, respectively). Probably a mouthbrooder.

F: C; large *Artemia*, *Cyclops*, *Daphnia*, mosquito larvae, *Mysis*, and flake foods.

S: This species was classified into the genus group Perissodini by POLL (scale-eaters).

T: 23°–28°C, **L:** 25 cm, **A:** 150 cm, **R:** m, **D:** 3

Hemichromis cerasogaster

(BOULENGER, 1899)

Syn.: *Paratilapia cerasogaster.*

Hab.: West Africa: Zaïre, in Lake Majindombe. The pictured animal was captured around Kinshasa in a tributary of the Zaïre River.

F.I.: 1984 by PÜRZL, HOFFMANN, and RADDA.

Sex.: Gender can only be distinguished in adults. ♂♂ grow larger and have more iridescent spots. Mature ♀♀ are fuller through the ventral region.

Soc. B.: Territories are energetically defended. Generally plant friendly. Digging activities are limited to within the confines of the territory. Small, bite-size fishes are preyed upon. Sometimes quarrelsome towards conspecifics and heterospecifics.

M: House in tanks subdivided with vegetation, rocks, and roots. Use a fine- to medium-grained gravel substrate. No particular demands are placed on water chemistry.

B: Open spawner. Rocks, roots, or plant leaves are used as spawning substrates. *H. cerasogaster* even spawn in hard, slightly alkaline water. The larvae hatch after about 2 days at 26°C and are free-swimming after an additional 4–5 days. Raise with *Artemia* nauplii. Nuclear family.

F: C, O; live, frozen, and dry commercial foods.

S: It is not clear whether or not the pictured animal is *H. cerasogaster* or a closely related species. *H. cerasogaster* reputedly has a black area in the dorsal fin, yet animals from Kinshasa do not.

T: 22°–26°C, **L:** ♂ 10 cm, ♀ 8 cm, **A:** 70 cm, **R:** m, b, **D:** 2–3

Haplotaxodon microlepis

Hemichromis cerasogaster

Fam.: Cichlidae

Hemichromis stellifer

LOISELLE, 1979

Syn.: None.

Hab.: West Africa: from Gabon to Zaïre.

F.I.: Not known.

Sex.: ♂♂ are somewhat larger and more elongated. They are wine red from the onset of courtship until the fry are free-swimming. Then the ♂♂'s color changes to a bright red which is maintained while they guide the mobile young. ♀♀ are fuller through the ventral area when laden with eggs and turn bright red during reproduction.

Soc. B.: Territorial. Sometimes slightly quarrelsome towards conspecifics and heterospecifics. Plant are ignored. Digging activities are confined to within the territorial boundaries.

M: Subdivide the aquarium with rocks and roots. Fine- to medium-grained gravel is an appropriate substrate. There are no set requirements in regard to water chemistry.

B: Open spawner, nuclear family. The small, transparent eggs are adhered along their side to rocks, roots, or plant leaves. Development is similar to that of *Hemichromis cerasogaster*. Hatched larvae are placed into a large depression in the substrate. Rear the young on *Artemia* nauplii. *H. stellifer* also breeds in hard, slightly alkaline water.

F: C; live, frozen, and dry foods.

S: *H. stellifer* is very similar to its close relative *H. guttatus*. The two species are so difficult to differentiate, the pictured animal may in fact be *H. guttatus*. Only after studying the pharyngeal dentition does the pendulum swing towards *H. stellifer*.

T: 22°–26°C, **L:** 8–11 cm, **A:** 60 cm, **R:** m, b, **D:** 1–2

Herichthys carpintis
Pearlscale cichlid

(JORDAN & SNYDER, 1899)

Syn.: *Cichlasoma carpinte, C. carpintis, C. cyanoguttatum, Neetroplus carpintis.*

Hab.: Central America: northern Mexico, e.g., in the Laguna Carpintero near the city of Tampico in the lower region of the Rio Panuco.

F.I.: Unknown.

Sex.: There is no clear sexual dimorphism. However, ♀♀ remain smaller than the ♂♂, which in extreme cases can grow to a length of 30 cm.

Soc. B.: This large cichlid has a bad reputation, but in comparison to other Central American cichlids, it is considered to be an amiable, even retiring charge.

M: Very adaptable in regard to water chemistry, as seen from the different waters it inhabits in nature. In captivity, water with a pH of around 7, a hardness of 15° dGH, and a temperature of 25°C is suggested. A large aquarium with roomy hiding places is needed. Plants may be summarily uprooted as they dig.

B: ♂♂ reach sexual maturity at a length of 11 cm, while ♀♀ are mature at 8 cm. This is a fecund open spawner which establishes its pair bond after intense jaw locking. Larvae hatch 4 days post-spawning and are free-swimming after another 4 to 6 days. Both parents tend the free-swimming young. When involved in custodial care, they are distinctively dark, almost black, with the exception of a right-angle triangular spot in the anterior dorsal half of the body.

F: O; all hardy fish foods. Juveniles seem to be susceptible to intestinal diseases.

T: 24°–26°C, **L:** ♂ up to 30 cm, **A:** 120 cm, **R:** b, **D:** 1–2

Hemichromis stellifer

Herichthys carpintis

Fam.: Cichlidae

Herichthys pearsei

HUBBS, 1936

Syn.: *Cichlasoma pearsei.*

Hab.: Central America: southern Mexico and northern Guatemala, along the Atlantic seaboard in the Rio Champoton and the Usumacinta Basin.

F.I.: 1983 by H. G. BREIDOHR, R. STAWIKOWSKI, and U. WERNER.

Sex.: ♀♀ have a dull matte yellow and brown rounded body. ♂♂ have a more vertical cranial profile and a shiny green-yellow body.

Soc. B.: Temperamental and sometimes slightly quarrelsome. Their behavior is comparable to large species in the *"C."* *synspilum* and *fenestratum* group.

M: Keep in spacious tanks with open caves and clearly delineated borders. Generally robust and undemanding.

Plants are inappropriate additions to aquaria housing this cichlid. Strong filtration and a frequent water turnover are necessary.

B: Has not been bred in captivity. Observations made in its natural habitat indicate that it is a very fecund open spawner.

F: O; voracious omnivore. All foods are accepted to fuel its explosive growth rate. Vegetable fare must be included in the diet, e.g., lettuce, spinach.

S: In Mexico and Guatemala, this fish is called "Sacatierra," meaning earth remover. It has a penchant for eating terrestrial vegetation it finds growing along the stream verge. Its large teeth are always visible. Juveniles have a particularly pointed snout.

T: 25°–29°C, **L:** exact information is unavailable, probably around 30 cm, **A:** 150 cm, **R:** b, m, **D:** 1–2

Hoplotilapia retrodens

HILGENDORF, 1888

Syn.: *Hemichromis retrodens, Haplochromis bicolor, Paratilapia retrodens, P. bicolor, P. polyodon, Cnesterostoma polyodon.*

Hab.: Africa: endemic to Lake Victoria.

F.I.: Unknown.

Sex.: Marked sexual dichromatism.

Soc. B.: Although *H. retrodens* is sometimes imported, information on its social interaction is scant. Its behavior should not be significantly different from other haplochromines. Rather tranquil.

M: Plants are ignored, so feel free to put these fish in planted aquaria. While it can be appropriately placed in community with other fishes, a large tank will be needed. Use a sand substrate and rock edifications along the back of the tank.

B: Unknown, but it can be assumed that *H. retrodens*, like all other haplochromines, are maternal mouthbrooders.

F: C; primarily molluscivores. However, examined stomach contents have also revealed insect larvae and small crustacea. All common foods are accepted in captivity.

S: There are two color morphs. The mottled form of ♀♀ is particularly common, similar to some Malawi cichlids.

T: 24°–27°C, **L:** 15 cm, **A:** from 80 cm, **R:** b, m, **D:** 3

Herichthys pearsei

Hoplotilapia retrodens ♀

Fam.: Cichlidae

Labidochromis sp. "yellow"

Syn.: *"Labidochromis tanganicae"* (commercial name).

Hab.: Africa: Lake Malawi.

F.I.: Ca. 1980 to Sweden.

Sex.: Full-grown ♂♂ have a cephalic hump and more luminous colors (blue- and black-edged fins). ♀♀ are paler. The majority of bred specimens are ♂♂.

Soc. B.: Older ♂♂ are bellicose towards equal-sized conspecifics. Juveniles can easily be kept in schools. Shy.

M: Undemanding. Good tankmates for other cichlids. Associating it with characins, barbs, and loaches posses no problems as long as they are not overly small. Water: pH 7.3–8.0; hardness 15°–30° dGH. Limit plants to robust species.

B: Pairwise set-up in aquaria over 80 cm long. Include caves. The nonadhesive eggs are laid on a stone. The ♀ takes the eggs into her mouth and broods them for 18 days at 24°–26°C. The fry are easily raised with *Artemia*, *Cyclops*, and ground flakes. Several broods can be raised simultaneously in an aquarium, since the parents do not molest their offspring.

F: C, O; small live foods and all types of flake and freeze-dried foods. Frozen bloodworms are particularly relished.

S: These beautifully colored animals make an appealing contrast to different colored cichlids—especially some of the more common blue cichlids.
L. caeruleus (Vol. 2, p. 920) is much lighter, almost white. The animal introduced here is probably a new species which is sold as *Labidochromis* sp. "yellow." It lives between the islands of Charo and Mbowe. This color morph was taken to Burundi at the beginning of the '80's by PIERRE BRICHARD and exported from there, creating the impression that the species came from Lake Tanganyika.
The truly gorgeous pure colors of this cichlid are rarely seen outside of marine reef aquaria.

T: 23°–28°C, **L:** 10 cm, **A:** 80 cm, **R:** m, b, **D:** 1–2

Continuation of *Melanochromis "lepidophage"* (p. 800):

minated. Raising the young is simple. Newly hatched *Artemia salina* nauplii, small flakes, and sieved pond plankton are suitable initial foods.

F: Undiscriminating, voracious omnivores which eagerly accept all foods offered, including live and frozen foods. A diet rich in fiber is important, as fiber-poor foods such as fish meat or beef heart foster intestinal diseases.

S: Stomach content analyses of newly captured specimens showed that *M. "lepidophage"* primarily lives off the scales of other cichlids (note the name). This parasitic behavior, however, has not been observed in the aquarium. It seems that *M. "lepidophage"* is a facultative scale-eater which prefers readily available offered foods to its natural fare.

T: 24°–26°C, **L:** 12 cm, **A:** from 120 cm, **R:** all, **D:** 2–3

Labidochromis sp. "yellow"

Nimbochromis livingstoni waiting for prey, Chisemulu Island, Malawi

Fam.: Cichlidae

Labidochromis pallidus   LEWIS, 1982

Syn.: None. However, some of the whitish *Labidochromis* species have been imported under the invalid names of *L. "fryeri"* and *L. "magaritae."*

Hab.: Africa: exclusively in Lake Malawi. Only found at the Maleri Island group (islands of Nankoma, Nakanthenga, and Maleri) on the southwestern coast of the lake. However, an additional population of this species is also known from the small island of Thumbi West in the southern part of the lake close to Cape Maclear. It is possible that this population was released there by an aquarium fish exporter (LEWIS, 1982). It colonizes the littoral zone, predominantly in shallow rocky regions. Infrequently found at depths of 25 m and more.

F.I.: Unknown, probably in 1986.

Sex.: Sexual differences are slight. ♂♂ grow larger and have more pronounced egg spots on their anal fin. Their sides are bluish while courting.

Soc. B.: Maternal agamic ovophile mouthbrooder. This species expresses minimal territoriality in large aquaria. ♂♂ are aggressive at spawning time, particularly towards congeners. In its natural habitat, *L. pallidus* is generally found singly, less commonly in small groups.

M: Very active fish. Include sufficient hiding places among rocks for subdominant animals. To decrease intraspecific aggressions, associate it with other mbunas. Best to keep one ♂ with several ♀♀. Water: pH 7.8–8.3; hardness 10°–20° dGH. Although plants are not found in its natural habitat, they can be included in the decor, since they are generally ignored. Partial water exchanges of 20%–30% of the tank's volume every 10 days is of visible benefit.

B: Simple. Mouthbrooder, maternal family. The egg spot method of fertilization is followed as the fish move in a circular pattern. After the ♀ has put the eggs into her throat sac, the ♂ is chased away. As long as the aquarium offers sufficient hiding places, some young will always survive. When the entire brood is desired, separate the ♀. After about 3 weeks, the young are free-swimming and released from the mother's mouth. Raising the young from this point forward is unproblematic and can be accomplished with newly hatched *Artemia salina* and small flake foods.

F: O; in its natural habitat, *L. pallidus* is a specialized aufwuchs feeder. However, under aquarium conditions, this cichlid has proven to be an unselective omnivore. Mosquito larvae, *Mysis,* small *Gammarus, Cyclops, Daphnia,* and various types of dry foods are readily accepted.

S: So far, three different totally white *Labidochromis* species are known. *L. caeruleus* with its characteristic pronounced black stripe on the dorsal fin hails from the area around Nkhata Bay. *L. careuleus,* in contrast to *L. pallidus* and *L. mylodon,* has monocuspid anterior teeth. The third white species is *L. mylodon.* It is only found at Mumbo Island. Unfortunately, *L. mylodon* cannot be differentiated from *L. pallidus* based on coloration or any other easily discernible characteristic. The pharyngeal dentition stands as the method of differentiation for these three species (LEWIS, 1982).

T: 24°–26°C, **L:** 8 cm, **A:** 100 cm, **R:** b, m, **D:** 2

Labidochromis pallidus ♂

Labidochromis pallidus ♂

Fam.: Cichlidae

Lamprologus callipterus
Callipterus

Syn.: *Lamprologus reticulatus, L. modestus nyassae.*

Hab.: Africa: endemic to Lake Tanganyika. Encountered in the rubble and rock littoral zone and the transition zone.

F.I.: Unknown.

Sex.: ♂♂ grow significantly larger than ♀♀.

Soc. B.: Very aggressive towards conspecifics. Each 15 cm ♂ seems to "own" several 6 cm ♀♀. The latter live above empty *Neothauma* shells, while ♂♂ cruise around either singly or in groups in the littoral zone (see photo on p. 798).

M: Provide plenty of hiding places. Keep one ♂ and several ♀♀. ♀♀ require empty snail shells as shelters for living and spawning. Use a sand substrate; the tank can contain plants.

B: 25° to 28°C; medium-hard and neutral to slightly alkaline water (10°–15° dGH and pH 7.0-8.5, respectively). Cave spawner. The ♀ adheres the spawn to the interior of the empty shell, while the ♂ releases his semen just above the shell's entrance. The ♀ cares for the spawn, and the ♂ defends the territory.

F: C; large *Artemia*, mosquito larvae, *Mysis*, and other hardy foods.

S: Imported as *Neolamprologus* sp. *"tembo,"* a name given by the African natives.

T: 23°–26°C, **L:** 6–15 cm, **A:** 100 cm, **R:** b, m, **D:** 2

Pair of *L. callipterus*. Its camouflage coloration is not very appealing. Rather than rearranging the snail shells to their liking, they are used as found.

Lamprologus callipterus ♂

Lamprologus callipterus ♀

Lamprologus callipterus. Schools of bachelors cruise through the sand and rubble zones of the lake.

Fam.: Cichlidae

Lepidiolamprologus cunningtoni. See p. 811.

Lestradea perspicax

POLL, 1943

Syn.: None.

Hab.: Africa: endemic to Lake Tanganyika. Inhabits the littoral zone.

F.I.: 1985.

Sex.: ♂♂ grow about 1 cm longer and have two clearly defined longitudinal lines on the dorsal fin. ♀♀ often just have one line on the dorsal fin.

Soc. B.: This relatively peaceful cichlid spends the day cruising the tank.

M: A spacious open swimming area is its main requirement. Since this species does not bother plants, vegetation can be included in the decor. Use a sand substrate so that *L. perspicax* can occasionally masticate through it. Various *Xenotilapia* species make eminently suitable tankmates.

B: Has not been successfully bred in captivity. However, wild caught specimens have shown this cichlid to be a mouthbrooder.

F: O; voracious omnivore.

S: *L. perspicax* contained the subspecies *L. perspicax stappersi* until POLL reclassified the latter as an autonomous species in 1986.

T: 25°C, **L:** 12 cm, **A:** 100 cm, **R:** t, m, **D:** 2

Melanochromis "lepidophage"

Syn.: None. This species was sold in the '70's as *Melanochromis "fuscus."* *M. "lepidophage"* is a temporary name until it is scientifically described.

Hab.: Africa: endemic to Lake Malawi. Exclusively found along the eastern coast near Makanjila Point above rocky substrates.

F.I.: 1970's.

Sex.: ♂♂ are light blue with larger and more numerous egg spots on the anal fins. ♀♀ are gray.

Soc. B.: One of the most pacific *Melanochromis* species. It even schools in its natural biotope. In small aquaria less than 1.2 m long, 1 ♂ can be kept with 2–3 ♀♀. Several ♂♂ with a corresponding number of ♀♀ can be maintained in large aquaria.

M: As found in their natural habitat, there should be sufficient hiding places for weak animals and brooding ♀♀, despite its relatively peaceful nature. The hiding places should be among stones or roots. Plants can be used in the decor, since the animals normally ignore them. Use a coarse sand or fine-grained gravel substrate. In regard to water chemistry, an alkaline pH (7.5–8.2) is of primary importance, while other water values are less significant, since *M. "lepidophage"* is a hardy adaptable fish. Other mbuna cichlids from Lake Malawi such as *Melanochromis, Pseudotropheus, Labidochromis,* or *Labeotropheus* make the best tankmates for these fishes.

B: Maternal mouthbrooders. Spawning is via the egg spot method in the typical T position. After about 20–25 days, the young are 10 mm long, totally developed, and ready to be released. The ♀ generally continues her custodial responsibilities for a few days after the fry are released, readmitting them into her buccal cavity at night and when danger threatens. Afterwards, brood care is ter-

Continued on p. 792.

Lestradea perspicax

Melanochromis "lepidophage" ♂

Microgeophagus altispinosa
Bolivian ram

(HASEMAN, 1911)

Syn.: *Crenicara altispinosa, Papilio-chromis altispinosus.*

Hab.: South America: Bolivia and Brazil, in the Rio Mamoré near the mouth of the Rio Guaporé at Trinidad, the Guaporé Basin at Santa Cruz, the Rio Quizer at San Ramón, flood plain below Todos Santos, and the mouth of the Igarapé at Guajara-Mirim.

F.I.: 1984 by H. LINKE and W. STAECK.

Sex.: Sexual differences are only discernible in full-grown, older specimens. ♀♀ are somewhat fuller at that age.

Soc. B.: Social, pair-forming species. Nuclear family. The task of rearing their brood is shared equally by both sexes.

M: Requires several dense plant groups, an open swimming space, and some hiding places (caves).

T: 22°–26°C, **L:** 8 cm, **A:** 80 cm, **R:** m, b, **D:** 2

B: Soft to medium-hard (10° dGH), neutral water with a temperature of 25°–28°C is suggested. Add peat. These open spawners lay up to 200 eggs on stones or, occasionally, in depressions.

F: C. O; live, freeze-dried, flake, and tablet foods.

S: In 1987, W. STAECK reported that parents sometimes protect their brood by taking it into their buccal cavity like a mouthbrooder.

Melanochromis "lepidophage" ♀, see previous page for text

Microgeophagus altispinosa ♂

Microgeophagus altispinosa ♀

Nannacara aureocephalus
Golden-head dwarf cichlid

ALLGAYER, 1983

Syn.: None.

Hab.: South America: French Guyana.

F.I.: Probably in 1982 by French hobbyists.

Sex.: ♂♂ are larger and more colorful with more elongated, sizable unpaired fins.

Soc. B.: Peaceful to the point of being shy when not engaged in sexual activities. Territorial and extremely aggressive when caring for eggs or young, particularly towards conspecifics.

M: The tank should be well planted and contain many hiding places (stones, roots).

B: Water needs to be medium-hard and slightly acid with a slightly elevated temperature in comparison to that suggested for maintenance (10° dGH, pH 6.2–6.5, 26°–28°C). The ♀ develops a contrasting checkerboard design when spawning. The 50–300 eggs are laid within a cave. The ♂ guards the territory, while direct brood care is the responsibility of the ♀.

F: C; exclusively feeds on live foods. Flake foods are rarely accepted.

S: Besides *Nannacara anomala* and *N. aureocephalus*, there seems to be an additional, as yet undescribed *Nannacara* species in French Guyana. Contrary to previous beliefs, *Nannacara taenia* (Brazil, Manaus-Belém) is not a synonym of *N. anomala,* but an autonomous species.

T: 22°–25°C, **L:** ♂ 9 cm, ♀ 5 cm, **A:** 60 cm, **R:** b, **D:** 2

Nannacara aureocephalus ♂

Nannacara aureocephalus ♀

Fam.: Cichlidae

Nanochromis sp. "Kisangani"
Silverspot nanochromis

Syn.: None.

Hab.: West Africa: Zaïre, near Kisangani.

F.I.: 1986 by Heiko BLEHER.

Sex.: ♀♀ have a shiny silver area in the middle of the body which extends to the base of the anal fin. Mature ♀♀ have an enlarged red-violet ventral area. ♂♂ have rows of dots on the caudal fin.

Soc. B.: Comparatively peaceful, but territorial. Plants are not harmed. When kept in pairs in small aquaria, hiding places have to be provided for subdominant animals.

M: N. sp. "Kisangani" needs an aquarium with plants and a fine sand or gravel substrate. Include an abundance of hiding places and caves. There are no specific water chemistry requirements.

B: Water should be soft and acid (pH 5.5) with minimal dissolved ions. From 30 to 50 yellowish eggs are adhered to the ceiling of a cave by their poles. At 26°C, the larvae hatch after 2 days and are free-swimming after an additional 5 days. Raise with Artemia nauplii. Patriarch-maternal family.

F: C; live, frozen, and dry foods.

S: In Zaïre, there is a similar fish which is occasionally called Nanochromis dimidiatus. Due to lack of information contained in the description, its appearance and behavioral characteristics are largely unknown. Aquarists should avoid crossing the various populations.

T: 23°–26°C, **L:** ♂ 6 cm, ♀ 4.5 cm, **A:** 50 cm, **R:** b, **D:** 3–4

Continuation of Neolamprologus buescheri (p. 808):

M: Hiding places and caves for subdominant animals are fundamental necessities for successful maintenance. The size of the aquarium is only important if other fishes are housed with them. Include plants in the decor.

B: Cave spawners. The eggs are usually laid and fertilized on the ceiling of a cave. ♂♂ play a very small role in brood care. All care is overseen by the ♀. After hatching, the larvae remain in the cave. Escapees are returned to the cave by the ♀. The territory is keenly defended by both parents.

F: O; wild caught specimens must be "convinced" to feed on live foods such as glassworms and mayfly larvae. They are finicky feeders that only accept small quantities of food at each meal.

S: Individuals from previous spawns not exceeding 4 cm in length can peacefully live within the parent's territory, even after the parents resume breeding activities.

T: 24°–28°C, **L:** 7 cm, **A:** from 40 cm, **R:** b, m, **D:** 3

Nanochromis sp. "Kisangani" ♂

Nanochromis sp. "Kisangani" ♀

Fam.: Cichlidae

Neolamprologus boulengeri
(STEINDACHNER, 1909)

Syn.: *Julidochromis boulengeri, Lamprologus boulengeri, L. kiritvaithai, L.* sp. *"vaitha", L. vaithae, L. vaithai, Neolamprologus kiritvaithai.*

Hab.: Africa: endemic to Lake Tanganyika.

F.I.: 1985.

Sex.: Differentiation of the sexes is difficult based on external characteristics. For example, black ventral fins signify health and well-being, not gender. ♂♂ grow larger than ♀♀.

Soc. B.: Territorial. Small territories are energetically defended, even against much larger fishes. Though it burrows, plants are not damaged. Cave spawner, paternal-maternal family.

M: Provide a 5–6 cm deep sand substrate with several empty snail shells scattered over its surface. (Open sand areas are of paramount importance!) Snail shells other than the Tanganyika snail *Neothauma* are also accepted, e.g., those of edible snails (*Helix* species). *Helix* shells can either be collected personally or bought in a deli. Use medium-hard (ca. 15° dGH), alkaline (pH 7.5–8.5) water. The aquarium can include several plants.

B: An extensive report concerning maintenance and reproduction by PUTT-BERG (1986) can be found in "Das Aquarium" **20**, 574–577. The ♂'s territory has up to 3 empty snail shells at its center and a shallow depression approximately 30 cm in diameter. While the depression is excavated by the ♂, the ♀ is responsible for arranging the snail shells at a certain angle in relation to their upward pointing opening and burying them on a small hill, frequently until merely the opening is visible. This is accomplished by three techniques: pushing, digging, and plowing (see STAECK, 1983: Aquarienmagazin **17**, 135–140). In contrast to *Neolamprologus ocellatus* (see Vol. 2, p. 942), the shells almost exclusively serve as the ♀'s sleeping and hiding place because of the respectable size of mature ♂♂, which prevents them from entering the snail shell. After spawning and as soon as the eggs, larvae, or young have to be defended, the aggressiveness of the parents increases significantly towards potential enemies. Since adult ♀♀ can lay over 60 eggs, the space in the snail shell is often insufficient to house the entire spawn. The spawn can often be seen from the outside because the eggs are adhered close to the opening. The young tend to quickly leave the protection of the territory, so the animals should be cared for in a species tank to ensure good offspring survival (see STAECK, 1988: DATZ **41**, 104–108).

F: O; all kinds of live, frozen, freeze-dried, tablet, and flake foods.

S: See B.

T: 24°–26°C, **L:** ♂ 7 cm, ♀ 5 cm, **A:** 80 cm, **R:** b, **D:** 2–3

Neolamprologus buescheri
Striped lamprologus
(STAECK, 1983)

Syn.: *Lamprologus buescheri.*

Hab.: Africa: Lake Tanganyika. So far, it has only been found in the southern section.

F.I.: 1982.

Sex.: Sexes cannot be differentiated based on external characteristics.

Soc. B.: *N. buescheri* exhibits strong intraspecific aggressions, which primarily originate with the ♂. Only very large tanks permit maintenance of more than one ♂. Heterospecific fishes are not bothered. Sometimes several ♀♀ establish small territories within the ♂'s territory.

Continued on p. 806.

Neolamprologus boulengeri

Neolamprologus buescheri

Fishing in the African lakes

Fish from Lake Malawi represent the most important source of protein for the human population living along the lake's shores.

Lepidiolamprologus cunningtoni
Black lamprologus

(BOULENGER, 1906)

Syn.: *Lamprologus cunningtoni.*

Hab.: Africa: endemic to Lake Tanganyika. Found above sandy substrates.

F.I.: ?

Sex.: ♂ are larger than ♀.

Soc. B.: These predators primarily feed on small shell-dwelling cichlids in nature. Larger cichlids and catfishes may make appropriate tankmates.

M: Use a large aquarium, potted plants such as giant vallisneria, and a high-volume filter. Decorate with dolomite rocks and use a mixture of crushed dolomite (e.g., Preis's Alfa Marin) and coarse sand at a ration of 1:3 as substrate. Water: pH 7.5–8.0; 25°–30° dGH; >15° dKH.

B: Has not been bred in captivity. Spawning occurs among and under rocks.

F: C; fish and large live foods. Nutrition is unproblematic, since all standard foods are accepted after acclimation.

T: 24°–27°C, **L:** ♂ 25 cm, ♀ 10 cm, **A:** 150 cm, **R:** b, m, **D:** 2–3

Neolamprologus caudopunctatus

(POLL, 1978)

Syn.: *Lamprologus caudopunctatus.*

Hab.: Africa: Zambia, endemic to Lake Tanganyika. Found in the southern section of the lake around Capes Kabeyeye, Chaitika, and Nundo.

F.I.: 1984.

Sex.: No definite external distinguishing characteristics are known. ♀♀ and ♂♂ are the same color, though the latter grow larger.

Soc. B.: Territorial, but the space requirements for each territory are easily satisfied in the aquarium. Hardly aggressive towards conspecifics or heterospecifics. Cave spawner.

M: A spacious aquarium is a basic condition for successful maintenance. Decorate the tank as for other small *Neolamprologus* species. Hiding places must

be offered. The water should be medium-hard to hard and slightly alkaline (ca. 15° dGH, pH 7.5–8.5, respectively). They can be housed with other cichlids as long as the tank is spacious.

B: Has not been bred in an aquarium.

F: C, O; predominately live foods, e.g., *Artemia, Daphnia, Cyclops,* and *Tubifex.* Flake foods are also accepted.

T: 23°–25°C, **L:** ♂ 7 cm, ♀ 6 cm, **A:** 80 cm, **R:** b, **D:** 3

Neolamprologus christyi

(TREWAVAS & POLL, 1952)

Syn.: *Lamprologus christyi.*

Hab.: Africa: endemic to the southern part of Lake Tanganyika. Found in rock and rubble shore regions.

F.I.: Unknown.

Sex.: Unknown.

Soc. B.: Extremely bellicose towards conspecifics as well as heterospecifics. Pair maintenance is recommended. They are territorial, monogamous cave spawners with a nuclear family structure. The ♀ cares for the spawn and young, while the ♂ guards the territory.

M: Requires an abundance of hiding places and a sand substrate. Plants can be included as part of the decoration.

B: Water should be medium-hard and neutral to slightly alkaline (10°–15° dGH and pH 7.0–8.5, respectively) with a temperature of 25° to 28°C. The 150 eggs are laid in a cave.

F: C; large *Artemia,* mosquito larvae, *Mysis,* and other hardy foods, either live or frozen. Flake foods are also consumed.

T: 23°–28°C, **L:** 12 cm, **A:** 120 cm, **R:** b, m, **D:** 2

Neolamprologus caudopunctatus

Neolamprologus christyi

Fam.: Cichlidae

Neolamprologus cylindricus

STAECK & SEEGERS, 1986

Syn.: Lamprologus "cylindricus."

Hab.: Africa: endemic to Lake Tanganyika. Encountered in the rocky littoral zone. So far it has only been found along the southeastern coast.

F.I.: 1983/84, Africa Aquarium.

Sex.: ♂ ♂ grow somewhat larger.

Soc. B.: Intolerant of conspecifics. Pair maintenance is recommended. The ♀ cares for the spawn and young, while the ♂ guards the territory. They are monogamous cave spawners with a nuclear family structure.

M: Offer hiding places and a sand substrate. Plants can be part of the decoration.

B: Water should be medium-hard and neutral to slightly alkaline (10°–15° dGH,

pH 7.0–8.5, respectively) with a temperature of 25° to 28°C. The 50 to 200 eggs are laid in a cave.

F: C; large *Artemia*, mosquito larvae, *Mysis*, and other hardy foods, either live or frozen. Flake foods are also eaten.

S: This species has been imported as *Neolamprologus* sp. "adriani."

T: 23°–28°C, **L:** 12 cm, **A:** 80 cm, **R:** b, m, **D:** 2

Neolamprologus kungweensis
Ocellated shell-dweller

(POLL, 1956)

Syn.: Lamprologus ocellatus POLL, 1952, L. kungweensis.

Hab.: Africa: endemic to Lake Tanganyika.

F.I.: Not precisely known; perhaps in 1985.

Sex.: No definite external differentiating characteristics are known.

Soc. B.: Like *Neolamprologus boulengeri.*

M: As for *N. boulengeri.*

B: There is no information available concerning breeding this species, but it should be similar to other shell-dwelling cichlids.

F: C, O; all kinds of very small live foods such as small crustacea, mosquito larvae, and worms. Flake foods are sometimes accepted.

S: The most conspicuous characteristic of this fish is its light-framed elongated

black spot on the last four hard rays of the dorsal fin. Some specimens have more than one spot. Only ♀ ♀ were available for the original description. ♂ ♂ were described as a different species, possibly *L. signatus.*

T: 24°–26°C, **L:** ♀ 4 cm, ♂ 7 cm, **A:** 60 cm, **R:** b, m, **D:** 2–3

Neolamprologus cylindricus

Neolamprologus kungweensis ♂, Maswa

Neolamprologus kungweensis ♀

Continuation of *Neolamprologus multifasciatus* (p. 817):

B: Use temperate, medium-hard to hard, alkaline water (26°C, ca. 15° dGH, and pH ca. 8, respectively). The ♀ buries its chosen snail shell deep into the substrate. Spawning occurs within the shell. The ♀ cares for the spawn and the hatched larvae until they are free-swimming. While not very prolific, they spawn at relatively short intervals. Offspring of previous spawns are tolerated within the spawning territory.

F: C; live foods such as *Artemia, Cyclops,* small *Daphnia,* microworms, and grindal worms. They can the trained to accept small flake foods.

S: *N. multifasciatus* is always found close to a snail shell. A large number of such shells should be placed in the aquarium. The more shells there are, the less likely it is that *N. multifasciatus* will bury the shells deep into the substrate.

T: 24°–26°C, **L:** ♂ 4.5 cm, ♀ 3.5 cm, **A:** 50 cm, **R:** b, **D:** 3

Neolamprologus multifasciatus   (BOULENGER, 1906)
Many-banded shell-dweller

Syn.: *Lamprologus multifasciatus.*

Hab.: Africa: endemic to Lake Tanganyika. Lives in colonies along the substrate at depths of about 10 m among groups of empty *Neothauma* snail shells which serve as hiding places and spawning caves.

F.I.: 1983.

Sex.: Usually only adult specimens can be differentiated. ♂♂ are about 1 cm larger and more intensely colored than their consorts. In addition, the upper edge of the dorsal fin is slightly reddish.

Soc. B.: Territorial. The animals are aggressive within their territories and vigorously defend their snail shell, even against much larger tankmates. They form colonies. Cave spawner. Their territory can have a diameter of up to 30 cm. Monogamous and polygamous lifestyles have been observed. Less aggressive than other shell-dwellers. This the smallest known shell-dwelling cichlid.

M: This species has only been found in Niamkolo Bay. The animals inhabit the sand zones and depend on the presence of empty snail shells. Small aquaria (30–40 l) are adequate for successful maintenance and reproduction. The finest sand must be used as substrate, since the fish are expert dredgers and excavators. Empty, cleaned shells of edible snails are a good substitute for *Neothauma* shells. The water should be medium-hard to hard (15°–25° dGH) and moderately alkaline (pH 8). Best kept in a species tank or associated with other small cichlids from Lake Tanganyika. The aquarium can be decorated with aquatic plants. Digging activity is indirectly related to the number of shells lying on the substrate: the more shells the less they dig.

Continued on facing page.

Mbenji Island, Lake Malawi

Rock and sand zone along the shoreline of an African lake.

Neolamprologus obscurus

Neolamprologus obscurus
Mottly lamprologus

(POLL, 1978)

Syn.: *Lamprologus obscurus, Paleolamprologus obscurus.*

Hab.: Africa: endemic to Lake Tanganyika. Found in rock and rubble littoral zones.

F.I.: 1984.

Sex.: ♂ ♂ are larger.

Soc. B.: Intraspecific aggressions are minimal. Pairwise maintenance is recommended. Monogamous cave spawners with a nuclear family structure. The ♀ cares for the spawn and the young, while the ♂ guards the territory.

M: Sufficient hiding places must be offered. The substrate should be of sand. Plants are optional.

B: Water should be medium-hard and neutral to slightly alkaline (10°–15° dGH and pH 7.0–8.5, respectively) with a temperature of 25°–28°C. Up to 50 eggs are laid in a cave.

F: C; large *Artemia*, mosquito larvae, *Mysis*, and other hardy foods, either live or frozen. Flake foods are also accepted.

T: 23°–28°C, **L:** 9 cm, **A:** 60 cm, **R:** b, m, **D:** 2

Fam.: Cichlidae

Lepidiolamprologus profundicola
Deep-water lamprologus

(POLL, 1949)

Syn.: *Lamprologus profundicola.*

Hab.: Africa: endemic to Lake Tanganyika. In the rock and rubble zone.

F.I.: 1980 (?).

Sex.: Have not been described.

Soc. B.: In nature, this species is a piscivorous loner. In the aquarium, it can be housed with large cichlids such as *Cyphotilapia frontosa*, which it associates with in its natural habitat.

M: This tranquil species requires an aquarium with a large surface area (from 120 x 50 cm) because of its size. So far, only large specimens have been imported, which is why nothing can be said about its intraspecific behavior.

B: For the above mentioned reason, no information is available concerning breeding this species in captivity. According to KONINGS, a specimen in the lake was observed at the outer fringes of the rocky biotope with a spawn that was hidden in a pit. According to this observation, only the ♀ guards the spawn and larvae.

F: C; hardy foods are indicated, since the animals feed on other cichlids in nature. As suitable substitutes, fish, mussel, and shrimp meat have proven acceptable as well as earthworms and fly grubs.

S: The northern population is indistinguishable from the southern population. However, DIECKHOFF discovered a lighter morph along the central Tanzanian coast.

T: 24°–26°C, **L:** 30 cm, **A:** from 120 cm, **R:** m, **D:** 3

Neolamprologus pleuromaculatus
Blotched lamprologus

(TREWAVAS & POLL, 1952)

Syn.: *Lamprologus pleuromaculatus.*

Hab.: Africa: endemic to Lake Tanganyika. Known habitats are located along the northern section of the lake. Sandy and muddy substrates are preferred.

F.I.: Could not be determined.

Sex.: There is neither sexual dimorphism nor dichromatism. It is impossible to distinguish the sexes from external characteristics. Adult ♂♂ are supposedly larger.

Soc. B.: *N. pleuromaculatus* is a territorial, tranquil species that is relatively peaceful towards conspecifics and heterospecifics. Predators. Plants are respected. Cave spawner with nuclear family. Pair maintenance is recommended.

M: The aquarium needs a deep layer of sand, some hiding places, and caves among rocks and roots. Water should be medium-hard and alkaline (15° dGH and pH 7.5–8.5, respectively). They can be kept with other *Neolamprologus* species. Plants can be included as part of the decoration.

B: Information on breeding in captivity could not be found. According to STAECK (1982): Handbuch der Cichlidenkunde, *N. pleuromaculatus* lays up to 300 eggs on rocks or, if possible, in caves in its natural habitat.

F: C; especially partial to live fishes, but other hardy live foods such as large *Artemia*, mosquito larvae, and *Mysis* are also accepted.

S: *N. pleuromaculatus* has 47–60 lateral line scales and 9–12 gill rakers.

T: 23°–25°C, **L:** 12 cm, **A:** 100 cm, **R:** b, m, **D:** 3 (C)

Lepidiolamprologus profundicola

Neolamprologus pleuromaculatus

Fam.: Cichlidae

Neolamprologus pulcher

(TREWAVAS & POLL, 1952)

Syn.: *Lamprologus savoryi pulcher, L. pulcher.*

Hab.: Africa: Lake Tanganyika (endemic). Limited to the rocky littoral zone of the lake.

F.I.: Middle of the '70's.

Sex.: Sexes are difficult to differentiate. The dorsal and anal fins of ♂♂ are reputed to be more elongated.

Soc. B.: Territorial. Normally a schooling fish, but they pair off for spawning. During that time they are relatively aggressive. Plants are tolerated. Suitable tankmates for *Neolamprologus, Julidochromis,* and *Telmatochromis* species. Cave spawner, nuclear family.

M: Decorate the tank with rock edifications, creating caves and other hiding places. Avoid heavy vegetation that interferes with their required free swimming space. While appropriate for community aquaria, a large tank (100–120 cm) will be needed to fulfill its territorial requisites. Water: hardness up to 18° dGH; pH 7.3–8.5.

B: More productive in a species tank. Keep pairs. A strong intersexual bond is established. Up to 100 eggs are laid in a cave. After about 6–7 days (at 25°C) the fry emerge from the cave and are essentially ignored from that point on. Feed the young *Artemia* nauplii and crumbled flake foods.

F: C, O; all kinds of live, frozen, freeze-dried, and flake foods as well as FD Menu.

S: *Neolamprologus brichardi* and *N. savoryi* have a horizontal black stripe behind the eye which extends over the edge of the anterior operculum. This stripe does not extend to the operculum in *N. pulcher;* instead it curves and follows the posterior edge of the anterior operculum.

T: 24°–26°C, **L:** 10 cm, **A:** 80 cm, **R:** m, b, **D:** 2

Neolamprologus marunguensis

BÜSCHER, 1991

Syn.: None. Previously sold as *N. "walteri."*

Hab.: Africa: endemic to Lake Tanganyika. Colonizes the rock and rubble littoral zones of the lake.

F.I.: 1984.

Sex.: Sexes are difficult to distinguish.

Soc. B.: Territorial; they usually live in large groups (extended families), but they pair off for spawning. Plants are not molested. Cave spawner, nuclear family.

M: As for *Neolamprologus pulcher.*

B: Similar to that of *N. pulcher.* However, *N. marunguensis* produces truly meager spawns, often only laying 10 eggs. In a seemingly compensatory exchange, the animals spawn repeatedly at surprisingly short intervals.

F: C; all kinds of live foods, but particularly small crustacea and insect larvae. Frozen and flake foods are also eaten.

S: The notorious striated design on the dorsal and deeply forked tail fin is characteristic for this species.

T: 24°–26°C, **L:** ♂ 6 cm, ♀ 5 cm, **A:** 70 cm, **R:** m, b, **D:** 2–3

Neolamprologus pulcher

Neolamprologus marunguensis

Ophthalmotilapia ventralis, Mpimbwe color morph

Ophthalmotilapia ventralis
Blue gold-tip cichlid

(BOULENGER, 1898)

Syn.: *Ophthalmochromis ventralis*.

Hab.: Africa: endemic to Lake Tanganyika.

F.I.: Ca. 1984.

Sex.: ♂♂ have noticeably long ventral fins which terminate in two spatulate tips. The ♀♀'s ventral fins are shorter and lack egg dummies.

Soc. B.: Nest builder. In nature, it constructs a depression in a sand substrate or builds a sand-rimmed pit on a rock. Its nest-building tendencies decline over time in captivity, where it builds a pit in sand substrates. Limit maintenance to one ♂ unless there are two that have been raised together. Pairwise maintenance is recommended. Perhaps a few calm, bottom-oriented fishes would make appropriate companions.

M: See *Ophthalmotilapia heterodonta* on p. 826 and Vol. 2, p. 960.

B: During courtship, the spatulate tips of the ventral fins are folded together to form an egg dummy. Like *O. heterodonta* (p. 826), *O. ventralis* is a mouthbrooder.

F: C, O; all kinds of live, frozen, and freeze-dried foods. Flake foods are accepted after acclimation. Young animals will eat TetraTips.

S: This is one of the most interesting cichlids of Lake Tanganyika. As evidenced by the photos on the facing page, there are several color morphs scattered throughout the lake. *O. nasutus* is a similar species (Vol. 2, p. 960). The "normal" morph of *O. ventralis* can be found in Vol. 1, p. 746.

T: 24°–26°C, **L:** ♂ 14 cm, ♀ 12 cm, **A:** 140 cm, **R:** m, b, **D:** 3

Ophthalmotilapia ventralis, Kabogo white cap

Ophthalmotilapia ventralis, Kachese

Ophthalmotilapia ventralis, Kapembe

Ophthalmotilapia ventralis, Maswa

Ophthalmotilapia ventralis, nominate form

Fam.: Cichlidae

Ophthalmotilapia boops

(BOULENGER, 1901)

Syn.: *Tilapia boops.*

Hab.: Africa: southern Tanzania, endemic to Lake Tanganyika.

F.I.: Not exactly known; perhaps imported in 1958.

Sex.: Clear sexual dimorphism. ♂♂ are more splendidly colored with significantly longer ventral fins that have spatulate bright tips (egg dummies).

Soc. B.: Like *Ophthalmotilapia heterodonta*. Ovophile mouthbrooder, maternal family.

M: See *O. heterodonta.*

B: As for *O. heterodonta.*

F: O; all kinds of live foods such as small crustacea, aquatic insects and their larvae, and molluscs as well as frozen foods, algae, and flake foods.

S: In 1981, LIEM dissolved the genus *Ophthalmochromis* and transferred its species into the genus *Ophthalmotilapia*, which at that time only contained *O. boops*. He justified his action by pointing out the great similarity between the species of the two genera.

T: 22°–26°C, **L:** 15 cm, **A:** 120 cm, **R:** b, m, **D:** 3

Ophthalmotilapia heterodonta

(POLL & MATTHES, 1962)

Syn.: *Ophthalmochromis ventralis heterodonta, O. heterodontus, Ophthalmotilapia ventralis heterodontus.*

Hab.: Africa: endemic to Lake Tanganyika. Lives in the rock zone, preferably in the transition zone where small sandy surfaces can be encountered among large rocks and rubble fields.

F.I.: Probably in 1958 with *Ophthalmotilapia ventralis.*

Sex.: Clear sexual dimorphism. ♂♂ are larger and beautifully colored with pointed dorsal and anal fins and significantly longer ventral fins.

Soc. B.: When sexually active, they are territorial and hostile towards both conspecifics and heterospecifics. They tend to dig at that time as well. They live in loose aggregations outside times of sexual activity. Ovophile mouthbrooder, maternal family.

M: Place loose groups of rocks upon the sand substrate and rock structures containing plenty of crevices and caves along the back of the tank. Plants are not necessary, but if included, use those that attach to rocks such as *Anubias* species or *Microsorium pteropus.*

B: Use medium-hard and moderately alkaline water (≥10° dGH and pH 7.5). ♂♂ are agamic; therefore, keep one ♂ with several ♀♀. This species is a maternal ovophile mouthbrooder. The approximately 60 eggs are fertilized by a modified egg spot method in which the ♀ is not stimulated by egg spots on the ♂'s anal fin, but by the yellow spatulate tips of the ♂'s ventral fins. All of the spawning sequence occurs in a shallow, previously constructed sandy depression (compare E. SCHOOP, 1986: DCG-Informationen **17**, 124–126).

F: O; primarily feeds on insects, molluscs, and plants. They also accept crustacea, fish flesh, and frozen, freeze-dried, and flake foods.

S: For a long time, *Ophthalmotilapia heterodonta* was considered to be a subspecies of *O. ventralis.*

T: 24°–26°C, **L:** 15 cm, **A:** from 120 cm, **R:** b, m, **D:** 3

Ophthalmotilapia boops

Ophthalmotilapia heterodonta

Fam.: Cichlidae

Oreochromis niloticus baringoensis
Baringo Nile tilapia

TREWAVAS, 1983

Syn.: None.

Hab.: Africa: Kenya, in Lake Baringo. This shallow lake is no deeper than 7.5 m at any point.

F.I.: 1983 by COOIJMANS, SEEGERS, and WILDEKAMP.

Sex.: ♂♂ are somewhat darker, particularly dorsally, and have a conspicuous genital papilla.

Soc. B.: Territorial. When engaged in sexual activity, ♂♂ are very intolerant of conspecific ♂♂ and heterospecifics. Ovophile mouthbrooder, maternal family.

M: Requires a substrate of gravel and/or sand and numerous secluded areas among rocks and roots. A planted aquarium is impossible since vegetation is either consumed or mercilessly up-

rooted as they constantly rearrange the decor. No major demands are placed on water quality, but avoid acidic pHs. Do not house with overly small fishes. Best kept in a species tank.

B: Probably not difficult, but to the best of our knowledge, it has not been bred in an aquarium.

F: O; all kinds of live, frozen, and freeze-dried foods as well as beef heart, flakes, and plant fare (lettuce, spinach, etc.).

S: The external tricuspid adult teeth, the relatively few vertebrae, and the dorsal fin arrangement of XVI 12 (16 hard rays, 12 soft rays) are distinctive characteristics for this subspecies of *O. niloticus*.

T: 24°–28°C, **L:** 36 cm, **A:** from 120 cm, **R:** b, m, **D:** 2

Oreochromis niloticus niloticus
Nile tilapia

(LINNAEUS, 1758)

Syn.: *Labrus niloticus, Chromis guentheri, Ch. nilotica, Ch. niloticus, Sarotherodon niloticus, Tilapia calciati, T. nilotica.*

Hab.: Africa and Asia: this species' broad distribution range extends from Syria and Israel to Tanzania, the Chad Basin, Senegal, Niger, and the Zaïre Basin. It inhabits stationary and flowing waters as well as brackish waters.

F.I.: 1902 by Dr. SCHOELLER, Alexandria.

Sex.: Recent studies have shown that differences between the genders are minor when spawning. The best differentiating characteristic is probably the dorsal and anal fins, which are pointed in the ♂ and rounded in the ♀.

Soc. B.: Territorial; the animals are aggressive when spawning and energetically defend their spawning pits against both conspecific and heterospecific fishes. Relatively peaceful species out-

side times of sexual activity. Ovophile mouthbrooder, maternal family.

M: As for *Oreochromis niloticus baringoensis.*

B: The fish do not have major water chemistry requirements. Breeding is not difficult. The ♂ digs a deep spawning pit where the ♀ lays up to 200 eggs and then takes them into her mouth. The eggs are pear-shaped, 3 mm in size, and yellowish brown.

F: O; all kinds of live, frozen, and freeze-dried foods as well as pieces of meat, flakes, tablets, and plant fare (algae, lettuce, spinach, etc.).

S: All offspring of the F_1 generation of ♀ *O. n. niloticus* crossed with ♂ *O. aureus* or *O. macrochir* are ♂♂. *O. niloticus* was frequently confused with *O. aureus*.

T: 14°–26°C, **L:** 35 cm, **A:** from 150 cm, **R:** b, m, **D:** 1–2

Oreochromis niloticus baringoensis

Oreochromis niloticus niloticus

Oreochromis pangani pangani

(LOWE, 1955)

Syn.: *Tilapia pangani, Sarotherodon pangani.*

Hab.: Africa: Tanzania, in the Pangani River. Cultivated in ponds, reservoirs, and Lake Singida.

F.I.: Unknown.

Sex.: In mature ♂♂ the tail fin may turn black with the exception of a red superior edge. Adult ♂♂ are larger and reputedly have a golden sheen on the cheeks, opercula, and sides. Ripe ♂♂ have a prominent genital papilla.

Soc. B.: Territorial; ♂♂ build spawning pits during spawning time and energetically defend them. Ovophile mouthbrooder, maternal family.

M: As for *Oreochromis urolepis urolepis.* A species tank is recommended because of its respectable mature size.

B: There is no information concerning breeding this fish successfully in an aquarium. Outdoors, the fish reach sexual maturity at a length of 20 cm. Large ♀♀ buccally incubate up to 1000 eggs.

F: O; all kinds of live, frozen, flake, and freeze-dried foods as well as pieces of meat and vegetable fare (algae, spinach, lettuce, etc.).

S: Besides the nominate form presented here, a subspecies from Lake Jipe, *O. p. girigan* (LOWE, 1955), has also been described.

T: 24°–28°C, **L:** ♂ up to 47 cm, ♀ up to 32 cm, **A:** from 150 cm, **R:** b, m, **D:** 2–3

Oreochromis spilurus niger

(GÜNTHER, 1894)

Syn.: *Oreochromis niger, O. athiensis, Tilapia athiensis, T. nigra, T. nilotica athiensis, T. spilurus nigra.*

Hab.: Africa: Kenya, in the Athi River and its tributaries above the Lugard Falls and the upper tributaries of the Tana River.

F.I.: Unknown.

Sex.: ♂♂ have beautiful courtship coloration.

Soc. B.: Territorial; the animals build and vigorously defend spawning pits. Ovophile mouthbrooder, maternal family.

M: As indicated for *Oreochromis niloticus baringoensis.*

B: There is no information concerning successfully breeding this species in an aquarium. In nature, the ♂♂ build a saucerlike spawning pit, which is where the ♀ lays the eggs in batches and the ♂ fertilizes them. Immediately thereafter the eggs are taken into the ♀'s mouth.

The eggs are pear-shaped with a longitudinal diameter of 2.5–3.0 mm. The number of eggs depends on the size of the ♀.

F: O; all kinds of live, frozen, freeze-dried, and flake foods as well as plant fare (algae, lettuce, spinach, etc.).

S: *Oreochromis spilurus* and its subspecies have been introduced into various regions of Africa by man (e.g., Madagascar).

T: 24°–28°C, **L:** 33 cm, **A:** from 120 cm, **R:** b, m, **D:** 2–3

Oreochromis pangani pangani

Oreochromis spilurus niger

Fam.: Cichlidae

Oreochromis spilurus spilurus

(GÜNTHER, 1894)

Syn.: *Chromis spilurus, Oreochromis d'anconai, Sarotherodon niger spilurum, Tilapia browni, T. nyirica, T. nigra spilurus, T. spilurus.*

Hab.: Africa: Kenya and Tanzania, in the coastal tributaries of the Mwena River near the Tanzanian border down to the Iwer Athi River below the Lugard Falls. In ponds and lakes of the Athi Plains and in coastal lagoons close to the mouth of the Athi.

F.I.: Unknown.

Sex.: Mature ♂♂ are more attractive than ♀♀.

Soc. B.: Territorial; sexually active ♂♂ build nests in the sand and energetically defend them against conspecific ♂♂ and heterospecifics. Ovophile mouthbrooder, maternal family (?).

M: As for *Oreochromis niloticus baringoensis*. Its size limits companions to conspecifics or large robust fishes.

B: There is no information available concerning breeding this fish in an aquarium.

F: O; all kinds of live, frozen, and freeze-dried foods as well as meat, flakes, and plant fare.

S: Two meristically different subspecies have been described (see TREWAVAS, 1983: Tilapine Fishes, p. 235, Table 56).

T: 24°–28°C, **L**: up to 40 cm, **A**: from 150 cm, **R**: b, m, **D**: 2–3

Oreochromis tanganicae
Tanganyikan tilapia

(GÜNTHER, 1893)

Syn.: *Tilapia tanganicae, Neotilapia tanganicae, Sarotherodon tanganicae.*

Hab.: Africa; Lake Tanganyika, in shallow shore zones above sand and rock substrates.

F.I.: Unknown.

Sex.: ♂♂ are larger with elongated fins and a beautiful pearl- to gold-colored body. ♀♀ have less extravagant colors.

Soc. B.: In its natural habitat, both juveniles and adults have been found in schools or small groups. One ♂ with several ♀♀ is suggested for aquarium maintenance.

M: Its large size and corresponding metabolism make a large tank, good filtration, and frequent water exchanges necessities. Restrict decorations to rocks and wood, since *O. tanganicae* is herbivorous. Provide a sand substrate.

B: Mouthbrooders. Brood care falls solely into the jurisdiction of the ♀. Detailed observations concerning reproductive behavior are not available. In nature, young up to a size of 2 cm have been seen repeatedly returning to the safety of their mother's buccal cavity.

F: O; based on stomach content analyses, *O. tanganicae* has been classified as a detritivore. In the aquarium, they accept all suitable-sized foods. Vegetable fare should always be provided.

T: 24°–26°C, **L**: 40 cm, **A**: from 120 cm, **R**: m, b, **D**: 2–3

Oreochromis spilurus spilurus, WC, Lillifi Creek, lower Athi River

Oreochromis tanganicae ♂

Oreochromis tanganicae ♀

Continuation of *Palaeolamprologus toae* (p. 836):

F: C; all kinds of live foods (mosquito larvae, *Tubifex,* small crustacea), various crustacea, and meat. Commercial diets are usually accepted.

S: The genus *Palaeolamprologus,* established by COLOMBE & ALLGAYER in 1985, is considered monotypic; that is, it only contains this species.

T: 24°–26°C, L: 11 cm, A: 80 cm, R: b, m, D: 2–3

Oreochromis urolepis urolepis, coastal zones of Tanzania, WC

Oreochromis urolepis urolepis (NORMAN, 1922)

Syn.: *Tilapia urolepis, T. adolphi* STEIN-DACHNER, 1916, not STEINDACHNER, 1909!

Hab.: Africa: Tanzania, found in the Kingani and Mbemkuru Rivers and two tributaries of the Rufiji River, the Kilombero and Great Ruaha Rivers, as well as the Rufiji itself. Brackish waters of the Rufiji Delta are avoided.

F.I.: 1979 by G. EGGERS and L. SEE-GERS.

Sex.: ♂♂ are larger, darker, and more intensely colored. In the Rufiji River, territorial ♂♂ may be black.

Soc. B.: Territorial, but not overly aggressive. Ovophile mouthbrooder, maternal family (?).

M: Requires a substrate of sand or gravel, some large flat stones for spawning, and shallow hiding places and caves among rocks and roots. Vegetation can and should be omitted, since plants are uprooted as the fish arrange the decor to their taste and needs. No particular demands are placed on water composition, but avoid acidic pHs.

B: There is no information concerning a successful aquarium spawn. In nature, the animals build spawning pits 75 cm in diameter and 15 cm deep. The eggs can be up to 3.1 mm in diameter. Depending on the size of the ♀, up to 500 eggs are laid.

F: O; all kinds of live, frozen, and freeze-dried foods as well as meat, flakes, and vegetable fare.

S: Juveniles of this subspecies are often found at temperatures of up to 38°C due to the influx of soda springs (52°C). *O. urolepis hornorum* (TREWAVAS, 1966) was previously considered to be an autonomous species (*Sarotherodon hornorum*) and was presented as such in Vol. 2, p. 980. However, TREWAVAS (1983) relegated it to the status of subspecies.

T: 22°–28°C, **L:** 38 cm, **A:** from 120 cm, **R:** b, m, **D:** 2–3

Fam.: Cichlidae

Oreochromis variabilis

(BOULENGER, 1906)

Syn.: *Tilapia variabilis, Sarotherodon variabilis.*

Hab.: Africa: Lake Victoria and its tributaries, Victoria Nile above the Murchinson Falls, and Lakes Kioga, Kwania, and Salisburg.

F.I.: Unknown.

Sex.: According to ALBRECHT (1968): Z. Tierpsychol. **25**, 377–394, ♂♂ and ♀♀ have differently colored irises, red with a black stripe and solid black, respectively. In addition, ♂♂ have a genital papilla that is several centimeters long when spawning.

Soc. B.: Territorial; sexually active ♂♂ build nests and vigorously defend them against conspecific ♂♂ and heterospecifics. ♂♂ actively dig during that time. Ovophile mouthbrooder, maternal family.

M: A thick layer of sand and a multitude of hiding places among rocks and roots should be provided. Plants in the tank would be futile, since these fish will ei-ther uproot or consume them. With the exception of a neutral to slightly alkaline pH, requirements are minimal.

B: The animals reach sexual maturity at a length of about 16 cm and are easily bred. The ♂ builds a shallow two-part nest in the sand substrate: a large depression with a circular, deeper pit in its center. The latter is where the ♀ actually lays her eggs. Fertilization takes place after the ♀ takes the eggs into her mouth and mouths the ♂'s genital appendage. The over 500 eggs are pear-shaped and 2.5–4.5 mm long. The young are independent at a length of 14–17 mm.

F: O; live foods of all kinds, frozen and freeze-dried foods, flakes, and vegetable fare.

S: A particular phenomenon of this species is the so-called "Maradadi" coloration of some animals, which means "beautifully colored." These animals have a black-spotted, pale orange dorsum.

T: 24°–28°C, **L:** 28 cm, **A:** from 120 cm, **R:** b, m, **D:** 2–3

Palaeolamprologus toae

(POLL, 1949)

Syn.: *Lamprologus toae.*

Hab.: Africa: endemic to Lake Tanganyika. Colonizes the rock and rubble littoral zones.

F.I.: 1984.

Sex.: There is neither sexual dichromatism nor dimorphism. Comparing the genital papillae is the only sure way to separate ♂♂ from ♀♀. ♀♀ have a round genital papilla, while ♂♂ have a dermal lobe above the genital opening (HERRMANN, 1986).

Soc. B.: Territorial. Intraspecific aggressions in this species are a daily occurrence. Cave spawner, paternal-maternal family.

M: Include many caves and other hiding places in the decor. Plants are left unmolested. The water should be clean and oxygen-rich with a hardness between 10° and 20° dGH and a pH of 7.2–8.5. Very soft water is detrimental.

B: A small aquarium (ca. 60 l) with caves, e.g., inverted flower pots, and a harmonizing pair are prerequisites for reproduction. The eggs are adhered to the wall of the spawning cave, and the ♀ guards and fans the spawn while the ♂ defends the vicinity against intruders. After 10 days, when the young appear for the first time at the cave's entrance, feed them *Artemia* nauplii. Juveniles are gray-brown with light spots.

Continued on p. 834.

Oreochromis variabilis, Lake Victoria at Muhoro, Kenya, WC ♂

Palaeolamprologus toae

Fam.: Cichlidae

Paracyprichromis brieni (POLL, 1981)

Syn.: *Cyprichromis brieni.*

Hab.: Africa: endemic to Lake Tanganyika. Found in the open waters of the rocky littoral zone.

F.I.: Unknown.

Sex.: ♂♂ are larger with a dark dorsal fin and yellow ventral fins. ♀♀ reputedly have a yellowish dorsal fin.

Soc. B.: Intraspecific aggressions and fights are occasionally seen, but do not lead to injuries. Agamic mouthbrooder.

M: Sufficient swimming space must be provided for this cichlid. If possible, keep a group of more than 10 specimens. Plant friendly.

B: Medium-hard, neutral to slightly alkaline water (10°–15° dGH and pH 7–8.5, respectively) with a temperature of 25°–28°C is appropriate for breeding. Five to ten young are produced each spawn. The ♀ assumes full custodial responsibility for 3 weeks. Agamic mouthbrooder.

F: C; large and small *Artemia, Cyclops, Daphnia,* and flake foods. Zooplanktivore.

S: *P. brieni* has been repeatedly confused with *Paracyprichromis nigripinnis*; however, the latter is probably only found in southern Lake Tanganyika.

T: 23°–28°C, **L:** 11 cm, **A:** 120 cm, **R:** m, t, **D:** 3

Continuation of *Paratheraps hartwegi* (p. 842):

B: Open spawner. Numerous small eggs are laid. They and the resulting offspring are almost exclusively cared for by the ♀. The larvae hatch four days postspawning at 25°–27°C and are freeswimming after an additional 5 to 6 days. They have a large head, a longitudinal stripe extending from behind the eye to the caudal peduncle, and a dark spot on the head. Even with *Artemia*, the parents feed their young by whirling up the sand.

F: O; all traditional cichlid foods are accepted. Plant fare must be included in the diet.

T: 24°–27°C, **L:** ♂ up to 16 cm, **A:** 100 cm, **R:** b, **D:** 1–2

Paracyprichromis brieni ♂

Paracyprichromis brieni ♀

Fam.: Cichlidae

Parananochromis longirostris (BOULENGER, 1903)

Syn.: *Pelmatochromis longirostris, Nanochromis longirostris.*

Hab.: West Africa: southern Cameroon and northern Gabon, in the Rio Muni.

F.I.: February 1987 by NUMRICH, LANDSBERG, and WUNDERLICH.

Sex.: Only adults or those animals near adulthood can be differentiated. The upper half of the caudal fin of ♂♂ is reddish and elongated. ♀♀ seem to be slightly stout with less iridescent spots on the flanks and shorter fins.

Soc. B.: Comparatively peaceful. Plant friendly. It likes to swim through the aquarium in groups. At breeding time, territories are established and defended.

M: Decorate the aquarium with plants, caves, rocks, and roots. Use a sand or fine-grained gravel substrate, since this species often sifts through the substrate searching for edibles. There are no notable requirements for water chemistry.

B: Because it is a recent import, breeding successes are few. Mouthbrooders. Water: hardness 5°–9° dGH; pH 5–6. The eggs are laid on the ceiling of a cave. It is unclear whether the eggs or only the larvae are cared for buccally. Oral incubation seems to be predominately the ♀'s job. The young are free-swimming after one week at the earliest. Raise the fry with *Artemia* nauplii.

F: O; live, frozen, and dry foods.

S: GREENWOOD placed *N. longirostris* into the new genus *Parananochromis* together with *N. gabonicus* and *N. caudifasciatus* in 1987. The type species *P. longirostris* is the only mouthbrooder in the genus.

T: 22°–26°C, **L:** ♂ 12 cm, ♀ 9 cm, **A:** 70 cm, **R:** b, **D:** 1–2

Paraneetroplus bulleri REGAN, 1905

Syn.: *Cichlasoma bulleri.*

Hab.: Central America: southern Mexico, in the upper Coatzacoalcos tributaries on the Tehuantepec Ismus (endemic): Rio Jaltepec, Rio Almoloya, Rio Sarabia, Rio Malatengo.

F.I.: 1983 by H. G. BREIDOHR, R. STAWIKOWSKI, and U. WERNER.

Sex.: No clear external differentiating characteristics are known. In nature, ♀♀ have bright golden scales behind the eye, while ♂♂ are an intense red.

Soc. B.: *P. bulleri* is an animated species that precociously starts defending territories and participating in low-level aggressiveness as a juvenile.

M: Requires large, roomy aquaria, a frequent water turnover, and surface movement. Rubble and its associated secluded areas should be arranged along the back of the aquarium. Plants are an accepted part of the decor. Water: pH 7.5; 5°–15° dGH; 5°–10° dKH; 25°–27°C.

B: Open spawners in their natural biotope. Eggs are deposited on or between pebbles in shallow flowing waters. Sites immediately above rapids are preferred. Though the amber eggs are few in number, they are quite large.

F: O; its diet should consist of easily digested foods: pond plankton, insect larvae, *Mysis*, and flake foods, including vegetable flakes.

T: 25°–27°C, **L:** 25 cm, **A:** 120 cm, **R:** b, **D:** 1–2

Parananochromis longirostris

Paraneetroplus bulleri

Fam.: Cichlidae

Paratheraps breidohri
Angostura cichlid

WERNER & STAWIKOWSKI, 1987

Syn.: None.

Hab.: Central America: southern Mexico, endemic to the highlands of Chiapas. Found in the Angostura Reservoir (Presa).

F.I.: 1983 by BREIDOHR, STAWIKOWSKI, and WERNER.

Sex.: Full-grown ♂♂ are blue-gray to burnished steel blue with a black throat, chest, and ventral region. ♀♀ are generally darker with an irregular long black spot on the dorsal fin and rust red areas on the dorsal and anal fins. Both sexes have horizontal spots on their sides.

Soc. B.: This lively, active cichlid is less aggressive than many of its close relatives.

M: The Angostura Reservoir has a rocky substrate that provides plenty of caverns and secluded areas. During the dry season its waters have the following values: temperature 30°C, 10° dGH, 12° dKH pH 7.5. Several close relatives, namely, *P. hartwegi* and *"C."* *grammodes* and two *Oreochromis* species, live

sympatrically with *P. breidohri*. Sexual maturity is attained at approximately $\frac{1}{4}$ to $\frac{1}{3}$ of its mature length of 21 cm.

B: Open spawner. *P. breidohri* lays its eggs on vertical substrates, usually rocks, in medium-hard water. The ♂ secures the spawning territory, while the ♀ assumes responsibility for direct brood care. Four days after spawning, the eggs hatch and the resulting larvae are moved into a pit and guarded. The ♂ places himself in the immediate vicinity of the young after they become free-swimming. The parents brood coloration is notorious. When engaged in custodial activities, the lips, inferior body, and posterior flanks turn jet black, while the head and dorsum, including the dorsal and caudal fin, become off-white.

F: O; the usual fare, but vegetable foods must be included in the diet.

S: With the description of *P. breidohri*, the original describers established a new genus, *Paratheraps*. *Paratheraps* was separated from the genus *Theraps*, which was redefined.

T: 22°–28°C, **L:** 21 cm, **A:** 120 cm, **R:** m, b, **D:** 2

Paratheraps hartwegi
Hartweg's cichlid

(TAYLOR & MILLER, 1980)

Syn.: *Cichlasoma hartwegi.*

Hab.: Central America: Mexico, highlands of Chiapas near Chiapa de Corzo in the Rio Grande de Chiapas/Rio Grijalva system and at Villa Flores in the Rio Santo Domingo and tributaries of the Angostura Reservoir.

F.I.: 1983 by H. G. BREIDOHR, R. STAWIKOWSKI, and U. WERNER.

Sex.: ♀♀ are smaller with fine dots and crossbands along their sides which begin short of the dorsum and extend down where they fuse into a black ventral area. Depending on their mood, the mem-

branes between the hard dorsal fin rays turn black. The head and dorsum turn lighter in direct proportion to how sexually active and aggressive the ♀♀ are.

Soc. B.: Temperamental and aggressive, especially towards adult conspecifics.

M: In its natural habitat, it is found in fast-flowing, clear to muddy waters which are usually cool (20°C) because of the altitude, but at times reach temperatures of 29°C. The water is usually hard to very hard, 10°–33° dGH, with a pH of 7.5. Although an active fish, numerous hiding places among roots and rocks should be available.

Continued on p. 838.

Paratheraps breidohri ♂

Paratheraps hartwegi ♂, additional photos on the following page

843

Paratheraps hartwegi ♂

Paratheraps hartwegi ♀

Petrochromis fasciolatus, BOULENGER, 1914

Petrochromis sp., Lake Tanganyika

Fam.: Cichlidae

Perissodus microlepis
Blue-spotted perissodus

BOULENGER, 1898

Syn.: *Perissodus burgeoni, P. gracilis.*

Hab.: Africa: endemic to Lake Tanganyika.

F.I.: Unknown; probably after 1980.

Sex.: No definite external differentiating characteristics are known.

Soc. B.: Loners. Probably not territorial. Maternal ovophile mouthbrooder. The fry are guarded by both parents.

M: Although *P. microlepis* accepts substitute foods, it never completely divorces itself from its natural feeding specialization, scale eating. Hence, it cannot be recommended for community aquaria. Perhaps they can be maintained in a species tank, though there is no guarantee that they will not consider each other's scales tasty appetizers. It is unknown whether or not this fish can subsist for long periods of time on foods other than scales.

B: There is a scientific article by YANAGISAWA & NSHOMBO (1983): Physiol. Ecol. Japan. 20, pp. 23–31, concerning courtship and reproductive behavior of *P. microlepis*. According to that publication, two behavioral customs radically separate this species from other mouthbrooders: the eggs are fertilized prior to the ♀ putting them into her mouth, and the pair bond lasts throughout custodial duties. Like open spawners, both parents guard the offspring. Behaviorally, *P. microlepis* is between a substrate spawner and the mouthbrooder. BRICHARD has seen this species guiding up to 350 young.

F: In nature the animals are highly specialized scale-eaters.

S: *P. microlepis* has two ovaries, whereas other cichlids only have one (POLL).

T: 24°–28°C, **L**: 11 cm, **A**: 100 cm, **R**: m, **D**: 4 (feeding specialist)

Petrochromis macrognathus

YAMAOKA, 1983

Syn.: None.

Hab.: Africa: Lake Tanganyika, Kalemie and the northwestern side of the lake. Along rubble littoral regions.

F.I.: 1984 by C. J. Aquarium.

Sex.: ♀♀ are usually smaller, and they often have light vertical lines on the body.

Soc. B.: Territorial. Very bellicose towards conspecifics. Other tankmates are not molested.

M: Roomy tank with hiding places amidst rock edifications. Feed a well-balanced, fiber-rich diet which includes large *Artemia, Daphnia,* glassworms and, of course, plant foods such as flake foods with a high proportion of vegetable matter and blanched spinach—avoid beef heart. Aquatic plants are consumed as well.

B: The lack of imports accounts for the fact that *P. macrognathus* has yet to be bred in captivity. Presumably these are agamic mouthbrooders with a maternal family. The fry are free-swimming 4–5 weeks postspawning.

F: O; fiber-rich foods such as *Daphnia, Artemia,* mosquito larvae and, of course, plant fare.

S: There are a number of *Petrochromis* which have yet to be scientifically studied. Many may be mere geographic color morphs.

T: 24°–26°C, **L**: 20 cm, **A**: 150 cm, **R**: m, **D**: 4

Perissodus microlepis, Kigoma, photographed in its natural habitat

Petrochromis macrognathus

Fam.: Cichlidae

Petrochromis orthognathus

MATTHES, 1959

Syn.: None.

Hab.: Africa: endemic to Lake Tanganyika. Found in the rock and rubble littoral zone.

F.I.: 1983.

Sex.: ♂♂ are usually monochromatic. ♀♀ have many crossbands along their sides.

Soc. B.: Agamic, territorial cichlids. Markedly aggressive towards conspecifics. There should always be several ♀♀ for each ♂ to distribute aggressions.

M: It is important that *P. orthognathus* is offered visual barriers and sufficient hiding places in the form of large rock caves. Other petricolous cichlids of Lake Tanganyika (e.g., *Tropheus, Simochromis*) make appropriate tankmates.

B: The ♂ lures the ♀ to a hard substrate (stones or similar) with body shimmies. Circling, they touch each other's genital region with their mouth. The eggs are immediately taken into the ♀'s mouth then fertilized. Brood care lasts for 4–5 weeks and is performed by the ♀.

F: O; fiber-rich foods: *Daphnia, Artemia*, mosquito larvae, and vegetable fare.

S: Juveniles are a beautiful yellow until a length of about 6 cm.

T: 24°–26°C, **L:** 14–16 cm, **A:** 150 cm, **R:** m, **D:** 2

Plecodus straeleni

POLL, 1948

Syn.: *Perissodus straeleni.*

Hab.: Africa: endemic to Lake Tanganyika. An uncommon species.

F.I.: Uncertain, but probably after 1980.

Sex.: No definite external differentiating characteristics are known.

Soc. B.: Like *Perissodus microlepis.*

M: As for *P. microlepis.*

B: To the best of our knowledge, this fish has not been successfully bred in an aquarium.

F: In nature, *P. straeleni* is a scale-eater.

S: *P. straeleni* can easily be differentiated from other scale-eaters by its deeper body and rounded head profile. *P. straeleni* is similarly colored to *Neolamprologus tretocephalus* and *Cyphotilapia frontosa*. Hypothetically, this may be a type of mimicry that allows it to approach unsuspecting fishes and parasitize off their scales. Further observations are required.

T: 24°–28°C, **L:** 16 cm, **A:** 100 cm, **R:** m, **D:** 4 (feeding specialist)

Petrochromis orthognathus ♂

Plecodus straeleni, Kigoma, photo taken in its natural habitat

Fam.: Cichlidae

Pseudocrenilabrus nicholsi (PELLEGRIN, 1928)

Syn.: *Paratilapia nicholsi, Haplochromis nicholsi, Paratilapia ventralis.*

Hab.: Africa: in the Zaïre Basin from Lake Upemba northward to Ankoro.

F.I.: 1985 (?) by H. BLEHER and accompanying travelers.

Sex.: Clear sexual dichromatism. ♂♂ are much more colorful that ♀♀, particularly while sexually active.

Soc. B.: Territorial. Aggressive towards conspecifics and heterospecifics. *P. nicholsi* digs while sexually active. Mouthbrooder, maternal family.

M: As for *Pseudocrenilabrus philander philander.*

B: Similar to other *Pseudocrenilabrus* species (see *P. philander philander*).

F: C; all kinds of live foods such as small crustacea, insects and their larvae, and worms.

S: *P. nicholsi* has notoriously long ventral fins.

T: 22°–25°C, **L:** 7 cm, **A:** 60 cm, **R:** b, m, **D:** 2–3

Pseudocrenilabrus philander philander (WEBER, 1897)
Dwarf Egyptian mouthbrooder

Syn.: *Chromis philander, Ch. ovalis, Ctenochromis philander, Haplochromis philander, Hemihaplochromis philander, Pseudocrenilabrus natalensis, Tilapia ovalis, T. philander.*

Hab.: Africa: Zimbabwe, Mozambique, and South Africa, from the upper to the lower courses of the Zambezi River and its tributaries in Mozambique, Lakes Kariba, Kafue, Malawi, and Tanganyika to the Uvongo River in Natal as well as the Oranje/Vaal Basin in South Africa.

F.I.: 1911 by the Vereinigte Zierfischzüchtereien Conradshöhe, Berlin.

Sex.: Pronounced sexual dichromatism. ♂♂ are significantly more colorful. Sexually active ♂♂ have a golden anal fin with numerous red spots, including one red spot on its lower tip.

Soc. B.: Territorial, aggressive, and quarrelsome. When spawning, extensive digging activities ensue. Agamic mouthbrooders with maternal family.

M: Requires a fine-grained sand substrate, free swimming space, and secluded areas and caves among large rocks and inverted flower pots. Plants must be tough-leaved varieties, preferably potted to deter *P. p. philander* from uprooting them. Medium-hard, neutral water (12° dGH and pH 7, respectively) is suggested.

B: Not very difficult. The water values listed under maintenance and a temperature of 24°–27°C satisfy its prerequisites for reproduction. ♂♂ build small nests in the sand for spawning. Up to 70 egg are laid, fertilized, and then taken into the ♀'s mouth. The ♀ protects the fry by readmitting them into her buccal cavity at night and during danger.

F: C; piscivore, but aquatic insect larvae, terrestrial insects, crustacea, and many other aquatic organisms are also accepted.

S: In comparison to the nominate form, the subspecies *P. philander dispersus* (TREWAVAS, 1936) has a smaller mouth and shorter premaxillae.

T: 22°–25°C, **L:** 9 cm, **A:** 60 cm, **R:** b, m, **D:** 2–3

Pseudocrenilabrus nicholsi, WC, Kisangani, Zaïre

Pseudocrenilabrus philander philander, WC, Lake Mweru Wantipa, Zambia

Fam.: Cichlidae

Pseudosimochromis curvifrons

(POLL, 1942)

Syn.: *Simochromis curvifrons*.

Hab.: Africa: endemic to Lake Tanganyika. Found in the upper rubble and rock littoral zone.

F.I.: Unknown.

Sex.: ♀♀ are not blue-gray but green-gray with a number of light lines on the flanks.

Soc. B.: Territorial. Very aggressive towards conspecifics. Agamic mouthbrooders with maternal family.

M: Requires a large aquarium and rock edifications with a multitude of caves and niches. *Simochromis, Tropheus,* and *Petrochromis* species make suitable tankmates.

B: These animals lay their eggs on a hard substrate. Immediately thereafter, the eggs are taken into the ♀ buccal cavity and then fertilized. For 3¹/₂ weeks the ♀ tends to the brood alone.

F: O; aufwuchs feeder. Feed a fiber-rich diet that includes vegetable fare (Tetra Conditioning Food, Sera Flora).

S: *P. curvifrons* is a fast, very difficult to catch species, both in its natural habitat and the aquarium.

T: 24°–26°C, **L:** 12 cm, **A:** 150 cm, **R:** m, **D:** 2

Pseudotropheus crabro
Hornet cichlid

RIBBINK & LEWIS, 1982

Syn.: None. However, this species was sold as *P.* "chameleo" before it was scientifically described.

Hab.: Africa: endemic to Lake Malawi. Known to inhabit various sites along the southern and central region of the lake. Animals destined for the aquarium trade predominately come from the Mbenji Islands. Rock or sand-rock substrates at depths of 10–20 m are preferred.

F.I.: Probably in the early '80's.

Sex.: Fully colored ♂♂ have an almost totally black body and fins. ♀♀ and inferior ♂♂ have a yellowish body with 4–5 broad black crossbands beneath the dorsal fin. However, dominant ♀♀ may also turn black—a fairly rapid process (hence the previous trade name, "chameleo"). ♂♂ have 2–4 clearly pronounced egg spots on the anal fin, while ♀♀ only have 1–2 egg spots.

Soc. B.: In nature, *P. crabro* predominantly lives singly or in small groups. ♂♂ are only slightly territorial. Keep either one ♂ with 2–3 ♀♀ or, if the aquarium is more than 1.5 m long, a small group of 5–6 animals. Agamic ovophile mouthbrooder with maternal family.

M: A basic condition to successfully care for this very active species is an aquarium with a large surface area. Hiding places among stones or bogwood for subdominant or brooding animals should always be present. Use a fine gravel or coarse sand substrate and robust, fast-growing plants such as giant vallisneria or various crypotocorynes rather than delicate species. The water should be alkaline (pH 7.5–8.2). Water hardness is of secondary importance. In respect to *P. crabro*'s voracious appetite, a powerful filtration system and regular water exchanges of 30% every 10–14 days are indispensable.

B: Relatively easy to bred. After spawning, which occurs by the egg spot

Continued on p. 854.

Pseudosimochromis curvifrons

Pseudotropheus crabro

Fam.: Cichlidae

Continuation of *Pseudotropheus crabro* (p. 852):

method, the ♀ has sole responsibility of the brood. Depending on water temperature, the young are released from the mother's mouth in 20–24 days. At that time, the young are approximately 10 mm long and can be fed newly hatched *Artemia* nauplii, small freshwater plankton, or finely ground commercial diets. Depending on the size of the ♀, between 20 and 60 fry are produced each spawn. The fry are occasionally readmitted into the mother's mouth for another 4–5 days after they are free-swimming. Brood care is terminated soon thereafter.

F: O; large foods are eagerly accepted by this gluttonous omnivore. Beware—it is easily overfed. Its hardy appetite is manifest by a rapid growth rate. All frozen, live, or commercial diets such as flakes or tablets are suitable. Diseases of the digestive tract are a consequence of a diet poor in fiber. Meat should only be fed in small quantities.

S: *P. crabro* has been seen cleaning the ectoparasite *Argulus africanus* from large catfish (*Bagrus meridionalis*) in Lake Malawi. Whether the sum of the relationship should be classified as beneficial or detrimental, however, is debatable, since *P. crabro* feeds on newly laid catfish eggs.

T: 24°–26°C, **L:** 12 cm (15 cm), **A:** 120 cm, **R:** all, **D:** 2–3

Continuation of *Pseudotropheus greshakei* (p. 855):

caught specimens. As for many other mbunas, a diet made up exclusively of meat frequently induces digestive tract diseases, which in turn often result in death.

S: *P. greshakei* is part of the *P. zebra* group, which is comprised of a number of closely related species. One of these is the as yet undescribed *P.* "red top zebra Mbenji" from the Mbenji Islands, a close relative of *P. greshkei*.

T: 24°–26°C, **L:** 10 cm, larger in aquaria, **A:** from 100 cm, **R:** b, m, **D:** 2

Pseudotropheus greshakei
Red top ice blue

MEYER & FÖRSTER, 1984

Syn.: None. Prior to its scientific description, the species was sold as *P.* "red top ice blue."

Hab.: Africa: endemic to Lake Malawi. Distribution seems to be very limited. So far, *P. greshakei* has only been found along a few underwater reefs at the southeastern arm of the lake close to Makokola.

F.I.: Beginning of the '80's.

Sex.: Pronounced sexual dichromatism. The pictured animal has the typical ♂ coloration. ♀♀ are a solid reddish brown.

Soc. B.: Agamic maternal mouthbrooder. Sexually active ♂♂ are territorial. Non-territorial, subdominant ♂♂ and ♀♀ are frequently found in groups. All genders and social ranks are aggressive among themselves in the aquarium.

M: Besides a large surface area, numerous hiding places are important. It is vital that the hiding places be arranged so that the animals cannot maintain visual contact with each other. Intraspecific aggressions can also be dampened by keeping other robust mbunas as tankmates. One ♂ with 2–3 ♀♀ seems to be best. Use water values given for other Lake Malawi cichlids and a coarse sand or fine-grained gravel substrate.

B: Simple. Mouthbrooder with maternal family. With the maintenance conditions described above, this species generally breeds without further ado via the egg spot method. All custodial duties fall to the ♀. Raise the young by the guidelines given for other *Pseudotropheus* species.

F: C, O; in its natural habitat, *P. greshakei* primarily feeds on aufwuchs it scrapes off the substrate. When available, plankton is also eaten. Though considered an unproblematic omnivore, a fiber-rich diet should be offered, particularly for wild

Continued on facing page.

Fam.: Cichlidae

Pseudotropheus hajomaylandi

IN'T VEEN, 1984

Syn.: None. Prior to its scientific description, this species was sold as *P. "greeberi."*

Hab.: Africa: endemic to Lake Malawi. Exclusively found near Chisumulu Island, where sand substrates with a scattering of a few large stones or smaller rocks at depths of 10–30 m are preferentially chosen.

F.I.: Unknown, but probably at the end of the '70's.

Sex.: In contrast to the pictured ♂, ♀♀ are dull gray-blue with dark crossbands. In addition, ♀♀ only have slightly visible egg spots on the anal fin and usually remain smaller.

Soc. B.: Agamic maternal ovophile mouthbrooder. ♂♂ are territorial. Subdominant, nonterritorial ♂♂, juveniles, and ♀♀ live singly and are intolerant of conspecifics.

M: Typical mbuna. The aquarium should be divided into numerous hiding places with rocks and/or roots to offer protection to subdominant or brooding animals. Best experiences have been achieved with one ♂ and 2 or more ♀♀. To limit intraspecific aggressions, *P. hajomaylandi* should be housed with other mbuna species. Use a fine-grained gravel or coarse sand substrate. Water: hardness 10°–20° dGH; pH 7.5–8.3.

B: The maintenance conditions listed above and a good diet are usually enough to induce this species to breed without further difficulties. After spawning, the ♀ should be carefully caught and transferred into a separate aquarium. In 20 to 25 days, the 1 cm long young are released from the mouth of the mother and can immediately be fed newly hatched *Artemia salina* or finely ground commercial diets. Remove the ♀ when she no longer admits the young into her mouth. From that point forward, rearing is uncomplicated.

F: All kinds of live and frozen foods such as mosquito larvae, shrimp, *Cyclops*, and *Daphnia*. Wild caught specimens are prone to diseases of the digestive tract and must be fed a fiber-rich diet as a preventive measure.

S: None.

T: 24°–26°C, **L:** 10 cm (15 cm), **A:** from 120 cm, **R:** b, m, **D:** 2–3

Pseudotropheus williamsi
Williams's mbuna

(GÜNTHER, 1893)

Syn.: *Chromis williamsi.*

Hab.: Africa: endemic to Lake Malawi. Predominately found along shallow rocky shore regions.

F.I.: Unknown.

Sex.: Pronounced sexual dichromatism. ♀♀ are plain gray with dark crossbands which change in intensity depending on mood. The pictured animal is a typically colored ♂.

Soc. B.: Agamic ovophile mouthbrooder. Sexually active ♂♂ claim territories. ♀♀ and juveniles usually live in aggregations.

M: Numerous hiding places should be included among rock edifications and roots. Robust plants can be used even though they are not found in their natural habitat. Coarse sand or fine gravel, as with most Malawi cichlids, is the recommended substrate. In comparison to other mbunas, intraspecific aggressions are not as pronounced. Nevertheless, keep one ♂ with several ♀♀ and other mbunas. Water: pH 7.8–8.3; 10°–20° dGH. Performing 20%–30% water exchanges every 2 weeks heightens the fish's well-being.

Continued on p. 860.

Pseudotropheus hajomaylandi

Pseudotropheus williamsi ♂

Fam.: Cichlidae

Ptychochromis oligacanthus
Madagascar cichlid

Syn.: *Tilapia oligacanthus, T. grandidieri, T. madagascariensis, Ptychochromis grandidieri, P. madagascariensis.*

Hab.: Africa: endemic to Madagascar.

F.I.: Unknown.

Sex.: Unknown.

Soc. B.: Little is known about this species. Its behavior is similar to other substrate spawners such as *Tilapia* or *"Cichlasoma"* species.

M: Requires a large aquarium with a fine sand substrate and rock edifications in the background. Plants should be waived. Warm temperatures are generally necessary, but according to literature, they can also be acclimated to cool water.

B: Several pits are constructed in each territory, but only one is selected for spawning. After 8 to 10 days the eggs hatch and are cared for by both parents.

F: O; feed hardy foods such as shrimp and perhaps crabs as well as insects and worms commiserate to their size.

S: This species has four geographically separated color morphs. In Madagascar, this is an important food fish.

T: 24°–30°C, **L:** 27 cm, **A:** 120 cm, **R:** b, m, **D:** 2–3

Ptyochromis sauvagei
Victoria mottled hap

(PFEFFER, 1896)

Syn.: *Ctenochromis sauvagei, Haplochromis sauvagei, Tilapia sauvagei.*

Hab.: Africa: endemic to Lake Victoria.

F.I.: After 1980.

Sex.: ♂♂ have egg spots on the anal fin and are sexually active at half their mature size, even though they still have the drab juvenile coloration. Only full-grown ♂♂ acquire beautiful blue colors (see photos).

Soc. B.: *P. sauvagei* can be a saint or a tyrant. If the latter is the case, the dominant ♂ will show extreme intolerance towards conspecific ♂♂, even in large tanks. ♀♀ are not particularly bothered; nevertheless, it is advisable to house several ♀♀ with one ♂. Towards heterospecifics, even ♂ haplochromines, there are occasional territorial disputes, though rarely violent.

M: A sand substrate and a pile of rocks form the basis of the tank's decor. To the best of our knowledge, plants are left unmolested. *P. sauvagei* should be housed with numerous other Lake Victorian cichlids in a large tank. Frequent water exchanges and filter maintenance prevent unwanted losses, since the animals are somewhat sensitive to dissolved metabolites.

B: Mouthbrooders; the ♀ alone broods the eggs after spawning.

F: C; in nature, this species mainly feeds on snails. All normal substitute foods are accepted in captivity. Occasionally frozen foods have to be vitamin enriched to maintain the fish's vitality.

S: The genus *Ptyochromis* was established by GREENWOOD (1980). It is closely related to the sister genera *Macropleurodus* REGAN, 1922 and *Paralabidochromis* GREENWOOD, 1956.

T: 24°–27°C, **L:** 13 cm, **A:** from 80 cm, **R:** m, b, **D:** 2–3

Ptychochromis oligacanthus

Ptyochromis sauvagei ♂, ♀ on following page

Ptyochromis sauvagei ♀

Continuation of *Pseudotropheus williamsi* (p. 856):

B: Maternal mouthbrooder. The eggs are fertilized by the egg spot method as the fish move in a circular pattern. Once the eggs are fertilized, the ♂ does not contribute to any phase of brood care. Raise the young as suggested for *Pseudotropheus hajomaylandi*.

F: C, O; *P. williamsi* is an aufwuchs feeder, but it can be easily trained to substitute foods in the aquarium. Mosquito larvae, shrimp, and *Daphnia* as well as all kinds of frozen and commercial dry foods are readily accepted. A diet rich in fiber is especially important for wild caught specimens. Feed meat in very small quantities, lest *P. williamsi*, like many other mbunas, falls prey to intestinal diseases.

S: The taxon *P. williamsi* represents a species group in Lake Malawi. Probably due to geographic isolation, several very new, closely related species have evolved. According to new findings (RIBBINK et al., 1983), 8 different species found in different locals have been distinguished. Detailed taxonomic work with scientific names for the individual species, however, is still pending. That is why they are still referred to by their habitat: *P. w.* "Chisumulu," *P. w.* "Khuyu," *P. w.* "Maingano," *P. w.* "Makanjila," *P. w.* "Maleri," *P. w.* "Mbenji," *P. w.* "Namalenje," and *P. w.* "Nkudzi." The species pictured here is *P. w.* "Namalenje" from Namalenje Island along the western coast of the lake.

T: 24°–26°C, **L:** 11 cm, **A:** from 80 cm, **R:** m, **D:** 2–3

Ptyochromis xenognathus ♂

Ptyochromis xenognathus   (GREENWOOD, 1957)

Syn.: *Haplochromis xenognathus.*

Hab.: Africa: endemic to Lake Victoria.

F.I.: Probably after 1980.

Sex.: ♀♀ are generally paler with color-less fins. ♂♂ have egg spots on the anal fin.

Soc. B.: In comparison to other Lake Victorian cichlids, *P. xenognathus* is very peaceful and can easily be associated with similar species. Even several conspecific ♂♂ can be kept together in large aquaria.

M: Use rock edifications to delimit territories and sand for the substrate. Like all fishes from the Rift Lakes of Africa, frequent water exchanges are needed for breeding and long term maintenance. Apparently they do not eat plants, so feel at ease including plants in the decor.

B: Mouthbrooder. After the eggs are fertilized, the brood is the sole responsibility of the ♀. For best offspring survival, it is usually necessary to transfer the brooding ♀ into a separate aquarium.

F: C; stomach contents have shown that this fish feeds on gastropods, insects, and detritus in nature. In the aquarium, all normal foods are accepted.

S: The beautiful blue acquired by courting ♂♂ is reminiscent of Lake Malawi cichlids. *P. xenognathus* is very similar to *Ptyochromis sauvagei.*

T: 24°–27°C, **L:** 15 cm, **A:** from 80 cm, **R:** m, b, **D:** 2–3

Fam.: Cichlidae

Reganochromis calliurus
Calliurus

(BOULENGER, 1901)

Syn.: *Paratilapia calliura, Lamprologus calliurus, Leptochromis calliura, L. calliurus.*

Hab.: Africa: endemic to Lake Tanganyika. Found at great depths.

F.I.: Large numbers were imported for the first time in 1984/85.

Sex.: No external differences are known.

Soc. B.: This relatively peaceful cichlid claims a territory at spawning time. Mouthbrooder, nuclear family. Intense brood care.

M: There should be open sandy surfaces as well as hiding places among rock edifications. Plant friendly.

B: Breeding is considered difficult. Water: hardness 10°–15° dGH; pH 7.0–8.5; 25°–28°C. Mouthbrooder. ♂♂ and ♀♀ take turns caring for the spawn. The animals retire into a cave to care for their offspring. The 50 or more eggs and fry are incubated for about 3 weeks.

F: C; crustacea, mosquito larvae, other animal fare (frozen foods), and flake foods.

T: 23°–28°C, **L:** 15 cm, **A:** 120 cm, **R:** b, m, **D:** 2–3

Retroculus lapidifer
Riffle eartheater

(CASTELNAU, 1855)

Syn.: *Chromys lapidifera, Acara lapidifera, Geophagus lapidifera, G. (Retroculus) lapidifera, G. (R.) lapidifer, Retroculus boulengeri.*

Hab.: South America: Brazil, Guamá, probably throughout the Tocantins Araguaia do Pará Basin.

F.I.: 1987 by A. WERNER, Brazil.

Sex.: Unknown.

Soc. B.: Extraordinarily peaceful large cichlid. Occasionally several specimens retire into a cave, or they calmly lie on the substrate or on an elevated site outside their hiding place. Sometimes *R. lapidifer* circles about with unpaired fins spread and throat lowered, simultaneously nodding their head. These actions may represent part of their courtship behavior.

M: Since this is an eartheater, avoid sharp-edged substrates; sand is best. Water chemistry is of secondary importance, but a hardness of 15° dGH and a pH of about 7 seem to be optimal. Breeding may require soft, acid water. The aquarium can contain plants, but they should be strongly anchored in the substrate or protected with stones.

B: Unknown. Their eggs, which are reminiscent of mustard seeds both in size and color, are laid in depressions they excavate (*lapidifer* = "stone carrier") within the substrate (CASTELNAU, 1855). It is unknown whether *R. lapidifer* is a substrate spawner or mouthbrooder.

F: C, O; despite the size of its mouth, this species seems unable to swallow large foods. Smaller foods such as mosquito larvae are chewed singly. Dry foods are accepted with great reluctance.

S: Members of this genus are rheophile cichlids, that is, they are specialized inhabitants of fast-flowing waters. Imported animals were captured in the immediate

Continued on p. 870.

Reganochromis calliurus

Retroculus lapidifer

Sarotherodon galilaeus

(ARTEDI, 1757)

Syn.: *Sparus galilaeus, Chromis lateralis, Chromis tiberianis, Tilapia galilea, T. lateralis, T. macrocentra, T. pleuromelas, T. macrocephala.*

Hab.: Middle East, Africa: from Jordan through all of east and central Africa to Liberia. Found in flowing and stationary waters. *S. galilaeus* all but disappeared from aquaria, but sporadic imports of wild caught specimens are again appearing.

F.I.: 1934 by Dr. AHL, Berlin.

Sex.: Very difficult to distinguish; there is no sexual dichromatism. ♀♀ are very full when ripe (eggs) and more active during courtship.

Soc. B.: Nonterritorial schooling fish. Pairs bond to variable degrees just prior to spawning. Quarrelsome and bellicose towards conspecifics, but peaceful towards heterospecifics. Plants are both eaten and uprooted. Nuclear family.

M: Tanks over 100 cm long suffice for a few animals. Numerous hiding places among rocks and hollow roots should be present. Use tough plants (*Sagittaria, Vallisneria*), a fine sand substrate, and a water temperature of 20°–25°C. *S. galilaeus* generally limits its activities to middle to lower water strata. Though they reach a length of 40 cm in nature, they remain significantly smaller in the aquarium, attaining sexual maturity at a length of 10 cm.

B: 24° to 28°C. Few demands are placed in regard to water chemistry. Up to 1,500 eggs are laid on stones then taken into the buccal cavity. Both parents participate in the first phases of brood care. Parents actively tending offspring separate from the school. The bond between the parents and brood is very weak. After the young are released from the buccal cavity, they are not readmitted, yet they continue to be guarded by the parents.

F: O; hardy live foods and vegetable supplements (e.g., lettuce, spinach, *Elodea*, filamentous algae, oats). Dry commercial diets such as flake and tablet foods are also eaten.

S: A highly rated food fish in its natural habitat. *S. galilaeus*'s eggs still have an adhesive organ that has vanished from the eggs of highly specialized mouthbrooders.

T: 22°–28°C, **L:** 40 cm, **A:** from 100 cm, **R:** m, b, **D:** 2

Satanoperca leucosticta

(MÜLLER & TROSCHEL, 1849)

Syn.: *Geophagus leucostictus, Satanoperca macrolepis* (has erroneously been called *Geophagus jurupari* commercially).

Hab.: Northern South America: Guyana and Suriname, found in Lake Amucu and the river systems of Essequibo and Corantijn. The description is based on specimens from Lake Amuco.

F.I.: Though repeatedly imported since World War II, it was always under the name *Geophagus jurupari*.

Sex.: Clear secondary sexual characteristics are lacking. There is neither sexual dimorphism nor dichromatism. At best, ♂♂ are a little larger.

Soc. B.: Peaceful and retiring. Because antagonistic actions are rare among conspecifics, a group can be kept in large aquaria.

M: Keep in roomy aquaria that have a large surface area, a few hiding places, and generous open regions which are covered with loose, smooth-edged gravel or sand. This substrate allows the fish to engage in its natural feeding custom of sifting and masticating through the substrate (eartheater). The aquarium can be decorated with tough plants. Soft to medium-hard, slightly acid water (≤10° dGH and pH slightly below 7, respectively).

Continued on p. 870.

Sarotherodon galilaeus

Satanoperca leucosticta

Fam.: Cichlidae

Satanoperca pappaterra

(HECKEL, 1840)

Syn.: *Geophagus pappaterra.*

Hab.: South America: Brazil and Bolivia. Described from the Rio Guaporé Basin.

F.I.: Unknown.

Sex.: Clear secondary sexual characteristics are absent. ♂♂ and ♀♀ are largely identical in color and shape. At best, ♂♂ are a little larger.

Soc. B.: Peaceful and retiring. Fights are rare, even between conspecifics. Several specimens can be kept in a large aquarium.

M: The aquarium should have a large surface area, a few hiding places, and open regions covered with loose, smooth-edged gravel or sand. The substrate allows the fish to engage in its natural feeding custom of sifting and masticating through the substrate (earth-eater). The aquarium can be stocked with hardy plants. The water should be soft to medium-hard and acid (≤10° dGH and pH <7, respectively).

B: Sexually mature at a length of 12–13 cm. Although we know that this is an ovophile mouthbrooder, more precise information concerning its reproductive behavior is unknown.

F: Small foods are readily accepted; *S. pappaterra* prefers to take its food from the bottom. Small worms and sunken mosquito larvae are a delicacy.

T: 24°–27°C, **L:** ♂ up to 25 cm, ♀ somewhat smaller, **A:** from 120 cm, **R:** b, **D:** 3

Serranochromis robustus robustus
Southern bass cichlid

(GÜNTHER, 1864)

Syn.: *Hemichromis robustus, Pelmatochromis tanganyicae, P. tanganicae.*

Hab.: Africa: Lake Malawi and the upper Shire River. *S. r. robustus* prefers to colonize sandy substrates that are overgrown with plants. Frequently found at the mouths of rivers and swampy shore regions, less commonly above rocky substrates.

F.I.: Unknown.

Sex.: No pronounced sexual dichromatism. Sexually active ♂♂ lose the longitudinal stripe seen on the pictured animal, becoming solid blue-green instead.

Soc. B.: Information is scant. Agamic mouthbrooder. *S. r. robustus* usually lives singly, less commonly encountered in small groups. In its natural biotope, the ♀ attends to all custodial duties for the brood. Piscivore.

M: Not an aquarium fish. This predatory large cichlid can only be kept in large tanks as a juvenile. In nature, *S. r. robustus* is said to reach a length exceeding 50 cm. Corresponding to its habitat in the lake, an aquarium with a large surface area and a thick layer of sand should be provided. Robust plants and some stone edifications are recommended to provide cover. A powerful filtration system and frequent partial water exchanges prove necessary. Water values recommended for other Malawi cichlids are suitable but not critical, since this species is found inhabiting waters with varying chemistry in nature. *S. r. robustus*'s occasional presence in the trade is owed exclusively to juveniles imported as by-catch.

B: There is no information concerning successfully breeding this fish in captivity.

F: C, O; voracious consumer of large foods. Live fishes are preferred, but it can be trained to substitute foods. Earth-

Continued on p. 872.

Satanoperca pappaterra

Serranochromis robustus robustus

Fam.: Cichlidae

Simochromis diagramma
Diagonal bar mouthbrooder

(GÜNTHER, 1893)

Syn.: *Chromis diagramma.*

Hab.: Africa: endemic to Lake Tanganyika. Found along the rocky littoral zone.

F.I.: Unknown.

Sex.: ♂♂ grow about 2 cm larger and have more brilliantly colored fins.

Soc. B.: Territorial. Very aggressive towards conspecifics and similar heterogeners (*Tropheus*). Agamic mouthbrooder.

M: Numerous hiding possibilities must be offered in the form of rock edifications. Maintain just one ♂ with several ♀♀ to distribute the aggressions. Plants should be excluded from the decor, since *S. diagramma* is apt to treat them like a salad bar.

B: In general, reproduction is similar to *Simochromis pleurospilus*.

T: 25°C, **L:** 18 cm, **A:** 150 cm, **R:** m, **D:** 2

F: O; a fiber-rich, vegetable diet is quintessential.

S: *S. diagramma* is widely distributed throughout Lake Tanganyika, so it is not surprising that there are different geographic color morphs. The pictured specimen comes from the southern part of the lake.

Simochromis pleurospilus

NELISSEN, 1978

Syn.: None.

Hab.: Africa: Lake Tanganyika, in the rocky littoral zones and the transition zones of the sandy littoral.

F.I.: Large numbers were imported in 1983.

Sex.: Only ♂♂ have salmon red dots on their flanks.

Soc. B.: Territorial and very aggressive towards conspecifics. Keep only one ♂ with a group of several ♀♀. Agamic mouthbrooder.

M: The aquarium should contain sufficient hiding places for subdominant animals. Various *Tropheus* and *Petrochromis* species make suitable tankmates.

B: ♂♂ build small pits in the sand at spawning time and, using strong body quivering, lure a mature ♀ into the depression. There the animals circle each other as part of their courtship before laying the eggs. The eggs are immediately taken into the ♀'s mouth then fertilized within her buccal cavity. Approximately 3½ weeks postspawning, the fry are released.

F: O; avoid fiber-poor foods, e.g., *Tubifex,* beef heart).

S: There seem to be two different size morphs in Lake Tanganyika, one 12 cm long and one 9 cm long.

T: 25°C, **L:** 9–12 cm, **A:** 120 cm, **R:** m, **D:** 2

Simochromis diagramma

Simochromis pleurospilus

Fam.: Cichlidae

Steatocranus gibbiceps
Blunt-head cichlid

BOULENGER, 1899

Syn.: None.

Hab.: West Africa: lower Zaïre River between Kinsuka and Inga.

F.I.: 1971.

Sex.: Gender is difficult to distinguish in juveniles. ♂♂ have a more elongated dorsal fin and a more pronounced cranial hump. In comparison to *Steatocranus casuarius*, the cranial hump is much less developed.

Soc. B.: Plant friendly. Well-behaved towards tankmates. Strongly bottom oriented, since it is a rheophile. However, it occasionally seeks the middle water column.

M: The aquarium should have a large surface area, a fine-grained gravel substrate, many hiding places, and vegetation. Decorate with stones, roots, and coconut shells. A strong water current is not necessary.

B: Breeding is also possible in hard, alkaline water. The pairs establish a strong bond and chase conspecifics from their vicinity. About 50 to 100 eggs are laid within a cave. At 25°C, the larvae hatch after 5 to 6 days and are free-swimming after another 5 days. *Artemia* nauplii are an appropriate first food, but the fry will probably have to be fed within the cave, since they rarely emerge.

F: O; stomach content analyses of wild caught specimens contained a large proportion of snails. They can be fed live, frozen, and dry commercial foods in the aquarium.

S: Similar to *S. casuarius*, but more slender. While *S. casuarius* has dark scales with a light edge, *S. gibbiceps* has light scales with a dark edge.

T: 24°–27°C, **L:** ca. 11 cm, **A:** from 60 cm, **R:** b, m, **D:** 1–2

Continuation of *Retroculus lapidifer* (p. 862):

vicinity of the rapids of the Rio Guamá near the town of Ourém. According to observations make in nature by BITTER and VON DRACHENFELS at the Oyapock River (the border of Brazil and French Guyana), *Retroculus septentrionalis* inhabits raging rapids as well. The third known species of the genus, *R. xinguensis*, has also been found in rapids.

T: 22°–27°C, **L:** up to 25 cm, **A:** 120 cm, **R:** b, **D:** 3 (4?)

Continuation of *Satanoperca leucosticta* (p. 864):

B: Larvophile mouthbrooder with nuclear family. The animals spawn on hard substrates such as leaves of aquatic plants, tree leaves, roots, or rocks. The first 24 hr of custodial duties are like those of any open spawner. Then the pair takes the hatched larvae into their mouth and carries them until they are free-swimming. Once they are mobile, they are still admitted into the buccal cavity at night or when danger threatens.

F: C, O; the species relishes small foods, preferably those it can eat from the bottom. Small worms and sunken mosquito larvae are considered delicacies.

S: In nature, this species seems to prefer spawning on transportable substrates which allow it to move its spawn into deeper water should the water level begin to fall (tidal influences).

T: 27°–30°C, **L:** around 20 cm, **A:** from 120 cm, **R:** b, **D:** 3

Steatocranus gibbiceps ♂

Steatocranus gibbiceps, juv. ♂

Fam.: Cichlidae

Steatocranus irvinei

(TREWAVAS, 1943)

Syn.: *Gobiochromis irvinei, Leptotilapia irvinei.*

Hab.: Africa: Ghana and Burkina Faso, in the Volta River.

F.I.: 1983.

Sex.: Difficult to distinguish. ♀♀ are smaller and have a less massive head. Ripe ♀♀ are fuller through the ventral region.

Soc. B.: Territorial. Its general demeanor is one of amicability with occasional outbursts of hostile behavior towards conspecifics. Plants are rarely bothered.

M: Vegetation, a large surface area, a fine-grained gravel substrate, and hiding places in the form of rock caves, coconut shells, flower pots, and roots are required. *S. irvinei* has maintained more of its faculty to swim than many of its congeners.

B: *S. irvinei* can be maintained and bred in hard water. On average, 200 yellow-green eggs are adhered along their axis to the substrate within a cave. The young are free-swimming after about 11 days and are guided in a school by the parents. *Artemia* nauplii are an appropriate initial food.

F: O; aufwuchs in nature. If food is not abundant, algae will be grazed from stones. It accepts live, frozen, and dry commercial foods.

S: This is the only *Steatocranus* species found outside the Zaïre River Basin.

T: 24°–27°C, **L:** ca. 15 cm, **A:** from 70 cm, **R:** b, m, **D:** 1–2

Continuation of *Serranochromis robustus robustus* (p. 866):

worms, fish flesh, beef heart, and other hardy foods are accepted.

S: A second subspecies, *S. r. jallae*, was described in 1896 by BOULENGER as *Hemichromis jallae*. *S. r. jallae* can be distinguished from *S. r. robustus* by its distribution (Mossamedes, Okowango, upper Zambezi River, and the Bangweolu region, among others) and yellow areas along its throat and stomach (from TREWAVAS, 1964).

T: 24°–26°C, **L:** over 50 cm, smaller in captivity, **A:** from 200 cm, **R:** b, m, **D:** 2–4

Steatocranus irvinei ♂

Steatocranus irvinei ♀

Steatocranus ubanguiensis

ROBERTS & STEWART, 1976

Syn.: None.

Hab.: West Africa: Mbomon River, a tributary of the Ubangi.

F.I.: 1986.

Sex.: ♂♂ have pointed dorsal and anal fins. ♀♀ are smaller and, when ripe, have a light-colored, round ventral region they use to seduce ♂♂.

Soc. B.: Relatively peaceful, but territorial animals. Plant friendly.

M: Decorate the tank with plants and include many hiding places amidst roots, rocks, and coconut shells. Use fine-grained gravel or sand as substrate. Water chemistry is not of prime importance for either maintenance or breeding.

B: Just 15–25 eggs are laid within a cave. Surprisingly, the ♂ has full responsibility of the brood and conceals the newly hatched larvae well until they are free-swimming at about 2 weeks of age. Once the fry are mobile, the ♀ begins to participate in brood care. Artemia nauplii make a suitable first food.

F: O; live, frozen, and dry commercial foods.

S: Smallest known Steatocranus species. ♀♀ are sexually mature at a length of 3 cm.

T: 24°–27°C, **L:** 6–7 cm, **A:** 50 cm, **R:** b, **D:** 1–2

Taeniacara candidi
Black-stripe dwarf cichlid

MYERS, 1935

Syn.: Apistogramma weisei.

Hab.: South America: Brazil, in the Amazon River near Manaus.

F.I.: 1914.

Sex.: Clear sexual dimorphism; ♂♂ are larger, more colorful, and have a lanceolate tail fin. ♀♀ have comparatively plain fins.

Soc. B.: Territorial and energetic cichlids which do not hesitate to attack significantly larger fishes, expelling them from their territory. ♂♂ generally form a harem and are aggressive among themselves. Cave spawner, patriarch-maternal family with a tendency towards a nuclear family.

M: This dwarf cichlid should not be kept in small aquaria. Good vegetation, plenty of hiding places, and a fine dark sand substrate are recommended. Small characins in the community serve two functions—to enliven the upper water strata and to act as target fish, drawing the ♂'s hostilities away from the ♀♀. Soft, acid peat water is best (ca. 5° dGH and pH 5.5, respectively). T. candidi is extremely intolerant of varying water values.

B: 28° to 30°C. Use water values listed under **M**. The breeding set-up can consist of one ♂ and 3 to 4 ripe ♀♀. Pairwise breeding is also possible. The 60–90 eggs are adhered to the ceiling of a cavernlike structure. At a temperature of 28°C, the eggs hatch after 48–60 hr. Unlike Apistogramma species which place their larvae into a pit on the cave's floor, T. candidi suspends its offspring from the ceiling. After another 6 days, the fry are free-swimming. Generally the ♀ assumes responsibility for direct brood care while the ♂ defends the supraterritory. But in pairwise breeding set-ups, the ♂ may participate in direct brood care. Feed the fry Artemia nauplii.

F: C; all kinds of live foods such as small crustacea, mosquito larvae, and Tubifex.

S: Taeniacara differs from closely related genera (Apistogramma, Apistogrammoides) by its unusually elongated body. The lateral line is absent in some specimens.

T: 25°–28°C, **L:** ♂ 7 cm, ♀ 5 cm, **A:** 60 cm, **R:** b, **D:** 3

Steatocranus ubanguiensis

Taeniacara candidi

Fam.: Cichlidae

Theraps irregularis   GÜNTHER, 1862

Syn.: *Cichlasoma irregulare.*

Hab.: Central America: *T. irregularis* has been described from Guatemala, where the species inhabits, among others, the Rio Saquiz and the Rio Chianaga, two tributaries of the Gulf of Honduras. A more colorful red-throated population is known from the Rio Chocoljá and Rio Chacalá of the Usumacinta system in southern Mexico.

F.I.: 1985 by H. G. BREIDOHR and U. WERNER.

Sex.: Full-grown ♂♂ have a nuchal hump, grow to more than 20 cm in length, and have colorful opercula and bright blue flanks. ♀♀ are smaller with pronounced contrasting colors and cross-bands along the body that extend into the dorsum. ♂♂ reach sexual maturity at a length of 14 cm, while ♀♀ attain this state at a length of 11 cm.

Soc. B.: The species appears delicate, but is extremely temperamental and potentially very quarrelsome, particularly towards conspecifics.

M: *T. irregularis* prefers flowing waters and can be considered a rheophile (current-loving) species. A powerful pump to provide a strong current proves ben-

eficial. Additionally, these temperamental, active fish need the space provided by long aquaria and a number of open caves. The water should be medium-hard and slightly alkaline (10°–20° dGH and a pH above 7, respectively).

B: Open spawner. Direct brood care is the ♀'s responsibility. These slender, fragile looking animals can stand their ground surprisingly well; consequently, a good pair hardly loses any young, even when housed with other cichlids.

F: O; easily digested algae and small crustacea probably make up the main part of their diet in their natural habitat. If high protein foods such as beef heart, worms, and mosquito larvae are fed, illness often results. Pond plankton like *Daphnia*, *Cyclops*, and fly larvae as well as fiber-rich frozen foods like *Artemia*, *Mysis*, and krill seem to be appropriate.

S: *T. irregularis* is the type species of the genus *Theraps*. The most important characteristics for this genus are the elongated body, a slender caudal peduncle, a somewhat protruding upper mandible, and very elongated clawlike mandibular bicuspid teeth.

T: 25°-27°C, **L:** ♂ up to 25 cm, **A:** 150 cm, **R:** b, **D:** 3–4

Theraps lentiginosus   (STEINDACHNER, 1864)

Syn.: *Heros lentiginosus, Astronotus lentiginosus, Cichlasoma lentiginosum, Cichlosoma lentiginosum.*

Hab.: Central America: southern Mexico, along the Atlantic seaboard from Pichucalco and Teapa to the Rio Grijalva and the Usumacinta Basin; Guatemala, in the Rio de la Pasión Basin.

F.I.: By WERNER and accompanying travelers.

Sex.: ♂♂ are larger with numerous brown dots densely covering the body and the anterior opercula. Old ♂♂ develop a cranial hump. Many ♀♀ do not

have any dots, but those that do lack dots on the anterior opercula, only having dots posterior to and including the second opercula. They also have a dark area on the dorsal fin.

Soc. B.: Lively and somewhat shy, though not particularly aggressive. Likewise towards conspecifics.

M: As for most fishes from flowing waters, clean, unpolluted water is absolutely essential. Frequent partial water exchanges must be performed! Lava flows and other volcanic rocks occur throughout their natural habitat. Se-
Continued on p. 878.

Theraps irregularis

Theraps lentiginosus ♀

Theraps lentiginosus ♂ from Guatemala

Continuation of *Theraps lentiginosus* (p. 876):

cluded areas are sought. Otherwise, follow suggestions given for *T. irregularis*. The aquarium can be planted without worries.

B: This cave spawner widens existing caves. Direct brood care is initially the ♀'s responsibility. When the young are free-swimming, the ♂ also stays with the family. Both parents are a luminous white-blue with dark bands while tending to their brood.

F: C, O; its diminutive mouth size makes large foods inappropriate. Feed easily digested fare: dry commercial foods (also vegetable-based), pond plankton, frozen *Artemia*, insect larvae, and *Mysis*.

S: Easily confused with *Theraps coeruleus*, a smaller species that only grows to 10–12 cm.

T: 24°–27°C, **L:** ♂ up to 25 cm, ♀ somewhat smaller, **A:** from 120 cm, **R:** b, **D:** 3

Theraps coeruleus ♀

Theraps rheophilus ♀, Palanque, Mexico

Cuatro Ciénegas, Coahuila, Mexico
Home of *Gambusia longispinis, G. marshi, Cichlasoma, Cyprinodon otrorus, Dionda,* and *Notropis.*

Thorichthys affinis ♂

Thorichthys affinis

(GÜNTHER, 1862)

Syn.: *Heros affinis, Astronotus affinis, Cichlasoma affine, Cichlosoma affine.*

Hab.: Central America: Guatemala, Mexico, Belize, in Lake Petén and smaller lakes in Petén, from western Guatemala to the Usumacinta Basin.

F.I.: Willem HEIJNS imported bred specimens from the United States to the Netherlands in 1984.

Sex.: ♂♂ are larger and more colorful. The dorsal and anal fins of full-grown specimens frequently have threadlike elongations. ♀♀ are fuller, particularly when in spawning condition.

Soc. B.: These territorial animals live in pairs. Plants are left unmolested, even though sexually active animals are inclined to dig. When not engaged in spawning activities, they are amiable towards heterospecifics. They are always bellicose towards conspecifics. Nuclear family with intense brood care.

M: Substrate of fine sand and gravel, hiding places among rocks and roots, and robust plants (such as *Sagittaria, Echinodorus, Vallisneria,* or *Microsorium*). It would be prudent to protect the latter with pebbles, since *T. affinis* sometimes excavates deep pits for its larvae. Open swimming areas are less important than well-defined territorial limits. In large aquaria, a group of six or more animals is recommended. Pairs will separate from the group and establish and defend small territories among each other.

B: Ideal water is medium-hard to hard, and neutral to slightly alkaline (>8° dGH and a pH of 7.0–8.5, respectively) with a temperature of 23°–27°C. *T. affinis* is an open spawner that lays its plaque of 100–500 eggs on previously cleaned rocks, roots, or dead leaves. Pits are dug and the larvae placed therein. The parents are capable of producing several spawns within one year.

Continued on p. 882.

Thorichthys aureus
Aureum

(GÜNTHER, 1862)

Syn.: *Heros aureus, Cichlasoma aureum, Cichlosoma aureum.*

Hab.: Central America: southern Belize, in Golden Creek, north of Punta Gorda and further south; Guatemala, in Rio Motagua and tributaries and Lake Isabel and its tributaries; Honduras, Rio Copán and tributaries of the Rio Motagua.

F.I.: Unknown.

Sex.: ♂♂ are bigger with larger dorsal and anal fins. ♀♀ have a dark zone on the dorsal fin.

Soc. B.: Calm, but territorial. Best kept in a group. Sexually active specimens pair off and defend a small territory. Rarely are hostilities so pronounced that serious injuries or death result. Occasionally shy.

M: *T. aureus* requires a tank with a large surface area and alkaline and soft to medium-hard water (pH above 7.5 and hardness of 2°–15° dGH, respectively). Perform small (20%), frequent water exchanges to ensure uniform water chemistry. Use bogwood, rocks, and plants to subdivide the tank into visually independent territories.

B: *T. aureus* is an open spawner that adheres its eggs on horizontal or vertical surfaces. The resulting fry are tiny. Rearing is unproblematic until a length of 3–4 cm. At that time losses are accrued, seemingly because of intestinal diseases. Minimize changes in maintenance conditions and avoid haphazard feeding practices.

F: C; feed easily digestible, fiber-rich foods such as pond plankton, large *Artemia*, freeze-dried mosquito larvae, commercial diets, and *Mysis*. Do not overfeed. Frequent small meals are suggested.

S: *T. aureus* is, depending on its origin, either intensely blue (Isabel tributaries) or golden (lower Rio Motagua).

T: 24°–28°C, **L:** 15 cm, **A:** 80 cm, **R:** b, m, **D:** 3–4

Continuation of *Thorichthys affinis* (p. 881):

F: C, O; all live foods save those that are too large, freeze-dried foods, tablets, and flake foods. Beef heart, bloodworms, and *Tubifex* should be fed guardedly!

S: In form and design, *T. affinis* is very similar to the well-known *T. meeki* (firemouth), but is generally more elongated. In 1986 and 1987, *T. meeki* was frequently mistakenly imported as *T. affinis* because of their orange coloration. Keep in mind that *T. meeki* is widely distributed and has a number of different populations which look very similar to *T. affinis*.

T: 21°–27°C, **L:** 14 cm, **A:** 60 cm, **R:** b, **D:** 2

Thorichthys aureus pair, ♂ above

Thorichthys aureus ♀

Fam.: Cichlidae

Thorichthys ellioti

MEEK, 1904

Syn.: *Cichlasoma ellioti, Heros maculipinnis.*

Hab.: Central America: Mexico. Described from the Rio Papaloapan Basin in southeast Mexico. According to MILLER, the *Thorichthys* population from the drainage basin of the Rio Coatzocoalcos and the population discovered by BREIDOHR, STAWIKOWSKI, and WERNER in 1983 west of the Papaloapan Basin in the coastal lowlands near Vera Cruz, though different, are *T. ellioti.*

F.I.: 1983 by BREIDOHR, STAWIKOWSKI, and WERNER.

Sex.: ♂♂ are larger and more colorful, and older ♂♂ have threadlike extensions on their dorsal and anal fins. ♀♀ are fuller when in spawning condition and have a clear black spot on the hardrayed section of the dorsal fin.

Soc. B.: Shallow shore regions of rivers and creeks with ample cover are choice areas for *T. ellioti* to establish breeding colonies. This behavior is probably common to all *Thorichthys.* The individual territories within the colony are relatively small, but wholeheartedly defended against conspecifics and large predators. However, it seems that conspecific juveniles from neighboring territories are permitted, even welcome, to transverse territorial boundaries. A 100 x 50 cm tank allows 3 pairs of *T. ellioti* to express their colony-style breeding activities in a captive environment.

M: *T. ellioti* requires a substrate of fine sand and gravel, hiding places among rocks and bogwood, and robust plants (e.g., *Sagittaria, Echinodorus, Vallisneria,* or *Microsorium*). Protect the plants from being uprooted by placing a few stones around their base, as the fish construct deep pits for their larvae. Open swimming areas are less important than visual barriers between territories.

B: Use temperate, medium-hard to hard, and neutral to slightly alkaline water (23°–27°C, ≥8° dGH, pH of 7.0–8.5, respectively). This open spawner lays its 100–300 eggs on previously cleaned stones, roots, or dead plant leaves. The larvae are placed in pits dug by their parents. Several spawns can be produced within a year.

F: C, O; live foods (with the exception of overly large items), freeze-dried foods, tablets, and flake foods. Feed bloodworms, beef heart, and *Tubifex* cautiously!

S: The different populations of *T. ellioti* should, if possible, be kept separately because of likely hybridization. This follows for forms found within a single river system as well (Papaloapan, Coatzacoalcos). In some upper Coatzocoalcos tributaries (e.g., Rio Almoloya), *T. ellioti* (?) lives with *T. callolepis,* another *Thorichthys* species of the so-called *helleri* subgroup. In early 1988, GARBE captured *T. ellioti* (?) from the Coatzacoalcos system where the water temperature was a mere 16°C!

T: 20°–27°C, L: 13 cm, A: 60 cm, R: b, D: 2

Thorichthys ellioti, Papaloapan, Mexico, WC

Thorichthys ellioti ♂

Fam.: Cichlidae

Thorichthys helleri (STEINDACHNER, 1864)

Syn.: *Heros helleri, Astronotus helleri, Cichlasoma helleri, C. champotone.*

Hab.: Central America: southern Mexico and Guatemala. Described from the Rio Teapa, a lowland river in the Rio Grijalva Basin in southern Mexico. Additional populations have been found in the western Grijalva Basin, the Usumacinta Basin (Rio Chacalá, Rio Chocoljá in southern Mexico, Rio de la Pasión in Guatemala), and the Rio Champotón and Rio Candelaria. In view of the widely differing coloration and morphology of the populations, there is speculation as to whether or not all populations are in fact *T. helleri.*

F.I.: 1979 by SCHULZ (Rio Candelaria population; sold at that time as *"Cichlasoma" aureum*).

Sex.: ♂♂ are larger and more colorful. Old ♂♂ have threadlike extensions on their dorsal and anal fins. ♀♀ have a conspicuous black spot on the soft-rayed section of the dorsal fin and are fuller when in spawning condition.

Soc. B.: Shallow shore regions of rivers and creeks with ample cover are choice areas for *T. helleri* to establish breeding colonies. This behavior is probably common to all *Thorichthys*. The individual territories within the colony are relatively small, but wholeheartedly defended against conspecifics and large predators. However, it seems that conspecific juveniles from neighboring territories are permitted, even welcome, to transverse territorial boundaries. A 100 x 50 cm tank allows 3 pairs of *T. helleri* to express their colony-style breeding activities in a captive environment.

M: *T. helleri* requires a substrate of fine sand and gravel, a few hiding places among rocks and bogwood, and robust plants (e.g., *Sagittaria, Echinodorus, Vallisneria,* or *Microsorium*). Protect the

Continued on p. 888.

Thorichthys helleri; Palenque, Mexico, photo taken in its natural habitat

Thorichthys helleri ♂

Thorichthys helleri ♂

Thorichthys pasionis (RIVAS, 1962)

Syn.: Cichlasoma pasione.

Hab.: Central America: Guatemala. Found in rivers and lakes of the Petén and Usumacinta Basins, including the white waters of the Rio de la Pasión (14° dGH, 10° dKH0, which is the type locality for this cichlid. Other areas of distribution include the muddy Laguna San Juan Acul west of Sayaxché (69° dGH (!), 11° dKH), the clean, fast-flowing waters of the Rio Subin (24° dGH, 11° dKH), the Rio Pucté (34° dGH, 14° dKH), and the Rio Achtinia (28° dGH, 11° dKH). The latter rivers are characterized as having light, round volcanic rocks along the substrate and alkaline water (pH 8–9). Water temperature during the dry season climbs surprisingly high with Pucté the coolest at 29°C and the Laguna San Juan the warmest with 34°C!

F.I.: 1985 by H. G. BREIDOHR and U. WERNER.

Sex.: ♀♀ have red dots on the ventral region and sometimes, especially in older animals, a dark spot on the dorsal fin. Under oblique lighting, ♂♂ are more bluish.

Soc. B.: Outside moments of sexual activity, they are calm and retiring. Keep a group of 6 to 8 animals in a spacious tank.

M: The aquarium should be rich in hiding places. Plants are left alone. Only sexually active animals dig.

B: It was successfully reproduced in soft water, 5° dGH, which speaks in favor of its ability to adapt to different water chemistry. Like other Thorichthys, they are open spawners with strong pair bonding. They courageously defend the spawning site, the small transparent eggs, the larvae, and the free-swimming young. T. pasionis has a distinct design—its crossbands only reach midbody where they terminate at the interrupted longitudinal band that runs the length of the body and encompasses the lateral spot and the spot on the caudal peduncle.

F: C; accepts all hardy foods, but should not be kept on a high fat/high protein diet.

S: The branchiostegal membranes are black, not red, and serve as a good identifying characteristic.

T: 25°–28°C, **L:** ♂ 16 cm, ♀ 14 cm, **A:** 100 cm, **R:** b, m, **D:** 1–2

Continuation of Thorichthys helleri (p. 886):

plants from being uprooted by placing a few stones around their base, since the fish occasionally construct deep pits for their larvae. Open swimming areas are less important than visual barriers between territories.

B: Use temperate, medium-hard to hard, and neutral to slightly alkaline water (23°–27°C, ≥8° dGH, pH of 7.0–8.5, respectively). This open spawner lays its 100–300 eggs on previously cleaned stones, roots, or dead plant leaves. The larvae are placed in pits dug by their parents. Several spawns can be produced within a year.

F: C, O; live foods (with the exception of overly large items), freeze-dried foods, tablets, and flake foods. Feed bloodworms, beef heart, and Tubifex cautiously!

S: The different populations (?) of T. helleri should be maintained separately, since they easily hybridize. The so-called helleri group (MILLER, 1984), is made up of T. ellioti, T. aureus, T. socolofi, T. callolepis, and T. helleri.

T: 22°–27°C, **L:** 16 cm, **A:** 70 cm, **R:** b, **D:** 2

Thorichthys pasionis ♂

Thorichthys pasionis ♀

Fam.: Cichlidae

Thorichthys socolofi

(MILLER & TAYLOR, 1984)

Syn.: *Cichlasoma socolofi.*

Hab.: Central America: southeastern Mexico, Rio Tulija, Grijalva Basin.

F.I.: 1983 by H. G. BREIDOHR, R. STAWIKOWSKI, and U. WERNER.

Sex.: ♀♀ are smaller. Some ♀♀ have a spot on the anal fin as well as the dorsal fin.

Soc. B.: Sexually active animals are strongly territorial. When not engaged in spawning activities, it is peaceful and can be kept in community with smaller fishes. Plant friendly. Brood caring open spawner.

M: Provide a fine substrate, hiding places, roots, and rocks. Open swimming areas are important.

B: Proper nitrogen cycle management must be observed. Water hardness is unimportant. This open spawner lays 100–200 eggs.

F: C; do not feed overly coarse foods. Hardy foods such as mosquito larvae, *Mysis,* and flake foods are appropriate. It "chews" the substrate like eartheaters.

S: If housed with aggressive fishes, they become shy and refuse to eat.

T: 22°–26°C, **L:** 14 cm, **A:** 80 cm, **R:** b, **D:** 2–3

Tilapia guinasana
Guinas tilapia

TREWAVAS, 1936

Syn.: None.

Hab.: Africa: northern Namibia, in Lakes Guinas and Otijikoto. These are deep, clear water lakes, each 1,000 m above sea level.

F.I.: 1938 under the arrangement of G. MERTENS, Windhoek, Namibia.

Sex.: ♂♂ and ♀♀ are not easily distinguished by color. The most indisputable characteristic is the shape of the genital papilla, which is pointed in ♂♂ and rounded in ♀♀.

Soc. B.: Territorial. Aggressive when spawning. When not engaged in spawning activities, the animals are relatively peaceful towards conspecifics and heterospecifics as long as their environmental requirements are taken into consideration. ♂♂ are monogamous. Open spawners, paternal-maternal family.

M: Community fish which need a large tank with many isolated hiding places among rocks and roots, a substrate of medium-grained gravel, and clean, clear water. *T. guinasana* readily eats vegetation, so save yourself some money and frustration and decorate the tank *sans* plants. Water: pH 7.0–7.8; hardness up to 15° dGH.

B: Not difficult. Open spawners that lay their approximately 200 eggs in pits where they are carefully maintained and guarded by the ♀ with the ♂'s help. Prior to spawning, the ♂ courts the ♀ and finds and cleans a spawning site. MEINKEN observed that the eggs were removed from the spawning site by the parents 3 days postspawning and placed in a rock crevice. The parents often transfer their young. After an additional 6 to 8 days, the free-swimming young are guided by the parents. The parents can spawn several times each year.

F: O, H; a lot of plant fare (e.g., lettuce, spinach, algae), all kinds of live foods, frozen foods, freeze-dried foods, flake foods, and tablets.

S: There are two morphs of *T. guinasana*: a light and a dark morph. The dark morph is more colorful.

T: 22°–26°C, **L:** 15 cm, **A:** 100 cm, **R:** b, m, **D:** 2

Thorichthys socolofi

Tilapia guinasana ♀♀

Fam.: Cichlidae

Tilapia (Coptodon) guineensis
Guinea tilapia
(BLEEKER, 1862)

Syn.: Chromis guineensis, Ch. affinis, Ch. latus, Ch. polycentra, Haligenes guineensis, Tilapia affinis, T. camerunensis, T. lata, T. polycentra, T. zillii guineensis.

Hab.: Africa: from Senegal to Angola, in freshwaters of coastal areas.

F.I.: 1908 by the Vereinigte Zierfischzüchtereien in Conradshöhe.

Sex.: Difficult to distinguish when not spawning. ♀♀ are generally smaller and fuller.

Soc. B.: Territorial. T. guineensis is capable of standing its ground against equal-sized cichlids when spawning. Even when not engaged in sexual activities, the pair bond endures. Usually only one pair can be kept in a tank. Open spawners, nuclear family.

M: A spacious aquarium sans vegetation is a necessity. The fish have their own ideas on how the aquarium should be decorated, shifting large quantities of sand in their bid to build spawning pits. This activity can be curtailed by judiciously arranging flat stones along the substrate to limit the pit's dimensions.

B: About 2 weeks prior to spawning, the pair digs a pit where the 600–1000 eggs are to be laid. Depending on temperature, the larvae hatch after about 2 days and are free-swimming approximately 7 days postspawning. Both parents zealously guard their school of free-swimming fry. Rearing the young is unproblematic, notwithstanding the large amounts of food that are required.

F: O; hardy foods and vegetable fare.

S: Considered a food fish in some areas.

T: 22°–26°C, **L:** 25 cm, **A:** 100 cm, **R:** m, b, **D:** 2

Tilapia rendalli
Rendall's tilapia
(BOULENGER, 1896)

Syn.: Chromis rendallii, Tilapia christyi, T. druryi, T. kirkhami, T. latifrons, T. mackeani, T. melanopleura, T. melanopleura rendallii, T. swierstrae, T. sykesii.

Hab.: Africa: from the Cunee and Zaïre Rivers to the Zambezi and Limpopo Rivers, Lakes Tanganyika and Malawi, and the Pongolo River in Natal, South Africa.

F.I.: Unknown.

Sex.: Sexes are difficult to differentiate. The genital papillae and the dorsal and anal fins are the characteristics that can be used with the most security. In ♂♂, the genital papilla is pointed, whereas it is more rounded in ♀♀.

Soc. B.: Territorial, but moderately peaceful despite their size. However, while spawning and caring for offspring, T. rendalli becomes very aggressive towards tankmates and digs extensively, placing plants in jeopardy. Open spawners, paternal-maternal to nuclear family.

M: Substrate of sand or gravel and many hiding places among rocks and roots. If vegetation is used, then limit it to tough, well-rooted species. No particular demands are placed on water chemistry, though the pH should not be acid. Due to its size, a species tank is suggested.

B: There are no breeding reports available regarding a successful spawn in the aquarium. Due to its size, reproducing this fish in a home aquarium is surely problematic. ♂♂ frequently build their spawning pit among depressions other pairs have established, forming small colonies. There the eggs are laid, tended, and strictly guarded by the parents.

F: O, H; plenty of plant fare and all kinds of live, frozen, freeze-dried, flake, and tablet foods.

S: In the cranium of T. rendalli, the mesethmoid does not point to the vomer, an exception within this genus.

T: 24°–28°C, **L:** 30 cm, **A:** from 120 cm, **R:** b, m, **D:** 2

Tilapia (Coptodon) guineensis, adult

Tilapia rendalli, TZ 88/16, Lake Kingiri

Fam.: Cichlidae

Tilapia sparrmanii
Sparrman's tilapia

SMITH, 1840

Syn.: *Chromis sparrmani, Tilapia fouloni.*

Hab.: Southern Africa: from Angola and Zaïre to South Africa. Exclusively found in freshwater.

F.I.: 1926 by A. DIETZ, Hamburg, Germany.

Sex.: Very difficult to sex. Differentiating the sexes by color has not been described. ♀♀ are fuller while in spawning condition (eggs).

Soc. B.: Relatively peaceful, but digs copiously and eats plants. ♂♂ are sometimes territorial. Open spawner, nuclear family.

M: *T. sparrmani* needs a deep substrate of sand, some large stones as spawning substrates, and hiding places among rocks and roots. Medium-hard, neutral water (10° dGH and pH 7.0, respectively) is suitable for both maintenance and reproduction. Cichlids make good tankmates for *T. sparrmanii* as long as they are not too aggressive.

B: A temperature of 26°–28°C is appropriate. Open spawner. Up to 500 eggs are laid on a previously cleaned rock. *T. sparrmanii* has been observed allowing its free-swimming young into its buccal cavity when threatened. Both parents participate in brood care, which lasts about 6 weeks.

F: O; all types of hardy live foods and plenty of vegetable foods such as algae, *Elodea*, and lettuce as well as flake foods and tablets.

S: None.

T: 22°–25°C, **L:** 20 cm, **A:** 100 cm, **R:** b, **D:** 1–2

Tilapia zillii
Zilli's cichlid

(GERVAIS, 1848)

Syn.: *Acerina zillii, Chromis andreae, Ch. faidherbi, Ch. menzalensis, Ch. tristrami, Ch. zillii, Coptodon zillii, Glyphisodon zillii, Haligenes tristrami, Sarotherodon zillii, Tilapia andreae, T. menzalensis, T. shariensis, T. tristrami.*

Hab.: Africa and Asia: inhabits Africa north of the equator. In Asia it lives in the Jordan River and its tributaries and in Lake Kinneret. Found in flowing and stationary freshwaters and brackish waters.

F.I.: 1903 by Dr. SCHOELLER, Alexandria.

Sex.: ♂♂ are more intensely colored than ♀♀, though the sexes are best differentiated based on their genital papilla, which is pointed in ♂♂ and blunt and rounded in ♀♀.

Soc. B.: Territorial and aggressive towards conspecifics and heterospecifics while engaged in sexual activities. Inclined to dig liberally and eat any vegetation you happen to include in the decor. Open spawner, nuclear family.

M: As for *Tilapia rendalli*.

B: Breeding is easy, and the animals are very fecund. Full-grown ♀♀ lay over 1,000 eggs on a previously chosen and meticulously cleaned rock. The spawn is excellently guarded by both parents. Depending on water temperature, the young hatch in 3–5 days. They are then carried to deep pits where they are carefully fanned and guarded. Both parents guard the free-swimming fry. Rearing is straightforward with small foods. Several broods can be produced each year.

F: O, H; plenty of plant food. All types of live, frozen, freeze-dried, flake, and tablet foods.

S: *T. zillii* is a species that has been introduced to many parts of the world for aquaculture. See Vol. 1, p. 778.
The variable coloration found in this species tempted us to present it once again.

T: 18°–24°C, **L:** 30 cm, **A:** from 120 cm, **R:** b, m, **D:** 1

Tilapia sparrmanii

Tilapia zillii adult ♂

Tropheus moorii, ♀, "Murago," Lake Tanganyika

Tropheus moorii, Ikola Kaiser Moori

Tropheus polli, juv., Ikola Island

See Vol. 1, p. 782 and Vol. 2, p. 1005.
The opposite page shows different color morphs of *T. moorii* and *T. polli* photographed in their natural habitat.

Tropheus moorii, Mtosi

T. moori, Kachese

T. moori, Kalambo

T. moori, Chipimbi, Katete

T. brichardi, Kipili

T. polli, Mkombe

T. polli, Mpimbwe

T. polli, Karilani

Fam.: Cichlidae

Tylochromis intermedius

(BOULENGER, 1916)

Syn.: *Pelmatochromis intermedius.*

Hab.: West Africa: Sierra Leone.

F.I.: If the species has been imported alive, it was one specimen imported by A. LAMBOJ.

Sex.: None known.

Soc. B.: Unknown.

M: There is no information available concerning care of this cichlid. Information gathered at its natural biotope in Sierra Leone by A. LAMBOJ is as follows: hardness below 2° dGH, pH 6.5–7.5, conductivity 15–110 μS.

B: To the best of our knowledge, this species has not been bred in captivity.

F: Probably either a carnivore or an omnivore.

T: 24°–28°C, **L:** 15 cm, **A:** 100 cm, **R:** b, m, **D:** 3

Xenotilapia flavipinnis
Yellow-finned xenotilapia

POLL, 1985

Syn.: None. Frequently confused with *Xenotilapia boulengeri.*

Hab.: Africa: northern Lake Tanganyika.

F.I.: Supposedly not until 1983, but the animals were being sold as early as 1980.

Sex.: The yellow hues are more pronounced, even extending into the ventral fins, in ♂♂.

Soc. B.: Social cichlids from sandy substrates. Keep in small groups. Pronounced pair formation. Normally peaceful, but aggressive when spawning.

M: As for other cichlids from the sandy substrates, the aquarium should have a fine sand substrate and a few plants and stones along the back of the tank. *X. flavipinnis*, like all featherfins and their relatives, demands good water quality for successful maintenance. Frequent water exchanges visibly heighten the animal's well-being. Water: medium-hard; pH above 7; 26°–27°C.

B: HERRMANN has observed ♂♂ and ♀♀ alternately take the brood into their buccal cavity 14–16 days postspawning. The ♀ initially broods the eggs. After one week, the ♂ takes the larvae for several days. The young are readmitted during danger by both parents. Newly hatched *Artemia* nauplii and other small foods can be fed initially.

F: O; food is predominantly taken from the bottom. Live foods such as mosquito larvae and frozen foods make up the bulk of its diet. Flake foods are accepted in an emergency.

S: This species was frequently confused with *Xenotilapia boulengeri* and *X. sima* in popular literature.

T: 24°–27°C, **L:** 8 cm, **A:** from 80 cm, **R:** b, **D:** 3

Tylochromis intermedius

Xenotilapia flavipinnis

Fam.: Cichlidae

Xenotilapia sima
Big-eyed xenotilapia

BOULENGER, 1898

Syn.: None.

Hab.: Africa: endemic to Lake Tanganyika. Found in large schools in the sandy littoral zone.

F.I.: Methodically imported since 1984.

Sex.: ♀♀ are smaller and paler than ♂♂. The anal and dorsal fins in ♀ animals are rounded, but pointed in ♂♂.

Soc. B.: Typical schooling fish that hardly shows any aggression towards conspecifics. Incapable of defending itself against robust cichlids. Agamic mouthbrooder.

M: A spacious large tank with open sandy surfaces. The sand should have rounded edges like that found in rivers, since the fish constantly masticate and sift through it as they search for food. *X.*

sima may be startled by sudden movements outside of the tank. As cichlids of the sand zone, *X. sima*'s response to danger is to flee long distances rather than seek cover.

B: ♂♂ dig shallow pits, but brood care is the sole responsibility of the ♀. The eggs and fry are buccally incubated for about 3 weeks.

F: O; food is preferably taken from the bottom.

S: Since these cichlids sleep on the open sand at night, nocturnal catfishes make totally inappropriate tankmates. *X. sima*, in contrast to most other cichlids, has three lateral lines.

T: 24°–26°C, **L:** 16 cm, **A:** 120 cm, **R:** b, **D:** 3

Xenotilapia spilopterus
Spot-fin xenotilapia

POLL & STEWART, 1975

Syn.: None.

Hab.: Africa: southern Lake Tanganyika (Zambia). Found in rocky zones and rock-rubble-sand transition zones.

F.I.: 1986.

Sex.: None.

Soc. B.: Pronounced pair bond when spawning. In its natural habitat, single specimens as well as small schools of up to 15 individuals have been observed.

M: Rock edifications in the background and a substrate of fine sand. Medium-hard water with a pH above 7.

B: Mouthbrooder. In the aquarium, they spawn on rocks and sand without constructing a pit. The larvae were first buccally incubated by the ♀, then the ♂. The small, slow-growing fry are cared for by both parents.

F: C; prefers animal-based foods. Food is taken from the open water and off the bottom.

S: Between the 9th and 13th ray of the dorsal fin there is an elongated black spot that is partially framed in white. This characteristic is not clearly visible in this photo.

T: 26°–27°C, **L:** 8 cm, **A:** 80 cm, **R:** b, m, **D:** 4

Xenotilapia sima

Xenotilapia spilopterus

Group 9

Fam.: Kurtidae (Humpheads)

Humpheads are small to medium-sized perchlike fishes with a maximal length of 60 cm. Their body is strongly compressed laterally and covered with small round scales. The head is almost naked, the anal fin is very broad with many rays, and the caudal fin is deeply forked. Beginning with the 5th vertebra, the ribs are strong and large, encasing the elongated swimbladder like armor, a unique and as yet unexplained feature among fishes. An additional characteristic of the Kurtidae is found in ♂♂. Sexually mature animals grow a serrated comb at their nape which ends posteriorly in a bony, forward-directed hook.

The family Kurtidae is comprised of only one genus with two species, *Kurtus indicus* and *Kurtus gulliveri*. The former attains a length of 14 cm and is distributed throughout the coastal waters and mouths of rivers of India, Thailand, Malaysia, and Indonesia to China. *Kurtus gulliveri* reaches a length of 60 cm and is found in freshwaters and brackish waters of New Guinea and North Queensland (Australia).

Badis badis siamensis
Siamese badis

KLAUSEWITZ, 1957

Syn.: None.

Hab.: Southeast Asia: Thailand and Phuket Island.

F.I.: 1987 by R. LATKA.

Sex.: ♂♂ are larger and more colorful and have a concave ventral profile. ♀♀ are pale with either a straight or, when mature, convex ventral line.

Soc. B.: Peaceful. However, each ♂ requires a cave and a small territory. An apt addition to community aquaria. Eggs are laid in a cave, and they and the resulting larvae are tended by the ♂.

M: The aquarium should have dense vegetation around the edges and a partial cover of floating plants. Numerous secluded areas among coconut shells and bamboo or beneath flat stones are important. The water should be clear and well-filtered, as organic pollutants are detrimental. Regular partial water exchanges are recommended. No particular demands are placed on water chemistry, but soft, slightly acid water is preferred.

B: Similar to that of *Badis badis badis*; see Vol. 1, p. 790. According to LATKA (DATZ 10, 1987, p. 442), the young have a distinct schooling behavior.

F: C; all kinds of live foods, e.g., mosquito larvae, *Daphnia, Cyclops, Tubifex,* and small earthworms. In exceptional cases, frozen and substitute foods such as liver or scraped meat are also accepted. Feed *Artemia* and cultured insects during the winter.

S: *B. badis siamensis* has different meristic values in regard to its scales than the other subspecies. See *B. b. badis* in Vol. 1, p. 790 and *B. b. burmanicus* in Vol. 2, p. 1,013 (photo on p. 1,011).

T: 22°–26°C, **L:** 6 cm, **A:** 70 cm, **R:** m, b, **D:** 4 (C)

Badis badis siamensis

Lates microlepis
Small-scaled Nile perch

BOULENGER, 1898

Syn.: *Lates mariae.*

Hab.: Africa: endemic to Lake Tanganyika.

F.I.: At the beginning of the '80's by Lothar SEEGERS.

Sex.: No external differentiating characteristics are known.

Soc. B.: Pronounced predators. Quarrelsome towards conspecifics. Smaller fishes are considered prey.

M: Only juveniles are suitable for home aquaria, as large specimens can only be adequately maintained in show aquaria. Use a gravel substrate, and provide hiding places and cover among rocks and roots. Vegetation can be waived. No particular demands are placed on water chemistry. Due to their predatory lifestyle, individual maintenance is recommended.

B: Probably impossible in an aquarium because of space limitations.

F: C; all kinds of hardy live foods, particularly fishes. However, frozen foods, meat, beef heart, etc., are also readily accepted.

S: *L. microlepis* is a food fish in its natural habitat.

T: 24°–28°C, **L:** 135 cm, **A:** from 150 cm, **R:** m, b, **D:** 4 (S)

Chanda sp. ♂, India, Assam

Chanda sp. ♀, India, Assam, Dibru River

Chanda baculis
Burmese glassfish

HAMILTON, 1822

Syn.: None.

Hab.: Asia: India, Burma, Thailand. The Dikuk, Menum Nana, and Bung Borapit Rivers in Thailand.

F.I.: Exact date unknown. Probably after 1970.

Sex.: Definite external sexual differences are unknown.

Soc. B.: Peaceful, shy (skittish) schooling fish. The animals prefer certain territories.

M: *C. baculis* requires well-aged water, a dark substrate (e.g., lava), dense vegetation, and hiding places among rocks and roots. The aquarium should be placed in a sunny local. Adding 1 to 2 tablespoons of salt per 10 l of water is beneficial. Limit tankmates to amiable fishes of equal size.

B: To the best of our knowledge, this species has not been bred. However, it is probably similar to that of *Chanda buruensis*.

F: All kinds of small live foods. The animals are difficult to train to flake foods.

S: *C. baculis* is the smallest *Chanda*.

T: 18°–25°C, **L:** 4.5 cm, **A:** 50 cm, **R:** m, **D:** 2–3

Creek around Edith Falls, Australia

Chanda buruensis
Buru glassfish

Syn.: *Ambassis buruensis.*

Hab.: Southeast Asia: Thailand, Malaysia, Philippines, Indonesia (Sumatra, Celebes, and other islands).

F.I.: Unknown.

Sex.: The posterior end of the swimbladder—pointed in ♂♂, round in ♀♀— is the best differentiating characteristic. Mature ♀♀ are fuller.

Soc. B.: Relatively calm. Only ♂♂ are occasionally aggressive among themselves. Small territories may be claimed. House with pacific fishes.

M: A dark substrate (lava, basalt), a cover of not overly coarse vegetation, and hiding places among rocks and/or roots should be offered. The animals appreciate direct sunlight. Mature water is recommended. Apparently, sea salt does not need to be added.

B: Not difficult. The temperature should not be below 24°C. Raising it to 28°–30°C stimulates the animals to spawn. Adding fresh water and separating the sexes for a few days further encourages spawning. Over 100 eggs are adhered to fine-leaved aquatic plants such

as *Cabomba*. Depending on temperature, the young hatch in 24–36 hr. They are free-swimming after another 24 hr. Rearing the young is not easy, as very small foods are required.

F: C; all kinds of live foods. A varied diet is required. Flake foods are insufficient for long-term maintenance.

S: The lateral line of *C. buruensis* is interrupted briefly under the anterior edge of the second dorsal fin.

T: 22°–30°C, **L:** 7 cm, **A:** 70 cm, **R:** m, **D:** 3

Continuation of *Etheostoma nigrum* (p. 920):

information concerning the reproductive biology of *E. nigrum* can be found in WINN (1958): Am. Midl. Nat. **59** (1): 190–212, pp. 205–207.

F: Almost exclusively subsists on live foods such as small crustacea, mosquito larvae, *Tubifex,* Enchytraeidae, and earthworms.

S: Adults have several irregular W-shaped spots on their sides (see photo). The genus *Etheostoma* is taxonomically complex and muddled.

T: 4°–18°C (coldwater fish), **L:** 6 cm, **A:** 60 cm, **R:** b, **D:** 2–3

Chanda buruensis ♂

Chanda buruensis ♀

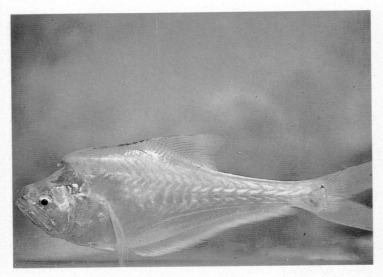

Kurtus gulliveri
Nursery fish

CASTELNAU, 1878

Syn.: *Cyrtus gulliveri.*

Hab.: New Guinea and Australia (northern Queensland); in rivers and estuaries.

F.I.: Probably has not been imported into Germany.

Sex.: Sexually mature ♂♂ develop a bony nuchal hook (see photo).

Soc. B.: The information on maintaining this species in an aquarium, although scant, affirms its amiable personality. In nature, they live in small schools.

M: There is no information available on how to care for this species in an aquarium. Should *K. gulliveri* be imported into Germany, specialists will be faced with investigating the biology of this extremely interesting fish.

B: To the best of our knowledge, this species has not been bred in an aquarium. There is no information concerning courtship and spawning in its natural habitat. After spawning, egg clumps are found hanging on the nuchal hook. The eggs are united in bunches and held together by a "rope" created from the adhesive threads of the eggs. The bunches are adhered to the ♂'s hook such that an egg clump hangs along each side of the head. The number of eggs laid, their time of development, developmental stages, and degree of parental care are still unknown. The smallest ♂ seen carrying eggs was 37.5 cm long.

F: C; all kinds of live foods, particularly small fishes and crustacea.

S: Extremely susceptible to fungal infections and shock when handled.

T: 20°–28°C, **L:** 60 cm, **A:** from 100 cm, **R:** m, **D:** 4

Polycentropsis abbreviata   BOULENGER, 1901

Syn.: None.

Hab.: Africa: Nigeria, Cameroon, Gabon, in slow-flowing rivers, stationary freshwater, and brackish water.

F.I.: 1906 by Hans STÜVE, Hamburg.

Sex.: Difficult to determine. ♂♂ reputedly have a straight ventral line, while ♀♀ have a slightly convex ventral line. ♀♀ are lighter colored when spawning.

Soc. B.: Pronounced predators. Nocturnal. The ♂ builds a bubble nest and assumes custodial duties (paternal family).

M: *P. abbreviata* requires a densely planted yet spacious tank with secluded areas among roots and rocks and an open swimming area. Dim the tank with a cover of floating plants. A species tank is recommended. Water: medium-hard and slightly acid (≤10° dGH and a pH of 6.0–6.5, respectively).

B: Difficult. Maintain a low water level (≤10 cm). Dense vegetation, floating plants, and a water temperature of 27°–30°C are suggested. The ♂ frequently builds a bubble nest on the water surface. Up to 100 eggs are laid and immediately fertilized amidst fervent spawning activity. Parents do not eat their spawn. Depending on temperature, the eggs need 2 to 3 days to hatch. Though the fry have a robust appetite, they are sometimes sensitive. MEINKEN recommends the addition of marine salt.

F: C; all types of live foods such as small fishes, mosquito larvae, Enchytraeidae, *Tubifex*, and small crustacea.

S: *P. abbreviata* is similar to its South American relative, *Polycentrus schomburgki* (Vol. 1 p. 806). The easiest way to differentiate these fishes is by the number of lateral scales: *P. abbreviata* has 31–35 per central longitudinal row, while *P. schomburgki* has 25–27.

T: 26°–30°C, **L:** 8 cm, **A:** 80 cm, **R:** m, b, **D:** 3–4

Pristolepis grooti
Small-mouthed leaffish

Syn.: *Catopra grooti.*

Hab.: Southeast Asia: Burma, Thailand, Cambodia, Vietnam, and parts of Malaysia and Indonesia.

F.I.: 1932.

Sex.: Not known.

Soc. B.: Territorial. Quarrelsome among themselves, but relatively peaceful towards other fishes, barring overly small specimens. Twilight-active species.

M: Large aquaria with secluded areas among roots and rocks. Use fine sand as the substrate. Plants are tolerated but delicate or pinnate vegetation is inappropriate. Clear water with a hardness of at least 10° dGH and a pH of about 7 is recommended.

B: Not known; has not been successfully bred in captivity.

(BLEEKER, 1852)
Sub-fam.: Pristolepidinae

F: O; besides hardy animal foods, e.g., Enchytraeidae, *Tubifex*, earthworms, and crustacea, vegetable fare is also accepted (boiled rice or oats). Flake and tablet foods are likewise accepted.

S: Unlike the other two *Pristolepis* species which have villiform (threadlike) dentition on their vomer, the teeth of *P. grooti* are spherical.

T: 23°–28°C, L: 21 cm, A: from 100 cm, R: m, b, D: 3

Polycentropsis abbreviata, p. 911

Pristolepis grooti

Coius campbelli (no text)

Etheostoma blennioides
Greenside darter

RAFINESQUE, 1819

Syn.: *Diplesion blennoides, D. blennioides, Diplesium blennioides, Hyostoma blennioperca, H. newmanii, Pileoma cymatogramma.*

Hab.: North America: eastern United States, Canada. Found in many creeks, rivers, and lakes of the United States, but only in Lake St. Claire and its tributaries in Canada.

F.I.: Unknown.

Sex.: Sexual dichromatism is present in mature animals. Sexually active ♂♂ are bright green and have a short, pointed genital papilla. ♀♀ are yellow-green and have a short, rounded genital papilla when spawning.

Soc. B.: ♂♂ establish a territory when ready to spawn. It is up to the ♀ to choose a spawning site within that territory.

M: As for *Etheostoma nigrum.* It is important that the aquarium has a strong pump to provide a continuous current.

B: Information concerning successfully breeding *E. blennioides* could not be found in German aquarium literature. Depending on latitude, the spawning season begins in either April or May. Algal mats of *Cladophora* or *Fontinalis*, an aquatic moss, are often chosen as spawning substrates. Spawning begins when the water temperature reaches 10.6°C (51°F)—lower temperatures will not support spawning activity. Between 460 and 1,830 eggs are released either during the morning or the day. Ripe eggs are adhesive and have a diameter of 1.8 mm.

F: C; all kinds of live foods, particularly aquatic insects and their larvae and small crustacea.

S: There are three subspecies of *E. blennioides* other than the nominate form: *E. b. gutselli, E. b. newmanii,* and *E. b. pholidotum.*

T: 4°–18°C (coldwater fish), **L:** 15 cm, **A:** 100 cm, **R:** b, **D:** 3

Etheostoma blennioides blennioides

Etheostoma blennioides newmanii

Etheostoma caeruleum
Rainbow darter

STORER, 1845

Syn.: *Astatichthys coeruleus, Poecilichthys coeruleus, P. versicolor, Poecilosoma erythrogastrum, P. transversum.*

Hab.: North America: eastern United States and southeastern Canada near the Great Lakes. A relict population has been found in the southern United States (Louisiana, Mississippi). Inhabits creeks and small rivers with coarse gravel or rubble substrates.

F.I.: Unknown.

Sex.: Sexual dichromatism—♂ ♂ are significantly more colorful and frequently have nuptial tubercles. ♂ ♂ and ♀ ♀ can, of course, be sexed by their genital papilla.

Soc. B.: ♂ ♂ are territorial when spawning. Intruding ♂ ♂ are kept at bay through intimidation.

M: As for *Etheostoma nigrum.*

B: Information concerning successfully breeding *E. caeruleum* could not be found in German aquarium literature. In nature, the animals achieve the apex of maturity when the water temperature reaches 17°–18°C. ♀ ♀ swim into the ♂'s territory and lay their eggs in the gravel substrate. Up to 800, 1.5 to 1.8 mm eggs are laid over the course of several days.

F: C; all kinds of live foods. Various aquatic insect larvae are especially relished as are snails and small crustacea. In nature fish eggs, for example, those of minnows, are consumed.

S: *E. caeruleum* is frequently confused with *E. spectabile* (AGASSIZ, 1854). However, unlike *E. spectabile, E. caeruleum* has a complete infraorbital channel (see drawings).

T: 4°–18°C (coldwater fish), **L:** 8 cm, **A:** 80 cm, **R:** b, **D:** 2–3

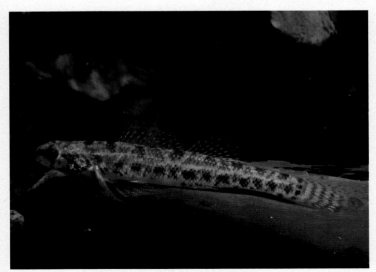

Etheostoma cf. *fusiforme,* Lake Bradford, nothern Florida.

Etheostoma caeruleum

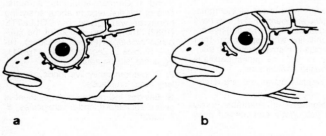

a

Etheostoma caeruleum

b

Etheostoma spectabile

Etheostoma flabellare
Fantail darter

RAFINESQUE, 1819

Syn.: Catonotus fasciatus, C. flabellatus, C. kennicotti, Etheostoma fontinalis, E. linsleyi, Oligocephalus humeralis, Poecilichthys flabellaris.

Hab.: North America: southeastern Canada (Quebec) and the central to eastern region of the United States. Usually inhabits gravel- or pebble-bottomed creeks and rivers.

F.I.: Unknown.

Sex.: Gender can be distinguished by the genital papilla. The ♂'s genital papilla is a flattened triangular tube, much smaller than that in most other Etheostoma species. In ♀♀, the genital papilla is round fleshy.

Soc. B.: ♂♂ are territorial when spawning.

M: As for Etheostoma nigrum.

B: Information concerning successfully breeding E. flabellare could not be found in German aquarium literature. In nature, the ♂ preferentially establishes his territory near stones and guards it against intruders. Their spiny dorsal fin is used to clean the lower side of a stone. There is where the ♀ will lay up to 450, 2.3 mm eggs. The pair positions their bodies head to tail while spawning. ♀♀ repeatedly breed with the same ♂ or different ♂♂. At a temperature of 21°C, the eggs need 21 days to hatch.

F: C; all kinds of live foods, especially mosquito larvae, aquatic insects, and small crustacea (Asellus, Gammarus).

S: Of all the known darter species, E. flabellare has the widest distribution. It presents a number of serious taxonomic difficulties.

T: 4°–18°C (coldwater fish), L: 8 cm, A: 80 cm, R: b, D: 3

Etheostoma fusiforme
Swamp darter

(GIRARD, 1854)

Syn.: Boleosoma fusiforme, Boleichthys fusiformis, Hololepis fusiformis.

Hab.: North America: United States, in bodies of water of the Atlantic coastal plains from southern Maine to North Carolina and Florida. Found in slow-flowing rivers, swamps, and bogs as well as artificial lakes, especially those rich in detritus and vegetation.

F.I.: Unknown.

Sex.: Though there is sexual dichromatism, it is little pronounced. ♂♂ may have nuptial tubercles on the rays of their ventral and anal fins when spawning. Their genital papilla is a small, flattened, triangular tube. In ♀♀, the genital papilla is a broad-based conical tube.

Soc. B.: Sexually active ♂♂ are territorial.

M: E. fusiforme is an adaptable, easily cared for fish. Water composition does

not play a major role in successful maintenance. Even warm water with extreme turbidity or a brown color is tolerated, as are acid pHs and low dissolved oxygen levels. Furnish the aquarium with a fine sand substrate, hiding areas among rocks, and many coldwater plants along the tank's fringes.

B: Information concerning successfully breeding E. fusiforme could not be found in German aquarium literature. One of the first reports about spawning behavior was given by COLLETTE (1962): The swamp darters of the subgenus Hololepis (Pisces, Percidae). Tulane Studies in Zoology 9 (4), 115–211. Eggs are laid on aquatic plants.

F: C; predominantly live foods, particularly small crustacea.

S: Besides the nominate form, there is also a southern (Florida) subspecies, E. f. barrati.

T: 14°–26°C, L: 6 cm, A: 60 cm, R: b, D: 2

Etheostoma flabellare

Etheostoma fusiforme

Etheostoma nigrum
Johnny darter

Syn.: *Boleosoma brevipinne, B. maculatum, B. mesaea, B. mesotum, B. nigrum, B. olmsteadi, B. olmstedi, B. olmstedi maculatum, B. mutatum, Poecilichtys beani, P. mesaeus.*

Hab.: North America: eastern United States, in rivers and creeks.

F.I.: Unknown. Only sporadically kept in Germany.

Sex.: ♂♂ turn dark and acquire faint iridescent spots when ready to spawn. Ripe ♀♀ have a fuller abdomen.

Soc. B.: At spawning time, ♂♂ form a territory and guard it against encroaching conspecifics as well as heterospecifics. Their personality turns quite quarrelsome at this time. *E. nigrum*'s reproductive behavior lies somewhere between an open spawner and a cave spawner. Paternal family.

M: *E. nigrum* will benefit from a sandy or fine-grained gravel substrate, hiding places among rocks, a slight current, good aeration, and cool, clear water. The rocks will also serve as spawning substrates. Several American coldwater plants can be placed along the sides and background. Water: up to 15° dGH; pH of 7.0. A species tank is best.

B: Probably has been bred in the United States but not in Germany. In its natural habitat, the spawning season extends from April to June. ♂♂ claim territories near oblique stones at spawning time. The underside of the stone is cleaned using ventral, anal, and tail fins. A ♀ is lured to the spawning territory where she adheres her eggs to the underside of the cleaned stone. After spawning, the ♀ leaves the territory while the ♂ stays behind and guards the spawn. Detailed

Continued on p. 908.

Etheostoma spectabile
Orange throat darter

Syn.: *Poecilichthys spectabilis, P. coeruleus spectabilis, P. spectabilis pulchellus, Etheostoma arcuscelestis, E. lepidum, E. variatum, E. varietum.*

Hab.: North America: United States from southern Michigan and northwestern Ohio to Nebraska, Wyoming, Texas, Arkansas, Tennessee, and Kentucky. Found in slow-flowing shallow headwaters above sand, gravel, and pebble substrates.

F.I.: Unknown.

Sex.: Mature ♂♂ have gorgeous colors. Nuptial tubercles may be present on the soft and hard rays of the fins, the ventral scales, and the caudal peduncle. Their genital papilla is flat and triangular. While mature ♀♀ lack the spectacular coloring of mature ♂♂, the hard-rayed section of the dorsal fin is yellow and part of their body is dark red. Their genital papilla is a short, tubelike appendage with a rounded tip.

Soc. B.: ♂♂ are territorial and very aggressive towards conspecific ♂♂ while sexually active.

M: As for *Etheostoma nigrum.*

B: There are no breeding reports in German aquarium literature. In nature, the species normally spawns in April and May in slow-flowing, shallow sections of creeks and rivers. A ♀ enters the ♂'s territory and buries herself in the gravel. The ♂ follows. There she lays several eggs during one spawning act. A total of up to 1,200 eggs may be laid during one spawning episode.

F: C; all kinds of live foods such as small crustacea, aquatic insect larvae, *Tubifex*, and Enchytraeidae.

S: Five subspecies of *E. spectabile* have been described, two widely distributed and two with a very limited distribution.

T: 4°–18°C (coldwater fish), **L:** 8 cm, **A:** 80 cm, **R:** b, **D:** 2–3

Etheostoma nigrum

Etheostoma spectabile

Gymnocephalus schraetser   (LINNAEUS, 1758)

Syn.: *Perca schraetser.*

Hab.: Europe: only in the Danube and its tributaries from Bavaria to its delta. *G. schraetser* is an uncommon benthic fish that inhabits deep water over sand and gravel substrates.

Sex.: There are no differentiating external characteristics, but ripe ♀♀ have a larger girth.

Soc. B.: This is a rare benthic fish that generally lives singly. Quite peaceful, but it adopts a more predatory lifestyle as it grows older. Larger fishes make appropriate tankmates.

M: Provide a substrate of fine sand, edge and background vegetation (e.g., *Elodea* or *Myriophyllum*), and some secluded areas among rocks or roots. The water must be clear, oxygen-rich, and cool. Water: 10°–15° dGH; pH of 7.0–7.5. Perform regular water exchanges.

T: 4°–18°C, **L:** 25 cm, **A:** 80 cm, **R:** b, **D:** 3

Associate with species that have similar demands, for example, *Gymnocephalus cernua* or *Gobio gobio*.

B: There is no information that indicates that this fish has been successfully bred in captivity. In nature, they spawn during April and May. Eggs are laid in broad bands on a hard substrate. Depending on water temperature, the young hatch after 6 to 10 days.

F: C; all kinds of live foods such as *Tubifex, Gammarus*, insect larvae, and small fishes. Meat of fishes and crustacea is usually accepted. Difficult to accustom to flake foods.

S: *G. schraetzer* is part of the red list of threatened species and is nearly extinct. *Gymnocephalus cernua* has more lateral line scales and more hard rays in the dorsal fin than *G. schraetzer.*

Stizostedion lucioperca   (LINNAEUS, 1758)
European pikeperch

Syn.: *Perca lucioperca, Lucioperca lucioperca, L. sandra, Sander lucioperca, Stizostethium lucioperca.*

Hab.: Originally distributed in central and eastern Europe and southern Scandinavia. Today it is much more broadly distributed. It lives in large rivers in the barb and chub regions as well as in lowland lakes. Usually inhabits turbid open waters and lower water strata.

Sex.: Sexes are difficult to distinguish. ♀♀ are stouter during the spawning season.

Soc. B.: Solitary predators. Only young animals live in schools.

M: Adults must be kept singly. Required aquarium maintenance conditions correspond to that of equal-sized perches, except *S. lucioperca* has an even more voracious appetite. A fish for advanced hobbyists.

B: In its natural habitat, it spawns between April and May. Their very adhesive eggs are laid in pits in gravel substrates or near the shore on aquatic plants or submersed limbs. They are attentively guarded by the ♂. At 4 years of age and a length of more than 25 cm, the animals are sexually mature.

F: C; juveniles feed on crustacea and fish eggs. Older specimens are piscivores and demand a diet of fishes.

S: Appreciated sport and food fish. Under favorable conditions, it grows to a length of 130 cm.

T: 6°–22°C, **L:** 70 cm, **A:** from 120 cm, **R:** m, **D:** 3

Gymnocephalus schraetser

Stizostedion lucioperca

Zingel zingel   (LINNAEUS, 1758)

Syn.: *Perca zingel, Aspro zingel.*

Hab.: Europe: Danube, Prut, and Dnjestr as well as their tributaries. Shallow, flowing waters are preferred.

Sex.: No external differentiating characteristics are known. However, ♀♀ have a significantly larger girth during the spawning season.

Soc. B.: This is a rare, nocturnal, benthic fish. Territorial predators. *Z. zingel* can only be housed with large fishes that are not overly disturbed by its nocturnal lifestyle (e.g., catfishes).

M: Needs a spacious tank with a substrate of fine sand or gravel and cover and hiding places among wood or rocks. Average water values are best. Only young specimens make suitable aquarium fish.

B: Probably has not been successfully reproduced in captivity. In nature, this species spawns from March to May. Eggs are released over gravel substrates.

F: C; all kinds of live foods e.g., benthic insect larvae, *Gammarus*, *Tubifex*, and fishes.

S: *Z. zingel* can tilt its head slightly laterally, a scarce ability among fishes. In addition, the eyes move independently. This species is just as rare as its close relative *Zingel streber* SIEBOLD, 1863. Unfortunately, both species have become extinct in many of their former habitats.

T: 4°–18°C, **L:** 20 (50) cm, **A:** 100 cm, **R:** b, **D:** 3

Siniperca chua-tsi
Chinese perch

BASILEWSKY, 1855

Syn.: None, but it is also spelled *S. chuatsi.*

Hab.: Asia: in the central and lower course of the Amur and its tributaries.

F.I.: Unknown; probably has not been imported into western Europe.

Sex.: Difficult to differentiate. ♂♂ are larger and darker, while ♀♀ have a greater abdominal girth during the spawning season.

Soc. B.: Solitary predators which can only be housed with larger fishes.

M: Plant the edges of the tank with robust vegetation, and arrange pieces of bogwood to provide secluded areas. Water: pH 7.0–7.4; hardness 2°–5° dGH. Drop the temperature to 2°–8°C during the winter to allow *S. chua-tsi* to hibernate; it does not feed during this time. This is one of the few freshwater groupers. Do not add salt to the water.

B: In nature, this fish spawns in June and July when the water temperature is 20°–21°C. For the first four weeks, the young exclusively feed on spawns of other fishes. Afterwards, the fry begin to feed on small crustacea and insect larvae. It needs approximately 2 years to grow to 15 cm in length in captivity. At 3 to 4 years of age and a length of 30–40 cm, the animals are sexually mature in nature.

F: C; all kinds of hardy live foods, but small fishes are preferred.

S: Juveniles are attractively colored with star-shaped black striations. The head is orange red. A well-liked aquarium fish in the former Soviet Union because of its beautiful juvenile coloration.

T: 4°–22°C, **L:** 30 (40) cm, **A:** 120 cm, **R:** m, b, **D:** 2–3

Siniperca chua-tsi

Lake Khanka (Amur Basin)

Vespicula sp.

A 5 m long show tank of cichlids and perches

Pingalla midgleyi
Black-blotch grunter

ALLEN & MERRICK, 1984

Syn.: None.

Hab.: Northern Australia: Arnhem Land, in the Katherine and Alligator River systems.

F.I.: Has probably never been imported into Germany.

Sex.: No external differentiating characteristics are known.

Soc. B.: Very active, social fish which can be kept in small groups. Nevertheless, they are easily startled and aggressive towards equal-sized fishes.

M: A roomy aquarium with dense vegetation around the tank's fringes, a substrate of fine-grained gravel, and some hiding places among rocks and roots should be offered. In nature, these animals inhabit acid to neutral water (pH 4.5–7.0). Any robust fish of respectable size will make an appropriate tankmate. However, best kept in a species tank.

B: To the best of our knowledge, this fish has not been successfully bred in captivity.

F: H, O; primarily feeds on benthic algae and detritus in its natural habitat. Small live foods and flakes make an adequate diet in captivity.

S: Several horizontal brown bands appear when startled.

T: 23°–35°C, **L:** 14.5 cm, **A:** from 100 cm, **R:** m, b, **D:** 3

Pool around the Mary River, Northern Territory, Australia. Fishes found here include *Melanotaenia trifasciata, Melanotaenia exquisita, Melanotaenia splendida*, and *Mogurnda mogurnda*.

Fam.: Anguillidae (Eels)

Eels are benthic fishes with a snakelike body that lacks ventral fins. The dorsal, caudal, and anal fins are fused, creating one fringe. The scales are either tiny or totally absent. Their blood contains a very poisonous neurotoxin (nerve poison). Most species of this family live in freshwater and spawn in the sea (catadromy).

Fam.: Comephoridae (Oilfishes)

This family has but two genera and two species, both of which are livebearers. Oilfishes are pelagic endemics of Lake Baikal, living at depths down to 1,000 m. All lack a postcleithrum and ventral fins. The area between the second suborbital and the preoperculum has degenerated. Oilfishes are famous for their highly unbalanced ratio of ♂♂ to ♀♀. ♂♂ are a mere 4 to 21 percent of the population. Almost all ♀♀ die after they bear young. The flesh from these fishes is very fatty, hence the name!

Fam.: Coregonidae

This small family encompasses two genera which in turn contain eight species and innumerable subspecies and populations. Most are slender, laterally compressed, and opaque with a small mouth that barely reaches below the eye. The dentition is weak to totally vestigial, and the scales are small, yet still larger than those of salmonids. The lateral line is complete, and the base of the dorsal fin is anterior to that of the ventral fins. Coregonids live in lakes and rivers and, depending on the species, are either migratory or nonmigratory. The multitude of shapes within this family confounds taxonomic classification, making those endeavors almost impossible. The Coregonidae are broadly divided into two ecological groups—the planktivores and those that prey on benthic organisms. The former group has adapted to their trophic level by developing numerous soft gill rakers, while the latter group has fewer gill rakers, each of which is coarse and short. Nevertheless, identification remains difficult because of numerous transitional forms. It is easier and more reliable to speak of morphological groups instead of species.

Pike (*Esox lucius*), p. 965

Fam.: Cottidae (Sculpins, Bullheads)

The majority of the members of this family live in the sea; few of its representatives live in brackish or freshwater. Though their body is devoid of scales, they occasionally have bony plates and spines. They are further characterized by superiorly placed eyes, lack of a swimbladder, and large, posteriorly positioned pectoral fins. ♂♂ often have a visibly protruding genital papilla.

Fam.: Esocidae (Pikes)

The genus *Esox* and its five species range over three continents—Europe, Asia, and North America. Pikes are long, slender predators with a large head and a deep cleft mouth. Their snout resembles a duck bill, but is equipped with strong teeth. The dorsal and anal fins are situated extremely posterior. They and the caudal fin make up the propulsion unit (ambush predator). Pikes are extremely voracious, swallowing anything they can tackle.

Fam.: Cottocomephoridae ("Baikal Sculpins")

This family is divided into two subfamilies—Abyssocottinae and Cottocomephorinae—and eight species. All are closely related to the family Cottidae, but differ in their cranial morphology and dentition. Each species deposits large benthic eggs which are guarded by the ♂. The Abyssocottinae are bottom-oriented fishes, while Cottocomephorinae are pelagic. Some species that inhabit Lake Baikal have economic importance because of their delicious flesh.

Various True Bony Fishes

Fam.: Indostomidae
The single genus and species of this family lives in Burma in Lake Indawgyi and one of its tributaries. It is vastly similar in appearance to the family Gasterosteidae, particularly to the genera *Spinachia* and *Aulorhynchus*. In fact, *Indostomus paradoxus* was just recently separated from the Gasterosteidae and placed in its own order and family (BANNISTER, 1970). Although the body of *I. paradoxus* is anteriorly enclosed in hard plates, it still maintains enough flexibility to allow it to be laterally bent into a complete circle. Their head can move up and down, a significant peculiarity. *I. paradoxus* is closely related to the Gobiesocidae (clingfishes).

Fam.: Lotidae (Cods)
Cods primarily inhabit the Northern Hemisphere; only a few species enter the southern hemisphere. All cods, with the exception of a single species, *Lota lota*, live in the sea. They are characterized by their toothed vomer, lack of major appendages on the anterior section of the swimbladder, independent caudal fin, single chin barbel, and anterior ventral fins which are not elongated to any degree.

Fam.: Pleuronectidae (Flatfishes)
Flatfishes are asymmetrical with their eyes predominantly located on the right side. The upper side of the body usually has ctenoid scales, while the inferior side is smooth. They are further recognized by their protrusile mouth, lack of a swimbladder, and very broad dorsal and anal fins. Newly hatched flatfishes are symmetrical; only later do they become asymmetrical. Pleuronectids are almost cosmopolitan. Freshwater species are rare, whereas brackish water inhabitants a bit more common.

933

Fam.: Salmonidae (Salmonids)

The nine genera of salmonids live in marine and freshwater habitats of the Northern Hemisphere. Some species are migratory, traveling between freshwater and the sea. Most salmonids are appreciated food fishes and of great economic importance. Without exception, salmonids need oxygen-rich, cool water. For some species, 15°C is the maximal tolerated temperature. They possess an adipose fin.

Fam.: Thymallidae

Members of this family differ from other families of the suborder Salmonoidei by having a large dorsal fin with more than 17 rays. These fish primarily inhabit waters of the foothills, preferably fast-flowing rivers with gravel substrates, but they may live in cool lakes as well. The family contains a single genus, *Thymallus*, whose representatives can be found in freshwaters of the temperate and cooler regions of the Northern Hemisphere.

Continuation of *Anguilla anguilla* (p. 935):

larvae (= Leptocephalus stage) migrate in the Gulf current, arriving in European waters within three years. The typical eel morphology is adopted as the larvae enter the coastal waters (elvers). The animals subsequently attain their pigmentation.

T: 4°–20°C (coldwater fish), L: ♀ up to 150, ♂ up to 90 cm, A: 100 cm, R: b, D: 1

Anguilla anguilla
European eel

(LINNAEUS, 1758)

Syn.: *Muraena anguilla, Anguilla acutirostris, A. bibroni, A. capitone, A. eurystoma, A. fluviatilis, A. latirostris, A. marginatus, A. microptera, A. vulgaris.*

Hab.: Europe: in coastal areas and freshwaters from the White Sea to the Mediterranean, the Black Sea, north and west coast of Africa, the Canary Islands, and the Azores. Does not inhabit the Volga region, Siberia, or Greenland.

F.I.: Native species.

Sex.: ♀♀ are much larger than ♂♂; otherwise, there are no external differences.

Soc. B.: Lives in loose schools when young. Later, it becomes a solitary predator.

M: Only juveniles are suitable for the aquarium. The substrate should consist of the finest sand so that the animals can bury themselves. While plants are optional, hiding places among stones and a tightly fitting cover to prevent the eels from escaping are absolute necessities. *A. anguilla* is extremely hardy and can adapt to a wide range of water compositions. Temperatures should be moderate to cool (max. 20°C). Maintain in either a species tank or a coldwater community aquarium.

B: Has not been successfully bred in an aquarium. Many questions concerning its reproductive biology in nature remain unanswered. Details can be found in TESCH (1973): Der Aal, Parey Verlag.

F: O; live foods, flake foods, and carrion. Large eels are very predacious (piscivores).

S: The European eel is a catadromous migratory fish. It migrates from freshwater to great depths of the Sargasso Sea (between 20°–30° N and 50°–68° W) to spawn. The smallest known larva is 6 mm long. To reach European waters, the crystal clear, willow leaf shaped pelagic

Continued on p. 934

Apteronotus leptorhynchus   (ELLIS, 1912)
Long-nosed black ghost knifefish

Syn.: *Sternarchus leptorhynchus.*

Hab.: South America: Brazil, Peru, and the Guianas.

F.I.: Unknown.

Sex.: Unknown.

Soc. B.: Very quarrelsome fishes. Often waspish among themselves. Twilight- and night-active.

M: Keep in a dim or dark aquarium that has numerous hiding places, a fine-grained substrate, plants, and an open area for swimming. Generally shy and skittish, especially until they are accustomed to their surroundings. With appropriate care, they frequently turn surprisingly tame (hand tame!). Large placid fishes make suitable tankmates.

B: Has not been successfully accomplished. Nothing is known concerning the reproductive biology of this species.

F: C, O; all kinds of live foods, chopped earthworms, small pieces of meat, frozen foods, freeze-dried foods, and flake foods.

S: These animals possess a weak electrical organ they use to navigate.

T: 24°–28°C, **L:** 40 cm, **A:** from 120 cm, **R:** m, **D:** 3

Continuation of *Coregonus lavaretus* (p. 944):

F: C; all kinds of live foods, e.g., crustacea, worms, mosquito and other insect larvae, and sometimes small fishes.

S: In the strictest sense of the word, we should not speak of a species, but of the morphological group *Coregonus lavaretus*. All the members of this group have 25–34 gill rakers, usually 30–34, and all distinguish themselves with their great ecological plasticity.

T: 4°–16°C, **L:** 57 cm, **A:** from 120 cm, **R:** m, t, **D:** 4 (extreme coldwater species)

Apteronotus leptorhynchus

Apteronotus albifrons

Telmatherina celebensis   WEBER & DE BEAUFORT, 1922

Syn.: None.

Hab.: Southeast Asia: Celebes (Sulawesi), only known from Lake Towoeti.

F.I.: Ca. 1991.

Sex.: ♂♂ have somewhat larger and more pointed fins. However, this characteristic is extremely variable.

Soc. B.: Peaceful schooling fish.

M: Requires a medium-sized to large aquarium with fresh water and aeration. Although a powerful filter should be used, a stong current is undesirable. Plants, including fine-leaved species, will be used as spawning substrates and as hiding places. Water: pH 6.0–7.5; 24°–26°C. Regular water exchanges are a necessity.

B: Following a short courtship, primarily in the morning sun, the pair spawns over fine-leaved plants.

F: O; *Artemia* nauplii, freshwater plankton.

S: Very sensitive to deteriorating water conditions. Due to its susceptibility to various diseases, maintenance in a species tank is recommended.

T: 24°–26°C, **L:** 8 cm, **A:** 80 cm, **R:** m, **D:** 3–4

Batrachus grunniens   (LINNAEUS, 1758)
Toadfish

Syn.: *Cottus grunniens, Halophryne trispinosus, Coetus grunniens.*

Hab.: Indian Ocean and the estuaries of its rivers.

F.I.: 1974.

Sex.: Not known.

Soc. B.: Voracious. *B. grunniens* is an inactive predator that lurks, waiting for its prey like anglerfishes or rockfishes. Its unsuspecting victims are inhaled into its mouth with a strong current.

M: This toadfish can only survive a few weeks in freshwater; successful maintenance demands seawater. Since it is often sold as a freshwater fish, acclimating it back to marine water should be done slowly over the course of a week. Provide hiding places. Water: pH 7.8–8.5; density 1.020–1.024 (2.5% to 3% salinity).

B: Not known.

F: C; hardy live foods such as fishes, shrimp, and earthworms.

S: Not a freshwater fish as is often assumed. When touched, the fish makes croaking noises (name!). Batrachoididae are a link between the Blenniidae (blennies) and the anglerfishes.

T: 23°–28°C, **L:** 20 cm, **A:** 80 cm, **R:** b, **D:** 4 (marine fish)

Potamorrhapis guianensis
Freshwater needlefish

(SCHOMBURGK, 1843)

Syn.: *Belone guianensis, B. taeniata, Potamorrhaphis eigenmanni, P. taeniata.*

Hab.: South America: Brazil (Amazon Basin), Peru, Bolivia, the Guianas, and Paraguay.

F.I.: 1935.

Sex.: Unknown.

Soc. B.: Little is known about these fish. The Wilhelma Aquarium in Stuttgart has had a small group for a long time. Other large fishes such as *Anostomus* species and cichlids make appropriate tankmates.

M: Does not seem to be difficult as long as it is kept in a large aquarium. Cover the aquarium well, since the animals are good jumpers. Very nervous until acclimated.

B: Has been unsuccessful in captivity.

F: Offer hardy floating foods.

S: Few *P. guianensis* have been imported. Their maintenance should be limited to specialists and public aquaria.

T: 23°–26°C, L: up to 40 cm, A: from 150 cm, R: t, D: 3–4 (C)

Coregonus oxyrhynchus (LINNAEUS, 1758)

Syn.: *Coregonus macrophthalmus.*

Hab.: Great Britain, Ireland, northern Europe and Asia, and the Alps: found in large lakes and as a migratory fish in large rivers.

Sex.: Sexes cannot be distinguished by external characteristics.

Soc. B.: Peaceful schooling fish. Few morphs pursue fry (Lake Peipus).

M: Somewhat less problematic to care for than *Coregonus lavaretus.*

B: See *C. lavaretus.*

F: C.; zooplankton. Fry are rarely eaten.

S: Many geographic morphs and similar species make up the *Coregonus oxyrhynchus* group. All *Coregonus* have an adipose fin. Some fast-growing large forms are released into other bodies of water, which explains the crosses that have cropped up in many lakes at the foothills of the Alps.

The *Coregonus* forms presented here only represent a small portion of the overall variety within this genus!
All species are in grave danger of extinction due to water pollution.

Additional species of this genus can be found on p. 944.

T: 4°–20°C, **L:** 30 (50) cm, **A:** 120 cm, **R:** m, **D:** 3

Comephorus baicalensis
Large oilfish

(PALLAS, 1776)

Syn.: *Callionymus baicalensis, Elaeorhous baicalensis.*

Hab.: Asia: former Soviet Union, endemic to Lake Baikal.

F.I.: Has not been imported into Germany.

Sex.: ♂♂ are smaller than ♀♀.

Soc. B.: Unknown. It is probably a schooling fish.

M: Unknown.

B: Has not been bred in captivity. Livebearers. The fry are born between July and October. ♀♀ rise to the upper water strata to give birth, while ♂♂ always remain at great depths. Almost all ♀♀ die after giving birth. The larvae stay in deep water during the day, only rising to 10 m at night.

F: C; live foods, predominately pelagic crustacea.

S: ♂♂ are merely 3% to 4% of the total population. *C. baicalensis* has larger eyes than its congener *C. dybowskii* and inhabits less significant depths (750 m).

T: 4°–18°C (coldwater fish), **L:** ♀ to 19 cm, **A:** 100 cm, **R:** m, **D:** 3–4 (deep water fish)

Comephorus dybowskii
Small oilfish

KOROTNEV, 1905

Syn.: None.

Hab.: Asia: former Soviet Union, endemic to Lake Baikal.

F.I.: Has not been imported into Germany.

Sex.: ♂♂ are smaller (80–90 mm) than ♀♀ (115–140 mm).

Soc. B.: Nothing is known about the social behavior of this species, but it is probably a schooling fish.

M: Not known.

B: To the best of our knowledge, this species has not been bred in an aquarium. Livebearer. It gives birth from February to the beginning of March. ♂♂ have been known to occasionally rise to the water surface. Almost all ♀♀ die immediately after giving birth. The larvae do not undergo daily vertical migrations.

F: C; live foods, predominantly pelagic crustacea.

S: ♂♂ only comprise 12% to 21% of the entire population. *C. dybowskii* is found at depths of more than 1,000 m. Both species of oilfish are very fatty (hence the name!). Both of the photos on the facing page were taken at the Moscow Aquarium.

T: 4°–18°C (coldwater fish), **L:** ♀ to 14 cm, **A:** 80 cm, **R:** m, **D:** 3–4 (deep water fish)

Comephorus baicalensis

Comephorus dybowskii

Fam.: Coregonidae

Coregonus autumnalis migratorius (GEORGI, 1775)

Syn.: *Salmo migratorius, S. autumnalis, S. omul, Coregonus migratorius, C. omul.*

Hab.: Asia: former Soviet Union, endemic to Lake Baikal. In September, the fish also enter tributaries.

F.I.: Has not been imported into Germany.

Sex.: No definite external distinguishing characteristics are known.

Soc. B.: Pelagic, migratory fish.

M: *C. a. migratorius* needs a spacious aquarium with cold, clear, oxygen-rich (well-aerated) water, a sand or gravel substrate, and a decor of rocks and/or root. Vegetation can be waived. Water: hardness up to 20° dGH; pH 7.0–7.5.

B: To the best of our knowledge, this fish has not been bred in an aquarium. Due to its size and environmental demands, it is probably impossible. From September to November the animals migrate to the shores of Lake Baikal and swim into its affluent waterways to spawn. The 15,000–47,000 demersal eggs are about 2 mm in diameter. They are typically released over gravel substrates in riffles. Some parents die after spawning. Immediately after hatching in the spring, the fish migrate downstream into Lake Baikal to feed.

F: C; all kinds of live foods, especially invertebrates such as cyclops (*Epischura baicalensis*), chironomid larvae, and amphipods. Eggs and young of perches, roaches (*Rutilus rutilus*), and Baikal sculpins (Cottocomephoridae) are preyed upon.

S: *C. a. migratorius* is divided into three races: northern Baikal (Nagra), Selenga, and Tschiwykui. Each has a distinctive growth rate and fecundity as well as other distinguishing features and characteristics such as the number of gill rakers and spawning and feeding grounds. This species and all its races are valuable food fish of Lake Baikal.

T: 4°–16°C, **L:** 56 cm, **A:** from 120 cm, **R:** m, t, **D:** 4 (extreme coldwater species)

Coregonus lavaretus (LINNAEUS, 1758)

Syn.: *Salmo lavaretus, Coregonus wartmanni.* There are a great number of additional synonyms and names, some of which are valid subspecies. This fish's taxonomy is very convoluted and difficult to comprehend, even for specialists.

Hab.: Europe and Asia: from central Europe and the British Isles to the Bering Straits in the east.

F.I.: Native "species."

Sex.: No definite external differentiating characteristics are known.

Soc. B.: Some specimens are pelagic migratory fish of riverine or lacustrine habitats, while others of this species are nonmigratory riverine fish (Siberia).

M: Requires cold, clear, oxygen-rich (well-aerated) water, a spacious tank, a substrate of sand or gravel, and stones and/or roots as decorations. Vegetation can be waived, but if desired, only use coldwater species. Water: hardness up to 20° dGH; pH 7.0–7.5. *C. lavaretus* is a fish for coldwater specialists.

B: To the best of our knowledge, this species has not been bred in an aquarium. It is probably impossible because of its size and requirements. In nature, a morph from Lake Constance, Germany, spawns between September and December, depending on water temperature. Open areas above great depths are the preferred spawning sites.

Continued on p. 936.

Coregonus autumnalis migratorius

Coregonus lavaretus

Spring biotope of Miller's thumb

Cottus gobio

Cottus gobio
Miller's thumb

LINNAEUS, 1758

Syn.: *Cottus ferugineus, C. microstomus.*

Hab.: Europe: from northern Spain, Wales, and England to Weichsel, Seeland, southern Sweden, the coastal region of the Baltic Bay, and south of the Alps to the Tiber and the Dalmatiens. Also found in the Crimea.

F.I.: Native to Europe.

Sex.: ♂♂ have more intense colors, a larger head, and a clearly visible genital papilla; ♀♀ have a very large girth when in spawning condition.

Soc. B.: ♂♂ are quarrelsome among themselves and territorial, obligating hobbyists to keep equal-sized animals. Twilight- and night-active. ♂♂ practice brood care (paternal family).

M: Sand or a fine-grained gravel substrate and hiding places among rocks. Vegetation can be waived. Ensure that the animals have clear, cool, well-aerated water (powerhead?) with a pH of 7.0–7.5 and a hardness of around 10° dGH.

B: Occasionally bred in aquaria (see STAWIKOWSKI (1978): Aquareinmagazin **12**, 234–239). They spawn from February to June in their natural habitat. Normally the ♀ lays a clump of up to 1,000 orange eggs on the underside of a cleaned rock overhang. There the eggs are guarded and fanned by the ♂ for 30 to 45 days until they hatch. Raise the young with small live foods (*Artemia* and *Cyclops* nauplii).

F: C; live foods of all kinds (e.g., *Tubifex* and *Gammarus*). The animals can be trained to accept raw meat and even flake foods. Sometimes they consume fish eggs and fry.

S: There are three subspecies: *C. gobio gobio* LINNAEUS, 1758 (areas of distribution listed above), *C. g. koshewnikowi* GRATZIANOW, 1907 (former Soviet Union: the Newa, Duna, Dnjepr, Volga, and Ural Rivers), and *C. g. jaxartensis* BERG, 1916 (western Asia: Jaxartes region in the Ugama and Zirzika Rivers).

T: 10°–16°C (coldwater fish), **L:** 15 cm, **A:** 80 cm, **R:** b, **D:** 2–3

Cottus gobio

Paracottus kessleri
Sand sculpin

Syn.: *Cottus kessleri, C. trigonocephalus.*

Hab.: Asia: former Soviet Union, in Lake Baikal and tributaries such as the Angara, Irkut, and Selenga. Found above sand, mud-sand, and stone-sand substrates.

F.I.: Has not been imported into Germany.

Sex.: Pronounced sexual dimorphism: ♂♂ are larger and have a flat head, thick fin rays, and dermal tubercles on the nape and back.

Soc. B.: These benthic fish are mostly twilight- and night-active. ♂♂ form territories and practice brood care (paternal family). *P. kessleri* has a voracious appetite.

M: Unknown. However, conditions suggested for *Cottus gobio* should suffice.

B: In their natural habitat, the spawning season extends from mid-May to the end of June. The 2,100–3,000 eggs are laid over sand-rock substrates, especially under stones, at depths of 3–5 m. There they are guarded by the ♂. Sexual maturity is attained at 3 years of age.

F: C; all kinds of live foods such as *Tubifex, Daphnia,* and insect larvae. In nature the larvae of *Cottocomephorus* are also eaten.

S: In comparison to *Paracottus kneri*, *P. kessleri* is larger and lives at greater depths. *P. kessleri* can be distinguished from other sculpins of the Palearctic region by their long anal fin.

T: 4°–20°C (coldwater fish), **L:** 14 cm, **A:** 80 cm, **R:** b, **D:** 2–3

Paracottus kneri
Rock sculpin

Syn.: *Cottus kneri.*

Hab.: Asia: former Soviet Union, in Lakes Baikal and Baunt and the Selenga, Angara, and Jenisei Rivers, tributaries of the two lakes. Only found above rock and coarse sand substrates.

F.I.: Has not been imported into Germany.

Sex.: ♂♂ are larger and have thicker fin rays.

Soc. B.: Benthic fishes of the littoral zone. ♂♂ guard the eggs (paternal family).

M: As for *Cottus gobio.*

B: In nature, the animals spawn from the end of May to mid-July at a maximum depth of 1.5 m. Up to 600 eggs are laid on and underneath stones. They look like light orange spots. The ♀♀ move into deeper water after they spawn (10–30 m), while the ♂♂ guard the eggs until they hatch.

F: C; live foods. In nature they primarily feed on *Daphnia* and chironomids.

S: *P. kneri* and *P. kessleri* can hybridize.

T: 4°–20°C (coldwater fish), **L:** up to 14 cm, usually 8–10 cm, **A:** 80 cm, **R:** b, **D:** 2–3

Paracottus kessleri, adult ♂

Paracottus kneri

Batrachocottus baicalensis
Large-headed Baikal sculpin

Syn.: Cottus baicalensis.

Hab.: Asia: former Soviet Union. Encountered at depths down to 130 m above rock substrates along the shores of Lake Baikal.

F.I.: Has not been imported into Germany.

Sex.: ♂♂ have slender fin rays and round white spots on their posterior body. ♀♀, in contrast, have thick fin rays and no spots on their posterior body.

Soc. B.: B. baicalensis is a benthic fish with a paternal family structure.

M: Hobbyists are totally bereft of information concerning maintaining this species in a captive environment. Imports of this or other members of the Baikal sculpins are needed to provide these data.

(DYBOWSKI, 1874)
Subfam.: Abyssocottinae

B: In March and April this species commences its spawning migration, often ending up at the mouth of the Kultushna River. There the demersal, 3 mm eggs are laid. Each has 3–10 oil droplets. The larvae are 10 mm long when they hatch and they metamorphose at a length of approximately 16 mm.

F: C; live foods, predominantly small crustacea.

S: Three Batrachocottus species live in Lake Baikal. Besides the one presented here, there is B. nikolskii (BERG, 1900) and B. multiradiatus (BERG, 1907).

T: 4°–20°C (coldwater fish), **L:** 19 cm, **A:** 100 cm, **R:** b, **D:** 3

Cottocomephorus comephoroides
Long-finned Baikal sculpin

Syn.: Cottus comephoroides, Cottocomephorus megalops, C. grewingki var. comephoroides.

Hab.: Asia: former Soviet Union, in Lake Baikal and the Angara River above Irkutsk.

F.I.: Has not been imported into Germany.

Sex.: ♂♂ have dark brown pectoral fins and dermal tubercles on the underside of the pectoral fin rays. ♀♀ have light brown pectoral fins.

Soc. B.: Pelagic fishes that inhabit the littoral zone down to a depth of 1,000 m. Almost the entire year is spent at depths of 300 m or more. During the summer they lead a solitary life. However, they school during the autumn.

M: There is no information concerning caring for this species in an aquarium.

B: Migrating to the littoral zone, C. comephoroides spawns at depths of 5–

(BERG, 1900)
Subfam.: Cottocomephorinae

10 m from February to the end of April. After laying approximately 2,100 eggs, the ♀ returns to depths of 100 m and more. The ♂♂ remain at the spawning site to guard the eggs until the fry hatch. Then they, too, migrate back to deeper water.

F: C; crustacea are the primary source of nourishment.

S: In comparison to Cottocomephorus grewingki, C. comephoroides has longer pectoral fins and different otolith (ear stone) morphology.

T: 4°–20°C (coldwater fish), **L:** 19 cm, **A:** 100 cm, **R:** m, b, **D:** 3

Batrachocottus baicalensis

Cottocomephorus comephoroides, juv.

Cottocomephorus grewingki
Yellow-finned Baikal sculpin

Syn.: *Baikalocottus grewingki, Cottus grewingki, C. inermis.*

Hab.: Asia: former Soviet Union, endemic to Lake Baikal.

F.I.: Has not been imported into Germany.

Sex.: ♂♂ are smaller and have shorter pectoral fins. During the spawning season, ♂♂ develop pearllike dermal knots on the underside of the pectoral fin rays.

Soc. B.: Pelagic inhabitants of the coastal belt of Lake Baikal. During the spawning season (March to June), they form dense schools near the shore. From July to August, hoards congregate close to the coast where they feed on plankton and their own offspring. In the fall, they slowly descend into deeper water strata (50, 100, 200 m) and overwinter at depths of more than 300 m. The ♂ practices brood care.

M: There is no information concerning maintaining this species in captivity.

B: *Cottocomephorus* spawn in shallow shore regions, usually on rock substrates. Between 900 and 2,400, 1.2 to

T: 4°–20°C (coldwater fish), **L:** 19 cm, **A:** 100 cm, **R:** m, b, **D:** 2–3

(DYBOWSKI, 1874)
Subfam.: Cottocomephorinae

1.8 mm eggs are laid. Newly hatched larvae are 7 mm long. At a length of 19 mm, they undergo metamorphosis. After guarding the spawn for 2–3 weeks, the ♂ dies, as do some ♀♀.

F: C; plankton makes up the bulk of their diet: *Epischura baicalensis,* the amphipod *Macrohectopus branickii*, and larvae of congeners.

S: There are two races of *Cottocomephorus grewingki,* an early spawner (March to mid-April) and a late spawner (May to June).

♀

Procottus jeittelesi
Red Baikal sculpin

Syn.: *Cottus jeittelesi.*

Hab.: Asia: former Soviet Union, endemic to Lake Baikal.

F.I.: Has not been imported into Germany.

Sex.: ♂♂ are larger and darker and have broader, longer fins with heavier fin rays. Their eyes are smaller.

Soc. B.: *P. jeittelesi* is a benthic fish with a paternal family structure.

M: Unknown.

B: There are conflicting reports concerning exactly when *P. jeittelesi* spawns in

(DYBOWSKI, 1874)
Subfam.: Abyssocottinae

its natural biotope. DYBOWSKI says they spawn between January and February, while TALIEV states that they spawn from the end of November to February. The size of the demersal eggs varies between 2.5 and 3.3 mm. After spawning, the ♀ has no further interest in her eggs and leaves. The ♂ stays and guards the spawn.

F: C; live foods, predominantly benthic crustacea.

S: The Russian ichthyologist TALIEV claims there are two subspecies: *P. jeittelesi minor* and *P. jeittelesi major*.

T: 4°–20°C (coldwater fish), **L:** 35 cm, **A:** 100 cm, **R:** b, **D:** 3

Cottocomephorus grewingki ♂

Procottus jeittelesi

Batanga lebretonis
Clay goby

(STEINDACHER, 1870)

Syn.: *Eleotris lebretonis, E. ornosema, Batanga lebretonis microphthalmus.*

Hab.: Western Africa: from Senegal to southern Angola, in brackish estuaries and lagoons and freshwater of lower river courses.

F.I.: 1905.

Sex.: In ♂♂, the last rays of the anal fin and second dorsal fin are longer. Their genital papilla is very large, flat, and pointed. Some ♂♂ develop a frontal hump at spawning time.

Soc. B.: Generally peaceful. Sexually active ♂♂ are territorial. In sparsely decorated tanks, the fish generally stay on the bottom, but they swim extensively throughout the tank if it is well-planted.

M: Needs a spacious tank with sections of dense vegetation. Dim the illumination with a layer of floating plants and provide hiding places and potential spawning sites as well as a few roomy caves and roots. Keep in slightly brackish water or alkaline freshwater. *B. lebretonis* can be associated with smaller

fishes, but slender small fishes such as guppies and barbs may be considered food by the gobies. *B. lebretonis* feeds on soft, dead plant leaves; live aquatic plants are generally not bothered.

B: *B. lebretonis* spawns in roomy caves or on plants in the aquarium. Sometimes 2 or 3 ♀♀ simultaneously spawn with one ♂. Newly hatched larvae are not very developed; until their swimbladder fills, they move up and down in the water column (actively and passively, respectively). Specific information on how to rear these fish is lacking. In their natural biotope, they spawn in river floodplains during the rainy season. Adults migrate from the estuaries into these freshwater zones, meaning it should be possible to rear the fry in freshwater.

F: O; small live, frozen, and flake foods and cooked vegetables.

S: *B. lebretonis* is a close relative of *Dormitator* species, yet it can easily be differentiated by its rectangular dark spots on the center of its sides. Otherwise, they are quite similar in color.

T: 25°C, **L:** 12 cm, **A:** 100 cm, **R:** all, **D:** 2–3

Butis gymnopomus

(BLEEKER, 1853)

Syn.: *Gobius gymnopomus, Eleotris gymnopomus, Stenogobius gymnopomus.*

Hab.: India to the Philippines, Indonesia, and the Solomon Islands.

F.I.: Unknown.

Sex.: In ♂♂, the last rays of the anal fin and the second dorsal fin are longer. Their genital papilla is very long and thorn-shaped.

Soc. B.: This is a reclusive, solitary abiding predator. *B. gymnopomus* has, like other members of this genus, the ability to hover in any water stratum. Usually

the fish sit motionless with their ventral area resting on a substrate such as roots or a plant leaf. There they lurk, well camouflaged, waiting for their prey. *B. gymnopomus* are aggressive among themselves.

M: Plant the aquarium heavily with large-leaved plants (e.g., Java fern). These, floating plants, and roots are all very important habitat aspects for this goby. Intricate, heavily decorated tanks with numerous hiding places will allow several animals to be kept together. They can be maintained in brackish water as well as relatively soft (8° dGH), neutral freshwater. Slender fishes up to about

Continued on p. 957.

Batanga lebretonis ♂, ♀ on p. 956

Butis gymnopomus

Batanga lebretonis ♀, see p. 954

Batanga lebretonis ♂, fright coloration

Continuation of *Butis gymnopomus*   (p. 954):

$^1/_3$ their length are swallowed. Hence, one requisite for appropriate tankmates is that they be larger than the aforementioned size. They should also have a tranquil, amiable nature.

B: HORSTHEMKE & EBERHARDT reported a successful aquarium spawn in Das Aquarium **19**, pp. 509–512. The tiny eggs were laid in an open area and guarded by the ♂. The larvae hatched after about 36 hr at a temperature of ca. 23°C.

F: C; hardy live and frozen foods e.g., mosquito larvae, *Gammarus*, small shrimp, and young fishes. These gobies may have to be fed live foods at first, but it should be possible to train them to sinking foods.

S: *B. gymnopomus* has occasionally been confused with *B. butis* in aquarium literature, but the former is easily identified by its dark corporal striations which *B. butis* lacks. *B. gymnopomus* does not have scales on its cheeks.

T: 25°C, **L:** 11.5 cm, **A:** 80 cm, **R:** all, **D:** 3

Dormitator maculatus ♀, see following page

Butis melanostigma

(BLEEKER, 1849)

Syn.: *Eleotris melanostigma, E. wolffii.*

Hab.: Asia: India to Indochina, Indonesia. Found in estuaries and lower river courses.

F.I.: Unknown.

Sex.: Like *B. gymnopomus.*

Soc. B.: As indicated for *B. gymnopomus.*

M: As for *B. gymnopomus*; this species grows larger and therefore requires a more spacious aquarium. Slightly brackish water (1–3 ppt) suffices for prolonged maintenance.

B: Unknown.

F: C; hardy live and frozen foods such as mosquito larvae, *Gammarus*, and shrimp.

T: 25°C, **L:** 14 cm, **A:** 120 cm, **R:** all, **D:** 3

Dormitator maculatus
Fat sleeper

(BLOCH, 1790)

Syn.: *Sciaena maculata, Eleotris mugiloides, E. grandisquama, E. sima, E. somnulentus, E. gundlachi, E. omocyaneus, Dormitator lineatus, D. gymnocephalus.*

Hab.: America: North Carolina (United States) through Central America and the West Indies, including the area from the Bahamas to Santa Catarina, Brazil. In brackish, fresh, and salt water.

F.I.: 1901.

Sex.: In ♂♂, the last rays of the anal fin and the second dorsal fin are longer. Their genital papilla is very long, flat, and pointed, and during the spawning season, they have a frontal hump. ♀♀ have a shorter, curved ovipositor and a larger girth when ripe.

Soc. B.: Generally peaceful. ♂♂ are territorial during the spawning season. If the aquarium is suitably decorated, the gobies are active swimmers and not very bottom-oriented. Though often erroneously classified as a predator in aquarium literature, it chiefly feeds on detritus, tender live plants, and invertebrates.

M: Requires a spacious aquarium that has heavily planted areas, floating plants, roots, and roomy caves. Both slightly brackish and freshwater, even relatively soft tap water (8° dGH), are appropriate. Amiable towards all but much smaller fishes. Sleeper gobies feed on dead or tender plant leaves; aquatic plants are otherwise not bothered.

B: In Central America, *D. maculatus* spawns during the rainy season in freshwater. In the aquarium, the fish spawn immediately following a water exchange. The eggs are laid in roomy caves or other hidden locations and are guarded by the ♂. After 11–15 hr, 1 mm long larvae hatch from the incredibly tiny eggs (0.29 mm Ø). Until their swimbladder fills, they move vertically in the water column. No information concerning raising the fry could be found.

F: O; flake foods and boiled vegetables as well as live and frozen foods such as mosquito larvae and *Tubifex*.

S: The genus *Dormitator* typically has a blue spot on the shoulder. Additionally, it has more hard rays in the first dorsal fin (7–9 instead of 6) than other American and west African sleeper gobies. *Batanga* is a very closely related genus.

T: 20°–27°C, **L:** 25 cm, **A:** 120 cm, **R:** all, **D:** 2–3

Butis melanostigma

Dormitator maculatus ♂, ♀ pictured on p. 957

Eleotris fusca (SCHNEIDER, 1801)

Syn.: *Poecilia fusca, Eleotris pseudacanthopomus, E. pisonis fusca, Culius fuscus.*

Hab.: Reportedly found in the Indo-Pacific between east Africa, Melanesia and Polynesia; however, frequently confused with other *Eleotris* species. Mainly found in freshwater.

F.I.: Unknown.

Sex.: See *E. melanosoma.*

Soc. B.: See *E. melanosoma.*

M: As for *E. melanosoma*; this species can be kept in freshwater.

B: The initially planktonic and marine larvae adopt a benthic lifestyle at a length of more than 2 cm.

F: C; live and frozen foods.

S: *E. fusca* differs from *E. melanosoma* primarily by the number and length of its rows of sensory papillae on its head.

T: 25°C, **L:** 26 cm, **A:** 100 cm, **R:** b, m, **D:** 3

Eleotris melanosoma
Brown sleeper (BLEEKER, 1852)

Syn.: *Culius melanosoma, C. macrocephalus, C. insulindicus, C. macrolepis, Eleotris macrocephalus, E. insulindica, E. macrolepis, E. fortis.*

Hab.: Indo-West Pacific: reportedly from east Africa to Tahiti and Samoa. Its exact distribution is unclear because it is frequently confused with other *Eleotris* species. Inhabits brackish water and freshwater.

F.I.: 1935.

Sex.: In ♂♂, the last rays of the anal fin and the second dorsal fin are longer. Their genital papilla is longer and more pointed.

Soc. B.: A solitary fish that tends to be aggressive towards conspecifics and other fishes which cross its path. Daylight hours are usually passed hidden among the decor or prowling among plant thickets or within caves. They are more active at night.

M: *E. melanosoma* can be maintained in either brackish water or freshwater. Plant thickets, hiding places among rock structures and roots, subdued illumination, and floating plants all contribute to

overcome the innate diurnal shyness of this goby. Heterospecifics can be housed with this goby as long as they are relatively equal in size if not larger than the goby and the aquarium is roomy. However, due to the bellicose personality of the brown sleeper, it is prudent to avoid other cave-dwelling benthic fishes. Some individuals seem to be fin nippers.

B: Until a length of slightly less than 2 cm, the larvae of *E. melanosoma* are planktonic inhabitants of estuaries and coastal waters. Afterwards they adopt a benthic lifestyle. Cave spawner, paternal family. The larvae have not been successfully reared in captivity.

F: C, O; live and frozen foods e.g., mosquito larvae, *Tubifex*, and *Gammarus*.

S: Many species of the cosmopolitan tropical genus *Eleotris* are very similar. Exact identifications are only possible when the fish's origin is known. The pictured specimen comes from Sri Lanka. *E. melanosoma* barely grows larger than 10 cm in captivity.

T: 25°C, **L:** 20 cm, **A:** 100 cm, **R:** b, **D:** 3

Eleotris fusca

Eleotris melanosoma

Hypseleotris swinhornis (GÜNTHER, 1873)

Syn.: *Eleotris swinhornis, Micropercops dabryi borealis, M. swinhornis, Percottus swinhornis, Sineleotris sauaharae.*

Hab.: Asia: China, north of Hong Kong in the Peh and Riao Rivers and the Sungari Basin.

F.I.: Has not been imported into Germany.

Sex.: ♂♂ have brighter colors, darker fins, and a longer second dorsal fin. See photos.

Soc. B.: Outside of spawning season, this is a calm, peaceful fish. When spawning, ♂♂ are aggressive. ♂♂ are responsible for brood care.

M: Needs an aquarium with a substrate of sand or fine-grained gravel and hiding places and cover among rocks. Light vegetation along the tank's fringes is acceptable. Overall, there are no special demands placed on water chemistry. However, the water should be medium-hard and neutral (≤15° dGH and pH 7.0, respectively) as well as clear and oxygen-rich.

B: Has not been bred in captivity. Likewise, its reproductive biology in its natural habitat is unknown.

F: C, O; all kinds of live, flake, frozen, and freeze-dried foods as well as tablets.

T: 18°–22°C, **L:** up to 8 cm, but generally smaller, **A:** 60 cm, **R:** b, **D:** 2

Mogurnda adspersa (CASTELNAU, 1878)
Purple-spotted gudgeon

Syn.: *Eleotris adspersa, E. striata, Krefftius adspersus.*

Hab.: Australia: the drainage basins of the Murray, Murrumbidgee, and Lachlan Rivers and tributaries of the Darlin River in New South Wales and eastern Australia, including northern Queensland.

F.I.: Since it has been frequently confused with *Mogurnda mogurnda*, the exact date is unknown.

Sex.: Sexually active ♂♂ are brightly colored and have a frontal hump. Their genital papilla is pointed. ♀♀ have dull colors and a short, broad ovipositor.

Soc. B.: Territorial. A small group is recommended to prevent aggressions from becoming focused on one or two conspecifics. Despite their hostilities towards one another, they have been bred in very limited confines (60 x 30 x 30 cm).

M: Furnish the tank with roots, stone caves, lateral and background vegetation, and a substrate of sand or fine-grained gravel. Use groups of plants to divide the aquarium (territorial delimiters). The water should be medium-hard to hard and neutral (10°–20° dGH and pH 7, respectively). Best maintained either in a species tank or a roomy community tank with calm, equal-sized fishes.

B: Sexual maturity is attained at a length of approximately 5 cm. The ♂ courts the ♀ by circling her with his fins and opercula spread. The eggs are 2.0–3.8 mm long and 1.1–3.0 mm wide and laid on a hard substrate such as a rock, glass pane, or cave ceiling. They are guarded by the ♂ until they hatch after 8–13 days (20°–29°C). The larvae are then 3.4 to 4 mm long and free-swimming. Rearing the fry is nonproblematic with a diet of *Artemia*. Information on maintaining and spawning *M. adspersa*, unfortunately under the name of *M. mogurnda*, was presented in DATZ **35** (6): 201–203, 1982 by ZIEHM.

F: C; live and frozen foods (mosquito larvae and *Gammarus*) and beef heart.

S: *M. adspersa* and *M. mogurnda* are very similar, yet this species has larger scales (lateral line 30–36 vs. 37–48) and can be differentiated based on such. (*Batanga lebretonis* was erroneously pictured under *M. mogurnda* in Vol. 2 on p. 1071).

T: 16°–20°C, **L:** 14 cm, **A:** 80 cm, **R:** b, m, **D:** 3

Hypseleotris swinhornis ♀

Hypseleotris swinhornis ♂

Mogurnda adspersa

Perccottus glehni
Amur sleeper

DYBOWSKI, 1877

Syn.: *Eleotris dybowskii, E. glehni, E. pleskei, Percottus pleskei.*

Hab.: Asia: former Soviet Union, China, northeastern Korea, in the Ussuri, Sungari, Zeya, central and upper Amur, Tungur, Tumen-Ula, and the Josen Rivers and Lake Chanka.

F.I.: Has not been imported into Germany.

Sex.: No definite distinguishing external characteristics are known. ♂♂ are said to be slightly larger than ♀♀.

Soc. B.: This relatively peaceful sleeper goby is suitable for community aquaria. The ♂ is responsible for broodcare.

M: Care is nonproblematic, and there are no particular requirements in regard to oxygen levels and water temperature. Its captive environment should not be cramped. Use a sand or fine-grained gravel substrate. A few hiding places and plants along the edges and back-

ground can be included. Maintain in a species tank or with other sleeper gobies or gobies that have similar requirements.

B: Has not been bred in an aquarium. In nature, the fish reach sexual maturity at 2 years of age. They spawn from May to July at temperatures of 15°–20°C. Up to 1,000 elliptical eggs are laid on items laying along the substrate (aquatic plant leaves, wood, etc.). The eggs are guarded by the ♂.

F: C; predominantly aquatic insect larvae e.g., chironomid, dragonfly, mayfly, and mosquito larvae as well as small crustacea, and small fishes.

S: Other than *Hypseleotris swinhornis* (GÜNTHER, 1873), *P. glehni* is the only Eleotridae found in the former Soviet Union. The species is not of great economic importance, but it is eaten by humans in some places.

T: 15°–30°C, **L:** 25 cm, **A:** 100 cm, **R:** b, **D:** 3

Esox lucius
Northern pike

LINNAEUS, 1758

Syn.: None.

Hab.: Throughout Europe and Siberia to the Kolyma River. Its distribution does not include the Iberian Peninsula, Iceland, Dalmacija, or Crimea. Also found in North America.

F.I.: Native to Europe and North America.

Sex.: With the exception of size, (♂ ♂ are much smaller than ♀ ♀), there are no external differences.

Soc. B.: Ambush predators. Pikes are pronounced loners.

M: Requires a large aquarium, a gravel or sand substrate, dense coldwater vegetation along the edges and background, and thick roots as hiding places and cover. The water's chemical composition is immaterial. In view of their cannibalistic lifestyle, maintain individually.

B: Not possible in an aquarium for spatial reasons. In nature, pikes spawn from February to the beginning of May. Up to several hundred thousand very adhesive eggs can be deposited on aquatic vegetation by one large ♀. Depending on temperature, the fry hatch after 2 to 3 weeks complete with a gluttonous appetite which should immediately be appeased with *Daphnia*, *Cyclops*, and other small live foods.

F: C; young pikes feed on small crustacea, mosquito larvae, etc., but they quickly convert to a piscivorous diet. Although large pikes also feed on small mammals and amphibians, using these creatures as foodstuffs in captivity should be considered cruel. Pikes will not eat flake foods.

S: Pikes cannot be confused with other fishes thanks to their distinctive mouth (resembles a duck bill) and the extreme posterior position of their dorsal and anal fins. The dorsal, caudal, and anal fins form the pike's "propulsion unit." The fish burst from cover to seize their prey; see RIEHL (1980): Aquarienmagazin **14** (7): 354–356.

T: 10°–22°C (coldwater fish), **L:** ♀ 150 cm, ♂ 90 cm, **A:** from 100 cm, **R:** all, **D:** 1

Esox niger
Chain pickerel

LESUEUR, 1818

Syn.: *Esox affinis, E. phaleratus, E. reticulatus, E. tridecemlineatus.*

Hab.: North America: southern Canada and the United States, from Nova Scotia south along the Atlantic slopes east of the Appalachians to Texas and the Mississippi Basin to southern Missouri, Tennessee, and Alabama.

F.I.: Probably has not been imported.

Sex.: No distinguishing secondary sexual characteristics are known. ♀♀ are larger than ♂♂.

Soc. B.: Like *Esox lucius.*

M: See *E. lucius.* Dense vegetation is important.

B: Aquarium breeding is probably impossible because of spatial limitations.

F: C; as for *E. lucius.*

S: *E. niger* and *E. americanus* were once considered synonymous. The fact that

these two pikes hybridize where their distribution overlaps further confounds the issue. It can be very difficult to identify these hybrids.

T: 10°–20°C (coldwater fish), **L:** 80 cm, **A:** from 100 cm, **R:** all, **D:** 1–2

Lota lota
Freshwater cod

(LINNAEUS, 1758)

Syn.: *Gadus lota, G. maculosus, Lota maculosa, L. vulgaris, Lotta lota.*

Hab.: Europe: north of the Balkans and the Pyrenees from the Rhone to northern Siberia, eastern England, the Po and Danube Basins, southeast and northern Norway, Sweden, and Finland.

F.I.: Endemic species.

Sex.: None known.

Soc. B.: Nocturnal solitary predator that eats anything it can tackle.

M: *L. lota* benefits from a fine sand substrate, caves and other secluded areas among rocks and roots, subdued illumination, and well-aerated, cool, clean water (≤18°C). Vegetation can be waived. Water: 10° dGH and above; pH ca. 7.5. Regular water exchanges should be performed. Only juveniles are suitable charges for hobbyists. Keep singly!

B: Has not been bred in an aquarium. In nature, these fish spawn from November through March (winter). The eggs have a large oil vacuole. Depending on temperature, the eggs take 6–10 weeks to develop.

F: C; live foods such as *Tubifex,* mosquito larvae, caddisfly larvae, small crustacea, and fishes. Difficult to train to flake foods.

S: In its natural habitat, this fish is a highly successful spawn predator. *L. lota* is easily recognized as a representative of the family Lotidae by its single barbel on its lower lip. It is the only freshwater cod, and like its marine brethren, its meat and liver are a gastronomical treat.

T: 4°–18°C (coldwater fish), **L:** 60 cm, **A:** from 80 cm, **R:** b, **D:** 3

Apeltes quadracus
Four-spined stickleback

(MITCHELL, 1815)

Syn.: *Gasterosteus quadracus, G. apeltes, G. millepunctatus.*

Hab.: North America: from Labrador to Virginia. Mainly in brackish and marine waters.

F.I.: 1933.

Sex.: During the spawning season, ♂♂ have red ventral fins, an olive-green dorsum, and a black ventral area.

Soc. B.: Schooling fish. During the spawning season, ♂♂ construct nests and energetically defend territories against other ♂♂. Paternal family.

M: Place the aquarium in a sunny local and stock it with European and/or North American coldwater plants. Hiding places among rocks and roots and a sand substrate should be provided. Aerate the aquarium well. *A. quadracus* can only be kept in brackish water (100 g of sea salt per 10 l of water).

B: Almost identical to that of *Gasterosteus aculeatus* except this species only breeds in brackish or salt water. One ♂ and several ♀♀ should be placed together. The ♂ delimits her territory and begins building a nest with plant fragments. Once the nest is finished, the ♂ entices a mature ♀ within to spawn. The eggs are fertilized after the ♀ leaves the nest. Remove the ♀ after she has spawned. The ♂ practices intense brood care.

F: C; all kinds of live foods (small crustacea, insect larvae, worms) and mussel meat. Difficult to train to flake foods.

S: *A. quadracus* has four hard spines in the dorsal fin, while *Pungitius pungitius* has nine, and *G. aculeatus* only has three.

T: 4°–20°C (coldwater fish), **L:** 6 cm, **A:** 60 cm, **R:** b, m, **D:** 2

Culaea inconstans
Brook stickleback

(KIRTLAND, 1841)

Syn.: *Gasterosteus inconstans, G. globiceps, G. micropus, Eucalia inconstans.*

Hab.: North America: southern Canada (Saskatchewan) and the northeastern United States to Kansas, Ohio, Illinois, and Indiana. Solely inhabits freshwater, preferably small creeks.

F.I.: Probably has not been imported into Germany.

Sex.: ♂ turn velvety black at spawning time. Ripe ♀♀ are fuller through the ventral area.

Soc. B.: Normally ♂♂ are moderately aggressive, but at the onset of the spawning season, they turn territorial and extremely bellicose. A schooling fish during the rest of the year. ♂♂ are polygamous, breeding with several ♀♀. A brood caring species. Paternal family.

M: Clear, cold freshwater with a hardness of up to 15° dGH and a pH around 7.0 is needed. Provide the tank with a substrate

of fine sand, hiding places among rocks and roots, dense vegetation along the side and background using American coldwater species (*Elodea, Myriophyllum*), and good aeration. The animals should be kept in a species tank.

B: 18°–21°C; water values given under **M** suffice for breeding as well. One ♂ should be kept with several ♀♀. The ♂ establishes a territory and builds a spherical nest out of algae, sand, and plant fragments. Secretions of the renal cortex are used to glue the nest together. Now the ♂ entices a ripe ♀ into the nest. As part of the highly ritualized spawning procedure, the ♂ nudges the ♀'s posterior end which is outside of the nest, inducing the release of the eggs. After the eggs are laid, the ♀ breaks out of the nest on the opposite side, while the ♂ swims into the nest and fertilizes the eggs. ♂♂ almost always spawn with several ♀♀. When spawning is concluded, the ♂ chases all

Continued on p. 970.

Apeltes quadracus

Culaea inconstans inconstans

Continuation of *Culaea inconstans* (p. 968):

♀♀ away from the nest and then guards and cares for the eggs. By fanning the eggs with his fins, the ♂ keeps them exposed to fresh water. At 20°C, the eggs need about one week to develop. After another few days the young are free-swimming. Brood care lasts until the young venture from the nest. Feed the young *Artemia* nauplii.

F: C; all kinds of live foods such as *Daphnia, Cyclops*, mosquito larvae, *Tubifex,* and young guppies. Sometimes scraped meat is accepted. Flake foods are rarely accepted.

S: There are three subspecies of *C. in-* constans: *C. inconstans inconstans* (KIRTLAND, 1841), *C. inconstans cayuga* JORDAN, 1876, from Lake Cayuga and other bodies of water of New York, and *C. inconstans pygmaeus* (AGASSIZ, 1850) from Lake Superior.

T: 4°–18°C (coldwater fish), **L:** 7 cm, **A:** 60 cm, **R:** usually b, **D:** 3 (C)

Culaea inconstans pygmaeus ♂ at the nest

Culaea inconstans pygmaeus

Nest of *Culaea inconstans pygmaeus*

Acentrogobius audax

J. L. B. SMITH, 1959

Syn.: *Acentrogobius ennorensis.*

Hab.: Indo-West Pacific: only known from Mozambique (Ibo) and the Ryukyu Islands. Found in estuaries.

F.I.: Ca. 1986.

Sex.: ♀♀ have three slender black striations on the anterior body.

Soc. B.: Benthic fishes. ♂♂ are territorial and may attack other bottom-dwelling fishes, particularly similar gobies.

M: As for *Acentrogobius viridipunctatus.* It can be housed with other gobies in large tanks. Fishes that inhabit the middle and upper water strata can easily be associated with *A. audax.*

B: Unknown.

F: C; live and frozen foods e.g., mosquito larvae, *Tubifex, Mysis, Gammarus.*

T: 25°C, **L:** 9 cm, **A:** 100 cm, **R:** b, **D:** 3

S: *A. audax* has large scales on its body (LR 28–29) and predorsum (8–10). It can easily be identified by the black band that extends from the eye to the chin. A second diagonal band crosses the operculum.

Acentrogobius viridipunctatus

(VALENCIENNES, 1837)

Syn.: *Gobius viridipunctatus, G. venenatus, G. chlorostigma, Acentrogobius chlorostigma, Rhinogobius viridipunctatus.*

Hab.: Indian Ocean and western Pacific: Pakistan to the Ryukyu Islands and northern Australia. In estuaries.

F.I.: Unknown.

Sex.: The ♂'s genital papilla is thorn-shaped and clearly visible on live as well as preserved specimens.

Soc. B.: Bottom dweller. When not involved in sexual activities, these fish are peaceful towards conspecifics and other fishes with the exception of those small enough to be considered food. ♂♂ are territorial when spawning.

M: *A. viridipunctatus* requires brackish water with a salinity of ca. 1 ppt, numerous shallow caves of flat stones or mussel shells, open areas, and vegetation along the sides or arranged in groups. Surface-oriented fishes make suitable tankmates.

B: Captive breeding has yet to be successfully accomplished. JONES (Proc. Ind. Acad. Sci. **85**: 261–289, 1937) has observed them spawning in caves, among rocks, and within empty oyster shells in their natural biotope. The spawn is guarded by the ♂ until the larvae hatch (5–7 days). Newly hatched larvae are 3.3 mm long and take to the open water.

F: C; hardy live and frozen foods such as shrimp, *Gammarus,* mosquito larvae, *Mysis,* and small fishes that are $\frac{1}{4}$ to $\frac{1}{5}$ of its length.

S: *A. viridipunctatus* can be distinguished from other *Acentrogobius* by its relatively small corporal (LR ca. 38) and predorsal scales (over 30 prior to the first dorsal fin). The dark horizontal stripe on its side curves at the eye, a species-typical feature.

T: 25°C, **L:** 16.5 cm, **A:** 150 cm, **R:** b, **D:** 3

Acentrogobius audax

Acentrogobius viridipunctatus

Awaous strigatus
Striated river goby

(O'SHAUGHNESSY, 1875)

Syn.: *Euctenogobius strigatus, Gobius kraussii, Awaous decemlineatus, Gobionellus strigatus.*

Hab.: Northern South America (Atlantic seaboard): from the Rio Atrato of Colombia to the Marajó Bay, Brazil. Lives in freshwater.

F.I.: 1985.

Sex.: ♂♂ have purple crossbands, more colorful fins, and a mouth in which the upper maxilla extends to the posterior edge of the eye, almost to the edge of the preoperculum. The last rays of anal fin and second dorsal fin are longer, and the genital papilla is long and thorn-shaped. ♀♀ have a short, blunt ovipositor.

Soc. B.: Benthic, inept swimmers. ♂♂ establish and defend territories against conspecifics and similar looking benthic fishes. Each territory has a centrally located spawning cave. ♂♂ intimidate competitors frontally with their yawning mouth, attempting to shove their adversary away. Since they respond to danger by burying themselves in the substrate, it should consist of sand or fine-grained gravel.

M: The aquarium should have a substrate of fine-grained materials and shallow caves where they can hide and spawn. Plastic pipes buried in the substrate are accepted as spawning caves. A large area of the substrate should remain open to allow the animals to dig. They can easily be housed with free-swimming fishes.

B: Cave spawner; extremely tiny eggs are laid on the ceiling of a shallow cave or tube and guarded by the ♂. After 13 hr, 1 mm, very immature embryonic larvae begin to emerge (the eyes are not yet functional, and the swimbladder is not filled). They drift pelagically with occasional vertical movements in the water column. Larvae immediately placed into seawater upon hatching live longer than those reared in freshwater, but neither method has proven successful.

F: O; these gobies sift and dig through the substrate, searching for organic components (*Tubifex,* algae). Food is also taken from the bottom or the open water. Small live, frozen, and flake foods are accepted.

S: Its systematic position within *Awaous* needs confirmation because it is a rather unique member of the genus, differing in dentition, mouth size, and design.

T: 25°–27°C, **L:** 10 cm, **A:** 80 cm, **R:** b, **D:** 3

Awaous strigatus

Awaous strigatus

Awaous taiasica

(LICHTENSTEIN, 1822)

Syn.: *Gobius taiasica, G. banana, G. martinicus, Chonophorus bucculentus, Rhinogobius contractus, R. bucculentus, Gobius dolichocephalus, Euctenogobius latus, Chonophorus taiasica, C. banana, C. mexicanus, Awaous mexicanus.*

Hab.: America, West Indies: Atlantic seaboard from Florida (United States) to southeast Brazil. In rivers and creeks from the lowlands to the headwaters.

F.I.: Not known.

Sex.: ♂♂ have a longer snout, a larger mouth, and a long, thorn-shaped genital papilla. The ♀'s ovipositor is short and blunt.

Soc. B.: *A. taiasica* is a benthic, territorial fish that generally lives in moderate current over sand substrates. When threatened, it buries itself. Always found alone in its natural biotope.

M: A spacious freshwater aquarium with large open areas of sand or fine-grained gravel is needed. Include caves to act as hiding places. House with fishes that swim in the upper or middle water strata. According to conditions in its native biotope, *A. taiasica* should be kept in clean, oxygen-rich water with moderate values (pH ca. 7.0, hardness 10°–20° dGH).

B: Diadromous freshwater species. The tiny larvae spend the first part of their life in the open waters of estuaries or coastal regions. Towards the end of the larval phase, large numbers migrate into the mouth of rivers. From there they proceed upriver. Nothing is known about breeding this species in captivity.

F: C; all normal hardy foods, including small live and frozen fare. The substrate is searched for food items

S: *A. taiasica* is a demanding benthic fish. Specimens not accustomed to their environment startle easily, often becoming frantic.

T: 22°–30°C, **L:** 30 cm, **A:** 150 cm, **R:** b, **D:** 4

Benthophilus macrocephalus

(PALLAS, 1787)

Syn.: *Gobius macrocephalus.*

Hab.: Asia: former Soviet Union, from the northern to the southern coast of the Caspian Sea. Common in the Volga Delta.

F.I.: Has not been imported into Germany.

Sex.: Mature ♂♂ are naked, larger, and have bigger dorsal and anal fins. ♀♀ and juveniles are covered with bony plates (modified scales).

Soc. B.: Calm bottom-dwelling species.

M: Keep in fresh or brackish water aquaria that have hiding places (rock caverns, mussel shells) and open areas with fine-grained substrate.

B: Has not been accomplished in an aquarium, but it should be similar to that of *Benthophilus stellatus*.

F: C; live foods such as molluscs, worms, crustacea, insect larvae, and small fishes.

Frozen foods are accepted in captivity.

S: Besides the nominate form, the subspecies *B. macrocephalus magistri* ILJIN, 1929 has been described. It inhabits the Sea of Azov and the estuaries of its tributaries.

T: 4°–20°C (coldwater fish), **L:** 12 cm, **A:** 100 cm, **R:** b, **D:** 3

Awaous taiasica, WC, SE Brazil

Benthophilus macrocephalus

Bentophilus stellatus

(SAUVAGE, 1874)

Syn.: *Doliichthys stellatus, Benthophilus macrocephalus* var. *maeotica, B. monstrosus, B. macrocephalus* var. *nudus, B. macrocephalus ponticus, B. macrocephalus maeoticus, B. maeoticus, B. stellatus stellatus, B. sellatus leobergius, B. stellatus casachicus.*

Hab.: There are three subspecies: *B. stellatus stellatus* (SAUVAGE, 1874), *B. stellatus leobergius* ILJIN, 1949, and *B. stellatus casachicus* RAHIMOV, 1978. The former lives in freshwater and brackish water areas of the Black Sea Basin and far upstream of rivers such as the Danube and the Svistov (Bulgaria) as well as muddy bottom rivers and brackish waters above mussel grass and sand. The latter two subspecies are found in the Caspian Sea.

F.I.: Unknown.

Sex.: Head and body of ♀♀ and juveniles are covered with bony plates and granules (modified scales); in contrast, sexually mature ♂♂ are naked. They also have a broader, flatter head, longer posterior rays on the anal and second dorsal fins, and larger pectoral fins.

Soc. B.: Calm bottom-dwelling species.

M: Keep in fresh or brackish water aquaria that offer some hiding places (stone caves, mussel shells) and open areas with a fine-grained substrate.

B: Annual species. Adults die after oviposition, which occurs between May and June in the Sea of Azov. The 5.5–8.5 cm long (standard length) *B. stellatus stellatus* ♀♀ lay ca. 700–2,500 eggs. In the Caspian Sea, *B. stellatus leobergius* lays between 500 and 3,100 eggs, each with a diameter of ca. 2.1 mm. Those that live in the northern part spawn in shallow water from April to August, while the southern population spawns from October to December and March to April at depths of 30 to 35 m.

F: C; molluscs, worms, crustacea, insect larvae, and small fishes are eaten in nature. In the aquarium, live and frozen foods are accepted.

T: 4°–20°C, L: 13.5 ♂, 11 cm ♀, A: 100 cm, R: b, D: 3

Brachygobius kabiliensis

INGER, 1958

Syn.: None.

Hab.: Asia: initially discovered in the estuary of the Kabili River, Sandakan, northern Borneo. Other areas of distribution are unclear.

F.I.: Unknown.

Sex.: ♂♂ have a pointed genital papilla. The ♀♀'s ovipositor is short and stout.

Soc. B.: *B. kabiliensis* have been observed swimming in shallow waters of small, occasionally brackish pools among mangrove roots (HERRE Philippine: Journal of Science 72, 1940, p. 363). The species leads a secluded benthic life in the aquarium when only a few animals are maintained.

M: This diminutive goby should be kept in a species tank. Include hiding places (stones, roots). Floating plants may reduce the fish's shyness. Slightly brackish water is recommended.

B: Probably similar to that of *Brachygobius doriae*; see Vol. 1, p. 836. *B. doriae* was identified in early editions of Vol. 1 as *B. nunus*.

F: C; small live and frozen foods, *Artemia* nauplii, *Tubifex*, and small mosquito larvae.

S: The genus *Brachygobius* is comprised of three diminutive species (*B. nunus, B. aggregatus,* and *B. kabiliensis*), none of which grow much more than 2 cm long. They differ from the "large" species which grow about 4 cm long (e.g., *B. doriae*) by their more numerous and much more slender dark crossbands. *B. kabiliensis* is similar to *B. aggregatus*, primarily deviating by having scales on the opercula and cheeks. The specimen pictured here has a length of 22 mm, which corresponds to *B. kabiliensis*; however, the design is rather similar to that of *B. aggregatus*. The systematics of *B. kabiliensis* has yet to be checked.

T: 25°C, L: 2.5 cm, A: 30 cm, R: all, D: 3

Bentophilus stellatus

Brachygobius kabiliensis

Evorthodus lyricus
Lyra goby

Syn.: *Gobius garmani, G. lyricus, G. parvus, G. wurdemanni, Evorthodus breviceps, Gobionellus costalesi, G. lyricus, Euctenogobius lyricus, Mugilostoma gobio, Smaragdus costalesi.*

Hab.: America: west Atlantic from Chesapeake Bay, Virginia, United States, through Central America and the West Indies to Porto Belo, Santa Catarina, Brazil; primarily in shallow and calm zones of estuaries above muddy to sandy substrates. Usually found in brackish water, though said to enter freshwater as well.

F.I.: 1905.

Sex.: ♂♂ have threadlike extensions on the rays of the first dorsal fin that extend to the caudal peduncle, a long tail fin with two or three ocelli on the dorsal half, and iridescent blue-green sides. ♀♀ have a shorter first dorsal fin, a shorter banded caudal fin, and less intense colors.

Soc. B.: This benthic goby lives in galleries within muddy substrates or concealed under various objects. A very tranquil fish in aquaria. ♂♂ are territorial and aggressive among themselves.

M: Use a shallow brackish water aquarium and a fine sand substrate. These gobies only take food from the bottom, filtering small organisms and organic components from sediment on the substrate. Searching for food is generally haphazard. Therefore, limit tankmates to calm fishes that will not present competition for these gobies.

B: FOSTER & FUIMAN (Bull. Mar. Sci. **41**: 27–35, 1987) lay claim to being the first to successfully breed this fish in an aquarium. More than 100 small (0.45 x 0.20 mm) elliptical eggs were laid on the underside of pieces of flower pots and guarded by the ♂. After 16–20 hr, immature 1.9 mm long larvae hatched. The authors failed to rear the young. Adults were kept in a 75 x 30 cm aquarium with 13 cm of water, a salinity of 6 ppt and a temperature of 26.5°C.

F: O; small particles of flake and tablet foods, small live and frozen foods, *Artemia* nauplii and small mosquito larvae. Food is only eaten off the bottom.

T: 20°–30°C, **L:** 10 cm, **A:** 70 cm, **R:** b, **D:** 4

Evorthodus lyricus

Evorthodus lyricus ♀

Glossogobius bicirrhosus

(WEBER, 1894)

Syn.: *Gobius bicirrhosus, Illama cacabet, I. bicirrhosa.*

Hab.: Asia: from the Ryukyu Islands, Philippines, and Indonesia to the tropical South Pacific. Primarily in brackish estuaries, but reportedly found in freshwater as well.

F.I.: Unknown.

Sex.: ♂♂ have threadlike extensions on the rays of the first dorsal fin and a pointed genital papilla.

Soc. B.: Because of its pronounced benthic lifestyle, it rarely leaves the substrate. ♂♂ are territorial and aggressive towards conspecifics and other gobies of similar size and shape.

T: 25°C, **L:** 8.5 cm, **A:** 100 cm, **R:** b, **D:** 3

M: Can be kept with fishes that swim in the middle or upper water strata as long as they are not so small the gobies consider them prey. In sufficiently large tanks, *G. bicirrhosus* can be kept with other benthic fishes. Maintain in either freshwater or slightly brackish water with a salinity of ca. 1 ppt. Include some areas where the fish can hide in the decor, such as caves beneath stones with a ground-level opening.

B: Unknown.

F: C; live and flake foods, mosquito larvae, small shrimp, *Mysis, Gammarus*.

S: *G. bicirrhosus* differs from other members of this species-rich genus by its two small chin barbels.

Glossogobius giuris
Flathead goby

(HAMILTON, 1822)

Syn.: *Gobius giuris, G. russelii, G. catebus, G. spectabilis, Glossogobius tenuiformis, Eleotris laticeps.*

Hab.: India (*terra typica*: Ganges): east Africa and the Red Sea to the western Pacific, found in brackish and fresh water, even far upstream of rivers.

F.I.: Unknown.

Sex.: ♂♂ are larger and have a long pointed genital papilla. ♀♀ have a round fleshy ovipositor (visible after the fish reaches a length of 60 mm). Ripe ♀♀ have darker ventral fins.

Soc. B.: Benthic predators.

M: Needs a brackish water or freshwater aquarium with an open substrate of sand or fine-grained gravel and numerous hiding places. Spawning sites in the form of shallow caves need to be present. Free-swimming fishes of comparable size make the best tankmates for these gobies.

B: In Bangladesh, the gobies spawn throughout the year in saline water as well as stationary or flowing freshwater. According to observations made in its natural biotope (Madras, southern India),

the eggs are laid in shallow water in caves beneath stones or in tunnels which are commandeered from crabs or other aquatic animals. The ovaries of ♀♀ between 119 and 154 mm long produce 11,000–30,000 eggs. The eggshell is club-shaped after the eggs are fertilized, ca. 0.25 to 0.5 mm in diameter, and 3 to 6 mm long. The larvae are 2.25 mm long and planktonic upon hatching. Apparently, the fry have not been successfully reared in an aquarium (SUNDRA RAJ, 1916 and DOHA, 1974).

F: O; omnivores in nature. Besides fishes (including conspecifics), it accepts invertebrates and vegetable material (green algae, diatoms, and blue-green algae). In some regions cannibalism is significant. Live and frozen foods as well as fish flesh and beef heart are acceptable foods.

S: Representatives of the genus *Glossogobius* are very similar to each other. The sensory papillae arrangement on the cheeks is of paramount importance for exact species identification.

T: 25°C, **L:** 42 cm, **A:** 150 cm, **R:** b, **D:** 3

Glossogobius bicirrhosus

Glossogobius giuris

Gobioides grahamae
PALMER & WHEELER, 1955

Syn.: *Gobioides unicolor.*

Hab.: Northeastern South America: Amazon Delta (Marajo Island), coastal region of Guyana and the Demerara River over muddy substrates.

F.I.: Unknown.

Sex.: Unknown.

Soc. B.: As for *Gobioides peruanus.* They spend the daylight hours hidden in shallow caves under rocks and, at night, swim above the bottom with snaking movements. This hyperactive species is smaller and less elongated in comparison to *G. peruanus.* Very waspish towards other fishes.

M: As for *G. peruanus*; sand or fine-grained gravel is excavated from under stones lying flat on the substrate until a rock-ceilinged cavern results. Keep in brackish water (salinity of 3 ppt).

B: Unknown.

F: O, C; small live and frozen foods such as mosquito larvae, *Tubifex,* and *Mysis.* All foods are exclusively eaten from the bottom.

S: *G. grahamae* primarily differs from *G. broussonnetii* and *G. peruanus* by its shorter body and significantly larger scales (LR ca. 70 to 75).

T: 25°C, **L:** 22 cm, **A:** 100 cm, **R:** b, **D:** 4

Gobioides peruanus
Peruvian goby
(STEINDACHNER, 1880)

Syn.: *Amblyopus peruanus.*

Hab.: Pacific Seaboard of America from Costa Rica to northern Peru, in bodies of water with muddy substrates. Adults are found far upriver.

F.I.: Unknown.

Sex.: The genital papilla of the ♀ is a large, hemispherical organ. The ♂'s genital papilla is smaller and flat.

Soc. B.: *G. peruanus* digs itself a cave under flat stones lying on the substrate and energetically defends it against conspecifics. It passes the day within the cave, emerging at night to swim or snake along the bottom. Acclimated animals will come out of their cave during the day as long as the aquarium's illumination is not too bright. Outside of their cave, the animals are quite amiable towards each other. Free-swimming fishes are ignored. Even the smallest of fishes or juveniles are in no danger of being eaten by *G. peruanus.* However, this species' penchant for digging makes it unsuitable for "normal" community aquaria.

M: Needs a roomy aquarium with a sand or fine-grained gravel substrate and sufficient hiding places (at least one per animal). If several specimens are kept, a separate rock cave for each, as the species demands, becomes too voluminous. Glass or plastic tubes with a diameter that just allows the fish to enter are preferred. They can be glued together. Put them on the bottom pane of the aquarium and add sand until the tube openings are all but covered save the upper edge. The caves can be hidden with stones or adhered sand. The gobies use their fins to keep the entrances and the caves themselves swept clean. Keep in either brackish water or freshwater. Tap water with a hardness of 8° dGH is sufficient for maintenance.

Continued on page 986.

Gobioides grahamae

Gobioides peruanus

Knipowitschia longecaudata
Long-tailed goby

(KESSLER, 1877)

Syn.: *Gobius longecaudatus, G. (Deltentosteus) longecaudatus, Knipowitschia longicaudata, P. knipowitschi, Pomatoschistus (Knipowitschia) longecaudatus, Knipowitschia georghievi.*

Hab.: Estuaries and enclosed bays of the Black, Azov, and Caspian Seas. Inhabits shallow freshwater and slightly brackish water over sand bottoms or among plants.

F.I.: Unknown.

Sex.: Adult ♂♂ have several vertical dark bands on the flanks and larger dorsal and anal fins; ♀♀ are smaller and have a dark spot on the chin.

Soc. B.: Benthic fish. ♂♂ are territorial at spawning time.

M: Fresh or brackish water aquarium with a substrate of sand or gravel; mussel shells should be included as spawning sites.
S. DAMIAN wrote an article dealing with maintenance and reproduction of *Knipowitschia caucasica*, a related species, in AQUARIEN MAGAZIN 1985, p. 122–125.

B: In nature, each year it spawns several times from March to the end of July. The 1.7 x 0.8 mm eggs are released under mussel shells (e.g., *Carsium, Unio*) or stones and guarded by the ♂. The larvae are planktonic. At 8 to 10 months of age and a length of 2 cm, the fish are sexually mature. Their life expectancy does not exceed 2 years.

F: C; small live and frozen foods (mosquito larvae, water fleas, etc.).

T: 4°–20°C, **L**: 4 cm, **A**: 50 cm, **R**: b, **D**: 3

Continuation of *Gobioides peruanus* (p. 984):

B: No reports are available dealing with successfully breeding this species.

F: O; *G. peruanus* is incapable of capturing foods from the open water because of its poor eye sight. It takes small live and frozen foods (mosquito larvae, *Tubifex*) from the bottom and finds food particles within fine sand substrates. In addition, small planktonic foods (*Artemia* nauplii) are sucked in with strong gulps of water. This species is probably a detritivore in its natural biotope.

S: *G. peruanus* differs from *G. broussonnetii* (see Vol. 2, p. 1091) by its more oblique mouth, larger exterior teeth, smaller eyes, and lack of broad dark bands and spots.

T: 25°C, **L**: 38 cm, **A**: 150 cm, **R**: b, **D**: 4

Knipowitschia longecaudata ♂

Knipowitschia longecaudata ♀

Lophogobius cyprinoides (PALLAS, 1770)

Syn.: *Gobius cyprinoides, G. cristagalli, Lophogobius androsensis.*

Hab.: Central America: west Atlantic from Bermuda and southern Florida to Venezuela, but absent from the northern Gulf of Mexico; in Panama it is advancing towards the Pacific side (Miraflores sluices). Inhabits estuaries and brackish lagoons. Though primarily found in calm water, it also inhabits open bay beaches with moderate wave action.

F.I.: Unknown.

Sex.: Adult ♂ ♂ are darker and have more pigment in their first dorsal fin. ♀ ♀ and juveniles have more spots.

Soc. B.: Unknown.

M: Brackish water aquarium with caves as hiding and spawning sites.

B: DELMONTE & RUBINOFF presented an article on breeding and rearing the fry of *L. cyprinoides* in Copeia 1968, **2**: 411–412. Pairs were kept in 40 l marine aquaria at 27°–28°C. There they spawned each week on the underside of unglazed tiles. Approximately 100 hr postspawning, the 1.5 mm larvae hatched and immediately commenced swimming in the open water. Successfully rearing the fry was conditional upon the size of the tank (320–570 l). Aerated outdoors seawater tanks with plants and plenty of algae proved adequate. At first the larvae were fed Liquifry 1 thrice a day. Five days later, the feeding regime changed to Liquifry 2 and unicellular green algae (*Dunaliella*). Filamentous algae and zooplankton were fed when the fry were 8 days old. *Artemia* nauplii were eaten 22 days postspawning. They metamorphosed into bottom-dwelling juveniles after 35 days. Penicillin was added to prevent spoilage due to Liquifry, hence maintaining water quality.

F: O; small crustacea and other invertebrates as well as detritus and filamentous algae. In captivity, the goby lived one year exclusively on rotting mangrove leaves (trial by ODUM & HEALD, 1972).

S: *L. cyprinoides* has a tall fleshy dermal fold between the eyes and the first dorsal fin. This fold is shorter in the east Pacific species *L. cristulatus*.

T: 24°–28°C, **L:** ca. 10 cm, **A:** 100 cm, **R:** b, **D:** 3

Mesogobius batrachocephalus
Toad goby (PALLAS, 1811)

Syn.: *Gobius batrachocephalus, G. batrachocephalus* f. *batrachocephalus, G. nonultimus.*

Hab.: Eurasia: Black, Azov, and Caspian Seas; in coastal regions during the summer at 20 to 60 m depth (occasionally down to 100 m). Found in brackish lagoons and estuaries, rarely in freshwater. There are two subspecies: *M. batrachocephalus nonultimus* (ILJIN, 1936) and the nominate form. The former inhabits the Caspian Sea, and its ♂ has a distinct courtship coloration. The nominate form is distributed in the Black Sea. It lacks a special courtship coloration.

F.I.: Unknown.

Sex.: ♂ ♂ are larger than ♀ ♀ and have a pointed genital papilla.

Soc. B.: This bottom-oriented fish is aggressive towards conspecifics; when several individuals are maintained together, a social hierarchy is established.

M: Requires a spacious tank, numerous hiding places in the form of caves, and an open substrate of sand, gravel, or crushed shell.
In nature, these fish migrate into shallow coastal regions between the end of February and the beginning of May to spawn. Eggs are only laid once per spawning season. MOISEYEVA & RUDENKO (1981, 1985) have described breeding and rearing procedures.

Continued on p. 994.

Lophogobius cyprinoides, WC, Cancun, Mexico

Mesogobius batrachocephalus

Mugilogobius chulae

(H. M. SMITH, 1932)

Syn.: *Vaimosa chulae,* *"Stigmatogobius hoevenii."*

Hab.: Asia: Thailand, Philippines, Taiwan, Ryukyu Islands. In brackish waters of estuaries.

F.I.: Unknown.

Sex.: ♂ ♂ have a larger mouth, a broader head, elongated posterior rays on the anal fin and second dorsal fin, and threadlike elongated hard rays on the first dorsal fin. ♀ ♀ have a larger girth when in spawning condition.

Soc. B.: ♂ ♂ are territorial while sexually active. They defend small territories against other ♂ ♂ and court passing ♀ ♀. Though bottom-oriented, it is often seen swimming in the open water.

M: *M. chulae* can be kept and bred in brackish water or seawater. A salinity of 1 ppt is sufficient for long-term maintenance. Rock caves, bamboo, or PVC pipes should be included as hiding places and spawning sites. This goby can be maintained and bred in community tanks.

B: The elliptical, 0.95 x 0.40 mm eggs are laid in shallow caves and guarded by the ♂ until they hatch. The larvae, which leave the egg membrane after 90 to 96 hr at 24°C, are about 1.8 mm long. Immediately upon hatching they drift in the open water. They are easily reared in salt water with *Euplotes* as their initial food and *Brachionus* and *Artemia* added later.

F: C; small live and frozen foods such as mosquito larvae, *Tubifex*, *Artemia*, *Mysis*, etc.

S: The genus *Mugilogobius* contains more than 30 nominate species, most of which have muddled systematics. It is unknown whether or not *M. chulae*—also known as *Stigmatogobius hoevenii* in aquarium literature—represents a valid species. This confounding situation needs to be addressed when the genus is revised.

T: 25°C, **L:** 5 cm, **A:** 50 cm, **R:** b, **D:** 2–3

Mugilogobius inhacae

(J. L. B. SMITH, 1959)

Syn.: *Stigmatogobius inhacae.*

Hab.: Western Indian Ocean: Mozambique, Seychelles.

F.I.: Unknown.

Sex.: ♂ ♂ have longer posterior rays on the anal fin and second dorsal fin.

Soc. B.: Unknown.

M: *Mugilogobius* species are euryhaline fishes; they primarily live in brackish regions of estuaries. Keep in a brackish water aquarium.

B: Unknown.

F: C; probably small live and frozen foods.

T: 22°–25°C, **L:** ca. 4 cm, **A:** 50 cm, **R:** b, **D:** 3

Mugilogobius chulae

Mugilogobius inhacae

Neogobius cephalarges constructor
(NORDMANN, 1840)

Syn.: *Gobio constructor, Gobius constructor, G. cyrius, G. platyrostris* var. *cyrius, G. weidemanni.*

Hab.: Asia: former Soviet Union, in rivers of the Caucasus (Kuban, Dachestan, Kura, Aras, Astara), Lake Yaskhan, and tributaries of the southern Caspian Sea.

F.I.: Has not been imported into Germany.

Sex.: None known.

Soc. B.: Nothing is known about the social behavior of this fish, but it is probably territorial like other gobies.

M: Requires clear, clean water, a gravel substrate, and hiding places among rocks or similar materials. Vegetation should be waived. Preferred water values (pH and hardness) are unknown.

B: Has not been bred in an aquarium. We are bereft of information concerning the reproductive biology of this fish in its natural biotope.

F: C; all kinds of live foods. Voracious feeders.

S: The subspecies *N. c. constructor* represents the stationary freshwater form of *Neogobius cephalarges.* The nominate form, *N. c. cephalarges,* inhabits the Black and Azov Seas above stone substrates where it achieves a length 24 cm.

T: 16°–22°C, **L**: 13 cm, **A**: 80 cm, **R**: b, **D**: 3

Neogobius fluviatilis
Fluvial goby
(PALLAS, 1811)

Syn.: *Gobius fluviatilis, G. lacteus, G. steveni, G. fluviatilis* var. *nigra, G. fluviatilis* f. *fluviatilis, G. (Neogobius) fluviatilis, G. fluviatilis fluviatilis, G. fluviatilis pallasi.*

Hab.: Eurasia: basin of the Black and Caspian Seas. There are two subspecies: *N. fluviatilis fluviatilis* (PALLAS, 1811) and *N. fluviatilis pallasi* (BERG, 1916). The former lives in the region of the Black and Caspian Seas in brackish water and freshwater, migrating far upriver in the Dniepr at least to Kiev. In 1972 it was reported from Lake Balaton. *N. fluviatilis pallasi* inhabits the Caspian Sea and was introduced into the Aral Sea. The species is found above sand and mud substrates.

F.I.: Unknown.

Sex.: ♂♂ are larger with bigger fins and have a pointed genital papilla. When spawning, they are totally black with yellow- orange fin fringes.

Soc. B.: Benthic, territorial fish (especially ♂♂ during the spawning season).

M: Freshwater aquarium with rock caves, halved flower pots, or similar hiding places. Sparse vegetation.

B: In Bulgarian rivers, it spawns from May to September, but only from May to July in the Sea of Azov. The approximately 1,000 to 1,450 eggs are laid on stones or aquatic plants and guarded by the ♂. Sexual maturity is attained at 2 years of age and a length of 9–12 cm for ♂♂ or 8.5–10.5 cm for ♀♀. This species has a life expectancy of 4 years and more.

F: C; primarily crustacea (amphipods), but worms, mussels, small fishes, and bloodworms are also part of its diet.

S: This fluvial goby is a valuable commercial fishery around the Black and Caspian Seas.

T: 4°–20°C, **L**: 20 cm, **A**: 150 cm, **R**: b, **D**: 3

Neogobius cephalarges constructor

Neogobius fluviatilis ♂

Neogobius fluviatilis ♀

Continuation of *Mesogobius batrachocephalus* (p. 988):

B: The eggs are laid in protected sites (e.g., the inferior side of a flat stone or tile) and guarded by the ♂. Fry hatch from very large eggs (2.4 to 2.6 mm Ø and 5.2 mm long) without passing first through a free-swimming larval stage. The 8.0–10.5 mm fry emerge 43–48 days post-spawning at temperatures of 6°–15°C, or 53–58 days at 6°–12°C. The ♂ stimulates the eggs to hatch by changing his fanning frequency. When the ♂ is not present to tend the eggs, not all embryos are capable of breaking through the egg's membrane. Strong aeration with the resulting current can replace the fanning stimulus and likewise trigger the embryos to hatch.

Raise with *Artemia* nauplii. After about one month, the spawn begins to cannibalize on each other. The fish reach a length of ca. 15 cm in the aquarium. In nature, they are sexually mature at 3 years of age and have a life expectancy of at least 4 years.

F: C; primarily a piscivore in its natural habitat. In captivity, half-grown specimens accept shrimp and fish meat, while large specimens eat whole, small fishes.

S: Due to their size, this goby is of commercial significance as a food fish.

T: 4°–18°C, **L:** 37 cm, **A:** 150 cm, **R:** b, **D:** 3

Neogobius gymnotrachelus (KESSLER, 1857)

Syn.: *Gobius gymnotrachelus, G. macropus, G. macrophthalmus, G. burmeisteri, Gobius (Babka) gymnotrachelus, Gobius (Babka) gymnotrachelus gymnotrachelus, Mesogobius gymnotrachelus, M. gymnotrachelus otschakovinus, M. gymnotrachelus macrophthalmus.*

Hab.: Eurasia: there are two subspecies—*Neogobius gymnotrachelus gymnotrachelus* (KESSLER, 1857) and *N. gymnotrachelus macrophthalmus* (KESSLER, 1877). The nominate form inhabits coastal regions and tributaries of the Black and Azov Seas, primarily in freshwater, rarely in mesosaline brackish water (5–18 ppt salinity). The latter is found in brackish waters of the Caspian Sea above sand or mud substrates.

F.I.: Unknown.

Sex.: ♂♂ are darker and have a pointed genital papilla.

Soc. B.: Benthic. ♂♂ tend to be territorial during the spawning season.

M: Fresh or brackish water aquaria with stone caves or other secluded locals as spawning sites.

B: In nature, this fish spawns in Bulgarian waters from April to the end of June. Between 1,500 and 2,000 eggs are laid either under rocks or mussel shells and guarded by the ♂. Sexual maturity is reached at 2 years of age.

F: C; small fishes and invertebrates such as *Daphnia*, mosquito larvae, worms, and molluscs are eaten in nature.

S: The Caspian subspecies only grows to 67 mm in length; it has larger eyes than the nominate form. *N. gymnotrachelus* and *N. kessleri* are known to hybridize.

T: 4°–20°C, **L:** 16 cm, **A:** 150 cm, **R:** b, **D:** 3

Neogobius kessleri
Kessler's goby

(GÜNTHER, 1861)

Syn.: *Gobius kessleri, G. platycephalus, G. (Ponticola) kessleri, Neogobius kessleri kessleri, N. kessleri gorlap.*

Hab.: Eurasia: there are two known subspecies: *N. kessleri kessleri* (GÜNTHER, 1861) and *N. kessleri gorlap* (ILJIN, in BERG 1949). The nominate form lives in freshwater and brackish lagoons in the northwestern region of the Black Sea. *N. k. gorlap* is found in the Caspian Sea and many tributaries thereof in the former Soviet Union and Iran. The species is found over rocky substrates or in sites offering dense vegetation.

F.I.: Unknown.

Sex.: The genital papilla of the ♂ is pointed.

Soc. B.: Benthic. ♂♂, at least during the spawning season, are territorial.

M: Freshwater or brackish water aquarium with rock caves or other hiding places.

B: Spawns between March and April in Romania and in May in the former Soviet Union. The ♂ guards the spawn.

F: C; primarily feeds on crustacea in its natural habitat (*Mysis* and amphipods), but small fishes are consumed as well. Live and frozen foods are accepted in the aquarium.

S: The Caspian form (*N. k. gorlap*) is paler with less pronounced dorsal bands and fainter reticulation on its cheeks.

T: 4°–20°C, **L:** 22 cm, **A:** 150 cm, **R:** b, **D:** 3

Neogobius melanostomus
Blackmouth goby

(PALLAS, 1811)

Syn.: *Gobius melanostomus, G. cephalarges, G. chilo, G. melanio, G. virescens, G. exanthematosus, G. affinis, G. sulcatus, G. lugens, G. grossholzii, G. (Apollonia) melanostomus, Gobius (Apollonia) melanostomus melanostomus, Neogobius melanostomus affinis.*

Hab.: Eurasia: Black, Azov, and Caspian Seas, in coastal regions and lagoons at depths to 20 m (60 m during the winter). Also found in freshwater of lower and middle river courses. A common, economically important species of the Black Sea region.

F.I.: Unknown.

Sex.: ♂♂ are larger and have a nuptial dress consisting of dark, white-edged dorsal and anal fins. ♀♀ are either striated or lack a design.

Soc. B.: Benthic. ♂♂ are territorial during the spawning season.

M: Fresh or brackish water aquarium with rock caves or other hiding places.

B: In nature (Romania), these fish spawn from April to September in fresh or salt water. Each 7–13 cm ♀ is capable of depositing 328–5,221 eggs. After 14–15 days, fry emerge from the large (3.9 x 2.2 mm) eggs without passing through a free-swimming larval stage. Raise with *Artemia* nauplii. In aquaria, ♀♀ spawn up to 6 times in 18 to 20 day intervals. The eggs are laid on stones and guarded by the ♂. Sexual maturity is attained 3–4 years postspawning for ♂♂ and 2–3 years for ♀♀. ♂♂ die after the first breeding season.

F: C; gobies primarily feed on mussels, amphipods, polychaetes, small fishes, and bloodworms in nature. Live and frozen foods are consumed in captivity.

S: The black spot on the posterior part of the first dorsal fin is a species-specific characteristic.

T: 4°–20°C, **L:** 25 cm, **A:** 150 cm, **R:** b, **D:** 3

Neogobius kessleri ♂

Neogobius melanostomus ♂

Parapocryptes serperaster
Slim mudskipper

(RICHARDSON, 1846)
Subfam.: Oxudercinae

Syn.: *Apocryptes serperaster, Boleoph-thalmus serperaster.*

Hab.: Asia: southern China through Thailand, Malaysia, and India (Madras). Found along muddy coastal regions and within estuaries, occasionally far inland.

F.I.: Unknown.

Sex.: Unknown.

Soc. B.: This benthic species is shy in lit environments—its activity level is inversely related to the illumination level in the aquarium. It is aggressive towards conspecifics and energetically defends its cave against them. Other fishes, with the exception of similar-appearing species, are largely ignored.

M: Brackish water aquarium with a fine-grained substrate and numerous caves

(flat rocks lying on the bottom or buried plastic pipes). The gobies can be housed without further ado with free-swimming species, including small fishes such as the golden-banded goby and bumblebee gobies.

B: Unknown.

F: O, H; small live and frozen foods, mosquito larvae, *Tubifex,* and dry commercial diets.

S: A relative of mudskippers and four-eyes, in nature it predominantly feeds on vegetable matter (diatoms or detritus). *P. serperaster* generally has a stronger bond to the water than those mudskippers, allowing them to be kept in normal aquaria.

T: 25°C, **L:** 22 cm, **A:** 150 cm, **R:** b, **D:** 3–4

Rhinogobius wui

(LIU, 1940)
Subfam.: Gobiinae

Syn.: *Ctenogobius wui, Tukugobius wui.*

Hab.: Asia: southern Chinese mountain ranges and the New Territories of Hong Kong, in creeks.

F.I.: Unknown. Ca. 1960.

Sex.: ♂♂ have intense red spots and lines on the branchiostegal membranes, longer posterior rays on the anal fin and second dorsal fin, and a broader head.

Soc. B.: Bottom-oriented, rheophilic species. ♂♂ are territorial when spawning. They excavate shallow caves (e.g., under flat stones) or occupy available locals (pieces of flower pots) and, defend the surrounding territory. ♂♂ impress and threaten by lifting their head and displaying their extended branchiostegal membranes which have pronounced red markings.

M: Requires a freshwater aquarium with flat rocks upon a fine-grained substrate to serve as hiding places. The tank can

have a strong current. Best kept in a species tank.

B: Ca. 10–50 eggs are laid on a cave ceiling and then intensely guarded by the ♂. Young are close to 8 mm long with developed fins when they hatch after 14–15 days at 24°C. They immediately start to feed after the yolk sac is assimilated. One to two days after the young hatch, *Artemia* nauplii can be fed. Chopped *Tubifex* can be fed soon afterwards. Simple to raise.

F: C; small live and frozen foods, mosquito larvae and other aquatic insect larvae, *Tubifex,* etc.

S: *R. wui* tolerates temperatures as low as 10°C. Allowing the temperatures to ambient during the winter may encourage the fish to reproduce the following spring. Avoid high temperatures over extended periods of time.

T: 15°–25°C, **L:** 4.5 cm, **A:** 50 cm, **R:** b, **D:** 2

Parapocryptes serperaster

Rhinogobius wui ♂, ♀ Vol. 2, page 1101

Sicyopus jonklaasi
Lipstick goby

KLAUSEWITZ & HEINRICH, 1986

Syn.: None.

Hab.: Southern Asia: Sri Lanka (Ceylon). The species inhabits fast-flowing mountain rivers of southwestern Sri Lanka.

F.I.: 1981 by Arend van den NIEUWEN-HUIZEN.

Sex.: ♂♂ have a red upper lip and a red caudal peduncle; ♀♀, in contrast, have a black upper lip.

Soc. B.: ♂♂ are territorial. Bottom regions or stone crevices are preferred.

M: A tank with a fine sand substrate, rock crevices, hiding places below stones, and a strong current-producing filter is recommended. Keep the fish in clear water that has a hardness of 5° dGH and a pH of 7.0.

B: Unknown. In nature, the animals spawn in mountain rivers after the rainy season.

The larvae hatch in freshwater and then drift about 100 km downriver to the sea at Kalutara. At a later, as yet undetermined stage, the young enter river deltas and migrate up mountain streams.

F: C; all kinds of small live foods such as *Daphnia, Tubifex,* and Enchytraeidae. Algae are not eaten.

S: *S. jonklaasi* is closely related to *S. multisquamatus,* but differs by having 5 instead of 6 dorsal rays, a naked nape, and different coloration.

T: 23°–25°C, **L:** 5 cm, **A:** 60 cm, **R:** b, **D:** 3

Stenogobius gymnopomus

(BLEEKER, 1853)

Syn.: *Gobius gymnopomus, G. richardsonii.*

Hab.: Asia: India and Indonesia. *Stenogobius* species inhabit estuaries and flowing freshwater.

F.I.: Unknown.

Sex.: ♂♂ have a longer tail fin, a taller first dorsal fin, and are more colorful than ♀♀.

Soc. B.: Bottom-oriented. ♂♂ are probably territorial during periods of sexual activity.

M: Provide a spacious freshwater or slightly brackish water aquarium with a fine-grained gravel or sand substrate and some caves. Free-swimming fishes make the best tankmates for this species.

B: Unknown.

F: O; *S. gymnopomus* primarily feeds on detritus, algae—diatoms, blue-green, and green filamentous—and small crustacea

in their natural biotope. In captivity, they can subsist on a diet of small live and frozen foods.

T: 25°C, **L:** 13.5 cm, **A:** 100 cm, **R:** b, **D:** 3

Sicyopus jonklaasi

Stenogobius gymnopomus

Hemirhamphodon chrysopunctatus
Gold-spot halfbeak

BREMBACH & KORTHAUS, 1978

Syn.: None.

Hab.: Southeast Asia: southern Borneo, Kalimantan, north and northwest of Benjarmasin. In inundated forests and, during the dry season, creeks and river basins.

F.I.: 1978 by Edith KORTHAUS.

Sex.: The anal fin of ♂♂ is modified into a gonopodium, a copulatory organ.

Soc. B.: *Hemirhamphodon* are surface-oriented schooling fish which can turn very aggressive towards conspecifics when maintained in close confines. Because it is a rare, sensitive species, a species tank is recommended. ♂♂ may have to be separated.

M: Extremely soft water (≤1° dGH) is found in its natural habitat. Water in its

captive environment should be slightly acid and soft (pH 6.0–6.5 and a hardness below 5° dGH, respectively). Cover the aquarium well, since this fish is an excellent jumper.

B: Unknown because the animals imported in 1978 died after a short period of time.

F: C; floating insects and other live foods. Try to train the animals to flake foods to prevent food shortages during the winter months.

T: 24°–28°C, L: 8.5 cm, A: 80 cm, R: t, D: 4

Dermogenys ebrardtii
Ebrardt's halfbeak

(POPTA, 1912)

Syn.: *Hemirhamphus ebrardtii, Nomorhamphus ebrardti.*

Hab.: Southeast Asia: southeast Celebes, Kabaena, Penango, and Rumbia Plain.

F.I.: About 1985.

Sex.: The anal fin of ♂♂ is modified into a gonopodium, a copulatory organ.

Soc. B.: Lives in loose groups. Limit tankmates to peaceful fishes that are either equal-sized or slightly larger. ♂♂ are very aggressive among themselves. Keep one ♂ with several ♀♀.

M: A long, wide aquarium with a volume of at least 100 l and a water depth of 20–30 cm suits this fish's surface-oriented lifestyle well. Strong filtration and regular partial water exchanges are mandatory. Plant the edges of the tank densely to provide hiding places. The water should be medium-hard and about neutral (5°–12° dGH and pH 6.7–7.5,

respectively). Cover the aquarium well, since *Dermogenys* are accomplished jumpers.

B: Twenty offspring with a length of 20 mm are born every 4 to 6 weeks (25°C, 5° dGH, pH 6.5). They must be separated from their parents and graded by size to decrease cannibalism.

F: C; live foods, particularly floating insects (*Drosophila*), spiders, etc. *Tubifex*, mosquito larvae, and flake foods are accepted as well.

T: 24°–26°C, L: 9 cm, A: 80 cm, R: t, (m), D: 3

Hemirhamphodon chrysopunctatus

Dermogenys ebrardtii

Indostomus paradoxus
Paradox fish

PRASHAD & MUKERJI, 1929

Syn.: None.

Hab.: Southeast Asia: upper Burma and Thailand, in a tributary of Lake Indawgyi and within the lake proper near Nyaungtin; Cambodia, Malaysia.

F.I.: 1978 by Arthur WERNER, Munich.

Sex.: ♀♀ have a larger girth during the spawning season. ♂♂ are lighter, and their dorsal fins have a broader black fringe.

Soc. B.: Calm, peaceful, and generally languid. The ♂ guards the eggs and larvae until they are free-swimming (paternal family).

M: Even the smallest tank is sufficient to maintain this diminutive species. The aquarium should offer a substrate of fine sand covered by a layer of dark puffed clay, floating plants to dim the illumination, a plenitude of fine-leaved plants, and small stones and wood arranged to form narrow crevices and caves. The water should be slightly acid and soft (pH 6.5 and a hardness of 6° dGH, respectively). These animals do best when kept in a species tank or with relatively indolent fishes such as small *Rasbora* (*R. maculata* or *R. urophthalma*).

B: B. WALLACH has successfully bred *I. paradoxus* (1986, DATZ **39**, 500–502). The above-mentioned water values and decor were used, and one ♂ and two ♀♀ were placed in the tank. Approximately 20, vitreous green eggs were adhered to the side of a stone. They had a diameter of about 1 mm. About 24 hr postspawning, the eggs turned milky green. The fry hatched 24 hr later and were free-swimming after 7 days. Both eggs and larvae were guarded by the ♂. The newly hatched fry were fed rotifers, newly hatched bloodworms, microworms, and *Artemia* nauplii.

F: C; very small live foods such as small crustacea, rotifers, infusoria, grindal worms, *Tubifex*, and mosquito larvae.

S: The family Indostomidae only contains the genus *Indostomus* which in turn only contains the species *paradoxus*. BANNISTER (1978) established the order Indostomiformes especially for this family. Members of the family Gobiesocidae are probably its closest relatives. These animals do not have a lateral line. *I. paradoxus* is one of the few fishes which can move their head both up and down.

T: 24°–28°C, L: 3 cm, A: 50 cm, R: b, m, D: 2–3

Indostomus paradoxus ♀

Indostomus paradoxus

Kneria sp., Shaba, Zaïre, WC

Fam.: Kneriidae

Kneria spekii

GÜNTHER, 1868

Syn.: None.

Hab.: Africa: Tanzania, Uzaromo, between the coast and Usangara.

F.I.: ?

Sex.: The ♂♂ has a bean-shaped, lamellae-covered adhesive organ behind the head (occipital organ). He uses to adhere himself to the ♀ when spawning.

Soc. B.: Peaceful, gregarious fish that can be housed with other peaceful species.

M: Substrate of fine sand. According to conditions in their natural habitat, the aquarium should have good filtration, a current, oxygen-rich water, and moderate temperatures. Provide soft to medium-hard, neutral water (5°–15° dGH and pH 7.0, respectively).

B: Not difficult to reproduce. Separate the sexes for about 10 days to heighten the animals sexual drive. One pair should be stocked in a moderate-sized tank (50 x 25 x 25 cm). The ♂ soon begins to pursue the ♀. After a while, the ♂ presses himself laterally to the ♀, adhering the two together. Thus united, the pair darts 10–30 cm through the tank. Just as rapidly the pair separates. This display is probably a pseudopairing. True spawning activities usually take place during the early morning hours. The eggs, which hatch about 4 days postspawning, are not guarded.

F: O; live foods, aufwuchs, algae, and vegetable fare.

S: The family Kneriidae contains two genera: *Kneria* and *Parakneria*. Only ♂♂ of the genus *Kneria* have an occipital organ. It serves as contact surface to stabilize the union of both spindle-shaped fish while pairing.

T: 20°–22°C, **L:** 5.5 cm, **A:** 60 cm, **R:** b, **D:** 2

Parakneria sp. aff. *tanzaniae*

POLL, 1984

Syn.: None.

Hab.: East Africa: Tanzania, in the Ruaha and Wami Basins.

F.I.: August of 1987 by B. KILIAN and L. SEEGERS from the Wami Basin.

Sex.: Difficult to determine. ♂♂ are slightly more slender, while ♀♀ are rounder.

Soc. B.: Peaceful fish that "graze" the substrate either alone or in small groups.

M: Unproblematic. Can be kept in a community tank as long as the other inhabitants are small fishes. The water should be soft to medium-hard with a pH around 7. Flat stones should be illuminated strongly when possible. This seems to be beneficial, as it helps ensure the presence of a good algae lawn. While they graze on these algae, they repeatedly lift their head and prop themselves up on their ventral fins. *P.* sp. aff. *tanzaniae* constantly scoots forward, searching for food. Its behavior is reminiscent of Characidae, another group that is very bound to their benthic environment.

B: Unsuccessful.

F: O; all offered foods are accepted, especially live foods, as long as they are not too large. It is unknown whether or not plant material is ingested when the algae are "grazed," but it seems likely.

S: *P. tanzaniae* was described from the upper courses of the Ruaha in Tanzania. It is unknown whether or not the animals from Wami (see photo) represent an autonomous species or even if *P. tanzaniae* is a valid species.

T: 22°–24°C, **L:** 7.5 cm, **A:** 80 cm, **R:** b, **D:** 2–3

Kneria sp. aff. *spekii*

Parakneria sp. aff. *tanzaniae*

Afromastacembelus flavidus (MATTHES, 1962)

Syn.: *Mastacembelus flavidus.*

Hab.: Africa: endemic to Lake Tanganyika. Found along shallow coastal regions.

F.I.: Unknown.

Sex.: No definite distinguishing external characteristics are known.

Soc. B.: Night- or twilight-active predatory benthic fish. The animals may be quarrelsome among themselves.

M: Requires a substrate of fine sand and large stone and rock edifications with many crevices, niches, and other hiding places. Plants can be waived. The water should be medium-hard to hard and alkaline (10°–20° dGH and pH 7.5–8.5). Regular water exchanges and good aeration are recommended.

B: To the best of our knowledge, this species has not been successfully bred in an aquarium.

F: C; live foods of all kinds such as worms, insects and their larvae, small crustacea, and small fishes.

S: The classification of this species into *Afromastacembelus* is not undisputed. It may change when newly captured specimens can be studied. *A. flavidus* is a very rare species.

T: 24°–28°C, **L**: 27 cm, **A**: 120 cm, **R**: b, **D**: 3

Afromastacembelus tanganicae (GÜNTHER, 1893)
Tanganyikan spiny eel

Syn.: *Mastacembelis tanganicae.*

Hab.: Africa: endemic to Lake Tanganyika. Inhabits shallow coasts with rocky substrates.

F.I.: Unknown.

Sex.: No certain external differences are known.

Soc. B.: Twilight- and night-active predators. The animals have been known to bite each other.

M: As for *A. flavidus*.

B: Has not been successfully accomplished in an aquarium.

F: C; live foods commiserate to its size e.g., small crustacea, mosquito larvae, worms (*Tubifex,* Enchytraeidae, small earthworms), and fishes.

S: *A. tanganicae* differs from *A. flavidus* by the design on the tail fin and other characteristics.

T: 24°–28°C, **L**: 19 cm, **A**: 100 cm, **R**: b, **D**: 3

Afromastacembelus flavidus

Afromastacembelus tanganicae

Mastacembelus circumcinctus   HORA, 1924
Belted spiny eel

Syn.: None.

Hab.: Asia: southeast Thailand.

F.I.: Unknown.

Sex.: Unknown.

Soc. B.: Aggressive towards conspecifics and heterospecifics. While small fishes will be eaten, larger individuals make appropriate tankmates.

M: A soft substrate of sand and peat is necessary because the animals bury themselves during danger. Use dense edge and background vegetation. Floating plants dim the light and help alleviate the fish's shyness. *M. circumcinctus* have a secluded lifestyle, often remaining invisible for days at a time. The animals appreciate regular water exchanges. The water should be soft to medium-hard and around neutral ($\leq 15°$ dGH and a pH of 7.0, respectively).

B: Has not been bred in an aquarium.

F: C; all kinds of live foods such as small crustacea, worms, mosquito larvae, and small fishes. The animals are hard to train to commercial diets, but frozen and freeze-dried foods are readily accepted. Since these animals generally only eat at night, feed them at that time!

S: The yellow form of *M. circumcinctus* is a variety in which the black pigment is either totally lacking or present in small amounts.

T: 24°–28°C, **L:** 16 cm, **A:** 80 cm, **R:** b, **D:** 3

Mastacembelus zebrinus   BLYTH, 1858
Zebra spiny eel

Syn.: None.

Hab.: Asia: Burma, in the Irrawaddy, Sittang, and Salween Rivers.

F.I.: Unknown.

Sex.: None known.

Soc. B.: Twilight- and night-active benthic fish with a predatory lifestyle.

M: As indicated for *Mastacembelus maculatus*.

B: This species has not been bred in an aquarium.

F: C; all kinds of live foods such as mosquito larvae, earthworms, *Tubifex,* small crustacea, and fishes.

S: The tip of *M. zebrinus*'s snout is covered with scales.

T: 23°–26°C, **L:** 31 cm, **A:** 100 cm, **R:** b, **D:** 3

Mastacembelus circumcinctus

Mastacembelus zebrinus

Chilatherina axelrodi
Axelrod's rainbowfish

ALLEN, 1980

Syn.: None.

Hab.: Papua New Guinea: distribution seems to be limited to a few creeks in the north near Bewani, e.g., the Yungkiri, a tributary of the Pual River.

F.I.: Has probably never been imported.

Sex.: ♂♂ have pointed fins and a higher back (see photo). Courting ♂♂ have a golden-brown dorsal band which they can turn on and off like a light.

Soc. B.: Peaceful schooling fish. With the exception of the smallest fry, suitable tankmates for all peaceful fishes.

M: House in moderate-sized tanks that have free swimming areas. Part of the aquarium should be planted densely so that inferior ♂♂ and ♀♀ can escape overzealous pursuits. Water: pH >7; hardness at least 15° dGH.

B: As yet unknown, but it should not be significantly different than that of C. bleheri (see Vol. 2, p. 1108). Since courting ♂♂ energetically chase ♀♀, more ♀♀

than ♂♂ should be placed in the breeding tank. The breeding tank only needs a clump of Java moss or a spawning mop. Remove the parents after 5 days. One to two days later the first young hatch. They are easily raised with very small flake foods.

F: O; floating foods, good flake foods, and vegetable fare. Food that sinks to the bottom is ignored. Overfeeding, a particular danger with older specimens, makes them susceptible to disease.

S: Its typical crossbands distinguish this species from all its congeners.
Unfortunately, it is very difficult to import fishes from Papua New Guinea, since Australia has closed its borders to imports from there to prevent released animals from crossbreeding with native rainbowfishes. Almost all rainbowfish crosses are fertile, which is why rainbow fishes should never be bred in community aquaria.

T: 27°–30°C, **L:** ♂ up to 10, ♀ up to 8 cm, **A:** 100 cm, **R:** m, t, **D:** 2

Chilatherina lorentzi
Lorentz's rainbowfish

(WEBER, 1908)

Syn.: Rhombatractus lorentzi.

Hab.: In creeks of northern Papua New Guinea, primarily the Tawarin River.

F.I.: Has not been imported.

Sex.: ♂♂ have a taller back with pointed, elongated dorsal and anal fins. The pictured fish is a ♀.

Soc. B.: Peaceful schooling fish that only pursues the smallest of fishes.

M: Large aquaria with dense vegetation, good filtration, and strong aeration are needed. Frequent partial water exchanges are mandatory. The pH should be around 7.5 and the hardness up to 15° dGH.

B: As with almost all other rainbowfishes, breeding is considered facile (see C. axelrodi).

F: O; floating foods, insect larvae, small crustacea (water fleas), and vegetable fare. Quality flake foods are also readily accepted.

T: 26°–30°C, **L:** ♂ up to 12 cm, ♀ up to 10 cm, **A:** 100 cm, **R:** m, t, **D:** 2

Chilatherina axelrodi ♂

Chilatherina lorentzi

Edith Falls, Northern Territory. A natural biotope of *Melanotaenia exquisita* and *Melanotaenia splendida*.

Melanotaenia lacustris
Lake Kutubu rainbowfish

MUNRO, 1964

Syn.: None.

Hab.: New Guinea: only known from Lake Kutubu in the Kikori Basin in the southern highlands.

F.I.: 1987 by H. BLEHER.

Sex.: ♂ ♂ are more intensely colored. Full-grown adult ♂ ♂ have more elongated, darker fins. ♀ ♀ are more simple.

Soc. B.: This peaceful schooling fish requires plenty of open swimming space.

M: House in large aquaria that have sufficient free swimming space. Water: pH 7–8; hardness up to 10° dGH; temperature around 22°C. When kept in tanks that are too small, these rainbows do not display their beautiful colors to their full potential. The pictured animals have yet to develop their full coloration.

B: Place a clump of Java moss or a spawning mop in the tank to serve as a spawning substrate. The young hatch after about 6 days and are easily raised with small flake foods. In contrast to many other rainbowfishes, *M. lacustris* has some coloration from a length of 3 cm.

F: O; other than the usual foods, a certain proportion of vegetable components (duck weed) is also required. Flake foods are adequate for both maintenance and breeding. Do not overfeed these fish.

S: After it was first imported, this rainbowfish underwent an almost explosive distribution. It is hoped that this trend continues and this beautiful, peaceful fish does not disappear from the market equally fast.

T: 20°–24°C, **L:** 12 cm, **A:** 100 cm, **R:** m, t, **D:** 2–3

Melanotaenia maccullochi
McCulloch's rainbowfish

OGILBY, 1915

Syn.: *Nematocentris maccullochi, N. sexlineata* (erroneous identification), *Melanotaenia sexlineata* (erroneous identification), *M. sexfasciata* (fictional name).

Hab.: Southern New Guinea and Australia: Cape York Peninsula and coastal plains south of Cairns. The pictured specimen comes from Sigabadurn on Papua New Guinea; however, this variant is found throughout southern New Guinea and at the extreme tip of the Cape York Peninsula.

F.I.: The geographical morph from the Brisbane region was imported in 1934 by "Aquarium Hamburg." The exact date of import of the variant presented here cannot be determined because it has almost always been imported under the wrong name.

Sex.: ♂♂ have slightly more elongated fins and brighter colors, while ♀ are fuller through the ventral area.

Soc. B.: Lively peaceful schooling fish.

M: Moderate-sized aquaria with a lot of free swimming space and fine-leaved plants in the background. These plants are used as spawning substrates. If possible, situate the aquarium so that it receives the morning sun. The Cape York population comes from very soft water with a pH around 5.5, while the water from southern New Guinea, although soft, has a pH between 6.5 and 7.5. These populations can be maintained and bred under almost all standard water conditions.

B: Very easy. A partial water exchange triggers spawning and generally results in better fecundity. Otherwise, McCulloch's rainbowfish, like all rainbowfishes, is a continuous spawner, spawning almost every morning and occasionally during other tiems of the day. The young can easily be reared with very small flake foods. See Vol. 1, p. 852.

F: O; avoid overly large pieces of food. Smallest fry of this and other species are eaten.

S: *M. maccullochi* has several color morphs. The variety presented here has distinctive, unconfusable black and white stripes on the dorsal and anal fins and is primarily found in southern New Guinea.

T: 24°–30°C, **L:** 7 cm, usually somewhat smaller, **A:** 60 cm, **R:** m, t, **D:** 1

Melanotaenia maccullochi ♂, Papua New Guinea

Melanotaenia maccullochi, Harvey Creek, Australia

Melanotaenia monticola
Mountain rainbowfish

ALLEN, 1980

Syn.: None.

Hab.: Papua New Guinea: the southern highlands in the upper Purari River System near Mendi.

Sex.: The dorsal and anal fins of ♂♂ are more elongated. The size difference seen in the photo is not typical.

Soc. B.: Robust schooling fish. It can be kept with similar-sized fishes.

M: Large aquaria with sufficient swimming space. Only a small part of the tank needs to be planted. If fine-leaved plants are included in the decor, they will be readily accepted as spawning substrate. Water conditions are unimportant, but the temperature should not exceed 22°C. Water in its natural biotope had a temperature of 18°C.

B: Simple. The only preoccupation is water temperature, as high temperatures result in unbalanced sex ratios. Because ♂♂ pursue ♀♀ very strongly, there should always be one ♂ and several ♀♀. Rear the young with the finest live foods or pulverized flake foods.

F: O; floating foods are appreciated, but other live foods, not necessarily floating, and good quality flake foods are also accepted.

S: The type locality is at an elevation of 1,600 m, the highest known altitude for a rainbowfish.

T: 18°–22°C, **L:** 9 cm, **A:** 80 cm, **R:** m, t, **D:** 3

Melanotaenia splendida tatei

(ZIETZ, 1896)

Syn.: *Nematocentris tatei, N. winneckei.*

Hab.: Australia: in central Australian rivers (Northern Territory, South Australia, Queensland, and New South Wales), most of which flow into the Lake Eyre Basin. Also found in the central eastern region of the Northern Territory.

F.I.: Unknown.

Sex.: ♂♂ have pointed dorsal and anal fins. Older ♂♂ develop a very high back. ♀♀ become more slender as they age.

Soc. B.: Lively, peaceful schooling fish.

M: Moderate-sized aquarium which, although offering plenty of free swimming space, contains robust plants along the back half of the tank. A small quantity of salt may prove beneficial. Water: pH 6–8; hardness up 30° dGH.

B: Simple. Very small eggs are laid daily (continuous spawner!) on suitable spawning media such as Java moss or a spawning mop. ♂♂ are very active when courting. The breeding tank should contain hiding places for the ♀♀.

F: O; any animal and vegetable fare that fits into its mouth, including occasional forays on tender aquarium plants. Do not overfeed these voracious feeders.

S: Besides this subspecies, *M. s. splendida, M. s. inornata, M. s. australis,* and *M. s. rubrostriata* are all members of the group. Differentiation of the individual subspecies is not an easy task, since each subspecies may have several color morphs.

T: 20°–30°C, **L:** 9–10 cm, **A:** 80 cm, **R:** m, t, **D:** 2

Melanotaenia monticola, ♂ top, ♀ bottom

Melanotaenia splendida tatei ♂, Monte Alline Bone

Campylomormyrus elephas
Blunt-jaw elephantnose

(BOULENGER, 1898)

Syn.: *Gnathonemus elephas.*

Hab.: Africa: Zaïre Basin.

F.I.: Unknown.

Sex.: No definite external distinguishing characteristics are known.

Soc. B.: This reclusive, twilight- and night-active fish has a weak electrical organ. The animals are frequently quarrelsome among themselves.

M: Provide a substrate of fine sand, some hiding places among rocks and roots, and dense edge and background vegetation. Maintain sufficient free swimming space. Occasionally add fresh water with a good water conditioner (e.g., AquaSafe). Juveniles make better aquarium pets than their adult consorts. A species tank is recommended.

B: To the best of our knowledge, this fish has not been bred in an aquarium. Due to its size, it is unlikely that this feat is possible in an aquarium. Very little is known about its reproductive biology in nature. The only information comes from MATTHES (1964): Ann. Mus. roy. Afr. Centr., Zool. ser., No. 126, p. 39. The animal's eggs are beige and approximately 1 mm in diameter.

F: C; all kinds of live foods such as *Tubifex*, Enchytraeidae, small crustacea, various types of mosquito larvae, and aquatic insects and their larvae.

S: The genus *Campylomormyrus* was established in 1874 by BLEEKER. The type species is *Mormyrus tamandua* GÜNTHER, 1864.

T: 26°–28°C, L: 40 cm, A: from 120 cm, R: b, m, D: 3–4

Mormyrus kannume

FORSKÅL, 1776

Syn.: None.

Hab.: Africa: the region of the Nile and many large lakes such as Lakes Victoria, Albert, Eduard, and George.

F.I.: 1934.

Sex.: None known.

Soc. B.: Twilight- and night-active animals. Frequently antisocial in front of conspecifics.

M: Only juveniles make suitable aquarium animals. Keep just one specimen per tank, since their electrical impulses annoy each other.

B: Has not been successfully bred in an aquarium. Information regarding the reproductive biology of this species is scarce. On p. 255 of *Das große Buch der Fische*, 1977, WHEELER voices his suspicions that these animals spawn in rocky wave-buffeted regions.

F: C; benthic insect larvae, particularly chironomid larvae.

S: In some regions *M. kannume* supports valuable commercial fisheries.

T: 22°–26°C, L: 50 cm, some individuals grow up to 80 cm, A: 120 cm, R: b, m, D: 3

Campylomormyrus elephas

Mormyrus kannume

Mormyrus rume proboscirostris

Syn.: *Mormyrus jubelini, M. proboscirostris.*

Hab.: Africa: Angola and Zaïre, in the upper Zaïre River.

F.I.: Unknown.

Sex.: No definite external differentiating characteristics are known.

Soc. B.: Nocturnal, electricity-producing fish. *M. r. proboscirostris* leads a secluded life.

M: As for other *Mormyrus* species.

B: Has not been successful in an aquarium.

F: C; predominantly live foods of all kinds, particularly benthic insect larvae.

S: None.

T: 24°–28°C, L: 60 cm, A: 120 cm, R: b, m, D: 3–4

Petrocephalus simus
Dorsal-band whale

Syn.: *Mormyrus simus, M. tenuicauda.*

Hab.: Africa: from Liberia to Zaïre.

F.I.: Cannot be determined.

Sex.: ♂♂ have a more concave anal fin.

Soc. B.: This lively schooling fish is peaceful towards heterospecifics, but quite aggressive among themselves. Active during night and twilight hours.

M: Needs a substrate of fine sand, some hiding places among rocks and roots, dense edge and background vegetation, and an open swimming area. The animals appreciate a slight pump-generated current. Occasional additions of conditioned fresh water are recommended. Best kept in a species tank.

B: To the best of our knowledge, this fish has not been bred in an aquarium.

F: C; all kinds of live foods such as *Tubifex*, Enchytraeidae, *Daphnia, Cyclops*, glassworms, bloodworms, and mosquito larvae.

S: The anterior rays of the dorsal fin are black.

T: 24°–28°C, L: 12 cm, A: 80 cm, R: b, m, D: 3

Mormyrus rume proboscirostris

Petrocephalus simus

Pollimyrus nigripinnis   (BOULENGER, 1899)
Dusky whale

Syn.: *Marcusenius nigripinnis.*

Hab.: Africa: Zaïre, in the central Zaïre Basin.

F.I.: Cannot be determined.

Sex.: No external differentiating characteristics are known.

Soc. B.: *P. nigripinnis* is a lively twilight- and night-active fish. Animals of equal strength are quite peaceful towards each other, but weaker animals are often suppressed.

M: Provide a substrate of fine sand, hiding places among rocks and roots, dense edge and background vegetation, and plenty of free swimming space. Occasional fresh water added with the accompaniment of a good water conditioner is recommended. Slight water movement may be beneficial. Water: up to 15° dGH; pH 7.0. Best kept in a species tank.

B: Unknown.

F: C; all kinds of live foods as long as they are small enough.

S: The genus *Pollimyrus* was established in 1971 by TAVERNE with *P. isidori* (VALENCIENNES, 1846) as the genotype. The genus is named in honor of the famous Belgian ichthyologist Max POLL.

T: 24°–26°C, **L:** 12 cm, **A:** 80 cm, **R:** b, m, **D:** 3–4

Papyrocranus afer
African featherfin

(GÜNTHER, 1868)

Syn.: *Notopterus afer, N. afer congensis.*

Hab.: Africa: western Africa and the Zaïre Basin. Neither found in the Nile nor the Chad Basin. Calm waters with dense plant growth are their habitats of choice.

F.I.: 1912 by BRÜNING.

Sex.: No definite external distinguishing characteristics are known.

Soc. B.: Night- and twilight-active fish. Antisocial and waspish among themselves. A progressively more solitary lifestyle develops as the animals age. *P. afer* practices brood care; paternal family.

M: Requires dense edge and background vegetation, plenty of free swimming space, hiding places among roots and/or rocks, and floating plants to dim the illumination. Water: pH around 6.5; hardness up to 10° dGH. Best kept in a species tank, since large individuals are antisocial.

B: ONG KAY YONG successfully bred this species (Tropical Fish Hobbyist, 1965).

F: C; all kinds of live foods such as earthworms, aquatic insects and their larvae, crustacea, snails, and fishes.

S: Notopteridae use their swimbladder as an accessory breathing organ, which allows them to breath atmospheric air.

T: 24°–30°C, **L:** up to 62 cm, **A:** from 120 cm, **R:** m, b, **D:** 3

Kiunga ballochi
Kiunga blue-eye

ALLEN, 1983
Subfam.: Kiunginae

Syn.: None.

Hab.: Papua New Guinea: in the upper Fly River System at Kiunga on the Tabubil Road.

and second dorsal fins. Its coloration is also very characteristic (see photo).

F.I.: Has not been imported.

Sex.: Unknown.

Soc. B.: Peaceful, somewhat shy schooling fish.

M: This species can be kept in small, densely planted aquaria. Water: pH around 7.5; hardness up to 15° dGH.

B: Still unknown.

F: O; small live foods and dry commercial foods.

S: The genus *Kiunga* differs from the related genera *Pseudomugil* and *Popondichthys* primarily by its very long anal

T: 24°–26°C, **L:** 3 cm, **A:** 40 cm, **R:** m, t, **D:** 3

Pseudomugil paludicola
Swamp blue-eye

ALLEN & MOORE, 1981
Subfam.: Pseudomugilinae

Syn.: None.

Hab.: New Guinea: in rivers flowing to the western coast of Papua New Guinea such as the Morehead, Pahoturi, and Binaturi River Systems.

F.I.: Has not been imported.

Sex.: Unknown. ♂♂ probably have a more elongated first dorsal fin.

Soc. B.: Peaceful, small schooling fish. A species tank is recommended.

M: The smallest tanks are suitable. A little salt in the water may prove necessary. The tank should offer ample vegetation. Water: pH 7.0–8.0; hardness to 20° dGH.

B: Still unknown. Probably similar to that of *Pseudomugil cyanodorsalis*, which is not presented here but is also one of the smallest members of this genus. That species lays its small eggs on plants. After 7 to 10 days, the tiny young hatch. They can be raised with very small flake foods.

T: 26°–30°C, **L:** 3–3.5 cm, **A:** 60 cm, **R:** m, t, **D:** 3

Kiunga ballochi

Pseudomugil paludicola

Retropinna semoni
Australian smelt

(WEBER, 1895)

Syn.: *Prototroctes semoni.*

Hab.: Australia: southern Queensland, New South Wales, Victoria, and South Australia.

F.I.: Has probably not been imported into Germany.

Sex.: ♂♂ have larger fins.

Soc. B.: Lively, peaceful schooling fish.

M: Best kept in raceway tanks (long tanks with a relatively low water level). Provide a substrate of sand or fine-grained gravel, sparse background vegetation, and plenty of free swimming space. Undemanding in regard to water chemistry. Best kept in a species tank.

B: *R. semoni* is best bred in a school (2 ♂♂ and 4 ♀♀). The animals are most likely to spawn when the aquarium is exposed to the morning sun and the water is totally still (i.e., both aeration and filter turned off). A spawning mesh should be present because the parents are very cannibalistic towards their spawn. At 22°C, the larvae hatch after nine days. They are easy to raise, though growth is exceedingly slow.

F: C, O; small live, freeze-dried, and flake foods.

S: In its natural habitat, *R. semoni* is an excellent biological control for mosquito larvae and is stocked into bodies of water for that purpose.

T: 10°–25°C, L: 8 cm, A: 80 cm, R: m, t, D: 2

Sternopygus macrurus
Variable ghost knifefish

(SCHNEIDER, 1801)

Syn.: *Gymnotus macrurus, Carapus macrourus, C. sanguinolentus, Sternopygus carapo, St. marcgravii.*

Hab.: South America: Brazil, Peru, Bolivia, and the Guianas.

F.I.: Unknown.

Sex.: ♂♂ are larger than ♀♀.

Soc. B.: Twilight- and night-active. Their predatory nature is directly proportional to their age. The animals mainly feed at night. Sometimes they can be quite shy.

M: The aquarium should have a substrate of sand or fine-grained gravel, some plants, hiding places in the form of roots, rocks, or clay pipes, good filtration, and floating plants to dim the light. Mature water seems to be preferred. Water: pH 6.0–6.5, soft to medium-hard (4°–15° dGH).

B: No one has reported a successful aquarium spawn.

F: C; all kinds of live foods. Young feed on crustacea and insect larvae, whereas larger specimens accept freshwater shrimp and fishes. However, all ages chiefly subsist on insects and their larvae. Flakes are reluctantly accepted, if at all.

S: In some regions, this is a food fish.

T: 22°–28°C, **L:** 90 cm, **A:** from 120 cm, **R:** m, b, **D:** 3–4

Hucho hucho
Danube salmon

(LINNAEUS, 1758)

Syn.: *Salmo hucho.*

Hab.: Europe: only in the Danube and its tributaries, particularly those on its right side. Not found in the lower river courses. *H. hucho* is a freshwater fish.

F.I.: Endemic to Europe.

Sex.: Mature ♂ ♂ have a hook-shaped lower mandible ("salmon hook") and a rindlike thickened skin.

Soc. B.: This rare sedentary fish prefers to live amid swift-flowing water. Often found in secluded locals because of its solitary lifestyle.

M: As indicated for *Oncorhynchus mykiss*. However, this fish requires a significantly larger tank. A powerful pump can provide the strong current needed to maintain the Danube salmon. Include some cover of roots and/or rocks. Cold, oxygen-rich water is appreciated.

B: Has not been successfully bred in an aquarium. In nature, this species spawns from March to May (spring). Some animals participate in extensive upriver spawning migrations. Its spawning sites are often located in small tributaries or on gravel banks of the rivers themselves. The spawn is laid in previously dug pits which are filled afterwards. Egg development parallels that of the salmon (70–200 days).

F: C; all kinds of live foods. Large specimens mainly consume fishes.

S: The young, like *Salmo salar,* have a different juvenile coloration. They are black and gray striped. This species has one row of 4 to 8 strong hook-shaped teeth along the posterior edge of the vomer.

T: 6°–18°C (coldwater fish), **L:** up to 150 cm, **A:** from 120 cm, **R:** all, **D:** 3–4

Oncorhynchus mykiss
Rainbow trout, steelhead trout

(WALBAUM, 1792)

Syn.: *Salmo gairdneri, S. irideus, S. iridia.*

Hab.: North America: from southern Alaska to southern Oregon and the lacustrine regions of the Frazer and Columbia Rivers. It has been introduced into many water systems in Europe.

F.I.: To Europe in 1880.

Sex.: Large ♂ ♂ have a hook on the lower mandible during the spawning season.

Soc. B.: Juveniles live in schools. Older specimens are solitary abiding predators. They are frequently aggressive and waspish among each other.

M: Provide a gravel substrate and hiding places among stones. Vegetation can be waived. While depth does not need to be great, the water should be clear and oxygen-rich (good aeration). Very sensitive to high temperatures, even a chiller may be required. Use a powerhead to provide the desired current. Due to the difficulties involved in maintaining this species, its

care should be limited to specialists.

B: Has not been successfully bred in an aquarium. In nature, these fish spawn from December to May (winter and spring). The animals fan out pits in the gravel with their tails. The eggs are laid in these pits, fertilized, and then covered with the excavated gravel. Egg development is slow (to 90 days).

F: All kinds of live foods (fishes, invertebrates). Rainbow trout also eat flake foods and trout chow.

S: Rainbow trout differ from the European brown trout (*Salmo trutta* f. *fario* LINNAEUS, 1758) by the lack of red spots on the body and the presence of a shiny pink longitudinal band along their side. The rainbow trout is an appreciated food fish cultivated in many aquaculture facilities.

T: 10°–20°C (coldwater fish), **L:** 50 cm, **A:** 100 cm, **R:** all, **D:** 4

Hucho hucho

Oncorhynchus mykiss

Salmo salar

Salmo salar, juv.

Salmo salar
Atlantic Salmon

LINNAEUS, 1758

Syn.: *Salmo brevipes, S. hamatus, S. nobilis, S. spurius, Trutta salar.*

Hab.: Europe, Iceland, southeast Greenland: along the coast of the Petschora to the Mino River, rarely encountered in the Douro. Widely distributed in the Baltic Sea. Anadromous, entering rivers from the sea to spawn.

F.I.: Native to Europe.

Sex.: Older ♂♂ have a hook-shaped lower mandible ("salmon hook").

Soc. B.: Juveniles live in groups. Older specimens become progressively more solitary and predatory. Mature animals unite into large schools.

M: As for *Salmo gairdneri*; however, *S. salar* needs a larger aquarium. A fish for specialists. The aquarium must be equipped with a chiller, as *S. salar* cannot handle warm temperatures or low oxygen levels.

B: Aquarium breeding is probably impossible because of their size. During the fall and winter months (September to February) the fish enter rivers from the sea to spawn (anadromous). To reach their spawning sites—gravel beds in fast flowing water— the fish overcome such obstacles as waterfalls. The ♀♀ fan out large pits and lay the 7 mm eggs within. The pits are then covered with gravel. Depending on temperature, the fry hatch after 70–200 days. Since salmon do not feed in freshwater, most fish die after spawning. The young live for 2–3 years in freshwater before migrating to the sea where they remain for 1–3 years, growing rapidly and accumulating fat. The cycle is then closed as they migrate to freshwater to spawn.

F: C; all kinds of live foods, particularly fishes, and special commercial salmon foods.

S: *S. salar* is a valuable commercial fishery. Its pleasant tasting flesh is highly appreciated and commands a high price. The vomer of this fish has teeth. Juveniles are differently colored than adults.

T: 6°–18°C (coldwater fish), **L:** up to 150 cm, **A:** from 120 cm, **R:** all, **D:** 4

Salmo trutta f. *fario*, juv.

Salmo trutta f. *fario*
Brown trout

Syn.: *Salmo fario.*

Hab.: Europe, northern Africa (Morocco and Algeria): found in almost all rivers that are appropriately clear and cool. Does not inhabit lentic (static) waters.

F.I.: Native to European waters.

Sex.: Mature ♂♂ have a variable-sized hook on their mandible.

Soc. B.: Juveniles live in groups. Older animals have a solitary predacious life–style. Among themselves, brown trout are quarrelsome and waspish. They are non-migratory freshwater fish of the upper courses of lotic (flowing) waters.

M: As for *Salmo gairdneri*, though *S. trutta* f. *fario* is more sensitive to warm temperatures and requires more oxygen. A fish for specialists. A chiller will be needed for warm summer days.

LINNAEUS, 1758

B: Has not been bred in an aquarium. In nature, they spawn from January to March. Spawning sites are located in cool, clear, fast-flowing creeks that have a gravel bottom. The ♀♀ fan out large pits, lay several thousand eggs, and then cover them with gravel. Approximately 3 months are needed for the eggs to hatch at 4°C.

F: C; predominately live foods such as insect larvae, crustacea, flying insects, and fishes. The animals can also be trained to special trout chows.

S: A number of subspecies have been described of *Salmo trutta*. Three of these are found in Germany: *S. trutta* f. *fario*, *S. trutta trutta* LINNAEUS, 1758 (sea trout; up to 100 cm long), and *S. trutta* f. *lacustris* LINNAEUS, 1758 (lake trout; rarely grows to 140 cm).

T: 2°–16°C (coldwater fish), **L:** 50 cm, **A:** from 100 cm, **R:** all, **D:** 4 (cool temperatures)

Salvelinus alpinus salvelinus ♂

Salvelinus alpinus salvelinus
Arctic char

(LINNAEUS, 1758)

Syn.: *Salmo alpinus, S. kundsha, S. leucomaenis, S. salvelinos stagnalis, S. stagnalis, S. umbla* var. *alpinus, S. salvelinus, Salvelinus alpinus alipes, S. alpinus arcturus, S. alpinus stagnalis, S. umbla stagnalis*.

Hab.: Europe: in deep lakes of the Alps north of the Alpine apex at elevations of up to 2,300 m.

F.I.: Native to European waters.

Sex.: ♂♂ are more colorful than ♀♀.

Soc. B.: Nonmigratory fish of deep alpine lakes. Juveniles are social; adults are solitary predators. Often aggressive towards conspecifics.

M: Provide clear, oxygen-rich water (good aeration), a gravel substrate, and stones and/or roots to provide secluded areas. Vegetation can be waived. In light of their need for cool temperatures, a chiller is imperative for warm summer days. A fragile aquarium fish.

B: Has not been successfully bred in an aquarium. In nature, the animals spawn in the winter or spring on rock or gravel substrates at depths of 20–80 m. The eggs are 4 mm in diameter, transparent, and yellow. Depending on temperature, the fry hatch after 65–72 days. Like all salmonids, they have a huge yolk sac which sustains them for a month.

F: C; predator! Fishes, crustacea.

S: Tasty food fish.

T: 4°–16°C (extreme coldwater fish), **L:** 25–40 cm, **A:** 250 cm, **R:** b, m, **D:** 4

Salvelinus fontinalis
Brook trout

(MITCHELL, 1815)

Syn.: *Salmo fontinalis, Baione fontinalis.*

Hab.: Eastern North America: from Labrador to the Savannah and French Broad Rivers. Today the species has been introduced throughout Europe, particularly in alpine regions.

F.I.: To Europe in 1884.

Sex.: No definite external differentiating characteristics are known.

Soc. B.: Nonmigratory freshwater fish that inhabits open waters. Juveniles live in groups, while adults are solitary predators. Very waspish among themselves.

M: As for *Oncorhynchus mykiss*, but *S. fontinalis* is more demanding in regard to temperature and oxygen than rainbow trout.

B: Has not been successfully bred in an aquarium. In nature, it spawns from October to March (winter spawner). Its reproductive behavior is largely similar to that of *O. mykiss*.

F: Live foods of all kinds (invertebrates, fishes), flake foods, pieces of meat.

S: Crosses between *S. fontinalis* and *Salmo trutta* f. *fario* LINNAEUS, 1758 (= "tigerfish") as well as *S. fontinalis* and *Salvelinus alpinus* (LINNAEUS, 1758) (= the so-called "Elsässer Saibling") are sterile.

T: 10°–14°C (coldwater fish), **L:** 40 cm, **A:** 90 cm, **R:** m, **D:** 4

Stream in the Odenwald. An appropriate biotope for trout.

Salvelinus fontinalis

Salvelinus fontinalis ♂ ♂

Doryichthys deokhatoides

(BLEEKER, 1853)

Syn.: ?

Hab.: Southeast Asia: Thailand, Malaysia, Indonesia (Sumatra, Borneo). Lives exclusively in freshwater.

F.I.: 1986 (?).

Sex.: The ♂ has two longitudinal ridges that jut out from his belly, forming a channel. Eggs are adhered within this channel.

Soc. B.: Peaceful, harmless fish. This species practices brood care (paternal family). Either keep in a species tank or, if placed in a community, associate with calm, peaceful fishes.

M: Use a fine sand or gravel substrate, plant a few *Vallisneria*, and place the aquarium in a sunny local. The tank should be weakly aerated. Water: hardness 10°–15° dGH; pH around 7. Do not add salt, since this is a true freshwater fish.

B: To the best of our knowledge, *D. deokhatoides* has not been successfully bred in an aquarium.

F: C; only live foods, primarily small crustacea such as *Daphnia, Cyclops,* and *Artemia,* but glassworms and an occasional very small guppy fry are accepted as well.

S: The organisms this fish feed upon are sucked into the buccal cavity rather than grabbed. Beneath the tubelike mouth, at approximately the height of the eyes, there is an extendible membrane. The hyoid bone is located here. If prey is to be taken, the hyoid is pushed downward to extend the membrane and simultaneously the opercula and the mouth are closed, creating a negative pressure inside the mouth which is equilibrated when the mouth opens and water rushes in. The prey is sucked into the mouth with the resulting water current.

T: 24°–28°C, **L:** 13 cm, **A:** 80 cm, **R:** m, b, **D:** 4

Syngnathus nigrolineatus
Black-line pipefish

EICHWALD, 1931

Syn.: *Syngnathus agassizi, S. bucculentus.*

Hab.: Europe and Asia: Azov and Black Seas and many tributaries thereof.

F.I.: Has probably not been imported into Germany.

Sex.: ♂♂ are smaller and have a conspicuous ventral channel which is converted into an incubation pouch after the fish spawn.

Soc. B.: Peaceful and harmless. ♂♂ practice brood care (paternal family).

M: As for *Doryichthys deokhatoides.* However, *S. nigrolineatus* is not a true freshwater fish. The animals appreciate salt being added to their water (1–2 teaspoons per 10 l). Soft, acid water plays havoc with the animals' health, ultimately resulting in death.

B: To the best of our knowledge, this species has not been successfully bred in an aquarium.

F: C; only live foods, mainly small crustacea, mosquito larvae, and small sinking worms.

S: There is an additional subspecies, *S. nigrolineatus caspius* EICHWALD, 1931, that inhabits the Caspian Sea.

T: 22°–24°C, **L:** up to 21.5 cm, **A:** from 100 cm, **R:** m, b, **D:** 4

Doryichthys deokhatoides

Syngnathus nigrolineatus

Chonerhinus modestus
Modest puffer

(BLEEKER, 1850)

Syn.: *Tetraodon modestus, Arothron modestus.*

Hab.: Southeast Asia: southern Thailand, Malaysia, and Indonesia (Borneo, Sumatra).

F.I.: Apparently in 1959.

Sex.: There are no sure external differentiating characteristics.

Soc. B.: Loners; quarrelsome towards conspecifics, especially newly introduced specimens. Prone to nipping the fins of larger fishes. Firm plants (*Echinodorus, Cryptocoryne*, etc.) are bitten but not eaten.

M: Clear, oxygen-rich water is necessary; water hardness is irrelevant. Hiding places among stones or roots should be created. The animals are active during day and twilight hours. They have to be given items to chew on (e.g., roots) to keep their teeth worn down. If allowed to go unchecked, its overgrown teeth make it impossible for the fish to feed.

B: There is no information concerning successfully breeding this fish in captivity.

F: O; live foods such as mosquito larvae, earthworms, *Gammarus, Daphnia*, flies and their larvae, and mussel meat; snail shells and tablet foods are particularly appreciated.

S: These animals produce quacking sounds when they are removed from the water.

T: 23°–28°C, **L:** 13 cm, **A:** 120 cm, **R:** m, t, **D:** 3

Tetraodon cutcutia
Sea frog

(HAMILTON, 1822)

Syn.: *Tetrodon cutcutia, T. caria, T. gularis, Leisomus cutcutia, L. marmoratus, Monotretus cutcutia.*

Hab.: Asia: Sri Lanka, Bangladesh, India, in the states of Orissa, Bengal, and Assam.

F.I.: 1903 by STÜWE.

Sex.: ♀♀ are smaller and lighter colored. ♂♂ have nuptial coloration.

Soc. B.: Juveniles are peaceful in comparison to the waspish and quarrelsome adults. Single maintenance is best, but if several specimens are kept, then they all must be the same size. ♂♂ practice brood care (paternal family).

M: Provide a sand or gravel substrate, edge and background vegetation, and hiding places among stones and roots. Ensure that there is an open area that allows swimming. Water should be medium-hard (from 10° dGH) and neutral (pH 7.0). *T. cutcutia* is a freshwater fish.

B: This species has been bred in captivity. Use large aquaria. The ♂ acquires breeding coloration and courts the ♀ by dancing. The eggs are laid on carefully cleaned flat stones and guarded by the ♂. Depending on water temperature, juveniles hatch after 6 to 10 days and remain on the substrate. Rearing is arduous because of their need of very small foods. After the fry hatch, remove the ♂ lest he pursues the spawn.

F: C, O; live foods, preferably snails, but also mosquito larvae, *Tubifex, Daphnia*, and earthworms. Mussel flesh, tablet foods, and sometimes vegetable supplements are accepted as well.

S: The body lacks thorns. The nasal openings are united into a short tube with but one opening. Animals removed from the water, expand into a sphere and make quacking noises. They are called "sea frogs" by the inhabitants of Malabar.

T: 24°–28°C, **L:** 8 cm, **A:** 80 cm, **R:** all, **D:** 3

Chonerhinus modestus

Tetraodon cutcutia

Fam.: Thymallidae

Thymallus thymallus
Grayling

Syn.: *Salmo thymallus, Thymallus gymnogaster, T. gymnothorax, T. vexillifer, T. vulgaris.*

Hab.: Europe: from western Wales and France to the Urals and Petschora as well as the Danube, Volga, and Dnestr regions. The southern limit of distribution is northern Italy.

F.I.: Endemic to Europe.

Sex.: ♂♂ are larger with longer dorsal, anal, and ventral fins. During the spawning season, ♂♂ have a shiny nuptial dress.

Soc. B.: Nonmigratory, peaceful, coldwater fish which, especially as juveniles, form small schools.

M: Use a fine sand or gravel substrate and roots and aquatic moss as decoration, leaving an open area for swimming. The water must be cool, clear, and oxygen-rich (good aeration) with a neutral to slightly alkaline pH (pH 7.0–7.5) and a hardness of up to 20° dGH. Current is appreciated (powerhead). On hot summer days, a chiller is required.

B: This species has not been bred in captivity. In nature, it spawns from March to June (spring) over gravel substrates. The ♀ excavates a pit using its tail fin. Here the eggs are laid and then covered with the gravel. Between 3,000 and 36,000 eggs are laid, with 10,000 being the norm.

F: C; all kinds of live foods such as aquatic and flying insects and their larvae, snails, worms, and small fishes.

S: *T. thymallus* has a species-typical tall multiradiated dorsal fin ("flag"). This is the most numerous fish of the Hyporithrons (= lower course of the salmonid region) of European rivers.

T: 6°–18°C (coldwater fish), **L:** up to 50 cm, **A:** 100 cm, **R:** all, **D:** 3–4

Thymallus thymallus

Grayling region, Tauber River

Dallia pectoralis

BEAN, 1879

Syn.: *Dallia delicatissima.*

Hab.: Limited to the Arctic and Subarctic freshwaters of the following regions: northeastern tip of Siberia, islands of the Bering Strait and the St. Lawrence, St. Mattews, and Nunivak Islands as well as Alaska.

F.I.: Unknown.

Sex.: The dorsal, caudal, and anal fins are light red in mature ♂♂, but white to clear in ♀♀ and sexually immature ♂♂.

Soc. B.: Juveniles are peaceful. They become more predatory as they age.

M: There is no information available concerning maintaining this fish in an aquarium. Much territory remains to be investigated. A chiller is probably required. Dense vegetation is important, since the animals like to live hidden among plants.

B: To the best of our knowledge, this fish has not been bred in an aquarium. In nature, the fish migrate upriver during the spring. This migratory action coincides with the water temperature reaching 6°–8°C. They spawn from May to August. ♀♀ simultaneously carry both mature and immature eggs with a diameter of 2 mm and 0.6–1 mm, respectively. The immature eggs most likely mature the following year. Depending on the size of the ♀, 40 to 300 eggs are released. Ripe eggs are demersal and extremely adhesive. At 12°C the young hatch after about 9 days.

F: C; all kinds of live foods such as mosquito larvae, small crustacea (ostracods, *Daphnia*), and snails. Large animals also feed on small fishes.

S: In nature, the animals bury themselves in the mud during the winter, frequently freezing. Experiments by BORODIN have shown that this fish is capable of living if merely frozen superficially, only dying if their visceral fluids freeze.

T: 4°–14°C (extreme coldwater), **L:** to 33 cm, usually smaller, **A:** 100 cm, **R:** b, m, **D:** 4

Umbra krameri
Eurasian mudminnow

WALBAUM, 1792

Syn.: *Aphrya lacustris, Cyprinodon umbra, Umbla krameri, Umbra canina, U. nattereri, U. umbra.*

Hab.: Europe: regions around the central and lower courses of the Danube (Vienna to its mouth), Lake Balaton, the Prut river, and the lower course of the Dnestr. Endangered and considered extinct in many regions.

F.I.: 1896.

Sex.: ♂♂ are generally smaller. ♀♀ are much more brightly colored during the spawning season.

Soc. B.: Quite peaceful outside of the spawning season. The ♀ is territorial during the spawning season. She tends the eggs and young (maternal family).

M: Requires a soft substrate (fine sand), a dense border of coldwater plants, free swimming space, and moderate illumination. Peaty soft, acid water (ca. 5° dGH and pH 6–6.5, respectively) is relished. Aeration can be waived. Bitterling, weatherfish, and Crucian carp make suitable tankmates.

B: 13°–17°C. Densely planted aquaria. The ♀ excavates a pit and energetically defends it against other fishes. While actually spawning, the ♀ is relatively congenial, only becoming belligerent after she lays her 200–300 eggs. These are guarded and kept clean by the ♀. Brood care terminates when the young hatch. The young are easily raised, even though they are very cannibalistic.

F: C; all kinds of live foods e.g., chironomid larvae, mosquito larvae, *Asellus*, and other crustacea, *Tubifex*. *U. krameri* relishes fish spawns.

S: *U. krameri* will learn to recognize its caretaker. These fish can almost meet all their oxygen requirements by breathing with their swimbladder (accessory respiration). See Vol., p. 870.

T: 10°–23°C (coldwater fish), **L:** 11.5 cm, **A:** 80 cm, **R:** b, **D:** 1–2

Dallia pectoralis

Umbra krameri

Index

In our index the genus- and species-names are printed in *italics*.
The family-and subfamily-names are printed **bold**.
The **bold** printed page-numbers will show you, where you'll find the
species description.
Normal printed page-numbers will show you it is a synonym.

Index

Index

Index

Index

Index

Index

Index

Index

Index

Index

Index

Index

Index

Index

Index

Index

Index

Index

Index

Index

Index

Index

Index

Index

Index

Index

Index

Index

Index

Index

Index

Index

Index

Index

Index

Index

Index

Index

Your AQUARIUM ATLAS
is in
good company

Enjoy your reading
The Authors

TEMPERATURE

$$°F = (°C \times 1.8) + 32 \qquad °C = (°F - 32) / 1.8$$

°C	°F	°C	°F	°C	°F	°C	°F	°C	°F
0	32	15	59	21	70	27	81	50	122
10	50	16	61	22	72	28	82	60	140
11	52	17	63	23	73	29	84	70	158
12	54	18	64	24	75	30	86	80	176
13	55	19	66	25	77	35	95	90	194
14	57	20	68	26	79	40	104	100	212

VOLUME

$$gal = l / 3.785 \qquad l = 3.785 \times gal$$

l	gal	l	gal	l	gal	l	gal	l	gal
1	0.26	15	3.96	70	18.5	250	66	550	145
2	0.53	20	5.28	80	21.1	300	79	600	158
3	0.79	30	7.93	90	23.8	350	92	700	185
4	1.06	40	10.57	100	26.4	400	106	800	211
5	1.32	50	13.21	150	39.6	450	119	900	238
10	2.64	60	15.85	200	79.3	500	132	1000	379

LENGTH

$$1m = 100 \text{ cm} = 1000 \text{ mm} \qquad 1yd = 3 \text{ ft} = 36 \text{ in}$$
$$in = cm / 2.54 \qquad cm = in \times 2.54 \qquad ft = m / 0.305 \qquad m = 0.305 \times ft$$

mm	in	cm	in	cm	in	m	ft	m	ft
0.5	0.02	1	0.4	30	12	1	3.28	70	230
1	0.04	2	0.8	35	14	2	6.56	80	262
2	0.08	3	1.1	40	16	3	9.84	90	295
3	0.12	4	1.6	45	18	4	13.1	100	328
4	0.16	5	2.0	50	20	5	16.4	200	656
5	0.20	6	2.4	60	24	10	32.8	300	984
6	0.24	7	2.8	70	28	15	49.2	400	1310
7	0.28	8	3.1	80	31	20	65.6	500	1640
8	0.32	9	3.5	90	35	25	82.0	600	1970
9	0.35	10	3.9	100	39	30	98.4	700	2300
		15	5.9	125	49	40	131	800	2620
		20	7.9	150	59	50	164	900	2950
		25	9.8	175	69	60	197	1000	3280

Literature

This bibliography is intended as a supplement to the literature listed in Volumes 1 and 2 of the Aquarium Atlas.

Adler, H. E. (1975): Fish behaviour: why fish do what they do. T.F.H., Neptune City, N. Y., United States.

Ahrens, H. (1984): Die Tiere zuhause. 2. A., Mergus-Verlag, Melle, Germany.

Alfred, E. R. (1961): The Javanese Fishes described by Kuhl and van Hasselt. Bull. Nat. Mus. 30: 80-88.

Allen, G. R. (1987): *Popondichthys*, a replacement name for the melanotaeniid fish genus *Popondetta*. Jap. J. Ichthyology 33: 409.

Annandale, N. (1918): Fauna of the Inlé Lake. Rec. Indian Mus. 14: 33-64.

Aquarienmagazin-Redaktion (Ed.) (1983): Kosmos-Handbuch Aquarienkunde. Das Süßwasser-Aquarium. 4. A., Stuttgart, Germany.

Arnold, A. (1990): Eingebürgerte Fischarten. Zur Biologie und Verbreitung allochtoner Wildfische in Europa. Wittenberg Lutherstadt, Germany.

Bade, E.: Die ausländischen Aquarienfische. Creutzsche Verlagsbuchhandlung, Magdeburg, East Germany.

Baensch, U. (1987): Bunte Zierfischwelt. Tetra-Verlag, Melle, Germany.

Baerends, G. P. & J. M. Baerends-Van Roon (1950): An introduction to the study of the ethology of cichlid fishes.

Bastock, M. (1969): Das Liebeswerben der Tiere. Fischer-Verlag, Jena, East Germany.

Barlow, G. W., Liem, K. F. & W. Wickler (1968): Badidae, a new fish family - behavioural, osteological, and development evidence. J. Zool., London 156: 415-447.

Bateman, G. (Ed.) (1988): Die Tiere unserer Welt, Band 9, Fische. Mosaik Verlag, Gütersloh, Germany.

Baur, W. & J. Rapp (1988): Gesunde Fische. Verlag Paul Parey, Hamburg, Germany.

Bech, R. (1984): Eierlegende Zahnkarpfen. Neumann-Verlag, Leipzig- Radebeul, East Germany.

Berra, T. M. (1981): An Atlas of Distribution of the Freshwater Fish Families of the World. University of Nebraska Press, Lincoln, United States.

Bloch, M. E. (1980, 1981): Naturgeschichte der Fische I + II. Harenberg, Dortmund, Germany.

Bone, T. M. & N. B. Marshall (1985): Biologie der Fische, Fischer-Verlag, Stuttgart, Germany.

Boulenger, E. G. (1946): Keep an Aquarium. Ward Lock, London, Great Britian.

Boulenger, G. A. (1902): Matériaux pour la faune du Congo. Ann. Mus. Congo 2 (1): 19-57.

Breder, C. M. & D. E. Rosen (1966): Modes of reproduction in fishes. How fishes breed. T.F.H., Neptune City, N. J., United States.

Brembach, M. (1979): Lebendgebärende Fische im Aquarium. Kosmos Verlag, Stuttgart, Germany.

Briggs, J. C. (1961): Emendated Generic Names in Berg's Classification of Fishes. Copeia (1): 161-166.

Brittan, M. R.: Rasbora. T.F.H., Neptune City, N. J., United States.

Brühlmeyer, A. (1985): Buntbarsche aus dem Malawisee. Franckh'sche Verlagshandlung, Stuttgart, Germany.

Brühlmeyer, A. (1987): Buntbarsche aus dem Tanganjika-See. Leipzig-Jena-Berlin, East Germany.

Burnand, T. (1967): Süßwasserfische und Süßwasser-Sportfischerei. Stuttgart-Zürich, Germany, Switzerland.

Bussing, W. A. (1987): Peces de las Aguas Continentales de Costa Rica. Editorial de la Universidad de Costa Rica, San José, Costa Rica.

Canestrini, J. (1861): Zur Systematik und Charakteristik der Anabantinen. o. O. 697-712.

Literature

Cantor, T. (1850): Catalogue of Malayan Fishes. Journal of the Asiatic Society **18** (2): 983-1443.

Caufield, C. (1987): Der Regenwald - in schwindendes Paradies. Frankfurt a. M., Germany.

Cihar, J. (1987): Süßwasserfische. Köln, Germany.

Cramphorn, J. (1983): Sungai Trengganu Fish Survey, 1980. Malaysian Naturalist: 16-21.

Cuvier, M. B. & M. Valenciennes (1828-1849): Histoire Naturelle des Poissons. 1-22. Paris, France.

Crapon de Caprona, M. D. & B. Fritzsch (eds.) (1986): Proceedings 3rd European Workshop on Cichlid Biology. Ann. Kon. Mus. Midden-Afrika, Zool. Wetensch. **251**: 1-173.

Daget, J., Gosse, J. P. & D. F. E. Thys van den Audenaerde (eds.) (1984-1988): Check-list of the freshwater fishes of Afrika (CLOFFA), Vols. 1-3. Institut Royal des Sciences Naturelles de Belgique, Brüssel, Belgium.

Deckert, G. & K. Deckert (1974): Verhaltensformen der Tiere. Köln, Germany.

Deckert, K., Freytag, E., Günther, P. & G. Sterba (1983): Die große Enzyklopädie des Tierreiches. Fische, Lurche, Kriechtiere. Wiesbaden, Germany.

Degen, B. (1986): Das große deutsche Diskusbuch. Bede-Verlag, Kollenburg, Germany.

Degen, B. (1986): Erfolg mit Diskusfischen. Bede-Verlag, Kollenburg, Germany.

Degen, B. (1988): Der Diskus im Gesellschaftsaquarium. Tetra-Verlag, Melle, Germany.

Duncker, G. (1904): Die Fische der malayischen Halbinsel. Mitteilungen aus dem Naturhistorischen Museum Hamburg **21**: 133-207.

Duncker, G. (1912): Die Süßwasserfische Ceylons. Mitteilungen aus dem Naturhistorischen Museum Hamburg **29**: 241-272.

Deraniyagala, P. E. P. (1952): A colored atlas of some vertebrates from Cexlon, Vol. 1: Fishes. The Ceylon Government Press, Colombo, Sri Lanka.

Eibl-Eibesfeldt, I. (1987): Grundriß der vergleichenden Verhaltensforschung. 7. A., München, Zürich, Germany, Switzerland.

Favré, H. (1971): Mein Aquarium. Köln, Germany.

Fink, S. V. & W. L. Fink (1981): Interrelationships of the ostariophysan fishes (Teleostei). Zoological Journal of the Linnean Society, London **72**: 297-353.

Forselius, S. (1957): Studies of Anabantid Fishes. I-III. Zoologiska Bidrag Fran Uppsala. **32**: 93-599.

Franck, D. (1964): Vergleichende Verhaltensstudien an lebendgebärenden Zahnkarpfen der Gattung *Xiphophorus*. Zoologische Jahrbücher für allgemeine Zoologie und Physiologie, **71**: 117-170.

Frank, S. (1969): Das große Bilderlexikon der Fische. Artia Verlag, Prag, Czechostovakia.

Frank, S. (1980): Welt der Aquarienfische in Farbe. Artia Verlag, Prag, Czechostovakia.

Franke, H. J.(1985): Handbuch der Welskunde. Landbuch Verlag, Hannover, Germany.

Freundlieb-Winkler, A. (1982): Vergleichende Analyse zum Schwarmverhalten junger Cichliden. Diss. Göttingen, Germany.

Frey, H. (1986): Das Süßwasseraquarium. 27. A., Quelle & Meyer, Heidelberg-Wiesbaden, Germany.

Fryer, G. (1959): The Trophic Interrelationship and Ecology of some Littoral Communities of Lake Nyasa with especial reference to the Fishes, and a discussion of the Evolution of a Group of Rock-Frequenting Cichlidae. Proc. Zool. Soc. London **132**: 153-281.

Fryer, G. (1977): Evolution of species flocks of Cichlid fishes in African lakes. Z. zool. Syst. Evolut.-forsch. **15**: 141-165.

Géry, J. (1972): Poissons Characoides des Guyanes. I. Généralités. II. Famille des Serrasalmidae. Zool. Verhand. **122**: 1-250.

Géry, J., Mahnert, V. & G. Dlouhy (1987): Poissons Characoids non Characidae du Paraguay (Pisces, Ostariophysi). Revue suisse Zool. **94**: 357-464.

Géry, J., Planquette, P. & P. Y. LeBail (1988): Nomenclature des espèces du group

Literature

Leporinus maculatus et formes affines du Guyanas (Pisces, Characoidei, Anostomidae). Revue suisse Zool. **95**: 699-713.

Goldstein, R. J. (1971): Anabantoids, Gouramis and Related Fishes. T.F.H., Jersey City, N. J., United States.

Greenwood, P. H. (1987): The genera of pelmatochromine fishes (Teleostei, Cichlidae). A phylogenetic review. Bull. Br. Mus. (Nat.Hist.), Zool. ser. **53**: 139-203.

Hamilton, F. (1822): An account of the fishes found in the river Ganges and its branches. Edinburg, Great Britian.

Hansen, M. (ed.): Das farbige Bilderlexikon der Fische. Hamburg, Germany.

Herrmann, H. J. (1987): Die Buntbarsche der Alten Welt - Tanganjikasee. Edition Kernen, Essen, Germany.

Hora, S. L. (1929): An Aid to the Study of Hamilton Buchanan's "Gangetic Fishes". Memoirs of the Indian Museum, Calcutta **9**: 169-192.

Immelmann, K. (ed.) (1974): Grzimeks Tierleben, Verhaltensforschung. Kindler Verlag, Zürich, Switzerland.

Inger, R. F. (1955): Ecological Notes on the Fish Fauna of a Coastal Drainage of North Borneo. Fieldiana: Zoology, Chicago **37**: 47-90.

Isbrücker, L. J. H. (1980): Classification and catalogue of the mailed Loricarrida (Pisces, Siluriformes). Verslagen en Technische Gegevens Instituut voor Taxonomische Zoölogie (Zoölogisch Museum) **22**: 1-181, Universiteit van Amsterdam, Holland.

Kahl, B. (1979): Süßwasser-Aquarienfische. Niedernhausen/Ts., Germany.

Konings, A. (1988): Tanganjika-Cichliden, Herten, Germany, und Zevenhuizen, Holland.

Konings, A. (1989): Malawi Cichlids, Zevenhuizen, Holland, und Herten, Germany.

Kottelat, M. (1987): Nomenclatural status of the fish names created by J. C. VAN HASSELT (1823) and some cobitoid genera. Jap. J. Ichthyology **33**: 368-375.

Kottelat, M. (1988a): Indian and Indochines species of *Balitora* (Osteichthyes: Cypriniformes) with descriptions of two new species and comments on the family group names Balitoridae and Homalopteridae. Revue suisse Zool. **95**: 487-504.

Kottelat, M. (1988b): Autorship, dates of publication, status and types of SPIX and AGASSIZ's Brasilian fishes. Spixiana **11**: 69-93.

Kottelat, M. & Ch. Xin-Luo (1988a): A synopsis of Chinese balitorine loaches (Osteichthyes: Homalopteridae) with comments on their phylogeny and description of a new genus. Revue suisse Zool. **95**: 181-201.

Kottelat, M. & Ch. Xin-Luo (1988b): Revision of *Yunnanilus* with descriptions of a miniature species flock and six new species from China (Cypriniformes: Homalopteridae). Env. Biol. Fish. **23**: 65-93.

Kullander, S. O. (1986): Cichlid fishes of the Amazon river drainage of Peru, Swedish Museum of Natural History, Stockholm, Sweden.

Kullander, S. O. (1988): *Teleocichla*, a new genus of South American rheophilic cichlid fishes with six new species (Teleostei: Cichlidae). Copeia (1): 196-230.

Kullander, S. O. (1989): *Biotoecus* EIGENMANN & KENNEDY (Teleostei: Cichlidae): Description of a new species from the Orinoco basin and revised generic diagnosis. J. Nat. Hist. **23**: 225-260.

Lacépède, B. G. E. (1801): Histoire Naturelle des Poissons. Paris, France.

Ladiges, W. (1963): Bärblinge und ihre Verwandten. Kernen, Stuttgart, Germany.

Ladiges, W. (1984): Der Fisch in der Landschaft. 3. A., Kernen, Essen, Germany.

Lamprecht, J. (1976): Verhalten. Grundlagen-Erkenntnisse-Entwicklungen der Biologie. Freiburg, Germany.

Last, P. R., Scott, E. O. G. & F. H. Talbot (1983): Fishes of Tasmania. Hobart, Australia (Tasmania).

Lazara, K. J. (1984): The Killifish Master Index. A checklist of oviparous Cyprinodontiform fishes. The American Killifish Association, Cincinnati, United States.

Lewis, D. S. C. (1982): A revision of the genus *Labidochromis* (Teleostei: Cichlidae)

Literature

from Lake Malawi. Zoological Journal of the Linnean Society, London **75**: 189-263.

Lewis, D., Rhenthal, P. & J. Trendall (1986): A guide to the fishes of Lake Malawi National Park. WWF, Gland, Switzerland.

Liem, K. F. (1963): The Comparative Osteology and Phylogeny of the Anabantoidei (Teleostei, Pisces). Illinois Biological Monographs: Nr. 30. Illinois, United States.

Liem, K. F. (1965): The Status of the Anabantoid Fish Genera *Ctenops* and *Trichopsis*. Copeia (2): 206-213.

Linke, H. (1987): Farbe im Aquarium. Labyrinthfische. 2. A., Tetra-Verlag, Melle, Germany.

Linke, H. & W. Staeck (1984): Amerikanische Cichliden I, Kleine Buntbarsche. Tetra-Verlag, Melle, Germany.

Loiselle, P. V. (1988): The cichlid aquarium. Tetra-Verlag, Melle, Germany.

Matschke, E. & K. H. Matschke (1986): Pflege und Zucht von Panzer- und Schwielenwelsen. Neumann Verlag, Leipzig-Radebeul, East Germany.

Matthews, W. J. & D. C. Heins (1987): Community and Evolutionary Ecology of North American Stream Fishes. University of Oklahoma Press, Norman, United States.

Maurus, W. (1976): All about bettas. T.F.H., Neptune City, N. J., United States.

Mayr, E. (1967): Artbegriff und Evolution. Hamburg-Berlin, Germany.

Mayr, E. (1975): Grundlagen der zoologischen Systematik. Hamburg-Berlin, Germany.

McGinnis, S. M. (1984): Freshwater Fishes of California. University of California Press, Berkeley-Los Angeles, United States.

Melzer, J.: Wunderwelt Aquarium. Tetra-Verlag, Melle, Germany.

Menni, R. C., Ringuelet, R. A. & R. H. Aramburu (1984): Peces marinos de la Argentina y Uruguay. Editorial Hemisferio Sur S. A., Buenos Aires, Argentina.

Merrick, J. R. & G. Schmida (1984): Australian Freshwater Fishes. Griffin Press Ltd., Netley/South Australia, Australia.

Merwald, F. (1977): Tiere der Welt. Band 2, Reptilien, Amphibien, Fische, 3. A., Linz, East Germany.

Meyer, M. K., et al. (1987): Contributions to the Knowledge of the Cichlid Fishes of the Genus *Aulonocara* of Lake Malawi (East-Africa). Courier Forschungsinstitut Senckenberg **94**, Frankfurt/M., Germany.

Mihálik, J. (1982): Der Wels. Ziemsen, Wittenberg Lutherstadt, East Germany.

Morrow, J. E.: The Freshwater Fishes of Alaska. Alaska Northwest Publishing Comp., Anchorage, United States.

Moser, H. G. (ed.) (1984): Ontogeny and Systematics of Fishes. Amer. Soc. Ichthyol. Herpetol., Special Publication No. 1, Lawrence/Kansas, United States.

Mowtschan, J. W. (1988): Fauna der Ukraine, Bd. 8: Fische. (in Ukrainian). Kiew Naukova Dumka, Kiew, Soviet Union.

Moya Meono, R. M. (1979): Estudio sistematico de los guapotes de America Central (Osteichthys, Familia Cichlidae, *Cichlasoma*). Universidad de Costa Rica.

Mühlberg, H. (1977): Vermehrung der Aquarienpflanzen. Urania Verlag, Leipzig-Jena-Berlin, East Germany.

Nichols, J. T. (1943): The Freshwater-Fishes of China. Natural History of Central Asia. Vol. IX.

Nieuwenhuizen, A. v. d. (1961): Labyrinthfische, Kernen, Stuttgart, Germany.

Nieuwenhuizen, A. v. d. (1986): Das Wunder im Wohnzimmer. 2. A., Kernen, Essen, Germany.

Nijssen, H., van Tuijl, L. & I. J. H. Isbrücker (1982): A catalogue of the type-specimens of Recent fishes in the Institute of Taxonomic Zoology (Zoölogisch Museum), University of Amsterdam, the Netherlands.

Norman, J. R. (1966): Die Fische. 2. A., Parey, Hamburg-Berlin, Germany.

Ostermöller, W. (1968): Die Aquarienfibel. Stuttgart, Germany.

Ostermöller, W. (1970): Fische züchten - nach Rezept. Stuttgart, Germany.

Ostermöller, W. (1976): Labyrinthfische im Aquarium. Stuttgart, Germany.

Ott, G. (1988): Schmerlen - wenig bekannte, aber interessante Pfleglinge. Philler Verlag, Minden, Germany.

Literature

Norman, J. R. (1966): Die Fische. 2. A., Parey, Hamburg-Berlin, Germany.

Ostermöller, W. (1968): Die Aquarienfibel. Stuttgart, Germany.

Ostermöller, W. (1970): Fische züchten - nach Rezept. Stuttgart, Germany.

Ostermöller, W. (1976): Labyrinthfische im Aquarium. Stuttgart, Germany.

Ott, G. (1988): Schmerlen - wenig bekannte, aber interessante Pfleglinge. Philler Verlag, Minden, Germany.

Paepke, H. J. & L. Seegers (1986): Kritischer Katalog der Typen und Typoide der Fischsammlung des Zoologischen Museums Berlin. Teil 1: Atheriniformes. Mitt. Zool. Mus. Berlin 62: 135-186.

Paul, G. & F. Walter (1987): Faszinierende Welt unter Wasser - sehen - hören - entdecken. Tetra-Verlag, Melle, Germany.

Petzold, H. G. (1988): Der Guppy. 3. A. , Ziemsen, Wittenberg Lutherstadt, East Germany.

Pfeffer, G. (1896): Die Fische Ost-Afrikas. o. O.

Piechocki, R. (1979): Makroskopische Präparationstechnik. Teil I, Wirbeltiere, Fischer-Verlag, Stuttgart-New York, Germany, United States.

Pinter, H. (1984): Labyrinthfische, Hechtköpfe und Schlangenkopffische. Verlag Eugen Ulmer, Stuttgart, Germany.

Pinter, H. (1988): Salmler. Verlag Eugen Ulmer, Stuttgart, Germany.

Ploeg, A. (1986a): The fishes of the cichlid genus Crenicichla in French Guiana (Pisces, Perciformes, Cichlidae). Bijdragen tot de Dierkunde 56: 221-231.

Ploeg, A. (1986b): The cichlid genus Crenicichla from the Tocantins River, State Pará, Brazil, with descriptions of four new species (Pisces, Perciformes, Cichlidae). Beaufortia 36: 57-80.

Ploeg, A. (1987): Review of the cichlid genus Crenicichla HECKEL, 1840 from Suri-nam, with descriptions of three new species (Pisces, Perciformes, Cichlidae). Beaufortia 37: 73-98.

Plöger-Brembach, K. (1982): Lebendgebärende. Kernen Verlag, Stuttgart, Germany.

Poll, M. (1971): Revision des Synodontis Africain (Familie Mochocidae). Annales Musee Royal de l'Afrique Centrale, Ser. In-8. Tervuren, Belgium.

Poll, M. (1986): Classification des Cichlidae du lac Tanganjika. Tribus. genres et espèces. Academie Royale de Belgique, Brüssel, Belgium.

Popta, C. M. L. (1906): Note I. Résultats ichthyologiques des voyages scientifiques de monsieur le professeur Dr. A. W. Nieuwenhuis dans le centre de Bornéo (1898 et 1900). Notes from the Leyden Museum 27. Leiden, Holland.

Popta, C. M. L. (1912): 4. Die geographische Verbreitung der Süßwasserfische zwischen Asien und Australien. "Die Sunda-Expedition" des Vereins für Geographie und Statistik zu Frankfurt am Main. Band II: 315-326.

Radda, A. C. & E. Pürzl (1981): Killifische aus aller Welt. Bd. 1: Feldführer der Cyprinodontiformes der Länder der Regenwaldlücke Westafrikas (Togo, Benin, SW-Nigeria). Verlag Otto Hofmann, Wien, East Germany.

Radda, A. C. & E. Pürzl (1982): Killifische aus aller Welt. Bd. 2: Feldführer der Cyprinodontiformes der Länder der Bucht von Biafra (SO-Nigeria, West-Kamerun). Verlag Otto Hofmann, Wien, East Germany.

Radda, A. C. & E. Pürzl (1983): Killifische aus aller Welt. Bd. 3: Feldführer der Cyprinodontiformes der Küstenländer Zentralafrikas. I. Ost-Kamerun. Verlag Otto Hofmann, Wien, East Germany.

Radda, A. C. & E. Pürzl (1985): Killifische aus aller Welt. Bd. 4: Feldführer der Cyprinodontiformes der Küstenländer Zentralafrikas. II. Gabun. Verlag Otto Hofmann, Wien, East Germany.

Radda, A. C. & E. Pürzl (1987): Colour atlas of Cyprinodonts of the rain forests of tropical Africa. Verlag Otto Hofmann, Wien, East Germany.

Radda, A. C. & R. H. Wildekamp (1986): Killifische aus aller Welt. Bd. 9: Synopsis der nearktischen Cyprinodontiformes. Verlag Otto Hofmann, Wien, East Germany.

Regan, C. T. (1904): A Monograph of the Family Loricariidae. Proc. Zool. Soc. London 17 (III): 191-351.

Literature

Regan, C. T. (1910): The Asiatic Fishes of the Family Anabantidae. Proc. Zool. Soc. London. 767-787.

Regan, C. T. (1921): The Cichlid Fishes of Lake Nyassa. Proc. Zool. Soc. London **49**: 675-727.

Reis, R. E. & L. R. Malabarba (1988): Revision of the neotropical cichlid genus *Gymnogeophagus* Ribeiro, 1918, with descriptions of two new species (Pisces, Perciformes). Rev. bras. Zool., Sao Paulo **4**: 259- 305.

Reiß, M. (1984): Erfolgreiche Aquaristik - Wasseraufbereitung und Wasserpflege. Verlag Manfred Reiß, Backnang, Germany.

Remane, A., Storch, V. & U. Welsch (1980): Systematische Zoologie. Fischer Verlag, Stuttgart-New York, Germany, United States.

Richter, H. J. (1979): Das Buch der Labyrinthfische. Verlag Neumann-Neudamm, Melsungen, Germany.

Richter, H. J. (1984): Aquarienfische im Blickpunkt. Leipzig-Jena-Berlin, East Germany.

Richter, H. J. (1988): Zwergbuntbarsche. Verlag Neumann-Neudamm, Melsungen, Germany.

Ridley, M. (1978): Paternal Care. Animal Behaviour **26**: 904-932.

Ripley, S. D. (1975): Tropisches Asien, Flora und Fauna. Rowohlt Verlag, Hamburg, Germany.

Roberts, T. R. (1978): An Ichthyological Survey of the Fly River in Papua New Guinea with Description of New Species. Smithsonian Contributions to Zoology **281**. Washington, United States.

Robinson, H. W. & T. M. Buchanan (1988): Fishes of Arkansas. University of Arkansas Press, Fayetteville, United States.

Roszak, K. H.: Die tropischen Zierfische. Berlin-Weimar, East Germany.

Sagar, K. & J. Swain (1976): Tropische Fische in Farbe. München, Germany.

Sands, D. (1985-1988): Catfishes of the World. vol. 1-5. Dunure Publications, Dunure/ Scotland, Great Britian.

Sands, D. (1988): Südamerikanische Welse. Tetra-Verlag, Melle, Germany.

Sawada, Y. (1982): Phylogeny and zoogeography of the superfamily Cobitoidea (Cyprinoidei, Cypriniformes). Mem. Fac. Fish., Hokkaido Univ. **28**: 65-223.

Schmettkamp, W. (1985): Die Namen unserer Aquarienfische. Landbuch Verlag, Hannover, Germany.

Schmidt, H. (1934): Der Garten im Glas. Frankfurt a. d. O.-Berlin, Dt.

Schöpfel, H. (1978): Schöne Aquarien - aber wie? 2. A., Leipzig-Jena-Berlin, East Germany.

Schröder, J. H. (1974): Vererbungslehre für Aquarianer. Stuttgart, Germany.

Schubert, P. (1984): Regenbogenfische. Neumann Verlag, Leipzig-Radebeul, East Germany.

Schulte, W. (1984): Piranhas - Wissenswertes über Verhalten, Pflege und Zucht. Philler Verlag, Minden, Germany.

Scott, W. B. & E. J. Crossman (1973): Freshwater fishes of Canada. Fisheries Research Board of Canada, Ottawa, Canada.

Scott, W. B. (1983): Freshwater Fishes of Eastern Canada. University of Toronto Press, Toronto-Buffalo-London, Canada, Great Britian.

Seegers, L.: Prachtgrundkärpflinge. Die Gattung *Nothobranchius*: Systematik, Vorkommen, Pflege und Zucht. DKG-Journal, 1: pp. 1-48.

Seegers, L.: Bemerkungen über die Sammlung der Cyprinodontiformes (Pisces: Teleostei) des Zoologischen Museums Berlin. I. Die Gattungen *Aphyosemion* MYERS, 1924 und *Fundulosoma* AHL, 1924. Teil 1. Mitt. Zool. Mus. Berl., **62** (2): 303-331.

Seegers, L.: Bemerkungen über die Sammlung der Cyprinodontiformes (Pisces: Teleostei) des Zoologischen Museums Berlin. I. Die Gattungen *Aphyosemion* MYERS, 1924 und *Fundulosoma* AHL, 1924. Teil 2. Mitt. Zool. Mus. Berl., **64** (1): 3-70, Taf. I-V.

Literature

Smith, C. L. (1985): The Inland Fishes of New York State. The New York State Department of Environmental Education, Albany, United States.

Staeck, W. (1985): Cichliden, Tanganjikasee. Engelbert Pfriem Verlag, Wuppertal-Elberfeld, Germany.

Staeck, W. (1988): Cichliden, Malawi-See. Engelbert Pfriem Verlag, Wuppertal-Elberfeld, Germany.

Staeck, W. & H. Linke (1985): Amerikanische Cichliden II, Große Buntbarsche. Tetra-Verlag, Melle, Germany.

Stallknecht, H. (1981): Freude am Aquarium. Urania Verlag, Leipzig-Jena-Berlin, East Germany.

Stallknecht, H. (1987): Seltene Sonderlinge. Neumann Verlag, Leipzig-Radebeul, East Germany.

Starmühlner, F. (1979): Urwaldinseln. Wien-München, East Germany, Germany.

Stawikowski, R. & U. Werner (1985): Die Buntbarsche der Neuen Welt - Mittelamerika. Edition Kernen, Essen, Germany.

Sterba, G. (1978): Handbuch der Aquarienfische. 2. A., München-Bern-Wien.

Sterba, G. (1987): Süßwasserfische der Welt. Urania-Verlag, Leipzig-Jena-Berlin, East Germany.

Sterba, G. (1988): Aquarienkunde. Urania-Verlag, Leipzig-Jena-Berlin, East Germany.

Stolk, A. (1980): Sprache der Fische. Landbuch Verlag, Hannover, Germany.

Studer, P. (1986): Nasse Welt. Basel, Switzerland.

Suvatti, C. (1981): Fishes of Thailand. Royal Institute, Bangkok, Thailand.

Taki, Y. (1974): Fishes of the Lao Mekon Basin. United States Agency for International Development Mission to Laos, Agriculture Division. United States.

Taliev, D. N. (1955): Groppen des Baikalsees (Cottoidei). (in Russian). Akademii NAUK SSSR, Moskau, Soviet Union.

Tembrock, G. (1984): Verhalten bei Tieren. Ziemsen, Wittenberg Lutherstadt, East Germany.

Tembrock, G. (1987): Verhaltensbiologie. Fischer Verlag, Jena, East Germany.

Teton, J. & R. Allgayer (1986): Encyclopedie du discus. Editeur Aquarama/Sopic, Strasbourg, France.

Tischler, W. (1984): Einführung in die Ökologie. 3. A., Fischer Verlag, Stuttgart-New York, Germany, United States.

Tönsmeier, D. (1989): Einheimische Fische im Aquarium. Verlag Eugen Ulmer, Stuttgart, Germany.

Trappl, W. (ed.) (1979): Das bunte Aquarienbuch. Klingbeils neue Aquarienkunde. München, Germany.

Ufermann, A., Allgayer, R. & M. Geerts (1987): Alphabetischer Katalog der Buntbarsche, Bd. 1. Imprimerie Martin, Brumath, France.

Uj, A. (1987): Les Cheirodontinae (Characidae, Ostariophysi) du Paraguay. Revue suisse Zool. **94**: 129-175.

Vaillant, L. M. (1902): Résultates Zoologiques de l'expédition scientifique Néederlandaise au Bornéo Central. Poissons. Notes from the Leyden Museum **24**: 1-202.

Vierke, J. (1986): Labyrinthfische, Arten - Haltung - Zucht. Stuttgart, Germany.

Villa, J. (1982): Peces Nicaraguenses de agua dulce. Coleccion Cultural, Managua, Nicaragua.

Villwock, W. (1960): Eierlegende Zahnkarpfen. Kernen, Stuttgart, Germany.

Vogel, Z. (1980): Taschenatlas der Aquarienfische. 8. A., Hanau/M., Germany.

Vogt, D. (1959, 1972): Salmler I, II, III. Kernen, Stuttgart, Germany.

Vogt, D. (1962): Welse. Kernen, Stuttgart, Germany.

Vogt, D. (1973): Schmerlen, Algenfresser, Flossensauger, Stachelaale. Kernen, Stuttgart, Germany.

Volz, W. (1904): Fische von Sumatra (Reise von Dr. Walter Volz). Zool. Jahrb. Syst. **19**: 347-422.

Literature

Volz, W. (1907): Catalogue of the Fishes of Sumatra. Natuurkundig Tijdschrift voor Nederlandsch-Indie. Deel LXVI, Tiende Serie, Deel X. Veltevreden, Holland.

Wainwright, N. (1979): Aquarienfische, Tropische Arten und ihre Haltung. München-Zürich, Germany, Switzerland.

Weber, M. (1917): Süßwasserfische von Neu-Guinea. Ein Beitrag zur Frage nach dem früheren Zusammenhang von Neu-Guinea und Australien. Nova Guinea. Zool. 5, 201-267.

Weber, M. & L. F. DeBeaufort (1911-1962): The Fishes of the Indo-Australian Archipelago, vols. 1-11. Brill, Leiden, Holland.

Weiss, W. (1979): Welse im Aquarium. Stuttgart, Germany.

Weitzman, S. H. & W. L. Fink (1983): Relationship of the Neon Tetras, A Group of South American Freshwater Fishes (Teleostei, Characidae), with Comments on the Phylogeny of New World Characiformes. Bulletin of the Museum of Comparative Zoology, 150 (6): Cambridge, United States, 339-395.

Wheeler, A. (1969): The fishes of the British Isles and North-West Europe. Macmillan, London, England.

Wickler, W. (1970): Stammesgeschichte und Ritualisierung, dtv, München, Germany.

Wickler, W. (1972): Verhalten und Umwelt. Parey, Hamburg, Germany.

Wildekamp, R. (1982): Prachtkärpflinge. Kernen Verlag, Stuttgart, Germany.

Willemse, H. S. (ed.) (1985): Cichliden van de wereld. Zuid Boekprodukties b. v., Best, Holland.

Xylander, W. & F. Nagelschmid (1985): Gewässerbeobachtung - Gewässerschutz. Stuttgart, Germany.

Zd'árek, J. (1988): Verständigung zwischen Tieren, Prag, Czechostovakia.

Zeiske, W. & J. Plomann (1976): Fisch- und Gewässerkunde. 3. A., Sportverlag, Berlin, East Germany.

Zukal, R. & S. Frank (1982): Balzspiele im Aquarium. Landbuch Verlag, Hannover, Germany.

Zukov, P. I. (1965): Fische von Weißrußland. (in Russian). Akad. NAUK BSSR, Minsk, Soviet Union.

Zupanc, G. K. H. (1982): Fische und ihr Verhalten. Tetra-Verlag, Melle, Germany.

Photo Credits

Dr. Gerald R. Allen: 1013 (3), 1017 t, 1019 (2).

Herbert Bader: 1041 t.

Hans A. Baensch: 7, 164, 288, 350, 362 (2), 363.

Rudi Bischoff/IKAN: 931.

Friedrich Bitter: 443 t, 457 t, 465 b, 467 t, 477 t, 485 t, 490, 497 t, 501 t, 563 b, 569 t, 917, 919 t, 921 b.

Otto Böhm: 137 b, 233 b, 265 b, 271 t, 291, 451 b, 453 b, 471 b, 479 b, 483 t, 491, 508 (2), 511 b, 535 t, 545 t, 548, 553 b, 561 b, 563 t, 570, 575 b, 589 t, 591 (2), 593 (2), 594, 601 (2), 607 (2), 619 t, 623 b, 628, 909 (2).

Horst Büscher: 849 t.

Helmut Debelius/IKAN: 895 b.

Horst Dieckhoff: 303, 399 b, 407 t, 408 (2), 700, 706, 710, 711 (2), 717 t, 759 t, 761 t, 763 t, 764, 781 b, 793 b, 796, 798, 810 b, 811, 815 b, 816, 818 t, 825 (4), 827 (2), 845 (2), 847 t, 849 b, 896 (2), 897 (8), 1009 t.

Dr. Walter Foersch: 111 t, 161 b, 191 t, 277 t, 295 (2), 299 (2), 317 b, 347 b, 364, 366, 367, 374, 375 (2), 377 t, 379 t, 389 (2), 391 (2), 392 (2), 393, 432, 457 b, 639 (2), 641 b, 643 b, 657 b, 663 t, 971 (2), 1003 t, 1004, 1005, 1039 t, 1041 b.

J. Geck: 645 t.

Hans-Jürgen Günther: 195 b, 199 b, 200, 209 t, 210, 257 b, 259 t, 261 t, 275 b, 913 t.

Hilmar Hansen: 81, 233 t, 422, 424, 1023 t.

Andreas Hartl: 163 b, 361, 679, 924, 970, 1034, 1035, 1045.

Horst Haunert: 364.

Steffen Hellner: 454, 533 b.

Hans J. Herrmann: 713 t, 763 b, 801 t, 847 b, 853 t, 869 (2), 901 t.

Harro Hieronimus: 225 b.

Hans Horsthemke: 671, 676, 927 t, 955 b, 956 (2), 959 t, 961 b, 963 b, 973 (2), 975 t, 979 b, 981 t, 983 t, 985 (2), 991 t, 999 t, 1001 b.

Burkhard Kahl: 180 b, 359, 419 t, 947, 1035, 1037 b.

Alexander M. Kochetov: 75 b, 77 (2), 79 (2), 83 b, 84, 85 (2), 107 t, 109 t, 125 t, 151 b, 159 b, 168, 171 t, 175 (2), 177 b, 196 b, 199 t, 203 b, 207, 217, 219 (2), 221 t, 236 (2), 237, 239 b, 245 t, 247 b, 249, 253 (2), 261 b, 267 (2), 269 (2), 271 t, 275 t, 279 t, 281 (2), 287 t, 313 b, 315 b, 323 t, 351, 394, 401 t, 427 b, 926 t, 937 t, 945 t, 964, 977 b, 979 t, 987 (2), 993 b, 994, 995, 997 (2), 1011 t, 1021 t, 1024, 1025, 1029 t, 1039 b, 1045 t.

Dr. Sergei M. Kochetov: 75 t, 80, 83 t, 171 b, 188 t, 235 t, 248, 279 b, 283 t, 311 b, 893 t, 913 b, 925, 926 b, 943 (2), 949 (2), 951 (2), 952, 953 (2), 963 (2), 989 b, 993 t, 1009 b.

Joachim Kollo: 779 b.

Edith Korthaus: 699.

Dr. Maurice Kottelat: 429 (2).

René Krummenacher: 653, 667 t.

Dr. Friedhelm Krupp: 203 t, 215 b, 216, 283 b, 285 (2), 551 (2).

Lagdon: 419 b.

J. Lake: 910.

Photo Credits

Anton Lamboj: 395 t, 787 b, 789 t, 873 b, 875 t, 899 t.

Horst Linke: 637, 648, 649 b, 677, 681 t, 687 b, 803 (2), 807 (2).

Dr. Volker Mahnert: 105 t, 113 (2), 115 b, 117 b, 122, 133 b, 137 t, 139 t, 141 b, 145 (2), 149 (2), 151 t, 155 b, 371 b.

Manfred K. Meyer: 421 b, 557 (2) 581, 585 b, 586, 587, 589 b, 590, 596, 597 (2), 599 (2), 603 (2), 604, 605 (2), 609 (2), 611 t, 613 (2), 615 (2), 616 (2), 619 b, 621 t, 623 t, 625 (2), 627 (2), 629 (2), 630, 632, 633 b, 701 (2), 702, 703 t, 705 (2), 736 b, 745 t, 765, 797 t, 809 t, 810 t, 813 t, 823 b, 880.

Friedrich Müller: 325 b, 458, 611b, 631.

Arend van den Nieuwenhuizen: 87 b, 88, 98, 101 b, 103 t, 117 t, 121 t, 131 t,152,155 t, 167 t, 178 b, 183 b, 187 b, 197 (2), 211, 221 b, 225 t, 228 b, 229, 263 b, 273, 277 b, 289, 305 b, 307 t, 333 b, 381 b, 433, 465 t, 480, 481 b, 505 t, 510, 519 t, 525 t, 561 t, 643 t, 703 b, 891 b, 915 b, 938, 1003 b, 1011 b, 1015, 1023 b, 1027t.

J. Nikolas: 651 b.

Aaron Norman: 119 t, 125 b, 127 (2), 129 b, 165, 196 t, 243 b, 255 t, 265 t, 779 t, 907 b, 919 b, 921 t, 966, 969 (2).

Roland Numrich: 841 t.

Gerhard Ott: 143 t, 287 b.

Kurt Paffrath: 15-71 (alle).

Klaus Paysan: 231 b, 290, 1021 b.

Alan Pinkerton: 335 t.

Helmut Pinter: 99, 146, 147, 157.

Eduard Pürzl: 191 b 447 t, 449 b, 475 (2), 489 b, 495 b, 503 (2), 535 b, 537 t.

Hans Reinhard: 119, 169, 172, 173, 177 t, 201, 204, 227 b, 239 t, 241 (2), 257 t, 289, 343 b, 360, 423, 923 (2), 935, 939, 946 (2), 965, 967, 1031 (2), 1032 (2), 1033, 1036, 1037 t, 1043 (2).

Günter Reitz: 818 b.

Hans-Joachim Richter: 11, 101 t, 115 t, 131 b, 133 t, 139 b, 153, 161 t, 296, 353 t, 638, 670, 683 t, 684 (2), 685, 805 (2), 875 b, 911, 929, 937 b, 1014.

Dr. Rüdiger Riehl: 678.

Uwe Römer: 683 b, 689 t.

Hans J. Rösler: 507 (8), 659 t.

Lucas Rüber: 809 b.

Mike Sandford: 206, 301 b, 323 b.

David D. Sands: 305 t, 307 b, 309 t, 311 t, 313 t, 315 t, 319 (2), 321 b, 327 t, 329 (2), 331 (2), 333 t, 335 b, 337 (2), 339 b, 345 t, 347 t, 349 (2), 353 b, 355, 357 (2), 368, 373 b, 385 (2), 387 b, 399 t, 401 b, 403 (2), 405 b, 407 b, 411 (2), 413, 415 (2), 417 (2), 421 t, 431.

Günther Schmelzer: 761 b.

Werner Schmettkamp: 111 b.

Gunther E. Schmida: 297, 907 t, 928, 1017 b, 1027 b, 1028.

Jürgen Schmidt: 167 b, 325 t, 365, 635, 636, 645 (4), 647 (2), 651 t, 655 (2), 656, 657 t, 661 (2), 663 b, 665 (2), 667 b, 669 (2), 673 (2), 675 (2), 903.

Photo Credits